CONFLICT IN THE CLASSROOM

CONFLICT IN THE CLASSROOM
POSITIVE STAFF SUPPORT FOR TROUBLED STUDENTS

SIXTH EDITION

Nicholas J. Long

William C. Morse

Frank A. Fecser

Ruth G. Newman

pro·ed
An International Publisher

8700 Shoal Creek Boulevard
Austin, Texas 78757-6897
800/897-3202   Fax 800/397-7633
www.proedinc.com

© 1965, 1971, 1976, 1980, 1996, 2007 by PRO-ED, Inc.
8700 Shoal Creek Boulevard
Austin, Texas 78757-6897
800/897-3202 Fax 800/397-7633
www.proedinc.com

Library of Congress Cataloging-in-Publication Data

Conflict in the classroom : positive staff support for troubled students /
[edited by] Nicholas J. Long ... [et al.].—6th ed.
     p. cm.
   Includes bibliographical references and index.
   ISBN 1-4164-0250-0
  1. Emotional problems of children. 2. Mentally ill
children—Education—United States. I. Long, Nicholas James, 1929-
     LC4181.C65 2007
     371.94—dc22
                              2007008222

Art Director: Jason Crosier
Designer: Cinqué Hicks
This book is designed in Lucida Sans and Adobe Garamond Pro.

Printed in the United States of America

1 2 3 4 5 6 7 8 9 10   12 11 10 09 08 07

We dedicate this revision of *Conflict in the Classroom* to our teacher, mentor, and personal friend, Fritz Redl (1902–1988). He was a most creative colleague whose insights came from his direct work with seriously disturbed children and youth in therapeutic camping and residential care. His national studies on delinquent youth took place at Pioneer House in Detroit and later in a special residential program at the National Institute of Mental Health in Washington, D.C. He was "Fritz" to everyone.

He once said that the more education a professional received, the more likely it would be further from the intimate daily life of disturbed youth.

When he would give one of his exciting presentations, be it in a college classroom or a national meeting, heads would nod in agreement: "He has been where I have been and now I understand better how and why to respond." Fritz was an ecologist before the term was common and used the life space of children with the interview to help distraught children and youth. Fritz recognized that helping youth on the spot was even more taxing than the classical therapeutic office interview. His innovative concepts included the nature of the therapeutic milieu, life space interviewing, psychology of kids in groups, roles members play, and the implications of various leadership styles. His critical insights into the dynamics of delinquent youth revolutionized their treatment. The concepts in his legacy are as fresh and pertinent as they were when he first shared them with us. We continue to strive to emulate his deep caring for even the most difficult child.

The path to his kind of caring is not a simple one: For most of us it involves transforming how we think about troubled students and about our efforts to help them. We encourage all who work with troubled children to enjoy Fritz Redl's *When We Deal With Children* and his two seminal books written with David Wineman, *Children Who Hate* and *Controls from Within* (Free Press). Much of what you will read in this revision of *Conflict in the Classroom* springs from his creative mind.

We also dedicate this revision to our wives, Jody, Sunny, and Mary Ellen, and our children.

CONTENTS

PREFACE

This sixth edition of *Conflict in the Classroom* is intended for use by all staff who work with troubled students. Troubled students no longer are the sole responsibility of special educators. Troubled students are in all classrooms and are the responsibility of all staff regardless of whether they received the necessary training to manage and educate these students. This edition addresses this reality by providing staff with the essential concepts and skills that will enhance their effectiveness with troubled students while also providing these students with a new experience of positive support and a caring adult relationship.

This edition also comes at a time of intense national criticism of public education. There are serious questions about the Individuals with Disabilities Education Improvement Act of 2004 (IDEA). In addition, 80% of schools have adopted some form of zero tolerance for trivial, minor, and serious behavior. Although the concept of zero tolerance of dangerous behavior is well intended, the automatic implementation of this concept has increased the frequency of school suspensions and dropouts. According to the Department of Education statistics, this concept has also singled out minority students, many of whom are at risk and troubled. The latest federal legislation designed to improve education is the No Child Left Behind of 2001. This act requires all states to improve the academic achievement of all students, including students with disabilities. The government's focus on academic improvement seems to deny the significant relationship between a student's emotional and cognitive needs. The ability to think and feel cannot be separated. Feelings influence learning, and learning influences feelings. A student who is upset cannot concentrate on lessons. During stressful times, this student more likely will react emotionally and not rationally.

Concurrently, a student who masters an academic skill feels better about him- or herself and others. If teachers, however, are forced to focus their primary energies on improving test scores, they are less likely to have the time to understand and meet students' social–emotional needs. We do not believe in an either/or approach to educating at-risk and troubled students. Instead, we contend that promoting both academic competence and the social–emotional needs of students is essential to the success of any school program.

Given these critical times and concerns, this sixth revision continues the psychoeducational fusion of current and effective educational and mental health practices that teachers can use to help troubled students. When our earlier editions were published, special education was preoccupied with such issues as identification criteria, emotional versus social maladjustment, proper settings and services, appropriate curricula, the nature of school therapy, and preparation of special teachers. There was much explication of contrasting theories. None of these matters has been resolved; they are all still with us. Meanwhile, the focus of the field is undergoing drastic revision in response to changes in U.S. society. These changes have put the United States at or near the top of the list of Western countries that have multiple indicators of family instability and disintegration. Schools are being expected to take the lead in helping to resolve a national crisis in child upbringing. There is a virtual revolution in educational practice as schools adjust to this new reality. This edition reflects these impending changes.

Several issues are altering the face of education for troubled students even as the schools struggle to restructure themselves to better meet the needs of all children. First, there has been a significant increase in the number of already troubled and seriously at-risk students in U.S. schools. It is estimated that 10% of school-age students have an identifiable mental health problem that interferes with their normal functions. No letup is in sight, and there are too many to accommodate in traditional special education programs. The presence of these special-needs students is daunting, as every regular and special teacher and administrator knows. Second, along with increased numbers of troubled students has come an awareness of the deeper and more profound nature of their personal and ecological difficulties. More students are deeply depressed, despairing, and suicidal; others turn defiant, angry, violent, and homicidal. Many will travel well-marked trails to gang membership, delinquency, drugs, or the occult. When we hear their stories, we wonder how many of them survived at all. Larger numbers of students are trying to cope with fearsome family and community conditions and are failing in life as well as in school. As a result, the schools reap the harvests of community poverty, neglect, and abuse. Inappropriate school programs and practices only add to the students' struggle when nurturing schools could contribute to a solution.

Even in the best of times, special education never included all of the disturbed and disturbing students and never was designed to include those at risk. Today, these students can be half the members of a given class. Special education services once awaited certification rituals for proper "fit" and were not geared to prevention or early intervention. But along with the current national thrust for school reorganization has come a profound change in special education philosophy regarding traditional exclusionary services. As a basic civil right and to the maximum extent possible, all special students are to be taught in the mainstream at their local school and with their age peers. This change makes all teachers responsible for educating all students, including the seriously troubled. The philosophy of full- and part-time inclusion presents special problems both for troubled students, who act out their struggles, and for their already overburdened teachers. Coping with individual differences and diversity takes on a new responsibility and implies new skills for teachers. As the wall between regular and special education is breached, all teachers become special teachers. The previously designated special teachers become team teachers in regular classrooms, collaborators, and consultants. When needed, they also continue their "hands-on" service for troubled students. This philosophical turnabout requires expanded teacher education and system reorganization to provide backup crisis support not only for the students but also for the teachers.

Another change that affects all teachers is the increased power parents and community representatives have in the educative process. As school reorganization brings local school autonomy, teachers find new faces at the decision-making table. Parents of special students continue to exercise their right to decide the content of their children's educational program. A few parents inevitably resort to the courts for new services. The fear of litigation has become a strong political force in some school systems. Concurrently, there is a new focus in working with families: Family preservation has become the central goal in providing support for distraught families and their children. Teachers are expected to reach out to families as intensively as possible, to accomplish conjoint efforts in helping all students to find school success.

Another far-reaching issue involves accountability. As though there were no multiple causes for students' troubles, the evaluation of the schools' programs is changing from "Are we doing the right things?" to "Are we getting the desired academic results?" In addition, stringent budgets for school and community agencies are resulting in fewer support services for teachers who teach troubled students.

We do not want to offer a bleak educational picture of the future, because we believe that well-trained teachers and nurturing schools can do much to meet the needs of at-risk and troubled students. We acknowledge the new realities of teaching, along with changes in our society. They are modifying education—particularly special education. Some observers think that special education will be unrecognizable in the future, but educators can still count on recognizing troubled students in their classrooms. The pace and nature of change are not uniform in the country's variegated schools. Indeed, there are competing and antagonistic directives in the proposals for change. For teachers, one of the most contentious conflicts in proposed educational goals is academic excellence versus equity-based meeting of needs. Programs in one school may differ drastically from those in another nearby school. We also realize that one textbook cannot cover all aspects of teaching and reclaiming troubled and at-risk students.

This sixth edition of *Conflict in the Classroom* has benefited from advice offered by teachers and from the editors' own experiences. Teachers have shared with us their trials in helping troubled students in their classrooms. They have suggested less theory and more practical strategies, especially strategies from other colleagues, to keep the book reality based. They do not want just a series of articles. Teachers proposed putting the individual pieces of each chapter into a meaningful context, so we have provided introductory essays and interfacing paragraphs. While keeping certain selections from the last edition, we have added much new material that is tuned to the current realities of the field.

In each chapter, the articles are bound together by the humanistic beliefs of psychoeducation, a concern for both inner life and external behavior. All students deserve teachers' caring and respect, and the most effective individualized interventions educators can learn. Educators still have a long way to go. Although the resources are not available to reclaim all of the troubled children, schools can get much better results than present practice is delivering. There is new hope in utilizing the power of the students' ecology and the effectiveness of positive teacher–student relationships. We believe all significant learning involves and revolves around the teacher. For us, the teachers have the potential of making lifelong changes in select students. Compared to teachers, what other trained professionals spend more time with students in their life space, using a wide variety of settings and activities? The goal of this revision is to help teachers make school time a more effective experience for these students.

The first chapter contains selections that describe how it feels to be emotionally upset. These stories have been a hallmark of *Conflict* since its first edition. When we read a case record—or better still, hear a student's story from his or her own lips—the youngster becomes transformed in our understanding. We become symbiotic in a common cause to reduce the troubles and the risks. This empathy may not make our task easier but it makes our work more meaningful. Great literature penetrates the life of an "other" and generates empathy for his or her plight, often with deeper effect than a case study. For that reason, the text opens with stories from literature to sensitize readers to the significance of the turmoil in troubled lives.

We want to thank the PRO-ED staff for their support and substantial help, which made this sixth edition possible. It is a distinct pleasure to be part of PRO-ED's expanding leadership in the field of special education publications.

Nicholas J. Long
William C. Morse
Frank A. Fecser

1 WALKING IN THE FOOTSTEPS OF TROUBLED STUDENTS:

How Classical Literature Portrays the Psychological Struggles of Troubled Children and Youth

STUDENTS' emotional problems are not a new phenomenon. Although psychologists argue about the causes of emotional problems and the relative importance of genetic, constitutional, and environmental factors, all agree their occurrence is in some degree dependent on the cultural and social values of the times.

Each of us contains the whole range of emotional health and illness within ourselves. Our nightmares, if they serve no other purpose, enable us to share the ways in which many people with psychoses experience life. If our legs "go to sleep" and refuse to behave as they should, we can briefly experience the helpless and often outraged feelings of someone with organic spasms. The sudden loss of temper we all have experienced gives us a momentary empathy with the feelings of uncontrollable rage, helplessness, confusion, and self-hate of a student who has no impulse control. Most of us have shared a variety of irrational symptoms. Because of a fear of something we know rationally should not in itself cause fear, we use the magical, protective cloak of knocking on wood, crossing fingers, counting to 10, holding our breath. We have the compulsive need to get one thing done, no matter how inane or how inconvenient, before we can do something more important or the piece of work that can never be finished because it is never good enough. We have headaches, stomach pains, or unexplained shortness of breath that often occurs at a family reunion, at exam time, or at the appearance of a certain person. We have the need to eat greedily though we are not hungry, or the inability to swallow a mouthful of food. We have the uncontrollable blush or stutter; the immobilizing lapse of memory; or the urge to take something, to break something, to say the very thing that will get us into trouble, or to be silent when speaking up might simplify our lives and reduce the hostility of others.

Such illogical behavior does not mean that we are disturbed—only that some emotional reactions are as much a part of everyone's life as the common cold. It is not surprising, therefore, that emotional problems play so great a role in childhood periods of dependence and change, in which the world and its demands are new and often confusing, conflicting, and frustrating.

Many literary writers have described the actions of troubled children and adults whose disturbances were rooted in their childhood. Writers were describing emotional illness long before Freud. Because good writers are skilled in conveying mental pictures and feelings, their descriptions often have greater emotional impact than the clinical descriptions in textbooks. Also, we have included some stories about adult behavior to show how they promote and reinforce childhood problems.

The chapter is divided into three parts. The first part describes basic internal difficulties that can be found anywhere, anytime. The second part presents certain aspects of society; its deprivations, restrictions, and human devaluations breed disturbing behaviors. Troubled children and youth react in different ways: by withdrawing into themselves, by separating their feelings from their thoughts, by resorting to body abuse, by getting headaches or ulcers, by becoming psychologically deaf or paralyzed, by eating compulsively to build a wall of fat between themselves and others, and by drinking to numb their pain. The third part discusses drug use. Many young people take drugs to such an excess that they delude themselves into a state of "nonfeeling" or believe they have grasped the importance of their lives or expanded their awareness of the world without having to be competent. Until helping staff can appreciate the plight of these students, they cannot show the compassion that is the beginning condition of a helping relationship.

HOW IT FEELS TO BE EMOTIONALLY TROUBLED

ARTICLE 1.1

THE first excerpt is a powerful story of a physician who is motivated to help an oppositional child and in the process becomes part of the problem. All of us who have worked with emotionally disturbed children can identify with this physician and say, "I have done something like this and I am not proud of my behavior."

THE USE OF FORCE
William Carlos Williams

They were new patients to me, all I had was the name, Olson. Please come down as soon as you can, my daughter's very sick. When I arrived I was met by the mother, a big startled looking woman, very clean and apologetic who merely said, Is this the doctor? and let me in. In the back, she added, You must excuse us, doctor, we have her in the kitchen where it is warm. It is very damp here sometimes.

The child was fully dressed and sitting on her father's lap near the kitchen table. He tried to get up, but I motioned for him not to bother, took off my overcoat and started to look things over. I could see that they were all very nervous, eyeing me up and down distrustfully. As often, in such cases, they weren't telling me more than they had to, it was up to me to tell them; that's why they were spending three dollars on me.

The child was fairly eating me up with her cold, steady eyes, and no expression to her face whatever. She did not move and seemed, inwardly, quiet; an unusually attractive little thing, and as strong as a heifer in appearance. But her face was flushed, she was breathing rapidly, and I realized that she had a high fever. She had magnificent blonde hair, in profusion. One of those picture children often reproduced in advertising leaflets and the photogravure sections of the Sunday papers.

She's had a fever for three days, began the father, and we don't know what it comes from. My wife has given her things, you know, like people do, but it don't do no good. And there's been a lot of sickness around. So we tho't you'd better look her over and tell us what is the matter.

As doctors often do I took a trial shot at it as a point of departure. Has she had a sore throat? Both parents answered me together, No … No, she says her throat don't hurt her. Does your throat hurt you? added the mother to the child. But the little girl's expression didn't change nor did she move her eyes from my face. Have you looked?

I tried to, said the mother, but I couldn't see. As it happens we had been having a number of cases of diphtheria in the school to which this child went during that month and we were all, quite apparently, thinking of that, though no one had as yet spoken of the thing.

Well, I said, suppose we take a look at the throat first. I smiled in my best professional manner and asking for the child's first name I said, come on, Mathilda, open your mouth and let's take a look at your throat. Nothing doing.

Aw, come on, I coaxed, just open your mouth wide and let me take a look. Look, I said opening both hands wide, I haven't anything in my hands. Just open up and let me see.

Such a nice man, put in the mother. Look how kind he is to you. Come on, do what he tells you to. He won't hurt you.

At that I ground my teeth in disgust. If only they wouldn't use the word *"hurt"* I might be able to get somewhere. But I did not allow myself to be hurried or disturbed but speaking quietly and slowly I approached the child again. As I moved my chair a little nearer suddenly with one cat-like movement both her hands clawed instinctively for my eyes and she almost reached them too. In fact she knocked my glasses flying and they fell, though unbroken, several feet away from me on the kitchen floor.

Both the mother and father almost turned themselves inside out in embarrassment and apology. You bad girl, said the mother, taking her and shaking her by one arm. Look what you've done. The nice man…

For heaven's sake, I broke in. Don't call me a nice man to her. I'm here to look at her throat on the chance that she might have diphtheria and possibly die of it. But that's nothing to her. Look here, I said to the child, we're going to look at your throat. You're old enough to understand what I'm saying. Will you open it now by yourself or shall we have to open it for you?

Not a move. Even her expression hadn't changed. Her breaths however were coming faster and faster. Then the battle began. I had to do it. I had to have a throat culture for her own protection. But first I told the parents that it was entirely up to them. I explained the danger but said that I would not insist on a throat examination so long as they would take the responsibility.

If you don't do what the doctor says you'll have to go to the hospital, the mother admonished her severely.

Oh yeah? I had to smile to myself. After all, I had already fallen in love with the savage brat, the parents were contemptible to me. In the ensuing struggle they grew more and more abject, crushed, exhausted while she surely rose to magnificent heights of insane fury of effort bred of her terror of me.

The father tried his best, and he was a big man but the fact that she was his daughter, his shame at her behavior and his dread of hurting her made him release her just at the critical moment several times when I had almost achieved success, till I wanted to kill him. But his dread also that she might have diphtheria made him tell me to go on, go on though he himself was almost fainting, while the mother moved back and forth behind us raising and lowering her hands in an agony of apprehension.

Put her in front of you on your lap, I ordered, and hold both her wrists.

But as soon as he did the child let out a scream. Don't you're hurting me. Let go of my hands. Let them go I tell you. She shrieked terrifyingly, hysterically. Stop it! Stop it! You're killing me!

Do you think she can stand it, doctor? said the mother.

You get out, said the husband to his wife. Do you want her to die of diphtheria?

Come on now, hold her, I said.

Then I grasped the child's head with my left hand and tried to get the wooden tongue depressor between her teeth. She fought, with clenched teeth, desperately! But now I also had grown furious—at a child. I tried to hold myself down but I couldn't. I know how to expose a throat for inspection. And I did my best. When finally I got the wooden spatula behind the last teeth and just the point of it into the mouth cavity, she opened up for an instant but before I could see anything she came down again and gripping the wooden blade between her molars she reduced it to splinters before I could get it out again.

Aren't you ashamed, the mother yelled at her. Aren't you ashamed to act like that in front of the doctor? Get me a smooth-handled spoon of some sort, I told the mother. We're going through with this. The child's mouth was already bleeding. Her tongue was cut and she was screaming in wild hysterical shrieks. Perhaps I should have desisted and come back in an hour or more. No doubt it would have been better. But I have seen at least two children lying dead in bed of neglect in such cases, and feeling that I must get a diagnosis now or never I went at it again. But the worst of it was that I too had got beyond reason. I could have torn the child apart in my own fury and enjoyed it. It was a pleasure to attack her. My face was burning with it.

The damned little brat must be protected against her own idiocy, one says to one's self at such times. Others must be protected against her. It is social necessity. And all these things are true. But a blind fury, a feeling of adult shame, bred of a longing for muscular release are the operatives. One goes on to the end.

In a final unreasoning assault I overpowered the child's neck and jaws. I forced the heavy silver spoon back of her teeth and down her throat till she gagged. And there it was, both tonsils covered with membrane. She had fought valiantly to keep me from knowing her secret. She had been hiding that sore throat for three days at least and lying to her parents in order to escape just such an outcome as this.

Now truly she was furious. She had been on the defensive before but now she attacked. Tried to get off her father's lap and fly at me while tears of defeat blinded her eyes.

EDITORS' COMMENTARY

DIAGNOSIS: Oppositional and defiant behavior that can lead to character disorder.

Mathilda has had many struggles with her parents. She has immobilized and terrorized them. She is the unhappy victor of her parents—unhappy because she would be greatly relieved to know she was not all-powerful, and to know that the adults on whom she *must* depend *can* be depended on to make and carry out decisions that she cannot make. A child feels helpless at best in the adult world, and when parents—and doctors or teachers—are rendered helpless, the result is increased child anxiety, panic, and rage. This rage often comes out in defiant, aggressive behavior. In turn, it makes adults more fearful or angry, and it further isolates the child. Thus, what develops is a circular pattern of control, helplessness, panic, and anger. For the child, the conflict spirals into misery, isolation, and trouble with the world.

Mathilda's parents, as the narrator says, are incompetent. Their words are ill-chosen, frightening, threatening, and shaming. They are effective only in arousing fear, not compliance. Even in a matter of life and death, they are so defeated by the child that they are unable to facilitate the throat examination.

The narrator's reaction to the child illustrates the feelings that such parental behavior arouses in other adults. He secretly admires the courage and determination of the little girl. At the same time, her defiance evokes rage in him, a need to counterattack, and a need simply for "muscular release." He is ashamed that such a little child can make him lose professional control and poise. His ambivalence in being both on the side of the willful and unhappy child and on the side of necessary adult behavior has increased his own hostility and therefore his consequent guilt and self-disgust. He has to complete the throat examination for the sake of the child's very life, and he is aware that his excuses or rationalizations to himself for the way he accomplishes this task are designed to cover up his own primitive rage.

As educators, what can we learn from this excerpt? Every teacher has a student like Mathilda in the classroom who has the ability to push the teacher's counteraggressive buttons. The pattern is predictable. The student refuses to do something that is requested and reasonable. When the teacher tries to help, the student becomes oppositional. The teacher is surprised by the way the student depreciates her help. The teacher becomes frustrated, and her feelings of concern turn into feelings of anger. After a few more unsuccessful attempts, her feelings of anger turn into counteraggressive behavior. This behavior often mirrors the student's oppositional behavior and escalates the conflict into a "no win" power struggle. The student is punished, and the teacher justifies her behavior by saying that the student deserves the punishment received.

This escalating pattern of student-versus-staff behavior is called the Conflict Cycle and explains why reasonable adults end up behaving in punitive and rejecting ways toward students they want to help. This paradigm is essential to learn if your goal is to help troubled students and is explained in detail in Chapter 6.

THE following excerpt is about peer loyalty. This dynamic interpersonal force needs to be understood and appreciated if you work with troubled adolescents.

THE DAY OF THE LAST ROCK FIGHT
Joseph Whitehill

Fallbrook Academy May 16, 195–

Dear Dad,

I expect this will be a very long letter, so I am sending it to your office marked Personal. I know you don't like to do family business at the office, but I wanted you to have a chance to read this all by yourself and I didn't want Mother or Sue reading it before you did.

Thank you for sending my allowance, and also for the subscription to the home paper. Thank you also for the nice new wallet for my birthday. I really needed it, as my old one was afflicted with rot and falling apart.

I apologize for not having written sooner. As you said in your last letter, "Something must have happened in the last two months worth writing down." I have been very busy with things here at school, but mainly I haven't written because I didn't know how to say what I wanted to say. I hope this letter will make up for the long delay.

You keep asking me what I think of Fallbrook Academy and if I'm happy here, and so on. Well, I don't like it here, and I want to come home. That's what this letter is for—to tell you that now it's all right for me to come back home. I guess I know why you sent me here, and I admit that I wanted very much to come when I did. It's not that the people here aren't nice or anything. They are. They're so nice it's phony. In all the catalogues of the school they call it a Special School, but the boys here call it Goodbar. (Mr. Goodbar is a chocolate bar full of nuts.) They all kid about it, and pretend they don't care about being put in a school for misfits and boys with emotional problems. I guess most of them like it here. Most of them say they hate their parents, one or both, and are really glad to get away from them. All the faculty are so sweet and kind and sympathetic that a lot of the boys get away with murder. (That last word was sort of a poor choice, I suppose, but I'll leave it there anyway.) But I don't feel like I belong here any more.

It is going to be very complicated to explain everything in just one letter, because there are lots of different ways of looking at that mess that happened there at home, and I suppose I am the only one who knows the whole story. I guess you sent me here because you thought I was terribly upset by Gene Hanlon getting killed out there at Manning Day School at home, and seeing his body lying in the creek, and so on. Well, that was part of it, but only a little part. The rest of it I couldn't tell anybody until Detective Sergeant Gorman put the story in the paper last week. I got that paper in the mail yesterday and I have been reading the story over and over, and feeling relieved and awful at the same time.

I'm sure you read the same story, so you already know that Gene Hanlon was murdered, instead of getting killed accidentally as they said at first. But neither you nor anybody else knows that I saw the murder done, and knew all the time who did it. I guess if I acted upset afterwards it was from knowing all this and not being able to tell anyone about it. I'm going to work on this letter all night, if it takes that long, because I have to get all this out of my system. (When you stay up after curfew around here they don't actually make you go to bed, but the doctor who is on duty looks in on you every half hour or so to see what you're doing, and to try to make you want to go to bed.)

I suppose the beginning is the best place to start, so I will tell you first about Gene Hanlon, the boy who got killed. He came to Manning Day School last fall as a senior. They said he was fired from his last school, but I don't know about that. I didn't like him just from looking at him. I know you hate judgments that way on first impressions, but I couldn't help it. I wouldn't ever bring him over to our house, but if I had, you might have seen what I was talking about. He was big and beefy, and he played on the first string last fall. He was also blond, and the girls thought he was cute and from what I heard they fought over him for dates. But he was a bully, and he cheated in the classroom and he borrowed your stuff without asking you and then left it some place where you had to go hunt it up for yourself.

In a school like Manning Day there are always a number of tight little groups—cliques, I guess you call them—that move around independently and generally stay out of the way of the others. I mean there is a football group, and a group of boys who drink beer, and a group who studies hard, and a group who loafs and tries to avoid everything that looks like work, and a group that meets in the locker room to talk about sex and tell dirty jokes. It was probably the same way when you yourself went to school, but you may have forgotten. When you go to a school like that, you pretty soon find the group that suits you best, and you stay there and don't try to mix with any of the others, because if you do you won't be let in.

What I am getting at in this long explanation is that Gene Hanlon was the Big Man in all the groups I wouldn't be seen dead in. He was tops among the football players and their fans. He could tell filthier stories and, he said, hold more liquor than anybody else. And he told stories about the things he had done to girls that you wouldn't believe if anybody else had told them, but with him telling them, you knew they were all possible. I guess he was feared more than he was liked, but one thing sure, he never went anywhere alone. There was always a loud bunch along with him horse-laughing and beating him on the shoulders.

I stayed out of his way. There is something about me that brings out the worst in bullies. That's what Peter Irish used to say. I guess it's because I'm slightly built, and because of those glasses I have to wear. Once, I was going upstairs to lab, and Gene Hanlon was coming down and we met halfway, and for no reason I could see, he belted me as hard as he could on my shoulder. My glasses flew off and bounced halfway down the stairs along with a whole armload of books and papers. I had to grab the banister to keep from following them down myself. Two other guys with him saw him do it and didn't say anything at first, but then they looked at Gene and knew they'd better laugh, so they did. So I sat there on the stairs all confused inside, holding my shoulder to make it stop hurting. Gene Hanlon and the others went on down the stairs laughing to beat all at how I looked there with everything scattered around me. On the way down, Gene kicked my physics book ahead of him, bouncing it all the way to the bottom. When I could stand up all right I went down and got it. When I picked it up it fell apart in my hands with its binding broken and I guess I started to cry. I hate to see books treated that way.

When I had about got everything picked up, Peter Irish came up to where I was and wanted to know what had happened. Peter being my best friend, I told him all about it. Probably there were still tears in my eyes about the physics book because Peter said, "Do you want me to get him for you?"

I thought for a minute how swell that would be, but then I said no. It was almost yes because Peter was the only one in school who could have whipped Gene under any rules, and it was a very satisfying thing to think about. But then I thought about afterwards, when Gene would have gotten over his beating and would begin to wonder why Peter had done it, and he would remember that Peter was my best friend. Then he would put one and one together and start out after me seriously. So I said no.

Peter Irish was a good friend to have. I suppose he was the strongest kid in school, but he didn't ever use his strength to bully people, but just for things that were fun, like squashing a beer can in one hand. You knew him pretty well because of all the times he came over to the house to study with me. I remember the time he beat you at Indian hand wrestling on the dining-room table, and you were a real good sport about it because Mother was watching and laughing at your expression. But anyway, you know how strong Peter was, and you can feature what he would have done to Gene if I'd told him to. Peter always stayed out of fights unless they were for fun, and if they ever got serious he'd quit because he didn't want to hurt anybody. But he would have torn Gene Hanlon apart if I had asked him to.

That was something I don't think you understood Peter and me, I mean, and why we hung around together. The simplest way to say it is that we swapped talents. I used to write a lot of his themes for him, and help him in labs so he'd finish when the rest of us did, and he'd show me judo holds and how to skin a squirrel, and such things. You would call it a good working agreement.

Now, there are just two more things you have to know about to see the whole picture. The first one is Peter Irish and Angela Pine. Peter and Angela went together all last year and the year before, and neither of them wanted anybody else. Both their folks made them date other kids because they didn't like to see them going steady, but everybody knew that Angela belonged to Peter, and Peter belonged to Angela, and that's all there was to it. He used to talk to me a lot about her, and how they were going to get married and run a riding stable together. And he told me that he would never touch her that way until they were married. They used to kiss good night and that was all, because Peter said that when the great thing happened, he wanted it to happen just right, and it could never be really right while they were both kids in high school. A lot of the fellows thought that more went on between them than I know did, but that's because they didn't understand Peter really. He had a simple set of rules he operated under, and they suited him very well. He was good to Angela and good to animals, and all he asked was to be let alone to do things his own way.

The other thing you have to know about is the noontime rock fights. From the papers and the inquest and all, you know something about them, but not everything. I guess most of the parents were pretty shocked to learn that their little Johnny was in a mob rock fight every day at school, but that's the way it was. The fights started over a year ago, as near as I can recollect, and went on all that time without the faculty ever finding out. The papers made a big scandal out of them and conducted what they called an "expose of vicious practices at select Manning Day School." It was comical, actually, the way everybody got all steamed up over the things we knew went on all the time, not only at Manning but in all the other schools in town. Of course, we all knew the rock fights were wrong, but they were more fun than they seemed wrong, so we kept them up. (That time I came home with the mouse under my eye, I didn't get it by falling in the locker room. I just forgot to duck.)

We had a strict set of rules in the fights so that nobody would really get hurt or anything, and so the little guys could get into them too without fear of being killed. All sixty of us, the whole school, were divided into two teams, the Union Army and the Confederates, and after lunch in the cafeteria we'd all get our blue or gray caps and head out into the woods behind the school. The faculty thought we played Kick the Can and never followed us out to check up on us.

Each team had a fort we'd built out of sapling logs—really just pens about waist high. The forts were about two hundred yards apart, invisible to each other through the trees and scrub. You weren't allowed to use rocks any bigger than a hazelnut, and before you pegged one at a guy in the opposite army, you had to go chk, chk with your mouth so the guy would have a chance to find where it was coming from and duck in time. We had scouting parties and assault teams and patrols, and all the rest of the military things we could think up. The object was to storm the enemy's fort and take it before recess was up and we had to quit.

These rock fights weren't like the papers said at all. I remember the Morning Star called them "pitched battles of unrelenting fury, where injuries were frequent." That was silly. If the injuries had been frequent, it wouldn't have been fun any more, and nobody would have wanted to keep doing it. You could get hurt, of course, but you could get hurt a lot worse in a football game with the grandstand full of newspaper reporters and faculty and parents all cheering you on.

Now I guess you know everything that was important before the day Gene Hanlon got killed, and I can tell you how it happened so that you'll know why.

After our last morning class, Peter Irish and I went down to the washroom in the basement to clean up for lunch. All morning Peter had acted funny—silent and sort of tied up inside—and it was worrying me some. At first I thought I had done something he didn't like, but if I had, he'd have told me. He'd hardly said two words all morning, and he had missed two recitations in English that I had coached him on myself. But you couldn't pry trouble out of Peter, so I just kept quiet and waited for him to let me in on it.

While he was washing his hands I had to go into one of the stalls. I went in and shut the door and was hanging up my jacket when I heard somebody else come into the washroom. I don't know why, but I sat down—being real careful not to make any noise.

Somebody said, "Hi, Pete, boy." It was Gene Hanlon, and he was alone for once.

"Hi, Gene." That was Peter. (I am trying to put this down as near as I can just the way they said it.)

"Oh, man!" Gene said. "Today I am exhaust pipe!"

"Tired?"

"You said the word, man. Real beat under." "Why so?"

"Big date last night. Friend of yours, Angela Pine." Just as if that stall door hadn't been there, I could see Gene grinning at Peter and waiting for a rise out of him. Peter didn't say anything, so Gene tried again. "You're pretty sly, Pete." "What do you mean?"

"I mean about Angela. You've done a real fine job of keeping her in drydock all this time."

"She dates other guys," Peter said, sounding like he ought to clear his throat.

"Aaaah. She goes out with those meatballs and then comes home and shakes hands at the door. What kind of a date is that?"

"Well, that's her business."

Gene said, giggling, "I don't know what her business is, but I got a few suggestions for her if she ever asks me."

"What are you getting at?"

"Real coy, boy. She's crazy for it. Just crazy. Real crazy hungry chick, yeah." "Are you through?"

"What? … Oh, sure. Hey! You sore or something?"

Peter said, "It's time for you to go eat lunch." "All right already. Jesus! You don't have to get that way about it. A guy gives you a compliment and you go and get sore. You are an odd ball. You and your screwy horses too. See you around." And Gene went out scuffing his feet along the floor.

When I came out of the stall Peter was hunched stiff-armed over the wash-basin. He didn't even know I was around. I wished right then that I could have gone back and unlived the last five minutes. I wished they had never happened, and that everything was back just the way it was before. I was hurt and mad, and my mind was whirling around full of all the stuff Gene Hanlon had said. Just to be doing something, I got busy combing my hair, wetting and shaking the comb and all, trying to find a way to say what I was feeling. Peter was very busy turning both faucets on and off again in a kind of splashy rhythm.

Finally, I said, "If you believe all that crap, you're pretty silly. That guy's a bragging liar and you know it." Peter looked up at me as though he had just noticed I was there. "I've got to believe it," he said. I jumped on him for that. "Oh, come on," I said. "Give Angela a little credit. She wouldn't give that pile of you-know-what the right time."

Peter was looking down the basin drain. "I called her this morning to say hello. She wouldn't talk to me, Ronnie. She wouldn't even come to the phone."

Now I knew what had been eating him all morning. There wasn't any more a friend could say to Peter, so I made him let go of the faucets and come with me to eat lunch in the cafeteria. All through lunch he just pushed dishes around on his tray and didn't say anything. As we scraped our plates I asked him if he was going out to the fight in the woods, and he surprised me by saying yes, so we got our caps and hiked out to the Confederate fort.

Almost everybody, Gene Hanlon too, was there before us, and they'd already chosen today's generals. Smitty Rice was General of the Armies of the Confederacy, and Gene Hanlon was the Union Commander. Gene took all his boys off to the Union fort to wait for the starting whistle, and Smitty outlined his strategy to us.

There was to be a feint at the south side of the Union fort, and then a noisy second feint from the north to pull the defenders out of position. Then Smitty and Peter Irish were to lead the real massed assault from the south, under the lip of the hill where the first feint had come from. When five minutes had gone by on my watch, we all got up and Smitty blew the starting whistle and we piled out of the fort, leaving only five inside as a garrison, and a couple of alarm guards a little way out on each side of the fort.

I got the job I usually got—advance observation post. I was to note enemy movements and remember concentrations and directions and elapsed times between sightings. Even though you couldn't see more than a hundred feet through the woods, you could always get a fair idea of the enemy strategy by the way they moved their troops around. So all I had to do was stay in one place and watch and listen and remember, and every so often Smitty would send a runner over from field headquarters to check up on what had happened lately. I had three or four good posts picked out where I could hide and not be seen, and I never used the same one twice running.

Today's was my favorite—Baker Post, we called it. It was a dense thicket of young blackjack oak on a low hill on the inside of a bend in the creek, and because nothing grew on the gravel bars of the creek, you could see a long way to each side. The creek ran generally south, cutting the fighting area between the forts right in two, and it made a good defense line because there were only a few places you could cross it in one jump and not get your shoes wet. The east bank of the creek, directly across from Baker Post, is a vertical bluff about ten feet high so that the ground up there is right on eye level with Baker, and the creek and the gravel bars are spread out between you and the bluff bank. I always knew that Baker Post was good, because every time I took it up I had to flush out a covey of quail or a cottontail.

It was always quiet in the woods during the first few minutes of those fights. Even the birds shut up, it seemed like, waiting for the first troop contacts. Out of the corner of my eye I saw somebody jump the creek at the North Ford, and I rolled over to watch. Because of the brush up there I couldn't see who it was, but I knew he was there because once in a while a bush would stir, or his foot would slide a little on the gravel. Pretty soon he came out to the edge of the underbrush and crouched there looking around and listening. It was Gene Hanlon. His eyes crossed right over me, without finding me, and after a minute he came out and ran low along the creek. When he got even with Baker Post, he went down to his knees and began filling his cap with rocks. I had to laugh to myself at how stupid that was. He should have collected his ammunition earlier, when he and his army were on their way over to their fort. He was wasting maneuvering time and exposing himself for no good reason. It makes you feel good when a guy you hate does something dumb like that.

I got ready to go chk, chk with my mouth just to scare him and see him run. But then I looked up at the bluff above him and my heart flopped over inside me. Peter Irish was there, down on one knee, looking over at Gene Hanlon. Gene never looked up. Peter moves like that— floating in and out of the brush as quietly as if he didn't weigh anything. Peter was a good woods fighter.

So instead of going chk, chk I hunkered down lower in my thicket and thought to myself that now it wasn't a game any more. Peter looked a long time over at where I was hiding, then he looked up and down the creek bed, and then he moved back a little from the edge of the bluff. He put all his weight pulling on a half-buried boulder beside him until it turned over in its socket and he could get a good grip on it. Even from where I was I could see the cords come out in his neck when he raised it up in his arms and stood up. I hadn't heard a sound except the creek gurgling a little, and Gene Hanlon scratching around in the gravel. And also the blood roaring in my own ears. Watching this was like being in a movie and seeing the story happen on the screen. Nothing you can do or say will change what is going to happen because it's all there in the unwinding reel.

Peter held the heavy stone like a medicine ball and walked to the edge of the bluff and looked down at Gene Hanlon. Gene had moved a few feet south along the creek, so Peter above him moved south too, until he was even with Gene. Peter made a little grunt when he pushed the rock out and away and it fell. Gene heard the grunt and lifted his head to look up, and the rock hit him full in the face and bent his head away back and made his arms fly out. He sat right down in the water with his red and dirty face turned up to the sky and his hands holding him up behind. Then he got himself up with his head still twisted back like that, so he was looking straight up, and he wandered a little way downstream with the water up to his knees, and then he fell out on a gravel bar on his stomach.

His legs and arms spread out like he was asleep, but his head was up rigid and his mouth was open. I couldn't look any more.

Peter hadn't made a sound leaving, but when I looked up, the bluff above was empty. As soon as I could move without getting sick I faded out of there and went up north a ways to Able Post and lay down in the foxhole there and held myself around the knees and just shook. I couldn't have felt more upset if I had dropped that rock myself. Just like a movie reel had the ends tied together, the whole scene kept rolling over and over in front of my eyes, and I couldn't stop the film or even turn off the light in the projector.

I lay there with my head down waiting for someone to find the body and start hollering. It was little Marvin Herold, Smitty's courier, who started screaming in his high voice, "Safety! … Oh, God! … Safety safety safety! … Help! … Help!" "Safety" was the call we used to stop the fights if anyone saw a master coming or somebody got hurt. I lay there for several minutes listening to guys running past me through the brush heading for Baker Post, then I got up and followed them. I couldn't move very fast because my knees kept trying to bend the wrong way.

When I came out of the brush onto the gravel bank, I was surprised that everything looked so different. When I had left just five minutes before, the whole clearing and the creek were empty and lying bright in the sun, and Gene Hanlon was there all alone on the gravel bar. Now, with all the guys standing around and talking at once with their backs to the body, the whole place was different, and it wasn't so bad being there. I saw little Marvin Herold go over and try to take the pulse of Gene Hanlon's body. Marvin is a Boy Scout with lots of merit badges, and I expected him to try artificial respiration or a tourniquet, but he didn't find any pulse so he stood up and shook his head and wobbled over to where we were. He looked terribly blank, as though the Scout Manual had let him down.

The assumption going around was that Gene had run off the bluff and landed on his head and broken his neck. I couldn't see Peter anywhere, so I finally had to ask Smitty where he was. Smitty said he had sent Peter in to the school to tell somebody what had happened, and to get the ambulance. Smitty was still being the General, I guess, because there was nothing less for him to do. I tried to think to myself what Peter must be feeling like now, sent off to do an errand like that, but I couldn't get anywhere. My head was too full of what I was feeling like, standing with the fellows on the gravel bar looking at Gene Hanlon spread out half in the water like a dropped doll, knowing just how he had gotten there, and not being able to say anything.

Then Smitty got an idea, and he said, "Ronnie, weren't you here at Baker Post all the time?"

I made myself look at him, and then I said, "No, damn it, I got to thinking their army might try a crossing up by Able Post, so I went up there instead."

He said, "Oh," and forgot it.

Not long after, we heard a siren. We all knew what it was, and everybody stopped talking to listen to it as it got nearer. It was the first time I ever heard a siren and knew while hearing it why it had been called, and where it was going. It was kind of creepy, like it was saying to us over the trees, "Wait right there, boys. Don't anybody leave. I'll be there in a minute, and then we'll see just what's going on." I wanted to run and keep on running, until I got away from all the things swarming around inside me. You always wish afterward you had never joggled the wasp ball.

Pretty soon we heard somebody moving in the woods on the bluff and then two big men in white pants, carrying a folded-up stretcher, and another man in a suit, carrying a black bag, came out to the lip of the bluff. They stood there looking at us a minute without saying anything until one of the stretcher-bearers saw Gene Hanlon lying there all alone on the gravel bar. The man said something to the other two, and they all three looked where he pointed. Then the doctor looked at us all bunched up where we were and said, "Well, how do we get down?" He sounded sore. None of us moved or said anything, and in a minute the doctor got tired of waiting and blasted us. "Wake up over there! How do we go to get down?" Smitty came unstuck and gave them directions, and they went back into the bush heading north.

From then on things got pretty crowded in the woods. Two uni-formed policemen and a photographer and a plain-clothes man showed up, and then Peter Irish came back leading almost the whole school fac-ulty, and later a reporter and another photographer arrived. Nobody paid any attention to us for a while, so we just sat there in a clump, not moving or saying much. I managed to get right in the middle, and I kept down, hiding behind the guys around me and looking between them to see what was going on. After the police photographer was through taking pictures of Gene Hanlon from all sides, the two ambulance men raised him onto the stretcher and covered him with a piece of canvas or something and carried him away. The photographer took pictures all around by the creek and then went up onto the bluff and took pictures of the ground up there too. The plain-clothes man poking around on the gravel bar found Gene Hanlon's blue cap half full of rocks and gave it, with the rocks still in it, to one of the policemen to save.

I finally got up nerve enough to look for Peter Irish. He was stand-ing with Smitty and Mr. Kelly, the math teacher, and they were talking. Peter didn't look any different. I didn't see how he could do it. I mean, stand right out there in plain sight of everyone, looking natural, with all that in his head. He looked around slowly as though he felt me watching him, and he found me there in the middle of the bunch. I couldn't have looked away if I had tried. He gave me a little smile, and I nodded my head to show him I'd seen it, then he went back to his talking with the other two.

Then the plain-clothes man went over to the three of them, and I got all wild inside and wanted to jump up and say that Peter couldn't possibly have done it, so please go away and let him alone. I could see the plain-clothes man doing most of the talking, and Peter and Smitty say-ing something once in a while, as though they were answering questions.

After a little the plain-clothes man stopped talking and nodded, and the other three nodded back, and then he led them over to where the rest of us were. Smitty and Peter sat down with us and Mr. Kelly collected all the other faculty men and brought them over.

The plain-clothes man tipped his hat back and put his hands in his pockets and said, "My name is Gorman. Sergeant Gorman. We know all about the rock fight now, so don't get nervous that you'll let on something that'll get you into trouble. You're already in trouble, but that's not my business. You can settle that with your instructors and your parents. Uh … you might think some about this, though. It's my feeling that every one of you here has a share in the responsibility for this boy's death. You all know rock fighting is dangerous, but you went ahead and did it anyway. But that's not what I'm after right now. I want to know if any of you boys actually saw this (what's his name?), this Hanlon boy run over the bluff." I was looking straight at Sergeant Gorman, but in the side of my eye I saw Peter Irish turn his head around and look at me. I didn't peep.

Then Sergeant Gorman said, "Which one of you is Ronnie Quiller?" I almost fainted.

Somebody poked me and I said, "Me." It didn't sound like my voice at all.

Sergeant Gorman said, "Which?" I said, "Me," again.

This time he found me and said, "Weren't you supposed to be lying there in this thicket all the time?"

"Yes," I said. All the kids were looking at me. "But there wasn't anything doing here so I moved up there a ways."

"I see," he said. "Do you always disobey orders?"

"No," I said, "but after all, it was only a game."

"Some game," said Sergeant Gorman. "Good clean fun."

Then he let me alone. There was only one person there who knew I would never have deserted the post assigned to me. That was Peter Irish. I guess, Dad, that's when I began to get really scared. The worst of it was not knowing how much Peter knew, and not daring to ask. He might have been waiting out of sight in the brush after he dropped that rock, and seen me take out for Able Post. I had always been his friend, but what was I now to him? I wanted to tell him everything was okay and I wouldn't for the world squeal on him, but that would have told him I knew he did it. Maybe he knew without my telling him. I didn't know what to do.

Sergeant Gorman finished up, "Let's all go back to the school now.

I want to talk to each of you alone." We all got up and started back through the woods in a bunch. I figured Peter would think it was funny if I avoided him, so I walked with him.

I said, "Lousy damn day." He said, "Real lousy."

I said, "It seems like a hundred years since lunch."

We didn't say any more all the way back. It took all afternoon to get the individual interviews over. They took us from Assembly Hall in alphabetical order, and we had to go in and sit across from Sergeant Gorman while he asked the questions. He must have asked us all the same questions because by the time he got to me he was saying the words like they were tired. A girl stenographer sat by him and took down the answers. "Name?" "Ronnie Quiller." I had to spell it.

"Were you at the rock fight this afternoon?" "Yes, I was."

"What side were you on?" "The Confederates."

"What were you supposed to do?" "Watch the guys on the other side." "After this whistle, did you see anyone?" "No."

"You sure?"

"No, I didn't. That's why I moved from Baker Post up to Able Post. There wasn't anything doing where I was hiding."

"In rock fights before, have you ever changed position without telling somebody?"

"Sure, I guess. You can't run clear back to the field headquarters to tell anyone anything. It's up to them to find you."

Sergeant Gorman squinted at me with his eyebrows pulled down. "You know that if you had stayed where you were supposed to be you would have seen him fall over that bluff there?" "Yes," I said.

"I wish you had."

Afterwards I ran into Smitty out in the hall and I asked him why all this fuss with the police and all. I asked him who called them.

"It was Peter, I think. He told Mr. Kelly to, and Mr. Kelly did."

"What do you suppose they're after?" I asked Smitty.

"Oh, I guess they're trying to get a straight story to tell Gene's parents and the newspapers. From what I get from Mr. Kelly, the school is all for it. They want everybody to know they weren't responsible."

"Do you think Gene fell over that bluff?" I couldn't help asking that one.

"I don't know. I suppose so." He cocked his head to one side and grinned a little at me. "Like they say in the papers, 'fell or was pushed,' huh?"

I said, "I guess nobody'd have nerve enough to do that to Gene—push him, I mean." All of a sudden I was thinking about something I had seen. Going back in my mind I remembered seeing Sergeant Gorman pick up Gene's cap half full of rocks. Gravel rocks taken from the low bank of the creek. Now, I figured that Sergeant Gorman wouldn't have been a sergeant if he was stupid, and unless he was stupid he wouldn't go on for long thinking that Gene had fallen from above—when the cap half full of rocks said he'd been down below all the time!

I got my bike and rode home the long way to give me time to think about Peter and what he had done, and what I should do. You were real swell that night, and I guess I should have told you the whole story right then, but I just couldn't. I put myself in Peter's place, and I knew he would never have told on me. That's the way he was. He hated squealers. I couldn't think about his ever learning I had squealed on him. That would put me right alongside Angela Pine in his book. To him, I would have been the second person he trusted who let him down.

I felt like a rat in a cage with no place to go and no way out. When you kept me home nights after that, I didn't mind, because I wouldn't have gone out after dark if I'd been paid to. I don't blame you and Mother for thinking I had gone loony over the whole thing. Every noon recess for two whole weeks they pulled us into Assembly Hall and one of the masters would give a speech about group responsibility or public conscience or something awful like that, and then, worst of all, they made us bow our heads for five minutes in memory of Gene Hanlon. And there I'd be, sitting next to Peter Irish on the Assembly Hall bench, thinking back to the day of the last rock fight, and how Peter had looked up there on the bluff with the cords of his neck pulled tight, holding that big rock like it was a medicine ball. I had the crawliest feeling that if anybody in the hall had raised up his head and looked over at us together there on the bench, he would have seen two great fiery arrows pointing down at us. I was always afraid even to look up myself for fear I would have seen my own arrow and passed out on the spot.

It was my nightmares that got you worried, I guess. They always started out with Peter and me on a hike on a dusty country road. It was so hot you could hardly breathe. We would walk along without saying anything, with me lagging a little behind Peter so I could always keep an eye on him. And then the road would come out on the football field there at school, and he would go over to the woodpile and pick up a thin log and hold it in one hand, beckoning to me with the other and smiling. "Let's go over to the drugstore," he'd say, and then I'd start running.

I would follow the quarter-mile track around the football field and I'd know that everything would be all right if I could only get around it four times for a full mile. Every time I turned around to look, there he'd be right behind me, carrying that log and running easily, just like he used to pace me when I was out for the 880. I would make the first quarter mile all right, but then my wind would give out and my throat would dry up and my legs would get heavy, and I'd know that Peter was about to catch me, and I'd never make that full mile.

Then I would jar awake and be sweating and hanging on tight to the mattress, and in a minute you'd come in to see why I'd screamed. Your face was always kind of sad over me, and there in my bed in the dark, with you standing beside, I would almost let go and tell you why things were so bad with me. But then as I'd come awake, and the hammering in my heart would slow up, and the sweat would begin to dry, all the things I owed Peter Irish would stand out again and look at me, and I would know that I could never tell you about it until my telling could no longer get Peter Irish into trouble.

I'm tired now, Dad—tired in so many ways and in so many places that I don't know where to begin resting. This letter took all night, as I thought it would. It's beginning to get light outside and the birds are starting up. I just reread the story in the paper where it says that Sergeant Gorman knew all along that Gene Hanlon had been murdered. I told you he wasn't stupid. He knew what that cap half full of rocks meant, and he knew what it meant to find a big damp socket in the earth on top of the bluff, and the rock which had been in the socket down below in the creek. And after he had talked to each of us alphabetically there in the school office, he knew the name of the only boy in school strong enough to lift up a seventy-pound rock and throw it like a medicine ball. He knew all of these things before the sun went down on the day of the last rock fight, but he was two months putting the rest of the story together so he could use it in his business.

As I read it in the paper, Sergeant Gorman went over to Peter's house last Monday and talked to him about the things he had learned, and Peter listened respectfully, and then, when Sergeant Gorman was through and was ready to take Peter along with him, Peter excused himself to go upstairs and get his toilet articles. He got his four-ten shotgun instead and shot himself. I suppose it was the same four-ten he and I hunted squirrels with.

There's only one good thing about this whole stinking lousy mess, Dad. Because Sergeant Gorman talked to Peter and Peter listened, there in the living room; when Peter Irish climbed up those stairs he did it knowing that I, Ronnie Quiller, had not squealed on him. That may have made it easier. I don't know.

Now please, Dad—please may I come home again?

RONNIE

EDITORS' COMMENTARY

DIAGNOSIS: Post-traumatic stress syndrome—severe anxiety reaction to a traumatic life event.

This story deals with the severe problems brought about by clashing feelings of loyalty and guilt. Ronnie was fully aware of the guilt of concealment he shared with Peter. Ronnie's conscience immobilized him. He was torn between society's demand to report a homicide to the authorities and his loyalty to his friend. Peter had many times protected Ronnie from the cruelty and bullying by other boys, particularly the star bully, Gene Hanlon. Ronnie's guilt was of shared hostility as well as concealment. Like Peter, he hated Gene Hanlon and at times may have wished the aggression that Peter acted out.

In the adolescent struggle for identity, Peter and Ronnie made up one whole person: Each compensated for the other's weaknesses and for using the other's strength. "We swapped talents," Ronnie said. Ronnie is the intellectual performer, and considers himself a natural scapegoat. With gratitude and respect, he sees Peter as the physical performer. Ronnie sensed that he must not, under any circumstance, betray his friend. His emotions were complicated by his partial hostility and jealousy toward Angela.

As a sensitive student, Ronnie was aware that Peter must be protected not only from the police or another betrayer, but also from knowing that he, Ronnie, knew of the crime. Thus, Ronnie felt trapped—"like a rat in a cage." His overt symptoms were deep depression, nightmares, sweating, and inability to be with his friends.

His letter, written to his trusted father as soon as the crime was exposed (without his having participated in its exposure), released him from his anxiety reaction. He was able to see his own part in the drama and to evaluate it realistically, and without blame. His trust in his father's ability to listen to him sympathetically indicates that Ronnie had a sound relationship and the capacity to overcome this incident.

As educators, there are several important psychological concepts to learn from this story. Never underestimate the power of peer loyalty. In our society we are taught to be loyal to our country, religion, family, friends, political parties, athletic teams, and even TV shows. Loyalty to our beliefs, people, and organizations is the interpersonal glue that holds our society together. However, there are degrees of loyalties. There are some loyalties we will stand up to protect and some loyalties we will die for. There are loyalties based on respect and loyalties based on fear.

Loyalty Based on Respect

Ronnie's loyalty to Peter is based on respect. This relationship is so important to Peter that he is willing to suffer psychologically for this friendship. It also represents the highest form of loyalty since Peter is unaware that Ronnie knows about the murder. Ronnie will protect Peter even under stressful confrontation. Ronnie will not rat, squeal, or be disloyal to Peter.

There are adolescent students in your classroom who belong to—and are loyal to—groups or gangs. No amount of adult pressure will change their loyalty to their friends. This is why any attempt to threaten and punish these students is ineffective. Instead, our approach to is acknowledge the importance of peer loyalty and in the process begin to establish a trusting relationship with troubled students so incidents can be examined and managed rationally. The establishment of a meaningful relationship with troubled students is central piece of our approach to helping. This is the reason why all of Chapter 2 is dedicated to this one significant concept of how to establish a trusting relationship with a troubled student.

Loyalty Based on Fear

Some parents tell their children never to reveal any family secrets. The children are told to be loyal to their family or face the wrath of their parents. They are made to promise never to mention, describe, or talk about any alcohol, drug, physical, or sexual abuse they witness in their family. The pressure of secrecy can become so intense that these children become depressed, anxious, and withdrawn. At times they are so angry at their parents and so overwhelmed psychologically that they come to school emotionally loaded and displace their feelings on their teachers and classmates. When crises occurs over insignificant school issues, the teachers find it hard to understand the students' explosive behaviors. We have identified this self-defeating pattern of behavior a Red Flag Reclaiming Interview. Chapter 8 describes the skills you need to learn to manage this type of student crisis.

Gene Hamlon also represents a classic picture of the school bully. Over the past decade, bullying of peers has become a national issue, and many principals have taken steps to "bullyproof" their school. We believe the long-term effects of being bullied are more emotionally damaging than anyone knew. A recent study found that 47% of sixth graders reported they were bullied at least once during a 5-day school week. As a result, we have included an article on understanding and managing a school bully in Chapter 6.

SOME REASONS WHY IT FEELS THE WAY IT DOES (ECONOMIC, RACIAL, AND ETHNIC CLASS DIFFERENCES)

THE next excerpt is a powerful example of impulsive group behavior and the different roles students play in a group. E. R. Braithwaite is a Black, Oxford-trained engineer. He cannot find a job and ends up teaching in the poorest slums in London with students who have been rejected by other schools. Braithwaite's understanding of group dynamics teaching is impressive.

ARTICLE 1.3

TO SIR, WITH LOVE
E. R. Braithwaite

Just about this time a new supply teacher, Mr. Bell, was sent to our school as supernumerary to the Staff for a few weeks. He was about forty years old, a tall, wiry man, who had some previous experience with the Army Education Service. It was arranged that he should act as relief teacher for some lessons, including two periods of P.T. with the senior boys. One of Mr. Bell's hobbies was fencing: he was something of a perfectionist and impatient of anyone whose co-ordination was not as smooth and controlled as his own. He would repeat a P.T. movement or exercise over and over again until it was executed with clockwork precision, and though the boys grumbled against his discipline they seemed eager to prove to him that they were quite capable of doing any exercise he could devise, and with a skill that very nearly matched his own.

This was especially true in the cases of Ingham, Fernman and Seales, who would always place themselves at the head of the line as an example and encouragement to the others. The least athletic of these was Richard Buckley, a short, fat boy, amiable and rather dim, who could read and write after a fashion, and could never be provoked to any semblance of anger or heat. He was pleasant and jolly and a favorite with the others, who, though they themselves chivvied him unmercifully, were ever ready in his defense against outsiders. Buckley was no good at P.T. or games; he just was not built for such pursuits. Yet, such is the perversity of human nature, he strenuously resisted any efforts to leave him out or overlook him when games were being arranged. His attempts at accomplishing such simple gymnastic performances as the "forward roll" and "star jump" reduced the rest of the P.T. class to helpless hilarity, but he persisted with a singleness of purpose which, though unproductive, was nothing short of heroic.

Buckley was Bell's special whipping boy. Fully aware of the lad's physical limitations, he would encourage him to try other and more difficult exercises, with apparently the sole purpose of obtaining some amusement from the pitiably ridiculous results. Sometimes the rest of the class would protest; and then Bell would turn on them the full flood of his invective. The boys mentioned this in their "Weekly Review," and Mr. Florian decided to discuss it at a Staff Meeting.

"The boys seem to be a bit bothered by remarks you make to them during P.T., Mr. Bell."

"To which remarks do you refer, Mr. Florian?" Bell never used the term "Sir," seeming to think it "infra dig." Even when he granted him the "Mr. Florian," he gave to this form of address the suggestion of a sneer.

"From their review it would seem that you are unnecessarily critical of their persons."

"Do you mean their smell?"

"Well, yes, that and the state of their clothing."

"I've advised them to wash."

"These are the words which appear in one review." The Headmaster produced a notebook, Fernman's, and read:

"Some of you stink like old garbage." His tone was cool, detached, judicial.

"I was referring to their feet. Many of them never seem to wash their feet, and when they take their shoes off the stink is dreadful."

"Many of them live in homes where there are very few facilities for washing, Mr. Bell."

"Surely enough water is available for washing their feet if they really wanted to."

"Then they'd put on the same smelly socks and shoes to which you also object."

"I've got to be in contact with them and it isn't very pleasant."

"Have you ever lived in this area, Mr. Bell?"

"No, sir."

"Then you know nothing about the conditions prevailing. The water you so casually speak of is more often to be found in the walls and on the floors than in the convenient wash basin or bath to which you are accustomed. I've visited homes of some of these children where water for a family in an upstairs flat had to be fetched by bucket or pail from the single back-yard tap which served five or six families. You may see, therefore, that so elementary a function as washing the feet might present many difficulties." Bell was silent at this.

"I've no wish to interfere, or tell you how to do your work; you're an experienced teacher and know more about P.T. than I ever will,"—the Old Man was again patient, encouraging—"but try to be a little more understanding about their difficulties." He then turned to other matters, but it was clear that Bell was considerably put out by the rebuke.

Matters came to a head that Monday afternoon. I was not present in the gym, but was able to reconstruct the sequence of events with reasonable accuracy from the boys' reports and Bell's subsequent admissions.

During the P.T. session he had been putting them through their paces in the "astride vault" over the buck, all except Buckley, who was somewhat under the weather and wisely stood down from attempting the rather difficult jump, but without reference to or permission from Bell, who was not long in discovering the absence of his favorite diversion.

"Buckley," he roared. "Yes, Sir."

"Come on, boy, I'm waiting." He was standing in his usual position beside the buck in readiness to arrest the fall of any lad who might be thrown off balance by an awkward approach or incorrect execution of the movement. But the boy did not move, and the master stared at him amazed and angry at this unexpected show of defiance by the one generally considered to be the most timid and tractable in the whole class.

"Fatty can't do it, Sir, it's too high for him," Denham interposed.

"Shut up, Denham," Bell roared. "If I want your opinion I will ask for it." He left his station by the buck and walked to where Buckley was standing. The boy watched his threatening approach, fear apparent in his eyes.

"Well, Buckley," Bell towered over the unhappy youth, "are you going to do as you're told?"

"Yes, Sir," Buckley's capitulation was as sudden as his refusal.

The others stopped to watch as he stood looking at the buck, licking his lips nervously while waiting for the instructor to resume his position. It may have been fear or determination or a combination of both, but Buckley launched himself at the buck in furious assault, and in spite of Bell's restraining arms, boy and buck crashed on the floor with a sickening sound as one leg of the buck snapped off with the sound of a pistol shot. The class stood in shocked silence watching Buckley, who remained as he fell, inert and pale; then they rushed to his assistance. All except Potter; big, good-natured Potter seemed to have lost his reason. He snatched up the broken metal-bound leg and advanced on Bell, screaming:

"You bloody bastard, you fucking bloody bastard."

"Put that thing down, Potter, don't be a fool," Bell spluttered, backing away from the hysterical boy.

"You made him do it; he didn't want to and you made him," Potter yelled.

"Don't be a fool, Potter, put it down," Bell appealed.

"I'll do you in, you bloody murderer." Bell was big, but in his anger Potter seemed bigger, his improvised club a fearsome extension of his thick forearm.

That was where I rushed in. Tich Jackson, frightened by the sight of Buckley, limp and white on the floor, and the enraged Potter, slobbering at the instructor in murderous fury, had dashed upstairs to my classroom shouting: "Sir, quick, they're fighting in the gym." I followed his disappearing figure in time to see Bell backed against a wall, with Potter advancing on him.

"Hold it, Potter," I called. He turned at the sound of my voice and I quickly placed myself between them.

"Let's have that, Potter." I held out my hand towards the boy, but he stared past me at Bell, whimpering in his emotion. Anger had completely taken hold of him, and he looked very dangerous.

"Come on, Potter," I repeated, "hand it over and go lend a hand with Buckley."

He turned to look towards his prostrate friend and I quickly moved up to him and seized the improvised club; he released it to me without any resistance and went back to join the group around Buckley. Bell then walked away and out of the room, and I went up to the boys. Denham rose and faced me, his face white with rage.

"Potts should have done the bastard like he did Fatty, just 'cos he wouldn't do the bloody jump."

I let that pass; they were angry and at such times quickly reverted to the old things, the words, the discourtesies. I stooped down beside Buckley, who was now sitting weakly on the floor, supported by Sapiano and Seales, and smiling up at them as if ashamed of himself for having been the cause of so much fuss.

"How do you feel, old man?" I inquired.

"Cor, Sir," he cried, smiling, "me tum does hurt."

"He fell on the buck. You should have seem 'im, Sir."

"Gosh, you should've heard the noise when the leg smashed."

"Mr. Bell couldn't catch Fatty, Sir, you should've seen him."

Most of them were trying to talk all at once, eager to give me all the details.

"Bleeding bully, always picking on Fats." This from Sapiano, whose volatile Maltese temperament was inclined to flare up very easily.

"If I'd had the wood I'd have done the fucker in and no bleeding body would have stopped me." Denham was aching for trouble and didn't care who knew it. Bell had slipped away unharmed after hurting his friend, and Denham wanted a substitute. But I would not look at him, or even hear the things he said. Besides, I liked Denham; in spite of his rough manner and speech he was an honest, dependable person with a strong sense of independence.

"Can you stand up, Buckley?"

With some assistance from Seales and Sapiano the boy got to his feet; he looked very pale and unsteady. I turned to Denham: "Will you help the others take Buckley up to Mrs. Dale-Evans and ask her to give him some sweet tea; leave him there and I'll meet you all in the classroom in a few minutes."

Without waiting for his reply I hurried off to the staffroom in search of Bell.

I was in something of a quandary. I knew that it was quite possible Buckley was all right, but there was no knowing whether he had sustained any internal injury not yet apparent. The Council's rules required that all accidents be reported and logged; the Headmaster should be informed forthwith, and in the light of what he had said to Bell so very recently, there would most certainly be a row.

I went up to the staffroom and found Bell washing his face at the sink.

"I've sent Buckley upstairs for a cup of tea," I said. "I suppose he'll be all right, anyway he was walking under his own steam."

"What happens now?" His voice was querulous.

"You should know as well as I do," I replied. "Shouldn't you see the Old Man and make some kind of report?"

"Yes, I suppose I'd better get over to his office right away. I should have attended to the Buckley boy, but the other one rushed me. Thanks for helping out."

"Oh, that's all right," I replied. "But why did you insist on the boy doing the vault?"

"I had to, don't you see; he just stood there refusing to obey and the others were watching me; I just had to do something." His whole attitude now was defensive.

"I'm not criticizing you, Mr. Bell, just asking. Buckley's a bit of a mascot with the others, you know, and I suppose that is why Potter got out of hand."

"I guess it was the way he jumped or something, but I couldn't grab him. He hit the buck too low and sent it flying."

"He's a bit awkward, isn't he; anyway I'm sure the Old Man will understand how it happened."

"He might be a bit difficult, especially after what he said the other day."

"Not necessarily. After all, it was an accident and thank Heaven it's not very serious."

He dried his hands and moved towards the door. "I suppose they'll really go to town on this in their weekly reviews," he remarked.

"I'll ask the boys to say nothing about it. I don't suppose Potter is now feeling any too pleased with himself at his conduct."

As he left Clinty came into the staffroom. "What's happening, Rick?" she asked. "I just saw some of your boys taking Fatty Buckley upstairs.

What's happened to him?"

I told her about the incident and added: "Bell has just gone to the Old Man's office to report the matter."

"Well, what do you know?" she chuckled.

"Fancy Potter going for Bell like that. I always thought that boy a bit of a softie, but you never know with those quiet ones, do you?"

"He was not the only one. Sapiano and Denham were just as wild, I think, but they were too busy fussing over Buckley to bother with Bell."

"He is a bit of a tyro, isn't he. This might make him take it a bit easier."

"I don't think the boys mind his being strict during P.T. It's just that Buckley's a bit of a fool and they resented his being hurt. If it had been Denham or someone like that, I'm sure they would have done nothing."

"Yes, I guess you're right. Bell is a good teacher. I wonder how long the Divisional Office will let him stay here. I hope he hasn't had too much of a fright."

"Oh, he'll get over that. Now I must go and have a word with my boys."

I left her. For some inexplicable reason I felt nervous about being alone with Clinty; I felt that there was something she wanted to say to me, and for my part I did not want to hear it.

In the classroom the boys were sitting closely grouped together, looking rather sheepish. I knew they were feeling aggrieved and, according to their lights, justifiably so; but nevertheless the matter of Potter's behavior had to be dealt with. "How's Buckley?" I asked.

"We left him upstairs with Mrs. Dale-Evans, Sir. He didn't want to stay, he kept saying he was all right. But she told him if he wasn't quiet she'd give him some castor oil, Sir. Ugh!" They all managed a smile at Seales' remark.

"Good," I replied. "I expect he'll be quite all right. But there is something I want to say to you about this unfortunate incident." I sat down on the edge of Fernman's desk.

"Potter, there is nothing I can think of which can excuse your shocking conduct in the gym."

Potter's mouth fell open; he looked at me in surprise, gulped a few times and stammered:

"But it was him, Sir, Mr. Bell, making Fatty fall and that." His voice was shrill with outrage at my remark.

"Mr. Bell was the master there, Potter, and anything that happened in the gym was his responsibility. Buckley's mishap was no excuse for you to make such an attack on your teacher."

"But Fatty told him he couldn't do it, Sir, and he made him, he made him, Sir."

Potter was very near tears. His distress was greater because of what he believed was the further injustice of my censure. The others, too, were looking at me with the same expression.

"That may be, Potter. I am not now concerned with Mr. Bell's conduct, but with yours. You came very near to getting yourself into very serious trouble because you were unable to control your temper. Not only was your language foul and disgusting, but you armed yourself with a weapon big enough and heavy enough to cause very serious harm. What do you think would have happened if everyone had behaved like you and had all turned on Mr. Bell like a pack of mad wolves?" I waited for this to sink in a bit, but Potter interjected:

"I thought he had done Fatty in, Sir, he looked all huddled up like, Sir."

"I see. So you didn't wait to find out but rushed in with your club like a hoodlum to smash and kill, is that it? Your friend was hurt and you wanted to hurt back; suppose instead of a piece of wood it had been a knife, or a gun, what then?" Potter was pale, and he was not the only one.

"Potts didn't think. He was naked, we was all naked, seeing Fatty on the deck. I wasn't half bleeding wild myself."

"You're missing the point, Denham. I think you're all missing the point. We sit in this classroom day after day and talk of things, and you all know what's expected of you; but at the first sign of bother you forget it all. In two weeks you'll all be at work and lots of things will happen which will annoy you, make you wild. Are you going to resort to clubs and knives every time you're upset or angered?" I stood up. "You'll meet foremen or supervisors or workmates who'll do things to upset you, sometimes deliberately. What then, Denham? What about that, Potter? Your Headmaster is under fire from many quarters because he believes in you—because he really believes that by the time you leave here you will have learned to exercise a little self-control at the times when it is most needed. His success or failure will be reflected in the way you conduct yourselves after you leave him. If today's effort is an example of your future behavior I hold out very little hope for you."

At this moment Buckley walked in, smiling broadly and seemingly none the worse for wear. I waited until he was seated then went on:

"I've no wish to belabor this matter, but it cannot be left like this. Potter, you were very discourteous to your P.T. instructor, and it is my opinion that you owe him an apology." Potter stared at me, his mouth open in amazement at my remark; but before he could speak Denham leapt to his feet.

"Apologize?" His voice was loud in anger. "Why should Potts apologize? He didn't do him any harm. Why should he apologize to him just because he's a bleeding teacher?" He stood there, legs slightly apart, heavy-shouldered and truculent, glaring at me. The others were watching us, but agreeing with him; I could feel their resentment hardening.

"Please sit down Denham, and remember that in this class we are always able to discuss things, no matter how difficult or unpleasant, without shouting at each other."

I waited, fearful of this unexpected threat to our pleasant relationship; he looked around at his colleagues indecisively, then abruptly sat down. I continued, in a very friendly tone:

"That was a fair question, Denham, although you will agree it was put a little, shall we say, indelicately?"

I smiled as I said this, and, in spite of his anger, Denham smiled briefly too. I went on:

"Potter, are you quite pleased and satisfied with the way you behaved to your P.T. teacher?"

Potter looked at me for a moment, then murmured, "No, Sir."

"But he couldn't help it," Denham interjected.

"That may be so, Denham, but Potter agrees that his own actions were unsatisfactory; upon reflection he himself is not pleased with what he did."

"How's about Mr. Bell then: How's about him apologizing to Buckley?" Denham was not to be dissuaded from his attitude.

"Yes, how about him?" echoed Sapiano.

"My business is with you, not with Mr. Bell," I replied.

This was not going to be easy, I thought. Denham was getting a bit nasty; the usual "Sir" had disappeared from his remarks, and Sapiano was following suit.

"It's easy for you to talk, Sir, nobody tries to push you around." Seales' voice was clear and calm, and the others turned to look at him, to support him. His question touched something deep inside of me, something which had been dormant for months, but now awoke to quick, painful remembering. Without realizing what I was doing I got up and walked to where he sat and stood beside his desk.

"I've been pushed around, Seales," I said quietly, "in a way I cannot explain to you. I've been pushed around until I began to hate people so much that I wanted to hurt them, really hurt them. I know how it feels, believe me, and one thing I learned, Seales, is to try always to be a bit bigger than the people who hurt me. It is easy to reach for a knife or a gun; but then you become merely a tool and the knife or gun takes over, thereby creating new and bigger problems without solving a thing. So what happens when there is no weapon handy?"

I felt suddenly annoyed with myself for giving way to my emotion, and abruptly walked back to my desk. The class seemed to feel that something had touched me deeply and were immediately sympathetic in their manner.

"The point I want to make, Potter," I continued, "is whether you are really growing up and learning to stand squarely on your own feet. When you begin work at Covent Garden you might someday have cause to be very angry; what will you do then? The whole idea of this school is to teach you to discipline yourself. In this instance you lost your temper and behaved badly to your teacher. Do you think you are big enough to make an apology to him?"

Potter fidgeted in his seat and looked uncertainly at me, then replied: "Yes, Sir."

"It's always difficult to apologize, Potter, especially to someone you feel justified in disliking. But remember that you are not doing it for Mr. Bell's sake, but your own."

I sat down. They were silent, but I realized that they understood what I meant. Potter stood up:

"Is he in the staffroom, Sir?"

"I think he should be there now, Potter."

Denham and Seales stood and joined Potter and together they went to find Bell. I called Buckley.

"How are you feeling, Buckley?"

"Okay, Sir," he replied, as jovial as ever.

"What will your parents say about all this Buckley?" I was being devious but, I thought, necessarily so.

"I shan't tell 'em, Sir. Must I, Sir."

"It's up to you, Buckley. If you feel fine there's no need to bother; but if in the next few days or weeks you feel any pain, it would be best to mention it so that they'd know what to do."

In a few minutes the boys were back, Potter looking red and embarrassed; behind them came Mr. Bell.

"May I speak to your boys for a moment, Mr. Braithwaite?" He came in and stood beside my desk and I nodded to him.

"I want to say to all of you," he began, "that I'm sorry about what happened in the gym a little while ago. I think that one way or another we were all a bit silly, but the sooner we forget the whole thing, the better."

"How're you feeling now, boy?" He addressed himself to Buckley.

"Okay, Sir," the boy replied.

"Fine. Well, I suppose we'll see each other as usual next week." And with that he was gone, having made as friendly a gesture as his evident nervousness would allow.

The boys seemed not unwilling to let the matter drop, so we turned our attention to the discussion of other things.

EDITORS' COMMENTARY

DIAGNOSIS: Impulse breakthrough—group acting-out by a socially and economically deprived student.

In this story, the behavior of Potter was clearly provoked. Potter's anger was aroused by his sense of injustice. Troubled students are committed to justice—even though their definitions at times may not coincide with society's. The crucial factor in Potter's case was not his anger but the way he handled his anger. Potter's anger turned into an overwhelming rage reaction and lead to his violent behavior.

Braithwaite is careful to make this point to the students as he details the precarious life ahead for students who are at the mercy of rage instead of being its master. His handling of the problem in this group of students, where all could hear and express themselves, displays the kind of skill that comes from psychological understanding. As a group leader, Braithwaite's revelation of his own deep personal feeling communicated real emotional understanding far more powerfully than intellectual reasoning. This feeling, more than the proper words, got across to the students. Students, even troubled ones, respond to genuineness. In many cases, the more troubled the student, the more therapeutic a teacher's genuine feelings can be, provided they are not overexploited or used to gain personal sympathy.

This selection also highlights the concept of group contagion among students. We believe teachers have been denied the essential concepts of group dynamics and management. It is ironic that classroom teachers primarily are group teachers, but all of their instructional training assumes they function on an individual basis. To compensate for this oversight on the part of teacher trainers, all of Chapter 5 is dedicated to presenting the essential skills teachers need to understand and manage group behavior in the classroom.

ARTICLE 1.4

THIS next excerpt highlights the teacher's lack of muticultural awareness, overinvolvement with a student, and unawareness of her own covert sexual messages.

DOCTOR JACK-O'-LANTERN
Richard Yates

All Miss Price had been told about the new boy was that he'd spent most of his life in some kind of orphanage, and that the gray-haired "aunt and uncle" with whom he now lived were really foster parents, paid by the Welfare Department of the City of New York. A less dedicated or less imaginative teacher might have pressed for more details, but Miss Price was content with the rough outline. It was enough, in fact, to fill her with a sense of mission that shone from her eyes, as plain as love, from the first morning he joined the fourth grade.

From *Eleven Kinds of Loneliness* by Richard Yates. Copyright 1961 by Richard Yates. Reprinted with permission of Monica McCall—International Famous Agency.

He arrived early and sat in the back row—his spine very straight, his ankles crossed precisely under the desk and his hands folded on the very center of its top, as if symmetry might make him less conspicuous—and while the other children were filing in and settling down, he received a long, expressionless stare from each of them.

"We have a new classmate this morning," Miss Price said, laboring the obvious in a way that made everybody want to giggle. "His name is Vincent Sabella and he comes from New York City. I know we'll all do our best to make him feel at home."

This time they all swung around to stare at once, which caused him to duck his head slightly and shift his weight from one buttock to the other. Ordinarily, the fact of someone's coming from New York might have held a certain prestige, for to most of the children the city was an awesome, adult place that swallowed up their fathers every day, and which they themselves were permitted to visit only rarely, in their best clothes, as a treat. But anyone could see at a glance that Vincent Sabella had nothing whatever to do with skyscrapers. Even if you could ignore his tangled black hair and gray skin, his clothes would have given him away: absurdly new corduroys, absurdly old sneakers and a yellow sweatshirt, much too small, with the shredded remains of a Mickey Mouse design stamped on its chest. Clearly, he was from the part of New York that you had to pass through on the train to Grand Central—the part where people hung bedding over their windowsill and leaned out on it all day in a trance of boredom, and where you got vistas of straight, deep streets, one after another, all alike in the clutter of their sidewalks and all swarming with gray boys at play in some desperate kind of ball game.

The girls decided that he wasn't very nice and turned away, but the boys lingered in their scrutiny, looking him up and down with faint smiles. This was the kind of kid they were accustomed to thinking of as "tough," the kind whose stares had made all of them uncomfortable at one time or another in unfamiliar neighborhoods; here was a unique chance for retaliation.

"What would you like us to call you, Vincent?" Miss Price inquired. "I mean, do you prefer Vincent, or Vince, or—or what?" (It was purely an academic question; even Miss Price knew that the boys would call him "Sabella" and that the girls wouldn't call him anything at all.)

"Vinny's okay," he said in a strange, croaking voice that had evidently yelled itself hoarse down the ugly streets of his home.

"I'm afraid I didn't hear you," she said, craning her pretty head forward and to one side so that a heavy lock of hair swung free of one shoulder. "Did you say 'Vince'?"

"Vinny, I said," he said again, squirming. "Vincent, is it? All right then, Vincent." A few of the class giggled, but nobody bothered to correct her; it would be more fun to let the mistake continue.

"I won't take time to introduce you to everyone by name, Vincent," Miss Price went on, "because I think it would be simpler just to let you learn the names as we go along, don't you? Now, we won't expect you to take any real part in the work for the first day or so; just take your time, and if there's anything you don't understand, why, don't be afraid to ask."

He made an unintelligible croak and smiled fleetingly, just enough to show that the roots of his teeth were green.

"Now then," Miss Price said, getting down to business. "This is Monday morning, and so the first thing on the program is reports. Who'd like to start off?"

Vincent Sabella was momentarily forgotten as six or seven hands went up, and Miss Price drew back in mock confusion. "Goodness, we do have a lot of reports this morning," she said. The idea of the reports—a fifteen-minute period every Monday in which the children were encouraged to relate their experiences over the weekend—was Miss Price's own, and she took a pardonable pride in it. The principal had commended her on it at a recent staff meeting, pointing out that it made a splendid bridge between the worlds of school and home, and that it was a fine way for children to learn poise and assurance. It called for intelligent supervision—the shy children had to be drawn out and the show-offs curbed—but in general, as Miss Price had assured the principal, it was fun for everyone. She particularly hoped it would be fun today, to help put Vincent Sabella at ease, and that was why she chose Nancy Parker to start off; there was nobody like Nancy for holding an audience.

The others fell silent as Nancy moved gracefully to the head of the room; even the two or three girls who secretly despised her had to feign enthrallment when she spoke (she was that popular), and every boy in the class, who at recess liked nothing better than to push her shrieking into the mud, was unable to watch her without an idiotically tremulous smile.

"Well—" she began, and then she clapped a hand over her mouth while everyone laughed. "Oh, *Nancy*," Miss Price said. "You *know* the rule about starting a report with 'well.'"

Nancy knew the rule; she had only broken it to get the laugh. Now she let her fit of giggles subside, ran her fragile forefingers down the side seams of her skirt, and began again in the proper way. "On Friday my whole family went for a ride in my brother's new car. My brother bought this new Pontiac last week, and he wanted to take us all for a ride—you know, to try it out and everything? So we went into White Plains and had dinner in a restaurant there, and then we all wanted to go see this movie, 'Doctor Jekyll and Mr. Hyde,' but my brother said it was too horrible and everything, and I wasn't old enough to enjoy it—oh, he made me so-mad! And then, let's see. On Saturday I stayed home all day and helped my mother make my sister's wedding dress. My sister's engaged to be married you see, and my mother's making this wedding dress for her? So we did that, and then on Sunday this friend of my brother's came over for dinner, and then they both had to get back to college that night, and I was allowed to stay up late and say goodbye to them and everything, and I guess that's all." She always had a sure instinct for keeping her performance brief—or rather, for making it seem briefer than it really was.

"Very good, Nancy," Miss Price said. "Now, who's next?"

Warren Berg was next, elaborately hitching up his pants as he made his way down the aisle. "On Saturday I went over to Bill Stringer's house for lunch," he began in his direct, man-to-man style, and Bill Stringer wriggled bashfully in the front row. Warren Berg and Bill Stringer were great friends, and their reports often overlapped. "And then after lunch we went into White Plains, on our bikes. Only we saw 'Doctor Jeckyll and Mr. Hyde.'" Here he nodded his head in Nancy's direction, and Nancy got another laugh by making a little whimper of envy. "It was real good, too," he went on, with mounting excitement. "It's all about this guy who—"

"About *a man who*," Miss Price corrected. "About a man who mixes up this chemical, like, that he drinks? And whenever he drinks this chemical, he changes into this real monster, like? You see him drink this chemical, and then you see his hands start to get all scales all over them, like a reptile and everything, and then you see his face start to change into this real horrible-looking face—with fangs and all? Sticking out of his mouth?"

All the girls shuddered in pleasure. "Well," Miss Price said, "I think Nancy's brother was probably wise in not wanting her to see it. What did you do *after* the movie, Warren?"

There was a general "*Aw-w-w!*" of disappointment, everyone wanted to hear more about the scales and fangs—but Miss Price never liked to let the reports degenerate into accounts of movies. Warren continued without much enthusiasm: all they had done after the movie was fool around Bill Stringer's yard until supertime. "And then on Sunday," he said, brightening again, "Bill Stringer came over to *my* house, and my dad helped us rig up this old tire on this long rope? From a tree? There's this steep hill down behind my house, you see—this ravine, like?—and we hung this tire so that what you do is, you take the tire and run a little ways and then lift your feet, and you go swinging way, way out over the ravine and back again."

"That sounds like fun," Miss Price said, glancing at her watch.

"Oh, it's *fun* all right," Warren conceded. But then he hitched up his pants again and added, with a puckering of his forehead, "Course, it's pretty dangerous. You let go of that tire or anything, you'd get a bad fall. Hit a rock or anything, you'd probably break your leg, or your spine. But my dad said he trusted us both to look out for our own safety."

"Well, I'm afraid that's all we'll have time for, Warren," Miss Price said. "Now, there's just time for one more report. Who's ready? Arthur Cross?"

There was a soft groan, because Arthur Cross was the biggest dope in class and his reports were always a bore. This time it turned out to be something tedious about going to visit his uncle on Long Island. At one point he made a slip—he said "botormoat" instead of "motorboat"—and everyone laughed with the particular edge of scorn they reserved for Arthur Cross. But the laughter died abruptly when it was joined by a harsh, dry croaking from the back of the room. Vincent Sabella was laughing too, green teeth and all, and they all had to glare at him until he stopped.

When the reports were over, everyone settled down for school. It was recess time before any of the children thought much about Vincent Sabella again, and then they thought of him only to make sure he was left out of everything. He wasn't in the group of boys that clustered around the horizontal bar to take turns at skinning-the-cat, or the group that whispered in a far corner of the playground, hatching a plot to push Nancy Parker in the mud. Nor was he in the larger group, of which even Arthur Cross was a member, that chased itself in circles in a frantic variation of the game of tag. He couldn't join the girls, of course, or the boys from other classes, and so he joined nobody. He stayed on the apron of the playground, close to school, and for the first part of the recess he pretended to be very busy with the laces of his sneakers. He would squat to undo and retie them, straighten up and take a few experimental steps in a springy, athletic way, and then get down and go to work on them again. After five minutes of this he gave it up, picked up a handful of pebbles and began shying them at an invisible target several yards away. That was good for another five minutes, but then there was still five minutes left, and he could think of nothing to do but stand there, first with his hands in his pockets, then with his hands on his hips, and then with his arms folded in a manly way across his chest.

Miss Price stood watching all this from the doorway, and she spent the full recess wondering if she ought to go out and do something about it. She guessed it would be better not to.

She managed to control the same impulse at recess the next day, and every other day that week, though every day it grew more difficult. But one thing she could not control was a tendency to let her anxiety show in class. All Vincent Sabella's errors in schoolwork were publicly excused, even those having nothing to do with his newness, and all his accomplishments were singled out for special mention. Her campaign to build him up was painfully obvious, and never more so than when she tried to make it subtle; once, for instance, in explaining an arithmetic problem, she said, "Now, suppose Warren Berg and Vincent Sabella went to the store with fifteen cents each, and candy bars cost ten cents. How many candy bars would each boy have?" By the end of the week he was well on the way to becoming the worst possible kind of teacher's pet, a victim of the teacher's pity.

On Friday she decided the best thing to do would be to speak to him privately, and try to draw him out. She could say something about the pictures he had painted in art class—that would do for an opening—and she decided to do it at lunchtime.

The only trouble was that lunchtime, next to recess, was the most trying part of Vincent Sabella's day. Instead of going home for an hour as the other children did, he brought his lunch to school in a wrinkled paper bag and ate it in the classroom, which always made for a certain amount of awkwardness. The last children to leave would see him still seated apologetically at his desk, holding his paper bag, and anyone who happened to straggle back later for a forgotten hat or sweater would surprise him in the middle, of his meal—perhaps shielding a hard-boiled egg from view or wiping mayonnaise from his mouth with a furtive hand. It was a situation that Miss Price did not improve by walking up to him while the room was still half full of children and sitting prettily on the edge of the desk beside his, making it clear that she was cutting her own lunch hour short in order to be with him.

"Vincent," she began, "I've been meaning to tell you how much I enjoyed those pictures of yours. They're really very good."

He mumbled something and shifted his eyes to the cluster of departing children at the door. She went right on talking and smiling, elaborating on her praise of the pictures; and finally, after the door had closed behind the last child, he was able to give her his attention. He did so tentatively at first; but the more she talked, the more he seemed to relax, until she realized she was putting him at ease. It was as simple and as gratifying as stroking a cat. She had finished with the pictures now and moved on, triumphantly, to broader fields of praise. "It's never easy," she was saying, "to come to a new school and adjust yourself to the level, the new work, and new working methods, and I think you've done a splendid job so far. I really do. But tell me, do you think you're going to like it here?"

He looked at the floor just long enough to make his reply—"It's alright"—and then his eyes stared into hers again.

"I'm so glad. Please don't let me interfere with your lunch, Vincent. Do go ahead and eat, that is, if you don't mind my sitting here with you." But it was now abundantly clear that he didn't mind at all, and he began to unwrap a bologna sandwich with what she felt sure was the best appetite he'd had all week. It wouldn't even have mattered very much now if someone from the class had come in and watched, though it was probably just as well that no one did.

Miss Price sat back more comfortably on the desk top, crossed her legs and allowed one slim stockinged foot to slip part of the way out of its moccasin. "Of course," she went on, "it always does take a little time to sort of get your bearings in a new school. For one thing, well, it's never too easy for the new member of the class to make friends with the other members. What I mean is, you mustn't mind if the others seem a little rude to you at first. Actually, they're just as anxious to make friends as you are, but they're shy. All it takes is a little time, and a little effort on your part as well as theirs. Not too much, of course, but a little. Now for instance, these reports we have Monday mornings—they're a fine way for people to get to know one another. A person never feels he has to make a report; it's just a thing he can do if he wants to. And that's only one way of helping others to know the kind of person you are; there are lots and lots of ways. The main thing to remember is that making friends is the most natural thing in the world, and it's only a question of time until you have all the friends you want. And in the meantime, Vincent, I hope you'll consider *me* your friend, and feel free to call on me for whatever advice or anything you might need. Will you do that?"

He nodded, swallowing.

"Good." She stood up and smoothed her skirt over her long thighs. "Now I must go or I'll be late for *my* lunch. But I'm glad we had this little talk, Vincent, and I hope we'll have others."

It was probably a lucky thing that she stood up when she did, for if she'd stayed on that desk a minute longer Vincent Sabella would have thrown his arms around her and buried his face in the warm gray flannel of her lap, and that might have been enough to confuse the most dedicated and imaginative of teachers.

At report time on Monday morning, nobody was more surprised than Miss Price when Vincent Sabella's smudged hand was among the first and most eager to rise. Apprehensively she considered letting someone else start off, but then, for fear of hurting his feelings, she said, "All right, Vincent," in as matter-of-fact a way as she could manage.

There was a suggestion of muffled titters from the class as he walked confidently to the head of the room and turned to face his audience. He looked, if anything, too confident: there were signs, in the way he held his shoulders and the way his eyes shone, of the terrible poise of panic. "Saturday I seen that pitch" he announced. "Saw, Vincent," Miss Price corrected gently.

"That's what I mean," he said; "I sore that pitch. 'Doctor Jack-o'-Lantern and Mr. Hide.'"

There was a burst of wild, delighted laugher and a chorus of correction: "Doctor *Jekyll!*"

He was unable to speak over the noise. Miss Price was on her feet, furious. "It's a *perfectly natural mistake.*" she was saying. "There's no reason for any of you to be so rude. Go on, Vincent, and please excuse this very silly interruption." The laughter subsided, but the class continued to shake their heads derisively from side to side. It hadn't, of course, been a perfectly natural mistake at all; for one thing it proved that he was a hopeless dope, and for another it proved that he was lying.

"That's what I mean," he continued. "'Doctor Jackal and Mr. Hide.' I got it a little mixed up. Any-ways, I seen all about where his teet' start comin' outa his mout' and all like that, and I thought it was very good. And then on Sunday my mudda and fodda come out to see me in this car they got. This Buick. My fodda siz, 'Vinny, wanna go for a little ride?' I siz, 'Sure, where yiz goin'?' He siz, 'Anyplace ya like.' So I siz, 'Let's go out in the country a ways, get on one of them big roads and make some time.' So we go out—oh, I guess fifty, sixty miles—and we're cruisin' along this highway, when this cop starts tailin' us? My fodda siz, 'Don't worry, we'll shake him,' and he steps on it, see? My mudda's gettin' pretty scared, but my fodda siz, 'Don't worry, dear.' He's tryin' to make this turn, see, so he can get off the highway and shake the cop? But just when he's makin' the turn, the cop opens up and starts shootin', see?"

By this time the few members of the class who could bear to look at him at all were doing so with heads on one side and mouths partly open, the way you look at a broken arm or a circus freak.

"We just barely made it," Vincent went on, his eyes gleaming, "and this one bullet got my fodda in the shoulder. Didn't hurt him bad—just grazed him, like—so my mudda bandaged it up for him and all, but he couldn't do no more drivin' after that, and we had to get him to a doctor, see? So my fodda siz, 'Vinny, think you can drive a ways?' I siz, 'Sure, if you show me how.' So he showed me how to work the gas and the brake, and all like that, and I drove to the doctor. My mudda siz, 'I'm prouda you, Vinny, drivin' all by yourself.' So any-ways, we got the doctor, got my fodda fixed up and all, and then he drove us back home." He was breathless. After an uncertain pause he said, "And that's all." Then he walked quickly back to his desk, his stiff new corduroy pants whistling faintly with each step.

"Well, that was very—entertaining, Vincent," Miss Price said, try-ing to act as if nothing had happened. "Now, who's next?" But nobody raised a hand.

Recess was worse than usual for him that day; at least it was until he found a place to hide—a narrow concrete alley, blind except for several closed fire-exit doors, that cut between two sections of the school build-ing. It was reassuringly dismal and cool in there—he could stand with his back to the wall and his eyes guarding the entrance, and the noises of recess were as remote as the sunshine. But when the bell rang he had to go back to class, and in another hour it was lunchtime.

Miss Price left him alone until her own meal was finished. Then, after standing with one hand on the doorknob for a full minute to gather courage, she went in and sat beside him for another little talk, just as he was trying to swallow the last of a pimento-cheese sandwich.

"Vincent," she began, "we all enjoyed your report this morning, but I think we would have enjoyed it more—a great deal more—if you'd told us something about your real life instead. I mean," she hurried on, "For instance, I noticed you were wearing a nice new windbreaker this morning. It *is* new, isn't it? And did your aunt buy it for you over the weekend?"

He did not deny it.

"Well then, why couldn't you have told us about going to the store with your aunt, and buying the windbreaker, and whatever you did afterwards. That would have made a perfectly good report." She paused, and for the first time looked steadily into his eyes. "You do understand what I'm trying to say, don't you, Vincent?"

He wiped crumbs of bread from his lips, looked at the floor, and nodded.

"And you'll remember next time, won't you?"

He nodded again. "Please may I be excused, Miss Price?"

"Of course you may."

He went to the boys' lavatory and vomited. Afterwards he washed his face and drank a little water, and then he returned to the classroom. Miss Price was busy at her desk now, and didn't look up. To avoid getting involved with her again, he wandered out to the cloakroom and sat on one of the long benches, where he picked up someone's discarded overshoe and turned it over and over in his hands. In a little while he heard the clatter of returning children, and to avoid being discovered there, he got up and went to the fire-exit door. Pushing it open, he found that it gave onto the alley he had hidden in that morning, and he slipped outside. For a minute or two he just stood there, looking at the blankness of the concrete wall: then he found a piece of chalk in his pocket and wrote out all the dirty words he could think of, in block letters a foot high. He had put down four words and was trying to remember a fifth when he heard a shuffling at the door behind him. Arthur Cross was there, holding the door open and reading the words with wide eyes. "Boy," he said in an awed half-whisper. "Boy, you're gonna get it. You're really gonna *get* it."

Startled, and then suddenly calm, Vincent Sabella palmed his chalk, hooked his thumbs in his belt and turned on Arthur Cross with a menacing look. "Yeah?" he inquired. "Who's gonna squeal on me?"

"Well, nobody's gonna *squeal* on you," Arthur Cross said uneasily, "but you shouldn't go around writing—" "Arright," Vincent said, advancing a step. His shoulders were slumped, his head thrust forward and his eyes narrowed, like Edward G. Robinson. "Arright. That's all I wanna know. I don't like squealers, unnastand?"

While he was saying this, Warren Berg and Bill Stringer appeared in the doorway—just in time to hear it and to see the words on the wall before Vincent turned on them. "And that goes fa you too, unnastand?" he said. "Both a yiz."

And the remarkable thing was that both their faces fell into the same foolish, defensive smile that Arthur Cross was wearing. It wasn't until they had glanced at each other that they were able to meet his eyes with the proper degree of contempt, and by then it was too late. "Think you're pretty smart, don'tcha, Sabella?" Bill Stringer said.

"Never mind what I think," Vincent told him. "You heard what I said. Now let's get back inside."

And they could do nothing but move aside to make way for him, and follow him dumbfounded into the cloakroom.

It was Nancy Parker who squealed—although, of course, with someone like Nancy Parker you didn't think of it as squealing. She had heard everything from the cloakroom; as soon as the boys came in she peeked into the alley, saw the words and, setting her face in a prim frown, went straight to Miss Price. Miss Price was just about to call the class to order for the afternoon when Nancy came up and whispered in her ear. They both disappeared into the cloakroom—from which, after a moment, came the sound of the fire-exit door being abruptly slammed—and when they returned to class Nancy was flushed with righteousness, Miss Price very pale. No announcement was made. Classes proceeded in the ordinary way all afternoon, though it was clear that Miss Price was upset, and it wasn't until she was dismissing the children at three o'clock that she brought the thing into the open. "Will Vincent Sabella please remain seated?" She nodded at the rest of the class. "That's all."

While the room was clearing out she sat at her desk, closed her eyes and massaged the frail bridge of her nose with thumb and forefinger, sorting our half-remembered fragments of a book she had once read on the subject of seriously disturbed children. Perhaps, after all, she should never have undertaken the responsibility of Vincent Sabella's loneliness. Perhaps the whole thing called for the attention of a specialist. She took a deep breath.

"Come over here and sit beside me, Vincent," she said, and when he had settled himself, she looked at him. "I want you to tell me the truth. Did you write those words on the wall outside?" He stared at the floor. "Look at me," she said, and he looked at her. She had never looked prettier: her cheeks slightly flushed, her eyes shining and her sweet mouth pressed into a self-conscious frown. "First of all," she said, handing him a small enameled basin streaked with poster paint, "I want you to take this to the boys' room and fill it with hot water and soap."

He did as he was told, and when he came back, carrying the basin carefully to keep the suds from spilling, she was sorting out some old rags in the bottom drawer of her desk. "Here," she said, selecting one and shutting the drawer in a businesslike way. "This will do. Soak this up." She led him back to the fire exit and stood in the alley watching him, silently, while he washed off all the words.

When the job had been done, and the rag and basin put away, they sat down at Miss Price's desk again. "I suppose you think I'm angry with you, Vincent," she said. "Well, I'm not. I almost wish I could be angry—that would make it much easier—but instead I'm hurt. I've tried to be a good friend to you, and I thought you wanted to be my friend too. But this kind of thing—well, it's very hard to be friendly with a person who'd do a thing like that." She saw, gratefully, that there were tears in his eyes. "Vincent, perhaps I understand some things better than you think.

"Perhaps I understand that sometimes, when a person does a thing like that, it isn't really because he wants to hurt anyone, but only because he's unhappy. He knows it isn't a good thing to do, and he even knows it isn't going to make him any happier afterwards, but he goes ahead and does it anyway. Then when he finds he's lost a friend, he's terribly sorry, but it's too late. The thing is done."

She allowed this somber note to reverberate in the silence of the room for a little while before she spoke again. "I won't be able to forget this, Vincent. But perhaps, just this once, we can still be friends as long as I understand that you didn't mean to hurt me. But you must promise me that you won't forget it either. Never forget that when you do a thing like that, you're going to hurt people who want very much to like you, and in that way you're going to hurt yourself. Will you promise me to remember that, dear?"

The "dear" was as involuntary as the slender hand that reached out and held the shoulder of his sweatshirt; both made his head hang lower than before.

"All right," she said. "You may go now."

He got his windbreaker out of the cloakroom and left, avoiding the tired uncertainty of her eyes. The corridors were deserted, and dead silent except for the hollow, rhythmic knocking of a janitor's push-broom against some distant wall. His own rubber-soled tread only added to the silence; so did the lonely little noise made by the zipping-up of his wind-breaker, and so did the faint mechanical sigh of the heavy front door. The silence made it all the more startling when he found, several yards down the concrete walk outside, that two boys were walking beside him: Warren Berg and Bill Stringer. They were both smiling at him in an eager, almost friendly way.

"What'd she do to ya, anyway?" Bill Stringer asked.

Caught off guard, Vincent barely managed to put on his Edward G. Robinson face in time. "Nunnya business," he said, and walked faster.

"No, listen—wait up, hey," Warren Berg said, as they trotted to keep up with him. "What'd she do, anyway? She bawl ya out, or what? Wait up, hey, Vinny."

The name made him tremble all over. He had to jam his hands in his windbreaker pockets to force himself to keep on walking; he had to force his voice to be steady when he said "Nunnya *business,* I told ya. Lea' me alone." But they were right in step with him now. "Boy, she must of given you the works," Warren Berg persisted. "What'd she say, anyway? C'mon, tell us, Vinny."

This time the name was too much for him. It overwhelmed his resistance and made his softening knees slow down to a slack, conversational stroll. "She din say nothin'" he said at last; and then after a dramatic pause he added, "She let the ruler do her talkin' for her."

"The *ruler?* Ya mean she used a *ruler* on ya?" Their faces were stunned, either with disbelief or admiration, and it began to look more and more like admiration as they listened.

"On the knuckles," Vincent said through tightening lips. "Five times on each hand. She siz, 'Make a fist. Lay it out here on the desk.' Then she takes the ruler and *Whop! Whop! Whop!* Five times. Ya think that don't hurt, you're crazy."

Miss Price, buttoning her polo coat as the front door whispered shut behind her, could scarcely believe her eyes. This couldn't be Vincent Sabella this perfectly normal, perfectly happy boy on the sidewalk ahead of her, flanked by attentive friends. But it was, and the scene made her want to laugh aloud with pleasure and relief. He was going to be all right, after all. For all her well-intentioned groping in the shadows she could never have predicted a scene like this, and certainly could never have caused it to happen. But it was happening, and it just proved, once again, that she would never understand the ways of children.

She quickened her graceful stride and overtook them, turning to smile down at them as she passed. "Goodnight, boys," she called, intending it as a kind of cheerful benediction; and then, embarrassed by their three startled faces, she smiled even wider and said, "Goodness, it *is* getting colder, isn't it? That windbreaker of yours looks nice and warm, Vincent. I envy you." Finally they nodded bashfully at her; she called goodnight again, turned, and continued on her way to the bus stop.

She left a profound silence in her wake. Staring after her, Warren Berg and Bill Stringer waited until she had disappeared around the corner before they turned on Vincent Sabella.

"Ruler, my eye!" Bill Stringer said. "Ruler, my eye!" He gave Vincent a disgusted shove that sent him stumbling against Warren Berg, who shoved him back.

"Jeez, you lie about *everything,* don'tcha, Sabella? You lie about *everything?*"

Jostled off balance, keeping his hands tight in the windbreaker pockets, Vincent tried in vain to retain his dignity. "Think I care if yiz believe me?" he said, and then because he couldn't think of anything else to say, he said it again. "Think I care if yiz believe me?"

But he was walking alone. Warren Berg and Bill Stringer were drifting away across the street, walking backwards in order to look back at him with furious contempt. "Just like the lies you told about the policeman shooting your father," Bill Stringer called.

"Even *movies* he lies about," Warren Berg put in; and suddenly doubling up with artificial laughter he cupped both hands to his mouth and yelled, "Hey, Doctor Jack-o'-lantern!"

It wasn't a very good nickname, but it had an authentic ring to it—the kind of a name that might spread around, catch on quickly, and stick. Nudging each other, they both took up the cry:

"What's the matter, Doctor Jack-o'-Lantern?"

"Why don'tcha run on home with Miss Price, Doctor Jack-o'-Lantern?"

"So long, Doctor Jack-o'-Lantern!"

Vincent Sabella went on walking, ignoring them, waiting until they were out of sight. Then he turned and retraced his steps all the way back to school, around through the playground and back to the alley, where the wall was still dark in spots from the circular scrubbing of his wet rag.

Choosing a dry place, he got out his chalk and began to draw a head with great care, in profile, making the hair long and rich and taking his time over the face, erasing it with moist fingers and re-working it until it was the most beautiful face he had ever drawn: a delicate nose, slightly parted lips, an eye with lashes that curved as gracefully as a bird's wing. He paused to admire it with a lover's solemnity; then from the lips he drew a line that connected with a big speech balloon, and in the balloon he wrote, so angrily that the chalk kept breaking in his fingers, every one of the words he had written that noon. Returning to the head, he gave it a slender neck and gently sloping shoulders, and then, with bold strokes, he gave it the body of a naked woman: great breasts with hard little nipples, a trim waist, a dot for a naval, wide hips and thighs that flared around a triangle of fiercely scribbled pubic hair. Beneath the picture he printed its title: "Miss Price."

He stood there looking at it for a little while, breathing hard, and then he went home.

EDITORS' COMMENTARY

DIAGNOSIS: Culturally and affectionally deprived student in a middle-class environment.

The story is a realistic description of how a new student in a strange environment tries to find his way. His clothes, manner, and speech make him different from the other students in his classroom. These differences are felt keenly by his classmates and teacher. His attempt to be like the others through lying or make-believe is understandable. Equally understandable is his well-intentioned teacher's overinvolvement with him. Her seductive and sympathetic behavior, although well meaning, singles him out and further alienates him from the class. Teacher's pet is a hard role, particularly when a student is starving for attention and expression.

Vincent's reaction to the teacher's moralistic, middle-class approach to him is confused. In despair, anger, loneliness, and a sense of isolation, he uses the very tools that shock middle-class society. He gets back at her by using street language and lewd sexual pictures.

Although a teacher's involvement with a student with special needs is encouraged, overinvolvement with a student often is not helpful and can lead to teacher disappointment and rejection. The dangers of being the teacher's pet are clear. What the teacher needed was to provide a gradual welcome that would give Vincent a chance to be accepted, and to understand that a weekend report from him was bound to be a fiasco.

Even teachers who come from the same ethnic groups as their students are not always trained in an awareness of their middle-class myopia. This condition of cross-culture training is improving, but it is still a major problem. Cultural differences between teachers and their students can have a negative effect on students. This issue is intensified as public education pushes the concept of inclusion of students with special needs. In select regular classrooms it is not unusual to see students who have mental challenges, physical disabilites, neurological impairements, emotional disturbances, and even autism in the same classroom. The concept of inclusion of all students is an admirable goal, but teachers will need additional training and support to make inclusion a meaningful practice.

SUBSTANCE ABUSE: WHAT SOME PEOPLE DO ABOUT THEIR FEELINGS AND WHAT THAT DOES TO THEM

Drugs

Anxiety is hard to bear, but none of us can live without learning to tolerate a certain amount of it. Anxiety arises from the self-preserving instinct of fear, in which we all react by either fleeing or fighting. Anxiety's basic purpose is to send us unmistakable alarms and warnings, alerting us to whatever is threatening, so that we can do something about it. There is a body of evidence to support the theory that, without some degree of anxiety, we would not learn to learn, and our very survival would be endangered.

As society grows increasingly complex, human-generated anxieties haunt us. Competition, anger, feelings of inadequacy and unworthiness, guilt, loneliness, confusion, problems of sexual identity, and dependence are just some of the anxieties that plague us, yet we live together and are by nature dependent on each other. When anxiety rises too high, it is sometimes more than we can handle. Immobilized, we may revert to the crudest, most primitive forms of combating danger and acute discomfort. In the moment of anxiety, everything we know can be forgotten and everything we have repressed may come pouring in. We may then give way to overwhelming bursts of anger and violence, or we may take flight. Anxiety is often the reason teenagers run away or students who have ability show apathetic lack of effort. Over the years, we all learn certain defenses, and sometimes they serve us worse than the anxiety they are combating. The particular defense we choose is determined by our nature and our environment, past and present. Some of us develop combativeness and irritability. For others, psychosomatic illnesses such as headaches, stomach aches, and hives are outward signs of the terror inside. Many of us choose escape, perhaps in books, films, or TV. Many people, especially preadolescents, use TV as a kind of drug. Some escape into alcohol, which can be as effective as any drug at damaging human relationships, job effectiveness, and physical or mental health.

To escape in anxiety and society's deficiencies and onslaughts, many young people today have turned to drugs, just as those in earlier generations turned to alcohol. The overuse of some drugs, such as amphetamines (stimulants), barbiturates (downers), or glue-sniffing, can cause long-term physical damage. Conclusive evidence suggests that hallucinogenics cause permanent physical harm. Other drugs are so addictive that they become the controlling force in a student's life. For the addictive drugs, the craving is both physical and psychological. Those addicted to alcohol, barbiturates, or opiates (such as heroin, opium, and morphine) suffer not only an overwhelming desire for the drug but also extreme physical discomfort upon withdrawal—shaking, stomach cramps, and wracking pain. They also incur a great risk of death from taking unknown mixtures or an overdose. Addiction brings helplessness, dependence, misery to oneself and others, and self-loathing.

More and more young people are using addictive drugs, and increasing numbers of them are very young. Some students begin drug use because resisting peer pressure is too much for their essentially conforming, infantile, and dependent social natures. Some young people take a hard drug once or twice and then leave it alone, but others become addicted with only a few exposures. Some young people may turn to drugs out of frustration at their inability to tell their parents about their unhappiness. It may be the normal unhappiness of any adolescent growing up, but it can seem especially acute in a world where so much is demanded, values often appear phony and hypocritical, and problems seem nearly insoluble. Given a sufficient sense of powerlessness, a young person in today's culture is often tempted to give up. Sometimes the adolescent then chooses an alternative life without knowing much about its terrors and consequences.

Some drug users have been disturbed for a long time; however, because their parents are insensitive, unprepared, or simply do not want to see, or because their teachers are afraid of alarming someone or "overstepping boundaries," drug use is left to go on until it is too late. These youngsters find no way to tell someone they are in trouble inside, except through actions that seriously limit their future. The disturbances have always been there; drugs make them manifest. Of course, drugs always make matters worse—at times irremediably worse. A familiar type of drug abuser is the gifted adolescent with middle- or upper-middle-class parents. Sensitive to the ills of the environment and unable to communicate with his or her family, the gifted adolescent sometimes shares a family tendency to avoid looking facts in the face. The drug abuser of the poor ghetto, like his or her wealthier counterpart, is dependent, frightened, and unwilling to grow up. Both may be disturbed in a psychiatric sense as well as for inappropriate social behaviors. Both have little sense of self and both share an inability to be direct or to communicate feelings. They have little ability to tolerate anxiety or to foresee that their future will largely derive from their present choices—for good or bad. The younger the child (and some are only 9 to 12 years old), the more the will is affected and training for coping with life is sacrificed.

Many adults are not nearly as learned as their children are about the varieties of pills, serums, powders, and plants that will take a person up, out, or down. But there is a terrifying ignorance about the actual effects of drugs among many young users themselves as well as among adults who ought to know better. The realistic handling of young drug abusers requires the active engagement of physicians, psychologists, researchers, lawyers, educators, and law enforcement officers in evaluating, preventing, and treating drug abuse—not simply in punishing it. Whatever other needs drug use may fill, its illegality has given it the added attraction among young people of being another channel for the common adolescent rebellion against authority. It is a very complicated issue, and we cannot begin to understand it without making a differentiation among the drugs, their effects, and the individuals and groups who use them.

Teachers and school officials seeking a sensible approach to student drug use will probably adopt at least one principle: Certain things are appropriate to do in school or during work hours, and others are not; some things are appropriate to bring to school, and others are not. A person does not drink in school or at work or come drunk to school or work without consequences. Likewise, a person does not get high on drugs in school. When a student fails to abide by this principle, as many do, it should be a major concern of the school to assist the drug abuser in coping with the sources of the problem. Fortunately, many teachers are now aware of certain signals of student drug use: large pupils and heavy eyelids, leaden or slack bodies, atypical or inappropriate speech, excessive giggling or tears, or reports of fantasies.

ARTICLE 1.5

ALTHOUGH heavy drug users often fantasize about great creations, they seldom act on those fantasies. The act of creation itself seems to require too much effort. The addictive drugs reduce the appetite, so that undernourishment and consequent lack of energy make productivity the exception rather than the rule among addicted users. The next excerpt describes this seductive and enervating state where, if the drugs take hold, particularly in children and youth, they can burn out a zest for learning and living.

DOWN THESE MEAN STREETS
Piri Thomas

I sat down on the edge of the roof ledge. My mind refused to get off its kick of reminiscing. Man, like how many times some cat's come up to me with his old man's watch or sister's coat and swap

Adapted from *Down These Mean Streets,* by Piri Thomas. Copyright 1967 by Piri Thomas. Adapted with permission of Alfred A. Knopf, Inc.

for a three-cent bag. Heh, a three-cent bag—like a grain of rice crushed to powder, that's how much it is for a cost of three dollars, and you couldn't beat down that hell-like look as the begging took place in exchange for that super-tranquilizing ca-ca powder. I sniffed back a tear that came out of my nose. And how about the time I plowed through that falling snow with no pride at all in my Buster Brown shoes—like brown on top and bustered on the bottoms—knowing without a doubt in the world that the only thing that would get me warm again so I could care about being cold was the connecting—the blending of my vein's blood and dogie drug.

Shit, man, how far can pride go down? I knew that all the help in the world could get that stuff out of my system, but only some kind of god would be able to get it out of my swinging soul and mind. What a sick murder scene! If you didn't get gypped outta your stuff, you'd get beat on some weak, cut-down shit. If you didn't get dead on an overdose, you'd get deader on a long strung-out kick. Everything in the world depended on heroin. You'd go to bed thinking about stuff and wake up in the morning thinking about it. Love and life took second place to it and nothing mattered except where, and how soon. It was like my whole puking system had copped a mind bigger than the one in my head.

I walked toward the roof landing. I was thinking. I was gonna kick for good. "I can do it. I swear ta God and the Virgin. Gonna get me li'l shit and cut down good. *I ain't no fuckin' junkie.*"

I went looking for Waneko. I found him in *El Viejo's* candy store. I put my want to him in fast words. "Help me kick, man?" It was a question. Waneko knew how it was. Even though he was pushing now, he wasn't using, but he'd been through that kicking road *mucho* times. Waneko nodded, "Sure, *panin—sure* I will." We walked into Waneko's place. He explained to his moms what was shaking. She smiled nice-like and said everything was gonna be all right. Waneko followed that assurance up with, "Moms helps most of the cats that want to kick and even some of the chicks. She should be some kind of church worker or something." He laughed. I tried a weak smile.

They put me in a room that just had a bed and chair and a window that had a metal gate across it to keep the crooks out and kicking junkies in. I laid down, and after a while Waneko brought in a small radio so I could dig some music, to take my mind off what was coming. Both he and I knew that the li'l taste of stuff I had shot up on the roof a while ago was gonna wear off and then World War III was gonna break out inside of me. Billie was wailing some sad song. I wailed along with her in a soft hum. Then some kinda time started to go by and my system was better than a clock. And then Judgment Day set in …

Man, talk about wantin' to die—everything started off as it should. First like always, the uncomfortable feeling as you knew your system wanted its baby bottle. And nose running ever so gently at first and the slow kind of pain building up not so gently. I tried hard to listen to some wailin' on the radio, but all I could hear was my own. I got up and went to the door. It was locked from the outside. "Hey, Waneko, open the door," I yelled.

"*Quotes?*"

"I feel real bad, like in bad, man."

"Man, lay down, you ain't been in there long enough to work up any kind of sweat. I'll tell you when, and only then I'll give you a li'l taste to ease you off. So cool it, *panin*."

I don't know how many hours ran crawling by. I just knew I couldn't make it. *But I hadda. I just hadda.* "Lemme out, Waneko—lemme out, you mother-fucker." I swam to the door and hit at it.

"Waneko is not home right now." It was Waneko's moms.

"Let me out, *senora*. I kicked already."

"He said not to let you come out until he comes back, *hijo*."

"Did he leave something for me?" My voice sounded like tears. I went back to bed and just rolled and moaned all alone.

I don't know how many hours ran crawling by. It was a lot of them. At one time I heard the lock being taken off the door and heard it fall from someone's hand. I felt Waneko's mom's voice—I felt her cool hand on my face and felt her wipe my cold sweating face. I heard sounds of comfort coming from her.

"No te apures, hijo, you weel soon be fine."

I tried to get up and make it, but she was faster. I felt the iron gates on the window. I shook them. I turned and flopped back on the bed. I was shaking. I was in bad pain. I was cold and I couldn't stop my snots from flowing. I was all in cramps and my guts wouldn't obey me. My eyes were overflowing real fast.

"Lemme out, Waneko—lemme out, you mother-fucker." Shit, I was like screaming out of veins. Nobody answered and I just lay there and moaned and groaned all alone and turned that mattress into one big soaking mopful of my sweat.

I don't know how many hours went crawling by. Millions maybe. And then a real scared thought hit me. Waneko wasn't coming back. He was gonna let me make it—cold-turkey—*a la canona*. I kept trembling and my whole swinging soul full of pain would make my body lurch up and tie itself up into one big knot and then ease itself almost straight and then retie itself. I felt like a puke coming afar. I thought, didn't I puke before? I felt it come out of my mouth like a green river of yellow-blue bile. I couldn't control nothing, and all the strength I had was enough just to turn my head away. I think I made some soft ca-ca on myself. I think I made some hard ones too.

Sometimes I think I heard Waneko telling me, "It's almost over, baby, it's almost over—we got it beat." But I couldn't answer. I'd just hold myself together with my arms holding me tight and rockabye baby myself to some kind of vague comfort. In a dream I'd eat mountains and mountains of sweet, sweet candy. I opened my eyes and Waneko had me sitting in a chair and I saw Moms cleaning the toilet I had made out of the room—and then I was back in the bed. I still had all the pain, all the cramps. I still had the whole bad bit, but I knew I was gonna make it. I rocked myself to and fro.

I don't know how many hours ran crawling by. Jillions maybe. At last the pain cut itself down. I felt all dried out. Waneko came into the room and rubbed my body down, like trying to work all the knots to straighten out. Waneko and his moms kept me with them for a week or so putting me into shape with hot pigeon soup, liquids, and later heavier stuff like I mean, rice and beans. They were great, Waneko and Moms. My body was kicked free from H—gone was dogie. They said it takes seventy or so hours to kick a habit. I think it seemed like seventy years. Now all I had to do was kick it outta my mind.

I left Waneko's house after really thanking them from way down. I hit the street thinking, "Wow, dying is easier than this has been. Never— *never—nunca mas*."

Alcohol

The use of alcohol by children and adolescents in the United States has increased alarmingly. It is becoming a more pervasive problem in schools than the use of other drugs and narcotics. Alcohol is easily available to children, although it is illegal for minors to buy or drink it. Youngsters can get liquor from people older than themselves, from illegal sales, through use of false identification cards, and at their own or friends' homes. Although liquor prices run high, the cost is small compared to the price of illegal drugs. What's more, liquor can be obtained by theft from businesses or homes.

Many children grow up seeing their parents drink, whether socially or heavily. The use of alcohol permeates American culture. A "happy hour" is frequently advertised by restaurants and bars, and liquor stores abound. The corner tavern, immortalized in the TV show "Cheers," is as much a part of the scenery to children as the gas station or drugstore. It is highly unlikely that a child could grow up today without seeing TV programs or movies depicting drinkers and drunks.

Many children whose families serve or drink alcoholic beverages are allowed to taste wine with dinner, beer with snacks, or hard liquor at parties. Some ethnic groups give children alcohol as a matter of course. Many of these children do not abuse alcohol, but some family practices may instigate its overuse. Although stereotypes are always dangerous, there are clinical observations that, given low-income and low-employment opportunities, some ethnic groups are more susceptible to alcoholism than others. For example, Irish and Native American people tend to find alcohol a particularly difficult chemical to handle. However, all ethnic groups are prone to misuse alcohol when their conditions in life appear to be or truly are overwhelming. Children from these families grow up considering alcohol a way to veil misery.

Children who drink too much may start for any reason: to be "one of the gang," or because they have seen their parents reach for drinks under stress, or because they found a bottle on the playground and found that drinking erased their problems temporarily. They may become severe drinkers if their home life is miserable, if they feel imprisoned in untenable situations by dependence on their parents or caretakers, or because they cannot yet fend for themselves in normal activities. Sometimes, a child is neglected or mistreated by one or more drunken parents. In an effort to erase the feelings of being uncared for, he or she proceeds to do what the elders do—opt for escape. In some ways, alcoholism is a contagious disease. It is so difficult to relate to an alcoholic family member that spouses and children may give up and join what they cannot fight. Sexual fears tend to be rampant at adolescence anyway, and they simply contribute to the teenage drinker's primitive neediness and sense of general inadequacy.

Like many drugs, alcohol numbs—it depresses the rigid controls most people live by. For a short while, it permits a child who feels lonely, unhappy, and unsure to feel okay, likable, affectionate, entertained, amusing, strong, and able. Yet, at the very moment liquor makes the child feel in control, he or she is usually most out of control. Illusion is the essence of excessive alcoholic intake. Often, drink gives youth an initial glow of ability to cope, and the numbness that follows momentarily loosens the pressures they feel and makes the world seem rosier, if unreal.

As different as alcoholics are from each other, there are some basic similarities. Whether adults or children, they are fundamentally very dependent, needy, and infantile, while presenting a facade that is often poised, charming, seductive, winning, indirect, and manipulative. They have great expectations of themselves, often because of explicit or implicit parental demands or because they want to prove to neglectful parents that they are worth loving. Their aspirations tend to be grandiose, and they are given to extremes of elation and despair. They are either the most wonderful or the most terrible, or they want to be one or the other, never in between, never ordinary. They must be special or nothing. Their need for reassurance and support is as bottomless as their thirst. Although they make demands for closeness, when push comes to shove they keep a wall or protective distance between themselves and others, because they feel so empty, so needy, so thirsty inside. They fear that others will discover their emptiness, what they see as their own fakery or deficiencies, and will despise them. They are therefore filled with self-hate and guilt. This self-hate is exacerbated by drinking, but to drown this feeling they drink more.

For alcoholics of every age, the symbol of a bottle is apt. Inside the alcoholic personality, no matter how sophisticated, is an infant needing the complete nurture one gets only at the breast. Underneath the grandiose goals or the "out-of-it" manner, there hides a fearful, self-critical, and pervasively guilty person who has unendingly voracious needs that are not met by what the world is offering.

Alcohol becomes a poison for a child even more, and sooner, than for an adult. It destroys not only liver and kidneys but also self-esteem, will, and motivation. It ultimately can affect the nervous system and the brain. It feeds on fantasy rather than fact. To drinking children, alcohol represents a return to the nipple or the bottle, a wish for the warm oblivion of infancy before expectations and demands became overwhelming. Often, alcoholism is an unspoken message that a child is not ready to grow up. This is particularly true where a child is under heavy pressure to act grown up or to undertake responsibility that he or she is not ready to bear. The escape from burdens that can't be shouldered is frequently through the bottle, which offers comfort and oblivion for a little while. Such a child often behaves and performs very well for periods, but mysteriously falls apart from time to time. The child has become a secret drinker (and secrecy and shame are part of the essence of alcoholism).

If a child comes to school drunk, it would be helpful for a teacher to know whether the home life is unsatisfying or whether the parents are modeling drinking behavior. Teachers can observe whether the alcoholic child fears other children in or outside the classroom, or fears being exposed as unprepared, ridiculous, or stupid in school. Both home and school have to be examined. Are the pressures and the rigidity of standards and expectations too great? When a pupil is drunk in school more than once, it is essential to take a good look at the youngster and the family, through interviews and, if possible, home visits. When teachers report that a child is drinking, parents may deny it and refuse to believe the facts until the habit is too far advanced to be easily curtailed. Often, a child is devastated to realize he or she is addicted and cannot stop drinking. Parents usually need help to acknowledge that, directly or indirectly, their habits, attitudes, pressures, or unrealistic dreams for their children have brought on addictive behavior.

Help can come through appropriate attention and recognition. Training can help the student to be comfortable with honesty and to develop more openness. Realistic expectations can be opened up along with opportunities for the pupil to relax and be childish when he or she needs to be. The family may need guidance in helping the child to order his or her social horizons. Finally, offering group therapy as a mode of treatment can ameliorate the student's drinking problem and the problems underlying it. Alcoholics Anonymous (AA) continues to be one of the very best organized groups dealing with alcoholics. The patient joins an

AA group, and his or her family joins an auxiliary Al-Anon group, which can help the families of alcoholics understand the problems of the alcoholic while drinking and while withdrawing from alcohol. It helps family members with their problems as well. Individual, group, or family therapy may also be used.

School personnel need to understand the part they can play in referral and in setting clear limits without overmoralizing or making unrealistic expectations. The parents or family of a drunk child must understand that the teacher attempting to deal with the child will try to furnish basic satisfaction of the youngster's needs while setting firm and clear limits on behavior. For example, the child will not be permitted to disrupt the class by becoming the center of attention. If too drunk to work, he or she may be allowed to sleep at the nurse's office and then be seen by an expert in the field of alcohol abuse. The counselor or other helping person needs to find out what factors in the child's life set off the desire to drink, and then guide the child and the family to recognition and appropriate treatment of the problem.

ARTICLE 1.6

INTERVIEW WITH A PATIENT—
The Voice of an Alcoholic Teenager

I began to drink when I was twelve when my parents went out, which they did often. I would raid the liquor cabinet. At first, it burnt and made me sick, but I kept trying—and I don't know why. It made me feel smart when I felt dumb. It made me laugh and made me forget things like bad report cards and the beatings I'd get for them. I made people laugh with me, or maybe at me, but anyway—Only then I couldn't do anything without a drink. It was like punctuation marks: I needed a drink to be with people, a drink to be alone, a drink before homework so I could tackle it, and another after, for reward. I carried vodka with me to school in my milk thermos, I chewed chlorophyll mints to keep away any smell. I'd steal liquor from my parents and put water in the bottles. They fired the maid because they thought she did it.

They found out when I was drunk and stole a guy's car and ran into a pole and I landed in the hospital. The social worker here saw my parents and the AA people came to see me. They said I

Printed with patient's permission.

could get well, and they'll help me, and my parents will go to Al-Anon, though I don't believe they'll go to their meeting. But I still want a drink right now so bad. You see when I'm drunk I know I'm good at things. I'm the best car designer. I'm the best basketball player like my father was. The girls are crazy for me instead of turning me down. Anything, everything looks good, and I don't even have to try—it just is there, one drink away … maybe.

A STUDENT'S REMINISCENCE ABOUT HER ALCOHOLIC MOTHER

I never told anyone, you see, that my mother was mostly drunk when I came home from school. Sometimes, she was very drunk and had fallen down in the house or even outside and, though I was little, I had to pull her into the bedroom so no one would find out—not my friends or the neighbors or the teachers who passed by. So, of course, I couldn't have friends over. I didn't have many friends. I tried to buy them things so they'd like me and make me feel like other people, but I couldn't invite them in. They would have seen my mother like that.

It was worse when she yelled or ranted. She wanted me with her all the time. The first time I stayed out overnight was in high school at a friend's. My mother got drunk and came and got me, yelling curses at my friend's family. My father left us when I was two, and there was never a man around I could count on. Oh, she'd bring drunk dates home from time to time, but no one lasted and in between she'd rave and rant about men and my father and how awful he was, so I grew up hating men. I still don't trust them. I always felt her drunkenness was his fault for leaving. But now I wonder if he left her because she was a drunk.

The worst was graduation day from the parochial eighth grade school I went to. For weeks, the nuns asked us to get dresses or have them made. My mother promised and promised—weeks went by and nothing happened. I had no money but I took little jobs and saved up and bought the material and my mother promised to sew it. When she was sober she could sew. Dress rehearsal came and went; the Sister was furious at me

Printed with student's permission.

because I had no dress. I promised I would have it on graduation day and pleaded with my mother to get it done. She began working on it the night before graduation, but then she got very drunk and as usual yelled and screamed at me because I wanted something. In her rage and drunkenness, she tore the dress in ribbons, and threw them at me.

All the long day of graduation the phone rang. My mother passed out and I knew it was one of the Sisters from school. I couldn't answer. I just cried and cried, and I never got to graduation. The one Sister in charge of my class was furious with me because I had spoiled her processional line, and called me to come in. She said I couldn't graduate because I'd been so unreliable. I went myself to see the head Sister—the Mother Superior—and burst into tears and, for the first time ever, told the truth about my mother. She was nice and put her arm around me, and I wept with shame and hurt. My mother couldn't come to explain. She got upset about what she had done, so she went out to a bar and got drunk. I never could think at school since I was busy worrying about what was happening to her and my worst thoughts always happened.

EDITORS' COMMENTARY

These previous two articles redirect this chapter from the dramatic power of literature to the painful realities of students in actual classrooms. Their voices need to be heard. We need to listen to their stories about what it is like to be labeled a student with behavior disorders or emotional disturbance in a special classroom. What do these students think about themselves and their problems? How do they perceive the teachers who are trying to help them? Here are some troubled teens' responses to these questions.

Bill: Others look at me and believe I am different. Sometimes, when I get angry and lose it, I feel I am different. They can control their anger and I can't. The teachers try to teach me anger management skills but they don't work.

Carol: I cannot concentrate when I am upset. When I get into a fight with my mother in the morning I am still mad when I come to school. I feel lonely. When I put my head down on my desk, my teacher thinks I am not being respectful. She yells at me and it only makes it worse. I yell back at her and now I have two problems.

Eric: I don't like being in a special class. It makes me feel different from the other students. I have no friends in the regular classes so I hang out with the other outcast students. The teachers think we are a gang and hell raisers but they are the only students who accept me. We also dress differently from the other students and that gets us another negative label. Sometimes I feel I am in a lose-lose situation.

Marcus: My teacher tries to help me but she usually get upset just like me. I try to calm down but if she touches me I go wild. Then I get into serious trouble. When I get upset I do not want to be told where to sit or where to go. I want her to speak softly and not be aggressive. Like, "Please relax and we will talk later."

ARTICLE 1.8

MANY troubled students find their teachers and the school experience to be a primary source of support and comfort. The next article is by Ryan Gauthier, a youth with a long history of traumatic life experiences, who describes how his experiences in an alternative school helped him to turn his life around. It is a wonderful story about the positive role a caring teacher and a flexible school program can have on the life of a troubled student.

FROM DOWN-AND-OUT TO UP-AND-COMING
Ryan Gauthier

Even when I was in elementary school, I had trouble with authority. Back then, I was disruptive—I was a kid with a short attention span and a school yard bully who got into a lot of fights. Letters were always going home to my mom, who was called to the

From *Reclaiming Children and Youth*, 7(4), 1999, pp. 197–199. Copyright by Reclaiming Children and Youth, Inc. Reprinted with permission.

school on a regular basis because of my behavior. At a very young age, I began to get a bad reputation.

By junior high, things had gotten out of hand. I started hanging out with a bad crowd, drinking heavily, and smoking pot. To get money to maintain this "going nowhere" lifestyle, I began stealing from businesses, homes, and even people in the street. I was also selling drugs. The police visited my home five or six times a month, and they sometimes took me down to the police station; I think this was to try to scare me into going "straight." It didn't work. The first time I was placed in the Youth Center (6 months for repeated breaking and entering [B & E]) I was 14 years old. Later that year, I was in the Center again (this time for only 7 days) for another B & E. It got worse: 14 months for yet another B & E when I was 16. Two months after being released from that incarceration, I got 21 months for robbery, B & E, assault, and drug possession. It was not a happy time, and I couldn't see anything good in my future.

One night, while serving the last sentence, I couldn't sleep. I heard the phone ring in the dead of night, and I had a premonition. When the counselor came to see me first thing in the morning, I already knew—my dad was dead. He had been killed in a car accident that involved alcohol. I started to wonder how long it would be before the same thing happened to me. To make matters worse, I didn't know if I would be permitted to attend his funeral: There was a concern that there would be drinking at the house afterwards and that I would get involved. I finally was allowed to go. I also decided that I was going to try to get out of my current lifestyle.

I was sincere in wanting to become more responsible and to make my life better; however, I didn't know where to begin. School was the only place I could think of. Because my track record was so bad and I had missed too much of the first semester, I wasn't admitted back into school right away. Luckily, the principal referred me to a program for high school dropouts called Lost Prizes. I hadn't even *gotten* to high school, let alone had the chance to drop out, so I was very nervous. The principal told me that if I did well there (taking career awareness, problem solving, and work experience courses), I could get some credits and enter the high school's mature student program for the second semester.

I attended classes regularly (which I had never managed to do before), worked hard (another first), earned my credits, and got back into the mainstream. It wasn't easy, but I finally graduated from high school in June 1995, at 19 years of age. To make matters even better, people had begun to notice and buy some of my artwork. I had never had an art lesson, but everybody said I had talent. I began to believe it when, in November of that year, I was one of seven students selected to present artwork at the National Association of Gifted Children Conference in Tampa, Florida. What excitement! It was my first flight, my first trip to the United States, and my first try at public speaking. My art appeared on the cover of a book about Lost Prizes, and people at the conference were asking me to autograph their copies. It was a better high than anything provided by drugs! Many of my sketches and paintings were sold, and I was asked to illustrate another book cover and do some work for a magazine. I now had a future. It wasn't where I had been that mattered, it was where I was going. I had come from nowhere and now was doing something productive.

Other good things started to happen. I had met my girlfriend, Carla Wise, on New Year's Eve of 1994. She believed in me and helped me stick things out during the tough times. I had someone to share things with. In April 1996, we had a little girl, Cheyanne Dakota, and on December 1st, 1997, our second daughter, Shawntae, arrived. We're a happy family!

There were some setbacks, of course. After high school graduation, I felt I was ready for more, so I enrolled in an advertising art course at the local community college. I thought I was ready, but I guess I wasn't. I couldn't handle the increased demands and dropped out after a few months. So much had happened so fast—I think I was still a little immature. I still believe that when I look at where I was and where I am now, I have accomplished a lot. There haven't been any miracles, I guess, but I have many achievements I'm proud of:

- I have stayed away from bad stuff for several years now. Now that I have the kids, I don't want any illegal activities going on. It's hard to believe, but I intend to be a good role model.
- I've plugged away steadily at jobs to support my family. I was employed at a bakery for a year and in Alberta on the oil rigs for a while. I now have a full-time job on a farm driving tractors and trucks (loading grain and canola) and helping with chores.
- Carla and I have stuck together and built a family. A few years ago, I didn't think I would ever be able to do that. We are taking good care of our girls and working for the future.
- I have graduated from high school and intend to go back to community college in September of 1999. I'll never be satisfied

until I get more art training and a diploma in that field—I want that real bad. Now I know the hurdles I have to get over to reach my dream, and now I think I have the self-discipline to do it. Carla will graduate from high school in January 1999, and she is planning to study nursing. Together we may be able to have careers and provide well for Cheyanne Dakota and Shawntae.

- I haven't done all I had hoped, but I have sold some paintings and had some of my artwork published. It hasn't been easy—we'll see how it works out.

- I now take much more pride in myself. We learned about non-verbal communication in one of our Lost Prizes courses, and I paid attention and followed through. I don't have many clothes (my dress outfit is khaki pants with a button shirt), but people have noticed how much better groomed I am now. I feel better about myself and I walk straighter!

- My attitude is better in general. I know what to expect, I'm better prepared, and I'm confident I can hang in there and make it. I have many people to thank for helping me, and I try to do that by giving them paintings. It has been quite a transformation, which I plan to continue working on!

SUMMARY

Not enough time, money, resources, trained staff, and effective programs are available to help troubled students. The mental health concept of treating psychopathology, deviancy, and deficits no longer is an effective concept to help the thousands of students who come to school with normal developmental problems, situational crises, and internalized chronic problems.

Our approach is to create a comprehensive psychoeducational program that results in promoting a student's strengths rather than weaknesses. This approach leads to the development of protective skills called *resiliency*—the ability to bounce back or negotiate stressful life experiences. To accomplish this, the student must be supported by adults who know how to connect with troubled students; who create proactive, supportive school programs; and who develop a relationship that indicates that the student is respected, is important, and can learn ways of being competent. This is what *Conflict in the Classroom* is all about.

2 CONNECTING WITH TROUBLED STUDENTS:
The Psychology of Helping

ALL teachers have relationships with their students, but not all these relationships are helpful. The ways professionals attempt to help troubled students range from a combination of tough love, punishment, and verbal guilt to the use of behavior modification, insight, and social skills training. During a teacher–student exchange, there is a surplus of hollow talk, most frequently by the teacher. The most likely way a student gets help is by seeing a therapist outside of school time in an office. Little wonder that the education of troubled students has been described by critics as generally ineffective.

Teaching troubled students saps the very core of a teacher's energy and is a major contributor to professional fatigue. The new and growing practice of inclusion only increases this stress. Further, the number and severity of student behavior problems continue to increase, reflecting new levels of poverty and family disintegration. Some teachers feel helpless to do anything significant for these students who have overwhelming life situations. This feeling is doubly frustrating because many teachers were attracted to the profession by the desire to do good things for students. There should be multiple community services available for troubled students and their families, but these are less and less the reality as social services are drastically reduced. As a result, the teacher remains the central figure for restorative possibility.

Little has been done, however, to present a comprehensive picture of the teaching role with troubled students (Morse, 1985). Because acting out behavior is the most common indicator of these students, the focus has been on the teacher's authority as a way to manage these behaviors, as if this single dimension were the cure. Unfortunately, teacher exercise of power easily becomes an end in and of itself. Sarason (1985) considered this an inadequate conceptualization of the modern teaching role. He included teaching in the mental health professions because teachers, for better or worse, must assess and respond to many troubled students in the course of a day. Sarason went on to say that such a view is seldom explicated in training; once the teacher is on the job, ethos emphasizes control. Fear of losing control permeates the field because the teacher is judged on the ability to manage, single-handedly, whoever is assigned to the classroom. Just conducting a classroom that includes such distraught students can be highly taxing. Although behavior control is necessary, control is not a sufficient raison d'être.

The aim of this chapter is to explore caring as one relatively neglected aspect of the teaching matrix for troubled students. The impetus came from visiting classrooms for these students where the teachers were considered by their supervisors as outstandingly effective. There was great respect and admiration for these teachers. After observing these teachers, it was easy to agree that real learning was taking place in these classrooms. To me, the striking observation was how different these classrooms were. Each teacher had a unique style. One might run a strict behavior modification point system, whereas another concentrated on Life Space Interviews and group work. Some teachers had students working together on worksheets, whereas others assigned individual self-selected projects. All classrooms included a wide range of activities. These classes did not always run smoothly. There were low-profile, quiet, modulated teachers and other teachers who were approaching manic. At times some of the teachers said and did things that were shocking.

What I was looking for were some common underlying attributes among these gifted teachers. Usually there was a time the teachers could talk about their kids, and here I discovered one common thread: They knew their students and had a deep empathy for the stress in their lives. They faced unacceptable behavior without panic. They were not permissive. They worked out what they considered was best for the student even when it caused pain and resistance. In short, these exemplary teachers all cared deeply about their charges, though they expressed that caring in different ways. Later, when I talked to the students and sometimes raised a question about certain teacher practices, the students would respond, "Yes, but my teacher cares about us students." The students were convinced that their teacher really was concerned about their welfare. This was the common thread. Such teacher commitment overrode moment-by-moment tactics, such as the sequence of testing that usually preceded acceptance. Not every teacher won over every child, to be sure, but for most of the students the level ground was teacher caring.

As we explore the essential role of caring in teaching troubled students, we would do well to remember that love alone is not enough. Without the presence of order, little will be accomplished. A teacher who tolerates chaos will be seen by the students as incompetent and thus uncaring. Students and adolescents who lack adequate internal control require assistance in managing their behavior at school. The issue is external control to what end? External control too often has become the ultimate goal of the reclaiming effort. Brendtro, Brokenleg, and Van Bockern (2002) believe that the raw use of adult authority only encourages these students to develop skills to outwit adults. But even if the students win, they lose. The system may be bested in a battle, but the system eventually wins the war even if victory means student exclusion. A few authors, such as Jones and Jones (1990), recommend management through interpersonal relationships instead of student management by power and system-based intimidation. These authors demonstrate how teachers can use student feedback to achieve a humanized behavior management program. Brendtro and Brokenleg (1993) worked from a base of attachment and American Indian ethos to present alternatives to a school culture of control. In her work Nichols (1991, 1992) faced the issue of compassion and control with an inclusive awareness. Even for oppositional students, recent recovery programs no longer rely on control alone but advocate behavior control with interpersonal caring.

The salient etiological condition most often mentioned in the histories of at-risk and troubled students is the lack of adequate adult caring. Increasing numbers of students come to school uncared for, neglected, and sometimes abused as a consequence of family struggles with poverty and dysfunction. Agewise, these students are developmentally unfinished, suffering from the absence of nurturing parenting. They suffer from low self-esteem and have not been taught impulse control. They are not ready for school, and school is not ready for them. The numbers of inadequately cared for students in some schools have reached epidemic levels. The school should face up to the need for a curriculum of caring and do whatever is possible to engender what students need. No teacher can be the central caring figure for all students, but perhaps each troubled student might have at least one school adult as an especially concerned personal advocate.

It is not enough for teachers to feel that they are caring professionals. Most of us believe we are. The task is to communicate our caring to our students so that they feel cared about. There is no single way to establish such a bond of trust. Those "exemplar" teachers each achieved this in a unique way, just as caring parents demonstrate their care in various ways. Perhaps teacher trainees should be selected from those with high profiles in two of Gardner's (1991) seven domains of intelligence. One he defined as *interpersonal intelligence,* or the capacity to sense and respond properly to the internal states of others. Thus, interpersonal interaction depends on understanding the other individual. It is the empathic ability to take the perspective of another and respond appropriately to the moods and motivations of that other. The other intelligence having a direct bearing on caring is what Gardner called *intrapersonal intelligence,* which is an awareness and knowledge of one's own feelings to be used in guiding one's behavior. This access to one's own feelings enables one to conduct honest dialogue. Gardner described different profiles of intelligence suited to given professions. Noddings (1991, 1992) had a slightly different slant, using the term *interpersonal reasoning,* which is an effort to cultivate relationships with engrossment and compassionate attention to others. Caring involves an active relationship. Rightly or wrongly, a common student complaint is, "The teachers just don't care, so why should I follow them?" While this may sometimes be a convenient defense, too often it is an accurate perception of the student's reality. On the other hand, when a teacher reaches out to troubled students, the students frequently respond.

In contrast to the helping professions of psychiatry, social work, and psychology, there is little in the training of teachers to expedite caring. The organization of schools also seems designed to frustrate caring activity. Persons drawn to teaching by a deep sense of caring for troubled students can face a cultural shock on entering some schools. The native caring, which should have been made more functional through training, is destroyed instead. *Caring,* however, is a difficult term to define. We know caring as the psychological condition that makes personal and social growth possible so that the infant becomes a human being. We recognize caring because we have experienced it at some level from parents, mates, friends, and teachers. The closest of human relationships is between the child and the parent, which is at the same time the most distant relationship because the adult and child live in separate psychological worlds. According to Goodlad, Soder, and Sirotnik (1990), caring in schools involves the whole life of the student in the setting. It is not just an atmosphere of being listened to with patience and nonrejection. Every learning task has both cognitive and affective components. Interpersonal caring is meeting the instructional, curriculum, and learning needs too, so that school is an exciting and fun place as well as a safe place. Teachers do provide, for some students, the only anchor of security and attachment.

Normal students are given to testing behavioral limits as part of growing up. Troubled students make a career of limit pushing and testing, which explains why many teachers are obsessed with control. However, teaching students, especially troubled students, puts the teacher in the center of students' need for caring and acceptance. The current modus operandi is to get immediate control, not as a stage but as the end point. Again we emphasize the need for an effective classroom management plan. Deeper than the surface management of behavior, teachers also hope to change the attitudes and values of these students. This requires the teacher to be a model, or a figure of identification, who interacts and can discuss meaningful issues with students. Caring facilitates identification and becomes a powerful force for the long-term impact teachers can have on students. Jones and Jones (1990) demonstrated how behavior management, based on caring relationships, can promote this goal.

Some students and adolescents are too emotionally damaged to respond to a caring teacher. As Noddings (1992) explained, it is difficult to keep caring when one is rejected, even though the rejecters are the very students most in need of caring. Much attention-demanding behavior can be recognized as resistance or the student's inappropriate way of seeking a caring relationship. If you don't know how to deal with it, the natural response is to drift into retaliatory resistance. Can the ability to reach out to these students continue if the teacher does not really know their life stressors?

If teachers are going to make long-standing inroads with troubled students, teachers must be convinced that they have a profound source of influence. Paul (Paul & Smith, 2000) created a method to bring home the power of caring to teachers in training or in the classroom. He had each teacher write two letters. The first was a letter of thanks to send to the teacher who had the greatest positive influence on that teacher. These were then read in the group. The interpersonal qualities of influential teachers became evident and explained why these teachers left an indelible mark on their students. Qualities of being cared about that these teachers reported include being respected, being listened to, feeling safe, being able to express their feelings and still be accepted, sharing lives, confirming accomplishments, and fostering students' power over their own lives. These helpful teachers shared the feeling that student and teacher were together on life's journey. The second letter proposed by Paul (Paul & Smith, 2000) was to the teacher who did the most personal damage to the individual. Most adults have vivid and disturbing memories of uncaring teachers, even to the point of reliving the personal humiliation and anger generated. This teaching method opens up the power of the student–teacher relationships for good or ill.

An additional exercise Paul (Paul & Smith, 2000) proposed is to have the teachers ask their students to write descriptions of teachers or adults who have helped them and who have frustrated them. He also had teachers write out episodes of "peak" experiences with students they liked and students they disliked, and explain why. Another activity is to have students recall any episodes of being punished in school. Paul also suggested that teachers write an account of a student with whom they feel they have done an outstanding job, and another student to whom they would relate in a different way, given a second chance. These personal accounts emphasize the unique nature of caring exchanges. I have asked high school teachers to describe situations where they have reached out to a student beyond the call of duty. Examples of such caring are almost universal, although the desired results were not always achieved.

Rogers and Webb (1991) wrote that it is not fair to encourage caring as a central feature of relating to troubled students unless teachers are given specific training to prevent codependent relationships. Students cannot be "adopted" by their teachers or even mentally taken home. It is not enough to want to help. The intent must be buttressed with deep knowledge of student development and pathology, as well as interpersonal relationships. Training is required to know how to understand and respond to the deep human needs these students express when they identify with their caring teachers. Without training, some teachers keep an emotional distance from students in order to avoid the intense feelings of interpersonal closeness.

Despite having individual relationships with students, teachers are primarily group workers (Hobbs, 1982). They will have to establish a positive relationship with the total class and potent subgroups in order to maintain a caring classroom.

Having caring teachers is a beginning but not comprehensive solution for troubled students. The overall neglect of our students is too acute. All social agencies will have to become more caring in their practice. The school can become the hub of service integration through the Full Service School concept, where relevant agencies function on the school campus and work under the monitoring of a case manager to bring appropriate services to the student and family. There is no implication in these introductory comments that caring teachers can do it all. The belief is that caring teacher relationships can be part of the solution rather than part of the problem.

TREAT ME WITH RESPECT

How do students feel about the ways adults respond to them? Are they sensitive to the overt and covert verbal and nonverbal messages teachers send as they interact with troubled students? The answer is obvious. Yes, not only are they sensitive to teachers' attitudes, but they also wish to be treated in a kind and caring way.

ARTICLE 2.1

STUDENTS at Our Lady of Lourdes Elementary School on the Pine Ridge Indian Reservation participated in "Child Abuse Awareness Month" with activities that stressed respect for students. Sister Rita Ostrey, counselor at the Porcupine, South Dakota, school, shared the following writing by two students.

AS I GROW
Echo LeBeaux (Grade 5)

Treat me with respect, the way you would to a person who you look up to.

Teach me things from right to wrong.

Understand me and have patience with me when I'm having hard times.

Be proud of me when I do things right.

When something does go wrong, show me the right way without getting mad.

When your anger flares up, put your hands in your pocket and don't use them on me.

Remember, I am a gift to you from God, and you are a gift to me from God, and His love is always there for us to share.

From *The Journal of Emotional and Behavorial Problems, 1*(4), 1993, p. 3. Copyright by The Journal of Emotional and Behavorial Problems, Inc. Reprinted with permission.

ARTICLE 2.2

RESPECT

Jerome His Law (Grade 7)

I want to be treated with respect and dignity. If you respect me, I will respect you. If you take pride in me, I will take pride in you. But if you treat me bad I will probably abuse myself by drugs, alcohol, and low self-esteem. This is going to all the parents on earth. If you do not abuse your children—good and don't start. Give us love and attention, listen to us when we have a problem and talk to us when you have a problem. Because when you ignore us it makes us feel stupid and mad.

It doesn't matter if you're white, black, or Indian, we are all human and humans have feelings. And it feels bad when we get hurt by bad names, teasing, taunting, and being ignored. So, talk it over with somebody, and tell your kid you love them and maybe he/she will say she/he loves you.

ARTICLE 2.3

TROUBLED youngsters most often do not or cannot control themselves during stressful situations. There remains a deeply ingrained notion that we can best help them by imposing adult control. As recent studies make clear, adult control dominates education. But the fear of loss of adult control still consumes many teachers and administrators. Polly Nichols has worked with troubled children in many capacities—teacher, administrator, teacher trainer, and author—but she has never lost her teacher viewpoint. Here, in a balanced discussion of the issues, she addresses the heart of the matter of control. What do we mean when we say a strategy "works." One attempt any teacher could use to answer this question is to apply the before-and-after self-esteem assessment that Nichols describes in this article.

THE CURRICULUM OF CONTROL: TWELVE REASONS FOR IT, SOME ARGUMENTS AGAINST IT

Polly Nichols

Classrooms of control—in these words, Jane Knitzer, Zina Steinberg, and Braham Fleisch (1990) characterize the school day world of children with emotional or behavioral disabilities and of their teachers: "For children labelled emotionally or behaviorally handicapped, control is … a central part of schooling … Too often the dominant curriculum is not the traditional academic curriculum, nor is it about concepts, thinking, and problem solving. Instead the curriculum is about controlling the behaviors of the children. The reward system is alike for teachers and students. A quiet class is highly regarded and few supervisors, administrators or even parents look much beyond this."

Their book, *At the Schoolhouse Door: An examination of programs and policies for children with behavioral and emotional problems,* published in 1990 by New York's Bank Street College of Education, is the report of a major study of programming for students with emotional or behavioral disorders (EBD). The report is exhaustive, the findings disturbing, but in no way more so than in their characterization of the EBD classrooms they studied as being dominated by a "Curriculum of Control."

"The curriculum emphasis is often on behavioral management first" with a central concern upon behavioral point systems. "Yet often, these seem largely designed to help maintain silence in the classroom, not to teach children how better to manage their anger, sadness, or impulses."

When we entered this field—we teachers, administrators, teacher-trainers, consultant—we had other dreams and purposes than to control children. Why do we all, to some degree or another, buy into this "curriculum of control"? The answers are complex and rooted so deeply in our beliefs about what children and grown-ups are about that they are hard to bring into the light for a close look. As someone who has worked in all of these job categories and has thought a good deal about our care of students with EBD. I have worried about a seeming overemphasis on "managing" our students, as though they were accounts or hirelings athletes. At least a dozen reasons for this preoccupation with control occur to me:

From *Beyond Behavior*, 3(2), 1992, pp. 5–11. Copyright by Beyond Behavior. Reprinted with permission.

- Controls are necessary for an orderly, productive existence. When we lose control, we are at risk for unpleasant or dangerous consequences. As we are grown-ups, we know these facts to be true from our own experience. As we are teachers, we devote our professional lives to the notion that we can teach children what we know that they do not already know, that they will be better off for it, and that they might even thank us for it sometime. So, since we know control is good, and we know EBD children are short of it, we make control the central point of our programming.

- Somewhere in the hearts of most of us is a desire, felt rarely or frequently, to show disobedient, mouthy children and teens just what authority is and who has it. We may genuinely believe that enforcing limits is the best lesson we can teach, or we may react that way only when we sense we are losing—our dignity, a battle, our touch.

- Everybody knows that controlling is what teachers are *supposed* to do. Teachers have known that from the time they were little girls (rarely boys) playing school. Remember the scoldings, the bossy directions, the hands on hips, the recesses denied, the principals sent to? Some teachers, the warmest, most easygoing people in the faculty lounge, are stricken with facial paralysis when they encounter students. They do not smile, they become severe, austere, bent on control. This seems to be a role, one of which they are scarcely aware. Note how much like playing school these descriptions by Knitzer and her colleagues sound:

  > But in many of the classrooms we visited, group work is not allowed, children's comments are squelched, and questions and answer format of the most teacherly kind is the only form allowed. If children talk, they lose points, if they exchange baseball statistics, the cards are taken away. Helping each other is called cheating—genuine excitement is rare.

- From the start, the degree to which boys and girls are or are not presumed to be "in control" is a primary factor in how sympathetically they are viewed and treated and where they are placed. There "lurks an implicit belief that somehow socially maladjusted children are able to control their behavior, while seriously emotionally disturbed or behaviorally disordered children cannot."

- Behavior modification techniques, when poorly understood and improperly applied, may lead the modifiers to rely most heavily upon external control for management. "In most behavior modification programs, obedience predominates over responsibility, punishment over logical consequences. Though children are placed in special (EBD) programs because of their behavioral difficulties, systematic, coherent attempts to help them gain control over their problems is the exception, not the rule."

- Society expects good teachers to have "excellent classroom control," perhaps above all else. When students misbehave, it reflects at least as poorly on their teachers as on themselves, a negative halo effect all EBD teachers have felt at one time or another, if not from their administrators, then probably from a regular education colleague or a faculty lounge clique.

- We think of control as something that can be and should be applied, rather like a behavioral ointment. When children in our care are neither self-controlled nor easily controlled by us, we may attribute their control deficiencies primarily to parents who have not applied enough control at home. Then it follows that the best thing for us to do is to slather on a lot of control at school. We may do this in the purest expectation that it will be helpful, or we may do it with some extra zeal, showing parents just how control can be and should be applied. We may extend this directly to parents themselves by setting up controls over their parenting behavior that can result in front office or social agency sanctions.

- Some published programs such as Assertive Discipline (Canter & Canter, 1976) or the Boys Town Model (Michael, 1987) are tremendously popular perhaps because they offer teachers completely prescribed, ready-to-operate methods of control. The skillful teacher is flexible and encouraging while using them, but their strongest appeal may be to teachers inexperienced or insecure about their ability to cope with students' misbehavior. In such programs, they may find a prescription for control that they sense they lack.

- Teachers fear their students. They are unsure what lengths students will go to if given an inch. If students were allowed free choice or free movement or free time to talk with friends, who knows if teachers would be able to regain control?
- Being controlling may be due to basic traits that are part of some individuals' personalities.
- Additionally, teachers may be struggling, isolated, depressed, or frightened and strong control in silent classrooms the only method they have found for dealing with what they fear otherwise would overwhelm them and be intolerable.

THE EFFECTS OF CONTROL

Control is not merely pepper in the pot, sometime there is enough, too much, or too little of according to one's taste. Neither is it intrinsically related only to harshness. In fact, many controlling behaviors are sweet indeed, from giving praise to giving M&Ms. A body of research has evolved from Edward Deci's cognitive evaluation theory which discriminates between rewards that are given in order to control children's behavior and those that are given in order to impart information to children about their behavior.

Deci and his colleagues (Deci, Nezlek, & Sheinman, 1981) note that most studies on the effects of rewards and constraints indicate that rewards actually work to *decrease* intrinsic motivation, clearly something to think about in a world which Knitzer and her colleagues describe as being preoccupied with the giving of points. Does this mean our behavior management systems are all to no avail? Not at all. "If rewards are administered in a way that does not emphasize control but rather signifies competence, the theory predicts a maintenance or enhancement of intrinsic motivation. The suggestion, therefore, is that rewards will not undermine intrinsic motivation if they are administered in a way that emphasizes positive competence rather than control."

Studying this theory, Deci et al. researchers predicted a correlation between teachers' attitudes toward control versus autonomy and children's feelings about the climate of their classroom. The more positive the students' views of the classroom climate, the greater their intrinsic motivation and the higher their self-esteem levels were likely to be.

Teachers were asked to choose among solutions for eight typical school problems—the playground bully, stealing, homework not done and such—which represented the following four basic orientations, two extreme and two moderate:

> *Highly Controlling:* teachers make decisions about what is right and use highly controlling sanctions to produce the desired behavior.

> *Moderately Controlling:* teachers make the decisions and emphasize that the children should perform the desired behaviors for their own good.

> *Moderately Autonomous:* teachers encourage children to compare themselves with others to see how to handle the problem.

> *Highly Autonomous:* teachers encourage children to consider the relevant elements of the situation and to take responsibility for working out a solution to the problem.

The self-esteem of the 610 fourth through sixth graders who participated in the study had their self-esteem measured twice, once at the end of the first six weeks of school, again near the end of the year. The prediction was that students in a classroom all year with either a control- or an autonomy-oriented teacher would change their original perceptions to develop either higher or lower self-esteem as the year went along. Instead, the researchers made a more startling discovery. There were meaningful differences between measures of children's self-esteem over the course of the year—the significant relationship between teachers' orientation toward control versus autonomy and students' self-esteem and intrinsic motivation occurred during the first six weeks of school and did not change markedly thereafter.

Vernon Jones and Louise Jones (1990) preface their book on classroom management with a reminder that in the 1960s, most teacher training went little beyond such simple prescriptions as "don't smile until Christmas" or "don't grin until Thanksgiving," homespun advice still passed along to neophytes. But the research by Deci and his colleagues suggests that in the first six weeks of the school year, the die is cast for development of student self-esteem for the year. Waiting until December to start to smile would be months too late for the affirmation and support youngsters need, sacrificed presumably to show no-nonsense control.

Perhaps many teachers are deliberately taught other aspects of the "curriculum of control" in their training programs. Certainly many administrators seem to have been. More than one principal in our Iowa town has launched his school year with an opening assembly speech which let everyone know the dire consequences that would befall students who did the rotten things that students had done the year before—and they soon had behavior to contend with they had not dreamed of, such as severe vandalism. *Should* that be so? Isn't firm limit setting from the start a maxim of behavior management? It seems reasonable enough an idea, but the results are predictable. As Jones and Jones comment:

"In short, the use of power is often effective at intimidating students who need control least and is seldom effective with students whose behavior is most unproductive."

So, it turns out that the curriculum of control is not only dreary; it is counterproductive. It tends to generate the very behaviors that EBD placement is designed to ameliorate. Even those who are successfully ordered by a classroom climate of quiet control may not be internally convinced it is the way to go. Have you experienced or heard tales of the ever-so-well-regulated classroom that no one can handle but the regular teacher? When his or her back is turned, or worse, when the substitute comes, the place turns upside down.

Even more pernicious are the findings reported by Allen and Greenberger (1980) of laboratory studies on the relation between hostility and defiance and perceptions of control over events. The less control a person has over objective events, the more satisfaction he or she draws from destructive acts; they create feelings of success that are unavailable elsewhere. Students who experience failures in school are more likely to act in deviant ways to increase, at least temporarily, their feelings of power and self-determination. One high schooler reported to an interviewer that each time he passed a locker he had smashed, he thought with pride, "There's my little destruction to this brand new school." He had made his mark of control on his environment.

So why, if the curriculum of control can be so damaging, is it so prevalent in EBD classrooms? In fairness, a twelfth cause of teachers' preference for it must be listed:

- The curriculum of control works. We can make our classrooms quiet—a mark of ourselves as good teachers in virtually everybody's book. But even more striking, we sometimes truly seem to shape up some kids by showing them the bottom line. We convince them that appropriate behavior is the only winning card and change their understanding of how the world works—at least it seems so while they are with us, and some youngsters' new behaviors do generalize to mainstream classes and to other environments very well.

Whether or not we choose to operate our classrooms along strictly behavioristic lines, the fact remains that everyone is subject to principles of operant conditioning. What is the most powerful schedule of reinforcement for maintaining a behavior? As we all learned in our first Intro to EBD courses, it is the intermittent schedule of reinforcement—and that is exactly the schedule we teachers are put on by our successes, no matter how rare, with our control-responsive students. If controlling techniques appear to be effective in changing children's lives for the better or improving our lives in the classroom or heightening our own feelings of competence even just once in a while, we will almost surely persist in using them. We will do so even in the face of irrefutable evidence that those control techniques are not bringing about improvement in the majority of situations with the greater number of our students and are instead causing dreadful confrontations or boredom or just chronic dissatisfaction.

When our controlling techniques—positive through our bestowal of rewards or negative through meting out of penalties—are effective, we attribute those successes to our effectiveness as teachers. When our techniques fail, we are likely to blame one or more factors lying within the students themselves. Failing to do this—and EBD teachers do like and defend most of their students as individuals, pointing out how "wonderful they can be on a one-to-one basis"—teachers next look for causes within their students' families. To look at our own teaching or management practices as blameworthy invites feelings of failure, and they may be intolerable.

IF NOT CONTROL, WHAT?

If studies have revealed such findings to us at least since the 1970s, why have we not all made use of them and created stimulating, effective classrooms that would have been a joy for Knitzer, Steinberg, and Fleisch to behold? Actually, they did find some that were:

But both in self-contained classrooms and in separate programs we saw and learned about alternatives that supplement more typical strategies (time-out rooms, point and level behavior management systems) with strategies to help students take responsibility for their own actions.

They tell of a fairness committee of EBD student representatives who discuss complaints and plan remedies; of a social skills project where students team with adults to discuss, practice, and try out strategies for use in their lunchrooms and playgrounds; of a "Time-In" room where students in difficulty are helped to relax, gain control, and work out solutions to their problems; of a sophisticated model of behavior management used in a girls' residential treatment facility called a Therapeutic Just Community; of an especially strong extra-curricular activity program involving coaches who teach social skills on the spot.

The common attribute of the programs Knitzer, Steinberg, and Fleisch admire is an innovative approach to designing meaningful, rewarding activities through which students will learn ways to fit into their real worlds with less stress, unhappiness, and conflict. In the academic domain where they generally found even less to admire, they sought alternatives to an impoverished life "defined by dittoed worksheets and isolation" but found few to describe.

A group of well-known theorists, researchers, and teacher trainers in the field of emotional or behavior disorders who call themselves the Peacock Hill Working Group, have recently produced a more encouraging account of the health and well-being of the EBD field in the United States (Cook et al., 1991). Noting that the authors of *At the Schoolhouse Door* have described existing problems "compellingly and comprehensively," they assert that less sweeping reforms than Knitzer and her colleagues call for may be needed:

> Effective school-based approaches for children or youth with emotional or behavioral disorders are presently available, but a lack of commitment to youngsters and families and the scarcity or resources have stymied their implementation. Indeed, much that we know can ameliorate the problems that have been described. To be sure, research is needed to address critical questions in many areas of practice, but current practices would be dramatically improved were the strategies and the programs known to be successful implemented with fidelity.

If so much is known and possible, why are so many teachers having such a difficult time with EBD classes that so much criticism is raining down on them? We know what the outcome of criticism is likely to be—lowered feelings of personal efficacy. It works the same way with adults as with children. With less sense of competence may come a greater need to exert external control over students which will, in turn, be likely to create more rather than fewer problems in the classroom (or on the sneak out of the classroom). Lowered self-esteem in teachers has even been shown to result in smaller academic gains in students over the course of a school year as compared to the progress made by children taught by teachers with high self-esteem (Aspy & Buhler, 1975). With such a discouraging set of outcomes likely, why do any teachers put up with it?

Many do not. The figure given in the Peacock Hill Group paper for teacher burnout is over a third of teachers surveyed saying that they expected to be doing something else within a year. They note one contributing reason to be the low levels of likability and social acceptability of youngsters with EBD. Others reasons are probably related to the unattractive working arrangements EBD teachers have in many schools. In a survey of EBD teachers' working conditions, Mary McManus and James Kauffman (1991) found that fully one-fourth of self-contained EBD class teachers dealt with disruptive behavior more than 22 times a day, one-fifth were verbally threatened daily, one-fourth were physically threatened monthly, and the mean numbers of physical attacks were nearly 14 per year, 47 per teaching career. And these teachers might well be in conflict with their superiors as well for, as the Peacock Hill writers point out, teachers and administrators tend not to agree about how to handle students whose behavior is extremely distasteful to them.

SKILL TRAINING—AND PERSONALITY TRAINING, TOO?

The Peacock Hill Group states that about 30 percent of teachers currently working in EBD programs are not trained and certified to be doing so; but that means that about 70 percent, a substantial majority, after all, are. We cannot blame the inadequacies that now exist only on a lack of training among the un- or under-certified. We must look at what happens within the actual certification programs. Besides teaching methodology skills, are there positive personality characteristics that can be taught to make a true master?

In a 1971 review of teacher effectiveness studies, Rosenshine and Furst identified 11 teacher variables that had shown the strongest relationships to student gains. The three strongest were clarity, variability, and enthusiasm. Anyone trained to think task-analytically could come up with training strategies to teach students to display these behaviors, even one as seemingly a part of built-in personality as enthusiasm. In fact, Rosenshine (1970) did exactly that. His observations of teachers revealed that components of enthusiasm were rapid speech, frequent movement, gesture, variation in voice, eye contact, appearing relaxed, asking varied questions, and praising frequently. Coleman (1977) comments:

> If the anxieties of teachers, particularly beginning teachers, and the boredom of students can be somewhat relieved by training teachers to be more enthusiastic or energetic, as the research suggests is possible, this could be a most useful contribution to teacher effectiveness.

Experiences I have had suggest to me that such training is possible and useful. Years ago, I taught in a program staffed by our children's psychiatric hospital and operated in a public junior high school. Our students registered typical complaints about the boringness or hardness or unfairness of various mainstream teachers, but one teacher escaped their criticism, the science teacher, Mr. Moeller. They thought he was great. When I looked at the homework they brought from his class, it did not appear to be especially stimulating nor geared to their individual learning abilities, nor did the students express any strong interest in the particular science they were studying. New to that school, I guessed that Mr. Moeller might be especially good-looking, young, with-it, but when I identified who he was I saw him to be middle-aged, balding, neither fit looking nor a snappy dresser. I pressed my questions, got a lot more "I don't know … he's just nice" answers, but finally got this description: "Well, whenever I go by him in the hall between classes, he always says 'Hi, Nick.' " So I checked the scene between classes. The rule in that school was that teachers were to be in their doorways between bells, watching students pass. A walk down the halls revealed teachers standing in pairs or alone, arms crossed, faces watchful, true standard bearers of the need for quiet and order in the halls. Mr. Moeller, by contrast, relaxed against his doorjamb and said such things as "Hi" or "How's it going," or he nodded, or he just smiled. As time went on and I spent more time in classes, I never discovered anything more remarkably charismatic or reinforcing about Mr. Moeller than that he was relaxed, looked at kids when they talked, smiled easily, used their names frequently, and spoke pleasantly. From that, I developed my first set of social skills steps for teachers:

- Use eye contact
- Smile
- Say the student's name
- Use pleasant words

I was thrilled with my discovery and taught this magic to good effect in a Methods class I was teaching in the evenings. Later I learned that I had only rediscovered some of Dale Carnegie's basic ingredients for winning friends and influencing people; later still, I recognized the same steps in various social skills curricula published for use with students. But it has never seemed less magic a discovery or less obvious a deficit among teachers who are having trouble with or hating their EBD classes.

It would be simple minded to suggest that all we need to do to help EBD teachers become effective and like their jobs is to teach them to smile more often, look at their kids when they talk to them, and quietly exchange everyday pleasantries. Yet when I consult in a classroom where the teacher is having trouble, these are the behaviors that are immediately conspicuous by their absence. Whether the stern faces, distance from students, and eyes focused on academic materials or point sheets except when surveying to pierce a bad actor with a piercing stare are the results of hard time or the results of having played teacher from the beginning, is impossible to say. Whichever, they are among the most obvious behaviors connected with the troubles at hand.

TRAINING FOR DOING

The most crucial part of teacher-training programs is experience in classrooms with experienced teachers. But what I wonder is this: What happens if a student teacher flunks adaptability or is only so-so on optimism, for instance, or manages only luke-warm relationships with students? It is a sure bet that he won't be flunked out of his program; and it is a sure bet that once alone in an EBD classroom instead of under the supervision and magic spell of a master teacher, those deficiencies will loom larger. It is then, when feeling uncertain and ineffective, that teachers seem to look to increased control for the structure *they* need. The conclusion is easily drawn that warm relationships are possible only after students have learned that the teacher is boss, and they must do what the boss says—don't smile until Christmas! But as efforts go on to establish control, those first crucial weeks during which the foundation for healthy self-esteem and positive personal expectations for the year pass by, and it is a cold and stormy year—for students and their teachers, too.

The key interaction, affect, and attitude variables that are listed as goals for teachers-in-training to acquire first appear as competencies not in course syllabi but on student teaching checklists. Who has taught these skills that are then to be practiced? Do we count on the supervising teachers alone to teach these critical elements of teaching children and teens with emotional or behavioral disorders? But what if the supervising teacher him- or herself lacks these skills? Certainly, one's impression from reading the criticism of EBD classrooms is that master teachers are rare. With many students to place for practice teaching, it seems inevitable that a majority will be placed with supervising teachers who themselves lack key skills and attitudes we urgently desire for our next generation of teachers in the field.

Shouldn't we offer to students in our teacher-training classes opportunities to develop the skills of interpersonal relationships just as we offer the youngsters in our EBD classes social skill training? Wouldn't it be possible to describe and demonstrate just what EBD teachers need to do and say to promote their students' sense of autonomy, control, and personal competence. Then have teachers-in-training practice, role play, receive feedback, and try out their new skills in real classrooms until they were truly confident and competent? Do we know how to teach the behaviors associated with enthusiasm or warmth, of giving quiet reprimands, offering instructional praise, assuming non-threatening physical postures, talking an out-of-control student down or a depressed student up, responding to lies, handling anger? What would you say to the oppositional child who would rather argue than agree no matter what? To the anxious child who couldn't handle stress? To the teenager who hated being in special ed? When is it better *not* to talk? Instead of discussing these problems, we might model, role play and practice things to say and do, when and how to say and do them.

We have cast a dubious professional eye on canned programs such as Assertive Discipline (Evans, Evans, Gable, & Kehlhem, 1991). Part of its huge success may be due to the implied control it gives to teachers by its use and even by its name, but part of its success is also undoubtedly due to its accessibility. A one-day workshop, a manual, some materials, and you are off and running. By having it offered as a school-wide program, the teacher not only knows what to do, he knows he has built-in administrative and peer support for doing it.

Teachers are not lazy, but we are often tired. All day teaching the same children, perhaps for years, consumes a lot of materials, and some EBD teachers must plan for students from first through sixth grades daily. Their cry in faculty rooms, at inservices and conferences, is, "Does it have anything in it I can use?" By use, they mean open up a manual, read the directions, copy a worksheet or gather some materials, and have a lesson set to go.

Rather than deploring this behavior, we need to think creatively about it. What can we package this way that will travel the farthest toward our goal of improving academic and behavioral instruction for EBD children and teenagers? An example of one such widely-traveled program is *The Walker Social Skills Curriculum* (1983). Not only does the teacher have "something she can use" ready with little extra planning beyond reading it through first, she actually has entire teaching scripts. Once the teacher has taught the program through according to the scripts, she will find that she has acquired a wonderful set of direct teaching, feedback, and encouragement skills that she can apply throughout her program.

SUPPORT FOR TEACHERS AND AN END TO ISOLATION

We say we cannot do enough in a one-day workshop to help teachers out substantially, so what can we do? In a world of video everything, surely there are ways to arrange two-way communication with far-off buildings to answer questions, model approaches, and share techniques. Instead of standing before crowds of people and delivering papers, we could lead remedial coping classes, dealing with nothing but the questions that usually are relegated to the last four minutes of a presentation. Perhaps we could convert state and national conferences, where often what one gains is a matter of serendipity, into focused training weeks, offering credit for advanced courses in the manner of a Berlitz blitz. Or remember those lab schools where teachers-in-training could work with real students every day?

What we cannot do is give up on our colleagues already in classrooms around the country. We are off and running, and we do not have the luxury of ordering a recall. But as we deal with the call for new kinds of service delivery to the students in our care, we must consider new means of service delivery to their teachers, too. No one went into teaching because he or she wanted to be boring, controlling, and miserable. We chose the field so that we could do good and change the lives of children—never were their needs greater, or ours.

REFERENCES

Allen, V. L., & Greenberger, D. B. (1980). Destruction and perceived control. In A. Baum & J. E. Singer (Eds.), *Advances in environmental psychology: Vol. 2, Applications of personal control* (pp. 85–109). Hillsdale, NJ: Erlbaum. Cited in Adelman & Taylor, 1990.

Aspy, D. N., & Buhler, J. H. (1975). The effect of teachers inferred self-concept upon student achievement. *Journal of Educational Research, 68,* 386–389.

Canter, L., & Canter, M. (1976). *Assertive discipline.* Los Angeles: Lee Canter & Associates.

Coleman, P. (1977). The improvement of aggregate teaching effectiveness in a school district. In G. D. Borich, *The appraisal of teaching: Concepts and process.* Reading, MA: Addison-Wesley.

Cook, L., Cullinan, D., Epstein, M. H., Forness, S. R., Hallahan, D. P., Kauffman, J. M., Lloyd, J. W., Nelson, C. M., Polsgrove, L., Sabornie, E. J., Strain, P. S., & Walker, H. M. (1991). Problems and promises in special education and related services for children and youth with emotional or behavioral disorders. *Behavioral Disorders, 16,* 299–313.

Deci, E. L., Nezlek, J., & Sheinman, L. (1981). Characteristics of the rewarder and intrinsic motivation of the reward. *Journal of Personality and Social Psychology, 40,* 1–10.

Evans, W. H., Evans, S. S., Gable, R. A., & Kehlhem, M. A. (1991). Assertive discipline and behavior disorders: Is this a marriage made in heaven? *Beyond Behavior, 2,* 13–16.

Jones, V. F., & Jones, L. S. (1990). *Comprehensive classroom management.* Boston: Allyn & Bacon.

Knitzer, J., Steinberg, Z., & Fleisch, F. (1990). *At the schoolhouse door. An examination of the programs and policies for children with behavioral and emotional problems.* New York: Bank Street College of Education.

McManus, M. E., & Kauffman, J. M. (1991). Working conditions of teachers of students with behavioral disorders: A national study. *Behavioral Disorders, 16,* 247–259.

Michael, A. (1987). A trip to Boys Town. *Behavior in Our Schools, 1* (2–7).

Rosenshine, B. (1970). Enthusiastic teaching: A research review. *School Review, 78,* 499–512.

Rosenshine, B., & Furst, N. (1973). The use of direct observation to study teaching. In R. Travers, Ed., *Second handbook of research on teaching.* Chicago: Rand McNally, Cited in Borich, G. D., 1977.

Walker, H. M., McConnell, S., Holmes, D., Walker, J., & Golden, N. (1983). The Walker social skills curriculum. Austin, TX: PRO-ED.

ARTICLE 2.4

IF you were to list the 10 predominant characteristics of troubled students, how many would be assets? The team of Larry Brendtro, an international figure in the field of reclaiming high-risk children, and Martin Brokenleg, a counseling psychologist who is bringing the very different view of Native American ideology to our awareness, shows how we can begin to think quite differently about helping troubled students. These authors propose an alternative to the curriculum of control. They take us back to our roots and reverse the negative preoccupations of our field. As they search for the positive, they suggest we avoid the "D" words (which are listed in Article 2.4). What Brendtro and Brokenleg give us is virtually a revolutionary ideology; they reject the belief system based on folk psychology. In restorative work, we are confronted with value differences. We react to troubled students as if they were negatively all-powerful, ignoring their available positive potentials. Thus, adult behavior fosters further alienation.

These authors contrast the Western culture of individualism with the American Indian child-raising assumptions, which teach children to move outside of themselves and contribute to others. We know that failure in our competitive arena results in a sense of powerlessness, hence the reactive aggressiveness that displays one kind of power. These authors describe what a milieu would be like if the Indian concepts replaced rampant individualism. How many current programs have "giving to others" as an essential ingredient in helping kids put their awry lives back together? Are we ready to entertain a new model? Brendtro and Brokenleg give numerous examples of things to start on Monday morning. Cooperation can replace individualistic competition in the classroom, and community service projects can transform the receiver-from-others to a giver-to-others.

BEYOND THE CURRICULUM OF CONTROL

Larry K. Brendtro and Martin Brokenleg

Augustana College

Existing approaches to children with emotional and behavioral problems are often little more than a rigid "curriculum of control," according to a recent study of educational and mental health programs in the United States (Knitzer, Steinberg, & Flesch, 1990). These researchers concluded that the widespread use of simplistic behavioral interventions contributes to a "bleakness" in the daily lives of troubled children.

Similar observations about this preoccupation with control were made by an international group of professionals who completed a year-long fellowship sponsored by ILEX (International Learning Exchange in Professional Youthwork). Reflecting on their experiences in North America, the visiting fellows from Europe, Australia, and Africa shared these poignant criticisms:

> *Control is the word I hear most often here and, to me, it is the opposite of creativity.*

> *I see "crisis intervention" as a reaction to the aggression that these children show, but also as a cause for some children to be aggressive.*

> *How can you teach youngsters to be independent when there is so much control on their behavior ... I had a feeling of heaviness and immobility.*

Knitzer and colleagues report that such obedience-training strategies are increasingly being called into question. However, without viable alternative models, many who work with troubled children and youth still assume the curriculum of control to be "necessary." In this discussion, we will examine ways in which traditional "treatments" have actually fostered greater alienation; and we will suggest the foundations for an alternative paradigm rooted in empowerment philosophy rather than obedience.

BEYOND DEVIANCE AND DEFICIT

Our current preoccupation with the management of "deviant" behavior is in stark contrast to the vision of the early pioneers in working with troubled youth. These Pygmalion optimists set out to find positive potentials in the most difficult youth. Pestalozzi gathered street urchins into his castle school, declaring that beneath their coarse exterior, he would find "precious faculties" waiting to be released. "Badness is misdirected energy," asserted Floyd Starr. "What makes delinquents unique," declared Jane Addams, "is their greater spirit of adventure!"

Goldstein (1991) notes that much of recent psychological literature addresses only the negative (disease, crime, psychopathology, aggression, etc.) and how it may be corrected. Rarely is the focus on strength and its facilitation. In fact, most of the terms used to describe emotional and behavioral problems are pejorative and demeaning. Youth are labelled as Disturbed, Disordered, Deprived, Deviant, Disadvantaged, Disruptive, Disrespectful, Dysocial, Disobedient, etc. A similar disparaging mindset is the labelling of parents and families as "Dysfunctional." "D words" focus on the negative. And, those who target what is wrong with a young person are apt to overlook strengths and resources.

Our fixation with deviance and its control is a vestige of a long cultural tradition in which human relationships were organized around dominance and subjugation. This authoritarian mindset has marked the relationship of children to adults in Western civilization, and schools are a product of that tradition. Scholars are just beginning to recognize how deeply our theories of human behavior are influenced by the "folk psychology" of our culture (Rogoff & Morelli, 1989). Each of us drags this belief system behind like a cultural tail a thousand years long.

In our book *Reclaiming Youth At Risk* (Brendtro, Brokenleg, & Van Bockern, 1990), we proposed a model of youth empowerment based on contemporary developmental research, the heritage of early youth work pioneers, and Native American philosophies of child care. Anthropologists have long known that these tribal peoples reared courageous, respectful children without using aversive controls. Nevertheless, Europeans in North America tried to "civilize" indigenous children in punitive boarding schools, unaware that Native Americans were using sophisticated child-care systems that were the product of advanced cultures.

Table 2.4–1 shows how Coopersmith's (1967) foundations of self-esteem compare with Native American and Western values. In a traditional Native American culture: (1) significance is nurtured in a community that celebrates the universal need for belonging, (2) competence is ensured by guaranteeing all children the opportunity for mastery, (3) power is available to all by cultivating each person's independence, and (4) virtue is embodied in the preeminent value of generosity.

These traditions contrast with Western patriarchal values, where (1) hyper-individualism replaces belonging as the measure of one's importance, (2) competition becomes a zero-sum game where enthroning "winners" ensures an abundance of losers, (3) those who wield power to dominate are depriving others of power, and (4) a society that equates worth with wealth provides its young with a script for selfishness.

Pioneer youth workers like Pestalozzi, Addams, Montessori, and Korczak advocated many ideas similar to traditional Native American philosophy. They were attacking the dominant patriarchal values of a culture that did not respect children. Today, the wisdom of these early educational pioneers and of indigenous tribal cultures are being validated by child research. Drawing on these sources, we propose replacing the "curriculum of control" with a new paradigm rooted in the core values of belonging, mastery, independence and generosity. This model, which we have called "the circle of courage," is portrayed in the medicine wheel, a sacred Native American symbol for the wholeness of life.

Foundation of Self-Esteem	Native American Empowerment Values	Western Civilization Patriarchal Values
Significance	Belonging	Individualism
Competence	Mastery	Winning
Power	Independence	Dominance
Virtue	Generosity	Affluence

TABLE 2.4–1

FROM ALIENATION TO BELONGING

Psychiatrist Karl Menninger warned that when the family, school, and community fail to meet the need to belong, youth will desperately pursue artificial belongings. Gangs and cults and promiscuous relationships are desperate attempts by some youth to meet the most basic human need— to be related to other human beings. Those most alienated have virtually abandoned the pursuit of belonging and become guarded, lonely, distrustful, and unattached.

Alienation between children and adults has reached massive proportions in modern society. Families are buffeted by a constellation of risk factors that now are converging dramatically to produce what Lisbeth Schorr (1988) calls "rotten outcomes." However, it is simplistic to blame the nuclear family for these problems.

Theologian Martin Marty argues that the core problem is the loss of the "tribe." From earliest times, biological parents were often too young, irresponsible, and overwhelmed; and short life spans made orphans abundant. However, the tribe was always there to carry on the culture. Today, says Marty, we have lost our tribes. Now, schools and youth organizations are being asked to become "new tribes" for our modern psychological orphans. But how do we go about creating such a culture of belonging?

Native American educator and anthropologist, Ella Deloria, noted that the spirit of belonging in Native American culture is expressed in these simple words: "Be related, somehow, to everyone you know." Treating others as kin forged powerful social bonds of community that drew all into relationships of respect. From earliest childhood, tribal youngsters experienced a network of human bonds where every older member of the tribe—adult or youth—felt responsible for the well-being of all younger members of the community. Wherever he or she strayed, a child was always at home, because all claimed relationships. Native American communities believed that all must be part of the circle of relatives. If a stranger entered the tribe, a rite of adoption ensured that he or she would feel part of the circle of relatives. This sense of belonging also extended to nature, in the belief that all of creation must live in harmony as relatives.

In this era of broken belongings, schools and youth organizations are being challenged to reclaim alienated young people. But our child-serving institutions are not always belonging places. The factory-school first comes to mind. These large, impersonal bureaucracies foster estrangement between teacher and child. Attachment theory research is expanding our knowledge of the powerful effects of human bonds. We once were taught that attention-getting behavior should be ignored and it would be extinguished. Now, it appears that at least some of this behavior may be understood better as an attempt to rebuild damaged attachments. Conventional wisdom in the control curriculum dictated "unbelonging" as the basis of discipline—suspend, exclude, isolate, expel. We now have discovered that children are most receptive to human attachment in such times of crisis and difficulty.

A comprehensive therapeutic approach for children with damaged attachments has been articulated by Vera Fahlberg (1991). She describes these children as having poor impulse control and weak conscience development. They often cannot appropriately manage feelings, especially anger, sadness, and frustration. Related cognitive problems include difficulty in understanding cause and effect and in planning ahead. Interpersonal relationships with these children may be marked by superficiality, distrust, hostile dependence, the need to control all situations, and continuous seeking of attention through attachment behavior.

Fahlberg describes three modes of building relationships for preventing and treating attachment problems:

- "Claiming" behaviors to foster inclusion. In any group there are markers that determine who is an insider and who is out, the "we" and "they." Addressing persons by relationship terms (e.g. "son"), claiming physical space with possessions and photographs, engaging in ceremonies and songs, adoption rituals, clothing styles and insignia shared by group members—all serve to include persons in the family, gang, or tribe. Fahlberg puts particular emphasis on claiming activities with children who have been buffeted around by the foster care system.
- Initiating positive interaction cycles. This includes engaging in pleasurable activities, expressing affection, supporting children in pursuing their outside interests and in achieving goals, and participating in fun and joyful living. Increasing positive social interaction has a reciprocal positive effect. The adult bonds to the child, while the young person is emotionally and intellectually stimulated and feels loveable and worthy.
- Support in periods of high arousal. These periods might include a range of crisis situations, such as grief, illness, frustration, being hurt or injured, etc. Even physical restraint in moments of

rage can serve to build positive ties. As the adult walks through these storms of life with the child and alleviates psychological or physical discomfort, bonding and attachment are enhanced. The caregiver develops feelings of efficacy for meeting the child's needs, while the child develops trust, security, and attachment to the caregiver.

The life space interview strategies initially developed by Fritz Redl provide a sophisticated application of support in periods of turbulence (Wood & Long, 1991). Instead of walling off the youth in crisis, the goal is to surround the young person at that opportune moment, using problems to teach new ways of solving life's problems. Another model of attachment building is being developed in Europe by Maria Aarts and colleagues (1990). Their Orion program uses videotapes of natural family interactions to teach parents to spot even those faint initiatives that signal the willingness of children to enter into positive communication with adults.

Two hundred years ago, Pestalozzi declared that the crowning achievement of education is to be able to criticize a young person and, in the same instant, convince the youth of our fervent love. But today, the typical adult response in times of conflict is to avoid youth, preach at or punish them, and, when that fails, kick them out. The professional must learn to view problems as critical moments for teaching. Thus reframed, a crisis becomes a window of opportunity for attachment rather than trouble requiring punishment or exclusion.

FROM INADEQUACY TO MASTERY

Children and adults strive for mastery of their environments. Some psychologists argue that the search for competence is the most basic motivation for all behavior, a phenomenon that Robert White of Harvard referred to as *competence motivation*. When the child's need to be competent is satisfied, motivation for further achievement is enhanced; deprived of opportunities for success, young people express their frustration through troubled behavior or by retreating into helplessness and inferiority.

Today, in the face of such major problems as school failure, dropouts, and dysfunctional, marginally skilled youth, there is a growing belief that we need another educational model for ensuring mastery for all our children. Long ago, traditional Native American culture refined just such a system.

The goal of traditional Native American education is to develop cognitive, physical, social, and spiritual competence in each child. Children are taught that wisdom comes from observing and listening to those with more experience. A person with more skill should not be seen as a rival but as a model for learning. While there is a strong emphasis on achievement, striving is for the attainment of personal goals, not for proving superiority to one's opponent. Adults ensure that each child has some opportunity for success, giving even the smallest child important daily tasks to master. The simple but profound wisdom of Native American culture is that, since all need to feel competent, all must be nourished in competency. One may generously celebrate the achievement of those who are the most skilled, but such honor must be accepted in humility. By sharing in the achievements of others, success becomes a possession of the many, not of the privileged few.

Fostering mastery has been a goal of forward-looking educators from the time of Pestalozzi. One little-recognized pioneer in mastery education was Sylvia Ashton-Warner (1963), who worked with Maori children in New Zealand. Her approach was a bellwether for the whole-language approach which challenges traditional paradigms of learning. She described the mind of the Maori child as "a volcano with two vents, destructiveness and creativeness." They arrive with no other thoughts than to take, break, fight, and be first. Without opportunity for creativity, they develop combat as their ideal of life. "To the extent that we widen the creative channel, we atrophy the destructive one."

Ashton-Warner rejected the tradition of authoritarian, competitive schools as contradictory to the nature of children. The "two worst enemies of teaching" are the children's interest in each other and their desire for expulsion of energy. Schools need to harness these "enemies" by going along with the nature of the child. Instruction in pairs and small groups where children learn from one another mixes learning with relationships and defeats the first enemy. An active, creative, experience-based curriculum outflanks the enemy of explosive energy.

Research synthesized by Nichols (1990) indicates that children in their natural state—not goaded by rivalry—are more preoccupied with learning from others than with trying to beat them. Yet traditional schooling pits students against one another, thwarting the natural tendency toward modeling and cooperative exploration. The result is that "how I measure up to others becomes more important than how I master a task." This is egoistic involvement instead of task involvement. These two orientations are compared below.

TWO COMPETING MODELS OF MOTIVATION FOR ACHIEVEMENT

Task Involvement	Egoistic Involvement
Fostered by highlighting value of work done, suggestions for future development	Fostered by competitive grades, praise, and comparing students with one another
The belief that school should make one competent fosters greater task involvement for all students	The belief that school should help one gain wealth and prestige fosters academic alienation for many students

Nichols also suggests that the cultural bias toward hyper-competitiveness is even reflected in the measurement of self-esteem. Many psychometric scales are dominated by questions about feelings of competence where children must believe that they are "above average" to score well. He suggests this is just the criterion one might expect from researchers in a competitive, meritocratic society.

Rather than trying to make all feel highly able and good about their ability (which will require delusional thinking by many), research suggests we should shift attention away from ability and toward the task at hand. Children can be taught that the lack of competence is good, because it motivates achievement. Often, we must first recognize our incompetence if we are to learn to do something about it (Sternberg, 1990). We do not advocate teaching failure for therapeutic reasons; however, perhaps we do need to teach children to fail courageously.

The hyper-competitive model of education, which developed from the patriarchal tradition, cannot be defended by scientific data or democratic values. While some youth become winners, a large group are relegated to the status of losers, the "forgotten half" who are placed at risk by schools unresponsive to their needs and life goals (William T. Grant

Foundation, 1988). At a time when we are recognizing the immense so-cial cost of "disposable" children, we need a new model for achievement. Carol Gilligan (1989) and colleagues question the kind of education that teaches us to trample others to win. A faculty member says: "To compete against another person, my students felt they needed to separate from that person. To beat you in competition meant that I could not know you or care about you." Competition must be redefined so that one can master skills, celebrate achievement, and enjoy the spirit and company of those with whom we share the quest. As we rediscover a more human and democratic form of competition, we become partners rather than enemies. We compete *with,* rather than *against,* one another. Our pedago-gies, games, and grading systems will never be the same again.

FROM IRRESPONSIBILITY TO INDEPENDENCE

Education in a democracy, said Horace Mann, is an apprenticeship in re-sponsibility. Yet too many of our youth are not responsibly independent. Fighting against feelings of powerlessness, some youth assert themselves in rebellious and aggressive ways. Those who believe they are too weak or impotent to manage their own lives become pawns of others. All of these young people need opportunities to develop the skills and confidence to assert positive leadership and self-discipline.

Traditional Native American culture places a high value on indi-vidual freedom. In contrast to "obedience" models of discipline, Native American education was designed to build "respect" and to teach inner discipline. From earliest childhood, children were encouraged to make decisions, solve problems, and show personal responsibility. To make a decision for a child was to make the child weak. This autonomy did not involve any lessening of the human attachments with adults. Adults would continue to model, nurture, teach values and provide feedback. But children were given abundant opportunities to make choices without coercion.

Children answered to self-imposed goals, not out of fearful obedi-ence to others. Children were never offered prizes or rewards for doing something well; the achievement itself was the appropriate reward, and to put anything above this was to plant unhealthy ideas. Likewise, harsh punishment was virtually nonexistent; but an errant youth would get many gentle "lectures" from his or her relatives. The focus of these talks was to set expectations and offer feedback on how the behavior was seen by others. Lakota writer Luther Standing Bear stated that he had never heard force with anger behind it until he met white teachers in boarding school. "My father would never say, 'You must do this.' Instead he would say, 'Son, someday when you are a man, this is what you will do.'"

Research by Benson (1987) and colleagues indicates the most dramatic developmental change during the middle years of childhood is an increase in autonomy, but this is not met with significant increases in responsibility. Knitzer (1990) and colleagues noted that the privileges attached to behavior modification systems "were the same for five-year-olds as they were for 14-year-olds." Students are expected to show their responsibility by being obedient. But, as W.E.B. DuBois once observed, only responsibility builds responsibility.

We have learned from research on peer-group processes that empowerment is reciprocal: adults who respect the autonomy of youth find youth more receptive to the legitimate authority of adults. However, adults caught in power struggles with youth only fuel a powerful negative counterculture. Wasmund (1988) researched the treatment climate in residential settings for delinquents. Adults in a control-oriented program believed they were in charge, but the *sub rosa* culture was actually chaotic and disorganized. Programs built on youth empowerment were actually better controlled, since youth shared—rather than sabotaged—the treatment goals of staff.

Summarizing child-development research, Martin Hoffman notes that there are only three ways of disciplining children: (1) power assertion, (2) love withdrawal, and (3) inductive discipline (e.g., learning how your behavior affects others) (1977). North American Indians practiced inductive discipline for thousands of years. The parent managing a small problem would quietly go to the child, whisper in Lakota the word "mistake," walk away, then allow the child to ponder the error. With really big problems, parents would talk more gently than usual, explaining that younger brothers and sisters look up to the child or that people who act like that won't have friends. Several grandparents might "gang up" on the most difficult youth, flooding him with these gentle conversations. Encircled by concerned friends—there is no more powerful human discipline system than being told how you are seen by people who deeply care about you. To paraphrase Carl Jung, "When love rules, there will be no will to power."

FROM EGOISM TO GENEROSITY

Unless the natural desire of children to help others is nourished, they fail to develop a sense of their own value and become absorbed in an empty, self-centered existence. Today we see many of these young people desperately pursuing empty pleasures in lifestyles of hedonism and narcissism. In fact, our society does not do a good job of nourishing the spirit of caring: research at the Search Institute on thousands of youth showed that the spirit of justice and concern for others reaches a peak at fifth grade and then declines! (Benson, Williams, & Johnson, 1987). The antidote for this malaise is to create opportunities for young persons to be of value to others.

A central goal in Native American child rearing is to teach the importance of being generous and unselfish. In *The Education of Little Tree,* Forrest Carter (1976) gives an account of his childhood reared in the mountains by Native American grandparents. The philosophy of his grandmother was "when you come on something good, first thing to do is share it with whoever you can find; that way, the good spreads out where no telling it will go." A person who accumulated property for its own sake was distrusted. One of the highest expressions of good values was to give away what one cherished the most. Native American writer Dr. Charles Eastman tells of his grandmother teaching him to give away his puppy so that he would become strong and courageous. Prestige was accorded those who gave unreservedly, while accumulation of property for its own sake was disgraceful.

At the end of the nineteenth century, William James wrote of the need of young people to move outside of themselves and contribute to some important cause. He saw community service as a means of replacing self-seeking behavior with civic discipline. The principles of James were embodied by Kurt Hahn in the Outward Bound programs developed in the 1930s in England. Hahn decried the malaise of youth who suffered from the "misery of unimportance." His prescription was to involve young persons in some "grande passion," allowing them to become committed to a cause outside of themselves.

The search for happiness through materialism and selfish pleasure is at the root of the alienation of many contemporary youth. Diane Hedin (1989) concludes that young people have never been more self-centered and consumed with money, power, and status. She cites research on the positive outcomes of volunteer service, including increased responsibility, self-esteem, moral development, and commitment to democratic values. The Carnegie Foundation has strongly supported the implementation of service-learning as part of the curriculum of all schools in the United States. Students are asked to spend time with the elderly, younger children, the sick, and the lonely. The benefits of such prosocial activity are particularly pronounced with troubled adolescents.

Our own earlier work on peer group treatment is in the tradition of empowering youth to care (Vorrath & Brendtro, 1985). Similar ideas have been used by many public schools in natural peer-helper programs. As youth decenter, they learn to empathize with others. In helping others, they create their own proof of worthiness; they have the power to make a positive contribution to another human life.

CONCLUSION

Maria Montessori said that a teacher must be humble enough to learn from the child. She was challenging a culture where childhood meant inadequacy by the standard of adult power. We still drag this cultural tail behind us. The word "child" is a pejorative in the English language. A racist calls an African-American man "boy," and a sexist addresses an adult female as "girl." Such words can be only pejorative in a society where children are of lesser value. In the Lakota language, one cannot insult a person by using the word "child," since the literal translation is "sacred being." One does not abuse, dominate, and control sacred beings; but rather, one learns spiritual truths from them.

The First Nations' cultures of North America have developed a wealth of core principles for rearing caring, confident, respectful, and generous children. These concepts are supported by the ideas of the great European youth work pioneers who challenged the authoritarian, patriarchal traditions of Western culture. Now, emerging research is validating this early wisdom.

In our pluralistic, "do your own thing" society, it has not been fashionable to suggest that there may be absolute values unbounded by history, culture, or circumstance. Some hold that this radical moral relativism is one of the great philosophical mistakes of our time. All values are expressions of either "wants" or "needs." Our wants are personal or cultural preferences and thus based on values that are relative. But human needs are universal, and absolute human values are those tied to absolute human needs.

The Native American "circle of courage" would seem to express absolute values. Children in every culture need to belong; therefore, depriving a child of caring is universally evil. Children by their nature are created to strive for mastery; thus, schools that sabotage this motivation to competence are wasting and maltreating children. Children from any background have inalienable rights to self-determination; to block this development of independence is to commit an injustice. Finally, children from the dawn of cooperative civilization have sought to give back to others the concern they have known; if we fail to provide opportunity for caring and generosity, we extinguish the human spirit.

WORKS CITED

Aarts, M., Lammerink, E., & Vostermans, M. (1990). Support by videoanalysis: Orion hometraining and early intervention. In F. Kool (Editor), *The power to change lies within the families.* Rijswijk, Netherlands: Ministry of Welfare, Health and Culture.

Ashton-Warner, S. (1963). *Teacher.* New York: Simon & Schuster.

Benson, P., Williams, D., & Johnson, A. (1987). *The quicksilver years: The hopes and fears of early adolescence.* San Francisco: Harper & Row.

Brendtro, L., Brokenleg, M., & Van Bockern, S. (1990). *Reclaiming youth at risk: Our hope for the future.* Bloomington, IN: National Educational Service.

Carter, F. (1976). *The education of Little Tree.* Albuquerque, NM: University of New Mexico Press.

Coopersmith, S. (1967). *The antecedents of self esteem.* San Francisco: W. H. Freeman.

Fahlberg, V. (1991). *A child's journey through placement.* Indianapolis, IN: Perspective Press.

Gilligan, C., Williams, N., & Hanmer, T. (1989). *Making connections: The relational worlds of adolescent girls at Emma Willard school.* Troy, NY: Emma Willard School.

Goldstein, A. (1991). *Delinquent gangs: A psychological perspective.* Champaign, IL: Research Press.

Hedin, D. (1989). The power of community service. *Proceedings of the Academy of Political Science, 37*(2), 201–212.

Hoffman, M. (1977). Moral internalization: Current theory and research. In L. Berkowitz (Ed.), *Advances in experimental psychology, 10.* New York: Academic Press.

Knitzer J., Steinberg, Z., & Fleisch, B. (1990). *At the schoolhouse door: An examination of programs and policies for children with behavioral and emotional problems.* New York: Bank Street College of Education.

Nichols, J. G. (1990). What is ability and why are we mindful of it? A developmental perspective. In R. Sternberg & J. Kolligan Jr. (Eds.), *Competence considered.* New Haven, CT: Yale University Press.

Rogoff, B., & Morelli, G. (1989). Perspectives on children's development from cultural psychology. *American Psychologist, 44*(2), 343–348.

Schorr, L. (1988). *Within our reach: Breaking the cycle of disadvantage.* New York: Doubleday.

Sternberg, R. (1990). Prototypes of competence and incompetence. In R. Sternberg & J. Kolligan Jr. (Eds.), *Competence considered.* New Haven, CT: Yale University Press.

Vorrath, H., & Brendtro, L. (1985). *Positive peer culture* (2nd ed.). New York: Aldine de Gruyter.

Wasmund, W. (1988). The social climates of peer group and other programs. *Child and Youth Care Quarterly, 17*(3), 146–155.

William T. Grant Foundation Commission on Work, Family, and Citizenship. (1988). *The forgotten half: Non-college youth in America.* Washington, DC: Author.

Wood, M., & Long, N. J. (1991). *Life space intervention: Talking with children and youth in crisis.* New York: PRO-ED.

ARTICLE 2.5

THE nature of the education–mental health collaboration is presented in depth in the following paper by William Morse. We must make collaboration effective. This paper offers some ways this can be accomplished.

MENTAL HEALTH PROFESSIONALS AND TEACHERS: HOW DO THE TWAIN MEET?

William C. Morse

EDUCATION–MENTAL HEALTH INTERPLAY, PAST AND PRESENT

The need for mental health–education liaison is not just a recent concern. Ekstein and Motto (1969) report that the history of such collaboration begins with teachers and analysts in the 1920s. A few teachers, Fritz Redl being our prime example, were provided a personal analyst. Their subsequent synthesis of the two fields made them the first educational therapists. A small group of teachers and analysts became committed to collaboration based on mutual respect, with each open to learning from the other since both disciplines utilized learning by repetition, by insight and identification. Prevention was an underlying goal. The early analysts respected the difficulties of teaching, even suggesting education was the impossible profession, more difficult than psychoanalysis. Sarason (1985) makes a strong case for including teaching in the clinical professions, saying that, after parents, teachers have the prime contact with children. He says that we expect more from teachers than any other professional and subject them to considerable unrealistic, inadequate and ultimately disillusioning training. So what is old is also new.

We have yet to resolve how the twain shall meet. The matter has become increasingly complex. We are especially interested in teachers of the behaviorally disordered, but there are other specialists, the regular class teachers and the school milieu to consider as well. Teachers may work in a wide variety of public or private settings. In addition, there are several mental health disciplines and each may reside in the school, community mental health or private practice.

But why the present intensification of concern about this relationship? It may stem from the state of recent studies from both education and mental health advocates which suggest that Behavior Disorders is the least effective area of special education. Parenthetically, there is not similar scrutiny of possible limitations in child mental health programs, perhaps because mental health is under no legal mandate to provide service for all children. The major papers on school collaboration focus mainly on the lack of and the need for symbiotic education–mental health collaboration. Students with behavioral disorders have access to mental health services in less than half of the educational programs serving such students, a percentage similar to the situation for the 6 to 8 million other children in the country who need such care. When mental health service is provided, little is known of the intensity or quality of such services. We are dealing with disturbed youngsters and yet our monitor, the Individualized Educational Program (IEP), often ignores pupils' emotional needs.

The National Needs Analysis in Behavioral Disorders (Grosenick et al., 1987) found a lack of mental health services among the program inadequacies commonly found in such programs. Forness (1989), in the mental health–special education coalition report, recommended increased liaison between such fields, a recommendation which found its way into P.L. 101-476. The law now makes social work related services generic (no longer prefixed by school), and provides grants to enhance education–mental health integration. While many current critics of BD special education see the better program solution in education and mental health collaboration, we best look beyond this shot gun marriage to the concept of an array of all service agencies from the various sources in working collaboratively on the school campus. It becomes clear that our goal must go beyond education–mental health to family centered, total community agency collaboration in the Full Service School if we hope to succeed with BD pupils.

No one denies that many education programs for BD youngsters are inadequate in various ways. We do have many successes and there are "points of light" but the drop out rate and concomitant employment histories as well as the quality of young adult lives depicts a shortfall. Whether the addition of mental health magic to special education magic will provide the solution remains to be seen. Interagency cooperation includes both formal agencies and natural support systems under the guidance of a case advocate. While the education–mental health combination is being emphasized, what is required is an integrated community service for these children, monitored by a case manager–advocate. Collaboration with law enforcement, health, social service, and recreation agencies or religious groups may be, in particular cases, more crucial than mental health services. Or the first need may be to generate new community services or augment particular services.

To accomplish community integration, a personally individualized service must replace categorical agency service. It reminds one of what we hoped for with the IEP! As a practical matter, children's mental health services have always been in short supply and are currently in stringent retrenchment.

That increased education and mental health cooperation will benefit our children is not a question, but there are several conditions ignored in the vision of a quick fix by liaison. First, regardless of professional input, it is extremely difficult to change the life course of many of our children with their multitudinous and severe problems. Fatigue rates in child helping professions, especially teaching, attest to the stress. The second obstacle is that both disciplines remain by and large still tied to notions of education and therapy not tailored to BD school programming. We are all in a common business of child upbringing regardless of labels and roles. Neither education nor mental health has adequately reconceptualized the generic aspects of helping let alone applied such concepts to programs for individual youngsters. There is still a great deal of yesterday's business as usual.

The third condition which limits effectiveness is the belated and limited recognition of the power of ecological factors as determinants in children's lives. The difficulty of altering negative ecological factors in communities, families or schools results in undue concentration on child change since the child is the only part of the total ecology easily available. There are ecological tactics which might be employed (Hobbs, 1982; Morse, 1991; Munger, 1991). Our "restorative oasis" programs still face the problem of sending the youngster back to the desert where he or she failed because of inability to cope.

Given the difficulties of the task and scarcity of resources, special teachers and mental health workers have a right to be proud of their considerable success. When things work out, we can expect to find at the center a very competent and dedicated teacher with creative mental health support. Very few disagree that improved collaboration with mental health will increase effectiveness, but it is fantasy to expect collaboration by itself will solve our many problems, especially if both parties are glued to traditional practice.

Pfeiffer (1982) has studied the value of collaborative team decision making. He points out that interdisciplinary evaluation and placement procedures are mandated in special education and his findings indicate that team decisions are less variant and more accurate than individual decisions, although it is difficult to understand the accuracy criterion. While many advocate team work, Pfeiffer (1980) does list several experts who see teams as increasing confusion, duplication, cost, territorial problems and ambiguous decisions. Stone (1988) holds that we cling to teams when all the necessary skills and experience may be possessed by a single member. After the reductionist operation of dividing the child into segments, meeting time is required to reconstruct the total child, if indeed that can be accomplished. Group decisions can also serve to diffuse responsibility. While the decisions are made jointly, execution is often left to a single member, usually the teacher.

Who actually collaborates in the most critical meeting of all for the special child, the needs at which the individualized education program is designed? Cruickshank, Morse, and Grant (1990) examined this team composition in over 600 such meetings. Mandated are a parent, a person from the diagnostic team, an administrator, and a teacher of the child. A parent attended 95% of the time. The average number of professionals attending was five, with two as the low and occasionally over seven the high. School mental health professionals attended 93% of the meetings (School Psychologist 93%, School Social Worker 47%, and School Counselor 18%), a special teacher 72%, and a regular teacher 30%. Non-school mental health personnel were not indicated. The school psychologist's diagnostic data generally carries considerable influence in these meetings.

It would be comforting if there were a simple answer to the enigma of how the twain shall meet—meet, that is, "to the maximum benefit for BD pupils." The fact is, almost every collaborative design works sometimes and almost every design fails sometimes. There are non-overt variables which enter in. We still dream of finding *the model* solution. While examples help, one still must work out how a given individual collaborative functions or malfunctions. To become informed participants in this cooperative team process, the areas to explore range from contracts to group dynamics.

Not parenthetically, mental health is a related service for BD pupils. Special education has the legal mandate to supply the services contained in the IEP contract. Mental health involvement is often left out because, as I was told again the other day by a social worker, it is often not politically wise to include this need. If included and yet not provided by an outside service, the IEP committee is to be reconvened to discover alternative means to provide the service. The right to psychotherapy or counseling for our clientele has not been adequately clarified by the courts. The result is wide variation from district to district. Osborn (1984) holds that the only BD related services expressly excluded are medical: social work and psychological counseling are clearly options, and psychotherapy when states permit the practice by disciplines other than the medical. But such mental health intervention can be required only if it is necessary in the effort to educate, a perplexing situation with considerable room for indiscretion. While both education and community mental health are public tax grant agencies, there is no universal right to mental health as there is to special education. With the rapid privatization of mental health, schools may have to contract with insurance agencies. How mental health participation can be considered ancillary for our clientele is a mystery.

COLLABORATION BY CONTRACT

As indicated above, there is a strong belief that liaison with mental health is the *sine qua non* for BD program improvement. This leads us to both interprofessional agreements and interagency contracts. There is the "one roof illusion" that when both professionals are under one budget or one administrator, there will be automatic collaboration. Unfortunately, this is often not the case under either mental health controlled with education ancillary or education controlled with mental health the foreign body. When budgets tighten, whichever agency is in charge tries to expurgate responsibility for the other. The first order is for intra-agency professional understandings. In mental health agencies the subspecialities may have trouble collaborating and in schools there can be conflicts between administrators, regular teachers, special teachers and school mental health workers. In-house agreements clarifying exchange of services and responsibilities precede interagency contracts. For example, where does the teacher get help in a crisis?

Each contract between mental health and education is unique. Some are brief memoranda of understanding while others are legal documents. I know of one over two years still in the making, now approaching book size. Perhaps this is a clue to the reluctance of one or both parties to integrate services. The old battles over turf have been replaced by strategies to avoid responsibility. Skrtic (1991) provides understanding as to why many interagency contracts end up impotent. By and large these are bureaucratic instruments, labored over pieces of paper. Both education and mental health are what he terms "machine bureaucracies" where technocrats rationalize and formalize rules and do task analysis—the 200 skills which make a BD teacher for example. Division of labor is central, dispersing ownership, prescribing specific worker task, and thus avoiding total responsibility. Contracts may come laden with red tape accountability forms to keep everyone honest. Interagency contracts negotiated in bureaucratic havens of national, state or county offices are usually brought about by external edict. In place of the past expanding turf efforts, now, to meet budget cuts, agencies try to avoid involvement as they are forced unwillingly to the bargaining table.

Skrtic holds that special education is not simple work and does not fit the mass production reductionist task analysis paradigm which dominates our contract agencies. Because of the complexity and individualistic nature of special education, what is required is not piece work but active problem solving by coupled service-providing workers. It is not the contract but how team members work together that becomes the focus. Such collaboration is required under P.L. 99-457 where intervention is organized around a lead agency and where a family plan replaces the IEP.

Interagency contracts are necessary for permission to collaborate. There are several patterns including merged budgets, and merged administration. Sometimes mental health and education contribute funds or stipulate personnel time to a new separate entity. Then, who has ultimate authority over the various personnel becomes critical: too many bosses can be an accerbation. In the long run budget control equals power.

What does this analysis suggest concerning effective contracts? We have learned that a good contract is only point zero and should not be taken as an actual cooperative program. A contract is permissive legislation. The test is the collaborative synergy at the work station level. The best way to insure either intra- or inter-professional cooperation is to give the personnel who are to be responsible for the delivery of integrated services a dominant role in contract development. Work from the bottom up rather than from the top down. We note too that there is not equality in the bargaining between mental health and education agencies. Special educators are in weaker position since there is no legal requirement for mental health to provide services. For special teachers, this may mean "Don't include in the IEP services not available in schools, lest, the school will have to pay." In spite of difficulties, many contracts do work out and enhance the programs for BD children. Failures can usually be traced to money, power disagreement, lack of clarity on responsibilities or interpersonal dissonance on the line. It would be interesting to give each BD teacher a time or money budget to purchase those mental health services on an open market which the teacher deemed most needed by the students.

RITUALS AND RITUALISM WHEN THE TWAIN MEET

We have the contract: Now how do the two professionals actually function in collaboration efforts? The answer requires attention to the nature of professionalism. Just as agencies follow the idiom of machine bureaucracies, so do professions. Both school mental health and special education are derived subspecialties and inherit much of their training and liturgy from very strong and different parent disciplines. As Erikson informed us, rituals are necessary to organize behavior lest every act become a complicated new decision. The danger comes when rituals ossify into ritualism so encapsulating that it stymies flexibility. Becoming a professional means becoming socialized into a given liturgy, part explicitly taught and part unconsciously absorbed. When rituals are diverse, team dissonance can result and team meetings become contests of these beliefs rather than problem solving. To work above these habits of thought requires training. Mental health workers usually get training only in working with other clinicians, while special educators are seldom trained in interdisciplinary work.

The pecking hierarchy between and within professions can produce contention. Like Orwell's animals, some are more equal than others. Professional prestige is an illusive phenomenon. One of our colleagues, seeking to elevate teacher status in a psychiatric setting, arranged for teachers to have white coat training and supervision in psychotherapy. While teachers at first anticipated the one-to-one engagement, many found they missed the group activity and did not prefer the "higher" calling. Paraprofessionals tell me how powerless they feel and we know they may sometimes be as effective as the certified personnel. Psychology and psychiatry are engaged in a nation-wide battle over prerogatives. In general, the time spent directly interacting with children is in reverse order of the amount of training required and pay scale. School mental health workers and school special teachers often suffer rejection from their parental disciplines. Thus the team dance is choreographed to some extent by prestige factors and defensive ritualism.

Sometimes our two professions forget their common cause because of role differences even though the professional codes of practice are quite similar. Both are anxious to do everything possible to rehabilitate the disturbed child. But they have been socialized into different professions, see the same youngster differently, have different concepts of helping and have different roles. Not only are there two disciplines but the fact is that each discipline within itself is not unitary in psychological orientation. The diversification of practice and ideology within a profession has become so great that stereotyping differences is misleading: Within-profession variation may be greater than between-profession variation when it comes to interventions. For example, educators generally put a high priority on external control of behavior while mental health personnel are more attentive to internal states. But in one instance the out-of-school mental health collaborators became so possessed with the need for external control that they violated pupil and parent rights. The contract was canceled in an acrimonious divorce. It is not an abstract matter of mental health and education collaboration: It is what brand of each profession is to collaborate. We must study the attitudes of the members of each specific team.

To appreciate what could go on in good and poor teaming it is helpful to examine general differences in professional socialization. When mental health workers leave the interview for the milieu (and especially the educational milieu), they experience a new set of demands often at odds with their training. The same is true of BD teachers who find themselves at odds with the dominating educational ethos of their school. What follows is, as they say, a story. It is a stereotype of professional dissimilarities and as such does not fit well. But it can serve as a check list to apply to local situations. Mental health professions have *clients* while teachers have *pupils*. In truth, both have *children*. Teachers focus on control and academic achievement by necessity. Traditionally, mental health emphasis has been concerned with the affective domain and inner control. Educators are mandated to take all comers, while mental health implies client initiation. Of course with children client initiation is not the case, it is coerced therapy vs. consensual. Both therapy in school and special education are coercive. Children can only "object" by being mute or acting out: Parents can directly refuse help or become no shows. The implications of coercion for school mental heath have largely been ignored. While both the classroom and the clinic are nonchoice, professionals often operate on the basis that the children should want my services and beyond their defenses really do. Thus neither discipline does well with the fundamentally alienated youngster.

Usually teachers are group workers regardless of the individualized IEP. They serve many roles in a day while mental health workers are usually single role and one-to-one. Generic education is designed to serve so-called "normals" in large, prepackaged, age level groups in public view. Mental health attends to the atypical who is having trouble meeting normal expectations, with provisions of confidentiality. Teachers spend long, consecutive hours with numbers of children. Mental health interacts episodically, usually on a single case basis. This contract makes for a significant difference in orientation, with BD teachers caught in the middle. Schools expect change on the basis of punishment and simple praise which produces complex systems of positive and negative contingencies. Teachers must remain on the line unless a substitute is provided, and thus are not free until the bus leaves. Criteria for progress may differ, teachers watching academics and manifest behavior and mental health workers watching for increased self-esteem and general coping capacity. BD teachers are more professionally isolated than the typical mental health person who uses cross-discipline consultation. These statements contrasting the two disciplines are true and untrue and serve only as points to consider in a specific team operation and as an aid for reflection on one's individual professional heritage. Better yet, one can compile a list of the differences between external and in-school mental health work, between BD teaching and other special education and regular teaching, and use these lists for sophisticated comparisons.

There is a sidebar to all of this. Youngsters often do not respect the assigned roles. They may not be moved at "interview" hour. Because of our definitions of therapy, the fact that the classroom can be a therapeutic place is often ignored. In helping distraught children there is really no division of labor. A mental health person may function more effectively in the classroom milieu, especially with young children. After being trained atomistically, the most effective professional may be those who cross over the lines of staid roles (Nichols, 1984). There are joint efforts in group counseling where both disciplines join together (Anderson & Marrone, 1977). Unfortunately "group" is too often institutionalized, becoming a mini course with a set time and agenda. Thus schoolized it has all the problems of the traditional curriculum.

There are signs of change in both professions which would make liaison more sibling-like, rather than of distant cousins. Mental health workers in schools are increasingly concerned with early intervention.

Screening for vulnerability and preventive intervention (Hughs & Hurth, 1984) replaces preoccupation with certification for special education services. Mental health personnel are training themselves for crisis intervention. Test kits are matched with observation, interviews and curriculum based assessment. Parent education and support groups supplement parent therapy. New styles of cooperative consultation (Friend & Cook, 1992) and active consultation (Newman, 1991) are making inroads on didactic interactions. Developmental considerations are countering method-driven intervention. Even old style social work reaching out in the community and homes has seen some return. Cognitive skill learning is being advocated, especially for the value deficient kids. Finding figures for identification in the community is recognized as essential. The mental health journals are as replete with "break out" articles as are journals in special education, so both professions are changing.

Generally speaking, special education for BD children seems to have a harder time moving from traditional academics and control to new patterns. But there is change here, too. I was once informed that teachers could do therapeutic things but never therapy. I have never figured this out, except to understand that "therapy" reflects a definitional guild matter and rights of practice. Woods (1986) strains to clarify the boundary between psychotherapy and therapeutic teaching, the teacher being tuned to the ego level and not to the unconscious, presuming the layers are discrete. Nichols (1984) has shown the limitations of this view. The role of educational therapist has been developed by Ungerlighter (1991) and Sapir (1985) to clarify the training and practice of a different BD teaching role. The Educateur is a different model, especially as practiced in parts of Canada (Hobbs, 1982; Linton, 1973; and Mitchell & Nicolaou, 1984). Nickerson and O'Laughlin (1982) show how teachers contribute through action oriented therapies in the curriculum. When Rhodes' pupil empowerment curriculum becomes available we will have another example of the merger of education and therapy. In short, both BD education and school mental health work show the potential for melting artificial boundaries. When we think of liaison, it should be in terms of new models.

TRAINING, SPECIALIZATION AND COLLABORATION

Just as agencies are structured along the idiom of machine bureaucracies, so are professions. Skrtic (1991) holds that the division of labor shapes the interdependencies and coupling of workers. Professional guilds are interesting entities. Each has to have some defined, unique specialization. A specific training curriculum may provide the rites of passage, but often there are also state or national exams. Legal status becomes registered in licensing. Then rights are jealously guarded and fought over. This a BD teacher can do, this only a psychiatrist, this a social worker. Teachers are not in the guilds permitted to provide psychotherapy and so on. Who can give individual intelligence and other psychological tests, take a family history and work with families, assess academic achievement? In special education does intervention dealing with the learning disability of a BD pupil require a different teacher? In this quagmire the strong professions lobby to maintain their identity and expand their roles. In general the longer and more exclusive the training, the greater the guild prestige. The more the guilds divide up the child, the more the need for collaboration and the more excruciating that collaboration. All of this aside, the studies show that so often the student has only the BD teacher who must serve all roles.

The fact is, while upbringers have common cause and often considerable shared knowledge base there is not common training. Even if we end up with common knowledge or skills, these must be learned in separate enclaves to perpetuate separate mystiques. Professions develop private languages and in-group code words. Krueger et al. (1987) have proposed a generic team approach which plays up the common functions. One special director explained that his psychologists, social workers and special teachers were taught through inservice the basic skills of all three. They could not afford the cost of shuttling children from one to the other and the time spent in subsequent integration. The higher the prestige of the specialization, the less willingness to engage in cross-disciplinary training and give away secrets, even if there are no secrets. Training institutions set up parallel courses for co-practicing professions rather than combining resources.

There are many who see conjoint multidisciplinary training as the road to improved collaboration. McCall (1990) holds that interdisciplinary training requires a broader integrating base than found in any present discipline. He proposes "children, youth and families." Bloom and Parad (1976) discuss this matter as well as interdisciplinary functioning in community mental health. In common with others, except for Sarason (1985), they do not include educators and see only membership of the Holy Trinity. Since all child upbringers have considerable common cause, they should by and large learn together in common curriculum. Actually, with increased specialization and certification structures, the trend is in the opposite direction except where personnel are in short supply and then anything goes, particularly in teacher accreditation.

It will not be enough to learn together: There will have to be joint practica together in settings where collaboration is active. There are settings where there is a meltdown of non-essential professional differences.

We can take measures to counteract training separatism for professionals engaged in a common task. We can lobby for joint training programs. Inservice and continuing education credits can be combined. Mental health workers can spend time helping in the classroom to see first hand the issues confronting the teacher. Teachers can participate in three-way conversations with the child and therapist to appreciate that mode of helping. This is with the goal of developing empathy and appreciation of the diverse contributions. Fenton et al. (1977) have discussed the implication of role expectations on interdisciplinary work in schools. All disciplines need to become familiar with emerging new concepts in other disciplines.

THE DYNAMICS OF COLLABORATION

Not all mental health special education collaboration is in team meetings. Often the interaction is in a consultative relationship where the mental health representative, on request or on schedule, meets with the BD teacher. Since many BD youngsters are in the regular classroom, consultation may be to apply the mental health approach in the mainstream least restrictive environment (Hughes & Hurth, 1984). Both system and individual consultation take place in a multitude of styles, which cannot be discussed here. Sufficient to say, professional role playing should be out. Consultation is a matter of co-equal status mutuality, to the end of problem solving. There are significant differences between one shot collaboration in an IEP versus sustained shared obligation on an on-going basis.

There is considerable slippery talk about teams and teaming the equality of disciplines. Understanding how teams really function takes us into the world of small group dynamics. There are roles to be played out that sometimes are like the dance of the wolves. Professional rituals may replace mutual problem solving as elaborated in Friend and Cook (1992).

But there is also a personal layer which can frustrate the efforts at problem solving. Beyond the professionalized role relationships are individual personal styles. One can find, in the same setting, mental health–education teams which flourish while others are perfunctory, meeting only to follow the rule. Incompatible personality styles can breed mistrust and disrespect, usually pasted over with a thin paper of civility. How a given member feels about the contribution of colleagues may stem from preordained stereotyped views carried into the "collaborative." "Teachers are rigid and do not understand therapeutic goals" or "Therapists don't make any real contribution: they just talk to kids." Which job is the more taxing? Who bleeds more profusely at day's end? It is particularly important for high status professions to function without arrogance. Reactions to team member participation get a going over with peers after the meeting but are seldom dealt with directly as team malfunctions. Also considerable interaction of the mental health and teaching professions takes place in a setting with parents, administrators and other disciplines. In such a mixed bag of lay and professionals, strange things may happen. In effective meetings expression is in basic English rather than professional lingo. While there are recognized role differences there is ideological similarity in both philosophy and psychology. Members all see the same youngster.

The study of team member roles is a fascinating and worthwhile exercise: Sometimes we learn to predict member roles and biases before they speak. Other team meetings are acts in the theater of the absurd, with each talking past the other. Small teams are usually the most effective. The gist of this is, collaboration at the service providing level is not simple. And yet we know that there are many examples of highly effective professional teaming. What does the literature say about effective teams and problem teams? Giangreco et al. (1991) review common practices which interfere with integrated delivery of services. Interfering processes include decisions made before consensus and from independent disciplinary perspectives, both major violations of proper team functioning. Larson and LaFasto (1989) found that successful teams had a clear and elevated goal, were driven by results, had competent team members, held a common commitment, produced a collaborative climate, enjoyed principled leadership and were given external support. Fenton et al. (1979) suggest trouble results from the fact that members do not agree on team goals and responsibilities.

Pfeiffer (1980) reviews four major conditions facing school-based professional teams: increasing parental and regular teacher involvement, selecting team relevant diagnostic information, getting the most meaningful decision and facilitating collaboration. Among his strategies for improving effectiveness we find: shared responsibility, rather than delegation to a single discipline; continuous support to the implementers; including a regular classroom teacher on the team; if necessary bringing in a process consultant to clear the air; and making provisions for program evaluation. He decries the current insular approach to training.

TACTICS FOR TEAM PROCESS IMPROVEMENT

There are times when the predominate issue to be solved is lost in ineffective group or two-person consultation. Implicit in the discussion above are many procedures for improving group effectiveness, both items of self-awareness and team involvement.

Because so many collaborations succeed or fail at the fusion point of group process, all of us must be students of how groups work and how to improve productivity. Few are comfortable in dealing with team conflict even when the child is ill-served by what goes on. Certain team members may be intimidating or hold power over others. Members not responsible for an intervention may propose actions alien to the one responsible for conducting the program. There is scapegoating—"He has been seen twice already and the little bastard is still impossible" or "We had it all worked out until the teacher got on his case again." Sometimes antagonists are open but frequently they are stifled until after the meeting when discussing the meeting with a friendly colleague. How can we introduce more honesty into group process without becoming hostile? Useful tactics follow analysis of the particular group dilemma. Post-meeting reaction blanks can help. Rotating chairmanship may be tried. In some instances the quality of collaboration can only be improved by the services of an outside "neutral" consultant. Specific training in collaboration may be necessary. The short of it is to face the necessity of working directly on ineffective collaboration. A personnel change may be the solution since frequently the team members are thoughtlessly assigned to work with each other.

The work of Friend and Cook (1991) is indispensable for dealing with team collaborative problems. While embedded in group process theory, there are concrete examples which identify various malfunctions followed by specific remedial actions. Particularly pertinent are sections on conflict and resistance in groups. This manual can be used by individuals or teams for training in the processes of collaboration.

The place for concentration is generally acknowledged to be common goal setting. If there is not agreement on goals, other problems are impossible to resolve. Often common goals are taken for granted when they need to be hammered out and prioritized. Participating in goal setting is the key to subsequent effort and commitment. Our division of labor requires not just cooperation: it requires *integration* of our work guided by the child and ecology. This is why the child study team is so important. Intensive child study takes the focus from disciplines back to the child and needs. The team members come to see the same child, albeit there are different facets.

Sometimes confounding differences of philosophy, psychology or methodology can only be resolved by substantive seminars. For example, cooperative learning or emergent teaching may be new to mental health workers. The role of cognitive therapies may need clarification for educators. Both disciplines may need to study pertinent new books and articles together. Given the diversity of training, we should not underestimate the time and energy that must be put into team exchange to reach a meeting of the minds. Worker divergency presents the same problem for our struggling pupils as does parental dissonance.

Speaking of promoting interdisciplinary work, McCall (1990) says that "the reputation, abilities, respect, sensitivity, selflessness, and energy of the staff are the ingredients which produce professional collaboration and hold them together during the process." It is such an overwhelming task that we might give up were there not so many examples demonstrating the possibilities of success.

REFERENCES

Anderson, N., & Marrone, T. (1977). Group therapy for emotionally disturbed children. *American Journal of Orthopsychiatry, 47,* 97–103.

Bloom, B. L., & Parad, H. J. (1976). Interdisciplinary training and interdisciplinary functioning: A survey of attitudes and practices in community mental health. *American Journal of Orthopsychiatry, 46,* 669–677.

Bray, N. M., Coleman, J. M., & Gotts, E. A. (1981). The interdisciplinary team:

Challenges to effective functioning. *Teacher Education and Special Education, 4,* 44–49.

Cruickshank, W. M., Morse, W. C., & Grant, J. O. (1990). *The individual education planning committee: A step in the history of special education.* Ann Arbor: University of Michigan Press.

Ekstein, R., & Motto, R. L. (1969). *From learning for love to love of learning.* New York: Brunner/Mazel.

Fenton, K. S. et al. (1977). *Role expectations: Implications for multidisciplinary pupil programming.* Washington: U.S. Dept. of Education.

Forness, S. R. (1989). *Statement of The National Mental Health and Special Education Coalition to Senate Subcommittee on the Handicapped.* Mimeographed Committee Report.

Friend, M. P., & Cook, L. (1992). *Interactions: Collaboration skills for school professionals.* New York: Longman.

Garner, H. (1982). *Teamwork in programs for children and youth.* Springfield, IL: Charles Thomas.

Giangreco, M. F., Edelman, S., & Dennis, R. (1991). Common professional practices that interfere with integrated delivery of related services. *RACE: Remedial and Special Education, 12,* 16–24.

Grosenick, J., George, M. P., & George, N. L. (1987). A profile of school programs for the behaviorally disordered: Twenty years after Morse, Cutler and Fink. *Behavioral Disorders, 12,* 159–168.

Hobbs, N. (1982). *The troubled and troubling child.* San Francisco: Jossey-Bass.

Hughes, J. M., & Hurth, J. L. (1984). *Handicapped children and mainstreaming: A mental health perspective.* U.S. Dept. of Health and Human Services.

Kauffman, J. M., & Wong, K. L. H. (1991). Effective teachers of students with behavioral disorders: Are generic teaching skills enough? *Behavioral Disorders, 16,* 225–237.

Krueger, M. A., et al. (1987). The generic team approach. *Child and Youth Care Quarterly, 16,* 131–144.

Larson, C. E., & LaFasto, F. M. J. (1989). *Teamwork: What must go right/what can go wrong.* Beverly Hills, CA: Sage.

Linton, T. (Ed.). (1973). The educateur: A European model for the care of 'problem' children. *International Journal of Mental Health, 2,* 1–88.

McCall, R. B. (1990). Promotion of interdisciplinary and faculty-service-provider relations. *American Psychologist, 45,* 1319–1324.

Mitchell, M. L., & Nicolaou, A. (1984). *From multidisciplinary to interdisciplinary: Training the educateur generalist.* Paper presented at 62nd Annual C.E.C. Convention, Washington, DC.

Morse, W. C. (1991). Ecological approaches. In T. R. Kratochwill & R. Morris (Eds.), *Handbook of psychotherapy with children.* Boston: Allyn and Bacon.

Munger, R. L. (1991). *Child mental health practice from the ecological perspective.* Lanham, MD: University Press of America, Inc.

Nichols, P. (1984). Down the up staircase: The teacher as therapist. In Grosenick et al. (Eds.), *Social/affective interventions in behavioral disorders* (pp. 43–68). Des Moines, IA: Iowa Dept. of Public Instruction.

Nickerson, E. T., & O'Laughlin, K. S. (Eds.). (1982). *Helping through action-oriented therapies.* Amerherst, MA: Human Resources Development Press.

Osborn, A. G. (1984). How the courts have interpreted the related services mandate. *Exceptional Children, 51,* 244–252.

Pfeiffer, S. I. (1980). The school-based interprofessional team: Recurring problems and some possible solutions. *Journal of School Psychology, 18,* 388–393.

Pfeiffer, S. I. (1982). The superiority of team decision making. *Exceptional Children, 49,* 68–69.

Sapir, S. (1985). *The clinical teaching model.* New York: Brunner/Mazel.

Sarason, S. B. (1985). *Caring and compassion in clinical practice.* San Francisco: Jossey-Bass.

Skrtic, T. M. (1991). The special education paradox: Equity as the way to excellence. *Harvard Educational Review, 61,* 148–206.

Stone, F. H. (1988). Reflections on multidisciplinary teams. *Maladjustment and Therapeutic Education, 6,* 93–97.

Ungerleider, D. (1991). An educational therapist is … *The Educational Therapist, 12,* 2–8.

Wellins, R. S., Byham, W. C., & Wilson, J. M. (1991). *Empowered teams.* San Francisco, CA: Jossey-Bass.

Woods, J. (1986). The boundary between psychotherapy and therapeutic teaching. *Journal of Child Psychotherapy, 12,* 67–78.

EDITORS' COMMENTARY

Mental health–education collaboration is not the only professional change in the offing. More services are likely to be delivered in tandem with colleagues. Because special teaching has historically been a teacher and a class of students, coteaching requires new skills. It can be great for the adults and the students, or it can be a disaster. Teaching teams are like marriages: not all turn out to be compatible, and divorce is difficult. Relationships have to be worked out rather than ignored. Students will work two teachers much as they work two parents. Special teachers will also become responsible for a variety of subject matters, adaptation of the curriculum, differential grading, and discipline processes. The descriptive "my students" becomes "our students," and "my class" becomes "our class."

There are impending roles where the specially trained teacher will serve as consultant to others who are doing the hands-on interventions—peers, parents, aides, teacher colleagues, and perhaps individuals from other disciplines. Old-style authoritarian consultation is no longer acceptable.

ARTICLE 2.6

IN the next article, Erik Laursen, the division director of residential services at United Methodist Family Services in Richmond, Virginia, reports on a study of 23 youths' perceptions of caring adults and the meanings they ascribe to caring relationships in helping them face adversity. The article describes seven characteristics of caring relationships: trust, attention, empathy, availability, affirmation, respect, and virtue. The results suggest a road map for self-reflection and skill development for those who seek to have a positive impact on the lives of challenging youth.

SEVEN HABITS OF RECLAIMING RELATIONSHIPS

Erik K. Laursen

In recent years, there has been an explosion of interest in strength-based perspectives in education, psychology, youth development, and human services (Cambone, 1994; Brendtro & Ness,

1995; Rapp, 1998; Seligman & Csikszentmihalyi, 2000; Saleebey, 2002). This is a shift away from preoccupation with pathology, stigmatizing jargon, and fix-it approaches to intervention. This new positive psychology is grounded in resilience research, which identifies specific strengths that enable children and adults to surmount adversity (Wolin, 1999; Wolin & Wolin, 1993, 1996).

A central theme in the resilience literature is that children who overcome difficult backgrounds have connections to caring adults who bolster their courage and determination to persist, despite difficult odds. While this finding is widely touted as the route to successful intervention, little has been said about the specific nature of successful helping relationships. This article seeks to identify specific competencies in caring relationships that can be taught to those who work with children and youth at risk.

RELATIONSHIPS IN RESILIENCE SCIENCE

Among the first to provide hard data about the key role of caring relationships in fostering successful outcomes among children of hardship was resilience researcher Norman Garmezy (Garmezy, 1991; Garmezy & Rutter, 1988). His findings augment a growing body of research that includes the most frequently cited study in the field, Werner and Smith's (1992) longitudinal study of the children of Kauai.

Over a forty-year period, Werner and Smith followed into adulthood a cohort of children born into poverty. Initially, one third were considered at particular risk because they were also burdened by multiple stresses such as family alcoholism, violence, divorce, or mental illness. This study documented the tug-of-war struggle between stressors and protective factors; stressful life events were often balanced with protective factors within their care-giving environments. The great majority of children initially designated as "vulnerable" developed personal strengths, self-reliance, and protective buffers, which enabled them to overcome the negative odds. Werner and Smith made a simple but profound observation about these survivors: Studies have shown that the most resilient youth all had at least one person in their lives who was absolutely crazy about them.

From *Reclaiming Children and Youth, 11*(1), 2002, pp. 10–14. Copyright by Reclaiming Children and Youth, Inc. Reprinted with permission. (*Note.* Dr. Laursen adapted portions of this article from a paper by Sybil Wolin presented at the 2001 Strength Based Services International's Annual Conference. Used with permission.)

Further clues about the nature of successful relationships can be gleaned from an evaluation of Big Brothers/Big Sisters of America conducted by Public/Private Ventures:

> Our research presents clear and encouraging evidence that caring relationships between adults and youth can be created and supported by programs and can yield a wide range of tangible benefits … The most notable results are the deterrent effect on initiation of drug and alcohol use, and the overall positive effects on academic performance that the mentoring experience produced. (P/PV, 1995, November, p. iv)

Reviews of this research identified two factors that marked effective helping relationships. First was intensity of contact. In effective relationships, mentors and youth met three times a month for an average of three to four hours per meeting. The second factor was a "developmental" perspective by the mentor. The adult was not a preacher but was to meet the developmental needs of youth by providing opportunities and supports. Effective mentors believed that the youth they served had strengths. They searched for those strengths and sought to build on them. They also saw risk as existing in the *environment* and not in *youth* themselves. In contrast, less successful mentors viewed the youth as deficient in morals and values and employed "prescriptive" strategies aimed to rectify the deficiencies in the kids. These flaw-fixing relationships were not likely to be effective (Benard, 1999; P/PV, 1995, May).

The strength-based perspective assumes that positive development is best supported by relationships in which youth feel that they are respected, that they have knowledge about what benefits them, and that they have strengths which enable them to make a difference in their own lives. But the mentoring research suggests that some attempts at relationships are unsuccessful. This implies that those who work with challenging youth need competencies in developing effective helping relationships.

YOUTH PERSPECTIVES ON EFFECTIVE RELATIONSHIPS

To further examine the nature of effective caring relationships, an exploratory ethnographic study was undertaken. Twenty-three youth, ages 13 to 19, who resided in four residential programs in Virginia and Michigan were interviewed in-depth about significant adults in their lives. The interviewers used a semi-structured interview guide to probe participants on their perceptions of what caring adults "do," i.e., what are the behaviors these youth ascribe to caring adults. All sessions were tape recorded, transcribed, and analyzed using HyperRESEARCH (2000), a qualitative software program designed to code and organize interview material.

Based on the foregoing analysis, we identified seven elements of caring relationships. These are: trust, attention, empathy, availability, affirmation, respect, and virtue. Each represents a pattern of behavior and beliefs that make an adult worthy of the trust of a young person. These are briefly described and annotated with excerpts from interviews with youth.

1. TRUST

Participants in the study identified trust as one of the building blocks of caring relationships. They suggested that trusting relationships bring safety, stability, and encouragement to their lives. While there is no single behavior that demonstrates trust between people, the participants expanded on this element in the following manner. For DeAndre, trust is demonstrated when "they [adults] make promises and they keep them. That gets you a lot of trust. If you are doing wrong on the trust, it's going to be hard for them to trust you." James described trust in the following way:

> She always did what she said she would do. Like if she told me she would talk with me, I could always count on her doing it. And if something came up, she would let me know she couldn't be there. You know, she was straightforward. So many other adults say they will do things, and they often never follow through. And then when you ask them, they always have a bunch of excuses, instead of just saying they couldn't do what they had promised. Mrs. Ghee was not like that; she always did what she said she would do.

Trevor emphasized that he would trust and confide in an adult who would keep this information confidential, "Whatever we talk about stays between the two of us. I know I can tell him anything, and he won't let anyone else know."

Participants agreed that trusted adults follow through on what they say they are going to do. These adults send the message: "I'm accountable to the kids I serve."

2. ATTENTION

Most participants discussed in depth that adults who listen to them convey support and interest, and they encourage dialogue and keep it going. Others pointed out that sometimes adults can attend to them by just "being with me" because it is comforting to "know that you are not here alone." Still others mentioned that adults who put distracting things aside and do what is best for the situation give them full attention. As John put it, "A caring adult listens to you 100% and wants to get the story from your point of view. At the same time, it's like they read between the lines and help you understand what's going on."

Shequetta's statement summarized the information given by many other participants. She said:

> She listens to us and tries to understand what we are saying. She responds by saying that she understands where you are coming from, and she avoids power struggles by not interrupting. She does not tell us how we should feel. She does not put us down. Ms. Johnson always paid me attention. You know, she always made me feel at the center of the world. Many other adults would read through their mail or flip through papers on their desks when they talk to kids. Or answer the phone and then when they hang up, they'd ask what we were talking about. Ms. Johnson was very different. She would let the phone ring and always give me full attention.

3. EMPATHY

Many of the young people interviewed expressed that they have a need to feel heard and understood. They said that when they do not feel heard, they tend to shut down and become weary of sharing information with adults in the future. Furthermore, they begin to feel that adults do not care about them. While most participants said that it is important for adults to listen and attend, it is equally important for adults to try to understand the story from the young person's point of view. According to Shawn,

> Mr. Turman always tried to understand me and then help me see things in another light. He asked a lot of questions to really try to understand

why you were thinking the way you did. He wouldn't tell you that you were wrong or what you said wasn't true.

Other participants described how adults helped them find different ways of interpreting life challenges. As James talked about a caring adult in his life, he said, "When he had heard your story, what you thought and felt about a situation, he would help you see the situation from another person's view. He would help you see how you sometimes misunderstand things, and that there is more than one side to a story."

4. AVAILABILITY

All the children who were interviewed expressed that they wanted to spend time with adults. Among the most powerful ways an adult can communicate interest is by offering time. A girl who calls herself "Cuzz" explained that her foster mother made an effort out of being available: "She is always able to stop what she's doing and make time for me to talk about whatever."

Another informant, Shine, said, "No matter what happens, no matter what I do, he's there for me. I can do anything, and he's still there for me."

John confirmed the importance of adults being available. He said:

Mrs. Hawkins would always make time for you. She would sit down and listen to you and would even stop what she was doing if you really needed it. If she absolutely had to leave you before you were finished talking, she would let you know from the beginning and would then find time to finish up our talk.

The participants also spoke of adults taking time to do special activities with them. LaQuinta said, "He does things that my father never did. I went to church with him last Sunday. He takes me to baseball games and spends time with me."

When adults make time for them, young persons find peace and gratitude in the midst of their struggle. They expressed that adults who give freely and unconditionally of their time convey that children are worthy and important.

5. AFFIRMATION

Most of the young people in the study pointed out that adults who care are always able to find something positive about them. Even in the midst of struggles, these adults convey that the youth has strengths and resources. This affirmation instills hope and gives a sense of worth. The children in the study talked vivaciously about the adults who affirm them.

Shine said, "When I'm down, she says, 'you gotta keep your head up and keep trying.' She keeps me going."

Tazz confirmed this by saying, "They encourage us a lot to do our work. They push you to do things even though you don't want to do it, because it lets you know who you are and what you're all about."

Other youth detailed how adults highlight their strengths and potentials. DeAndre said, "Mr. Stark always said I can make something out of myself. He saw the talents that each one's got, and he took us to visit a college. Now some people here plan to go to that college, because he took us there."

John illustrated the same behavior by saying:

> I still remember him saying to me: "I understand you are struggling right now, but it will get better. You are a great person, and I know you'll be doing great things in the future. You are so talented with your writing that you'll make something out of this one day." He always found the best in every kid in the program.

The participants agreed that anyone who works with children should practice accepting children for who they are and appreciating their differences. They stressed that adults should not excuse inappropriate, unacceptable behavior but rather affirm that they are willing to help them change. Further, the participants observed that when they feel appreciated, they are provided a source of strengths to face daily challenges.

6. RESPECT

Several participants mentioned adults who respected young persons enough to involve them in making decisions about their lives. These adults helped them develop a sense of power over their choices and options and instilled in them a sense of control over their lives. They described how adults enabled them to discover the resources and tools within them and around them.

Shequetta expressed how her caseworker and foster mother involved her in decisions:

> They always asked what I thought. The caseworker drove me crazy at times because she always said: "You are the expert on your own life, so what do you think?" But it was great to feel that you had a say in your own life.

DeAndre described the respect he received from adults in these words:

> They guided me, but the decisions I was making were mainly my own. They accept me for who I am, and they don't blame me for the things I do. They sat me down like a man and talked to me. If you give them respect, then they give you respect.

Youth felt that adults who enlist their suggestions send a clear message that they value their abilities, strengths, and resources. These adults believe that young people should and can be part of making decisions for themselves. Other participants felt that adults who behave in this manner teach children to help themselves and prepare them for adult life. Adults who work with them in this collaborative manner respect their opinions in developing solutions and achieving change.

7. VIRTUE

The participants described caring adults as good role models. These adults practice what they ask kids to do. Tweety said, "She is a positive role model. When I have a problem, she listens to me. She helps me use coping skills."

John was even more specific as he talked about the importance of role modeling. He said:

> He does what he asks us to do! He helps us with homework and talks to us about being responsible, like you shouldn't drink, you shouldn't smoke ... things like that. He walks you through the consequences of your actions so you can see for yourself what choices you have. He

doesn't tell you what to do, but it's clear what he believes is right and wrong.

Several youth said that it is important that adults set limits and hold them accountable when necessary. They stressed that boundaries assure that their environment is emotionally and physically safe. Caring adults create a safe environment where they can learn from reasonable rules, limits, and consequences. They felt that in this way they could best learn to internalize rules and behaviors that they can act upon in a thoughtful, reflective manner, even if the adult is not present. The youth appreciate respectful guidance.

Tweety said, "When someone yells at me, I get mad. But when someone tells me when I've been bad, I'm happy 'cause I know that they're trying to help me."

DeAndre sounded a similar theme:

I get held accountable. Show respect. Take responsibility for your actions. Do things like in reality—don't be fake. They negotiate with you. They debate and they educate you—make sure you got a smile on your face every day. That's great. You know you can make something out of yourself.

THE SEVEN HABITS OF RECLAIMING RELATIONSHIPS

This exploratory study identified seven elements of caring relationships as perceived by youth in residential treatment settings. The findings have clear implications for staff training and future research. In their own words, the youth described concrete ways in which caring adults can engender resiliency.

The goal of this study was to specify the components of effective relationships in a format useful to practitioners. Borrowing a metaphor from Stephen Covey's seven habits of the heart, we have labeled these patterns as "seven habits of reclaiming relationships." In Table 2.6–1, we summarize the specific adult behaviors and beliefs associated with each of these patterns.

An examination of this table makes it apparent that caring is not just a "feel-good" relationship. Rather, effective caring involves specific adult behaviors and beliefs, which provide the catalyst for positive youth

SEVEN HABITS OF RECLAIMING RELATIONSHIPS

TABLE 2.6-1

	Behaviors	Beliefs
1. Trust	Doing what you say you are going to do	I'm accountable to the young persons I serve
2. Attention	Putting the young person at the center of concern	Children and youth are valuable and worthy
3. Empathy	Seeing the world through the young person's eyes	There are many versions to same story
4. Availability	Making time for children and youth is a top priority	Young people are important and worth an investment of my time and energy
5. Affirmation	Saying positive things to and about a young person and meaning it	Even troubled youth have positive qualities and constructive behaviors which can be acknowledged
6. Respect	Giving young people a say in decisions which affect them	Feelings are valid and young persons are the best experts on themselves
7. Virtue	Holding young persons accountable for their behavior without blaming; being a role model	Children must learn self-discipline, and those who teach them must practice what they teach

Note. John Seita, the lead author of this list, was a troubled boy who had sabotaged a dozen court-ordered placements by the time he was 12 years old.

development. It [is] not enough for adults to contend that they care; the task is to convincingly demonstrate caring to youth who have not always found adults deserving of their trust.

By clarifying the components of successful caring relationships, we take the first steps on the road to developing a competency-based training program for relationship building. These seven clusters of behaviors and beliefs were drawn from interviews with youth in treatment settings. They complement resilience research and best practices in strength-based interventions. While this is not a formal instrument, these patterns sketch a road map for self-reflection and skill development for those who seek to have a positive impact on the lives of challenging youth.

REFERENCES

Benard, B. (1999). Mentoring: New study shows the power of relationship to make a difference. In N. Henderson, B. Benard, & N. Sharp-Light (Eds.), *Resiliency in Action* (pp. 93–99). Gorham, ME: Resiliency in Action, Inc.

Brendtro, L., & Ness, A. (1995). Fixing flaws or building strengths. *Reclaiming Children and Youth, 4*(2), 2–7.

Cambone, J. (1994). *Teaching troubled children: A case study in effective practice.* New York: Columbia University Press.

Garmezy, N. (1991). Resiliency and vulnerability to adverse developmental outcomes associated with poverty. *American Behavioral Scientist, 34*(4), 416–430.

Garmezy, N., & Rutter, M. (Eds.). (1988). *Stress, coping, and development in children.* Baltimore, MD: The Johns Hopkins University Press.

HyperRESEARCH [Computer Software]. (2000). Randolph, MA: Research-Ware, Inc.

Public/Private Ventures. (1995, November). *Making a difference: An impact study of Big Brothers/Big Sisters.* Philadelphia, PA: Author.

Public/Private Ventures. (1995, May). *Building relationships with youth in program settings.* Philadelphia, PA: Author.

Rapp, C. A. (1998). *The strengths model: Case management with people suffering from severe and persistent mental illness.* New York: Oxford University Press.

Saleebey, D. (Ed.). (2002). *The strengths perspective in social work practice* (3rd ed.). Boston: Allyn & Bacon.

Saleebey, D. (1996). The strengths perspective in social work practice: Extensions and cautions. *Social Work, 41*(3), 296–305.

Seligman, M., & Csikszentmihalyi, M. (2000). Positive psychology: An introduction. *American Psychologist, 55*(1), 5–14.

Werner, E. E., & Smith, R. S. (1992). *Overcoming the odds: High-risk children from birth to adulthood.* Ithaca, NY: Cornell University Press.

Wolin, S. (1999). Easier said than done: Shifting from a risk to a resiliency paradigm. *Reaching Today's Youth, 3*(4), 11–14.

Wolin S., & Wolin, S. J. (1996). The challenge model: Working with strengths in children of substance-abusing parents. *Adolescent Substance Abuse and Dual Disorders, 5,* 243–256.

Wolin, S. J., & Wolin, S. (1993). *The resilient self.* New York: Villard Books.

SUMMARY

This chapter has expanded on the importance of reaching out to troubled students and attempting to develop a significant relationship with them. The ability to connect emotionally with others or to empathize with others is a psychological quality that defines being human. It is the capacity to sense another's feelings without words. The potential of empathy begins when the 1-year-old can understand there is a "me" and "others." Empathy is apparent when a 2-year-old boy kisses the dog's tail after he steps on it. He wants to make it better just as his mother has done when he was hurt. Later, empathy allows the child and youth to reach out and develop new friendships in a caring way. Unfortunately, too many of our troubled students feel alienated from others and lack the trust that good things will happen if they open up to new relationships. Some of our troubled students have never experienced significant caring. In fact, some students will bite the hand that reaches out to them. This resistance to forming new relationships becomes the professional challenge of all teachers of troubled students. The comments and articles in this chapter highlight the essential skills needed to facilitate this professional goal. We believe the art of having a dialogue or listening to a student's perception of his or her life begets adult empathy. In the process it changes the feeling a teacher has toward this student and transforms the student into a real person who is struggling with unmet needs and a powerful life story. Only then can the process of building a new relationship with this student begin.

EDITORS' REFERENCES

Baden, A. D., & Howe, G. W. (1992). Mothers' attributions and expectancies regarding their conduct disordered students. *Journal of Abnormal Student Psychology, 20,* 476–485.

Brendtro, L. K., & Brokenleg, M. (1993). Beyond the curriculum of control. *Journal of Emotional and Behavioral Problems, 2,* 5–11.

Brendtro, L. K., Brokenleg, M., & Van Bockern, S. (2002). *Reclaiming youth at risk.* Bloomington, IN: National Educational Service.

Gardner, H. (1991). *The unschooled mind: How students think and schools should teach.* New York: Basic Books.

Goodlad, J. I., Soder, R., & Sirotnik, K. A. (Eds.). (1990). *The moral dimensions of teaching.* San Francisco: Jossey-Bass.

Hobbs, N. (1982). *The troubled and troubling student.* San Francisco: Jossey-Bass.

Jones, V. F., & Jones, L. S. (1990). *Classroom management.* Boston: Allyn & Bacon.

Morse, W. C. (1985). *The education and treatment of socioemotionally impaired students and youth.* Syracuse, NY: Syracuse University Press.

Nichols, P. (1991, May). Through the classroom door: What teachers and students need. *Mountain Plains Information Bulletin.* Des Moines, IA: Drake University.

Nichols, P. (1992). The curriculum of control: Twelve reasons for it, some arguments against it. *Beyond Behavior, 3,* 5–11.

Noblit, G. W. (1993). Power and caring. *American Educational Research Journal, 30,* 23–38.

Noddings, N. (1991). Stories in dialogue: Caring and interpersonal reasoning. In C. Withrell & N. Noddings (Eds.), *Narrative in dialogue as a paradigm for teaching and learning* (pp. 157–170). New York: Teachers College Press.

Noddings, N. (1992). *The challenge to care in schools.* New York: Teachers College Press.

Paul, J. L., & Smith, T. J. (2000). *Stories out of school memories and reflections on care and cruelty in the classroom.* Westport, CT: Greenwood.

Rogers, D., & Webb, J. (1991). The ethic of caring in teacher education. *Journal of Teacher Education, 42,* 173–181.

Sarason, S. B. (1985). *Caring and compassion in clinical practice.* San Francisco: Jossey-Bass.

3 CONNECTING WITH THE WORLD OF TROUBLED STUDENTS:
Their Family, School, and Community

THIS chapter is concerned with the student's ecology. There was a time when the treatment of troubled students focused only on the individual student in a school classroom or in the counselor's office. The famous works of Eric Bronfenbrenner, William Rhodes, and Nicholas Hobbs changed the application of ecological awareness to educational work with troubled students.

In this chapter we use the term *ecology* to refer to the total interactions of a student in multiple environments and the term *milieu* to indicate treatment strategies. What makes for reclaiming and preventive milieu in the three critical life spaces where student interactions take place: community, family, and school? We start by using Hobbs's developmental schema to sensitize us to the ecological changes that take place relative to a student's developmental age.

Hobbs's Developmental Approach to Student Ecology

A teacher needs to relate to more than the individual student in the classroom. Often, ecological impacts are evident in subtle ways, such as the way a student enters the classroom. For example, some teachers make it a habit to respond to a student's nonverbal behavior by quietly saying, "You seem to look happy/angry/tired/depressed this morning. Do you want to talk about it?" Hobbs (1982) presented a developmental view to students' ecology in *The Troubled and Troubling Child* and illustrated it with the three diagrams shown in Figure 3.1.

Hobbs wrote that the study of students' ecology is important to understanding their psychological world. For teachers, this means having a personal picture of their daily lives to determine what interpersonal hazards exist and which of these can be altered in the students' ecological system.

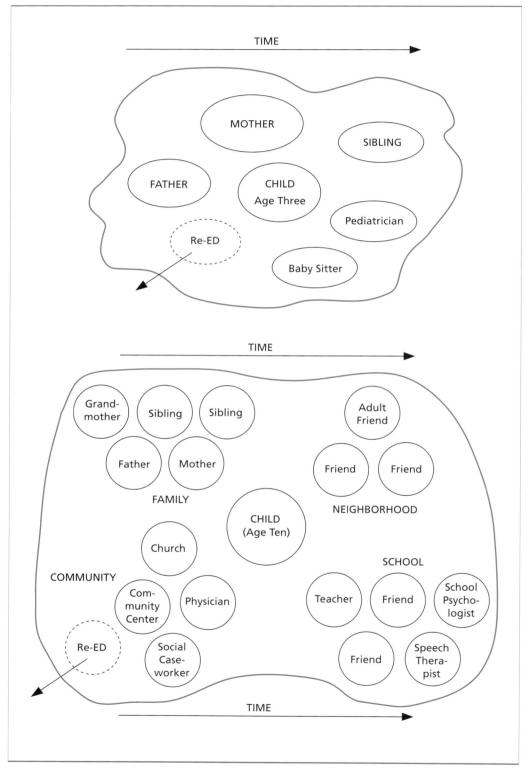

Figure 3.1. Hobbs's Developmental View of Students' Ecology. *Note.* From *The Troubled and Troubling Child,* by N. Hobbs, 1982, San Francisco: Jossey-Bass.

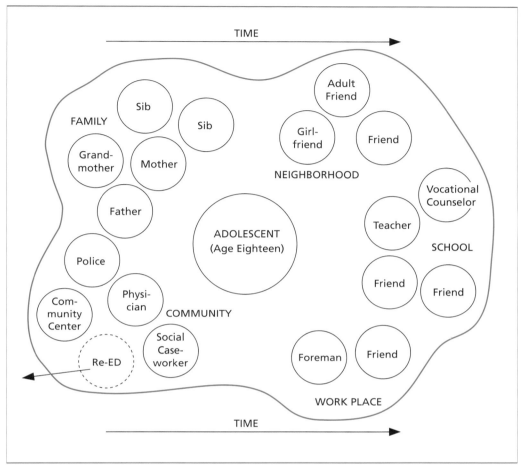

Figure 3.1. *Continued.*

What Makes a Setting Therapeutic?

A therapeutic experience with students is no longer the sole province of highly specialized, licensed professionals from psychology, social work, or psychiatry talking with students in an office. Therapeutic help can take place in all of a student's life spaces. The question is what makes a school and a classroom a therapeutic milieu? A therapeutic classroom or school is one that offers a climate of care, protects students from physical and psychological danger, respects students as individuals, offers freedom from prejudice, and provides a responsive and stimulating environment.

To understand the concept of a therapeutic milieu, we suggest consulting the work of Fritz Redl, who developed the concept. His insights in milieu therapy come from establishing a therapeutic environment called the Pioneer House in Detroit and from consulting at a therapeutic camp for disturbed boys in Michigan. Later, he was asked to replicate his residential study on aggressive delinquent boys at the National Institute of Mental Health at Bethesda, Maryland. We recommend reading his original 1959 article, "The Concept of a Therapeutic Milieu."

We now turn to the ecological systems that are of direct concern to troubled students: their families, schools, and communities. Although some students have difficulty negotiating in all three systems, others experience conflict in only one.

TEACHER LIAISON WITH FAMILIES

The first task of a teacher is to put aside the illusion of the family as a mother, father, and perhaps some siblings living in a home where all commingle in mutual support and closeness. Even in the fantasized good old days, few families were that simple. Now, half the students in a school may come from single-parent families. Even in families with two parents, the face-to-face time of parent and child may be limited if both parents are working. Further, as in any intense and intimate human relationship, the family is not always a supportive unit. For one thing, sharing responsibility for child rearing has never been easy even between parents. For parents of children with emotional problems, these difficulties are intensified. In our experience, their first request was for emotional support from someone who understands, followed by help with child care and financial assistance. These findings validate the importance of a helping teacher in a supportive relationship.

Families: All Shapes and Sizes

The families of Americans are becoming more diverse each year. Of the 105 million households in America, nearly 70% are defined as families. Approximately 35 million of these households include children under age 18. Racially, the population breaks down as follows: 73% White, 14% Hispanic or Latino, 13% Black, and 4% Asian. Of the children, 21% live in families headed by single mothers, and 5% live in families headed by single fathers. Among African American families, 51% are headed by single mothers. One million children live with adoptive parents. Probably the most disturbing fact is that 34% of single-mother families with children under the age of 18 have incomes below the poverty line. Approximately 2.4 million grandparents are the primary caregivers for the children in their families. In addition to all these other factors, 50% of marriages end up in divorce (U.S. Census Bureau, 2004).

Today's teachers are involved with the total range of family styles, some of which may lead to stereotyping. For example, because the impact of divorce in general is negative, a teacher may suspect that a child from a divorced family has some mental health problems. But this is not always the case. Too many things happen in students' lives for a single event to produce a predictable cause. There is no easy way to understand the impact of events on a student until one knows the meaning of the event to the individual. One needs to consider questions such as the following: Does a student think his behavior caused the divorce? What has changed since the divorce? Is the student still able to see and love both parents? Does the child become the parent? Does this student have the common wish for a reunion of the family? Similar stereotypes may come to mind when a teacher learns, for example, that a student has lived in six foster homes. This fact alone, however, does not indicate what these placements meant to the child. Did the placements get progressively worse or better? And how much of the student's view of "family" is objective and how much a fantasy?

Given all these factors, building a collaborative relationship with a parent is far from easy. It requires the same psychological effort as with a student. Seldom is there a single problem. Instead, problems come in clusters. Some parents, for example, are mentally ill or addicted to alcohol or drugs. The parents may be abusive, overly permissive, or in denial about their child's difficulties. Whatever the family composition, teachers need to develop collaborative relationships, capitalizing on any assets possible to aid their students and assisting the family with referrals when requested. For instance, teacher empathy should include the recognition that a student's fight at school may have a low priority to a family facing eviction.

The school–home relationship becomes a formal process starting with the Individualized Education Program (IEP) meetings. In most school–family contacts, the teacher talks with the mother or mother surrogate, but fathers also should be encouraged to attend. Although the IEP meeting is the place where multiple expectations are exchanged and goals are set, teachers should never forget that the ultimate power rests with the parent. Parents sometimes bring an advocate to an IEP meeting if they feel inadequate or expect to have difficulty in getting a satisfactory plan. Parents' behaviors range from cowed to demanding, and many expect a magical cure from special education regardless of cost. Some parents have become scholars of their child's problem and are as well versed about educational policies as are professionals. They may belong to a parent organization concerned with the child's problem. Whatever the case, the teacher will eventually be the main school contact. This initial meeting often determines the school–home relationship. We also advocate that the student should be included in the IEP meeting, particularly if the student is an adolescent.

A teacher's focus on student misbehavior is usually perceived as parental chastisement, and the fact that the parental effort to raise the child has culminated in low success, or even denial, is a stigma on the parents in the eyes of the public. The most effective program for parents of troubled students is to help them find ways to deal with their children effectively. Even little successes give parents hope. Many parents are open to any realistic help in understanding the behavior of their children.

Teacher and Parent Support for Troubled Students

One of a teacher's functions is to supply needed information while being aware that some parents may be using the Internet, library, and parent associations in their quest for knowledge. In their desperation parents may be gullible to the latest cures described in the Sunday paper and even move through legal channels so their child can get a given treatment. It is interesting that parents say the most help comes from other parents facing the same issues. If a teacher hopes to develop parent support groups, arranging for transportation and child care is essential in order to encourage parents to attend. Even scheduling a time may be problematic. Meetings are best sponsored by both parents and the teacher. Having the invitation extended by both a parent and the teacher is important. Encouraging parents to come in pairs rather than alone often reduces anxiety. One experienced administrator increased parent turnout by arranging for their children to put on a short performance prior to the meeting. He also had the students write the invitation as part of their language lesson and mentioned some of their achievements to replace the stream of comments about the problems their offspring had committed on any given day.

ARTICLE 3.1

IN the following article Naomi Karp takes a realistic view of school–family collaboration, recognizing that collaboration is a two-way street. Most families, Karp suggests, expect to be supported and not supplanted. The dual checklist she proposes could be useful in the initial teacher–parent meeting. Karp challenges the diagnosis of "dysfunctional family," a common label that tells teachers nothing. Instead, she suggests specific ways to increase parental involvement.

COLLABORATION WITH FAMILIES: FROM MYTH TO REALITY
Naomi Karp

Over the past decade, the field of children's mental health has undergone a series of changes that is upgrading the quality of services delivered to children who have emotional, behavioral, and mental disorders, and their families. Gradually, mental health service providers are shedding traditional roles and are examining the ways in which they approach and communicate with families. Instead of "we" and "they," professionals and families gradually are becoming partners in the therapeutic process.

From *The Journal of Emotional and Behavioral Problems,* *1*(4), 1993, pp. 43–46. Copyright by The Journal of Emotional and Behavioral Problems, Inc. Reprinted with permission.

The Federation of Families for Children's Mental Health grew out of a 1988 "Next Steps" conference, convened by Portland State University and the U.S. Department of Education. The goal of that conference was to set an agenda for children's mental health. Subsequently, 17 family members decided to meet again to form a national organization. That was the beginning of the Federation of Families for Children's Mental Health, the first advocacy organization dedicated solely to children's mental health and family-support issues. Four years later, the Federation has a strong impact on improving services, policies, and laws affecting children with mental health disorders and their families.

Unfortunately for families and children, educators often do not live up to legislative requirements to collaborate with families, and persons who deliver mental health services have no mandate to form partnerships with families. Therefore, families would like to have the professional disciplines understand what is meant when families talk about "partnerships" and "collaboration."

COLLABORATION CHECKLIST FOR PROFESSIONALS

_____ Do I really believe that parents are my equal, and, in fact, are experts on their child?

_____ Do I show the same respect for the value of families' time as I do for my own time by educating myself about an individual child's case before appointments or group sessions?

_____ Do I speak plainly and avoid professional jargon?

_____ Do I actively involve parents in developing a plan of action and then review, evaluate, and revise the plan with the family?

_____ Do I make appointments and provide services at times and places convenient for the family?

_____ Do I share information with other professionals to ensure that services are not duplicated and that families do not expend unnecessary energy searching for services and providers?

COLLABORATION CHECKLIST FOR FAMILIES

_____ Do I believe I am an equal partner with professionals and do my share of problem solving and planning to help my child?

_____ Do I clearly express my own needs and the needs of my family to professionals in an assertive manner?

ARTICLE 3.1

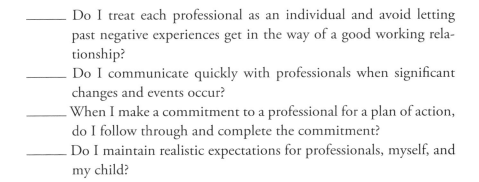

_____ Do I treat each professional as an individual and avoid letting past negative experiences get in the way of a good working relationship?

_____ Do I communicate quickly with professionals when significant changes and events occur?

_____ When I make a commitment to a professional for a plan of action, do I follow through and complete the commitment?

_____ Do I maintain realistic expectations for professionals, myself, and my child?

The preceding checklist challenges both professionals and families to approach each other in ways that embody values of respect, consideration, and empathy for others. A Vermont parent perhaps best summarizes why family–professional collaboration, based on family-centered principles, is important: "Parents should be thought of as scholars of experience. We are in it for the distance.... We have our doctorate in perseverance. We and the system must be in concert or the vision shrinks" (D. Sylvester. Cited in Thousand and Villa, 1989).

The composition of the American family is no longer the stereotypical "mom, dad, and two kids, and a dog." Rather, a family may be a single parent who relies on a maternal grandmother for child care; a teen-age couple who speak little English; or any configuration of people living under the same roof. Therefore, it is essential that mental health providers think about "parent" collaboration in new ways. One of the first steps toward a new way of thinking is to use new language. The term "parents" should be replaced with "family," since so many children do not live with both parents or, in many cases, with either parent. A comprehensive, inclusive definition of "family" should be used when mental health professionals are trying to collaborate with adults who are responsible for a child's well-being. The following definition was adopted by family leaders from across the country at a recent Office of Special Education and Rehabilitative Services (OSERS) conference:

> A family is a group of people who are important to each other and offer each other love and support, especially in times of crises. In order to be sensitive to the wide range of life styles, living arrangements, and cultural variations that exist today, the family in OSERS programs can no longer be limited to just parent/child relationships.... Family

involvement.… must reach out to include: … mothers, fathers, sisters, brothers, grandparents, neighbors, and other persons who have important roles in the lives of people with disabilities (Family and Integration Resources, 1991).

Support is a key ingredient for family success and coping. Families of children with emotional and behavioral problems would like to see the term "dysfunctional family" erased from the vocabularies of professionals. Service systems are inflexible and not responsive to families' individual needs. They create unnecessary stress and overwhelming responsibilities for families. Professionals often misperceive families as being "dysfunctional" when these families are, in fact, experiencing normal reactions to the serious lack of appropriate affordable accessible community-based services and supports. It is service systems that are dysfunctional when they do not respond to families' needs. The term "dysfunctional family" is the system's way of blaming someone else and must not be used.

Additionally, families would like professionals to not "assess the family's deficits" and dwell on them. Rather, they would like professionals to talk with them and to find out what types of services and supports would build on the family's strengths and really make a difference in the lives of the whole family. Further, families want professionals to share their visions and expectations for children. Daring to dream about what might be, in terms of services and outcomes, is an essential part of a sound, collaborative partnership.

True family–professional collaboration can be built only on a shared set of values about children and families. Here are some examples of values that teams may want to affirm jointly:

All children and youth are to be valued as people.

All children and youth have strengths and can learn to make positive contributions to their families, friends, and society.

All families have a variety of strengths and coping styles that should be identified and enhanced.

Diversity and individual differences are to be valued and respected.

The values, choices, and preferences of families should be respected.

Families are sources of wisdom and knowledge about their
children and should be recognized as experts.

After professionals have jointly developed a set of values about children and families, displaying them in a place where families can see them
will help lay the foundation for collaborative partnerships. The next task
is to put our values into practice. It is of paramount importance to develop strategies that will include families from all cultures and all walks of
life as equal partners in their children's treatment programs.

As a final note, families increasingly are asked to serve on local, state,
and national policy-making boards and councils. Most family members
are delighted and honored to be asked to serve. However, families across
the country are voicing a number of common complaints. These problems and our timelines for solutions are listed below:

- Only one family member is invited to serve on a board. This can
  be intimidating to the solitary "nonprofessional" in the group.
  Tokenism of any kind cannot be tolerated. Therefore, balanced
  representation on boards and councils is desired ...
- Conferences frequently have a "family theme," but no family
  members are invited to plan the conference, present their views,
  or participate in a major or minor way. To have a meeting about
  families and to not include families is like studying anatomy
  without a body.... Families [need] to be equal partners in conferences and meetings.
- Families participate on boards and councils but are not compensated for their time. Child care, transportation, time away
  from one's job, and a host of other factors are not considered
  when families are asked to devote countless hours to improving systems and policies. Families' consulting skills have to be
  recognized and paid for just as any professional is compensated
  for her or his time.
- Families participate on boards and councils, but their ideas and
  opinions frequently are discounted. For example, large numbers
  of families said that they took part in developing their states'
  P.L. 99-660 Plans. However, many families' ideas never appeared
  in the finished proposals. This is another form of tokenism that
  families would like to see obliterated long before the year 2000.

REFERENCES

Family and integration resources. (1991). Second Family Leadership Conference. Washington, DC: U.S. Dept. of Education.

Thousand, J. S., & Villa, R. A. (1989). Enhancing success in heterogeneous schools. In S. Stainback, W. Stainback, & M. Forest (Eds.), *Educating all students in the mainstream of regular education.* Baltimore: Brookes.

ARTICLE 3.2

MYRNA Olson speaks in the next article from both professional and personal experience in her discussion of strategies teachers can use to respond to single-parent families. Because she has been on both sides of the teacher–parent exchange, she is in a position to dispel common myths about the impact that having only one functioning parent has on students. Reading her work helps dispel the stereotypes about one-parent families that most of us have hidden somewhere in our belief systems. The author also suggests specific teacher strategies to support both parents and students in these families.

FIVE WAYS TEACHERS CAN HELP CHILDREN FROM SINGLE-PARENT FAMILIES
Myrna Olson

My interest in single-parent families grew out of my own experience as a single parent. I also have conducted research that included interviews with more than 30 other single parents. The strategies offered in this article came out of my personal experience, the interview data, and my own conviction that schools need to make some adjustments to meet the needs of children from single-parent homes.

From *The Journal of Emotional and Behavioral Problems, 2*(4), 1993, pp. 27–30. Copyright by The Journal of Emotional and Behavioral Problems, Inc. Reprinted with permission.

MAKE NO ASSUMPTIONS

While many studies have sought to compare the behavior and well-being of children from intact homes with those from single-parent homes, none are conclusive. Recent family research emphasizes that family behavior determines a child's self-concept, not family structure. Furthermore, there is clear evidence that income, not family structure, is responsible for many of the differences seen between these two groups of children. Finally, we know that children tend to see themselves, and consequently act, in ways consistent with the expectations of people important to them.

While single parent families may seem to have more problems than "traditional" families, it is important to remain open-minded when one searches for an explanation to problems children are having. One mother in my study related the following to me:

> My son was four years old and had been enrolled in a local preschool program. After two weeks of tears, I went in to discuss his unhappiness with the director. My son's explanation for his unhappiness was that he was there with the "babies." I mentioned this to the director, and she told me that the time slot I had chosen for my son happened to be for 18-month to three-year-old children. However, she felt certain his needs were being accommodated within the program. She then told me that if my son was unhappy, she was confident it related to my recent divorce from his father. I was furious with her lack of sensitivity and disappointed that an expert in early childhood education could overlook the importance of socialization with same-age peers.

Teachers are very important to children. It is imperative that teachers not stigmatize children for residing in single-parent homes. A good beginning is for teachers not to use the term "broken home" when referring to the homes of these children. "Broken" implies that something is defective, not to be valued, and even discarded.

Every child from a single-parent home is unique and comes from a unique set of circumstances. *Just* a few dimensions on which single parents differ are the following: (1) reason for single parenting (that is, death of spouse, prolonged separation, divorce, abandonment, never married, single adoption); (2) time elapsed since becoming a single parent; (3) number of children and their respective ages and personalities; (4) age and personality of parent; (5) relationship with other parent, if alive;

(6) financial situation; (7) occupational demands; (8) experiences from family of origin and family of construction; (9) self-esteem and attitude; and (10) support received from family, friends, and institutions.

Obviously, there is no single template for understanding or making assumptions about children from single-parent families. It is imperative that teachers remain open-minded about all children—affirming and supporting them for who they are.

TEACHING ABOUT DIFFERENCE

At the beginning of each school year, it is important to teach a unit on difference. Such a unit will set a background for discussing that there are many ways of being in the world—including the kind of family structure within which one lives.

Teachers must model acceptance of difference and give examples of it. With respect to single-parent families, it is important to acknowledge that not everyone has a mom and a dad living in the home. Children must be given opportunities to talk about and write about their families. Teacher-selected books that feature different kinds of family structures might be shared with children at this time.

Preschool/Elementary

- Williams, V. B. (1982). *A chair for my mother.* New York: HarperCollins.
  Child lives with mother and grandmother.
- Steele, D. (1989). *Martha's new daddy.* New York: Bantam.
  Child of divorced parents experiences remarriage of her mother.
- Christiansen, C. B. (1989). *My mother's house. My father's house.* New York: Penguin Books.
  Parents are divorced and child lives with both.
- MacLachlan, P. (1985). *Sarah, plain and tall.* New York: HarperCollins.
  Two children anticipate the remarriage of their father after their mother dies.

Junior/Senior High

- Wilson, B. (1988). *Breakdown.* New York: Scholastic Books.
  Two children experience a change in their father after their mother dies.

- Klein, N. (1972). *Mom, the wolfman and me.* New York: Avon Books.
  A girl whose mother never married deals with the change in her life as her mother becomes serious about a man.
- Klein, N. (1988). *Now that I know.* New York: Bantam Books.
  A young girl living with both parents after a divorce deals with each parent having a new partner.
- Paterson, K. (1988). *Park's quest.* New York: Puffin Books.
  A young man searches for information on his own when his mother refuses to talk about his father, who died in the Vietnam War.

Finally, at gift-making time, teachers have the opportunity to introduce the concept of "who is special" to each child. By encouraging children to share who the special people in their lives are, the focus on moms and dads is somewhat broadened. Children should subsequently be allowed to make the number of gifts they deem appropriate.

FACILITATING PARENTAL CONNECTION TO THE SCHOOL

We all know that it is in the best interest of children to have their teachers communicate effectively with their parents. Many single parents have limited financial resources and are unable to provide food or money for school activities. Furthermore, their jobs may preclude them from volunteering in the classroom or from attending conferences at assigned times. Unless a teacher is aware of such difficulties, he or she may interpret the single parent's lack of involvement as disinterest in the child's education.

A phone call made to every parent at the beginning of each school year will provide a valuable link to all parents. It is possible that a single parent can come in and share a hobby, chaperone a field trip, or assist with a party. On the other hand, it is important to find out that a parent's schedule will not accommodate traditional ways of being involved with schools. It is possible that even the parent–teacher conference will have to be accomplished over the telephone to allow for a single parent's particular set of circumstances. The purpose of phone conversations is to help the parent feel a connection to the teacher, to the school, and to the child's education within the school. The parent must feel valued regardless of his or her ability to be physically present in the school.

A child who has lost a parent by death may need increased support on the anniversary date of that parent's death. The parents I interviewed appreciated teachers who asked for this information and were prepared before the school year got under way.

SHARING GOOD NEWS WITH PARENTS

When our son, Nathan, started kindergarten, there were custodial proceedings still taking place. As his father and I sat down with his kindergarten teacher at the end of the first reporting period, the air "dripped" with tension. The teacher's first remark was, "I realize that the two of you are probably not very comfortable being here, considering all that you have been going through. I appreciate that you both came and must begin by complimenting you. Nathan is a very happy, well-adjusted little boy. Despite your differences, you have both obviously done something right!" The tension in that room was immediately reduced. She had affirmed us as parents and told us that something was going well in our otherwise difficult lives. It is rare that teachers cannot find a single good thing to say to parents. I think it is fair to say that most of us do not set out to be ineffective parents, though we may make mistakes along the way.

ALTERING WRITTEN COMMUNICATION AND RECORD KEEPING

Without teachers realizing it, children from single parent families often suffer discomfort related to written notices and school records. There are two situations responsible for the discomfort.

Often, only the custodial parent receives report cards, school bulletins, and letters written to parents. This practice not only causes stress for the parents but also puts the child in the middle of his or her parents. When the custodial parent and the noncustodial parent do not get along, the child often is made responsible for keeping both parents informed about school events and progress reports. Teachers can alleviate any problems in this area by simply sending all written communication to everyone who parents a child.

The school directory is another potential source of trouble for children from single-parent homes. These children may have names different from those of their parents, and they often have parents living at different addresses and responding at different phone numbers. A simple remedy for teachers is to request that the office send out forms with ample space for listing custodial and noncustodial parents or two parents who share custody equally but reside apart. The school directory (which often is compiled from these forms) can then designate biological parents with a star and custodial parents with an underline—giving all pertinent addresses and phone numbers for each. Again, allowing parents to feel valued, regardless of their custodial status, can serve to enhance the lives of their children.

If we want to advocate for children from single-parent families and nurture their emotional well-being, we must first *make no assumptions about these children.* Further, it is important to *teach children about difference,* to subsequently help children understand different types of families, and to model acceptance of those families. Teachers are in a position *to facilitate parental connection to the school* by arranging for conferences and school visits that are scheduled around work and child-care obligations. Too often parents hear from teachers only when children are doing poorly. It is crucial that teachers *share good news about children* as well. Finally, parents will feel more valued by the school if teachers try to *alter written communication and recordkeeping.* This means sending all school correspondence to everyone who parents a child and making school directories that properly acknowledge these individuals as well.

EDITORS' COMMENTARY

Several conditions of poverty that students might experience as they grow up can have negative consequences on their later lives. One major condition is growing up deprived of basic parental love and caring, which can result in feelings of mistrust and blunted relationships in the future. The teacher, often in the role of the surrogate parent, reaps the harvest of these feelings, including endless testing of authority. Another deprivation is growing up in material poverty—that is, without the basic necessities. In general, society prefers to ignore these issues, but teachers cannot. The material deprivation is hydra-headed because it reaches into so many aspects of students' lives. This deprivation can mean hunger, no bed of one's own, substandard housing and neighborhoods, life-endangering communities, risk-laden opportunities for recreation, no health or dental care—the list goes on and on. Comparison with the affluent can breed hopelessness and a sense of frustration. It is surprising how many poor students still struggle even when the country is experiencing good economic times. Many poor families sacrifice other things to send their kids to school well dressed. When poverty destroys the American dream, it often saps children's motivation to learn.

Lott (2002) wrote of our society's efforts to ignore the so-called underclass. A more recent book on this topic is David Shipler's (2005) *The Working Poor*. He reveals the nightmare underlying the honest, hard-working American Dream for the poor. While living in decaying homes, lacking health care, and experiencing social discrimination, they perform the low-paying, dead-end jobs that are essential to our economy but that no one else wants. This situation demonstrates that the class system operates in our country; the poor are classified as inferior.

IN the next article, John Seita writes about growing up in an unstable family living with poverty, alcoholism, and madness in an inner city.

ARTICLE 3.3

GROWING UP WITHOUT FAMILY PRIVILEGE
John R. Seita

> The first thing that happened to him was that he was abandoned by the people who were supposed to love him most.
>
> —Will's therapist in *Good Will Hunting*

I too was abandoned. Many times. At age eight, I became the property of the Juvenile Court in Cleveland, Ohio. I was separated from my mother whose lifestyle included excessive drinking, promiscuity, and inner city squalor. Over the next four years, I repeatedly ran away from or was kicked out of a long string of foster homes and juvenile centers. For the most part, I grew up without the privilege of a family. The man I called father was prone to violence. He nearly beat my mother to death, and that marriage ended. I also had a half-brother Jimmy and a half-sister Maria, but the court took them away, too. I

From *Reclaiming Children and Youth*, 10(3), 2001, pp. 130–132. Copyright by Reclaiming Children and Youth, Inc. Reprinted with permission.

wish that I could remember Jimmy and Maria better, but I don't. I have no idea what ever happened to them.

Ours was the world of poverty, alcoholism, deprivation, decay, and madness of the inner city projects. We constantly moved, sometimes living in transient hotels. Often our utilities were disconnected and we went hungry. A report in my case file reads: "When the women's bureau investigated the home, there was no food; there were broken beer bottles strewn on the floor and the place was in a state of utter dishevelment. The mother had been leaving the children unsupervised most of the time. The children were all very undernourished."

On the worst day of my young life, my mother brought us three kids with her in a dirty cab to the court building in downtown Cleveland. She said she had to talk to a judge and told me I was the oldest and should watch over Jimmy and Maria. Some people whom I had never seen before took us from my mother to sit on a wooden bench outside of the courtroom. In a few minutes I heard my mother screaming, "No, no, no, no, no!" I ran to the room and looked inside to see who was hurting her. I saw her lying on the floor rolling around, crying, "I love my babies, please don't take my babies away!" I tried to rush to her aid, but the workers restrained me. I never lived with my family again.

FAMILIES ON THE EDGE

Contemporary society is producing packs of kids detached from adults. Some roam wild as "mall orphans," while others are banished from our schools and communities. Children who do not bond to a caring adult come to believe they are unwanted and unlovable (Bowlby, 1982). The result is anger and aggression, often mixed with shame and depression. They target their rage at adults, who failed to meet their need for love, and at themselves for not deserving that love. Defiant and distrustful, they are society's unclaimed kids. They are forever biting the hand that didn't feed them.

Troubled behavior results when children are deprived of the ingredients for positive development. In a healthy family, children receive emotional nurturance and guidance. In a healthy school, supportive teachers instill academic and social competence. As youth gain independence, their peers provide belonging and healthy values. The broader community also provides positive support and standards through churches, employment, and social organizations. These positive connections inoculate youth against a wide range of risks. But a lack of these positive connections produce what Lisbeth Schorr calls "rotten outcomes" (Schorr, 1989).

In the film *Good Will Hunting,* Will was an unparented youth who grew up in abusive foster homes. We aren't told what happened to Will's family or why he is an orphan and so alone. Maybe Will's parents were killed in an accident. Perhaps his mother was a young, single parent who gave him up for adoption, or his parents simply got divorced and neither wanted Will. Maybe he was taken from his home due to neglect or abuse. Whatever happened, Will is deeply wounded, and his feelings of rejection ooze out of his very being. Will has experienced the deepest of human loss: he is missing the basic kinds of privileges that are provided by stable families and environments.

FAMILY PRIVILEGE

Family Privilege is defined as the benefits, mostly invisible, that come from membership in a stable family. Most people cannot even imagine what life might be like without Family Privilege. Only as we recognize the power of Family Privilege can we begin to grasp how its absence hinders development. Bill Buford (1955) notes that family is the essential presence—the thing that never leaves you even if you have to leave it.

Family Privilege is an invisible package of assets and pathways that provides us with a sense of belonging, safety, unconditional love, and spiritual values. With Family Privilege, children observe parents or older siblings to see the effort it takes to be successful in life. Family Privilege provides the chance to hope and to dream.

Parents who provide consistent affection and discipline foster the development of Family Privilege. A variety of stressors, however, can interfere with normal parenting and the growth of family privilege. These stressors include hurried lifestyle, work pressure, poverty, divorce, illness, disability, criminality, substance abuse, and physical abuse. Adults who are extremely stressed or who lack parenting skills cannot form the secure bonds necessary for their children to develop social skills, self-control, and conscience.

Economist Theodore Schultz (1974) coined the term "human capital" and rooted it squarely in the family. Like financial resources, human capital accumulates over generations and is passed from parents to children. Human capital includes the social and educational skills that allow young people to follow rules, solve problems, and communicate at a high level.

Family Privilege is a form of human capital that compounds its benefits over time. However, large numbers of youth today operate without the support of stable parents, an extended family, or even minimal traces of Family Privilege. Even in traditional families, Family Privilege is not a given. It must be intentional, not simply hit or miss or hope and pray. Those of us with Family Privilege take it for granted. Like oxygen, we would never notice its absence unless we were suffocating.

LOSS OF PRIVILEGE

The idea of Family Privilege hearkens to Peggy McIntosh (1997) who coined the concept of "White Privilege" which is strongly influencing multicultural understanding. McIntosh suggests that prejudice is more than active discrimination; it is also an undeserved status coming from unearned privilege. Powerful benefits come with membership in a dominant group. For example, men do not worry about the possibility of rape when traveling in a new environment, but this is an ever-present concern of women. In this nation founded by European Americans, few whites feel they risk rejection each time they enter a typical classroom, but such stresses are common to those of other cultures. McIntosh provides the following example of how white privilege affects her life:

> I have come to see white privilege as an invisible package of unearned assets that I can count on cashing in each day, but about which I was "meant" to remain oblivious. White privilege is like an invisible weightless knapsack of special provisions, assurances, tools, maps, guides, co-debooks, passports, visas, clothes, compass, emergency gear, and blank checks. (McIntosh, 1997)

Other examples of white privilege abound: If I am white, I can, if I wish, spend most of my time in the company of people of my race. I can be fairly sure that my children will not come home from school devastated by racial harassment. I can be pretty sure that my children's teachers will tolerate them without concern about their race. When I see police, I am usually certain that they are here to protect me.

McIntosh suggests that we cannot understand the barriers faced by "minorities" unless we first understand the benefits of whiteness. Likewise, in order to understand the barriers faced by those without Family Privilege, we must first recognize the benefits of those with Family Privilege. Here are a few examples of what it might be like to grow up without Family Privilege:

- As a small child, when I call out at night, I cannot be sure anyone will hear me. The people who come and go through my house frighten me. I never know if tomorrow I will live in this same home. I can never be sure if there will be anything to eat.

- When I start school, my parents don't attend conferences with the teacher, and I would be embarrassed if they did. If I am sick, they can't find my mother. There is no one to help me with my homework or even to wake me on time.

- As an adolescent, I can't bring friends home without being embarrassed. When I get in trouble, no one speaks for me. It wouldn't matter because people in authority like principals, police, and judges don't listen to or respect my parents.

- As a young adult, no one helps me plan for college and career. If life gets hard, I can't ask for a loan or move back home. I don't know my relatives or my genetic heritage, and I have no family medical history. I can never be sure that I am unconditionally loved.

Family Privilege is best secured in the family. When that is not possible, or even the best plan, then Family Privilege becomes a community issue. Peter Benson (1997) notes that "all kids are our kids." As long as there are any children at risk, then all our children reside in *at-risk communities.* Ironically, those children who most need Family Privilege from the school and the community are those who are the first to be expelled, rejected, or relegated to substandard services.

Those who thoughtfully examine their own Family Privilege may come to some disquieting conclusions. Perhaps their accomplishments are as much a product of unearned privileges and circumstances as of individual effort and capacity. Even goals and dreams may be the result of Family Privilege.

As a society, we place high expectations on young people for achievement and prosocial behavior. However, establishing standards without understanding privilege and handicap is like expecting all youths to run a 100-meter dash in twelve seconds. One runner must jump over hurdles, a second runs uphill, a third attempts to run the race on crutches. Meanwhile, three other runners in the same race have a smooth, dry, and obstacle-free track and come out ahead of the rest. Many applaud the three winners and look down on the others as losers. Only as we recognize their individual obstacles can we remove those barriers or help the runner overcome them. When youth lack Family Privilege, then schools, churches, and neighborhoods need to help fill this gap. Often that is not the case.

REFERENCES

Benson, P. (1997). *All kids are our kids: What communities must do to raise caring and responsible children and adults.* San Francisco: Jossey-Bass.

Bowlby, J. (1982). *Attachment and loss.* New York: Basic Books.

Buford, B. (Ed.). (1955). *The family.* New York: Granta Books.

McIntosh, P. (1997). White privilege and male privilege: A personal account of coming to see correspondences through work in women's studies. In Margaret L. Andersen and Patricia Hill Collins (Eds.), *Race, class, and gender* (pp. 76–87). Belmont, CA: Wadsworth.

Schorr, L. (1989). *Within our reach.* New York: Anchor.

Schultz, T. (1974). Marriage, family human capital, and fertility. Cited in James Traub, What no school can do. *New York Times Sunday Magazine* (2000, January 16).

EDITORS' COMMENTARY

Teachers recognize there are possible ethnic issues to be aware of in family relationships. For example, some Latino families take great pride in family bonds and the closeness of children and parents. The family takes care of its own and expects the school to do the education job. Consider as well the possible preconceptions that might be lurking when a teacher first meets a struggling poor Black or White mother who has several children and is overwhelmed by problems. The mother has to arrange for transportation, child care, and so on, only to discuss an aggressive student and what the home might do. Relationships must start with the teacher identifying with the parent, recognizing what life is really like in the parent's shoes, and determining which resources beyond the school may be needed.

SCHOOLS AND RACISM

Few teachers believe they are prejudiced and most claim that they treat all students alike. However, pervasive attitudes supported by the culture at large do not evaporate. Race is a huge educational issue that is rarely discussed with fellow staff members.

The overrepresentation of Black students, especially of troubled and at-risk Black students, is one of the scandals of special education. One result is that Black families also are overrepresented in education family liaison efforts. Establishing relationships with Black families brings up issues for Black, White, and Latino teachers. It would be an error to attribute the numbers solely to race when socioeconomic conditions are considered, although adult fear and prejudice may affect referrals of Black male students. The country has made great progress since the Civil War, but social equality is still evasive and, for many Black and Latino families, there is no economic parity.

THE next article is about racism. Although the article is about growing up as a Black youth, it should be read as a prototype of prejudice against all ethnic minorities. One can go even further and imagine what happens to any student who does not fit in the mythical mainstream.

The target of racism can experience feelings of fear and shame. Fear is an automatic personal response that protects one from dangerous situations. In this article, Jamie Chambers tells how racism, like cancer, has both overt and covert manifestations. He uses his personal experience of being a Black student in a White parochial high school to describe these conditions.

ARTICLE 3.4

UNMASKING THE TERROR
Jamie C. Chambers

In the late 1960s when I was growing up, one word that would strike fear and terror in the toughest of hearts was *cancer*. In my private logic, I had the notion that people were fine until the doctor opened them up to discover that this molecular weed of cancer had ravaged their insides. During those same years, I had to live daily with the terror of another dreaded word. For some time after I was enrolled in a White parochial high school in Denver, I would carry a short bat in my book bag, ever vigilant lest one of the racist students were to speak the terrifying "N" word, and I would have to act to defend my dignity.

Today, I work with youth of many races. Most keep the problem of racism concealed, denying any symptoms they might feel within. Others cannot conceal their pain and wounds. And, a growing number of youth who are brought to our counseling center flaunt their racism as a counterfeit badge of superiority. Racism today is like a form of a slow-growing cancer, but although we have the science of oncology to help diagnose and treat cancer, most of us are afraid to even utter the name of the illness from which we all suffer.

FACING THE TERROR

RACISM DEFINED

What is this malady called racism? I believe it is a disease with which we all have been injected and by which we are all severely affected. No one has immunity from this illness. James Cone (1991) said, "Racism is deeply embedded in American religion and society.... Racism is a cancer. To get rid of this deadly disease requires radical surgery that cuts deep into the 'body politic.' " Racism is a disease, a pathology whereby one race is preoccupied with establishing and maintaining its superiority over another. It is also characterized by a compulsive pursuit of control and power over another race or ethnic group.

In the United States, the dominant race is consciously and/or unconsciously interested in maintaining its place. Which means members of the majority expend untold amounts of energy trying to preserve their status—that is, to get what they want and keep what they have. The presence of outsiders, those of us who appear different, seems to drive this compulsive need to hoard and to bar the door to resources. Outsiders use popular terms such as "hitting the wall or glass ceiling" to describe what it is like to encounter racism. Racism can change its appearance, so youth today can often be caught and tangled deep within its web before they realize they have been infected.

HUES OF RACISM EXPOSED

Like cancer, this disease has both overt and covert manifestations. Painfully, our youth still are subjected to "good ole" bigotry and hatred based on skin tone and ethnicity. The signposts for overt racism are blatantly verbal and/or physical violence. Or, on the other hand, they may be social and/or economic segregation. An example in the midwest is kids who are subjected to overt racism because of their hip-hop style or preference in music. Suburban, European youth are being called "whiggers," which has a tragic similarity to the word *nigger*. It also has the word *nigger*'s power to separate and degrade. Blindsiding and kneebuckling overt racism is an obvious and ominous force that seeks to intimidate and impose inferiority on its victim and witnesses alike.

The underbelly of overt racism is covert racism, the invisible entity that quietly but tenaciously seeks to secretly oppress and subjugate a race. The covert racist hides in a maze of social convention, sarcasm, innuendo, and emotional reasoning. But these only serve to conceal his or her trap; once racism is inside, the victim is poked, stabbed, and robbed, then left for dead. But the assailant is cloaked, as that old song goes, "smiling faces, smiling faces tell lies!" Toni Morrison stated, "Racism [both overt and covert] is a scholarly pursuit, it's taught, it's institutionalized" ("Toni Morrison Now," 1987, p. 336). We are all taught the harsh lessons of racism! Covert oppression is invisible; sometimes you can feel it, you can smell it and even taste it, but you rarely see it. Youth with whom I work talk to me about being stunned and then confused by the covert racist's tactics. Joni, a caramel-skinned 16-year-old youth, revealed, "you just know it, you walk into a room and there it is. Its presence is unforgettable, 'cause people change right in front of your face and you're not sure why." That is probably the pain of covert racism—one never knows if it is the color of your skin, your talent or lack of talent, or something else that attracts rejection. Because it is taught and institutionalized, it has the ability to influence us invisibly, quietly, and below most of our "radar."

Today, our youth have to deal with neutrality, a new ally of racism. Multiculturalism and postmodernism have given us an appreciation of difference but also a kind of apathy. This position of neutrality numbs the souls of our youth to the fight and need to take a position. If one takes neutrality plus a tiny dose of tolerance, it will erode our youths' ability to clearly distinguish which way to go or whom to trust. Consequently, I find an odd trend happening: Youth are passionately defending another's right to be a bigot or racist. This phenomenon has become part of the locomotion that now moves racism!

Racism is real today and today's youth would be greatly served by the adults who have the courage to name it when they see it.

Adults who are willing to acknowledge being either a perpetrator or victim can effectively defeat racism.

FEAR UNMASKED: THE MOTIVATOR OF RACISM

You tend to be afraid when someone seems foreign to you. But if you aren't careful, that can lead to bigotry.
—Jasmine Guy (1993, p. 144)

All humans, including children and youth, have at least three competing motivational systems that propel us toward different courses of action. These dimensions of our humanness are so universal that they must be hard-wired on the hard drive of our minds and souls. These may be referred to as the sacred, the profane, and the force of fear.

THE SACRED

Native American psychologist Martin Brokenleg tells us that the Lakota word for child is *sacred being*. This view of children as sacred is shared by many tribal cultures around the world. In *Reclaiming Youth at Risk,* Brendtro, Brokenleg, and VanBockern (1990) have described what might be seen as four sacred passions, positive motivators for human life. They suggested that we are endowed in our DNA with these basic life forces, which cause us to seek to belong, to be independent, to develop mastery, and to be generous. These needs are not fully met in youth at risk. They are also the needs of all humanity. Each of us has an instinctual drive to love, to create, to manage our lives, and to contribute something of value to others. When children are given opportunities to follow these passions, life is in balance. When these sacred passions are missing, life is out of balance.

THE PROFANE

However much we may wish to celebrate the positive side of human nature, there is a darker part of our existence. Often it is that side of ourselves that we try hard to suppress. Or, sometimes we choose to let it run wild. An extreme example is seen in the videotapes of Eric and Dylan, the two youth who planned and carried out the Columbine High School massacre in Colorado. In a videotape, Eric said that he purposely stopped taking medication so that he could nurture his rage against those he saw as violating him. He described how he chose to avoid his parents so that he could unleash himself from the restraining bonds of their love. This conscious choice of darkness over light is described in the ancient sacred writings of all major faith traditions, and it is as current as our daily lives. The profane side of humanity drives in harsh competition—to allow hate and destruction to have their way, to segregate and separate, to hoard, and to subjugate or dominate others. We live in a time where this side of humanity heavily stains the airwaves with echoes of human destruction and devastation. We live in a day where most of us try to move away, push underground, or banish that which is a reminder of our profane side.

THE FORCE OF FEAR

This leads to the third motivating force underlying human experience. We all experience anxiety, those times when something or someone is not quite right. At the same time, we have all been frightened at one point or another. Whether on a scale from anxiety to true terror, fear is the experience that tells us that we're vulnerable. It is an alarm that sounds when our sacredness has been threatened or when our profane side has been exposed. Its job is to warn us of impending doom or a close threat.

Race-based fear is a response that can potentially devour both offender and offended. The racist therefore has to remain hypervigilant, always on the prowl for someone to dominate or devour. Coercion and contempt become his or her sweet nectar and help him or her hide from the reality of his or her own fear. Likewise, the hunted is also hypervigilant, but weary from being targeted. Denial and codependence become the armor he or she wears in the heat of battle. Regardless of one's position, what makes people sacred has to be disregarded, that is, their cultural creativity and unique ways of interacting. To make matters worse, that which is profane becomes a primary focus, that is, life organized around detecting the presence or absence of racial violence.

As a victim of racism, I find myself leery of opening myself to new relationships, for fear that it will only permit another "pounce" on my already tattered spirit. What I have witnessed and experienced is this: The very thing that makes you and me sacred racially has become the reason and justification for separation and segregation.

THE SHAME OF IT ALL

George Bernard Shaw confirmed what those of us who have been marred and maimed by racism live daily—"We live in an atmosphere of shame. We are ashamed of everything that is real about us" (cited in Andrews, 1989). Healthy shame reminds me of my limits and finiteness. It is a reminder that no matter how lofty my ambitions and accomplishments, I still roam this planet with feet of clay. Race-based shame proclaims that inherent in the fibers of my being is a malignancy that makes me an outcast, worthy of being treated like a leper. And when race-based shame grows up, it turns on its victim. Like a parasite, it feeds on the innards of its host.

So it goes: Race-based shame becomes the gong that sounds at the anticipation of being hunted; it is the fear of being found, discovered, or seen. But with my suede skin tone, how and where do I hide? Even if I can get you not to really look, my swagger, my enunciation, my determined glare, or my unique flare might give me away. And if you don't get me, I will. Race-based shame as it moves around inside turns me against me. At best, I begin to edit and silence the parts of me that racists seem to hate most. At worst, I segregate and "lynch" myself—at least then I get me before they do.

BANISHING OF TRUST

Race-based fear plus shame leaves one with few alternatives—hide or commit suicide. Both solutions foster the banishment of one fundamental desire, which is the ability and willingness to trust humanity. Without trust, where can I go to belong and have a place, and to whom do I give my creativity? Our communities are full of people hiding their treasure under a basket for fear it will not be regarded, and there are others who have ceased dreaming about the new dance or cures for disease. In *The Joys of Motherhood* (1979), Buchi Emecheta stated:

> In Nigeria, you are simply not allowed to commit suicide in peace, because everyone is responsible for the other person. Foreigners may call us a nation of busybodies, but to us an individual life belongs to the community and not just to him or her. So a person has no right to take it while another member of the community looks on. He must interfere, he must stop it from happening. (cited in Riley, 1993, p. 69)

Real community is the balm for healing racism; it is the place where belonging, independence, mastery, and generosity intersect. But community is not community if it is closed; Howard Thurman (1971) has asserted that genuine community can only flourish as we invite others from beyond, as we welcome our formerly unknown and undiscovered brothers and sisters. The process of developing community can begin when we do the following:

Provide youth with the opportunity to experience the affirming of their sacredness. Seek to give opportunity for belonging, mastery, independence, and generosity.

Teach youth how to regard the profane in life and themselves.

Acknowledge and validate race-based fear, touch and be willing to explore it from a position of curiosity.

Race-based shame is only healed in the contexts of long-term friend-ships and mentorships, where each student's creativity and longings are explored and then treasured. Remember that it does take a village of real people who are willing to expose their struggles in dealing with the sacred, profane, and fearful sides of themselves to raise a child.

REFERENCES

Andrews, R. (Ed.). *The concise Columbia dictionary of quotations.* New York: Avon.

Brendtro, L. K., Brokenleg, M., & VanBockern, S. (1990). *Reclaiming youth at risk: Our hope for the future.* Bloomington, IN: National Educational Service.

Cone, J. (1991). *Martin, Malcolm and America.* Marycarroll, NY: Orbis Books.

Emecheta, B. (1979). *The joys of motherhood.* New York: Braziller.

Guy, J. (1993). Spotlight: Jasime Guy. In D. W. Riley (Ed.), *My soul looks back, 'less I forget: A collection of quotations by people of color* (p. 144). New York: Harper Perennial.

Morrison, T. (1993). Toni Morrison now. In D. W. Riley (Ed.), *My soul looks back, 'less I forget: A collection of quotations by people of color* (p. 336). New York: Harper Perennial.

Riley, D. W. (Ed.). (1993). *My soul looks back, 'less I forget: A collection of quota-tions by people of color.* New York: Harper Perennial.

Thurman, H. (1971). *The search for common ground.* New York: Harper & Row.

ARTICLE 3.5

OVER the next two decades, remarkable demographic changes will take place in our country and the importance of cross-cultural differences will be seen in every classroom. In the following article Martin Brokenleg lists 13 suggestions for teach-ers, counselors, and administrators to address this change.

BRIDGING CULTURES
Martin Brokenleg

In the next generation, the United States will undergo the most remark-able demographic shift since the Whites began to outnumber Indians in the colonial era. Already many schools and youth agencies are populated with children whose cultural backgrounds are unlike those of the adults who work with them. With a limited number of persons of color in preprofessional training programs, this imbalance may not be redressed for some time. In any case, all of us will need to develop competence to connect across cultural differences. Here is short list of suggestions that can help teachers, counselors, and others who work with culturally diverse populations.

1. Don't view the unknown as pathological. The more we under-stand a young person, the more his or her behavior, however counterproductive, will be seen as a means of coping. My favorite example is a new teacher who had moved from Florida to South Dakota. As winter approached, she wondered why some of the kids had a twitch when they went out on the play-ground. Actually, the children who did not have gloves were pulling their hands up inside their coat sleeves. As they did so, they made a movement with their shoulders that appeared to be what the teacher recognized as a twitch. In South Dakota winters, this is a survival technique, not some type of hyper-activity.

2. Don't withhold interventions because you are uncertain what to do. Doing nothing will accomplish nothing, except per-haps to communicate to the young person that you are wary or disinterested. Try some intervention and, if you do make a mistake, you can apologize, which may do wonders for your relationship.

3. Don't let common conditions become stereotypes. We can very easily overgeneralize from something that seems typical. The

best definition for stereotype was one I got from a 7-year-old: "All Indians walk single file, at least the one I saw did."

4. Know how to incorporate cultural factors into the diagnostic code for your profession. In cultures where showing superiority is shameful, students might say they don't know the answer because this might make them appear better than their peers; this does not mean they are clueless—rather, they are actually very socially perceptive. In another case, a counselor reported to me that a Lakota girl described talking to her deceased mother in a dream. This may be referral material for a White kid, but this youth was describing a blessing.

5. Be a friend before there is a need. Most communal cultures in the world are relationally based. Young people will turn to you only if they know who you are. Most teenagers in the United States live in a relational culture. If a fight takes place on the school parking lot after school, most kids will know about it long before teachers or the principal.

6. Guard confidentiality in communal cultures. In those environments we must be very conscientious about confidentiality, not only because it keeps private information private, but because it shows that we are trustworthy.

7. Use elders and their advice. In a relational culture, people tend to go to the oldest persons in the community, those who have the longest tenure. In a gang, the leader might be the "elder." In a Native American community, it would be the chronological elder, perhaps someone who is 70 or 80 years old. The elders know the oral stories. Someone not connected to the community will not know the oral tradition.

8. Be involved in the community that you serve. A White teacher reported that after he moved into the minority community where he teaches, he started attending funerals and other cultural events, and his discipline problems declined dramatically.

9. Trust your intuition. If your feeling is respectful and makes sense, you are unlikely to spoil your relationships. There is powerful therapeutic value in kindness, and children will notice small things you do that are beyond expectations for your job.

10. Help those with minority backgrounds work with the larger cultural system. Just as you can learn about other cultures from youth and families you serve, so you can help them navigate the dominant culture if they are unsure in this respect.

11. Integrate rituals and symbols from the cultures of young persons into the milieu of school or agency. For example, judicious use of art and paintings can help youth feel comfortable (but remember that the goal is not to prove that you are a connoisseur of their culture).

12. Work through historic distrust. Generally a person of color will not immediately trust a White person. Like it or not, we represent our race until we become known as a person. Until youth feel safe in a relationship, they may be wary of you for fear you might be like others who have diminished their race or culture. Trust takes time, and relationships can't be "microwaved."

13. Help students or clients meet their own goals. Some youth expend great effort opposing persons they see as adversaries. When you are seen as an advocate helping them develop their interests and potentials, resistance is transformed into cooperation.

TEACHER AND THE COMMUNITY AS A RESOURCE

The Community as an Aid to Reclaiming Students

As Hobbs's diagrams illustrate (at the beginning of this chapter), it is typical for community involvement to expand at adolescence. A starting point for determining how to use the community as a resource to reclaim students is to examine the quality and availability of community life activities to offer students. It is hardly a surprise that participation in wholesome after-school activities facilitates reclaiming. Some schools sponsor recreation programs and even after-school and Saturday remedial schooling.

Each teacher should consider the following questions: How would you rate your school's neighborhood and the extended community as a supportive place for students to grow up? How does it compare with where you were raised? What are the assets and risks? Are peer group associations available?

If the teacher can provide information about community offerings, students' lives might be enriched rather than put at risk. It may be necessary for the teacher to become a community advocate, along with other adults, to get services for kids. The teacher might contact service clubs about student scholarships to the Y, a Boys' and Girls' Club, or Big Brothers/Big Sisters. Service clubs often have in their charters an obligation to youth. Also, a useful project would be for a class to explore getting these services.

Community Foster Care

The most common pseudo-home a teacher may face is the foster home, where there is no legal family or there is such disintegration that family rescue is deemed impossible and the student is declared a ward of society. The essential problem for foster parents is the cost in money and emotional concern of substituting for a child's family. Parenting, never easy, is more difficult with foster children. Attempts to provide a satisfactory second family are very costly for states, and states occasionally lose track of some students within the bureaucracy. Although many foster homes are caring and do quite well as surrogate families—an estimated 80% of foster placements are supportive and not providing this service for the money—there are cases in which foster parents exploit the situation for the money. Social work surveillance sees that minimum standards are met, but there is no way to assure continuity of care even in cases that turn into adoptions.

Exploring Community Religious Resources

The separation of church and state can cause educators to overlook religious institutions as community resources. Some students' families have significant attachment to a faith, and all of these institutions have a concern for students and youth. Sometimes a student has or could find support there. Not only do some churches have organized sports activities, but many have counselors who can take a personal interest in a student. It is the one place in the community where morality is the central purpose. Teachers should explore this possibility with families.

SUMMARY

Teachers rarely have the opportunity to learn about the sociological changes that may be taking place in our society and in their classrooms, although they may be experiencing these changes in painful ways. This chapter has invited teachers to look at these significant demographic changes. Teachers are exposed to various visions of family life, which often are alien to them, and to families of all styles, sizes, interpersonal relationships, and ethnic backgrounds.

Teachers need to better understand the role of racism in their classrooms and recognize any conscious and personal experiences that promote racism. At one time, racism focused predominately on Blacks, but now it has expanded to include Latinos, Asians, Muslims, and various other cultural groups. In addition to racism, teachers need to be aware of the damaging impact of poverty, alcoholism, and other factors on the lives of their students. Teachers can benefit troubled students by gathering information about community resources available to them.

EDITORS' REFERENCES

Hobbs, N. (1982). *The Troubled and troubling child.* San Francisco: Jossey-Bass.

Lott, B. (2002). Cognitive and behavioral distancing from the poor. *American Psychologist, 57,* 100–110.

Redl, F. (1959). The concept of a therapeutic milieu. *American Journal of Orthopsychiatry, 29,* 721–736.

Shipler, D. (2005). *The working poor.* New York: Vintage Books.

U.S. Census Bureau. (2004). *Current population survey.* Washington, DC: Author.

4 THE THERAPEUTIC CLASSROOM:
Strategies and Skills of Successful Methods and Social–Emotional Curricula

IN the 10 years since the last edition of *Conflict in the Classroom,* unprecedented events have influenced the landscape of public education. School shootings, especially the shocking devastation at Columbine High School in Littleton, Colorado, in 1999, have forced educators to acknowledge the importance of establishing environments where students are known by adults—where there is an effort to establish some sort of connection or relationship. There is a lesson to be learned from the Columbine incident: It is that we do not know our young people. Profiles of the student shooters often reveal rejected, isolated loners who have no sense of belonging anywhere in the formal structure of the school. The fact that these students can go virtually unnoticed by adults is testimony to the reality that the field of education has not kept pace with the changing society. Of course, the students who rise to this level of violence are at the extreme edge of the bell curve, but we can only wonder how many students feel similarly isolated from the mainstream and remain unknown to the school staff. Patricia Hersch (1998), in her riveting book *A Tribe Apart,* notes,

> Today's teens have grown up in the midst of enormous social changes that have shaped, reshaped, distorted, and sometimes decimated the basic parameters for healthy development. They have grown up with parents who are still seeking answers about what it means to be an adult man or woman. They have lived in families that seldom coincide with the old ideal, and in a culture where the traditional wisdom of how to raise children has been replaced by a kind of daily improvisation as parents try to fit child rearing into their busy lives. At a time when adolescents need to emulate role models, the adults around them are moving targets. Nobody seems to know what is "normal" anymore. (p. 18)

Slowly, our public schools are beginning to realize that their role has to change. To support the mission of academic learning, we cannot ignore the very real social–emotional needs of students. The No Child Left Behind Act of 2001 (NCLB) contains several relevant guidelines. NCLB requires that schools offer students a broad array of services and youth development activities, drug and violence prevention programs, counseling, and character education programs that are designed to reinforce and complement the regular academic program. Under NCLB, schools must establish plans for

- being safe and drug-free, including reporting school safety statistics to the public
- closing the achievement gap between high- and low-performing children and between disadvantaged children and their more advantaged peers
- preventing at-risk youth from dropping out of school
- providing delinquent youth with a support system to ensure their continued education

Under NCLB, schools are also required to implement prevention programs that are grounded in scientifically based research and to provide evidence of effectiveness. NCLB brings a host of hotly contested issues, particularly with regard to expectations for student academic performance and the impact it has relative to entitlement to funds. However, it is significant that NCLB acknowledges that social–emotional factors influence learning.

Perhaps the most well-known approach to developing schoolwide proactive intervention is Positive Behavioral Interventions and Supports (PBIS), developed by Sugai and Horner (1999). PBIS, sometimes known as Positive Behavior Supports (PBS), addresses the areas of discipline, academic performance, and social–emotional development. The model is based on the assumption that students have three levels of need, which should be addressed through a planned process. All students need primary (i.e., universal) supports, which are taught and reinforced uniformly by staff. About 80% of students have basic needs met through this level of support when systems are positive, consistent, and well established. Fifteen percent of students require secondary (i.e., individualized) supports. Programs such as social skills groups, counseling, peer tutoring, and other interventions address identified needs of this at-risk group. Tertiary (i.e., comprehensive) supports are required for 5% of students who have significant, well-established needs. Some of these students qualify for special education services. Repeated studies have demonstrated the effectiveness of PBIS in reducing office referrals for discipline and creating a more stable school climate. Detailed information about PBIS can be found at the Web site (www.pbis.org).

To support schoolwide efforts to identify and connect with students, a broad spectrum of evidence-based social–emotional learning curricula have been developed. It is now widely recognized that academic learning is enhanced when students' social–emotional needs are addressed. Over 250 social–emotional learning programs have been developed for students from kindergarten through Grade 12. These programs address a variety of issues, including social skills, cultural competence, conflict resolution, life skills, and more. The Collaborative for Academic, Social, and Emotional Learning (CASEL) at the University of Illinois at Chicago has released a comprehensive guide, *Safe and Sound: An Education Leader's Guide to Evidence-Based Social and Emotional Learning (SEL) Programs.* The manual reviews 80 social–emotional learning programs and offers guidance on selection and implementation. (The guide can be downloaded from www.edutopia.org.)

When teachers and school leaders invest in such programs, they send a message to students and parents that is just as important as the content of the program. These efforts demonstrate that the staff care for students as individuals, that the students are worth the time and effort to get to know, and that they have value. The skilled teacher knows that students, especially troubled and troubling students, will regularly test whether teachers care. Therefore, creating a classroom environment that is safe, predictable, structured, and nurturing sets the stage for learning, both academic and otherwise. This is no small task. As special education teachers become intervention specialists, general education teachers are challenged to include all learners regardless of disability. According to the *Study of Personnel Needs in Special Education* (U.S. Department of Education, 2002), 75% of special education students spend most of their day in regular education classes. The study further states that regular education teachers express confidence in their ability to work with these students; 96% of the general educators taught students with disabilities or had some experience with them in the past. Yet, according to a study on teacher preparation, knowledge and skills bases once confined to school psychologists are now considered critical to the functioning of effective teachers (Wilson, Floden, & Ferrini-Mundy, 2001). Having once taught special education or having had minimal experience with students receiving special education services can hardly equate to formal training. In addition, the same report notes that experienced teachers describe behavior management and teaching students with exceptionalities as areas in which they felt least prepared by their professional preparation programs.

The articles included in this chapter were selected to provide a sampling of issues, ideas, and reflections on the challenges that students with social–emotional–behavioral problems bring to the classroom. Although many factors combine to make the school experience positive or negative, it is the classroom teacher who has the most influence over a student's attitude about learning. From the tone of the interpersonal relationship to management and instructional style, the teacher daily shapes the probability of the student's success or failure.

For many students struggling with emotional problems, school has been a persistent failure experience. Early in the elementary grades, some students have already decided that they are failures in school and continue to act out that self-fulfilling prophecy year after year. They arrive at the conclusion that it is pointless to try to succeed because the outcome is predictable. However, most students do not enjoy failing and privately wish they could find a way to be successful. Collins and Tamarkin (1982) stated, "Often a problem in the classroom lies with the child but in the relationship between the child and the teacher" (p.112). A skilled teacher can use his or her position to great purpose and create a lifelong change in what a child believes about him- or herself. Ginnot (1972), in his classic book *Teacher and Child* described the power a teacher has:

> I've come to the frightening conclusion that I am the decisive element in the classroom. It's my personal approach that creates the climate; it's my daily mood that makes the weather. As a teacher, I possess a tremendous power to make a child's life miserable or joyous. I can be a tool of torture, or an instrument of inspiration. I can humiliate or humor, hurt or heal. In all situations it is my response that decides whether a crisis will be escalated or de-escalated or a child humanized or de-humanized. (pp. 15–16)

It is easy for us as teachers to get caught up in the intensity and daily demands of the classroom. Sometimes the greater purpose of our mission gets lost in the details. It is important that we remind ourselves of the tremendous responsibility with which we are charged and the powerful influence we can have on the lives and futures of students.

ARTICLE 4.1

IN the following article, Bridget Walker and Frank Fecser outline the structural elements of an effective, comprehensive classroom for students with emotional–behavioral disorders. They define four platforms, including a clear philosophic orientation, a predictable structured environment, positive classroom climate and strong group cohesion, and individualized interventions. Within each platform are research-based components, which, when combined, create the optimal circumstances for students' academic learning and social–emotional growth.

ELEMENTS OF AN EFFECTIVE RE-EDUCATION PROGRAM FOR THE 21ST CENTURY

Bridget A. Walker and Frank A. Fecser

The National Agenda to Improve Results for Children and Youth with Serious Emotional Disturbances reiterated the need for evolution in the field of special education and mental

From *Reclaiming Children and Youth,* *11*(2), 2002, pp. 110–115. Copyright by Reclaiming Children and Youth, Inc. Reprinted with permission.

health. Professionals who serve troubled children and their families are challenged to keep abreast of developments in the field and implement best practices (Osher & Hanley, 1996). Nicholas Hobbs (1982), the founder of Project Re-ED, recognized that practice is dynamic and is always in a state of "becoming." As Re-Education enters the 21st century, it is appropriate to examine current research and implications for practice.

Effective Re-ED classrooms integrate diverse strategies and approaches into a comprehensive and dynamic therapeutic learning environment. This article identifies four critical areas of best practice in successful classrooms: (1) program foundation and philosophy, (2) structure and predictability, (3) classroom climate, and (4) individual programming. Figure 4.1–1 diagrams these elements and their components. By organizing essential elements in this way, we can provide a template to assist in program self-assessment. When considering the extent to which these elements and best practices are present in a setting, it may be helpful to imagine what a program visitor might find if he or she were to walk in tomorrow unannounced.

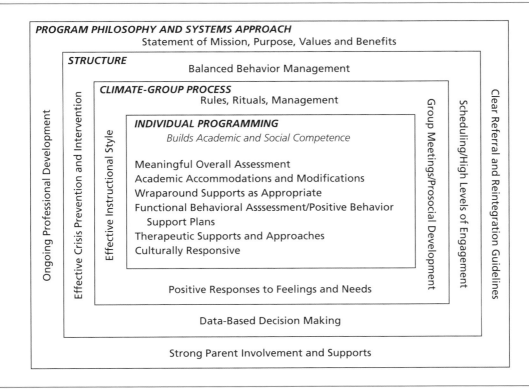

Figure 4.1–1. Elements of an Effective Re-Education Program for the 21st Century.

ELEMENT 1: PROGRAM FOUNDATION AND PHILOSOPHY

Ecology means the study of the complex interaction of energies in natural systems. It seems an apt term to express our concerns for children in settings and for mobilizing the natural resources of a system in the service of a child or an adolescent. (Hobbs, 1982, p. 189)

VALUES, BELIEFS, AND GOALS

The foundation of any program lies in its orienting philosophy. Re-Education believes in the importance of work within the child's ecology. Re-ED focuses on the strengths inherent in each child, employing a variety of perspectives and approaches to problem solving. Staff, students, and families involved in a program must have a common understanding of its purpose and goals in order to be able to fulfill them everyday. As Fecser (1993) summarized, "A clearly stated values system is the foundation of any community, be it an entire school or a single classroom. Our values system establishes the ethics of good practice and provides a standard against which our actions and decisions can be measured" (p. 15). When a program's mission statement, vision, and objectives are evident throughout the program, they serve as a solid base for decision making and program planning.

PURPOSES SERVED

Another critical feature is clear delineation of when and how children and families enter a particular program, as well as when and how they are supported in reintegrating into other settings or services. Clear referral and reintegration processes address such questions as: (a) What challenges are these programs designed to address? (b) How do we know if we are effectively meeting a child's needs? (c) How do we help a child reintegrate into another school and/or community setting? With these issues understood, staff and families have a clear sense of role, direction, and purpose, lending a significant positive momentum to day-to-day experiences.

CHILD AND FAMILY FOCUS

Meaningful involvement of parents and caregivers is fundamental to making a positive impact on the natural ecology of each child. "In Re-ED,"

Hobbs (1982) said, "parents are no longer viewed as sources of contagion, but as responsible collaborators in making the system work" (p. 28). Programs encourage greater involvement by recognizing parents and caregivers as essential partners in supporting and serving each child. Parents and caregivers are moving from the role of passive consumer into active roles as advocates or trainers, establishing networks of support for other families facing similar challenges. This network of support transcends the "formal" setting of the program, reaching families in their homes and communities and resulting in positive changes for the family as well as the individual child (Cheney & Osher, 1997).

INVESTING IN STAFF

Serving troubled children and their families is highly challenging and demanding, and staff need access to abundant professional development opportunities to promote skills and morale. Unfortunately, the realities of tight budgets and full schedules often result in sacrificing staff training. Inadequate training then contributes to a cycle of decreasing morale and effectiveness, burnout, and high turnover, leading to increased error and risk. Skilled and motivated staff are a program's most valuable resource, deserving of continued investment.

ELEMENT 2: PROGRAM STRUCTURE

Learning occurs in the context of well-planned, purposeful, and meaningful days. (Cantrell, Cantrell, Valore, Jones, & Fecser, 1999, p. 16)

Children with emotional or behavioral problems require a structured and predictable environment. They respond best when expectations are clear and consistent with changes in routine kept to a minimum. However, interpreting the optimal degree of structure is tricky business. Well-meaning staff may create a rigid structure, overly concerned with external control and reduction of behaviors at all costs, thereby losing the natural reinforcement inherent in a dynamic and interactive learning community. Steinberg and Knitzer (1992) refer to this tendency as the "curriculum of control." They found that overly controlled settings tended to produce poor academic and behavioral outcomes. Responsiveness to emerging student needs and interests is just as essential as consistency. Skilled teacher/

counselors understand that consistent classroom structure can and should evolve to encourage the emerging development of the child.

BUILDING POSITIVE STRUCTURE

Effective behavior management is fundamental. Ideally, adults can consistently develop a clear system of both positive and negative consequences. Perhaps most importantly, they must provide much higher rates of positive reinforcement than negative consequences in their interactions with students. Well-designed point systems, level systems, and token economies can be helpful management tools. However, staff who readily use social reinforcement such as praise, proximity, and attention, rather than relying primarily on external types of reinforcement, tend to have fewer behavior problems and see greater academic and social gains in their students.

LIMIT SETTING

Strong behavior management also includes the ability to use effective limit setting when necessary, intervening early in emerging problems, rather than waiting to react when the problem behavior has become a crisis. The front-line staff should handle most behavior problems. External administration or agencies (such as police) become involved only in connection with serious offenses, and then, as part of a planned strategy, rather than as a reactive response to a significant disruption. This assures that students understand that they remain accountable and connected to their front-line staff, even under the most difficult circumstances.

PLANNING THE DAY

Scheduling and pacing activities to promote active student involvement and success throughout the day reduces opportunity for bored students to get into trouble. High levels of positive interactions between staff and students and well-planned "unstructured" time can do much to keep everyone on track. A consistent daily schedule lends a sense of order and stability. More difficult or less interesting tasks are followed by activities of higher interest. For example, if a challenging academic task is followed by a group game or other interactive activity, this naturally motivates students to maintain positive behaviors.

USING DATA FOR DECISION MAKING

To determine if the program is generating desired outcomes, effective data collection techniques need to be used to drive program planning, evaluate student progress, and monitor daily functioning. Daily individual student data and aggregated classroom data may reveal trends and patterns that suggest adjustments in level of structure and behavioral supports. In order to be useful, any data collection system needs to be efficient, easy to maintain, and meaningful to staff, students, and families. Keeping parents and caregivers informed about a child's progress through daily notes, home/school passports, report cards, or other means helps them become more effective members of the child's team.

PREVENTING AND MANAGING CRISES

Even in a well-managed environment, students with emotional or behavior problems are still likely to display behavior problems. Thus, teacher/counselors use effective crisis prevention and early intervention strategies. This includes a clear process for addressing the early emergence of problem behavior, as well as for responding to the various levels of escalating behaviors with appropriate intervention strategies (Walker, Colvin, & Ramsey, 1995). Staff who are competent in crisis intervention strategies, verbal de-escalation techniques, and therapeutic physical interventions are best prepared to turn a student's crisis into an opportunity for teaching and learning. An understanding of the Conflict Cycle (Long, Wood, & Fecser, 2001), which describes how adults can be unintentionally drawn into power struggles with students, is a critical skill. The physical layout can hinder or support effective crisis intervention. The setting should provide a safe, private area away from the center of activity for students to regain control, talk privately with helping adults, and solve problems effectively.

DEBRIEFING CRISES

Supportive post-crisis intervention techniques such as debriefing, problem solving, and reintegration discussions maintain student dignity and repair staff/student relationships. Since crisis situations provide powerful teaching moments, teacher/counselors must be prepared to take advantage of these opportunities. Strategies such as Life Space Crisis Intervention

(LSCI) (Long, Wood, & Fecser, 2001) help staff understand the hidden or disguised issues driving a child's problem behavior. The goal is to help the student gain insight into and accountability for self-defeating patterns of behavior. To assure that crisis interventions are utilized effectively, safely, and consistently, it is also important that staff routinely debrief crisis situations. This relieves staff stress and suggests adjustments in management strategies.

ELEMENT 3: PROGRAM CLIMATE AND GROUP PROCESS

The constant challenge in a Re-ED program is to help groups build cultures that sustain children and adolescents in their efforts to manage their lives in ways satisfying to themselves and satisfactory to others. (Hobbs, 1982, p. 332)

A healthy program climate provides its members a sense of belonging, identity, and cohesion, encouraging more appropriate behavior and facilitating success. A program where the overall climate is not well-developed often experiences a higher level of disruption, sees less cooperation, and requires more external controls.

GROUP DEVELOPMENT

A positive group climate does not emerge spontaneously. This requires an understanding of the stages of group development, the nature of group functioning, and a great deal of planning. Staff must employ the dynamics of effective group management as the group progresses through its formative stages. Establishing a group identity (perhaps by selecting a name and mascot), contributing productively to the group, determining group goals, and developing group strategies for accomplishing those goals all help bring the group together and establish a sense of belonging, interdependence, and mutual interest.

RULES, RITUALS, AND ROUTINES

Positive group process is maintained through the use of meaningful rules, rituals, and routines. These are integrated into the schedule and environment in a way that promotes student success, minimizes opportunities for disruptive behavior, and builds group identity and cohesion. Rules that are developed with input from every group member have greater meaning and power to influence student behavior. Rules are most effective when they are visibly posted, positively stated, easily understood, consistently enforced, and clearly identify behaviors for success.

Meaningful routines are "essentially good habits" (Fecser, 1993, p. 17) that are established and practiced to facilitate transitions and classroom activities, handle disruptive behaviors, and manage emergencies such as fire and earthquake drills. Consistent signals and cues, such as "give me five" or "take a quiet minute," are used by staff and students for communication. These promote a sense of predictability and order, as well as personal involvement and responsibility.

In a positive group climate, rituals involving both staff and students mark significant events, such as acknowledging student progress, birthdays, or a staff or student joining or leaving the group. Rituals help students establish a sense of group membership and acknowledge the many expectations and responsibilities that come with being a part of the community.

GROUP MEETINGS

Prosocial skill development is enhanced when staff and students participate together in well-managed group meetings. Such meetings focus on problem solving, goal setting, group business, or positive feedback. Students are taught the steps and elements of effective group meetings and participate in facilitating meetings. When a student or staff member joins the group, experienced members orient the newcomer about the operation of and expectations for a meeting. Group meetings allow students to experience the impact they can have when they contribute as a member of a community.

PROSOCIAL PRACTICE

Targeted, direct instruction on prosocial skills, such as self-management, effective communication, making and keeping friends, is also necessary. This includes opportunities for students to practice new skills in realistic but supported social situations. Students learn to give and receive feedback. For example, in a daily "goal meeting" students identify and discuss their progress towards a specific goal for their day, receiving feedback on their successes from other students in the group. Although many excellent social skills or curriculums are available, these are most effective when integrated into ongoing teaching in natural day-to-day situations.

STAFF RESPONSIVENESS

A healthy program climate imparts an overall sense of positive responses to feelings and needs. This is one of the most important features in an effective Re-ED program because "trust between child and adult is essential" (Hobbs, 1982, p. 245). Teacher/counselors are sensitive to student needs and aware of the importance of their interactions. They respond to feelings and issues that may underlie the eruption of a particular behavior, not just to the surface behavior itself.

For example, if a student arrives one day visibly distracted and non-compliant, a sensitive staff member would talk with the student in an attempt to understand what might be driving the behavior, rather than simply relying on consequences. As students find words to express what they feel, the adult gains a window on their world outside the classroom. Staff look for "teachable moments," which link the student's feelings with the problem behaviors. Together they generate more appropriate ways to manage feelings and behavior. These interactions build positive relationships between students and staff and provide a series of real life, in-the-moment lessons in interpersonal skills.

COMMUNICATION ENHANCEMENT

Children need to learn interpersonal communication strategies, such as active listening, conflict mediation, and "I" statements. Staff provide cues and reinforcement until these strategies become a more natural part of the student's behavior. To create a tone of mutual respect within the group, students listen to the perspectives and opinions of others and acknowledge the contributions of others within the group. These are not just "hot-house" skills but will serve students well throughout their lives. To enhance generalization, teacher/counselors also continuously model respectful communication with one another and when interacting with students and family members. Children learn what they live.

EFFECTIVE INSTRUCTION

Success is a powerful change agent for children with a history of academic failure. Effective teacher/counselors support student success in academic, vocational, behavioral, and social learning. In the spirit of the true teacher/counselor, each staff member needs to understand the basic components of effective instruction and use them successfully in a variety of activities from outdoor education experiences or social skill groups to regular math lessons.

Implementing a variety of instructional strategies throughout the day (varying cooperative or experiential learning, direct instruction, group and individualized instruction) creates a rich and naturally rewarding learning climate. Lessons and activities are developmentally and cognitively appropriate, keyed to individual interests to provide frequent success and foster intrinsic motivation. Creative, alternative activities teach academic skills without focusing narrowly on traditional paper and pencil tasks. For example, when a class plans and builds a small greenhouse, grows plants and sells them in order to buy new equipment for the gym, such projects teach science, math, and interpersonal skills. A student who is unfamiliar with academic success is led "step by step to a successful encounter with learning" (Hobbs, 1982, p. 255). In turn, students who are actively involved in learning and experiencing success tend to exhibit far fewer behavior problems.

INTEGRATED PROGRAMMING

Blending academic and therapeutic modalities is analogous to a pianist playing a lovely piece of music. The movement of each hand across the keyboard is critical to the expression of the piece. At times the notes and chords of one hand may sound with more emphasis. Moments later those played by the other hand may do so, but it is this ongoing interplay of notes, sounds, and cadence played by each that comes together to express the melody beautifully. To the listener, the different movements of each hand are unimportant, because they blend together to create a powerful musical experience. So also a seamless blend of meaningful learning and therapeutic experiences in a Re-ED classroom creates a powerful climate supporting change and growth for children and families.

This blending also creates some of the most significant systematic challenges for Re-ED programs. Because of funding and regulatory issues for educational and mental health services, many barriers to meshing these services exist. Returning to the analogy of the pianist, many state and federal funding systems are structured so that the pianist is required to play with each hand on a separate piano, and never to play with both hands at the same time—even though they want to hear the same piece of music performed. As a result, those involved in effective Re-ED programs must constantly work to educate and inform regional, state, and federal agencies on the critical importance and the effectiveness of integrating learning and therapeutic approaches to meet the needs of troubled children and their families.

ELEMENT 4: INDIVIDUALIZED PROGRAMMING

Important helper strength in the education and treatment process lies in decoding, reframing, and pulling out the dormant potential and searching for strengths where some might see only weakness. (Cantrell, Cantrell, Valore, Jones, & Fecser, 1999, p. 20)

EDUCATIONAL AND BEHAVIORAL ASSESSMENT

While the first three components of best practices address the ecology within which the child is served, the core of every program lies in meeting the individualized needs of each child. The first step in individualizing a program involves a thorough assessment of strengths and needs. This includes identifying a student's unique learning styles, along with social/emotional and developmental needs.

ECOLOGICAL ASSESSMENT AND PROGRAMMING

An ecological assessment identifies the roles and involvement of family members, other care providers, and relevant community connections. In many areas today ecological planning is referred to as a "wraparound model." Most commonly the wraparound process is used to support the child whose needs are so significant that they impede multiple life domains and/or require the involvement of other agencies (Eber & Nelson, 1997; Eber, Nelson, & Miles, 1997). In order for teacher/counselors to contribute to ecological planning, they must be familiar with available options and develop contacts with other agencies that can provide specific types of support for the student and/or family (such as public health, child care, or employment services). Staff must also have a schedule that allows them time to make contact or attend necessary meetings.

Many Re-ED programs address ecological needs through the role of the liaison teacher/counselor, whose primary responsibility is providing support to the home and community agents involved. Some programs allow flexible scheduling and extra duty pay to compensate staff for attending evening meetings. However this need is met, effecting positive change throughout the ecology of the child must extend beyond the traditional program boundaries and the hours of the school day.

FUNCTIONAL BEHAVIORAL ASSESSMENT AND PLANNING

New expectations about assessment have been thrust into the spotlight as a result of the 1997 reauthorization of the Individuals with Disabilities Education Act (IDEA). Functional Behavioral Assessment (FBA) is used to understand the purpose of problem behaviors and build an individualized Positive Behavior Support (PBS) plan. A PBS plan emphasizes strategies to support the academic and social success of a child by directly addressing skill deficits and other needs that interfere with appropriate behavior (O'Neill, Horner, Albin, Sprague, Storey, & Newton, 1997). Professionals and families have become increasingly aware of the need to utilize the FBA/PBS process when shaping a student's individualized program, although there are many questions about how it should be implemented and supported. Resources to assist professionals and family members in understanding and implementing the FBA and PBS process include: The Center for Positive Behavior Interventions and Supports at the University of Oregon; www.pbis.org) the Center for Effective Collaboration and Practice (www.cecp.air.org); the BEACONS Project at the University of Washington; and the Kentucky Behavior Homepage (www.state.ky.us/agencies/behave/homepage.html).

SOCIAL/EMOTIONAL DEVELOPMENT

Just as with education, the therapeutic portion of a child's program is individualized as well. Intervention does not usually involve psychotherapy, but instead focuses on techniques and modalities that strengthen the child's social and cognitive development, such as teaching problem solving, increasing social awareness, and enhancing self-control. The goal of these strategies is to help children come to understand how their thoughts, feelings, and perceptions may be contributing to problem behaviors.

Just as effective instructional techniques are used in all classroom activities, therapeutic intervention is infused in all daily activities, including academics. Play, art, drama, and music offer opportunities for therapeutic expression and growth. Cognitive behavior modification strategies can become integrated into a child's daily program in both group and individual experiences. For example, exploring and expressing feelings can be incorporated into a language arts unit on poetry in which students are introduced to a variety of feeling words and expressive poetry, then supported in writing and publishing their own poetry, utilizing their favorite feeling words. In this manner, academic, therapeutic, and behavioral goals can be met within a single engaging learning experience.

The goal of therapeutic support is not for the child to gain deep personal insight into the origin of their difficulties, but rather that they "learn that they can think about their behavior, about their relationships with other people, about their future. They learn that they do not need to be the victims of impulse or the persuasion of others—in sum, that they can take thought and control their behavior here and now" (Hobbs, 1982, p. 266).

CULTURAL RESPONSIVENESS

All aspects of the child's program should be culturally responsive. Staff members, volunteers, and family members need to have ongoing training in multicultural issues and awareness, and access to information, curriculum resources, and materials related to a variety of cultural perspectives. Additionally, a climate of mutual respect must be developed within the program that supports a meaningful ongoing dialogue between program staff, students, family, and community members regarding diversity issues and needs. In this way, existing or emerging problems can be identified and addressed before they interfere with the success of a child's program.

IN CONCLUSION

> *The many competencies acquired in the Re-ED experience may permit a child or adolescent to accurately say, "I am a competent person."* (Hobbs, 1982, p. 257)

The challenge of meeting the needs of our troubled and troubling children is formidable. Thankfully, our profession continues to benefit from the research, advocacy, and the practical experience of committed professionals, community, and family members throughout the world. Because of their efforts, we continue to come to a better understanding of which strategies and approaches can make a difference in the lives of children in need.

Through the balanced implementation of the elements outlined in this article, a dynamic and effective program can be developed that meets the needs of troubled children and their families, while creating a reasonable working environment for staff members and volunteers. By regularly reviewing a program's progress in all four critical areas, administrators and staff can assure that they are creating a strong and viable program that has the potential to make a significant impact for years to come in the lives of the troubled children and youth whom they serve.

REFERENCES

Cantrell, M. L., Cantrell, R. P., Valore, T. G., Jones, J. M., & Fecser, F. A. (1999). A revisitation of the ecological perspectives on emotional/behavioral disorders. In L. M. Bullock & R. A. Gable (Eds.), *The third mini-library series: What works for children and youth with E/BD: Linking yesterday and today with tomorrow.* Reston, VA: The Council for Children with Behavior Disorders.

Cheney, D., & Osher, T. (1997). Collaborating with families. *Journal of Emotional and Behavioral Disorders, 5*(1), 36–44.

Eber, L., & Nelson, C. M. (1997). School-based wraparound planning: Integrating services for students with emotional and behavioral needs. *American Journal of Ortho-Psychiatry, 67*(3), 385–395.

Eber, L., Nelson, C. M., & Miles, P. (1997). School-based wraparound for students with emotional and behavioral challenges. *Exceptional Children, 63*(4), 539–555.

Fecser, F. A. (1993). A model Re-ED classroom for troubled students. *Journal of Emotional and Behavior Problems, 1*(4), 15–20.

Hobbs, N. (1982). *The troubled and troubling child.* Cleveland, OH: American Re-Education Association.

Long, N. J., Wood, M., & Fecser, F. A. (2001). *Life space crisis intervention: Talking to children and youth in crisis.* Austin, TX: PRO-ED.

O'Neill, R. E., Horner, R. H., Albin, R. W., Sprague, J. R., Storey, K., & Newton, J. S. (1997). *Functional assessment and program development for problem behavior: A practical handbook.* Pacific Grove, CA: Brooks Cole Publishing.

Osher, D., & Hanley, T. V. (1996). Implications of the national agenda to improve results for children and youth with or at risk of serious emotional disturbance. In R. J. Illback & C. Michael Nelson (Eds.), *Emerging school-based approaches for children with emotional or behavioral problems* (pp. 7–36). Binghamton, NY: Haworth Press.

Steinberg, Z., & Knitzer, J. (1992). Classrooms for emotionally and behaviorally disturbed students: Facing the challenge. *Behavior Disorders, 17*(2), 145–156.

U.S. Department of Education, Office of Special Education Programs. (1997). *Nineteenth annual report to Congress on the implementation of the Individuals with Disabilities Education Act.* Washington, DC: Author.

U.S. Department of Education, Office of Special Education Programs. (1994). *National agenda to improve results for children and youth with serious emotional disturbances.* Washington, DC: Author

Walker, H. M., Colvin, G., & Ramsey, E. (1995*). Antisocial behavior in school: Strategies and best practices.* Pacific Grove, CA: Brooks Cole Publishing.

ARTICLE 4.2

NOTHING exists in a vacuum, and even the most sophisticated classrooms must operate according to the increasing regulations that schools are mandated to meet. The next article neatly summarizes the tenets of the No Child Left Behind legislation. Charles Chrystal and Lenore Luciano note the impact of the law on special education but also observe opportunities for special education teachers to exercise their skills. The authors identify how regular educators can gain from working more closely with special educators and how students are the ultimate beneficiaries.

NO CHILD LEFT BEHIND AND THE CHANGING ROLE OF THE SPECIAL EDUCATOR: IS THE GLASS HALF EMPTY OR HALF FULL?

Charles A. Chrystal and Lenore B. Luciano

The No Child Left Behind Act (NCLB) was signed into law by President George W. Bush in 2002. The avowed purpose of NCLB is to ensure that all students attain satisfactory academic proficiency. Under NCLB, states are encouraged to use scientifically based methods to promote achievement and are able to use available federal funds in a flexible manner to meet student needs. Furthermore, parents of students in schools found to be underachieving are granted access to other educational programs, including charter schools and private tutoring, to help their children master basic skills.

When it was signed into law, NCLB had good support from both major political parties and was perceived by most Americans as a positive step toward improving public schools. Since that time, however, it has come to be seen as an "unfunded mandate" that has imposed many hardships upon public education. Many states and districts report that federal funds are inadequate to carry out all the provisions of NCLB, and qualified staff are also lacking (Center on Education Policy, 2006). Some have seen NCLB as an attempt to discredit public schools and to support private educational initiatives (Kohn, 2004). Provisions for special education students have come under fire (Center on Education Policy, 2006). The failure of NCLB to address the unique needs of students with emotional and behavioral difficulties is especially troubling. There is certainly reason to look at NCLB and conclude that the glass is "half empty."

ACADEMIC PROFICIENCY

The perceived need for the United States to remain competitive within the global economy underlies the interest in student academic proficiency under NCLB. As jobs in manufacturing and service industries have disappeared in this country, concern that the United States develop a viable, "knowledge-based" economy has grown. Such a knowledge-based economy depends on workers with highly sophisticated skills in science, mathematics, and technology, as well as the capacity to communicate clearly both verbally and in writing. Within an egalitarian society, the thinking goes, all students should have equal opportunity to achieve at the highest possible level. Unfortunately, equal opportunity is a myth: funding of the educational playing field has not been level for decades, and NCLB does little to correct what is a deeply rooted social problem.

NCLB imposes annual, "high-stakes" tests upon students in the elementary grades in an effort to determine how well students are performing academically. It also imposes ever-increasing disciplinary sanctions upon schools that fail to make adequate yearly progress (AYP) on those tests. This double-edged approach to holding districts accountable for student achievement has created hardships for many districts, especially for those that were struggling even before NCLB was signed into law. Because student achievement correlates highly with family income, districts where family income is low are not likely to realize great success on high-stakes tests (Hursh, Whitney, & Hawn, 2003). Some educators are highly critical of the law. "NCLB is designed to humiliate and hurt the schools that, according to its own warped standards, most need help," writes Kohn (2004, p. 573).

In fact, NCLB was implemented quickly and caught many schools and districts up short. First, demands for annual evaluation were made in the absence of baseline measurement and initially without the government supplying resources for districts to improve instructional practices. (Suggestions for research-based methods have since been made.) As Asa Hilliard puts it, "[NCLB] is really focusing on the symptoms, which is whatever a child's test performance is, rather than the substance of the problem, which has to do with the provision of appropriate instruction" (cited in Chamberlain, 2004, p. 101). Second, although the federal government has introduced slightly relaxed standards for special education students, students with disabilities as a group have had a hard time succeeding on the high-stakes tests mandated under NCLB (Gloeckler & Daggett, 2006). Some educators have questioned the reliability and validity of the tests used for diverse populations and students with disabilities (Chamberlain, 2004). In the meantime, special education teachers are scrambling to help their pupils attain satisfactory scores on the flawed tests.

Students with emotional and behavioral problems face particular challenges when it comes to high-stakes tests. Many such students lack the academic skills needed to achieve satisfactory scores, are unmotivated to perform on *any* test, and lack the frustration tolerance necessary to complete the required evaluations. To make matters worse, some schools have become so rigidly focused on improving test scores that teachers and administrators have become intolerant of students whose attitudes or behavior are at variance with that mission. Some teachers have developed what McEvoy and Welker (2000) termed "survivalist tendencies," adopting "a besieged attitude towards students, parents, and their profession" (p. 10). Rimer (2004) noted, "Schools are increasingly sending students into the juvenile justice systems for the sort of adolescent misbehavior that used to be handled by school administrators." There is evidence that some students are being pushed out of schools into alternative programs so their poor performance will not impact negatively upon their districts' aggregate test scores (Hursh et al., 2003). Other students are simply giving up and dropping out of school. The highest proportion of dropouts consists of minorities (Bridgeland, Dilulio, & Morison, 2006), who are already overly represented among students classified as emotionally disturbed.

HIGHLY QUALIFIED TEACHERS

Special education teachers as a group have also seen their responsibilities change under NCLB. Although all special education teachers are highly qualified in their area of certification, under NCLB regulations they may not be able to teach academic courses, even within self-contained classrooms. Unfortunately, the edict that teachers be "highly qualified" to teach core subjects such as English, reading, mathematics, science, art, and music has caused many veteran special educators to feel like second-class citizens in their schools. It also means that many students previously taught in self-contained classrooms are being moved into the general education program.

Criteria for attaining "highly qualified" status under NCLB include certification in a core subject. Those teachers who are dually certified in special education and some other area may already meet the standard. Otherwise, a special education teacher may be deemed highly qualified in a core subject matter area by meeting criteria through High Objective Uniform State Standard of Evaluation (HOUSSE) procedures. Under HOUSSE, moreover, "consultant" special education teachers need not be highly qualified in any core subject. Consultant special education teachers may work shoulder to shoulder with teachers who meet the standards to teach core courses.

Some special education teachers who previously taught core subjects are upset by what they view as a change in their status and may leave teaching altogether. It is also likely that, with NCLB's emphasis on inclusion, some students with disabilities, lacking support from special education teachers, will find themselves drowning in the mainstream (Gloeckler & Daggett, 2006). General education teachers who are deemed highly qualified under NCLB may find that, although they are able to deliver academic instruction, they are unprepared to deal with students who have learning, emotional, and behavioral problems. The bottom line is this: Being "highly qualified" to teach social studies means little if the teacher lacks the skills needed to deal with even a few defiant and disruptive students in the classroom.

Despite these restrictive provisions of NCLB, there is room for optimism: Special educators understand that crisis brings opportunity (Long, Wood, & Fecser, 2001) and that the consultant teacher models supported by NCLB give them freedom to work with both students and colleagues in new, creative, and significant ways. For example, consultant special education teachers may act as important bridges between students with disabilities and subject matter teachers. As expectations for student academic proficiency increase, consultant teachers will become critical to student survival in mainstream classes, because NCLB gives scant consideration to the *human* enterprise that is education. Relationships between adults and students are of paramount importance to student motivation and scholastic achievement (Erwin, 2003; Hall & Hall, 2003).

Special educators bring unique skills to the classroom that may make the difference between success and failure for students with learning, emotional, and behavioral problems. These include therapeutic listening and communication skills; the ability to provide brief and targeted academic assistance, or "hurdle help"; the capacity to build and sustain durable relationships with students; sensitivity to the social limitations many possess; and skills needed to deal effectively with frustrated, upset, and agitated students. Provision of Life Space Crisis Intervention (LSCI) by consultant teachers is an attainable reality. Assessing and dealing with group process concerns is also feasible. Ironically, NCLB may bring out the very best that special education has to offer.

Another potentially positive effect of NCLB is that it may force educators to develop collaborative professional relationships, drawing upon the unique skills each person brings to the instructional equation. In the past, many special education teachers have reported that they and their students have felt peripheral to the life of the school; now, under NCLB, they and their students will be thrust squarely into the limelight. The necessary partnerships between general and special educators may at times be uneasy but in the end may benefit everyone involved.

NCLB certainly brings a challenge to special educators, but as it evolves under new federal leadership, it may reduce the perceived differences between students and teachers that have created tension in the past. In the meantime, teachers who work with students with learning, emotional, and behavioral problems have the opportunity to examine new ways they may relate productively to their students and colleagues, and to hone skills that have not been used recently, or at all. Special educators are "special" because they are optimists, after all. And really, isn't it best to see the glass as "half full"?

REFERENCES

Bridgeland, J. M., DiIulio, J. J., & Morison, K. B. (2006, March). *The silent epidemic: Perspectives of high school dropouts* (a report by Civic Enterprises in association with Peter D. Hart research associates for the Bill & Melinda Gates Foundation). Retrieved October 26, 2006, from http://www.civicenterprises.net/reports.php

Center on Education Policy (2006, March). *From the capital to the classroom: Year 4 of No Child Left Behind.* Retrieved October 26, 2006, from http://www.cep-dc.org/nclb/Year4/Press

Chamberlain, S. P. (2004). An interview with Asa G. Hilliard, III and Alba A. Ortiz: The effects of the No Child Left Behind Act on diverse learners. *Intervention in School and Clinic, 40,* 96–105.

Ewin, J. C. (2003). Giving students what they need. *Educational Leadership, 61,* 19–23.

Gloeckler, L., & Daggett, W. (2006). *NCLB: A crossroads for special education.* Retrieved from http://www.daggett.com

Hall, P. S. & Hall, N. D. (2003). Building relationships with challenging children. *Educational Leadership, 61,* 60–63.

Hursh, D., Whitney, B., & Hawn, K. (2003). "No child left behind": An attack on equality and public education. *The SAANYS Journal, 32,* 12–14.

Kohn, A. (2004, April). Test today, privatize tomorrow: Using accountability to "reform" public schools to death. *Phi Delta Kappan,* pp. 569–577.

Long, N. J., Wood, M. M., & Fecser, F. A. (2001). *Life space crisis intervention* (2nd ed.). Austin, TX: PRO-ED.

McEvoy, A., & Welker, R. (2000). Antisocial behavior, academic failure, and school climate: A critical review. *Journal of Emotional and Behavioral Disorders, 8,* 130–140.

No Child Left Behind Act of 2001, 20 U.S.C. § 6301 *et seq.*

Rimer, S. (2004, January 4). Unruly students facing arrest, not detention. *New York Times,* p. 1.

ARTICLE 4.3

BOTH special and general education teachers are required to meet the needs of a diverse student population. In the past decade more children who exhibit challenging behaviors have been diagnosed with psychiatric disorders. In fact, the alphabet soup of diagnoses has become commonplace in school parlance: ADHD, ODD, PTSD, to note a few. These and other disorders, as well as their treatments, are not well understood by many teachers. Psychotropic medications are often combined with social–emotional–behavioral interventions in treatment of such disorders, and medications remain a mystery to many educators. In the next article, Steven Forness, Hill Walker, and Kenneth Kavale review the most common disorders diagnosed among students with emotional disturbance, including oppositional defiant disorder, attention-deficit/hyperactivity disorder, depression, and anxiety disorders. The diagnostic characteristics of each is discussed, along with treatment strategies including prescribed medications and their effects and side-effects.

PSYCHIATRIC DISORDERS AND TREATMENTS: A PRIMER FOR TEACHERS

Steven R. Forness, Hill M. Walker, and Kenneth A. Kavale

Children who have social or emotional problems require understanding and support from teachers and family members and may occasionally require counseling to help the child deal with his or her feelings and explore ways of coping. Psychiatric disorders, on the other hand, are generally much more disabling, more difficult to diagnose correctly, and sometimes require very specific therapeutic or medical treatments, meaning treatment with psychopharmacology (medications used to help the child control his or her emotional or behavioral symptoms).

Child psychopharmacology is a controversial field that is often sensationalized in the popular media. Coverage in the media often suggests that large numbers of children are being prescribed medication for only minor problems. Studies suggest that only a small fraction of children with serious psychiatric disorders are actually receiving such medication (Jensen et al., 1999; Zito et al., 1998). In the hands of a competent pediatrician or child psychiatrist, moreover, these medications are not only effective but an essential component of an overall treatment program for many, if not most, children with psychiatric disorders.

Careful treatment with these medications has been shown not only to effect dramatic improvement in behavioral or emotional responses of these children, but also to improve their social and academic functioning. Specific behavioral and related therapies are also critical. These may be used alone, prior to, or concurrent with psychopharmacologic treatment; and combined behavioral and psychopharmacologic treatments are often better than either used alone (Forness & Kavale, 2001; Forness, Kavale, & Davanzo, 2002).

Psychiatric disorders are classified in the fourth edition of the American Psychiatric Association's *Diagnostic and Statistical Manual* (*DSM–IV;* 1994). *DSM–IV* is used primarily by psychiatrists and psychologists to diagnose mental health problems in both children and adolescents. The diagnostic information contained here is taken directly from *DSM–IV,* and treatment issues are referenced separately. All of these disorders were diagnosed only after a thorough evaluation that included

1. Screening for health, vision, or hearing problems.

2. Review of the child's developmental history.

3. Interviews with the parents and the child.

4. Review of information from teachers or school records.

5. Careful consideration of context and occurrence of symptoms.

Psychiatric disorders are likely to be prevalent in children or adolescents receiving special education (Garland et at., 2001). Educators working with these children should be familiar enough with such disorders so they can readily detect and refer children to mental health professionals and collaborate with these professionals in ongoing treatment. These disorders are discussed in the following paragraphs in terms of definition or diagnosis and therapeutic and psychopharmacologic treatment.

OPPOSITIONAL DEFIANT AND CONDUCT DISORDERS

DIAGNOSIS

Both oppositional defiant and conduct disorders involve disruptive behavior. Oppositional defiant disorder often seems developmentally to precede a later diagnosis of conduct disorder. Both disorders probably occur in at least 4% of children or adolescents (Forness, Kavale, & Walker, 1999). Children with oppositional defiant disorder are those who have persistent patterns of negativistic, hostile, or defiant behavior directed primarily toward adults. Children with conduct disorder show consistent patterns of behavior in which they violate the rights of others or transgress age-appropriate social norms.

In oppositional defiant disorder, symptoms may include

- Persistent temper tantrums.
- Arguing with adults.
- Refusing to comply with reasonable adult requests.
- Annoying others.
- Vindictiveness.

The symptoms of an oppositional defiant disorder bother adults but are not considered as troublesome as conduct disorder, in which symptoms usually cluster into more serious patterns of

- Overt aggression toward people or animals.
- Destruction of property.

- Deceitfulness or theft.
- Serious violations of rules such as staying out all night and truancy from school.

As is the case with all psychiatric disorders, oppositional defiant disorder and conduct disorder are diagnosed in *DSM–IV* when the child meets a set number of symptoms from among a list of several symptoms typical of the disorder. Children must have 4 from a list of 8 symptoms to be diagnosed with oppositional defiant disorder and at least 3 from a list of 15 symptoms to be diagnosed with conduct disorder. These symptoms must also meet the criteria of causing significant impairment in social, academic, or related functioning. In conduct disorder, presence of only 3 symptoms is termed *mild conduct disorder,* whereas moderate and severe conduct disorder are characterized by increasing numbers of symptoms and increasingly greater harm to others.

TREATMENT

The primary treatment for both oppositional defiant disorder and conduct disorder is behavioral therapy (Kavale, Forness, & Walker, 1999). Usually this takes the form of a reward or a reinforcement system in which the child earns points for appropriate behavior and is ignored or even given time-outs for inappropriate behavior. Points are usually exchanged for privileges or tangible awards at home or school. A major part of such behavioral therapy is parent or teacher consultation, so that adults can learn how to praise or reward good behavior and ignore inappropriate behavior. Social skills training is also helpful for children who do not seem to know how to behave or interact appropriately.

Unlike most psychiatric disorders, medication is not usually used to control symptoms of oppositional defiant disorder or conduct disorder directly. Both disorders, however, are very likely to co-occur or be comorbid (more than one condition existing at the same time) with a wide range of other psychiatric disorders (Forness, Kavale, & Walker, 1999). Psychopharmacology for these disorders (such as attention-deficit/hyperactivity disorder, depression, or anxiety disorders) may often improve symptoms of oppositional defiant disorder or conduct disorder, as well.

ATTENTION DEFICIT/HYPERACTIVITY DISORDER

DIAGNOSIS

This disorder is found in 3%–5% of children or adolescents (Forness & Kavale, 2002). It is diagnosed when a child has persistent problems in inattentive or in hyperactive–impulsive behavior. At least some of these symptoms must have appeared prior to 7 years of age. The symptoms must also persist to a degree that markedly impairs the child's functioning in two or more settings, such as home and school.

Symptoms of inattention include

- Failing to give close attention to details in school work or related activities.
- Difficulty in sustaining attention.
- Seeming not to listen.
- Difficulty in organization.
- Distractibility.

Symptoms of hyperactivity or impulsivity include

- Excessive fidgeting.
- Inability to sit still in the classroom or other situations when this is expected.
- Running about or even climbing things excessively.
- Extreme restlessness or talkativeness.
- Difficulty waiting for turn.
- Interrupting conversations.

The child must usually meat criteria in *DSM–IV* for six of nine symptoms in inattention or six of nine symptoms of hyperactivity–impulsivity. Children can thus be diagnosed with three subtypes of attention deficit/hyperactivity disorder (ADHD): predominantly inattentive, predominantly hyperactive–impulsive, or combined. It is usually important to rule out other psychiatric disorders (such as depression, anxiety disorder, schizophrenia, or autism) before diagnosing ADHD, since these diagnoses may be more serious and usually take precedence. In many cases, a child may have both ADHD and one or more of these other disorders.

TREATMENT

The most effective treatment for ADHD generally combines both psychopharmacologic and behavioral interventions (MTA Cooperative Group, l999a, 1999b). Stimulant medications such as Ritalin, Adderall, or Dexedrine are. usually the first medications considered. While it often seems paradoxical to treat an overactive child with stimulants, these drugs stimulate brain chemicals, called neurotransmitters, to work more effectively, thus allowing the child to slow down and concentrate. Children not responding to stimulant medications have sometimes been treated with other psychopharmacologic medications, such as antidepressants like Tofranil or Wellbutrin. There are other medications that can be used if the child does not respond to these drugs or when ADHD co-occurs or is comorbid with certain other psychiatric disorders.

Selecting the appropriate medication involves a process called titration (see box). Table 4.3–1 depicts some of the primary stimulants and the approximate length of time each drug lasts or has noticeable effects in the child being treated. Some of the primary side effects (see Table 4.3–1) may occur only during the titration phase of treatment and may disappear in all but a few children.

Children with ADHD may also respond to psychosocial or behavioral treatments (Forness & Kavale, 2002). Behavioral interventions include establishing predictable routines and expectations for children, both at home and at school, and reinforcing the child for meeting these expectations. By increasing goals gradually, the child does not have to be "perfect" at the outset but can accomplish small steps over a period of days or weeks. Parent education and teacher consultation can help adults in the child's

STIMULANTS

Generic (and Trade) Name	Duration
Methylphenidate or MPH (Ritalin)	3–4 hours
Dextroamphetamine (Dexedrine)	6–8 hours
Amphetamine (Adderall)	7–10 hours
Sustained MPH (Concerta)	10–12 hours

Side effects: appetite loss, stomachache, headache, insomnia.

TABLE 4.3–1

TITRATION

The process of determining the right dose of medication, called *titration,* requires close collaboration between child, parents, and teachers (Wilens, 2001). The goal of titration is to use the lowest effective dose of medication while avoiding unwanted side effects.

Side effects occur because these medications, while very helpful, are still imperfect. Although stimulants target certain areas of the brain, they sometimes also spill over into other areas for which they were not intended, thus causing side effects such as loss of appetite, insomnia, dizziness, or irritability. These side effects may occur only at higher doses for some children or may occur with some children for some stimulants and not for others. At other times, these side effects may diminish as time goes by or as the child gets used to the drug. For some children, they may persist to the point where another medication or treatment must be tried instead.

In recent medication studies, researchers present side effects that occur on the drug as well as side effects that occur on placebo pills that contain no active medication. Interestingly, many children with ADHD seemed to show problems with irritability, insomnia, and poor appetite even when not on medication. Medication side effects are usually only slightly more frequent than problems that, upon careful observation, existed previously in these children before they were placed on medication.

Titration is somewhat easier with stimulants because these medications usually act within an hour or so and generally wash out of the body within a few hours or by the end of the day. The process of finding the right dose or switching to another medication may be accomplished within a few days or weeks.

Antidepressant medications, on the other hand, may take at least 3 or more weeks to obtain a full therapeutic effect. Other medications such as antipsychot-

life to set reasonable expectations, reinforce effective behavior, ignore hyperactive or distractible behavior, use time-out effectively, and collaborate by developing consistent expectations and reinforcers between home and school.

Research evidence on treatment of ADHDs comes both from a re-analysis of 115 recent medication studies (Forness, Kavale, Sweeney, & Crenshaw, 1999) and from a long-term nationwide study of nearly 600 children funded by the National Institute of Mental Health (NIMH; MTA Cooperative Group, 1999a, 1999b). This evidence suggests that psychopharmacologic treatment seems to be a critical factor in effective intervention for ADHD. The message from this research is also clear that ics or neuroleptics for schizophrenia or other treatment-resistant disorders may take weeks to establish the most effective regimen. Thus, effective titration for these medications may commonly take weeks or even months. The side effects of these medications are also likely to be more debilitating and may also include

- Sedation.
- Dizziness.
- Problems in heart rhythms, especially in children with a family history of heart disease.
- Tremors.
- Significant weight gain.

Prescribing physicians should warn patients and their families about what to look for in terms of both therapeutic effects and adverse side effects. Physicians should also schedule regular follow-up visits to assess and monitor both the effects and the side effects of each medication. Competent physicians do careful patient and family education to prepare the child and his or her family for the titration process. During titration, they will usually provide the family and the child's teachers with checklists of symptoms and side effects so that significant adults in the child's environment can also monitor and provide regular feedback to the physician on how the medication is working.

Certain medications require more careful screening and monitoring of health status or drug effects through blood work, electrocardiograms, and the like. Physicians should give families careful instructions for regular administration of these medications, as well as numbers to call in case of unexpected emergencies.

best practice is a combination of medication and behavioral therapies (Swanson et al., 2001). In the NIMH study, combined treatment also tended to improve scores on reading tests and on ratings of social skills on long-term follow-up, if children remained on medication (Arnold et al., 2000).

Evidence suggests that the presence of co-occurring or comorbid psychiatric disorders in children with ADHD may influence treatment outcome (Jensen et al., 2001). Children with ADHD and no other disorders tend to respond best, sometimes with only medication. Children with ADHD and comorbid anxiety disorders seem to respond almost as well, either to medication or to behavioral therapy.

Children with ADHD and comorbid oppositional defiant disorder or conduct disorder also respond relatively well but only if combined psychopharmacologic and behavioral treatments are used.

DEPRESSION OR OTHER MOOD DISORDERS

DIAGNOSIS

Although childhood onset of depressive or other mood disorders does not occur as frequently as ADHD, it is not uncommon and may affect more than 2% of children and at least twice that number of adolescents (Birmaher & Brent, 1998). There are essentially three major types of mood disorders: depression, dysthymia, and bipolar or manic–depressive disorder. Depression is diagnosed in *DSM–IV* when the child has depressed or irritable mood or loss of interest or pleasure in most activities. Other symptoms may include

- Unexplained fluctuations in weight.
- Insomnia.
- Loss of energy.
- Diminished ability to think or concentrate.
- Feelings of excessive guilt or worthlessness.

Of nine different symptoms, at least five must occur nearly every day during a 2-week period for depression to be diagnosed.

Dysthymia is diagnosed by a depressed or irritable mood on most days for at least a year and must also be accompanied by at least two of six other symptoms, including

- Insomnia.
- Low energy or fatigue.
- Low self-esteem.
- Poor concentration.
- Feelings of hopelessness.

The diagnosis of bipolar or manic–depressive disorder depends on fluctuations in mood, from depressed episodes, as noted previously, to manic episodes. Manic episodes are characterized by distinct periods in which the child or adolescent has an abnormal and persistently elevated or expansive mood and in which three of seven other symptoms are present, such as

- Decreased need for sleep.
- Excessive talkativeness.
- Distractibility.
- Psychomotor agitation.

All of these disorders must cause significant distress or functional impairment and require that certain other disorders, such as schizophrenia or substance abuse, be ruled out before making the diagnosis. Bipolar disorders in children are relatively rare and may be difficult to diagnose because of less distinct patterns of cycling than occur in adults; however, they become more common during adolescence and early adulthood.

TREATMENT

Treatment for depression usually involves cognitive behavioral therapies and psychopharmacologic treatment. Psychopharmacology for dysthymia is less predictable because symptoms may not always be consistently present, but it may be used depending on the child's or adolescent's age and presentation of symptoms (Wagner & Ambrosini, 2001).

In medicating for depression, physicians usually begin with one of the drugs known as selective serotonin reuptake inhibitors (SSRIs), such as Zoloft, Prozac, or Paxil. If the child or adolescent fails to respond to two or more of these medications, tricyclic antidepressants such as Tofranil or atypical antidepressants, such as Wellbutrin, may be tried.

In bipolar or manic–depressive disorder, physicians may begin with lithium and, in some cases, attempt a trial of other mood stabilizers such as Depakote. Examples of these medications in each classification are provided in Table 4.3–2, along with the approximate time it may take to obtain a full therapeutic effect. Table 4.3–2 also lists some of the most frequently occurring side effects.

Psychopharmacologic treatment in each of these disorders, however, can be quite complex because large numbers of children or adolescents may not respond favorably enough to continue treatment or may suffer from side effects that tend to lead to discontinuation of the drug. In a significant number of cases, more than one medication may be required for effective treatment. Pediatricians usually do not have sufficient train-

TABLE 4.3-2

ANTIDEPRESSANTS/MOOD STABILIZERS

Class (Examples)	Full Effects
SSRI (Zoloft, Paxil, Luvox, Prozac)	2–4 weeks
Tricyclics (Tofranil, Elavil)	2–4 weeks
Atypicals (Wellbutrin, Effexor, Serzone)	2–4 weeks
Stabilizers (Lithium, Depakote)	7–10 days

Side effects: stomachache, agitation, headache, dry mouth, dizziness.

ing to manage such treatment effectively, so most children with these disorders should be referred to board-certified child or adolescent psychiatrists for the best outcome.

Cognitive behavioral therapies may also be effective for treatment of depressive disorders (Asarnow, Jaycox, & Tompson, 2001). Such treatment focuses on the child or adolescent monitoring his or her mood, involvement in activities, stress, or other symptomatic behaviors and is then taught to coach himself or herself through "self talk," which is designed to give a sense of control over the symptoms and negate feelings of despair, low self-esteem, helplessness, and the like. Supportive therapy and education about the nature of the child's particular disorder can help and may assist in better outcomes for psychopharmacologic treatment, if warranted.

Monitoring suicidal symptoms is especially critical in children or adolescents with these disorders. These disorders also sometimes tend to have a diagnostic progression, with dysthymia putting a child at higher risk for depression and depression putting a child at higher risk for bipolar or manic–depressive disorder. Early detection and treatment is therefore very critical.

ANXIETY DISORDERS

DIAGNOSIS

Anxiety disorders occur in approximately 4% of children and in a slightly larger percentage of adolescents (Bernstein & Shaw, 1997). *DSM–IV* lists several types of anxiety disorders, including obsessive–compulsive disorder, generalized anxiety disorder, separation anxiety disorder, and posttraumatic stress disorder. Obsessive–compulsive disorder is marked by obsessions or compulsions that cause marked distress, are excessively time consuming, or significantly interfere with the child's or adolescent's functioning or social relationships. Obsessions are recurrent and persistent thoughts or impulses that seem to have no relationship to real-life problems or that the child or adolescent seems unable to ignore or suppress, despite the fact that he or she recognizes these as merely a product of his or her own mind.

Compulsions are repetitive behaviors (such as hand washing, ordering of objects, checking on things) or mental acts (such as counting objects or repeating words silently) that, according to rigid rules, the child or adolescent feels driven to perform and are aimed at preventing or reducing some imagined distress. These behaviors or mental acts do not seem to be connected in a realistic way to this distress or are clearly excessive.

Children or adolescents may be diagnosed with generalized anxiety disorder when they demonstrate excessive worry about events or activities (such as social functioning or school performance) and find it difficult to control these responses. Worrying must cause clinically significant impairment in social or academic functioning and also be associated with at least three of six anxiety symptoms:

- Restlessness.
- Fatigue.
- Concentration problems.
- Irritability.
- Muscle tension.
- Sleep disturbance.

Separation anxiety disorder is diagnosed when a child has developmentally inappropriate and excessive anxiety concerning separation from home or family. This must cause clinically significant distress or impairment and be accompanied by at least three of eight symptoms, such as

- Excessive worrying about injury or loss of a major family member.
- Anxiety about separation from family through being kidnapped or getting lost.
- Persistent refusal or reluctance to attend school because of fear of separation.
- Sleep disturbance.

- Complaints of physical symptoms whenever separation from a major family member occurs or is anticipated.

The diagnosis of posttraumatic stress disorder is made when a child or adolescent has experienced or witnessed a traumatic event that involved intense fear, helplessness, or horror. Subsequently, following that actual event, other symptoms have to occur. The traumatic event has to be persistently re-experienced in terms of at least one of the following:

- Intrusive recollections.
- Recurrent dreams.
- Feeling that the event is actually recurring.
- Intense distress upon exposure to cues that remind the child of the event or a physiologic reaction to such cues, like shaking or sweating.

There must also be persistent avoidance of at least three things that remind the child or adolescent of the traumatic event, such as

- Avoiding thoughts or situations.
- Inability to recall important details of the trauma.
- Feeling detached from others.
- Restriction of emotional range.

Finally, the child must demonstrate at least two of five symptoms of increased arousal, such as

- Sleep disturbance.
- Irritability.
- Difficulty concentrating.
- Hypervigilance.
- Exaggerated startle response.

TREATMENT

Treatment for each of these anxiety disorders varies, depending on the specific diagnosis, but generally involves cognitive or behavioral therapies and possible psychopharmacologic treatment (Ollendick & King, 1998). The cognitive therapies generally focus on providing the child both with ways to monitor his or her own internal anxieties and with a sense of control through "self talk." For example, a young child with an obsessive–compulsive disorder may be taught to pretend that his or her obsessions or compulsions are like a "little monster" trying to trick him or her into performing these rituals. The child is then shown ways to make the monster less threatening or powerful.

Other cognitive or behavioral approaches focus, in similar ways, on the unreality of the anxiety and how to anticipate responding in a more adaptive way. Reinforcement schemes may also be employed to assist or motivate the child in establishing a sense of control and participating more gradually over a period of time in anxiety-provoking events.

Psychopharmacologic treatment may involve anxiolytic or antidepressant medications (Green, 2001). The anxiolytic or anxiety-breaking medications are drugs such as Klonopin, Ativan, or Buspar. These medications are relatively fast-acting and must often be taken two or three times per day. Their major side effects include sedation or drowsiness and, in a few children, may cause a sudden onset of agitation, silliness, talkativeness, or even increased anxiety, a response that usually wears off within a couple of hours.

Stopping these drugs abruptly may also lead to increased agitation or anxiety, so their use should be withdrawn gradually, as is the case with most other psychopharmacologic medications discussed. Usually anxiolytics are used in children on a short-term basis only. The antidepressants that have been found most helpful for anxiety disorders are SSRI medications (such as Paxil or Luvox) or atypical antidepressants (such as Effexor). For children and younger adolescents, SSRIs and atypical antidepressants have become the first choice for treatment of most anxiety disorders.

SCHIZOPHRENIC OR OTHER PSYCHOTIC DISORDERS

DIAGNOSIS

These disorders are exceedingly rare, especially in children—the rate is probably less than a tenth of a percent (McClellan & Werry, 2000). *DSM–IV* diagnoses children or adolescents with schizophrenia when at least two of the following symptoms are present:

- Delusions (such as thinking one has special powers or feeling that people are out to do one harm).

- Hallucinations (such as hearing voices or seeing things that no one else experiences).
- Disorganized speech.
- Grossly disorganized behavior.
- Certain symptoms of social withdrawal.

These symptoms must generally be present over a period of at least 6 months and must markedly affect one or more areas of functioning, like school or interpersonal relationships. Separate diagnoses exist for brief or atypical psychotic disorders, which last less than a month or do not meet full criteria.

TREATMENT

Treatment is usually a combination of behavioral training (including social skills training) and psychopharmacology (Vitiello, Bhatara, & Jensen, 1999). Medications for schizophrenia are currently the new or atypical neuroleptic or antipsychotic drugs such as Risperdal, Zyprexa, and Seroquel. These medications may diminish agitation almost immediately but take days to diminish hallucinations. After several weeks, these medications will improve disorganized thinking and social withdrawal. Side effects, however, can be severe, including sedation or even abnormal facial or motor movements.

These side effects tend to limit their use especially in children but, in rare cases, are seen as unavoidable or preferable in the face of full-blown psychosis, which can be devastatingly frightening to children or adolescents with the disorder and to those around them. In some instances, these newer neuroleptic drugs are also being used for treatment-resistant depression and anxiety disorders.

AUTISTIC SPECTRUM DISORDERS

DIAGNOSIS

These disorders also occur quite infrequently but may not be as rare as childhood-onset schizophrenia (Volkmar, Cook, Pomeroy, Realmuto, & Tanguay, 1999). Autistic spectrum disorder is diagnosed by at least six symptoms across three areas:

1. Social impairment, such as

   - Lack of eye contact.
   - Failure to develop peer relationships.
   - Lack of sharing enjoyment or interests with others.
   - Lack of social or emotional give and take.

2. Communicative impairment, such as

   - Delays in spoken language.
   - Inability to initiate or sustain conversations.
   - Repetitive or odd use of phrases.
   - Lack of make-believe or social-imitative play.

3. Restrictive or repetitive behavior, such as

   - Intense preoccupations with restricted patterns of interest.
   - Inflexible routines or rituals.
   - Repetitive motor mannerisms such as hand- or finger-flapping.
   - Preoccupation only with parts of objects.

At least some of these symptoms must have occurred prior to 3 years of age. About three of every four children with autism may also have severe cognitive delays as well.

Asperger's disorder is diagnosed if at least three symptoms are present from the social impairment and restricted or repetitive behavior lists above but there are no significant delays in language or cognitive development. Pervasive developmental disorder may be diagnosed if it is not clear that symptoms were present prior to 3 years of age or if sufficient symptoms are not clearly present.

Treatment for children with autistic spectrum disorders relies primarily on developing basic language and social skills using behavioral strategies and reinforcement systems. Academic skills are taught according to the child's cognitive or intellectual levels. Community agencies and regional centers often provide education for parents in using behavioral approaches to further develop social and functional skills at home. There are as yet no recognized psychopharmacologic medications to treat autism directly. Some children with autism may also be at risk for other psychiatric disorders or symptoms, however, and they might be responsive to psychopharmacologic medications for such disorders (Sweeney, Forness, & Levitt, 1998).

OTHER DIAGNOSES IN *DSM–IV*

DSM–IV includes learning disorders, mental retardation. and communication disorders. Although they are not strictly considered mental health disorders, they are sometimes closely associated with certain psychiatric disorders. Children with these disorders are also at significantly higher risk for comorbid or co-occurring psychiatric disorders (Beichtman, Cantwell, Forness, Kavale, & Kauffman, 1998; King, DeAntonio, McCracken, Forness, & Ackerman, 1994). Eating disorders such as anorexia nervosa are listed as psychiatric disorders in *DSM–IV* and involve refusal to maintain normal weight for height and age (usually defined as less than 85% of expected weight), coupled with an intense fear of gaining weight and a disturbance of body image related to weight. This disorder affects primarily adolescent girls who are often apt to focus obsessively on academic achievement, in addition to their obsession with weight or diet (Lewis, 2002).

Tourettes disorder is also listed in *DSM–IV* and involves chronic motor and sometimes vocal tics occurring many times a day, usually in bouts. This disorder is often treated by SSRI or antihypertensive medications such as Clonidine (Sweeney et al., 1998).

Substance-related disorders, such as alcohol or drug abuse are listed in *DSM–IV* as psychiatric disorders and involve recurrent substance use that results in poor work or school performance, hazardous behavior such as impaired driving, or recurrent social or personal problems.

FINAL THOUGHTS

This is neither an exhaustive list nor a comprehensive description of childhood psychiatric disorders but, rather, an introduction for teachers and other school professionals to some of the major diagnoses that can impair school learning or classroom behavior. Detection and treatment of these disorders may sometimes greatly improve academic progress and social adjustment of children with more serious school learning or behavior problems. A behavioral checklist for teachers and parents has therefore been developed that is based on *DSM–IV* and provides both primary and possible comorbid psychiatric diagnoses (Gadow & Sprafkin, 1994). Introductory materials to further educate teachers and parents about psychopharmacology have also been developed for those interested in particular medications (Konopasek, 2002; Wilens, 2001).

REFERENCES

American Psychiatric Association. (1994). *Diagnostic and statistical manual of mental disorders* (4th ed.). Washington, DC: Author.

Arnold, L. E., Jensen, P. S., Hechtman, L., Hoagwood, K., Greenhill, L., & MTA Cooperative Group. (2000, October). *Do MTA treatment effects persist? New follow-up at 2 years.* Paper presented at the annual meeting of the American Academy of Child and Adolescent Psychiatry, New York.

Asarnow, J. R., Jaycox, L. H., & Tompson, M. C. (2001). Depression in youth: Psychosocial interventions. *Journal of Clinical Child Psychology, 30,* 33–47.

Beichtman, J. H., Cantwell, D. P., Forness, S. R., Kavale, K. A., & Kauffman, J. M. (1998). Practice parameters for the diagnostic assessment and treatment of children and adolescents with language and learning disorders. *Journal of the American Academy of Child and Adolescent Psychiatry, 37*(10 Supplement), 42S–62S.

Bernstein, G. A., & Shaw, K. (1997). Practice parameters for the assessment and treatment of children and adolescents with anxiety disorders. *Journal of the American Academy of Child and Adolescent Psychiatry, 36*(10 Supplement), 69–84.

Birmaher, B., & Brent, D. (1998). Practice parameters for the assessment and treatment of children and adolescents with depressive disorders. *Journal of the American Academy of Child and Adolescent Psychiatry, 37*(10 Supplement), 63-83.

Forness, S. R., & Kavale, K. A. (2001). Ignoring the odds: Hazards of not adding the medical model to special education decisions. *Behavioral Disorders, 26,* 269–281.

Forness, S. R., & Kavale, K. A. (2002). Impact of ADHD on school systems. In P. S. Jensen & J. R. Cooper (Eds.), *Attention deficit hyperactivity disorder: State of the science best practices* (pp. 1–20, 24), Kingston, NJ: Civic Research Institute.

Forness, S. R., Kavale, K. A., & Davanzo, P. A. (2002). Interdisciplinary treatment and the limits of behaviorism. *Behavioral Disorders, 27,* 168–178.

Forness, S. R., Kavale, K. A., Sweeney, D. P., & Crenshaw, T. M. (1999). The future of research and practice in behavioral disorders: Psychopharmacology and its school treatment implications. *Behavioral Disorders, 24,* 305–318.

Forness, S. R., Kavale, K. A., & Walker, H. M. (1999). Identifying children at risk for antisocial behavior: The case for comorbidity. In R. G. Gallimore, C. Bernheimer, D. L. MacMillan, & D. Speece (Eds.), *Developmental perspectives on children with high incidence disabilities* (pp. 135–155). Mahwah, NJ: Lawrence Erlbaum.

Gadow, K., & Sprafkin, J. (1994). *Child Symptom Inventory manual.* Stony Brook, NY: Checkmate Plus.

Garland, A. F., Hough, R. L., McCabe, K. M., Yeh, M., Wood, P. A., & Aarons, G. A. (2001). Prevalence of psychiatric disorders in youths across five sectors of care. *Journal of the American Academy of Child and Adolescent Psychiatry, 40,* 409–418.

Green, W. H. (2001). *Child and adolescent clinical psychopharmacology* (3rd ed.). New York: Guilford Press.

Jensen, P. S., Hinshaw, S. P., Kraemer, H. C., Lenora, N., Newcorn, J. H., Abikoff, H. B., March, J. S., Arnold, L. E., Cantwell, D. P., Conner, C. K., Elliott, G. R., Greenhill, L. L., Hechtman, L., Hoaz, B., Pelham, W. E., Severe, J. B., Swanson, J. M., Wells, K. C., Wigal, T. & Vitiello, B. (2001). ADHD comorbidity findings from the MTA study: Comparing comorbid subgroups. *Journal of the American Academy of Child and Adolescent Psychiatry, 40,* 147–158.

Jensen, P. S., Kettle, L., Roper, M. T., Sloan, M. T., Dulcan, M. K., Hoven, C., Bird, H. R., Bauermeister, J. J., & Payne, J. D. (1999). Are stimulants overprescribed? Treatment of ADHD in four U.S. communities. *Journal of the American Academy of Child and Adolescent Psychiatry, 38,* 797–804.

Kavale, K. A., Forness, S. R., & Walker, H. M. (1999). Interventions for ODD and CD in the schools. In H. Quay & A. Hogan (Eds.), *Handbook of disruptive behavior disorders* (pp. 441–454). Now York. Plenum.

King, B. H., DeAntonio, C., McCracken, J. T., Forness, S. R., &. Ackerman, V. (1994). Psychiatric consultation to persons with severe and profound mental retardation. *American Journal of Psychiatry, 151,* 1802–1808.

Konopasek, D. E. (2002). *Medication "Fact Sheets": A medication reference guide for the non-medical professional.* Anchorage, AK: Arctic Tern.

Lewis, M. (Ed.). (2002). *Child and adolescent psychiatry: A comprehensive textbook* (3rd ed.). New York: Guilford Press.

McClellan, J., & Werry, J. (2000). Summary of the practice parameters for the assessment and treatment of children and adolescents with schizophrenia. *Journal of the American Academy of Child and Adolescent Psychiatry, 39,* 1580-1582.

MTA Cooperative Group. (1999a). A 14-month randomized clinical trial of treatment strategies for attention-deficit/hyperactivity disorder. *Archives of General Psychiatry, 56,* 1073–1086.

MTA Cooperative Group (1999b). Moderators and mediators of treatment response for children with attention-deficit/hyperactivity disorder. *Archives of General Psychiatry, 56,* 1088–1095.

Ollendick, T., & King, N. (1998). Empirically supported treatments for children with phobic and anxiety disorders: Current status. *Journal of Clinical Child Psychology, 27,* 156–167.

Swanson, J. M., Kraemer, H. C., Hinshaw, S. P., Arnold, L. E., Conners, C. K., Abikoff, H. B., Clevenger, W., Davies, M., Elliot, G. R., Greenhill, L. L., Hechtman, L., Hoza, B., Jensen, P. S., March, J. S., Newcorn, J. H., Owns, E. B., Pelham, W., Schiller, E., Severe, J. B., Simpson, S., Vitiello, B., Wells, K., Wigal, T., & Wu, M. (2001). Clinical relevance of the primary findings of the MTA: Success rates based on severity of ADHD and ODD symptoms at the end of treatment. *Journal of the American Academy of Child and Adolescent Psychiatry, 40,* 168–179.

Sweeney, D. P., Forness, S. R., & Levitt, J. G. (1998). An overview of medications commonly used to treat behavioral disorders associated with autism, Tourette's disorder, and pervasive developmental disorders. *Focus on Autism and Other Developmental Disabilities, 13,* 144–150.

Vitiello, B., Bhatara, V. S., & Jensen, P. S. (1999). Special section: Current knowledge and unmet needs in pediatric psychopharmacology. *Journal of the American Academy of Child and Adolescent Psychiatry, 38,* 501–565.

Volkmar, F., Cook, E. H., Pomeroy, J., Realmuto, G., Tanguay, P. (1999). Practice parameters for the assessment and treatment of children, adolescents, and adults with autism and other pervasive developmental disorders. *Journal* of the *American Academy of Child and Adolescent Psychiatry, 38*(12 Supplement), 32–54.

Wagner, K. D., & Ambrosini, P. J. (2001). Childhood depression: Pharmacological therapy/treatment (Pharmacotherapy of childhood depression). *Journal of Clinical Child Psychology, 30,* 88–97.

Wilens, T, E. (2001). *Straight talk about psychiatric medication for kids.* New York: Guilford Press.

Zito, J. M., Safer, D. J., Riddle, M. A., Johnson, R. E., Speedie, S. M., & Fox, M. (1998). Prevalence variations in psychotropic treatment of children. *Journal of Child and Adolescent Psychopharmacology, 8,* 99–105.

ARTICLE 4.4

WORKING successfully with emotionally disturbed children and youth in the schools requires a great deal of knowledge and skill. One often hears teachers new to the field question how they can even begin academic instruction when behaviors are disruptive. It is a common myth that behavior must first be just right in order for learning to occur. In fact, as Claudia Lann Valore describes in the following article, academics can be therapeutic as well as inseparable from social–emotional learning. The author demonstrates how a master teacher competently blends her pedagogical and behavioral management skills to enhance academic instruction and maintain a smooth flow of activity in the classroom.

SPITTING FROM WINDMILLS: THE THERAPEUTIC VALUE OF EFFECTIVE INSTRUCTION

Claudia Lann Valore

> To do well in spelling or arithmetic, especially for students who expect and dread failure, is to know a sharp delight. It is like spitting from the top of a windmill.
>
> —Nicholas Hobbs

From *Reclaiming Children and Youth, 11*(2), 2002, pp. 85–89. Copyright by Reclaiming Children and Youth, Inc. Reprinted with permission.

The schedule indicates an academic period—it's right there on the wall, prominently displayed with cute, color-coded clocks showing the start and stop times for math. The noise level in the room is only a few decibels below that of the previous free time period. A few students are industriously working on a black-line worksheet. The teacher's aide hovers. Waiting for their time with the teacher, two others are giggling, kicking each other under the table they share in a dance, that if not interrupted, will soon erupt into a pushing match or full-blown fight. One student sits off by himself in a corner, immobile, surrounded by a sea of crumpled papers, strewn books, food wrappers, and a coat that he uses as a pillow with the hood pulled over his head. Three others sit at their desks, workbooks out, pencils in hand, eyes everywhere but on their work. Occasional insults, looks, giggles, or small items are tossed back and forth among them. One student is wandering the room, muttering about a lost book and stupid math. The teacher is crouched at William's desk, showing him yet again how to compute a problem. Not completely tuned out to the class, she looks up, scans the room. She says, "John, sit down." To the two at the table, she says, "Hands and feet to self, please!" Regarding the sleeper, she fleetingly decides to leave him alone. She goes back to William and his worksheet.

THE DILEMMA

An exaggeration? An anomaly? Sadly not. According to Walker, Forness, Kauffman, Epstein, Gresham, Nelson, and Strain (1998), "Substantial numbers of educators seem to ignore the concept of best practices and rely upon a hodgepodge of activities, unplanned curricula, and conceptually incompatible interventions to accomplish teaching, learning, and management goals" (p. 8). Though there are pockets of excellence and many effective classrooms with highly skilled and dedicated teachers and supportive staff, far too many classrooms for behavior disordered/emotionally disturbed (B/ED) students look like the opening scenario. Some are in regular school buildings. Others can be found in a variety of alternative settings from special schools and treatment centers to locked facilities. It is no wonder that teachers burn out and leave the field, transfer to regular education, or worse, become numb to chaos and return every morning to just make it through another day. It is no wonder that far too many students fail to learn, fall further behind, and often eventually drop out. Only a third of them complete school (Gunter & Denny,

1998). It is no wonder that principals and others responsible for student success feel ineffective, frustrated, annoyed, and even embarrassed. Parents are blissfully ignorant, or detached and unconcerned, or worried but helpless or hopeless, or battling the staff and system for something better on behalf of their child. Scenarios like these are lose-lose situations. No one is happy, feeling competent, or satisfied with the outcomes. Everyone wants change, but the question of "Where to start?" seems impossible to answer.

A SOLUTION

Many, if not most, troubled and troubling children are underachieving, experiencing learning difficulties or disabilities, or at best are making painfully slow progress in a curriculum several grade levels below their peers. In 1966, Nicholas Hobbs wrote, "Underachievement in school is the single most common characteristic of emotionally disturbed children" (p. 1110). In more recent years, the connection between low achievement and serious behavior problems has been well documented (Epstein, Kinder, & Barstuck, 1989; Kauffman, 1997; Walker, Colvin, & Ramsey, 1995). When charged with educating these students who also present challenging and sometimes overwhelming behavior and/or emotional problems, a teacher and other school professionals often do not know which to tackle—behavior or academics. Popular practice seems to support the idea that classroom behavior must be "brought under control" before academic instruction can occur. Re-ED programs have long held the belief that both behavior and academic learning require direct, effective, and rigorous attention simultaneously. Add to these group process strategies and techniques, and you have the three major elements of an effective and therapeutic Re-ED classroom.

In 1982, Hobbs wrote in *The Troubled and Troubling Child:*

> Research evidence today underscores the importance of academic competence in a child's achievement of personal integration and social effectiveness, and it contradicts the long-held assumption that the seriously disturbed child must be treated for his illness before he can become an effective learner. All our experience suggests that the causal direction of the relationship between emotional disturbance and learning competence may be, for many children, the reverse of that traditionally posited. The most probable relationship is interactional, so that early

and continuing address to both adjustment and learning problems is indicated. (p. 23)

More recently, the nature of the relationship between achievement and behavior problems has been declared as clearly reciprocal (Kauffman, 1997; Scott, Nelson, & Liaupsin, 2001; Walker et al., 1998). Other recent work in the area of functional behavioral assessments supports this reciprocal or interactional relationship by showing clear patterns of inappropriate behavior that maintain academic and social failure (Dunlap, Kern, Dunlap, Clark, & Robbins, 1991; Lewis, Sugai, & Colvin, 1998; Skiba & Peterson, 2000). It would seem that the research and current body of literature concurs with what Re-ED has long held to be true.

COMPETENCE AS A THERAPEUTIC GOAL

Re-ED's third principle states, "Competence makes a difference; children and adolescents should be helped to be good at something, and especially at schoolwork" (Hobbs, 1982, p. 251). In 1966, Hobbs shared an early version of the *Principles of Re-ED* in a presentation to the 74th Annual Convention of the American Psychological Association. Of this principle, he said:

> It means first and foremost the gaining of competence in school skills, in reading and arithmetic … If a child feels he is inadequate in school, inadequacy can become a pervasive theme in his life …We regard it as sound strategy to attack directly the problem of adequacy in school. (p. 1110)

Dr. Hobbs is often also quoted among those in Re-ED as having said, "Schoolwork is the business of children." Teacher/counselors have always held the status of being the most critical professional in Re-ED programs, as they are the ones working day-in and day-out with the children and must carry out the program minute by minute, using every opportunity to engage the children in successful, purposeful endeavor. This is no easy task; Hobbs went on in his address to say:

> It requires utmost skill and finesse on the part of the teacher/counselor to help a disturbed child move into an area where he has so often known defeat, where failure is a well-rooted expectancy, where a printed page

can evoke flight or protest, or crippling anxiety. The teacher/counselor need make no apologies to the psychotherapist with reference to the levels of skill required to help a disturbed child learn. (p. 1111)

FROM FAILURE TO SUCCESS

By the time children or adolescents reach Re-ED programs, they have often experienced a lifetime of failures across a variety of settings. But school is often the place where their behavioral and/or emotional problems first become manifest and their downward spiral of failure takes on momentum (Hobbs, 1982). At school, children and adolescents are faced with expectations they are unable to meet. They cannot sit still, or their poor reading becomes painfully public, or they cannot keep pace with their peers on even simple tasks because they are so disorganized. These failures bring on disapproval and criticism from within and without. Highly stressed, the children feel incompetent, stupid, angry, or depressed. Teachers, parents, and peers censure and punish. Such negative interactions often lead to more frequent or intense maladaptive responses. Discipline problems may escalate or students may withdraw into themselves, both reactions often driven by the function of avoidance. Disruptive, challenging, or depressed behavior often invites rejection. All of this creates or affirms in the student a self-concept of incompetence and inadequacy, and a pattern of living in which failure breeds failure.

Re-ED programs strive to reverse this downward, destructive spiral by teaching children new ways of living, by operationalizing in our work the belief that *successful living is healing.* A promising place to start this healing process is with academics. There is an arsenal of knowledge regarding effective instructional practices that can be used to almost guarantee task success and thus, academic learning. Though too little attention is paid to academics in the B/ED literature (Gunter & Denny, 1998; Ruhl & Berlinghoff, 1992), there still exists more than enough information and knowledge regarding effective instruction. We know how to effectively plan, manage, implement, and evaluate instructional programs (Ysseldyke & Christenson, 1993), if only we use it. Further, a body of literature is emerging regarding specific, promising instructional strategies and practices to use with children who have emotional and/or behavioral disorders (Cegelka, Fitch, & Shaughnessy, 2001; Shaughnessy, 2001). We can combine diagnostic-prescriptive or precision teaching with sound design and effective instruction to plan well, teach well, arrange the environment, and set expectations that put children in situations that are "just manageably difficult" (Hobbs, 1965). By using this Just Manageably Difficult (JMD) principle familiar to Re-ED, asking children to engage in learning at a pin-pointed level of appropriate challenge, the learner not only "gets it right," but also experiences a true sense of success, accomplishment, and growth. Every successful incident can be used to create new feelings of capability and to provide multiple opportunities to receive praise, recognition, and approval. Motivation is positively channeled, and when enough of these experiences have occurred, they eventually serve to reduce fear, anxiety, and hostility. No longer do children and adolescents seek to avoid school or find schoolwork inherently aversive. A willingness to risk emerges as trust is established between student and teacher/counselor, allowing the student to fully participate, engage, and learn. As skills, knowledge, and successful learning experiences accumulate, the child's concept of self changes from "failure" to "competent individual." Success breeds success!

EFFECTIVE, THERAPEUTIC INSTRUCTION

It is beyond the scope of this article to explore in detail the complex question: What is effective instruction for students with B/ED, and how is it done? It is both a science and an art; one that affects the heart as much as the head of both teacher and learner. Hobbs spoke of "the skillful hand and responsive heart" of teacher/counselors (1982, p. 253). Providing effective instruction requires a firm grasp of theoretical knowledge regarding principles of learning and instruction, as well as the nature and needs of children and adolescents with severe behavior and emotional problems. It requires procedural skills in application, and the ability to adapt and adjust for and to specific situations and students. If "teaching children to read is rocket science" (NRP video, 2000), then teaching troubled and troubling children and adolescents is quantum physics!

Madeline Hunter equated teaching with decision making, based on the combined knowledge of research-based principles of learning and a keen sensitivity to the individuality of students (1982). These decisions, in their simplest form, address three questions: What to teach? How to teach? What will students do? The ever-repeating cycle of instruction can be viewed as a four-step planning and implementation process: what to teach (content), how to teach (methods and strategies), teaching (implementation), and monitoring progress (evaluation). Within each step is a multitude of considerations, choices to be made, and professional knowledge to employ. It can be, and usually is, a rather overwhelming and daunting challenge to even the most seasoned and experienced professional. It cannot be done well without careful planning, reflection, and a commitment, in our field, to the belief "that children who are disturbed can be helped by the process of re-education" (Hobbs, 1982, p. 82). We know that helping includes rigorous attention to the building of academic competence and learning efficacy.

A TRANSFORMATION

So what might that math class look like in a Re-ED classroom? Experienced, skilled teacher/counselors know that time is a valuable asset not to be wasted, and the lesson must be carefully planned and executed in order to create a therapeutic learning environment:

> If each moment of a child's day can be programmed with exciting and relevant behavior changing, skill building, competence enhancing activities, there is less opportunity and need to engage in the old maladaptive, inappropriate, unproductive habits; and sound, constructive learning and growth can occur. (Hobbs, 1969, p. 6)

The cute, color-coded clocks indicate that it is time for math. The teacher/counselor has already informed the students that Choice Time was nearing its end, and the previously taught and well-practiced routine for transitioning into math is underway. As she gathers materials for two different lessons that will be directly taught this day, she comments on positive behaviors observed during the choice time period and reinforces appropriate behavior by thanking students who are getting ready. She's reminded them that the Puzzle Corner will be available during the last ten minutes of the period to those who finish their (carefully individualized) tasks to criteria. She approaches the sleeping student and quietly informs him that he'll be working on the computer today (a last-minute change of plans to encourage engagement), and asks him to go "fire it up." She directs the students' attention to today's math groupings and assignments on the blackboard, which were written there before school started.

One student goes to the "Think Tank" (a corner area blocked off with a bookcase) to take a test under the watchful eye of the associate teacher/counselor who can monitor the area from where she sits during this period. Students at their desks are working at independent practice, having already demonstrated a clear understanding and mastery of the process of long division. Three other students are assigned to engage in continued guided practice with the associate teacher/counselor, who has asked them to bring their math boxes (manipulatives) to the table. They are given a quick task to work on together so she can briefly excuse herself because a student working at his seat raises his hand for help. William hands over one of his question cards and asks, "Is this right?" After asking whether or not he really wants to spend the card (building independence is a goal), she checks the problem, smiles, and says, "We knew you could do that." She goes back to the table and provides feedback to the students on their successful completion of the task and tells them she appreciates their patience.

On her way over to the three who have moved their desks together for a lesson with the teacher/counselor, she unobtrusively makes tally marks next to several names on a well-used laminated chart that reads "Academic Bonus Points." John sees this, changes course from his wandering and goes directly to the shelf that houses the math books, gets his, and heads toward his desk. The teacher puts a tally mark next to his name. She says, "John, you'll be timing yourself on the facts today, so please get the stopwatch and the answer sheet envelope, so you can check your work when you're done." After the lesson she is about to deliver to the small group is finished, she'll send them off to the Puzzle Corner because they won't be quite ready for independent practice of the skill taught today. She goes to the student working on the computer, rests her hand on his shoulder, and watches quietly for ten seconds. She proceeds to monitor John, while he graphs his results on his ongoing line graph, and will introduce how to represent the same information in a bar graph. She'll then have him pull specific flash cards for the facts he missed for immediate review and homework practice. While he's doing that, she checks on the work of the independent workers and provides immediate feedback with instructions to correct any errors before going to the Puzzle Corner, time permitting. There's grumbling, but not much because it is what they expected. Correcting work is as much routine as is the schedule or rules, and the teacher strategically ignores their complaints.

About two minutes before the end of the period, one of the teacher/counselors will warn the group that math is almost over. Materials will be *put away, papers collected, and a quick evaluation of the period will occur. Students will be asked to comment on how they performed, and the next period will begin with the day's student group leader calling for a "quiet 30 seconds" and a review of the classroom rules and procedures for group meeting.*

SPITTING FROM WINDMILLS

Achieving academic competence is healing. For any student, especially those who do not necessarily expect it, success is exhilarating, motivating, and joyful. "It is like spitting from the top of a windmill" (Hobbs, 1982, p. 287). Effective instruction for the pursuit of student learning and achievement is more than a task of this honorable profession we call "teaching." It is a primary therapeutic intervention and one taken most seriously by teacher/counselors who believe and truly understand the philosophy and practices of Re-ED. Teacher/counselors know, from Re-ED training and experience:

> School is the very stuff of a child's or adolescent's problems, and, consequently, a primary source of instruction in living, in the achievement of competence. Special therapy rooms are not needed; the classroom is a natural setting for a constructive relationship between a disturbed youngster and a competent, concerned adult. (Hobbs, 1982, p. 252)

Dr. Hobbs said it simply, and best, from the earliest years, "So in Re-ED, school keeps. It is not regarded, as it is in many mental health programs, as something that can wait until the child gets better" (1966, p. 1111; 1982).

REFERENCES

Cegelka, P. T., Fitch, S., & Shaughnessy, M. (2001, November). *Developing effective instructional practices with BD teachers: A data-based teacher supervision model.* Presented at the TECBD Conference, Tempe, AZ.

Dunlap, G., Kern, L., Dunlap, L., Clarke, S., & Robbins, F. (1991). Functional assessment, curricular revision and severe behavior problems. *Journal of Applied Behavior Analysis, 24,* 387–397.

Epstein, M. H., Kinder, D., & Barstuck, B. (1989). The academic status of adolescents with behavioral disorders. *Behavioral Disorders, 14,* 157–165.

Gunter, P. L., & Denny, R. K. (1998). Trends and issues in research regarding academic instruction of students with emotional and behavioral disorders. *Behavioral Disorders, 24,* 44–50.

Hobbs, N. (1965). *The professor and student or the art of getting students into trouble.* Paper presented at the 48th Annual Meeting of the American Council on Education, Washington, DC.

Hobbs, N. (1966). Helping disturbed children: Psychological and ecological strategies. *American Psychologist, 21*(12), 1105–1114.

Hobbs, N. (1969). The philosophy of re-education. *Mind over Matter, 14*(1), 5–8.

Hobbs, N. (1982). *The troubled and troubling child: Re-EDucation in mental health, education, and human services programs for children and youth.* San Francisco: Jossey-Bass.

Hunter, M. (1982). *Mastery teaching.* El Segundo, CA: TIP Publications.

Kauffman, J. M. (1997). *Characteristics of emotional and behavioral disorders of children and youth* (6th ed.). Columbus, OH: Merrill.

Lewis, T. J., Sugai, G., & Colvin, G. (1998). Reducing problem behavior through a school-wide system of effective behavioral support: Investigation of a school-wide social skills training program and contextual interventions. *School Psychology Review, 27,* 446–459.

National Reading Panel. (2000). *Teaching children to read* [videotape]. (Available from NICHD Clearinghouse, www.nichd.nih.gov/publications /nrppubskey.cfm)

Ruhl, K. L., & Berlinghoff, D. H. (1992). Research on improving behaviorally disordered students' academic performance: A review of the literature. *Behavioral Disorders, 17,* 178–190.

Scott, T. M., Nelson, C. M., & Liaupsin, C. J. (2001). Effective instruction: The forgotten component in preventing school violence. *Education and Treatment of Children, 24*(3), 309–322.

Shaughnessy, M. R. (2001, November). *Effective academic instructional practices for students with behavioral disorders: A review of the research literature.* Presented at the TECBD Conference, Tempe, AZ.

Skiba, R., & Peterson, R. (2000). School discipline at a crossroads: From zero tolerance to early response. *Exceptional Children, 66,* 335–346.

Walker, H. M., Colvin, G., & Ramsey, E. (1995). *Antisocial behavior in school: Strategies and best practices.* Pacific Grove, CA: Brooks/Cole.

Walker, H. M., Forness, S. R., Kauffman, J. M., Epstein, M. H., Gresham, F. M., Nelson, C. M., & Strain, P. S. (1998). Macro-social validation: Referencing outcomes in behavioral disorders to societal issues and problems. *Behavioral Disorders, 24,* 7–18.

Ysseldyke, J., & Christenson, S. (1993). *TIES–II: The instructional environment system–II.* Longmont, CO: Sopris West.

ARTICLE 4.5

CHOREOGRAPHING learning and behavioral interventions to create the ideal environment for growth is a skill that requires time and energy to perfect. Given the pressure to have all students pass achievement tests, teachers are also faced with the question of how to have an impact on both areas in the already full school day. One answer is to use social–emotional curricula to blend academics and social learning into a single activity.

In the next article, Felicia Fago Demchuk and Elaine Harper describe their creative and innovative bibliotherapy program developed at Positive Education Program in Cleveland, Ohio. A full lesson plan is included, as well as the template for developing additional lessons. The lessons include directions for teaching language arts elements as well as for guided group discussion. Each of the books used in the program identify characters who are struggling with developmental and other issues familiar to the students. As students safely discuss how the character perceives, thinks, feels, and behaves, they begin to share their own experiences with the group and to explore ways of managing their own personally stressful situations.

BIBLIOTHERAPY: THE INTERSECTION OF LITERACY AND SOCIAL–EMOTIONAL INTERVENTION

Felicia Fago-Demchuk and Elaine Harper

By the time a student is identified as having an emotional disturbance, it is likely that he or she is already at least 1 year behind in grade-level performance, often manifested in the area of reading (Greenbaum et al., 1996; Nelson, Benner, Lane, & Smith, 2004). A number of factors contribute to this problem: exclusion from classroom programming because of disruptive behaviors; self-inflicted withdrawal from frustrating experiences; language and processing deficits; anger management problems; the inability to recognize, understand, and control feelings; and mental illness. Although the key reason for referral to special education services for a student with emotional disturbance stems from social–emotional issues, it is clear that academic challenges are often highly correlated with behavioral challenges (Nelson et al., 2004) Therefore, the integration of clinical and academic programming is essential to maximize the opportunity to impact both learning and adjustment.

However, in a world where mental health and educational programming often must be provided in discrete settings, and time with students is limited, the challenge becomes finding ways to help students achieve success. For this purpose, Positive Education Program[1] designed the Intervention-based Bibliotherapy Program.

Bibliotherapy, as a clinical concept and intervention, refers to the use of literature to help people cope more successfully with emotional problems, mental illness, or life changes, or to produce effective change and promote personality development. Bibliotherapy lies at the clinically fruitful intersection of literacy (academics), mental health (social–emotional) intervention, and therapeutic group work in the classroom (Lann Valore, 2004). This program offers an important advantage over other clinical interventions, because literature confronts life from a "once-removed" viewpoint, allowing the student to more comfortably confront emotional and behavioral issues that are too difficult to explore with a more direct approach. The process allows the student to "try out" new ways of perceiving, thinking, feeling, and behaving (Long & Fecser, 1997) within the relative safety of a character in a story.

The Intervention-based Bibliotherapy Program is designed to provide both social–emotional instruction and reading intervention simultaneously through "imaginative" literature. As the students are drawn into the literature by way of interesting characters, they barely recognize that, through the process of discussing the characters' struggles, they are often confronting their own social–emotional issues. By learning targeted

---

[1]Positive Education Program is a special education/mental health program serving children and youth in the Greater Cleveland area. For more information, visit the Web site (http://www.pepcleve.org).

vocabulary words and rereading key sections of a story, they are gaining reading skills, and through the model present in the literature, they are learning how to express their feelings in a socially acceptable manner. To make certain that text is understood and therapeutic gain is maximized, the book is read aloud (Pardeck, 1990). The need to account for compliance, participation, and reading comprehension in bibliotherapy is addressed (Ackerson, Scogin, McKendre-Smith, & Lyman, 1998). A key component of the program is the lesson plan template, which identifies both social–emotional and academic objectives for every lesson. The social–emotional objectives, drawn directly from the students' Individualized Service Plans, often address issues such as recognizing and verbalizing feelings, facing and overcoming adversity, dealing with issues of violence, developing decision-making skills, and creating new personal plans to use when facing similar conflicts. In addition, the students receive concrete instruction in connecting cause and effect and in recognizing that actions have consequences. Instruction is dynamically interactive to maintain the integrity of the process (Gladding, 2005).

Academic objectives are identified directly from Ohio's Academic Content Standards and are based on best practices as cited in the *Report of the National Reading Panel* (National Institute of Child Health and Human Development, 2000). Objectives focus on vocabulary, decoding, comprehension strategies, reading applications, and fluency. Comprehension activities are targeted toward understanding the therapeutic instructional theme via characterization and character issues, as well as the creation of visual timelines to help students understand cause–effect relationships. Interestingly, important concepts required for social–emotional growth, such as recognizing cause and effect in addition to action and consequence relationships, are embedded within the Academic Content Standards. The paired-objective approach flows seamlessly.

Another critical component of the program is the consistent process by which instruction is provided. Templates follow a structured cycle designed to help the students recognize issues and generalize them to their own personal experiences. In primary-level classroom, the following 5-day continuum is used:

> Day 1: The theme or feeling is introduced and presented in a generic fashion.

> Day 2: The theme or feeling is presented specifically, as it relates

to the character(s) in the story. The student begins connecting events to feelings as experienced by a character.

Day 3: The student recognizes the feelings of others via a character, and acknowledges how that character benefits from the expression of feelings.

Day 4: The student recognizes the similarities between what the character experiences and his or her own experiences. The cause–effect relationships of events and feelings are highlighted, and a personal plan for dealing with similar issues is discussed.

Day 5: The student understands and describes the benefits of expressing his or her own feelings, and identifies or practices healthy ways of expressing feelings.

In secondary-level classrooms, the continuum is presented differently. Longer, more mature works of literature are used, along with four cycles of lesson plans. Although the basic paradigm is the same, older students delve deeper into a character's motivations, and ultimately the students are assisted to recognize and synthesize information, comparing the character's conflict to their own. In this way the students come to a greater understanding of how to deal with personal conflict, emotions, or feelings, in order to generate and practice more appropriate personal solutions. The process supports Shrodes's (1955) claim that "as a character works through a problem, the reader is emotionally involved in the struggle and ultimately achieves insight about his or her own situation" (p. 24).

The following is an example of one of Positive Education Program's Intervention-based Bibliotherapy lesson plans. The plan described here was *Wings,* a book written by Myers (2000). This book has a reading level of approximately 3.4, and the interest level targets students in Grades 1 through 3. Note that the template can be applied to a wide range of children's literature, and the theme would reach older students.

LESSON PLAN: WINGS

Wings (Myers, 2000) is a beautifully written and illustrated story about a new boy who moves into the neighborhood. His name is Ikarus, and he has beautiful wings. In spite of this beauty, he is ridiculed by everyone, from the people in the neighborhood to the students and teacher at school. He is appreciated by only one person, a quiet girl who is also teased and kept isolated from the community. She is finally able to find her courage and her voice when she stands up for Ikarus and silences all those who would reject them.

The story has the following social–emotional themes:

- Celebrating one's uniqueness
- Embracing differences
- Rejection
- Bullying/teasing
- Isolation
- Friendship

LESSON PLAN FOR DAY 1

Objectives and Academic Content Standard

The following language arts (LA) objectives are targeted:

1. The student will be introduced to the themes.

2. The student will gain interest in the story.

3. The student will be introduced to key vocabulary.

Mental Health Objectives

The following mental health (MH) objectives are targeted:

1. The student will define what it means to be unique.

2. The student will acknowledge both positive and negative feelings related to being unique.

3. The student will express thoughts and feelings through verbal, artistic, and/or physical activity.

Mental Health Progress Note (template/assistance)

During a bibliotherapy session (*Wings*, C. Myers) that focused on feeling identification and social interaction, staff and students discussed how they and others respond to people who are different. The student was (was not) able to identify one characteristic about herself that is unique and to describe her feeling related to this quality. The student said … (she felt accepted by peers because of the unique quality, she felt rejected by peers because of the unique quality, etc.) and explained why.

Necessary Materials
- Teacher text only
- Vocabulary word list and sentences

Direct Instruction (Teacher should directly state those items in bold print.)

This week we will be talking about a boy named Ikarus who is different from everyone else. Although his difference is really beautiful, people are very mean to him because he is unique, and doesn't look or act like everyone else.

1. **What does it mean to be unique?** Staff should help students define *unique*. (MH)

2. **Tell me one thing about yourself that is unique.** Staff should help students identify something they recognize as unique. (MH)

3. **How do peers and adults treat you since you have this unique quality?** Answers may be both positive and negative. (MH)

4. Show the students the cover of the book *Wings,* and ask them to identify what is unique about the boy on the cover. (LA)

5. Have students look closely at the cover and identify where the title of the story is and where the name of the author is. (LA)

6. Have the students describe the artwork on the cover and try to explain how it was created.

7. **I wonder what this story might be about. Based on what you see on the cover, and knowing that we are talking about what makes us unique, what do you think it might be about?** A boy who has wings, which is unique.

8. **How do you think people will treat a boy who has wings?** They think he is cool, weird, an angel, etc.

Vocabulary Procedure

1. Write each word on the board, using large print.

2. Read each word aloud for the students.

3. Have them repeat the word.

4. Repeat each word, enunciating the syllables.

5. Repeat, and have the students clap the syllables.

6. Using the words on the board, draw lines to separate syllables.

7. Read each syllable part, then the full word.

8. Use each word in a sentence, and ask students to identify the meaning.

Vocabulary

Word	**Sentence from book using word**
strange	Look at that strange boy with wings.
neigh-bor-hood	Everyone who lived in our neighborhood was watching.
I-ka-rus	His name is Ikarus Jackson.
tongues	The students had staring eyes and wagging tongues.
whis-per	The whole school watched and whispered about his wings.
pi-geons	He sat on the edge of the building, with the pigeons.
whis-tle	The policeman blew his whistle.
trou-ble	He told Ikarus he would get in trouble.
beau-ti-ful	I told him, "Your flying is beautiful."
a-maz-ing	Ikarus is an amazing boy.

Compound Words

rooftops, blackboard, basketball, handball, policeman

Final Activity

• Read the first page of story to build anticipation for next lesson.

LESSON PLAN FOR DAY 2

Objectives and Academic Content Standards

1. The student will listen attentively to the story *Wings*.

2. The student will identify characters, events, and setting in the story.

3. The student will ask questions for clarification.

Mental Health Objectives

1. The student will identify events that caused Ikarus and the narrator to feel isolated as a result of their differences.

2. The student will identify how Ikarus expressed his feelings.

3. The student will identify the conflict felt by the narrator.

Mental Health Progress Note (template/assistance)

During bibliotherapy session (*Wings*, C. Myers) that focused on feeling identification and expression of feelings (or social interaction, etc.), staff and students discussed events that caused Ikarus and the narrator to express feelings of isolation and (sadness, anger, etc.). Student was (not) able (with prompting) to connect events to feelings, identifying that (story event) made the characters feel (sad, angry, isolated, lonely, rejected, etc.).

Necessary Materials

- Books for teacher and students.
- Markers and chart paper or board to make list.

Direct Instruction

Today I will be reading the story *Wings*, by Christopher Myers. As I read the story aloud, I want you to follow along silently in your book. I want you to listen to find out about the things that happen to the main character, Ikarus, as well as the girl who is narrating (or telling) the story. Think about how the other people they meet treat them, and think about how this makes them feel. When I am finished, you will be able to ask questions

about the story. Then we will work as a group to make a list of things that happen to the main characters.

1. Read the story aloud. Have the students look at the photos and try to identify who the narrator is (the yellow girl).

2. Allow students to ask questions about the story.

3. **Who are the main characters in the story?** Ikarus, the narrator. **How do you know they are the main characters?** Because the story is about Ikarus and his wings, and the narrator is the one who (tells about her feelings in the story, helps Ikarus, stands up for Ikarus, etc.). **Who are some of the other characters in the story?** The people in the neighborhood, kids and adults, the teacher. (LA)

4. **Can someone identify some of the settings of this story?** Staff should help students review the meaning of *setting* if necessary. Settings include the neighborhood, the classroom, the playground. (LA)

5. **We have already identified that Ikarus has a unique quality, which causes people to treat him differently. Let's make a list of events that happened, and describe how people responded when each event occurred.** (MH) Select students to reread pages aloud, or read aloud for them, pausing to add events to the chart.

   - Ikarus is flying above rooftops—neighbors call him a strange boy
   - Ikarus is new to the school, and has wings—kids whisper about his wings, hair, and shoes
   - Ikarus went to the classroom—the teacher complained that his wings blocked the board, and blamed Ikarus for causing other kids to be unable to pay attention
   - The teacher told Ikarus to leave the class—a kid laughed at Ikarus
   - Ikarus went to the playground—the big group made fun of his wings
   - Ikarus tried to play ball with the kids—kids didn't want to play with him, called him a show-off

- Ikarus left the playground—the narrator felt sorry for him, and understood his loneliness
- Ikarus flew to the top of a building and sat down—the police officer yelled at him for being dangerous
- Ikarus got the direction from the police officer—the narrator worried that he might be put in jail for being different, and this caused the kids to laugh at Ikarus
- Ikarus fell to the ground—the narrator told everyone to stop laughing at him, she stood up for him
- Ikarus flew to the narrator—she told him he was beautiful
- The narrator told Ikarus he was beautiful—he kept flying and smiled

6. **Why did the people make fun of the narrator, and what do you think she was thinking and feeling during these events?** The people teased her because she was quiet and shy. She felt really bad, and she felt sorry for Ikarus. She wanted to stand up for him but did not have any confidence, because everyone had done the same kind of teasing and mean behavior to her. (MH)

7. **What did Ikarus and the narrator have in common regarding how they expressed their feelings?** They both withdrew and didn't react with aggression. **Is this always the best way to react?** Not necessarily, because even though they are not fighting, they are getting very sad and they are lonely (depression). (MH)

8. **Why did these situations cause the narrator to feel uncomfortable?** Because she really wanted to do something to help, but she didn't have the courage to stand up for what she knew was right when everyone else was doing the wrong thing. **What did she finally decide to do?** Once she had enough, she finally stood up for Ikarus. By helping him feel better, she made herself feel much better and stronger. (MH and LA)

LESSON PLAN FOR DAY 3

Objectives and Academic Content Standards

1. The student will identify events in a story and establish a feelings timeline.

2. The student will compare information and recognize similarities with personal experiences.

3. The student will reread sections of the story to build fluency.

Mental Health Objectives

1. The student will acknowledge and identify with the thoughts, feelings, and needs of others via characters in a bibliotherapy story.

2. The student will connect events to feelings, using illustrations as well as text, and identify cause-and-effect relationships in reference to feelings.

3. Via bibliotherapy, the student will understand the benefits of expressing one's feelings in a safe environment.

Mental Health Progress Note (template/assistance)

During a bibliotherapy session (*Wings,* C. Myers) that focused on expression of feelings, staff and students discussed events that caused Ikarus and the narrator to express their feelings of loneliness, isolation, and (other feelings). The student was (not) able (with prompting) to match events to feelings, identifying that (event) made Ikarus and the narrator feel (feeling). The client identified (an illustration, quote from the story) that expressed what the character felt (feeling).

Necessary Materials

- The list that was created yesterday that charted all of the things that happened to Ikarus (You may want to have it saved on the board or chart paper, or you may want to have it on individual sheets for the students.)
- Books for teacher and students

Direct Instruction

Yesterday we talked about some of the mean and hurtful things people did to Ikarus and the narrator because they were different. The narrator described for us how she felt, which helps us understand how Ikarus might be feeling. Today we are going to reread some parts of the story and look at the illustrations of Ikarus and the narrator to try to figure out what they are feeling when each of these things happens to them.

1. Determine ahead of time whether you will ask about feelings for all or only some of the events. Have each student reread portions of the text, either on their own (if they are able) or using echo reading or choral reading. (MH and LA)

2. Pause at the end of each page or section, and have a student identify the event listed on the chart and explain how it might have made Ikarus feel. (MH and LA)

3. Ask students to identify any of the illustrations as you are reading that give body language cues as to how Ikarus or the narrator is feeling. (MH)

4. Write the feeling(s) identified for each event next to the event on the original chart, to create a feeling timeline. Discuss how and why that event might cause that feeling. [Feelings appear in brackets.]

   - Ikarus is flying above rooftops—neighbors call him a strange boy [confusion, hurt]
   - Ikarus is new to the school, and has wings—kids whisper about his wings, hair, and shoes [nervous, shy]
   - Ikarus went to the classroom—the teacher complained that his wings blocked the board, and blamed Ikarus for causing other kids to be unable to pay attention [embarrassed, hurt, confused, angry, afraid]
   - The teacher told Ikarus to leave the class—a kid laughed at Ikarus [embarrassed, hurt, angry]
   - Ikarus went to the playground—the big group made fun of his wings [embarrassed, hurt, angry]
   - Ikarus tried to play ball with the kids—kids didn't want to play with him, called him a show-off [hurt, isolated, lonely, frustrated, angry]
   - Ikarus left the playground—the narrator felt sorry for him, and understood his loneliness [hopeless, sad, lonely]

- Ikarus flew to the top of a building and sat down—the police officer yelled at him for being dangerous [scared of getting in trouble, feels like he has no options, hopeless]
- Ikarus got the direction from the police officer—the narrator worried that he might be put in jail for being different, and this caused the kids to laugh at Ikarus [scared, feeling like there is no solution or options, lonely, confused]
- Ikarus fell to the ground—the narrator told everyone to stop laughing at him, she stood up for him [embarrassed, angry, lonely, friendless]
- Ikarus flew to the narrator—she told him he was beautiful [hopeful, joyful, happy, excited, confident]
- Ikarus kept flying, and smiled [happy!]

5. **What are some of the things that caused Ikarus and the narrator to feel lonely, isolated, and angry?** (MH)

- The kids made fun of them and laughed at them.
- The teacher said he was ruining the learning of others because he was blocking the board with his wings. (*Counseling Note:* This concept has a lot of potential carryover for troubled students. During their school careers, they may have been identified as the key problem child in a classroom. This could tap into feelings of failure and rejection. You could create a group meeting on feelings related to this issue.)
- The kids refused to play with him, told him he was a show-off, and laughed at him, which caused him to feel like he was not part of the group. (*Counseling Note:* This is also a good topic for a group meeting. Ask students how isolation and lack of acceptance sometimes cause students to become part of a negative group. If the typical kids don't accept someone, sometimes "bad" groups of kids, like gangs, are the only ones willing to accept them.)
- Ikarus and the narrator were just trying to be themselves and were not bothering anyone on purpose, but the others still harassed them with their rude and unaccepting behavior.

6. **How might Ikarus and the narrator have expressed their feelings and needs differently, so they would not have remained isolated for so long?** (Accept any reasonable answer:

The narrator could have introduced herself earlier so they could have become friends right away, they could have sought help from a caring adult, Ikarus might have asked to have a parent talk to the teachers about his wings, etc. This question is a little tricky, because people's interactions with Ikarus at every level were so devastating. You may have to provide a lot of guidance for the group.) (MH)

7. **How do you think the narrator finally found her voice to stand up for Ikarus?** Everyone gets to a point of frustration where they have to stand up for what they believe in. The narrator finally got to that point. **How did this change her life?** She finally felt confident and felt like she had a friend. (MH)

LESSON PLAN FOR DAY 4

Objectives and Academic Content Standards

1. The student will reread sections of the story to build fluency.

2. The student will provide his or her own interpretation of the story using information from the text.

3. The student will identify setting and events in the plot.

Mental Health Objectives

1. The student will identify events that caused him or her to feel the same feelings and frustrations as Ikarus and the narrator.

2. The student will identify and label the personal feelings experienced during these events.

3. The student will consider and plan an alternative, healthy mechanism for dealing with similar personal experiences that cause feelings such as rejection, loneliness, isolation, and anger.

Mental Health Progress Note (template/assistance)

During a bibliotherapy session (*Wings,* C. Myers) that focused on expression of feelings, staff and students discussed a plan for developing alternative, healthy mechanisms for dealing with rejection, loneliness, and anger. The client was (not) able (with prompts) to identify that she has felt (feeling) when (event) occurred. Her new plan for dealing with conflict related to this event is (describe plan).

Necessary Materials
- Books for teacher and students
- Markers and board

Direct Instruction

We have been reading about Ikarus and the narrator, and how other people made them feel because they are unique and a little bit different from everyone else. Yesterday you created a feeling timeline and identified some of the things that people did to Ikarus and the narrator, and how these events made the characters feel.

1. **Can anyone tell me some of the settings where Ikarus and the narrator heard things that made them feel bad? Try to find pages in the story that tell you the answer to this question, and we will read them aloud.** Students should use their story as the source for identifying these events. They should read the section aloud, if they can, or the teacher can help them read using echo reading techniques. After reading, they should identify the place where the event occurred as the setting. Answers include "in the neighborhood," "on the playground," "at school." (LA)

2. **We have all felt lonely, isolated, and teased, and we have also done this to others. Today we will identify one thing that others have done to us that made us feel hurt and like we are not part of the group. We will talk about who can help us when we feel this way, and talk about a plan for handling these feelings differently. We will also talk about trying to stand up for what is right when everyone around you is doing something mean.** During a group session, have each student discuss an event in real life that caused him or her to feel hurt or isolated. Staff should guide this discussion to help students identify an event that is an easily identified problem area. (*Counseling Note:* If this is a very problematic issue for a student—for example, if the student is the recipient of a lot

of teasing or is isolated from the class group—you may want to talk to the student ahead of time, and let him practice talking about what hurts him before he is in front of the large group that teases him. Tell the student that this will be a big challenge for him, and encourage him to be assertive. You might want to consider arranging a contract or reward for him if he is able to remain with the group and deal with the discussion.) Talk to the group about various ways of dealing with either their own feelings of isolation, or if a student is the victimizer, discuss a plan for interacting with others in a way that is not teasing or mean. This discussion will be the basis of the role-play event on Day 5. (MH)

3. A staff member should take notes on each of the plans for the role-play activity on Day 5. (MH)

LESSON PLAN FOR DAY 5

Objectives and Academic Content Standards

1. The student will classify words or groups of words into categories.

2. The student will identify at least one alternative way of reacting to events that cause feelings of loneliness, isolation, or rejection.

Mental Health Objectives

1. The student will understand the benefits of expressing one's feelings appropriately.

2. The student will practice an alternative, healthy mechanism for dealing with personal experiences that cause feelings of isolation, loneliness, or rejection, and the anger that may result. The student will use role-play as a means of practicing this mechanism.

Mental Health Progress Note (template/assistance)

During a bibliotherapy session (*Wings*, C. Myers) that focused on expression of feelings, the student role-played alternative, healthy methods for dealing with personal experiences that cause feelings of isolation, loneliness, rejection, or anger. She role-played a reaction to (event) using (appropriate, alternate method of dealing with event). She said she learned (insight).

Necessary Materials
- Books for teacher and students
- Copies of plans for dealing with frustrating events

Direct Instruction

Today we will use our role-play activity to practice using the plans we made yesterday for dealing with frustrating events. If you were not able to come up with a plan, you can participate in a role play with a peer.

1. Pass out the plans to each student. When determining which student should go first, try to make sure it is a higher level student or someone who is more comfortable with role plays. If the students are not sure about how to do role plays, a staff member should be the second person in the role play. If students are comfortable with the process, the teacher should coach other students to be the second person in the role play. (MH)

   - Staff should set up each role play by describing the event and the setting, and introducing who the "characters" are. If the student wants to play himself, he can be one of the characters. If the student is not comfortable playing himself, he may become a "fictional" character.
   - Have as many students as possible complete their role-play activities. This may take more than one day. During this session or at another group meeting, the staff and students may give each other feedback on the role play. In addition, students should be encouraged to use their role play in real settings, and report o.n their success at future group meetings.

2. **What was the most important thing you learned about being unique, from the story *Wings* as well as from our role plays?** Probe for answers from students that focus on their own

unique needs. Encourage students who have been victimizers to share incidents in which they have been rejected, and discuss how that sometimes leads a person to become "mean" to others. (MH)

Culminating Unit Activity

Have the students create an image of their unique characteristics, using the same art media used by the author/illustrator of *Wings*. This activity can be used as a therapeutic art activity, part of an oral presentation activity, or part of a descriptive writing activity. (MH and LA)

Culminating Vocabulary Activity

1. Have students classify words into categories.

   - Identify categories of feelings for these phrases: strange boy, strong, proud wings, staring eyes, wagging tongues, whisper about, complained, dragging his feathers, snickered at, laughing at, show-off, glaring eyes, pointing fingers, lonely, wings drooped, amazing.
   - Category titles for these phrases might include rude behaviors, mean behaviors, compliments, etc.

2. Ask children to identify the categories, and why they would put certain words in each category.

REFERENCES

Ackerson, J., Scogin, F., McKendree-Smith, N., & Lyman, R. D. (1998). Cognitive bibliotherapy for mild and moderate adolescent depressive symptomatology. *Journal of Consulting and Clinical Psychology, 66,* 685–690.

Gladding, (2005). *Counseling as an art: The creative arts in counseling.* Alexandria, VA: American Counseling Association.

Greenbaum, P. E., Dedrick, R. F., Friedman, R. M., Kutash, K., Brown, E. C., Lardierh, S. P., et al. (1996). National Adolescent and Child Treatment Study (NACTS): Outcomes for children with serious emotional and behavioral disturbance. *Journal of Emotional and Behavioral Disorders, 4,* 130–146.

Hobbs, N. (1982). *The troubled and troubling child.* San Francisco: Jossey-Bass.

Lann Valore, C. (2004). [Re-ED illustration of Positive Education Program's Intervention-based Bibliotherapy Program]. Unpublished raw data.

Long, J. J., & Fecser, F. A. (1997). *Advanced instruction in Life Space Crisis Intervention: The skill of reclaiming children and youth involved in self-defeating patterns of behavior. Trainer's manual.* Hagerstown, MD: LSCI Institute.

Myers, C. (2000). *Wings.* New York: Scholastic Press.

National Institute of Child Health and Human Development. (2000). *Report of the National Reading Panel. Teaching children to read: An evidence-based assessment of the scientific research literature on reading and its implications for reading instruction* (NIH Publication No. 00-4769). Washington, DC: U.S. Government Printing Office.

Nelson, J. R., Benner, G. J., Lane, K., & Smith, B. W. (2004). Academic achievement of K–12 students with emotional and behavioral disorders. *Exceptional Children, 71,* 59–73.

Pardeck, J. T. (1990). Using bibliotherapy in clinical practice with children. *Psychological Reports, 67,* 1043–1049.

Shrodes, C. (1955). Bibliotherapy. *The Reading Teacher, 9,* 24–30.

EDITORS' COMMENTARY

The articles by Lann Valore and by Fago-Demchuk and Harper illustrate sophisticated approaches to maximizing classroom time for students challenged by emotional disturbance. They illustrate that academics and behavior are two sides of the same coin; when balanced appropriately, learning goes on and behavior is controlled. Yet, anyone who has ever worked in a special education classroom knows the job is not easy. Even the most interesting lessons will never work if behavior is out of control. What are the fundamentals of "management" that must be in place to create the kind of predictable and safe environment discussed by Walker and Fecser?

THE final article in this chapter is by Paul Filipek, who has more than 20 years experience working with students with serious emotional disturbance at the Positive Education Program in Cleveland, Ohio. He captures the soul of what it means to dedicate a career to helping troubled students and demonstrates the great satisfaction one can derive from having been a meaningful and significant person in the life of a child.

ON BEING A TEACHER–COUNSELOR
Paul Filipek

There is a story told that when Michelangelo was asked how he was able to create his magnificent statue of David from the badly marred piece of marble that so many other sculptors had rejected, he replied, "I simply chipped away everything that was not David." In his humble view, Michelangelo recognized that a potential masterpiece was locked inside the marble; he just needed to use his skill to uncover it. I think this is similar to what a teacher–counselor (TC) does. TCs help to uncover everything in a troubled and troubling child's behavior that is not part of the masterpiece that is the whole child, freeing the child to then begin successful movement toward his or her goals. If there were a thirteenth Re-ED principle, I believe it might read, "Sometimes we must look beyond the facts to see the truth." Just as there is something in a sculptor (part talent and part training) that enables him to look beyond the marble to see a masterpiece, there are qualities or perhaps values that are shared by many, if not all, TCs that enable them to see the whole child amid the rough exterior of troubling behaviors. While the tools or skills of TCs are many, two of the most important are their powers of observation and description.

I believe that the most effective teacher–counselors are good observers who can communicate their findings in simple, clearly understood language. This is particularly crucial to the treatment process because students with problem behaviors are highly diverse individuals who come with a variety of troubles, but all appear to share in common some form of receptive and/or expressive language deficit or difficulty. The TC serves initially as the narrator of his or her students' lives, providing an external voice that reports unmistakable observations of how a student behaves and what consequences result from that behavior. TCs describe actions and outcomes, both positive and negative, until students can do this for themselves. This approach generally begins supportively, with the TC drawing the student's attention to something that he or she is doing well, regardless of how seemingly insignificant the action might appear. TCs strive to "catch" the child being appropriate or making a good choice. These observations are frequently delivered in the form of praise, and nearly always emphasize action and outcome.

TCs also observe and describe how a student appears to feel following a particular action. This feedback is a necessary precursor to the goal of helping the student learn that one's thoughts control the way one feels. This process is repeated over and over until a student has internalized the feeling–behavior connection well enough to begin using positive self-talk to change the way he or she is are feeling. Over time, as students slowly learn through experience to trust the TC, they begin to see themselves as more than just their referral behaviors. Students begin to look beyond their own troubles to recognize themselves as individuals who are deserving and capable of success and happiness.

Through verbalizing or reflecting observations, teacher–counselors teach their students to become skilled observers of their own lives. Many clients are already somewhat skilled at observing others. Some are especially skilled at recognizing vulnerabilities in others that can be pushed, like buttons, to yield a desired and frequently negative reaction. These same children, however, are often poor observers of themselves in their social interactions. To them, life seems unpredictable, full of random and often unfair events over which they have little control. To counter these perceptions, treatment days are filled with rich experiences and skill-building activities designed to increase the probabilities for their individual and group successes. The TC stands ready and alert for opportunities to facilitate successes when needed and, perhaps more important, to act as a verbal historian lest a student's success be inaccurately self-attributed to luck or to the activity's just "being easy." TCs are always on the lookout for those priceless teachable moments that are like the tiny fissures in marble that, when struck precisely, will yield a desired form or outcome. When students can observe and describe for themselves what they do and what results, even in the most rudimentary terms, life is no longer something that just happens to them. They can begin to take some responsibility for their experiences and begin to choose what their lives will be. They are well launched on their journey toward becoming Re-EDucated. The masterpiece begins to more fully emerge.

Teacher–counselors are a highly diverse and resilient lot. We wear a variety of hats because this "calling" is not so much tied specifically to a degree or particular educational background as it is dependent on a commonly held philosophy founded on the principles of Re-ED. All who serve troubled and troubling children in a Re-ED program are considered to be teacher–counselors, custodian and coordinator alike. We communicate diversity and resilience by living and modeling them, and in so doing we help our students recognize and value their own diversity, and discover that they too are resilient. We meet problems with a positive attitude, whether the students' or our own, viewing difficulties as opportunities for new growth and success. We are teaching much more than mere optimism or that every glass is "half full." We are teaching that sometimes the glass is "empty" and we may be thirsty for a time, but we will learn skills to survive.

A unique opportunity was presented to me a few years ago when my 21-year-old son worked as a TC in a summer one-on-one aide position in the youngest classroom at my center. After one particularly trying day, he came home frustrated and exhausted, asking me, "Why would you ever want to do this for a living?" Remarkably, a few weeks later, he came home still exhausted but also excited as he announced that his little charge "didn't spit on me or pee on himself! More important, he tied his shoes when I asked him to because he finally understood that he would then be able to go outside and play!" Then he added, "How could you not love a job like this?" Why would a TC choose to do this hard and, at times, unrewarding work? Perhaps, like the sculptor who painstakingly labors over a badly marred piece of marble to carve a masterpiece, TCs are gifted with the ability to hold the vision of a masterpiece hidden within the marble (or troubles) and to communicate that image to students until each can hold the vision for him- or herself.

EDITORS' REFERENCES

Collaborative for Academic, Social, and Emotional Learning. (2003). *Safe and sound: An educational leader's guide to evidence-based social and emotional learning (SEL) Programs.* Chicago: Author.

Collins, M., & Tamarkin, C. (1982). *Marva Collins' way.* Los Angeles: Jeremy P. Tarcher.

Ginott, H. (1972). *Teacher and child*: A book for parents and teachers. New York: Macmillan.

Hersch, P. (1998). *A tribe apart: A journey into the heart of American adolescence.* New York: Ballantine Books.

No Child Left Behind Act of 2001, 20 U.S.C. § 6301 *et seq.*

Sugai, G., & Horner, R. (1999). Discipline and behavioral support: Practices, pitfalls and promises. *Effective School Practices, 17,* 10–22.

U.S. Department of Education. (2002). *Study of personnel needs in special education.* Washington, DC: Author

Wilson, S. M., Floden, R. E., & Ferrini-Mundy, J. (2001). *Teacher preparation research: Current knowledge, gaps, and recommendations.* Seattle: University of Washington, Center for the Study of Teaching and Policy. (Research report prepared for the U.S. Department of Education and the Office for Educational Research and Improvement, No. R-01-3).

5 THE DYNAMICS OF GROUP FORCES IN THE CLASSROOM:

Strategies and Skills for Promoting Positive Group Behavior

EXCEPT for the rare hermit, people are immersed in groups of one kind or another. Many times people need the stimulation of a group; at other times they seek escape to nourish their individuality. In their pursuit of group contact, students range from virtual addicts to those with a take-it-or-leave-it attitude. For students, group life is a laboratory for exploring the fundamental nature of self, the sense of belonging, and their roles. Group membership has highly individual values for particular students. A teacher may think of the classroom as a place for academic learning, but some students see that same class as a convenient place for making social contacts. Teachers usually find that dealing with a troubled student on an individual basis is simple compared to dealing with this same student in a peer setting. Students who are amenable as individuals may join the resistance when they are in a group. It is important to remember that the teacher is a minority of one in a classroom, and the assumed power of the teacher can sometimes be an illusion.

Simply stated, a group is an aggregate of persons who are related in some way and who are joined by a social structure. The family is a group, as are half a dozen teenagers independently watching their favorite TV show, all preparing to participate in tomorrow's peer group activity at school. Schools themselves are group agencies. They consist of a variety of formal and informal peer groups. Teachers direct their instruction to individual students, but most of this teaching takes place in a group setting. Incidentally, much educational research on learning yields little benefit for classroom teachers because powerful group forces that are not taken into account confound the results.

To appreciate the impact of groups in our lives, we suggest the following exercise. (This activity is also appropriate for your students.) First, list all groups you were involved in during the past week and indicate the time you spent within those groups. What benefits did you derive from each group? Did you attend any groups where you felt like an outsider rather than a participant? What roles did you play in each group? How many ways could you classify these groups (age, purpose, elected or required, etc.)? Exploring one's own group life is the best preparation for this chapter.

Group life is a consuming force for most students of all ages. It does not await adolescence, as some have thought. If students are restricted to working in booths, they will look out or sometimes make holes to see what their neighbors are doing. In classrooms, students conduct surveillance scans to see who is doing something they need to appraise. Any noise is a signal for alert. Schools create classroom groups for academic learning, but at the same time the give-and-take of group life is the setting for significant social learning. Feedback from the group reaffirms students' sense of acceptance. The group is so important to adolescents that some mental health personnel consider group therapy the treatment of choice to reach adolescents.

Although there are many types of groups, there is a distinction between a primary and a secondary group. The most significant imprinting takes place in primary groups. The prototype is the family, which is relatively permanent, intimate, and safe. Because the child is dependent, the family is expected to provide for his or her physical and psychological needs. Family interaction is the channel for developing and sustaining values, nurturing a healthy self-concept, and enforcing social behavior standards. The obvious problem today is that many troubled students come to school feeling neglected and rejected because they have never had a satisfactory primary family experience. The school, expecting to build on the socialization gained in the family, instead finds itself in the business of creating the ethical values and standards of society. Fortunately, a caring classroom for troubled students can become a surrogate primary group that will have a deep and lasting impact on students.

A student who profits from a primary family group is ready for secondary group participation. This expanded group life is exciting, though not always easy to achieve. The usual classroom, with peers, activities, and a caring adult leader, is an excellent example of a secondary group. Young children often have a difficult time sorting it all out; sometimes, they even call the teacher "Mother." Then there are all those sibling-like peers to get along with, and a student hopes some of them will become friends. Year after year, a school group can be heaven or hell. Each new classroom group is different. Nevertheless, group membership is mandated, particularly for special education students. Schools also offer many group affiliations beyond the classroom: playground, lunchroom, hall group, sport groups, study groups, and ethnic groups. Most groups develop an "in" and "out" group stratification well known to the students. Amid all the hustle and activity of a large middle or high school, it is hard to remember that many of our troubled students are lonely and miss out on healthy peer associations.

In spite of the fact that schools are group agencies and teachers are group leaders, the power of group dynamics in the classroom is shortchanged in professional education. Teachers rarely receive any course on group management even though they are group teachers. The real shock occurs when a beginning teacher has to manage the interaction of 30 students for 6 hours. Suddenly, the teacher becomes aware that he or she knows very little about what makes this class function and even less about how to select proper group strategies and skills to modify and redirect disruptive group behavior. Without training, teachers end up using three dysfunctional group techniques. The first technique is to deny the existence of a group. This is accomplished by arranging the desks in rows and columns so the students cannot speak to each other, resulting in a minimum of peer interaction. The teacher also maintains control of conversation by imposing one-way communication. This form of communication goes from the teacher to a student and from a student to the teacher. The rest of the class is to remain silent. Leadership is not shared but held exclusively by the teacher. By these decisions, the teacher denies the dynamics of group life in the classroom. The second way of misusing groups is to divide the classroom into competing and rival subgroups. For example, the teacher may resort to comments such as, "Will the girls or the boys receive the highest group score on the spelling test?" or "Which row will be the first to put away all their books?" The technique of using subgroup competition does not enhance group cohesion and cooperative learning. If anything, it depreciates these two concepts by dividing the class into winners and losers. The third technique for mismanaging groups is to use peer pressure to control a student's disruptive behavior, using statements such as, "If Calvin continues to talk, the entire class will stay indoors today," or "We cannot leave this room until Jason sits in his desk and is quiet." These threats will work, but they will not promote positive group behavior.

Teachers have the opportunity to change unhealthy group conditions and create classes that are caring, inclusive groups. A classroom group can become an important and meaningful experience for students. In a rare quiet moment, for instance, one special-class student spoke out as follows:

> This class is like a family. We spend lots of time here. Teach, you are like a parent trying to help us. And all of these others are like my brothers and sisters. We do lots of things together. We eat here. We have parties, and we go on trips together. Only we don't sleep here.

No one added anything more, and the group went back to its work.

Often, special education classrooms are saturated with negative peer roles, such as clowns, bullies, negative instigators, and seekers of attention. As we know, these students are referred because of the negative effect their behavior has on their own learning and that of others. One class finally explained why they could not have successful group meetings. The "hard gels" (the tough, antisocial, and delinquent members) would have nothing to do with the "soft gels" (the anxious, nervous students). The "hard gels" did not consider themselves to be in the same class psychologically, regardless of their physical placement.

Feuding subgroups may bring an outside conflict into the classroom. The class may have a student who plays the role of the conflict generator or the problem solver. Sometimes, a student becomes the junior cleric and announces the sins of others, earning their considerable consternation. Some high-power students can assume a coteaching role and control other students' attention. A teacher's life would be easier if school groups were internally balanced with complementary roles that led to harmony and productive activities. But in a group of troubled students, there are seldom enough positive roles to balance the negative ones. Most of our students crave affiliation even in the face of negative feedback. Life in adolescent peer groups can be cruel.

The challenge for a teacher is to find ways of teaching rejected and ignored students new social skills that will improve their chances of being accepted. To complicate these responsibilities, a teacher assumes many different roles in a day or even in an hour—listener, dispenser of information, caregiver, adviser, lawyer, limit setter, police officer, jurist, and judge—all the while modeling values and positive behavior.

We also recognize the power of a peer group and how it can influence a student's behavior and self-esteem. This is especially true for troubled students. The more a student is attracted to a group, the more cohesive the group becomes and the greater the group power. In a worst case scenario, a class may become cohesive through common dislike of a teacher. Some groups send clear messages to a student who does not support the group. The message is, "Shape up and accept the group standards or be cast out." If "just passing" is accepted as the group academic standard, those who outperform others are labeled "teacher's pet" or "smart ass" and are expected to dumb down or suffer peer isolation. This can be a problem for high-performing students and might explain why girls' math and science scores drop when they reach middle and high school. In this case, to be smart might mean the student is less likely to be accepted by a desired peer group.

Groups also develop their own code of rights. This code often is quite different from the teacher-imposed code posted in the classroom. Students have norms regarding how authorities should treat them and what punishments are fit for breaking what rules. A teacher who tries to trace the cause and effect of an incident often is stymied by the group norm that reads, "No squealing on a member."

There are several common group phenomena that need to be understood. For example, Redl introduced the group concept called "group contagion" (Redl & Wineman, 1966). This occurs when a student juices up the group by acting-out behaviors that are far beyond the usual limits of acceptance. Group members spontaneously join the behavior, such as defying the teacher or punishing the group scapegoat as school lets out, and become intoxicated by the excitement. The behavior spirals up until it reaches an intensity that shocks some of the perpetrators. They then call a halt and usually turn on the initiator. The initiator loses power and becomes "the bad guy," and the other peers take refuge in their newfound holiness. The behavior becomes "all his fault," and the others are guiltless.

Another type of instantaneous group behavior happens when a subgroup of students functions like one person. Redl called this group behavior the "pie phenomenon." Each member contributes only one piece of the group act, and chaos results. Each member does his or her own specific thing without feeling guilty. The cumulative activity beckons other members to add their bit until the chaos spreads and the group act is completed. Each member thus feels blame-less for the total act. For example, one member is "the idea man" who says, "I know where we could steal some stuff." The second produces the strategy for an escapade. The third is the lookout, and two others carry out the loot. No one feels guilty because each played only a partial role in a larger act proposed by someone else (see Article 5.3).

Groups also develop rituals or games that can go on undetected in the midst of a class. One such game is "playing the dozens." First, the players signal they are in. Then the teasing starts. The taunters know the vulnerability of the other players. The words may only be mouthed and not spoken, or gestures may be used (e.g., the finger), but the players know what is meant. Every member tries to "stay cool" during the teasing, but finally someone can't stand it any longer and reacts. Once this happens, the other players usually subside as if nothing had happened. Other group games to upset the teacher are the "you're not fair" game and the "our other teacher doesn't make us" game. Every substitute teacher has experienced these psychological games.

This brief overview of group dynamics demonstrates the challenge of teaching a group of troubled students. It is a professional task requiring both the knowledge of group dynamic concepts and the skills to carry out effective group programs. These concepts and skills are rarely taught at teacher training programs, so we will do our best to make up for their limited view of teacher preparation by summarizing them for you.

ESSENTIAL GROUP DYNAMIC CONCEPTS FOR TEACHERS

We believe the dynamics of a classroom group is similar to the character of an individual.

1. Every classroom group, like an individual, has a distinct personality. How would you characterize your class's personality? Is it a submissive group personality; an aggressive group personality; a silly, regressive group personality; a serious, compulsive group personality; an anxious group personality; or some other type?

2. Every classroom group, like an individual, has moods. What are the moods of your group? Is the mood of the group influenced by the lesson or activity? During a science lesson is the mood one of excitement, anxiety, or boredom? Does the group mood change as the activities change, such as during music or social study lessons?

3. Every classroom, like an individual, has values and standards for acceptable and unacceptable behaviors. What behaviors in your group are sanctioned, and what behaviors are unacceptable? To what extent are these peer values and behaviors consistent with your values and expectations?

4. Every classroom group, like an individual, has select tastes and aversions. There are certain activities, people, and routines groups enjoy and others they will try to avoid. Can you identify them?

5. Every classroom group, like an individual, has a self-control system. If any student's behavior deviates too far from the norm of the group, the group will use a variety of social pressures to get the deviant student to conform to the group standard. If the student does not change, the student will be rejected and isolated from most peer activities. Have you observed this group process?

6. Every classroom, like an individual, uses a variety of defense mechanisms to justify negative group behaviors. Many groups are skilled in rationalizing why they rejected a new student, treated a peer as a scapegoat, or joined a contagious and inappropriate group behavior. The teacher needs to identify these group defenses and confront the group benignly so students can understand the real reasons behind their rationalizations.

Characteristics of Subgroups in the Classroom

Although there is a parallel between the dynamics of a group and the character of an individual, every group breaks down into subgroups and cliques. The covert behaviors of these subgroups have considerable influence over what happens in the classroom. Some subgroups are more powerful than others. Some subgroups set up rival conflict situations. Some of these cliques are organized by gender, race, and social class. Some of these subgroups support your goals, whereas others passively resist.

Characteristics of Group Roles

1. Once a subgroup is formed, an unconscious social pecking order develops in the classroom. Social psychologists Lippett and Gold (1964) documented that elementary students beginning in the first grade can describe with consensus which students belong where in the social pecking order in the classroom. The data from their study show the social pecking order not only forms rapidly but also maintains its stability. A student with high social power receives more acceptance over the year, whereas a student with low social power receives more rejection and peer isolation. In addition, the group assigns negative labels to these students, such as fatso, stupid, ho, queer ball, and jerk. Other roles assigned to group members include the rebel, the clown, the mascot, the goody-two-shoes, the nerd, the party boy, the jock, the conscience, and the lawyer. These group labels have a life of their own. One way of validating the power of group roles is to attend your 25th high school reunion and listen to the conversation about your classmates!

2. Long developed a sociometric test (1962) to assess the social power of troubled students in a self-contained classroom. Each student is asked to select three students in the class he or she likes, three students in the class he or she likes the least, and three students in the class who can make other students frightened of them. An analysis of these peer group ratings can provide the teacher with four significant group roles:

- The *Significantly Preferred Student* (SPS) receives only positive peer choices, no negative choices, and no fear choices. This is the ideal high-power student for the teacher. The teacher's strategy is to get the SPS to take a leadership role in the class and model the positive attitudes and behaviors the teacher wants to promote. When the SPS speaks, the other students will listen and follow.

- The *Significantly Ignored Student* (SIS) receives no positive, negative, or fear peer choices. This student attends class but is psychologically absent, has no social power in the classroom, and has made no close friends. Often the student is shy and anxious, and would profit from learning new social skills on how to initiate conversation. One helping strategy is to pair the SIS with the SPS whenever possible.

- The *Significantly Rejected Student* (SRS) receives only negative peer choices, no positive choices, and usually no fear choices. This student has only negative social power in the classroom. He is the student the other students like to hate. While the SRS can be disruptive in the group, this student can also become the group scapegoat. The group feels this student deserves what he gets and has little or no guilt about the way they treat him.

- The *Significantly Split Student* (SSS) is an important role for the teacher to identify. This student receives many positive peer choices, many negative peer choices, and many fear choices. This student creates significant peer conflict in the group. The SSS is a leader of some students, is rejected by other students, and is feared by the majority of the group. If there is one SSS in the classroom, then there is usually another. These two SSS students set up rival subgroups and vie for control of the social climate and social power of the class. Whenever the members of these two rival subgroups are asked to work together on a project, peer conflict will develop. As a result, considerable bickering occurs and very little cooperative learning takes place. The teacher with these students often will report that this is one of the most difficult classes he or she has ever had to teach. The teacher usually has no awareness of why this class is so difficult or of the underlying peer rivalry that interferes with the learning process and contributes to the teacher's feelings of competence.

ARTICLE 5.1

TO reinforce the importance of these group dynamic concepts, the following three articles have been selected to provide in-depth knowledge and understanding of these ideas. The first two articles are by Ruth Newman (1921–1994). She was a lifelong friend, one of the original editors of *Conflict in the Classroom,* and a creative group therapist. Her book *Groups in Schools* (1974) was ahead of its time. Her insights into the dynamics of classroom groups are as meaningful today as they were in 1974. Like good wine, the ideas in her writings have grown better with time. We are pleased to publish two of her articles on classroom groups.

FIVE PSYCHOLOGICAL GAMES CLASSROOM GROUPS PLAY
Ruth G. Newman

Here are five typical games pupils play in classrooms, cafeterias, or playgrounds, in the waiting room or the office of the principal or within therapeutic groups. Feel free to translate them into adult group activities in or related to the school, or, for that matter, any place where groups meet in order, presumably, to get a job under way.

GAME 1: THE "WHO DID IT FIRST" SYNDROME

Called out by a parent, a seventh grade teacher leaves her room with a monitor.

"Hey, Dick," says Sam, "you got that picture from *Playboy* in your desk. Show it here."

"Nah," says Dick, "you guys'll tear it. It belongs to my brother, I ripped it off of him."

"Come on, Dick," plead a few voices.

From *The Pointer, 26*(3), 1982, pp. 16–24. Reprinted with permission.

The monitor makes initial threatening sounds, writes names on a list, is glared at, and subsides for good!

"I bet you're hiding it 'cause you don't want Kathy to be jealous," taunts Fay. (Giggles from the girls.)

By this time Henry has jumped over to Dick's desk and opened it; he gets out the picture and holds it high.

"Wow," he says. "Wow, what boobs! Bet none of you'll ever have boobs like that!"

He waves the picture so no one can see anything and dances about the room, mimicking a sexy walk and making lewd gestures.

"They just get shots to make 'em big. That's all, it's not real," shouts Willa.

"You gonna get those shots, Willa baby?" Jimmy taunts. "You can be my gal if you get those shots."

Leo is now fighting with Henry to get hold of the picture and Dick is shouting: "Don't tear it. Jeez, it's my brother's. Look out, you'll ruin it."

The girls are either pretending to be shocked or showing off, and the boys are so high they've lost all sense of where they are. The teacher walks in. At first no one notices her angry, cold face and stiff presence. A curtain of silence descends. Miraculously the somewhat torn picture disappears.

"What exactly is going on here?" the teacher asks. (Silence.) "Leo, Sam, Dick, Mary, Sue, what were you doing?" Sam invokes the magic. "Henry started it, Miss Richards," he says, waving the invisible wand.

"I did not. Dick had the picture," says Henry, trying to avoid the victim role.

"Can't a guy have a picture?" says Dick. "I didn't start anything."

"You did, you creep," says Henry.

"That's enough," says Miss Richards. "Henry, I don't want to hear a word."

This may be because she herself, despite sophisticated awareness of children's sexuality, is uncomfortable with sexual material, or it may be simply because the excitement caused by sexual discussion among pre-adolescents and early adolescents has made the children too high to settle down to work.

"Henry, you will go to Mr. Davis's office and you will go to Detention Hall after school. I can't trust you to behave when I leave you for fifteen minutes. The class will take out geography books."

Henry walks out, giving a finger sign to the other boys and muttering, but not too unhappy at the prospect of getting some free time in the principal's office to indulge in sexy daydreams.

That's the short form of the game. The scene could last hours, with each one blaming the others, and each one passing the buck. So long as the teacher colludes and accepts her role in dealing with the perpetrator of the initiatory act as an individual, and not as speaking for the group and their sexual interests and concerns, the underlying dynamics will be buried. One class member will be selected to be the sacrificial lamb; the game will be played and no one will learn anything about why what happened did happen, and how the whole group was involved, and what different things the incident meant to each member.

Let us consider the specifics of this example:

Dick often had sexy pictures in his desk. Dick was worried about his body in comparison to those of other boys of his age and dreaded the shower room after gym which was the next class period. He wanted to talk about his worries but could not do so, fearing ridicule from others, fearing ignorance, and fearing his fears. The other boys were also preoccupied in one way or another with their changing bodies, particularly the genital areas, and were mightily relieved to find in Dick's picture an outlet for being preadolescently sexy in a group, in a schoolroom, where clearly no one was going to have to go too far, or have to reveal his own doubts, fears, and wishes. It was a tax-free safe activity.

The girls, who were of course more developed than the boys, were enjoying the titillations and the fantasies as much as the boys. Each of them used the attitudes of all the others—Sue's giggles, Fay's guffaws, Mary's prudish disgust, Linda's pretense of being shocked, Judy's honest bewilderment. They also used the boys' hilarity for their own needs to talk about sex, to imagine, to learn.

The excitement that the subject of sex had aroused might have been a cue for the teacher. If she were more comfortable, she might have commented on the preoccupying interest in sex and the probable factual confusion of the group. She might have taken note of it, and at a later date—perhaps the next day—she might have brought about a class discussion at a time when the class could handle it more coolly. Or, she might have scrapped her lesson plan and at once brought the discussion up in an orderly fashion. Instead, especially since she wanted to avoid seeing the provocative picture and having to deal with it, she fell smack into the "Henry-did-it-first" trap. If the class was then in fact able to calm down and get back to work, maybe that was for the best. A lot of needs were taken care of. But the probability that they got much from their work right then is small. Another possible handling might have been a couple of moments of silence brought about by Miss Richards, then a comment: "You people certainly got carried away. If sexy pictures go to your head like that, I guess all of you have a lot of feelings and questions about sex. Maybe we can talk about it tomorrow. Now do you think we are ready to travel to South America by way of our geography books? Henry, why don't you tell us something you found out about the Andes?"

What is it that makes a youngster feel better when someone else "does it first"? A partial answer is, as Redl points out in *When We Deal With Children,* that the one who "does it first" often reflects the acting-out of impulses others in the class were wishing or thinking or repressing so hard they didn't even dare to wish or think them. When someone "does it first," the others can keep a picture of themselves as noble, clean thinking, courteous, peaceful beings and pile all the evil on the First Doer. The fact that they did not hesitate to follow does not seem to besmirch their self-image too much or for too long. And since one dynamic of punishment is that it underlines the misdeed, it becomes absolutely necessary, in order to keep the self-image relatively clear, that not "I" but "he" should get punished or scolded. His getting punished is confirmation that "I" wasn't guilty.

In the typical case above, it is hard to say whether Dick or Henry or Sam was the prime doer, since any one of the three would have served the group's need. But since it was Henry who made active Dick's more passive holder-of-the-picture role, it was he who represented the needs of most of the boys and girls in the group to express sexual preoccupation. As for the teacher, abdication of leadership in that instance to "Henry did it first" satisfied her need to deny sexual issues. All then colluded in letting Henry be the bad one so they could deny their own impulses. All could hang the unacceptable behavior on Henry.

There is nothing wrong in using such an economical method of taking care of inside dynamics that are indeed group dynamics—so long as Henry doesn't always get himself victimized, the sacrificial-lamb role gets passed around, and the "bad" feelings don't all get dumped on one person all the time. For example, the Black Sheep of the Family (no matter how it is defined) is kept very black so that the others can think of themselves as very white. If he reforms, the whole family goes into a tailspin until they either take some of the "sinfulness" into themselves or elect another member of the family—wife, husband, youngest brother—to be a new Family Black Sheep.

GAME 2: THE FAIRNESS SYNDROME

The obvious is often overlooked, especially when it parades in group clothing. No one would have any question, when dealing with individuals, that all our fuss about fairness originally derives from struggles in childhood to get as much attention as one can from mother or father and that as soon as brother or sister enters the scene, the struggle to get one's share—or the lion's share—is intensified. One can predict the struggle among siblings. A little less obvious is the struggle between the adults of the family or between adult and child for the most attention.

> **Father:** You are always busy with that child. You never have time to sit and talk with me.

> **Mother:** As soon as you come home, you're reading the comics with that child. You never ask about my day.

> **Both:** It isn't fair.

What usually goes unstated here is that while the rivalries among children are par for the course, and even rivalries between child and parent are known to any wife or husband who has been the subject or object of envy, the "dealer out of goods" is often more caught up in being meticulously fairer than the rivals themselves demand. This fact lurks behind the scenes prompting the Fairness Game; it has to be played out as "haute" drama, simply because it does so often stay beneath the level of awareness. The Fairness Game derives, of course, from the same source as sibling rivalries; it is living proof of unresolved feelings about being treated fairly and about one's own sibling or parental rivalries. It comes as often to those who secretly recognize they have been the favorite ones as it does to those who have suffered from being the non-getters of preference, the ones thought to be able to go without, the neglected ones. The former group—the favored—are burdened by guilt from the past and are fearfully waiting to get their "punishment" for having been favored. The latter, of course, suffer from resentment, bitterness, and injustice-collecting.

People in both categories find it nearly impossible to deal out decisions for fear of being unfair. Thus they are sometimes immobilized—trapped, that is, into playing the fairness game. It is a sure sign that the players have never resolved their own problems about having "gotten" or "not gotten" and about the revenge or retribution they fear must follow.

For a teacher to be so trapped can bring to a halt any work on the primary goal. If the conflict is a severe one, it can also ensure that few individual needs will be cared for—all will be sacrificed on the altar of utter fairness and equivalent favors, turns, attentions, helps, praise—whatever may be required. A group can get a leader to play the Fairness Game any time it wants to see a little excitement, avoid the task, or see the teacher or leader squirm.

Every child wants the teacher to be fair; a class will jump on any favoritism before the teacher even knows he is feeling it. Usually the child picked as favorite will be picked out by the group to be disliked or even ostracized. The question then becomes: what's fair? Is fairness a question of each child's getting the same amount and kind of time, help, material, reward, or punishment? Or is fairness a question of giving each child what he needs—that is to say, as far as that is feasible? Can a child understand that difference? Answer: Yes, if the adult can. Any hole in the adult's understanding lets the whole flood of injustice pour in.

EXAMPLE 1

The Open Trap

Lucy: Mr. Trent, Karen always gets to sit next to you in reading class. That's not fair.

The Fall-in

Mr. Trent: Why, Lucy, Karen didn't sit next to me yesterday or the day before.

Lucy: But she did three times last week. Karen's your pet.

The False Solution

Mr. Trent: No, she isn't, Lucy, and I think you've counted wrong. I like all of you just the same. (This is a grievous lie, unless Mr. Trent is a computer in disguise.) We'll take turns and everyone in the class will sit next to me by alphabetical order.

Now in all probability at least fifteen children in the class would much prefer to be as far as possible from Mr. Trent so they can daydream, write notes, wriggle without criticism, doodle without seeming to be rude. Lucy is simply testing. Presumably, Mr. Trent has two sides, and if he moves, it is possible for him, without going into numerical counts, to move in such a way as to be able to say, "Lucy, if you need to sit next to me today, why don't you sit on the other side of me?" This maneuver, however, won't solve anything if what Lucy wants is to get Karen out and herself in or if the idea is really just to put Mr. Trent on the spot. A more realistic solution might be for Mr. Trent to say: "It's fair, Lucy. Karen needs to sit next to me today because she's having a hard time concentrating. You need a chance to read out loud, so why don't you begin today's story?"

This answer implies that there are different needs in the group, and that Mr. Trent is aware of many of these needs and will try to attend to those he sees. He doesn't fall into the trap of defending himself against an accusation of favoritism; he doesn't take on responsibility for dealing omnipotently with all the needs he imagines.

EXAMPLE 2

Mike is the class mess. He wanders about disrupting every activity because he can't get started on anything. Once started, he can't stop. Transitions from one activity to another are difficult for him, but in Mike's case response to transition tension makes life harder for the rest of the class.

Mrs. Kern's supervisor has told her to stick close to Mike in transition times and help him get started. But Mrs. Kern has not been able to carry out this advice successfully because she believes that it is unfair to the rest of the children to spend so much of her time with one individual. In addition to being annoyed by Mike, she is getting to dislike him because to her mind he is putting her in the unholy position of discriminating and being unfair.

She herself introduces the "that's not fair" game: "Mike," she says after two or three minutes of helping him, as she sees the hands of two other children aloft calling for her help, "I can't spend all my time with you. It's not fair. The others have as much right to my help as you. Just go on and do the best you can."

"Yeah," says Dave, "he's always first getting help. It's not fair."

"You never help me," whines Rosie. "You always help Mike."

By then, between Mrs. Kern's statement and the gathering cloud of group resentment, Mike is embarrassed. He feels even more inadequate and anxious than usual and is about as able to do his short division as if he were asked to do calculus. He begins to chant to himself and roams over to the aquarium, wishing he were a tadpole instead of a boy. As he stands near the tank, he drops the fishfood and knocks over a bowl of water. Now, Mrs. Kern is really angry, and the class is divided between giggling and glaring at Mike. No one is working.

"Get out of this room," Mrs. Kern says between her teeth, "and don't come back until you can take care of yourself." (This is patently impossible for Mike at this moment.) "It's not fair." This time she's more honest, for she means it's not fair to her.

Instead of announcing to the class, as she had, "It's time to play the fairness game," thus putting both Mike and herself on the spot, she might have said, if challenged by the class, "Yes, I know it seems as if I help Mike a lot, but Mike needs help getting started and as soon as I have got him settled, I'll try to help you others. In the meantime, why don't you try to help each other quietly? We've got a lot of good dividers in the class who can help those who get stuck. Jim, Jeff, Bert, and Louise, why don't you be the helpers while I'm busy?" No one would have minded, and while Mike would have been singled out, as indeed he needed to be, the group would not have been disturbed by the symptoms of his misery—his roaming, breaking things, etc. In that situation Mike would not have been elected The Stupid One—he would have been seen as simply needy at the beginning of things which might have allowed him to do his job—and so to feel more adequate—and the group to do theirs. It was Mrs. Kern's own fear of being unfair and her own resentment of Mike's inept way of getting attention that created the situation.

To complete the discussion of the fairness syndrome it need only be said that this syndrome is one of the major reasons why people are fearful of leading groups. What they are afraid of is being immobilized by their old unresolved personal problems of who gets what, when, and how much. Fairness becomes so mixed up with doling out equal portions of love that leaders begin to feel they are "undemocratic" when they treat people as individuals each with his own special requirements at special times. "Why, it nearly seems anti-American, anti-democratic not to treat everyone the same," one hears. Yet it is precisely in the realm of caring for individual differences while living in a group that actual democracy, not its self-destructive facsimile, can be practiced. Jefferson had no such nonsensical thought as that each person needs the same thing. What he and Lincoln and John Dewey—to name only three proponents of true democracy—cared about was that a society be formed in which individuals with different needs and talents could be served differently and still find room for one another while working together in groups. The Fairness Syndrome, while pretending to be "democratic," in fact neglects individual differences, condescends to the unneedy in certain areas, and fails to care adequately for the needy. Since groups are made up of individuals who, if they lose their individualness, lose their ability to be self-determining within the group, the Fairness Syndrome in reality caters to unresolved emotional problems appropriate to the first years of group life but not afterward. It can become dangerous to democratic ideas rather than supportive of them, as our societal myths would have it. Like so many of the group games we play, the Fairness Game can and does contribute to the infantilizing of everyone, especially in schools—not only the children in our schools but the staff as well.

GAME 3: THE DO-GOODER SYNDROME

Miss Manning is a good young teacher. She is imbued with many ideas about how she is going to use the group to help her with class management. Indeed, by dint of her efforts, her third grade is already far more of a group than any of the other sections in the school. She has brought them far enough to be able to deal with Frank's noisy fidgets by letting him be mobile during a class while the others sit still; thus, she and they have overcome the "fairness syndrome." A subgroup has managed to take care of Beth's tears and timidity so that Beth, now sitting between Amy and Lois, is comparatively dry-eyed and can now speak a bit above a whisper without the boys' yelling "Louder in front." Miss Manning has indeed mobilized her group to take care of some disturbing symptoms in her class.

But there is Arnold. Arnold has titanic tantrums in which he tears up other people's work, kicks, bites, turns red easily any time he's not first or best in nearly anything and any time something new comes up. Moreover, Miss Manning herself can hardly abide Arnold. His tantrums are bad enough, but his whine goes right through her nervous system, and when he isn't roaring, he's whining. She has, conscientiously, gotten in touch with his mother. (His father is living in another city.) The mother was rude and irritated by the teacher's calls. For a while Miss Manning

havior modification principles, Miss Manning was rewarding acceptable nondisruptive behavior rather than disruptive behavior. She did it with a group reward in which Arnold could share, not an individual one. True, by May there weren't enough pennies to buy the volleyball they all wanted, but there were enough to get a ring-toss game, and Miss Manning had learned: first, that to lead a group you don't elicit phoney responses you yourself don't feel and secondly, that you get a group to help only when you take your own role in the group. For her the role was to be the adult leader, not the instigator of good deeds. The group had learned that they were there to learn and live together, not to minister to Arnold. As for Arnold—he learned he was there to learn about living in a group, not either to lead or mislead it.

GAME 4: THE "WILLING SUCKER" SYNDROME

Dr. Fritz Redl has called one familiar group maneuver "The Case of the Willing Sucker." The idea of master-sleuthing suggested by the title is fitting, for it takes some fast eye-ear- and foot-work to determine who is in fact the originator or director of the play, and why Bob or Kit or Mary has been selected for the role of star actor or actress in it.

The drama according to Dr. Redl's script goes this way:

> There are twelve to fifteen kids sitting around a table at lunch time. Barry is bored or would simply like to maneuver some excitement. Containers of milk and spoons are convenient props. Barry is fully aware that the adult (teacher or paraprofessional or whoever) sitting at the table is involved in a conversation with Tony and Jill. By merely picking up his spoon and flicking the spoon-end down and up, down and up, he catches Bob's eye. He says nothing and in fact does nothing except flick the spoon with one hand and move his milk nearer. He is absolutely pure of overt ill doing, but Bob, rising to the bait as soon as it is offered, connects the spoon flicking and the milk—just as he is meant to do. Bob nudges Patty and flicks some milk first at Lucy, then at Mark, and is becoming quite skilled when, of course, Mark avenges himself in like manner; Patty whirls round and wipes her dress. Lucy swears and the table is in pandemonium. Milk is flying, containers are being thrown, and spoons are banging. The adult sees Bob as the central figure—as indeed, in a way, he is—and it is Bob who gets punished. Either Barry is completely ignored, or, if the teacher,

experienced with the Barrys of this world, turns to him asking, "Barry, what are you doing?" his answer is, with injured innocence: "Nothing, I'm not doing nothing. Jeez, can't a guy touch his spoon?" The adult is left feeling helpless. If he is a wise teacher, he knows full well that it's Barry again, with Bob in the role of Barry's puppet. How is he to make Bobby and his multitudinous ilk immune from taking on such willing suckerdom time after time?

If the drama were translated to adult groups, it might well give off an odor more of hostility and less of mischief, but it would still be recognizable. It might go like this:

Setting: A school board meeting. Because of urgent phone calls the night before, Mr. Jay is aware that Mr. Beal is determined to put through a wage raise for the Pupil Personnel staff. Knowing how limited the funds available for raises are and being committed to getting more slots for a Remedial Reading Program, Mr. Jay makes use of something else he happens also to know: the superintendent has to leave the meeting promptly because his wife's sister is to be married that very day. The superintendent's subliminal agenda will be to get essential business under way at once; he will brook no diversions. Mr. Jay reasons that anyone who tries to take the group afield today will be a dead duck. He knows also that Mr. Beal is one of the world's easiest people to seduce into rambling, especially when led into discussion of his present favorite topic, Behavior Modification. He knows that today's agenda will be read alphabetically, that Pupil Personnel comes directly before Remedial Reading, and that both come late in the day after Language Arts, Mathematics, etc.

Being a good politician, he would rather be the first on the agenda for tomorrow's meeting than last for today's. All he has to do is to see to it that Mr. Beal gets involved in his favorite topic. At the meeting, Mr. Jay sits back, lighting a pipe or two, gallantly getting Mr. Beal a cup of coffee when he starts to get himself one. Just as Mrs. Stillman's discussion of the needs of Mathematics is drawing to a close, Mr. Jay slips a clipping headlined "New Methods of Behavior Modification in Psychological Assessment" beneath Mr. Beal's eyes. It has a friendly note on top: "Jake, thought this would interest you."

Mr. Beal, who is always bored by Mrs. Stillman's reports, smiles gratefully; innocent that he is, he does not know he is being led to the sacrificial altar and surreptitiously reads the clipping.

So engrossed is he that when the superintendent turns to him with "Well, now, Beal, Pupil Personnel is next and we have just twenty minutes. I have to leave at four today, remember," Mr. Beal jumps and rouses from dreams of professional glory.

"Sir, I simply must share with you the importance of bringing more Behavior Modification techniques into our system. I have been reading how an entire system was rejuvenated by its use"—and off he goes down his favorite road. Mr. Jay looks on with seeming fascination.

The superintendent shuffles his papers nervously, packs them away in his brief case. Twice he intervenes in polite fashion—"But, Mr. Beal ..."—"Mr. Beal, please, the clock ..." After ten minutes he angrily insists that Mr. Beal get to his specific budget requests. Seeing his irritated face, Mr. Beal flushes and gets to work, but it is too late. He cannot get through on time to give his justifications. The superintendent says irritably, "Well, Beal, time's up. We'll get back to Pupil Personnel Budget at the end of tomorrow's meeting after the Remedial Reading, Social Science, and Social Work Programs. I advise you to confine yourself to figures, not theories, at that time. Mr. Jay, please prepare to begin with purely budgetary reading needs in the morning." Quietly Mr. Jay nods his assent; he is careful to conceal his inner triumph.

The dynamics of this game is a sophisticated sense of the meaning behind power, a kind of Svengali knowledge of how to manipulate those more vulnerable than yourself to your own ends. The attempt is to conceal one's maneuvers by protecting oneself from open hostility or open attack but still to get one's desires acted upon by others. The power implicit here is heady and for the skillful next to irresistible, if one gets away with it. The best technique a teacher and leader can use to prevent such manipulation in the classroom is to try to catch the manipulator in the act and bring the matter out in the open. This will not only give the teacher or leader satisfaction but help the child or adult manipulator grow to be able to risk himself and his own feelings out front—to develop his acuteness in using leadership directly instead of hiding his feelings and wishes and needs behind someone else. "Getting away with it" is often a Pyrrhic victory.

GAME 5: THE DARE

We are told that, notwithstanding Cecil B. DeMille and television spectaculars, nothing has ever offered a more dramatic spectacle than the duel, that holdover from the days of chivalry. (Undoubtedly the Romans, Greeks, and Early Egyptians had their own forms of this game.) As time went on, the duel became more and more formalized, more and more rigid in structure. The result could still be, and often was, a corpse. In Europe and in America, dueling went on through the nineteenth century, killing one of our newborn nation's brightest luminaries, Hamilton, and indirectly ruining the career of his opponent, Aaron Burr.

Today's version is not half so glamorous and choreographic as the ancient duel, but we still have our feuding mountaineers, our street gangs, our fights in the alley, our revengers in the night. In cases where gangs and their leaders are involved, the dare and the conclusion are nearly as much a way of life as dueling used to be, and often as lethal. A common and dangerous form of the modern Dare-and-Die Game is the game of "Chicken" played with cars, racers, or motorcycles. There are the challenge, the appointed place, the encounter, and the fact that some people in the group may not come out alive. However, being more groupy than the duelists of old, we tend, like Samson Agonistes, to take others with us when we act on personal or group gripes.

Those who participate by watching are often present at the moment of decision as audience, just as in the duels of the Middle Ages. Spectator participation—in actuality or imagination—has much to do with the outcome, with the need to carry through the dare without negotiation. No matter how much the elected opponents may want to forget the whole thing or have done with it peaceably, they have become representatives of their groups; they are onstage and the show must go on. Neither representative feels he can go back to his own peer group without proving his "honor," no matter how inane the definition of honor may be and no matter how great his reluctance to proceed. It is as if he could not live without that image of himself, which is, or which he thinks is, the only acceptable one. If that effort fails, a man (this is as a rule a syndrome of males) feels he has lost his identity or his manhood and therefore has no right to live. The Japanese samurai with their hara-kiri stabbing of themselves in defeat have exactly the same formulation of values, except that they only do themselves in—they do not shoot it out with their opponents or race it out with 180-horsepower engines.

One has to say "opponent" rather than "enemy" in these circumstances, for in fact the participants in a duel or even in a rumble or roadway confrontation may not be enemies at all. It is all a matter of "honor" and has little to do with intrinsic relationships or points of view.

The dynamics in such group games center upon identity, including sexuality, upon the concept of machismo and honor as a man or boy, and upon the question of how one can live with oneself if one has failed to live up to the ideals and attitudes of one's peer-society. Failure comes not from losing, as in a war, but from not being willing to play the game. It is for this reason indeed that we call this activity a "group game"; though dead is dead, a "game" does not have the same motivation as a fight to the finish or a war. It comes less from hatred than from vanity. Girls have their own form of dare and double dare and their own feuds, but their feuds have tended in our culture to be less lethal—except as they become the focus of many of the boys' duels or feuds. Women are traditionally assigned the role of raison d'etre for many of the duels.

A teacher may get caught in the acting out of the "dare" phenomenon. In or just before adolescence, there is often an identity crisis—a crisis that involves a shifting ego-stability. The more shifting there is, the more frequently dare-battles are likely to occur. For instance, a familiar form of that potentially dangerous game is this: a teacher is marking papers, unaware of certain millings-about in the classroom. The children's talk may have to do with a subgroup that is insisting that Cal has a crush on the teacher. There is hot denial.

The dialogue might then go: "Cal wouldn't say nothing fresh to her—his lovey-dovey pussycat. It's all 'Yes, Miss Keller; no, ma'am; sure, Miss Keller,' with him."

The accusations mount, taunting Cal, who considers himself tough. Then someone drops the gauntlet: "You call other people plenty names, but betcha wouldn't call her a name."

"What kinda name?"

"Well, a name."

Now everyone has suggestions: "Betcha wouldn't call her a mother ..." "Betcha wouldn't say you're a no-good wiggle-ass."

Roars of laughter greet each suggestion till they diminish to more real possibilities.

"Betcha wouldn't dare even say when she calls on you, 'Miss Keller, I just don't want to say, and I ain't going to tell you.' " Since this is in the realm of possibility, they all dare him to say this.

When it is time for seventh-grade English class, Cal looks frantically at Miss Keller, pleading with her not to call on him. Miss Keller sees a strange look, but she doesn't get the message.

"Cal, will you tell us about what John Steinbeck was saying in *Of Mice and Men?*" He shakes his head no.

She pushes, with a "But Cal, you gave the book back yesterday and you said you liked it. What did ...'"

He catches the eye of one of his dare-tormentors. Dilemma. Which should he obey? She's here now—but they're here too, and they'll be outside at 3 P.M., and he can't risk their jeering—he can't risk seeming a sissy. A dare is a dare. So he says the words.

She is startled. "Cal, that's impudent. What's going on with you?" Cal glares and sulks. "Answer me, Cal." Cal is silent. She is amazed. "Cal, you will stay in an hour after school in detention hall today and write fifty times 'I'm impertinent and I'm sorry.' Do you hear me?" Cal, in misery, nods his head yes. She makes it worse. "Cal, speak up." Cal refuses and is sent to the assistant principal.

Now it is a fact that Cal likes Miss Keller, not passionately, as the boys have said, goading him, but he just likes her. He doesn't want to be rude. He doesn't want to be punished. But where honor beckons, and where loyalty and pressure weigh most heavily, he has had to choose. Peers are more important to him. He has been challenged and he has accepted. His social identity is preserved. Punishment and a "bad deportment" mark on his record cannot really compete with the approval of his peers.

A teacher's best hope of handling this sort of activity is in having sensitivity in differentiating behavior, the ability to recognize when someone is being impudent and challenging, let's say, because of internal forces or in relationship to the task or the adult authority, when it is a case of responding to an explicit or implicit dare in which the child is being put into jeopardy with his group by a given demand or task. If the latter is the case, it is a wise teacher who can let it go and not get trapped. The dare has virtually nothing to do with the teacher who is only a deus ex machina who exists to make it all happen. To become entangled at such a moment with one's own personal hurt or one's specific teaching mission is only to complicate and obfuscate. Moreover, it may be an entire neighborhood that one is dealing with rather than the particular youngster in question.

The rest of the daring, tormenting gang may not even be in the school-room. The reason the boy before the teacher is behaving as he is may derive from a week-end confab among his neighborhood group, a defeat at the hands of his taunters, a need to establish or reestablish himself in his own eyes as well as in theirs. Such behavior becomes nearly doubly obnoxious to the adult, but a sensitive teacher can sense a powerful group in the wings of the child's life and avoid a futile and sometimes destructive confrontation.

How can the teacher sense what the situation really is? Teachers can tell by being their own barometer and trusting their own perceptions. If Cal, for instance, has generally been pretty easy to work with, if he has not disliked the teacher, if his customary demeanor is not usually rude or provoking, one may guess that it is inner turmoil of some sort that makes him act in this atypical way. Though he may play his part to the hilt, there is often something that is a giveaway of the fact that this is a necessary act rather than a natural expression. It is more useful to listen to one's own inner messages and dismiss the behavior with a firm comment that such language or actions don't go in here (the setting of a limit) than to go into the counter-productive "I am the Authority, and I will show you my power group." A talk alone outside of class often may get things back in focus if the youngster is not too intimidated by his group. If the talk works, it may confirm one's hunch that his is a case of Honor-at-Stake, not one of hatred or malice.

EDITORS' COMMENTARY

The five psychological games classroom groups play occur in all classrooms at one time or another. Perhaps you can remember playing or observing these games when you were in school. At the time they seemed like a reasonable thing to do. However, with age and knowledge comes insight. Now when you observe these games in your classroom, you can smile and know what to do.

ARTICLE 5.2

THE concepts of group contagion and contamination have been presented previously. In the next article Ruth Newman discusses the dynamics of group contagion by using the examples of the Giggles and the Language of the Inner Circle. She also offers four useful strategies you can employ to manage group contagion in the classroom.

GROUP CONTAGION: NO TEACHER IS IMMUNE!

Ruth G. Newman

There are certain underlying, pervasive phenomena that may beset any group in or out of school but that particularly affect the teacher. These phenomena have something of the character of viruses in that they are difficult to isolate and deal with. Like viruses, they involve the danger of group contamination and contagion.

THE GIGGLES

Commonest among group contagions is the well-known "fit of giggles." Dotty looks at Laurie, puts her hands over her mouth and begins to shake, emitting sporadic squeals. Laurie joins in. Max says, "Hey, Teach, what are them dopey girls laughing at?" Before anyone has a chance to say or do anything, Peg and Judy and Ann join in, and then Arthur and Bob and Peewee. The teacher might just as well put away the homework assignments, for until the giggles have been giggled out no work will be done. She can, of course, send everyone involved (a good half of the class!) to the principal's office, but then she'd look foolish. So whether she greets them pleasantly, indulgently, humorously, or with rage, the giggles eat away seven minutes of the lesson time. They may take care of a number of needs. To guess at a few: tensions or tiredness have mounted in the group, too much time has been spent in sedentary, concentrated activity, and it is normal release time; the giggles may take care of anxiety, for they often act as a calm follow-

From *The Pointer, 26*(3), 1982, pp. 13–15. Reprinted with permission.

ing a storm. If someone—the teacher, let's say—has been very angry at a child, if something genuinely solemn or sad or even tragic has happened, the giggles are a common phenomenon and one of the most contagious diseases in the world.

Awkward, indeed miserable and shocking to everyone, is the contagious burst of giggles that comes after the announcement of a tragedy, a sickness, or a death. There are many grown-ups who dread being caught in such an act. Children hate it, too. "I laughed when I heard my favorite aunt died; my God, I laughed. I was so afraid I would laugh at the funeral. How could I do anything so awful? I liked her. Yet I laughed. I am terrified of hearing of anything really bad happening to anyone. I am so afraid I'll smile or laugh when I ought to cry." Why do we do things like that? The cause is surely anxiety in the face of helplessness. It comes from inability to handle what one fears. It is a way to cover over fright. We have been told time and time again as children that it is better to laugh than cry, to smile than look sad, so we translate tears to laughter, sorrow to smiles. To please relatives and teachers, we have learned to hide genuine feelings so well that when real emotion is evoked, the wrong one may often come out. Such phenomena are far more likely to occur in public—in a group—than when alone. The group forces the inappropriate reaction rather than helping individuals come to terms with the painful feelings that most people would prefer those around them to conceal.

Similar to the giggle are the yawn, the burp, the stomach rumble, and the fart. Skillful performers can use them to express hostility. Each may come as relief, as activity versus passivity, as the satisfaction of a genuine physiologic need, or as reaction to stress and anxiety.

How do these phenomena perform these functions? Here is an example: Mr. Zell has just launched forth on a description of medieval battles. He likes the subject and is soon lost in a verbal description of the colorful costumes of the participants. Larry yawns or burps or does both. Billy picks it up and produces some louder yawns; Jim then comes up with a prize yawn. Now the general oxygen intake and output cannot be ignored. Mr. Zell might react by getting insulted and sending Larry or the whole yawning subgroup out; if he feels his vanity particularly attacked, he might keep the whole class in from recess. But wouldn't it be better to recognize that though he may be entranced by the subject he is discussing, the class is not? He's gone on too long and it's too soon after lunch. If at this sleepy post-lunch hour he had the class act out a battle or improvise the costumes he is describing, the yawning disease might be cured. Instead it is likely to become a favorite part of the class repertoire, used to get Mr. Zell's goat and to put him down from his ego trip—not too roughly—rude but not too bad. Such noises may be heard as signals to the teacher that whatever he's doing is unlikely to work. One yawn or burp is physiological, two may be, but when yawning or burping gets to be a group activity, it's as clear a signal as a stop sign to do just that.

THE INNER CIRCLE LANGUAGE (THE LINGO)

Another not too serious contagious group disease is The Inner Circle Language or The Lingo. This phenomenon is as common in groups as inventing a password, a handshake, an oath of allegiance; all express group in-ness. We adults, too, have a Lingo in the jargon of our trades, one trade as clubby and exclusive as another. In Washington, for instance, it is possible to go to a cocktail party and hear a whole dialogue consisting of little more than initials, pronouns, and simple verbs: "Did you know he was riffed from the OAD after FTC lost part of its budget to the BLS?" This statement is seriously answered by: "Why, no, I thought his wife had got a job with HEW and that he had transferred to the AIS until the assistant secretary reestablished ONI."

A phrase comes in and is used again and again until it means everything and nothing, and then it disappears. But while it is in use, it delimits and bounds a group as strongly as a national border. It is as contagious to aspirants and ins as the common cold. If, as an adult, you don't understand the Lingo, you're out of it; but if you overuse it, you're thought, often accurately, to be regressively juvenile, or to be trying to con the young by seduction. For the Lingo is an age-group language; it catches on like fire in dry timber. Anyone who doesn't talk that way—whatever the way is for the moment—is considered queer. There are groups who as part of their unity against the outside world have developed a private, often graphic, group language all their own; the homosexual group, for instance, has idioms and phrases of its own. Sometimes a word, such as "gay," becomes public property, but often other words—"fag-hag," for example—are kept mostly within the inner circle. Likewise, there is the language of the drug group: they push or deal, trip down or out, shoot up, and freak in or out. Their names for the different drugs make up a dictionary in themselves. The Lingo is as transient as age itself and changes year to year. Since the lingo of special groups, including adolescents, is both contagious and exclusive, it is inclined to be ambiguous. A non-in adult, who deals with the group using it, first has to know which group is using which words and how, and how much of the lingo he as an outsider can be permitted to use before being seen as intrusive, as a group-language gate-crasher. The sin of knowing too much is held nearly as bad as the sin of knowing too little. Both extremes keep the outsider out—which is precisely what a special language is meant to do for the group it represents.

The strength of the lingo virus is explained by the needs it seeks to care for. It is part of the identity struggle and attempts to define who one's contemporary group is, as apart from the adults one is struggling to become independent of. For this reason, it is especially appropriate to adolescents, and particularly virulent during adolescence, since both identity and separation problems are being worked out by its use. The struggle is now to be a whole individual, on one's own, incorporating what one has learned from one's parents but no longer dependent on their approval or disapproval, their economic or emotional nurture, for one's course in life or one's decisions. Moreover, an even more primitive problem than identity is also alleviated by use of the Lingo—that of loneliness: use of the Lingo mitigates loneliness and makes one feel less isolated and more belonging. These three areas of need, then—identity, separation, and loneliness—are all partially cared for by the use of Lingo and account for the contagion it presents.

SOME WAYS TO HANDLE CONTAGION IN THE CLASSROOM

To help teachers feel more comfortable with group contagion, let's review four psychological and behavioral strategies that can be used to cope with group contagion in the classroom.

The first strategy is to be aware of the conditions that are necessary for group contagion to occur.

A. The group must be experiencing some common stress and feelings such as anger, sadness, fear, joy, boredom, etc.

B. The group member who gives expression to this feeling must be perceived by the group as having some status in the social structure of the classroom. For example, if a preferred pupil initiates the behavior, his social power in the classroom makes it safer for the other group members to imitate his behavior. This explains why pupils who are scapegoated, rejected, or ignored rarely have the manifest power to initiate contagion within a group.

c. The group member who initiates the contagion must behave in a manner which instantaneously communicates the message to the entire group, such as expressing group anger by dropping a book on the floor, expressing silliness by coughing, or expressing sadness by crying.

The second strategy is to decode group contagion by verbalizing to the group the underlying stress that initiated it, e.g., "It's clear to me that the group is telling me how angry, upset, bored, etc., it is about what happened when …" If the contagion continues, the third strategy is to walk over to the pupil who initiated the behavior and quietly but clearly escort him out of the classroom while telling the group what positive behavior you want, e.g., "I expect each one of you to turn to page 122 and answer the first four questions."

The fourth strategy is a function of the teacher's self-control. It is extremely important for the teacher not to threaten or yell at the group to stop this behavior immediately. This tactic frequently has the opposite effect of encouraging the acting out behavior. After all, group contagion is more irritating and upsetting than destructive and dangerous to the teacher. If group contagion doesn't succeed in creating teacher panic and confusion, its power will dissolve within five minutes into individual responses, which can be managed in the teacher's usual way.

Once again we note the importance of understanding the forces of group dynamics in the classroom. While no teacher is immune to group contagion, psychological insights provide the teachers with active choices instead of being overwhelmed by feelings of confusion, counter-aggression, or passivity.

ARTICLE 5.3

THE next article is by William Morse, who was founder and director of Fresh Air Camp (FAC), the University of Michigan's experimental therapeutic summer camp for delinquent preadolescent boys. This 8-week-long camp provided graduate students in psychology, social work, and special education with first-hand interdisciplinary counseling experience with delinquent youth, along with weekly individual supervision. It was a boot camp experience wrapped in a mental health climate. Counselors learned to live with the boys' disturbing behavior without becoming punitive or counteraggressive toward the youth. The goal was to understand the underlying concerns of these troubled campers and not to threaten them or moralize.

Graduate students who survived this camp felt it was the determining experience that influenced and directed their professional lives. Observing the experts in the field—including Fritz Redl, David Wineman, William Morse, Ralph Rabinovitch, Lee Saulk, and Elton B. McNeil—in action with delinquent campers raised expectations of what counselors needed to learn to be effective with these troubled boys. Unfortunately, this camp no longer exists. It was the beacon of professional innovation for approximately 15 years. This intense and personal clinical and educational experience created a fellowship among all the graduate students who attended this program.

Whenever colleagues discover that others also attended FAC, an instant interpersonal bond develops and old stories are exchanged. The one story all FAC counselors remember is the Mailbox Episode, which became a part of the FAC folklore. In the next article, William Morse describes the incident so readers can share the excitement of what it was like to be at this camp and observe the dynamic process of a group interview with these troubled preadolescent boys.

THE MAILBOX EPISODE: A DELINQUENT GROUP ACT
William C. Morse

Children learn very early to have individual and group lives that are not shared with adults. Therefore, parents, teachers, and staff often are oblivious to what goes on in delinquent group life.

The following incident was reported in a group therapy camp for emotionally disturbed boys. All the counselors were graduate students at the University of Michigan. The peer power hierarchy of the 11- and 12-year-old campers was established, so all seven boys knew the pecking order of their peers. Josh, a charming, bright, and very delinquent leader, had a close-knit subgroup of three followers, Ralph, George, and Pete. They were willing "privates" to Captain Josh, and the four boys did everything together. Billy and Hal were a separate twosome. Together they messed with no one, and the other peers did not mess with them. The final member was Raymond, a boy who had low self-esteem and who depended on adult attachment for his survival. He was slight of build and sometimes was even treated as a group mascot by Josh's group.

The group incident began on a hot, muggy July afternoon. The campers in Cabin 4 were scheduled for a 2-mile hike to the general country store. There was not great enthusiasm for the project. The boys asked for a truck ride rather than hiking, but with the inducement of getting ice cream, they started walking down the country road with their two counselors. Billy and Hal were out ahead, Raymond was with the counselors, and Josh's group was trailing behind. As the hike continued, the group got more strung out along the road, and the counselors periodically stopped to bring the campers together. However, Josh's group continued to lag behind and at a slight bend in the road they were out of sight. What they did as a group was learned by the staff much later.

This group—Josh, Ralph, George, and Pete—amused themselves by whatever means they could discover. When they passed a house, they would whack the trees on the side of the road with sticks. It made some noise and didn't hurt the trees, which were given profane titles as the enemy.

When they came upon three mailboxes for cottages along the road, Josh made a simple observation: "O, see dem three mailboxes." He later explained that all he did was make an observation, that free speech is the right of everybody. He commented, "What's wrong with that? Geezus." Josh insisted that it is not a crime to report an observation. He didn't do anything, suggested nothing, and didn't even touch any of the mailboxes. He didn't tell anyone to do anything. He merely saw the mailboxes and pointed them out to his friends.

But Ralph correctly interpreted Josh's comment as an invitation to look in the mailboxes. According to Ralph, he didn't do anything either. He just opened the boxes and reported their contents. He didn't touch any of the letters. He hadn't even see the boxes until Josh pointed them out. Otherwise, he would never have known the mailboxes existed. Ralph had his own anxieties. He knew about B&E (breaking and entering) and considered it to be a big-time crime that could send a person to prison. Now these two boys were convinced they did not do anything. All Ralph did was to open the boxes and report there was nothing in number one, a bunch of letters in number two, and nothing in number three.

This behavior is called the pie phenomenon. Each group member contributes a small piece to the incident, and nobody feels guilty about the total group behavior. There were two more pieces to the pie. George would never do B&E because he would be sent back to juvenile detention, which was a frightening experience. But because the B&E had been accomplished by the other boys, George was free to take out the letters and open them as Pete egged him on.

Josh, being the leader of this group, stepped in to take the contents of the open letters from George. Although Josh had been in Juvenile Court for stealing a welfare check, he distributed two checks to his friends and kept the largest one for himself. The torn envelopes were thrown by the roadside. Josh warned the group not to show the checks at the local general store and told them they would have to figure out how to find someone to act as a fence. This entire incident happened in less time than it takes to read the story. The counselors came in sight and stopped. Josh and his subgroup joined the others, and the group walked to the store to get their treats.

At the store, the wily proprietor would only let in two boys at a time plus the two counselors. There was no trouble at the store, but there was considerable bragging about what the boys had stolen when they returned to camp.

On the way back to camp, another pie phenomenon took place. Josh looked again at his check. It was written for over $10, and his fingerprints were on it. He told the others that stolen goods worth over $10 were tickets to prison. (Like many delinquents, he had a number of irrational beliefs.) He knew his smudgy hands left vivid fingerprints. He told his group he was going to destroy the evidence, so he tore up the check and threw the pieces along the roadside. Now he was totally free. He didn't do anything, and the evidence that might have caused him trouble had been destroyed. This started a group contagion chain: The other boys did the same. This brought closure to the event in their young minds, and they went swimming as soon as they were back in camp. There was not a shred of guilt now. Any latent anxiety and excitement was over. Now the slate was clear.

As the boys joked about this incident, a counselor overheard and reported it to me. I called the four boys and their counselors into our crisis room and began a Life Space Group Interview. As the timeline of the event became clear, the staff were surprised at how comfortable the boys were talking about the incident. When we raised the question about their involvement in taking the checks, the boys had a ready answer: "You would be crazy not to take money offered to you by a friend. What are you supposed to do? Do nothing?" After this 2-hour session, staff were sent to find any pieces of the checks.

Fortunately, a neighbor saw the pieces of the checks by the roadside. She reported it to the local mail carrier and to a neighbor whose name was on a check. Meanwhile, I learned the neighbor's name and met with her. It turned out she was a retired teacher from the city where many of the boys lived. She had taught many such students and understood their problems. She said if we could arrange for a replacement check, that would be the end of it. I thanked her for her sympathetic attitude and assured her we would confront the responsible campers. But that was not the end of the incident.

The call to the local post office had started another sequence of events. Previously, the local postman had asked that the camp be closed when he heard a camper let off a stream of foul language at a female counselor. He believed that she should never have to hear such abusive language, that this camp had no place in their rural countryside, and that these delinquents should be sent back to the city where they belonged. Our talks with him about the purpose of the camp were to no avail. Now he had an opportunity to do something about it.

Because tampering with mail is a federal offense, the postman reported the event to the Federal District Office. They turned the matter over to the Michigan state police. Two days later, two uniformed police officers came to the camp and asked to see the boys. It was obvious to us that this meeting was a duty they had to perform as quickly as possible and that they were at a loss as to what to do. I was asked to sit in on the meeting. In our initial conversation it was clear the police were after group contrition, repentance, and an assurance the boys would never steal again. All of the boys were to demonstrate they had learned a lesson because they were all involved in the incident. Individual roles were ignored.

The session started with the two officers, the seven boys, and me (the camp director). The boys paid no attention to me. The opening gambit was initiated by Josh and his group. They began questioning the police while the others sat quietly in their chairs. They gathered around the towering troopers and asked about their guns, if they had shot them and killed anyone. The boys asked to see the guns. At this point the officers took over, told them to sit down, and warned them that if they didn't pay close attention, they all would be sent home today. This changed the tone of the meeting; the kids could see they were faced with a real problem even if they had "done nothing." They listened to the lecture on their crime and what could happen to them if they didn't change.

At this time Raymond started to cry and wanted to call his social worker. He was told he would have to wait. After this crime and punishment lecture, the police said they were going to go outside for 5 minutes and wanted everybody to think about what they had done. While they were out of the room, the four culprits started to talk among themselves. What could they do? Josh had cased the situation and told them to tell the police how sorry they were and that they would never do it again.

When the police came back, all four boys repented. The other boys who were not involved said nothing. This caused another serious talk by the police. The police gave them a second chance to repent. Once the police left the room again, Josh took over. He told the boys there was nothing to worry about. He told them that even if they were not involved, they should pretend that they were and say they had learned their lesson. When the police returned, George and Pete said they had learned their lesson. Ray did not say anything, was tearful, and kept asking to call his social worker. The officers said that all or none of them could stay in camp. Josh got on his knees in front of Ray, held his hands as if in prayer, and pleaded in a kindly way. He sounded very sincere instead of threatening. Josh pleaded, "We know you didn't do nothin'. You ain't going to get in no trouble. We will protect you. But the only way is to tell them you are sorry." Ray protested that it would be a lie. Josh said it would not really be a lie because he would just be helping his friends. Nothing bad would happen. All Ray had to say was that he was sorry and would never do anything like that anymore. Then it would be over, they could all go swimming, and Ray could call his social worker. Josh said that the director knew that Ray was a good kid and would talk to his social worker.

It worked. Ray recited the catechism, there was another lecture, and the police let them go, but not before they gave one more warning. The boys again wanted to know about the guns and if the police had ever had a car chase. The boys then were excused to go swimming or make a phone call. The police said they would write up the report and commented, "These are just a sad bunch of little kids."

Later the staff held both individual and group sessions with the boys. We reviewed the way the group had worked and the roles the campers played. We also had the boys recall other negative examples of group experience. We had them think of their own group roles. With Josh, who was an effective leader, we encouraged his talent but worked with him about positive ways he could use it. There were interesting talks about their lives and the delinquent role models they had. Ray got to talk with his social worker. In the absence of any realization that they could have been in serious trouble, and with no feeling of having done anything wrong, the boys demonstrated no obvious anxiety. Considerable time was spent with each individual camper to make sure he understood the group process. Did any of these reclaiming efforts make a difference in their lives? We had doubts. But it did make a difference in our understanding of group dynamics and the need to appreciate their peer culture with a keener awareness of their world. These boys were teachers for the whole staff on the need to combine vigilance with awareness when helping delinquent youth.

EDITORS' COMMENTARY

This delinquent group act broke the law. Although adults were inconvenienced, no one was killed or injured. But this is not always the case. We are aware of several group killings in which this same group dynamic concept was at work. In those instances, gang members of one group attack, beat, and in the process kill a member of a rival gang. These acts of homicide cannot be understood by examining the behavior of individual gang members. In fact, no group member will take responsibility for the murder. It can only be explained by realizing how each gang member contributed to the "group act of murder."

After-the-murder comments by individual members might sound like this: "I only saw Juan and pointed him out to my friends." "I was walking along minding my own business when Juan was pointed out to me. I only said, 'Isn't he a member of that gang we hate?' " "I did not do anything but I said, 'Someone ought to teach him a lesson. This is our area!' " "All I did was walk up to him, call him a name, and tell him to get the f— out of here because he was in our territory." "I heard Juan bad-mouth my friend like he was disrespecting us. I told him to shut up. He didn't, so I pushed him." "I saw this guy trying to run away from my friend so I tackled him." "I saw my buddy rolling on the ground with this other gang member so I jumped in to help him."

Then the group obviously became excited, and group contagion took over. One member hit Juan, another kicked him, a third struck him in the head, a fourth punched him, and so on. Juan was unconscious and bleeding, the excitement was over, and each gang member walked away. Not one of them later believed he was responsible for the death of Juan.

This example shows the destructive power of the pie phenomenon and why some gang behaviors need to be viewed as group phenomena rather than the acts of individual group members.

CLASSROOM GROUP PROGRAMS THAT WORK

As described in this section of this chapter, various group programs can be effective in the classroom. Nicholas Hobbs's name is associated with the importance of group programs for troubled students. He was one of the leading mental health and educational pioneers to advocate the significant role that group life plays in the development and re-education of troubled children and youth. His book *The Troubled and Troubling Child* (1982) provided the theoretical and practical guidelines for the development of the American Re-EDucation Association. Hobbs believed that group experiences should be intrinsic and continuous in order to help each member of the group grow in competence, self-esteem, and compassion. According to him, the task of the teacher–counselor is to build a culture of group safety, acceptance, and new social skills for these students.

Hobbs proposed an additional group experience within his Re-ED milieu called the "Pow-wow," or Classroom Meeting. This group meeting provides students with different ways of understanding and resolving daily classroom issues and has become an essential part of the treatment program. The Classroom Meeting is an effective group concept that we believe should be a part of any strength-based reclaiming educational program.

IN the next article, Tom Valore, the director of training at the Positive Education Program (PEP) in Cleveland, Ohio, describes the characteristics of the Classroom Meeting. PEP is based on Hobbs's 10 principles of re-education and is one of the most comprehensive and successful Re-ED treatment programs in the country. The Classroom Meeting is a direct approach to helping troubled students and is scheduled on a regular basis. A student learns

ARTICLE 5.4

that he or she is not the only one who has troubles. Members discuss various classroom and personal problems and employ problem-solving skills to find acceptable group solutions. Proposed behavioral changes are tried out and reassessed at subsequent sessions.

CREATING COHESIVE GROUPS IN RE-ED SETTINGS: THE CLASSROOM MEETING
Thomas G. Valore

Group work in Re-ED programs has been a foundation of intervention since 1962 when the first of the two Re-ED schools, Cumberland House Elementary School and Wright School, opened their doors (Cantrell, Cantrell, Valore, Jones, & Fecser, 1999; Freeman et al., 1971; Hobbs, 1982; Rousseau, 1971). Hobbs (1982) believed that group work with troubled and troubling children was so important that he included it as one of his 12 Re-ED principles: "The group is very important to young people; it can be a major source of instruction in growing up" (p. 22).

FORMING POSITIVE, COHESIVE GROUP CULTURES

A major goal of Re-ED groups is to form healthy, positive, cohesive cultures that help troubled and troubling children and youth change their behavior. A significant factor in achieving this goal is the development of group cohesion. Group cohesion is defined as "the attraction to the group, including resistance to leaving it" (Shaw, 1981, p. 213).

Group cohesion was found to be a significant factor in a variety of contexts, including therapeutic groups (Bednar & Lawlis, 1971; Yalom, 1995), task groups (Cartwright, 1968), living units (Moos, 1976, 1979), and classroom settings (Long, Morse, & Newman, 1996; Schmuck & Schmuck, 1983; Valore, 1991; Vorrath & Brendtro, 1985). Moreover, group cohesion has also been identified as a salient factor in group processes, for example,

Printed with permission of the author.

in the achievement of established group goals (Lodahl & Porter, 1961; Rose, 1998), conformity to group norm requirements (Back, 1951; O'Keefe, Kernaghan, & Rubenstein, 1975), and behavior change (Grotjahn, 1981; Yalom, 1995).

THERAPEUTIC ADVANTAGES

Members who participate in highly cohesive groups experience several therapeutic advantages. For example, cohesive groups engage in a greater frequency of social interaction (French, 1941; Lott & Lott, 1961), engage in more positive interactions (Schachter, Ellertson, McBride, & Gregory, 1951), exert greater influence over their members (Back, 1951), are more effective in achieving goals (Shaw & Shaw, 1962), and have higher member satisfaction (Gross, 1954).

Schmuck and Schmuck (1983) claimed that group cohesiveness among students is a central feature in the development of a positive classroom climate. They wrote that a cohesive classroom group is "made up of students who are actively involved with one another, who care about one another, and who help one another" (p. 153).

It is clear that group cohesion is a powerful force wherever youth function in small groups. According to Yalom (1995), group cohesion is "a necessary precondition for other therapeutic factors to function optimally" (p. 49). He further stated that "cohesiveness in group therapy is the analogue of relationship in individual therapy" (1995, p. 47). Cohesive groups facilitate therapeutic relationships among the teacher–counselor, the group members, and the group as a whole. These relationships provide members with a feeling of acceptance that enables them to safely share their feelings and inner thoughts and to help one another. Guiding the development of this necessary component of group process is the teacher–counselor.

RE-ED COHESION BUILDING STRATEGIES

Developing a group of youth into a cohesive unit requires not only the specific skills and knowledge of the teacher–counselor but also specific cohesion building strategies. Group cohesion building strategies have been, as Rousseau (1971) stated, "borrowed, created, structured, and refined" (p. 10) beginning with the earliest pioneers of Re-ED. These strategies can be seen in the early writings of Doncaster (1972), Freeman et al.

(1971), Hobbs (1982), Kaset (n.d.), and West, Albright, Jones, Ransom, and Richman (1980), as well as in the *Group Process Manual* (1983). Over the years the list of strategies has grown and become more formalized, structured, and teachable, resulting in the 12 cohesion building strategies Re-ED programs use (Valore, 1992). The 12 strategies follow.

1. ***Name the group.*** This first strategy is critical in the creation of a cohesive and healthy group identity. Because of the importance of a name, groups often take up to a week or more to decide on one. Deciding on a positive and healthy name helps in guiding the group to a positive and healthy group identity, whereas negative names tend to promote a negative, unhealthy group identity. Teacher–counselors guide the process of naming the group with the goal that a positive theme (e.g., sports, animals, nautical, aviation, acronyms) can naturally grow from the name and be used to reinforce the group's identity. With continual attention, these themes become pervasive, infiltrating most systems and activities of the group. Such themes can be used to name positive behavior management systems; for special academic or behavioral awards or recognition; to provide visuals to set up a group behavioral contract; and for group ceremonies, rituals, and routines.

2. ***Refer to the group by name.*** For group members to feel a connection to or ownership of the name, it has to be used. Teacher–counselors should use the group's name throughout the day when addressing the group, as in, "Okay, the Navigators need to get ready for …," "TEAM (Together Each Achieves More) 68 will be going to the museum today," "Let's see the Mountaineers line up for bathroom break," or "Looks like it's time for the All Stars group meeting." Teacher–counselors should also encourage and reinforce all members to use the group name.

3. ***Generate group traditions.*** As Re-ED groups spend time together, many traditions evolve. These are special group-specific activities, rituals, objects, ceremonies, and so on, that lend uniqueness and provide an emotional connection to the group. Traditions help to establish a culture and convey the group's legacy by celebrating current and past events. Groups accomplish this by creating and maintaining diaries, photo albums, bulletin boards, and other types of records that describe significant group events. Traditions also help to celebrate accomplishments. Secret handshakes, rhythmic and synchronized hand clapping, special cheers, and so forth, are used to acknowledge academic achievement, behavioral progress, and family and other successes outside school.

4. *Develop group rules and values.* Another way to foster a cohesive group is to develop rules and values. Rules clarify *what to do* and *how to behave*. Rules should be few in number and stated positively, informing the students what to do rather than what not to do.

Values explain *why* the rules are created. Values provide the energy and motivation for following specific rules. One without the other loses impact, especially with troubled and troubling youth. Students are more likely to follow specific rules if they are connected to values. For example, one value for the rule "Follow teacher's directions" may be that school is a place where people learn. Likewise, the rule "Keep hands and feet to self" would be connected to the value of students' feeling and being safe at all times in school. Additionally, the value behind the rule "Participate with the group" would be to encourage everyone to be responsible for helping each other. Developing and encouraging values also help to create a culture of caring.

The process of discussing rules and values takes time and is important for several reasons. In younger groups, it may be the students' introduction to learning rules, values, and their interrelationship. In older groups, students know the basic rules of a classroom; however, they typically lack an understanding of the connection between rules and values. The development of rules and values articulates the group's code of conduct. Establishing rules also avoids the problems associated with an absence or lack of focus on rules, which students can construe as an opportunity to construct their own less desirable and nontherapeutic rules. Lastly, having students participate in the development of rules reduces their opposition to them.

5. *Set group goals.* Hobbs (1982) stated that "a group goal was a task that the group as a whole would strive to achieve" (p. 339). Group goals are worked on every moment of the day by every member. Each group member is responsible for his or her behavior and for the behavior of all other members. The primary group goal of every Re-ED group is to improve the overall functioning of the group, leading to successful transition from the program. Setting group goals is akin to a mission; group members should strive to articulate their purpose for being a group. The group addresses questions such as, "Why are we here?" and "What are we individually and as a group trying to accomplish?" There are also less formal goals that the group identifies and explores. Teacher–counselors facilitate discussions around less conventional goals like learning to laugh, play, share, and find joy in each day.

6. *Establish group norms.* Group norms are expectations for behavior but are different from rules. Rules govern what members should or should not do. Norms are less defined—they also govern behavior but in a less structured way. They are more like road maps that guide decisions as to how group members should think and act because of values and beliefs. Norms promote prosocial, responsible, caring behavior and improved self-esteem. In Re-ED groups, the underlying objective of discussing norms is to provide opportunities for altruism and hope. Norms typically discussed and adopted include members' dissatisfaction with their existing behavior and the eagerness to change it by learning new behaviors. Other guiding norms include experimentation with new behaviors, supporting others, and providing helpful and nonjudgmental interpersonal feedback.

7. *Promote teamwork.* Teacher–counselors promote teamwork by recognizing, encouraging, and reinforcing behavior that cultivates collaboration and cooperation among members. Teamwork is encouraged during academics (e.g., cooperative learning groups), group meetings, outdoor education/recreational therapy, leisure activities, and mealtimes. Each day, teacher–counselors consider the schedule of tasks to be accomplished and design opportunities for teamwork to occur. As a result, throughout the day members work together to complete academic assignments on time and to improve the group's overall accuracy; increase the group's daily behavior rating average; help each other earn goal activity, choice time, and field trips; help prepare and serve meals; and assist with many other instances created by the teacher–counselor.

8. *Engage members in various group activities.* Although group activities, projects, and camping experiences occur less frequently, they have a powerful effect on increasing the cohesiveness of groups. For the most part, group activities occur during structured recreational periods, outdoor education lessons, and camping trips. Group activities such as team building games and initiative tasks are designed to increase the ability of the group to work together cooperatively. Team building games are noncompetitive activities ranging from using paper and pencil (e.g., a blank coat of arms symbol to describe and share qualities about themselves) to initiating low-risk physical exercises (e.g., engaging in noncompetitive volleyball where both sides receive a point for each successful volley across the net).

Initiative tasks are more intense physical challenges. In these efforts, the teacher–counselor produces a problem or obstacle that can only be resolved or conquered successfully by the synergistic engagement of all group members. There are two types of initiatives used with Re-ED groups: natural and organized. Natural initiatives can happen spontaneously (e.g., the river that the group is to cross is running higher than expected) or they can be planned with the creative assistance of the teacher–counselor (e.g., challenging the group to scale the large stepped wall of the limestone quarry). Organized initiatives are developed for the specific purpose of challenging kids. These are typically found in Boy Scout camps and are arranged in a manner similar to an obstacle course, ranging from least to most difficult. The initiative courses are demanding, requiring group members to work as a unit to overcome each obstacle (e.g., helping each member over the imagined "electric fence" until all are on the other side).

Not only do initiatives build cohesiveness, but they also allow the teacher–counselor to periodically assess the group's level of cohesiveness—the stage at which the group is functioning—and the roles of individual members. To better understand the dynamics of their group (especially less cohesive groups), teacher–counselors pay particular attention, especially during the beginning initiatives, to the following patterns: (a) making an initial haphazard attempt at overcoming the obstacle, (b) exhibiting play behavior and argumentation as a result of frustration, (c) responding to the emerging leader or leaders, (d) solving problems and planning as a group, (e) exerting peer pressure to include all members, and (f) engaging in a cohesive group effort.

Group projects are employed by the teacher–counselor to increase the cohesiveness of the group. One of the most popular Re-ED group projects is the enterprise unit. The enterprise unit is "a group activity designed to make learning relevant and meaningful" (Hobbs, 1982, p. 336). The idea for any enterprise unit initially emerges from the interest of the group members. Enterprise units take many forms, from a simple small business of selling snacks in school, to growing a vegetable garden for the local hunger center, to recording and producing music albums. As the group's idea takes form through planning meetings, the teacher–counselor begins the process of merging academic content into the project for each member, thereby supporting the academic program. The rallying and interdependence of group members to achieve the goals and objectives of the enterprise unit increases the cohesiveness of the group.

9. *Use group contingencies.* A group contingency is an understanding or contract among all members in which the consequences for all members of the group depend on the behavior of each individual member. The consequences of group contingencies can be either punishing or reinforcing. Needless to say, Re-ED's focus is on the latter. Using reinforcing group contingencies can help turn a negative culture around because it engages the group in prosocial behavior. It can change the thinking of troubled and troubling members from, "How can I *not* get caught doing _____ (something harmful, offensive, etc.)?" to "How *can* I get caught doing _____ (something appropriate, responsible, etc.)?" There are several ways group contingencies are implemented; some examples follow.

Teacher–counselors use group contingencies to improve daily rituals and routines (e.g., "As soon as the Navigators are quiet, we can line up"). Kitchen timers set at random time intervals can be used to "catch the group being good" for general classroom behavior improvement. To support the academic program, the group enlists members to encourage one another to improve their overall percentage on class assignments. Group contingencies are also used to reduce and extinguish those annoying and disruptive surreptitious behaviors such as spitballs and specific disturbing noises. Instead of engaging in the "whodunit" game, teacher–counselors will award points to the group for every X number of minutes that pass without incident. Members are rewarded after accumulating a specific number of points. Over time, the teacher–counselor gradually increases the number of minutes until the behavior has been extinguished.

10. ***Make group meetings part of the daily schedule.*** The use of group meetings is probably the most powerful cohesion building technique. Through group meetings the teacher–counselor can immerse the members in a feeling of *groupness* and togetherness. Most group theorists and practitioners concentrate on either the individual or the group as the focus of behavior change. In Re-ED, the basis of group work is ecological, focusing on the individual, the group as a whole, and the home and community that affect each member. There are four basic types of group meetings: the Planning, Positives, Problem-Solving, and Evaluation meetings. A more in-depth look at these four meetings follows this list of cohesion building strategies.

11. ***Model to facilitate cohesive interaction and participation.*** Through the work of Albert Bandura (1971) and others, a solid research base exists supporting the elements, procedures, and effectiveness of modeling. The application of modeling in the formation of cohesive groups cannot be overlooked. Teacher–counselors model that the group is impor-

tant by attending all meetings, showing interest in group meetings and activities, and exhibiting energy and enthusiasm. Teacher–counselors are very aware that if the adult lacks enthusiasm, so will the members. Some incredibly touching, poignant, even "corny" but fun and healthy activities and behaviors have worked beautifully because of an adult's genuine enthusiasm, participation, and caring.

*12. **Reinforce cohesive behavior.*** Cohesive behavior is not typical of students in programs for troubled and troubling youth. Students who learn new behaviors, or relearn appropriate and responsible behaviors, require shaping, prompting, and cuing. Teacher–counselors are continually watchful that rules are being followed, norms are taking hold, and traditions are being practiced, and they use these moments as opportunities to reinforce members' cohesive group behavior. It is through the teacher–counselor's constant attention and reinforcement of cohesive behaviors that group members directly and vicariously learn what desirable group behavior is and then engage in it.

RE-ED GROUP MEETINGS

Within Re-ED programs, the use of group meetings is one of the most powerful cohesion building strategies. Through group meetings the teacher–counselor can immerse the members in a feeling of belonging and togetherness. Group meetings, of which there are several types, are the most frequently used strategies in Re-ED to harness the power of the group for therapeutic and instructional purposes.

For the past several decades, group work has played an important role in the treatment of troubled youth. Through group meetings, therapy has aimed to help children gain awareness of their problems; express feelings, wishes, and conflicts; and develop a healthy personality leading to appropriate socialization (Kazdin, 1985). Successful group work is performed in the context of an ongoing therapeutic group milieu (Valore, Cantrell, & Cantrell, 2006) as opposed to the more traditional weekly group therapy meetings or informal peer groups (e.g., Boy Scouts, YMCA groups) that Dishion, McCord, and Poulin (1999) found ineffective. The following is an overview of the structure, format, and purpose of the four types of meetings. It should be noted that the therapeutic power comes from the culture developed through the norms, cohesiveness, and, most important, the therapeutic alliance between the teacher–counselor and group members.

Teacher–counselors incorporate group meetings into their daily schedules to provide opportunities for students to develop several skills and to address their irrational thinking or cognitive distortions. Youth practice communication, interpersonal, and intellectual skills that lead to behavior change and emotional growth. Students also learn to identify effective solutions and appropriate behavioral choices through problem solving in group meetings. In groups, students learn to plan and to organize in order to become more productive and to have more manageable and less anxiety-producing lives (Hobbs, 1982). Students are able to focus on their positive accomplishments, thereby raising their concepts of themselves and their capabilities (Gallagher, 1979; Hobbs, 1982).

Four types of group meetings have remained central and pivotal throughout Re-ED's history: Planning, Positives, Problem-Solving, and Evaluation. Other topic-specific meetings, such as anger control, social skills, and character development, can occur or be woven into one of the four meetings, depending on the needs of the group.

PLANNING MEETING

The Planning meeting is held to prepare and plan for the group's daily and weekly activities (e.g., scheduling outdoor activities, writing letters, developing a food menu for a camping trip, arranging transportation, buying supplies). In Re-ED residential settings, the Sunday night Planning meeting is reserved for the evening activities of the coming week and is conducted by the night teacher–counselor. The day teacher–counselor is responsible for the Monday morning Planning meeting, during which the group develops plans for the daytime activities of the week. In nonresidential settings the Planning meeting is used to plan for the week's activities as well.

As the least complex and demanding of the four meetings, the Planning meeting serves to enable the novice teacher–counselor to increase skills and gain experience in group work. This meeting is also a helpful way to introduce new or low-cohesive groups to the group experience, because it is the least emotion-laden of the four meetings. Skilled teacher–counselors frequently engage new or low-cohesive groups in brief Planning meetings prior to most activities, thereby increasing the probability of success in an activity and offering multiple opportunities to practice group skills that will generalize to other meetings.

POSITIVES MEETING

The Positives meeting was originally a major part of the Evaluation meeting held at the end of the day. Because of its importance, however, it has become a separate meeting. The Positives meeting enhances the self-concept of each member by drawing attention to successes, providing a format and forum for peer reinforcement, and developing communication skills. This meeting typically occurs at the end of each day prior to dismissal to home in community-based settings, or just before bedtime in residential settings or on camping trips. Many possible formats can be used during the Positives meeting. The traditional format begins with one group member stating something positive (an act, deed, accomplishment, etc.) that he or she did that day and one specific "positive" about someone else in the group. After he or she finishes, other members can volunteer a positive statement to the member. Following the volunteered positives, the member chooses someone else to continue the process. This format continues until every member has participated (including the teacher–counselor).

PROBLEM-SOLVING MEETING

The Problem-Solving meeting is designed to teach group members the processes and techniques needed to resolve problems and conflicts effectively and peacefully. This type of meeting may be requested when any situation creates a problem for one or more group members, affecting the group. The teacher–counselor may call a meeting if he or she determines that a situation calls for a group solution to a group problem (e.g., the increasing classroom disruption during nonacademic periods) or that a difficult situation requires a group decision (e.g., how to help the local hunger center during a time of need). Re-ED Problem-Solving meetings are solution based. When a problem exists between group members or with the behavior of one member that affects the group, the emphasis is on solutions leading to responsible, caring behavior, rather than solutions based on punishment.

The procedure begins with a request for a Problem-Solving meeting. The group identifies or defines the problem and decides whether it requires a group decision. If the problem does require group input, the group assembles. A typical beginning ritual includes a call to order, leader selection, and review of the daily schedule as well as academics and other tasks that need to be completed despite schedule interruption. Following the beginning ritual, there is a statement of the problem from the "complainant" and a defense statement from the "defendant" (if relevant). Next, the group focuses on the solution. The group may also evaluate whether to apply the consequences of breaking existing rules. Lastly, before expectations are set for schedule recovery and the closing ritual, group members vote or reach consensus and commit to the solution. Depending on the age, stage, and cohesion of the group, Problem-Solving meetings can be simple "solution-seeking" activities or highly complex and powerful therapeutic group work. A highly cohesive group of adolescents, for example, may engage in problem-solving discussions around difficult issues in their lives. Such discussions require a safe and trustworthy setting, which the Problem-Solving meeting provides.

EVALUATION MEETING

The last type of group meeting, the Evaluation meeting, provides daily feedback to members regarding their overall progress. An individual goal procedure is one central structure for providing feedback. The method is devoted primarily to formulating or evaluating a behavior goal and plan for each member. The procedure calls for each member to formulate a short-term goal and to develop a plan that will assist the member in achieving that goal. Teacher–counselors lead members to state their goals positively. Goals are set to accelerate strengths or to build new ones that address needs.

During the meeting, each member states his or her goal and plan, evaluates his or her progress, and receives feedback from other group members, who may be asked to say how they can help the member meet his or her goals. If the member is making progress and the plan is working, the member will continue working on the goal until he or she achieves it (using criteria set by the group). If sufficient progress is not made, then the meeting is used to discuss how to adjust the goal or plan. After the member attains the goal, a new goal and plan are developed. A more indepth look at the individual goal procedure is described in other Re-ED writings on group work (Valore, 1992; Valore et al., 1992; Warren & Maxwell, 1983).

CONCLUSION

In Re-ED, the foundation of group work is ecological, focusing on the individual, the group as a whole, and the outside forces that affect each member. The teacher–counselor is continually assessing the group from an ecological perspective. Guiding the group involves knowing each student's individual strengths and needs (academic, social–emotional, behavioral, and cultural) and how those strengths and needs will affect the individual, the group, and the individual's ecosystem.

Group work is complicated and labor intensive. Guiding a group of individuals into a positive, healthy, and cohesive unit takes patience and hard work, but the benefits are tremendous, as one can glean from the following vignette.

AN EXAMPLE OF A CLASSROOM MEETING

Following a Problem-Solving meeting in a highly cohesive group of older adolescents, the group was quiet and somber as they returned to their seats. The meeting was called because a music compact disc was missing from a student's desk. There was strong circumstantial evidence that Monica, the new student in the group, had stolen the disc. The group had come together, discussed the problem, and presented the evidence, but Monica denied stealing the disc. The group's discussion centered around the topics of trust, what they valued, and how long and hard they had worked to develop their culture. During the meeting, there was no yelling or screaming, except for Monica's loud cry of denial. The members stated their disappointment that this theft had taken place, that there were no consequences, and that they could do nothing more about the situation because there was no direct proof. They also said they were saddened that this would set the group back because trust had been broken and they would now have to be watchful of their possessions. The group discussion ended, and daily activities resumed.

The next morning, Monica called a Problem-Solving meeting. She began by admitting to the group that she had stolen the disc, by apologizing to the group, and by returning the stolen item. She stated that she disliked stealing, but in her former classroom everyone took what they wanted because that was the way things were. She said that even the teachers in her former classroom told students, "Better watch your stuff in here." No one seemed to care or to encourage trust.

The group accepted Monica's apology and further discussed the group's history and reputation. Near the end of the discussion, one member stated, "When I first came to this classroom from being kicked out of my high school, I was handed trust. I was amazed that I didn't have to earn it. No one ever had given me such a gift before. Today, I think we can give that gift to you."

The meeting ended and students resumed their activities, satisfied this time. Dr. Hobbs would also be satisfied and proud to know of this victory in human relatedness, in which the outsider accepted the invitation to join the group.

REFERENCES

Back, K. W. (1951). Influence through social communication. *Journal of Abnormal and Social Psychology, 46,* 9–23.

Bandura, A. (1971). *Social learning theory.* New York: General Learning.

Bednar, R. L., & Lawlis, G. (1971). Empirical research in group psychotherapy. In A. E. Bergin & S. L. Garfield (Eds.), *Handbook of psychotherapy and behavior change* (pp. 812–838). New York: Wiley.

Cantrell, M. L., Cantrell, R. P., Valore, T. G., Jones, J. M., & Fecser, F. A. (1999). A revisitation of the ecological perspectives on emotional/behavioral disorders. In L. M. Bullock & R. A. Gable (Eds.), *The third mini-library series: What works for children and youth with E/BD: Linking yesterday and today with tomorrow.* Reston, VA: Council for Children with Behavioral Disorders.

Cartwright, D. (1968). The nature of group cohesiveness. In D. Cartwright & A. Zander (Eds.), *Group dynamics research and theory* (3rd ed., pp. 91–109). New York: Harper & Row.

Dishion, T. J., McCord, J., & Poulin, F. (1999). When interventions harm. *American Psychologist, 54,* 755–764.

Doncaster, J. (1972). *The self government system: The therapeutic use of group process.* Unpublished manuscript, The Pressley Ridge Schools, Pittsburgh, PA.

Freeman, R., Henon, J., Hogan, E. J., Kohl, J., Rousseau, F., Slagle, R., et al. (1971). *Group process in the Re-Education school.* Unpublished manuscript, The Information-Dissemination Office, Tennessee Re-Education Program, Tennessee Department of Mental Health.

French, J. R. P., Jr. (1941). The disruption and cohesion of groups. *Journal of Abnormal and Social Psychology, 36,* 361–377.

Gallagher, P. A. (1979). *Teaching students with behavior disorders: Techniques for classroom instruction.* Denver: Love.

Gross, E. (1954). Primary functions of the small group. *American Journal of Sociology, 60*(1), 24–29.

Grotjahn, M. (1981). Group cohesion as a factor in the therapeutic process. In H. Kellerman (Ed.), *Group cohesion* (pp. 247–253). New York: Grune & Stratton.

Group Process Manual. (1983). Unpublished manuscript, The Pressley Ridge Schools, Pittsburgh, PA.

Hobbs, N. (1982). *The troubled and troubling child: Re-Education in mental health, education and human services programs for children and youth.* San Francisco: Jossey-Bass.

Kaset, L. (n.d.). *Group process, goals, and evaluation rap.* Unpublished manuscript.

Kazdin, A. E. (1985). *Treatment of antisocial behavior in children and adolescents.* Homewood, IL: Dorsey.

Lodahl, T. M., & Porter, L. W. (1961). Psychometric score patterns, social characteristics, and productivity of small industrial work groups. *Journal of Applied Psychology, 45*(2), 73–79.

Long, N. J., Morse, W. C., & Newman, R. G. (Eds.). (1996). *Conflict in the classroom: The education of at-risk and troubled students* (5th ed.). Austin, TX: PRO-ED.

Lott, A. J., & Lott, B. E. (1961). Group cohesiveness, communication level, and conformity. *Journal of Abnormal and Social Psychology, 62*(2), 408–412.

Moos, R. H. (1976). *The human context: Environmental determinants of behavior.* New York: Wiley.

Moos, R. H. (1979). *Evaluating educational environments.* San Francisco: Jossey-Bass.

O'Keefe, R. D., Kernaghan, J. A., & Rubenstein, A. H. (1975). Group cohesiveness: A factor in the adoption of innovations among scientific work groups. *Small Group Behavior, 6,* 282–292.

Rose, S. D. (1998). *Group therapy with troubled youth.* Thousand Oaks, CA: Sage.

Rousseau, F. (1971). *Behavioral programming in the Re-Education school.* Unpublished manuscript, The Information-Dissemination Office, Tennessee Re-Education Program, Tennessee Department of Mental Health.

Schachter, S., Ellertson, N., McBride, D., & Gregory, D. (1951). An experimental study of cohesiveness and productivity. *Human Relations, 4,* 229–238.

Schmuck, R. A., & Schmuck, P. A. (1983). *Group processes in the classroom* (4th ed.). Dubuque, IA: Brown.

Shaw, M. E. (1981). *Group dynamics* (3rd ed.). New York: McGraw-Hill.

Shaw, M. E., & Shaw, L. M. (1962). Some effects of sociometric grouping upon learning in a second grade classroom. *Journal of Social Psychology, 57,* 453–458.

Valore, T. G. (1991). The group meeting cohesion profile: A reliability and validity study. *Dissertation Abstracts International, 53*(8), 2770A. (UMI No. 9238107)

Valore, T. G. (1992). *Group process in Re-ED.* Unpublished manuscript, Positive Education Program, Cleveland, OH.

Valore, T. G., Cantrell, R. P., & Cantrell, M. L. (2006). Competency building in the context of groups. *Reclaiming Children and Youth, 14*(4), 228–235.

Valore, T. G., Fecser, F. A., Valore, C. L., Bockmiller, S., Siemen, K., & Warren, R. S. (1992). *Group process.* Unpublished manuscript, Positive Education Program, Cleveland, OH.

Vorrath, H. H., & Brendtro, L. K. (1985). *Positive peer culture.* Chicago: Aldine.

Warren, R. S., & Maxwell, M. L. (1983). *Group meetings.* Unpublished manuscript, Positive Education Program, Cleveland, OH.

West, F., Albright, L., Jones, J. M., Ransom, L., & Richman, E. (1980). *Group process.* Unpublished manuscript, Positive Education Program, Cleveland, OH.

Yalom, I. D. (1995). *The theory and practice of group psychotherapy* (4th ed.). New York: Basic Books.

EDITORS' COMMENTARY

Another way to build group cohesion is to plan projects. The group selects a common goal and works together on an art project, a music presentation, a dance performance, a holiday play, a community project, or planning an exciting "fun event" together to create good memories. A class project that involves doing something for others can also enhance positive togetherness. Selecting a class name, flag, or insignia and posting individual pictures may foster positive belonging. Action-oriented activities can engender a positive feeling about the class as a group. Camping trips (with snapshots) can reveal why individuals have differential social power and whether this power is used in a healthy way.

ARTICLE 5.5

IN the next article, Steve Parese demonstrates how to use a group behavior modification strategy to promote group cohesion with a group of troubled students.

AN EXAMPLE OF PROMOTING GROUP COHESION AND POSITIVE GROUP BEHAVIOR IN AN EMOTIONALLY DISTURBED CLASSROOM

Steve Parese

In a one-on-one, individualized treatment program for emotionally disturbed (ED) students, special educators sometimes overlook the potential of the classroom group itself as a motivator and a behavior management tool. The same elements that can influence a group of ED students toward inappropriate, undesirable behaviors can, when properly focused, be used to help establish and maintain desirable behaviors.

Emotionally disturbed students are often described as self-centered, impulsive, unable to interact successfully with others, and lacking in social competence. The groups they form are often

From *The Pointer, 33*(3), 1989, pp. 36–38. Reprinted with permission.

transitory, fragmented, and competitive rather than cooperative. At times, these classroom groups come together or become cohesive by resisting the authority or source of help, the teacher. The purpose of this article is to describe one method used within an already-existing behavior modification program to increase the cohesiveness of just such a group, focusing their strength upon a common goal rather than a common enemy.

At The Rose School, a psychoeducational program of the D.C. Department of Mental Health: Children and Youth Services, the behavior management program integrates strategies based on psychodynamics, behavioral, and social learning theories. The behavior modification program includes a level system. As a result, daily point sheets are used to record appropriate behaviors on a half-hourly basis. Expected standards are clearly and operationally defined, and each student earns points based upon his or her behavior. At the end of each school day the points are tallied to determine which of four levels the students achieved. For instance, the highest level, Level 4, requires 300 points; Level 3, only 275; and so on. The reinforcement of this individual achievement is reflected in the color of the next day's point sheet and in the placement of the student's name in a prominently displayed achievement board. Students must earn new levels each day, so the opportunity for improvement and recognition always exists. Higher levels are rewarded both daily and at week's end with various privileges and activities.

Although this system provides for individual reinforcement of appropriate behaviors, it does little for the development of group cohesion or individual cooperation. However, it does lend itself easily to the implementation of a program designed with that purpose.

To reinforce positive behavior and encourage group cohesion, it was necessary first to identify effective group reinforcers. A class meeting was held in which the students generated a list of tangible and social rewards that they would be willing to work toward, ranging from a root beer float party to a hamster for a class pet. The teachers selected the options most feasible and described the system through which the students would have the opportunity to earn these rewards *as a group.*

Daily behavior levels were assigned a direct exchange value: Level 4 was worth 4 points, Level 3 was worth 3, and so on. Individuals having a difficult day, or choosing not to cooperate with the system, could still contribute at least 1 point; *everyone's* involvement counted. With 10 students in the class, the group might earn as many as 40 points in a day or as few as 10. These points were recorded at the end of each school day on a 3-foot "thermometer" displayed in the front of the room [see Figure 5.5–1]; as group points were added in, the "mercury" rose steadily each day. The highest scoring student for each day had the privilege of filling in that day's progress.

Rewards were scheduled into the chart for reinforcement. The group earned the root beer float party after earning 100 points, and immediately they became more enthusiastic about progressing toward the next goal. Discussions at class meetings centered around the group's present level and ways to move the mercury even faster. Students soon discovered that encouraging one another's positive behavior resulted in higher individual levels and thus greater group progress toward the next reward. Even the group scapegoat made valuable contributions and thus improved his status.

The daily charting became a focus of group attention and conversation and continued until the end of the marking period, about 6 weeks after its inception, when the class had earned a trip to the pet store to choose their new pet—a golden hamster they dubbed Fuzzy!

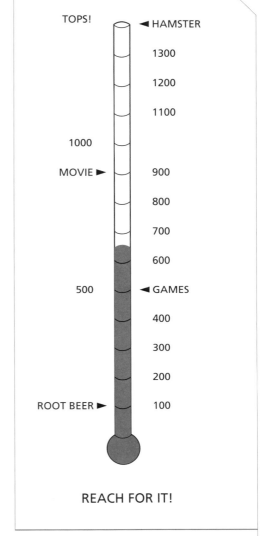

Figure 5.5–1. Example of Group Goal Thermometer.

During this 6-week trial, teachers noticed an increase in the class's cooperative, prosocial behavior and a small corresponding improvement in individual achievement. Most important, the students felt that they had earned their rewards as a group and so enjoyed them with less selfishness than with individual rewards. Although by no means an objective measure, the encouraging results of this method indicate a strategy through which common motivating goals might be used within an already existing behavior modification system to promote group cohesion, which, in turn, may help to establish and maintain desirable, prosocial behavior.

EDITORS' COMMENTARY

Group cohesion is the social glue that holds a group together. A highly cohesive group exists when the members are welded together by a common identity and attraction to the group. It is not enough to be cohesive. Sometimes, a group is anything but placid: Strong opinions are voiced, and disgruntled members threaten to leave. When a member of a truly cohesive group threatens to leave, a reinclusion effort is launched to induce the unhappy group member back. One caution should be recognized when employing Parese's methodology of total group awards: With so much depending on the group's performance, any member can sabotage a group effort. In a few cases, a student will do just that. When saboteurs are prevalent in a group, the use of a strategy other than total group performance to achieve the group goal should be considered.

ARTICLE 5.6

THE last example of an effective group program is provided by Martin Henley. This program is an excellent example of making an enjoyable group activity by taking an important and necessary psychological concept—in this case self-control—and breaking it down so it is understandable, teachable, and useful.

TEACHING SELF-CONTROL: A CURRICULUM FOR RESPONSIBLE BEHAVIOR
Martin Henley

Students spend most of the school day in group situations. What is a teacher to do when confronted with students who lack basic social skills for controlling impulses and getting along with others? The solution is simple and direct: Teachers can do what they do best—teach. By embedding the Self-Control Curriculum into academic lessons and classroom procedures, teachers help students acquire the social skills they need to successfully participate in group activities.

Although troubled youngsters present a range of behavioral and emotional difficulties, it is their lack of self-control that causes the greatest difficulty in school. Traditional discipline practices do not work with students whose life histories have hardened them to threats and punishment. Such youngsters present a challenge to the most sanguine teacher. The meager doses of discomfort doled out by school discipline codes barely make a dent in these students' armor-plated personalities. Confront them and they fight back; punish them and they grow resentful; suspend them and they are back on the streets, where they continue to learn all the wrong lessons for getting along in life.

Flawed thinking is at the core of self-control problems. Misperceptions, rationalizations, and lack of reflection form the bedrock of flawed thinking and subsequently undermine development of self-control. Troubled youngsters are limited in their ability to anticipate consequences before acting, they fail to learn from past experiences, and their need for immediate gratification impedes their ability to accommodate to the most basic social constraints. The following examples illustrate how flawed thinking leads youngsters to draw unreliable conclusions and make bad decisions.

> *Misperception*—Monique is walking down a high school corridor between classes. She passes two students who are whispering and laughing. They look in her direction and turn around. Monique is sure they are making fun of her and vows to get even.

> *Rationalization*—On his way home from school, William walks past a luxury SUV idling in front of a convenience store. He hops in the driver's seat and takes off. Two hours later, he is picked up by the local police. When they ask him why he stole the vehicle, William replies, "Hey, it's not my fault the guy was so dumb as to leave his car running when he wanted a loaf of bread."

> *Unreflective*—Mateo returned to the alternative high school after a month in juvenile detention. He told the principal he hated lockup

Adapted from *Teaching Self-Control: A Curriculum for Responsible Behavior* (2nd ed.), by M. Henley, 2003, Bloomington, IN: National Educational Service. Copyright by Martin Henley. Adapted with permission.

and he would never go back. Three days later, in violation of his parole, Mateo made lewd comments to a female student. He was sent back to the juvenile lockup.

Youngsters can learn to change their behavior by learning to change the way they think about themselves and their relationships with others. The Self-Control Curriculum is an educational program to redirect students' thinking and support the development of constructive behavior.

WHAT IS SELF-CONTROL?

Self-control is the ability to monitor impulsive behavior and consider reasonable alternatives before acting (Goleman, 1995; Henley & Long, 1999; Redl & Wineman, 1951). Self-control is learned behavior. When raised in a functional family, children acquire the social skills that comprise self-control during the formative years from infancy to adolescence. With appropriate guidance these youngsters gradually acquire the ability to cope with impulses, manage stress, and solve social problems. Other youth are not so fortunate. Their hardscrabble life experiences cultivate impulsive thinking and behavior. A dysfunctional upbringing teaches young people to get what they need, when they can get it. The "get mine now" imperative reinforces nonconstructive behaviors for meeting such basic needs as affiliation, success, and control.

SELF-CONTROL CURRICULUM

The Self-Control Curriculum is a cognitive model for teaching students to think more clearly about themselves and the world around them. It includes 20 discrete social skills organized into five domains: controlling impulses, adapting to school routines, managing group situations, managing stress, and solving social problems (see Table 5.6–1). The skills that comprise the self-control curriculum were identified during a 3-year field-based research project during which behavioral outbursts in elementary and secondary classrooms were observed, analyzed, and categorized (Henley, 1994).

The Self-Control Curriculum provides guidelines for merging self-control skills with academics and classroom management procedures. Because self-control acquisition is a progression from fundamental to higher level skills, each of the 20 Self-Control Curriculum skills is subdivided into several more basic skills. Table 5.6–2 outlines the subskills for the

Managing Group Situations domain.

ACADEMIC INSTRUCTION

The academic curriculum provides myriad opportunities to weave social skill development into lessons. Meshing social with academic skills helps students understand how every aspect of human culture, including mathematics, science, history, and literature, is immersed in thought, feelings, and behavior. Coping with frustration, anticipating consequences, and demonstrating patience are as essential to success in math and science as analytical and logical thinking. History, politics,

TABLE 5.6-1

THE FIVE DOMAINS OF SELF-CONTROL

Control Impulses
- Manage situational lure
- Demonstrate patience
- Verbalize feelings
- Resist tempting objects

Manage Group Situations
- Maintain composure
- Appraise peer pressure
- Participate in group activities
- Understand how behavior affects others

Solve Social Problems
- Focus on the present
- Learn from past experience
- Anticipate consequences
- Resolve conflicts

Follow School Routines
- Follow rules
- Organize school materials
- Accept evaluative comments
- Make classroom transitions

Manage Stress
- Adapt to new situations
- Cope with competition
- Tolerate frustration
- Select tension-reducing activities

and literature present an infinite array of opportunities to discuss how individuals work together to solve social and personal problems. Furthermore, integrating social and academic content enhances generalization of skill development without the necessity of setting aside valuable instructional time for social skill lessons.

Embedded self-control lessons are not a quick fix for behavior problems. A student's reading level does not improve after one lesson, and neither do self-control skills suddenly improve after exposure to one or two lessons. Behavior change follows cognitive change. As students begin to change the way they think, they will gradually begin to adjust their behavior accordingly. Even as change becomes evident, regressions will occur. Rather than following a smooth upward curve, behavior

TABLE 5.6–2

MANAGING GROUP SITUATIONS DOMAIN

Skill	Subskills
Maintain composure	To ignore classroom distractions
	To independently select a classroom activity
	To behave appropriately when the teacher is out of the room
Appraise peer pressure	To evaluate a situation in terms of personal beliefs about good and bad choices
	To act in accordance with personal beliefs
	To identify peer situations where student should say "no"
Participate in group activities	To help others
	To cooperate
	To contribute to group discussions
Understand how behavior affects others	To explain how media, culture, and social situations influence behavior
	To identify personal behaviors influenced by others
	To identify ways of improving the lives of others

change follows a curve of ascending spirals. Like a baseball player who experiences periodic slumps, students will exhibit lapses in recently acquired self-control skills. The following are sample lessons for subskills of the self-control skill "Participate in group activities."

> Subskill: To help others.
> *Mathematics/Social Studies*—Distribute sections of recent newspapers to students working in pairs. Have students circle events that portray acts of helping. Have students underline events that describe hurtful acts. Have each pair count the number of helpful and hurting acts. Compare the data and discuss. Ask probing questions (e.g., What is the effect of catastrophes on people's behavior? What conditions sustain helping and hurtful behaviors?).

> Subskill: To cooperate.
> *Language Arts*—Read a story aloud. Stop at various points and ask

students to comment on events in the story that illustrate cooperation or lack of cooperation. Ask students to improve the storyline.
Ask them how the story would unfold differently if the protagonists
cooperated.

Social Studies—Review a social studies instructor's manual to identify sections that highlight cooperation. Select topics such as building pyramids, great battles, legislation, and major construction
projects. Discuss specific ways that individuals needed to cooperate.
Have students conduct interviews with adults about ways they need
to cooperate in their jobs.

> Subskill: To contribute to group activities.
> *Mathematics*—This activity begins with any lesson that requires
> students to participate through class discussions or questions and
> answers. Before the lesson begins, give each student a "discussion
> counter" (i.e., a slip of paper on which they tally observations by
> writing check marks). Instruct students to put a check on the coun-
> ter each time they observe a student making a positive group con-
> tribution. At the end of the lesson, have students tally their check
> marks. Compare scores. Have students reflect on the following
> questions: Did some students have more checks than others? What
> type of behaviors warranted checks? What was the effect of positive
> group contributions on the entire lesson? What was the effect of
> negative behavior on the lesson? How can discussions or lessons be
> altered to promote positive group contributions?

CLASSROOM PROCEDURES

Classroom procedures are the routines that provide structure to daily
classroom activities. Procedures that promote collaboration teach positive
group participation skills. Collaboration requires students to reflect on
their beliefs and think through options before acting. The following recommendations are a synopsis of classroom procedures that bolster group
participation skills.

> Utilize Interactive Lessons. How much time do teachers waste try-
> ing to limit student socializing? The basic need for affiliation can
> be constructively channeled through cooperative learning and peer
> tutoring. Highlight creative ideas rather than "the right answer" by
> emphasizing brainstorming and critical thinking. Include movement

in classroom activities. Movement strengthens neural connections and increases alertness. Designate specific areas of the classroom for learning centers, quiet reading areas, and discussion groups.

Example: Cooperative Learning. Often used in schools, cooperative learning enhances group work by teaching skills for working with others. Students with self-control deficiencies need to learn to discriminate between behaviors that enable and behaviors that hinder group activity. Ask students to brainstorm and list actions that hinder and help groups. Give names to helping behaviors (e.g., the "engineer" keeps the group on track; the "detective" asks questions that move the group forward; the "lawyer" summarizes key points; the "coach" encourages feedback). After the list of helping roles is complete, organize a cooperative group activity. Write the helping labels on index cards and give each student a card. No one knows what name card each student holds. The students play the role listed on the card. After the group activity, students guess what role each was playing. Follow with a discussion about how individual behavior influences group harmony and productivity.

> Personalize Activities. Student engagement supports self-control. Students are most engaged with activities they can connect to on a personal level. Find ways to blend students' daily experiences into the curriculum. Nothing strains inadequate self-control more than a boring lesson. Conduct regular class meetings, which allow students to express their opinions. Pay attention to group dynamics. Arrange classroom activities to minimize cliques and draw in isolates.

Example: Class Meetings. Classroom meetings help students develop a sense of community. Feeling that one is a part of a classroom community improves academics and behavior. Use meetings for collaborative planning, summarizing daily events, setting group goals, and establishing class priorities. Set an agenda to avoid wandering conversations. Emphasize noncritical responses, as well as such nonverbal communication as eye-to-eye contact. Teach active listening by establishing a rule that no one can speak unless he or she can summarize what the previous speaker said.

> Empower Students. Powerlessness produces apathy; self-determination increases motivation. Provide opportunities for student choice. Allow students to participate in group decisions about such mainte-

nance tasks as decorating the classroom and establishing classroom rules. Analyze the curriculum, and ask students to prioritize their interests, strengths, and weaknesses. Give students responsibilities; don't limit these to the well-behaved students. Students who have the most social and behavioral difficulties have the greatest trust needs.

Example: Establishing Class Rules. The number one procedural concern for most teachers on the first day of school is delineating classroom rules.

> Include a Helping Component. Encouraging students to help each other is an affirmative method for fostering compassion. Helping others moves students beyond the egocentric thinking that underlies many self-control deficiencies. Arrange activities such as community service projects that enable empathy and require student cooperation.

CONCLUSION

School activities that promote success help develop student confidence and inspire the will to persevere. Troubled students have more right than wrong about them. Enabling their strengths reduces their deficiencies. Meaningful school activities take into account students' basic needs and life experiences. Lessons that students see as meaningful provide an infrastructure for preventing classroom disturbances and building self-control.

REFERENCES

Goleman, D. (1995). *Emotional intelligence.* New York: Bantam Books.

Henley, M. (1994). A self-control curriculum for troubled youngsters. *Journal of Emotional and Behavioral Problems, 3,* 40–46.

Henley, M., & Long, N. (1999). Teaching emotional intelligence to impulsive-aggressive youth. *Reclaiming Children and Youth: Journal of Emotional and Behavioral Problems, 7,* 224–229.

Redl, F., & Wineman, D. (1951). *Children who hate.* New York: Free Press.

SUMMARY

Most teachers have not had the opportunity to learn the essential group dynamic concepts and skills that are necessary for reclaiming troubled students. In this chapter, contributors have summarized these concepts and skills and described effective group programs that teachers can use in the classroom. We urge teachers to seek additional training in this area.

EDITORS' REFERENCES

Hobbs, N. (1982). *The troubled and troubling child*. San Francisco: Jossey-Bass.

Lippett, R., & Gold, M. (1964). *Classroom human relations program*. Ann Arbor: University of Michigan, Institute for Social Research.

Long, N. (1962). Groups in perspective: A new sociometric technique for classroom teachers. *Bulletin of the School of Education, Indiana University*.

Newman, R. (1974). *Groups in schools*. New York: Simon & Schuster.

Redl, F., & Wineman, D. (1966). *The aggressive child*. New York: Free Press.

6 PROMOTING POSITIVE STUDENT BEHAVIOR:

Essential Concepts and Skills
for Effective Classroom Discipline

NO other topic in education receives greater attention or causes more concerns for teachers, parents, and students than classroom discipline. This is not a new problem for public schools or to classroom teachers. The lack of effective classroom discipline or positive behavior management skills is the major stumbling block to a successful career in teaching. A study of first-year teachers found that 65% of this group were anxious about their ability to maintain classroom order and wondered if their students viewed them as competent authority figures. A similar finding was reported by the National Education Association in its 2002 survey of teacher concerns. Teachers ranked classroom discipline as their number one problem, and those teachers who experienced more disruptive student behavior felt their classrooms were more difficult to manage. Students who disregarded classroom rules, challenged teachers' authority, interfered with the instructional program, used obscene language, were apathetic to learning, and were verbally and physically threatening to the staff and peers caused teachers to report feeling less safe in their classrooms than they did in the past.

Students also are concerned about their physical and psychological safety. The majority of students want a safer and more secure school and classroom and become anxious when a few students act up in a frightening way. The majority of students are not ambivalent about the need for adult protection and the importance of clear, reasonable, and enforceable rules. However, in select schools, students are questioning the staff's ability to protect them against peer bullying and assaults. Perhaps this is one reason why some students bring weapons to school—not as an aggressive act, but as a last resort of self-protection. As one student reported, "I spend more time watching my back than planning for my educational future."

Parent groups, PTAs, and community leaders are voicing the same concern as teachers and students. These groups are alarmed by the growing reports of school violence, drugs, gangs, guns, and shootings. They are demanding their school board members to restore safety, order, and discipline to public schools and to stop the trend of having public schools reflect the destructive values of life on the streets. Parents also want the school principal to be in charge of the students and the staff. They want stricter student rules and want the staff to be less tolerant of the rights of deviant students. They believe that the prerequisite to classroom learning is classroom order and that classroom order can only be achieved by classroom discipline.

When schools have chronic disciplinary problems and the staff seem helpless to resolve them, staff competence emerges as the central issue in subsequent discussions. More principals and teachers are dismissed or leave public education because of their ineffective disciplinary skills than for any other reason. If this trend continues, teachers and administrators will become the new educational "dropouts."

How can we explain why there has been so little improvement in this area when there is a consensus among school board members, administrators, teachers, students, and parents that classroom discipline needs to be more effective? One explanation is that there are no easy or simple solutions to this complex problem. A school-based classroom discipline program does not function in the vacuum of college textbooks, nor can it be divorced from the social, ethnic, economic, political, professional, and personal values of the community, the school board, principals, teachers, and students. Each of these groups frequently holds different, and at times conflicting, views, values, beliefs, and expectations regarding what are appropriate school policies, rules, acceptable behaviors, and consequences. In our consultation with public schools, we have found that the following five interrelated reasons have contributed to this dilemma.

1. The Multiple Meaning of Classroom Discipline. *Classroom discipline* is a spongelike term that soaks up a variety of different meanings and attitudes. For some educators, discipline means the power of teachers to control the behavior of their students. It is a set of skills that makes students obedient to their authority. The locus of control is external, and the goal is to maintain a strict code of law and order. Teachers who operate on this definition frequently have students who perceive discipline as an act of punishment they receive for breaking school rules.

For other educators, discipline means an opportunity to teach students a set of values about how people can live together in a democratic society. This would include the values of honesty, fair play, the rights of others to learn, respect for property, respect for multicultural differences, and so on. Discipline is perceived as the process of helping students to internalize these values and to develop self-control over their drives and feelings. The locus of control is internal, and the goal is to help students learn responsible behavior. For these students, discipline is perceived as a chance to learn self-control or self-discipline from their personal experiences based on the natural consequences of their behavior. This definition fosters a developmental view of discipline in which students learn how to behave responsibly in various situations over time. Our definition of discipline reflects this point of view.

When staff meet to discuss ways of improving classroom discipline, they rarely pause to acknowledge and work out the different beliefs they attach to this term. As a result, these group deliberations frequently end up creating more staff frustration and confusion than staff consensus and direction.

2. The Growing Social–Emotional Needs of High-Risk and Troubled Students. More students are entering public schools without the benefits of ongoing, positive parental bonding and attachment. Many of these students already have been damaged emotionally by the debilitating effects of poverty, neglect, abuse, divorce, drugs, and rejection. They have not internalized a sense of trust in other adults or developed the necessary prosocial skills necessary for group instruction and personal learning. Consequently, these students have low frustration tolerance, misperceive social interactions, and have limited attention span and low self-esteem. Their social–emotional needs dominate their behavior and disrupt the learning process. Teachers who are motivated by the academic goals of teaching may not be prepared to recognize and meet the social–emotional needs of these students. A few of these teachers defend their educational position by saying, "I have an excellent program, but the wrong students come to my class."

3. The Needs of Multicultural Students. The public schools are serving an increasing number of multicultural students, resulting in significant and different racial, religious, sexual, gender, and socioeconomic issues, values, and norms. Teachers brought up on middle-class American values may have little direct experience with or knowledge of the importance of these multicultural values and can inadvertently deny or misread the behavior of some students. For example, a student's particular style of dress, language, and manners can become an ongoing cultural battleground for some teachers. This is particularly true when the cultural norms and values of the community are different from the social and academic norms and values of the school. Under these conditions, the issue of school discipline can spark powerful, multicultural school–community conflicts.

4. The Top-Down Administrative Solutions to Classroom Discipline. When school violence erupts, the community puts pressure on the local school board to implement new and more restrictive policies on deviant behavior. Occasionally, these policies are rigid, absolute statements that become unrealistic to implement with any degree of fairness. Although the intentions of these school board policies may be honorable, the actual enforcement of these policies becomes self-defeating. For example, murder in our society is viewed in three degrees. Let's assume for a moment the government decided to get tough on murder and have a zero tolerance toward killing others. The new policy immediately collapses the three degrees of murder to just one degree of murder. As a result, murder is murder and is an unacceptable act regardless of the circumstances. How long would this new policy last before it would be contested legally? However, a local board of education expects their administrators and teachers to carry out their policies or risk losing their jobs. For example, some city school systems have initiated a policy of zero tolerance toward any student who brings a weapon to school. This policy includes an automatic 5-day suspension and an immediate transfer to a different school. In order to guarantee a citywide standard of objectivity, the policy lists all the objects defined as weapons, from hat pins, scissors, and knives to guns. If any of these weapons were found on a student, there would be no further discussion of this incident. The principal must file a report to the superintendent, and the student is automatically suspended without exceptions. No one can disagree with the goal of keeping weapons out of school. This goal is uncontestable!

However, a rigid policy that operates in a robotic fashion and does not involve any meaningful student discussion only succeeds in depersonalizing any respect for the student. For example, the following incident was reported in the *Herald Mail* (Hagerstown, Maryland) newspaper. A 5-year-old boy found a razor blade at his bus stop. He picked it up and showed it to the bus driver, who in turn reported it to the principal. Because the razor blade was on the list of weapons, the principal was obligated to suspend the student and file the appropriate forms to transfer him out of his community school. These are the types of nonthinking, automatic policies that cause some teachers and administrators difficulty in supporting top-down discipline policies regarding student crimes and punishments.

5. The Limitations of Preservice Teacher Education Skills in Classroom Management. A survey of first-year teachers in New York City documented that 70% felt their preservice training in classroom management was naive and ineffective. The psychological concepts and marginal skills they learned were restricted to a part of a course in educational psychology or student teaching. Often, they were taught only one theoretical approach to behavior management and received little or no training in group management. The assumption seems to be that classroom management is an interaction that takes place only between a student and the teacher, independent of group forces. However, many classroom teachers must manage groups of 35 to 40 students with limited space and little administrative support. One first-year teacher summarized her preservice training as follows:

I was not prepared to survive in the real world of classroom life. It was like learning to swim without ever going into the water. I was long on theory but short on skills. The first time I tried to manage a class on my own, it was a disaster. I almost drowned!

Our experience with teachers confirms that many first-year teachers are not adequately prepared to manage student behavior successfully.

When these five reasons interact, it is understandable why there is so much confusion and frustration in developing and agreeing on the concepts and skills of promoting effective classroom discipline.

Our Definition of Effective Classroom Discipline

Our definition of effective classroom discipline involves four interrelated concepts and skills.

1. Classroom Discipline Begins with the Teacher and Not the Students. The teacher's level of self-awareness and the quality of his or her relationships with students directly influence the effectiveness of his or her behavior management skills. This important but poorly understood concept of classroom discipline is rarely appreciated, but it is the basis of our belief that all significant student learning involves and revolves around the personality of the teacher. No teacher enters the classroom with a history of no social–emotional problems or has a perfect psychological fit to work successfully with all the students assigned to the classroom. This fact can be used to motivate teachers to gain greater insights into helping troubled students. The journey begins by digging through one's developmental past and uncovering those powerful and buried life events that have affected the teacher's attitudes and behaviors toward select students. The question the teacher needs to answer is why he or she is compassionate and caring toward some students, tolerant and tactful toward others, and rejecting and renouncing toward still others. The image of the "perfect or great teacher" is an educational myth. The only reason the concept of the "ideal teacher" flies is because it is filled with hot air. In reality, each teacher carries his or her personal history, like a locked briefcase, into the classroom every day. Unfortunately, a few students have discovered the key to the teacher's psychological briefcase and they take some pleasure in exposing the teacher's unfinished business to the class. The nature of the teacher's unfinished psychological business explains why some teachers can help certain troubled students, such as the clinging, helpless, infantile behavior of a dependent student, while other teachers would react to the same students with anger and repulsion. If these two groups of teachers used the same behavior management skills on the same dependent students, the results would probably be significantly different. Effective classroom discipline cannot be successful when a teacher is stirred up emotionally. What a teacher can handle intellectually far exceeds what he or she can tolerate emotionally. This is why the first cornerstone of classroom discipline begins with the teacher's level of self-awareness and interpersonal skills, and not the behavior of the students.

2. Classroom Discipline Involves Long-Term Goals. The long-term goal of effective discipline is to teach students the basic democratic values and standards of our society, such as equality, work, fairness, and honesty, which lead to self-control and personal accountability. This is a gradual and ongoing learning experience for students based on their internal locus of control. The teacher can play a meaningful role in promoting long-term goals by providing opportunities (a) to move students from a point in time where adults make most of their decisions to a point in time where the students make most of their decisions, (b) to move students who have little responsibility for their behaviors to a point in time where they have maximum responsibility for their behaviors, and (c) to help students who are motivated by immediate and narcissistic goals to become motivated by long-range altruistic goals. These three examples of long-term goals reflect how a teacher can advance the second cornerstone of effective classroom discipline by facilitating students to become responsible, self-directed, and productive members of our society.

3. Classroom Discipline Also Involves a Multitude of Short-Term Skills that Maintain Classroom Order and Effective Student Instruction and Learning. A teacher needs a variety of daily intervention skills to maintain the ongoing educational program. These "on-the-spot" teacher skills are used for three different reasons. One set of skills is used to prevent problem behaviors from developing by increasing desirable student behaviors. This would include such techniques as rewarding positive behavior, using descriptive praise, and developing cooperative group norms and standards of appropriate behavior. The second set of short-term skills is aimed at teaching students the necessary prosocial skills they will need in order to cope with a stressful school incident. These skills include entering a group, developing friendship skills, managing frustration, managing peer rejection, and so on. The third set of skills is intended to decrease inappropriate student behavior by direct teacher intervention. This set involves using a variety of surface management skills ranging from planned ignoring to physical restraint. The goal of these short-term skills is to deter any minor student problem from becoming a major school crisis. These three subsets of skills are necessary and learnable.

4. Classroom Discipline Is Not a Bag of Tricks or Gimmicks a Teacher Uses During a Crisis. Our definition of classroom discipline is a thoughtful and purposeful way of interacting with students on a daily basis. It is a style and a philosophy of relating to others, and not a switch to be turned on and off in times of need. It is a professional way of modeling the values and the behaviors a teacher wants students to learn. It flourishes in an atmosphere where a teacher respects the students' dignity and self-esteem and has the maturity and skill to set realistic expectations and limits on student behaviors.

When the four definitions of discipline are combined, the new concept of schoolwide Positive Behavior Support (PBS) emerges. PBS integrates the various behavior management skills into a consistent schoolwide program. The rationale for this program is that it reduces the differences between teachers regarding their expectations and norms for student behavior while promoting staff cohesion. In addition, it creates a positive learning climate for all students based on strength-based interventions. There seems to be an explosion of published PBS programs (e.g., McCurdy, 2003; Rosenberg, 2003; Warren, 2003).

ARTICLE 6.1

ALL of the articles selected in this chapter have been classroom tested. They demonstrate successful ways of translating psychological theory into effective teacher practices. The first selection, by Nicholas Long and Frank Fecser, is an example of an effective PBS program. They describe a schoolwide competency-based certification program based on three levels of prevention and intervention. All staff are required to participate in the training, and if the staff demonstrates the required competencies, the school becomes recognized as a Safe and Reclaiming School.

BUILDING SAFE AND RECLAIMING SCHOOLS: A CERTIFICATION PROGRAM OF THE LSCI INSTITUTE

Nicholas J. Long and Frank A. Fecser

The Life Space Crisis Intervention Institute has developed a comprehensive schoolwide strategy for building positive learning climates for all students and providing effective interventions for students presenting challenging problems. This model contains three levels of prevention and intervention. All staff members in a school are given primary prevention skills, and teachers and classroom personnel receive early inter-vention strategies for difficult students. Finally, a school crisis reclaiming team is trained in the advanced strategies of Life Space Crisis Intervention. Training of trainers is also avail-able so that schools may maintain this program in a cost-efficient manner.

NEW CHALLENGES TO SCHOOLS

Problems in families and communities have created new and more de-structive levels of student deviancy and disturbances. General Colin Powell, the founder of the Alliance of Youth, reported that 15 million students, or one quarter of the population of students under the age of 18, are identified as at risk and troubled emotionally. Each day a sig-nificant number of these students arrive at school loaded with active and unresolved interpersonal conflicts related to gangs, guns, racism, divorce, death, poverty, abandonment, abuse, and victimization. These students are unable to leave their personal problems on the doorsteps of the school; instead, they carry them into the hallways and classrooms. They are so flooded by their consuming thoughts of anger, fear, anxiety, depression, and revenge that some of them cannot concentrate on their classroom assignments, accept reasonable staff member directions, or tolerate the slightest peer teasing and rejection. As a result, they often are only one minor frustration away from blowing up and creating a school-wide crisis that would endanger their peers, staff members, and themselves.

The needs of these students cannot be denied; passed on to special education; or managed by being reprimanded, punished, and labeled as a troublemaker or a misfit who does not belong in school. These students are not restricted to inner-city schools—they can be found in all regions and at every socioeconomic level. We believe that the massive media at-tention given to violent school incidents creates a groundswell of anxiety and consensus among parents and community groups, teacher unions, principal associations, boards of education, and state and federal govern-ments that the acts of school violence must be stopped and given priority status for funding.

From *Reclaiming Children and Youth*, 9(4), 2001, pp. 229–233. Copyright by Reclaiming Children and Youth, Inc. Reprinted with permission.

STAFF MEMBERS NEED SKILLS TO SUCCEED WITH DIFFICULT STUDENTS

A common strategy among organizations struggling with a painful reality problem is to manage the problem by blaming or projecting responsibility onto other groups or social conditions. The public school system is no stranger to this maneuver. The difficult question—"What changes can we make to prevent the acts of student violence or to promote a safer school environment?"—is avoided. Any discussion usually ends by highlighting a lack of parental involvement and values; the absence of after-school programs for latchkey kids; the ethnic diversity of the students; and the poisoning impact of movies, television shows, music groups and songs, video games, teen magazines, and pornography on the Internet that model and encourage primitive sexual and aggressive behaviors in students. Although these factors are real and contribute to irresponsible student behavior, they function outside the public school's immediate circle of influence. There is one factor contributing to student violence over which the school system does have control: A public school system is responsible for setting the professional standards for appropriate teacher and student behavior.

For example, when a first-year teacher is in a conflict situation with a student, what teacher behaviors does the school system promote, tolerate, or define as unacceptable? What is the school system's response if this teacher's behavior does not meet the minimum standards of professional acceptability? Is the teacher reprimanded, punished, labeled a troublemaker, or even banished from the school? Not likely. The most predictable scenario is to gloss over the problem and blame the student or the teacher-training institutions for graduating teachers who are not adequately prepared to manage disruptive student behavior.

Let's suggest an analogy. Would a city hire lifeguards who didn't know how to swim for their public swimming pools? We don't think so. But what if the city couldn't identify applicants who could swim, and the pools had to be open on time? The only reasonable answer is to hire the applicants and teach them to swim before going on duty. The public school system, however, continues to hire new teachers who have not been taught to help students who are drowning emotionally. Instead of providing these teachers with life-support skills that could keep them and their students afloat, the school leaves them on their own until they are carried out by the tides of fatigue, anger, and depression.

A second and more serious problem is the fundamental differences among school staff members regarding the definition of "problem student behavior." Any principal or supervisor can attest to the discouraging fact that a student's behavior in one teacher's classroom can be viewed as normal, irritating, and age-appropriate but in another teacher's classroom will be interpreted as a deliberate act of disrespect, defiance, and deviance. How is it possible for a faculty to tolerate such divergent and individual interpretations of the same student behavior? Would the public tolerate a policeman who has his or her personal view of law and order or a physician who has his or her own personal interpretation of what constitutes a normal temperature? Absolutely not, because the law enforcement and medical professions have clear professional standards to uphold.

Perhaps this sounds as if we are being too critical of teachers. We are not. We have great compassion for classroom teachers, who are confronted daily with student stresses and conflicts, and we understand why their psychological armor wears thin at times. Students in conflict stir up normal feelings of counteraggression in teachers; if the teachers are not trained to understand and manage these feelings, they will surface as hostility and escalate a student's conflict into a crisis situation. It should be noted that teachers *do not initiate 80% of student crises,* but in most situations their spontaneous anger and righteous indignation usually end up fueling or reinforcing a crisis. The solution is not to focus on blame but to provide teachers with specific strength-based intervention skills so they feel supported and empowered to reach out and help these students. Our work with the New York City School System, District 75 Alternative Programs, is a rewarding example of how providing strength-based skills to school staff members can make a significant improvement in the frequency, duration, and intensity of student crises. Staff skills, not staff blame, make a difference.

NEW SOLUTIONS REQUIRE FRESH THINKING

Most school systems have a central staff development department complete with a director and training staff. These individuals' task is enormous, but their status and value in a school system often are compromised by various conditions. The number of staff development days during a school year are limited by the district or by negotiated contracts. Existing staff development days often consist of passive learning, large-group settings, and simplistic single-focus issues that have the lasting effect of a psychological aspirin. When attempts at complex staff training in the areas of prosocial learning skills, peer mediation skills, or alternative learning styles are made, much of the time this training is not integrated into other educational strategies or reinforced by the administrators. Training effects disappear. Finally, there is an unstated assumption among many school board members that although staff training is necessary, it is probably ineffective, a waste of time and money, and a failure at changing staff members' behavior. This assumption is demonstrated whenever schools have to make financial cuts in the school budget.

THE LSCI SAFE AND RECLAIMING SCHOOLS PROGRAM

Under the leadership of these authors, the Life Space Crisis Intervention Institute has developed cost-effective, school-wide, competency-based safe school programs for public school systems. The following is a list of the outcome goals for this type of program:

- To guarantee the physical and psychological safety of all students and staff members in a school.
- To enhance staff members' competencies at connecting and supporting all students by modeling positive, strength-based behavior management skills.
- To serve select students and reduce the level of violence at home and in the community by connecting with other community agencies, including mental health agencies; the police department; the juvenile justice system; parent groups; and human resource agencies involved with physical and sexual abuse, neglect, drugs, alcohol, and teen pregnancy.
- To create a "training of trainers" program so the school system can maintain program effectiveness with new staff members at a minimal cost.

The LSCI Safe and Reclaiming School Program is organized around three levels of training that combine to create a pyramid model. This model illustrates a hierarchy of training needs based on the role and function of each staff member and employee at a school. Each training level has an independent set of specific outcome competencies, learning activities, and evaluation measures (see Figure 6.1–1). The relationship between the complexity of a student's behavior and the corresponding levels of advanced training is demonstrated in the figure.

LEVEL 1: PRIMARY PREVENTION—SCHOOL-WIDE STRATEGIES

Level 1 consists of baseline training for *all* staff members and employees in a school. This total school experience is essential to achieving a common group purpose, and it provides specific concepts, skills, and terminology for staff members and employees to use in their interactions

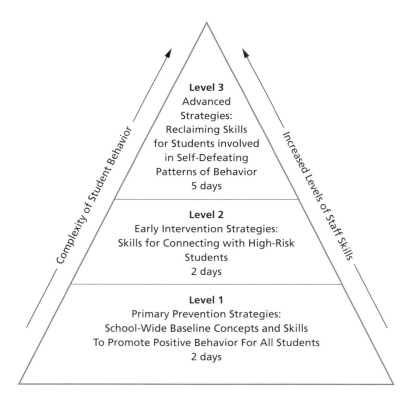

LEVELS OF TRAINING

Figure 6.1–1. The Pyramid Model of the LSCI Safe and Reclaiming School Program.

with students. The training competencies of this level are grouped around three concepts:

Management Begins with Us, Not with Our Students

- the awareness of how we think about our students
- the skill of identifying problem behavior in students
- the knowledge of the Conflict Cycles and student/staff member power struggles
- the knowledge of staff counteraggression
- the ability to demonstrate anger-management skills
- the ability to demonstrate eight skills for reducing staff stress

Create a Predictable School Environment

- the importance of rules, rituals, and structure
- the ability to use "I" rather than "you" messages
- the ability to use skills to deescalate a crisis involving an upset student
- the ability to demonstrate eight effective surface management skills to maintain positive student behavior

Create a Positive School Climate

- the ability to demonstrate the pairing of staff interventions with positive school values
- the ability to demonstrate the skills of positive talk and meaningful praise
- the ability to demonstrate the skill of decoding and affirming student feelings and behaviors

LEVEL 2: EARLY INTERVENTION STRATEGIES— SKILLS FOR CONNECTING WITH HIGH-RISK STUDENTS

Level 2 provides training for all classroom teachers and support staff members. The majority of students with special needs are in a general education classroom rather than a special education one. The classroom teachers who are responsible for these students often have not been taught the skills necessary for identifying, connecting with, and supporting them. This additional training is intended to provide teachers and staff with these skills.

Training Competencies

- the skill of identifying, connecting with, and supporting a student who is aggressive
- the skill of identifying, connecting with, and supporting a student who is passive-aggressive
- the skill of identifying, connecting with, and supporting a student who is depressed
- the skill of identifying, connecting with, and supporting a student who is anxious and withdrawn

Also provided at this level are an overview for the LSCI process for the school crisis reclaiming team and the skills of identifying carry-in problems, deescalating the crisis, and connecting the student with a member of the school crisis reclaiming team.

LEVEL 3: ADVANCED RECLAIMING STRATEGIES— SKILLS FOR THE CRISIS RECLAIMING TEAM

Two or more staff members in each school constitute the *crisis reclaiming team*. These individuals are selected for training in advanced reclaiming skills that enable them to work on crisis situations in a safe and productive manner. This is a 5-day certification program in Life Space Crisis Intervention based on 26 competencies designed to respond to a student crisis and to turn it into a learning opportunity for personal insight, new social skills, and improved staff member relationships. The types of persons usually selected for a crisis reclaiming team include a school counselor, social worker, psychologist, special education teacher, or administrator who works with troubled students. LSCI is an essential skill for any school committed to reducing school violence. Certification in LSCI represents the most sophisticated and successful way of helping difficult and alienated students who are the most likely to create a school crisis. LSCI skills provide the crisis team with the ability to respond successfully to a student crisis, regardless of the pattern.

Some of the types of students a crisis team might work with include

- stressed-out students who take home/community problems and act them out in school,
- frustrated individuals who misperceive other intentions and distort reality events,
- self-centered youth who bully and hurt others without remorse or regret,
- low self-esteem students who berate and punish themselves for normal mistakes,
- socially rejected students who act inappropriately when they try to fit in, and
- naive students who are easily set up by more manipulative students.

WHERE TO BEGIN

An effective program needs the support of the school board, superintendent, principals, teacher unions, and parents. It must be adequately funded and have a built-in evaluation component. Results must be measurable and based on sound psychoeducational concepts and skills. We find that it is best to begin with schools that volunteer or actually compete to have this new program. The teaching process must be active, powerful, and realistic, with immediate application to the students. The training must empower staff members to model what they have learned, and they must get clear feedback on their effectiveness in using these skills. Schools must be able to certify select staff members as trainers who can maintain this program without relying on outside consultants.

The Life Space Crisis Intervention Institute offers a network of senior trainers; however, in order for programs to be cost effective, we recommend that school districts train their own trainers in this curriculum. Training-of-trainers certification is also provided by the Institute.

Just as school boards are raising the academic standards for advancement to the next grade level and for graduation, the LSCI Institute is elevating the professional standards of schools to help meet the new social realities of students. The LSCI Safe and Reclaiming School Program represents an effective method for developing a school-wide, competency-based program that not only prevents acts of student violence but also builds a nurturing school environment.

When school staff members agree to participate, they make a commitment to volunteer additional time and effort to master the program's competencies. The LSCI Institute awards a plaque to those schools that have successfully completed the program. This plaque documents that the staff members have demonstrated the necessary skills to develop a safe and reclaiming school program. In addition, the names of these schools will be published in *Reclaiming Children and Youth* to highlight the community's recognition and appreciation of the school staff members' professional dedication.

If your school wants to be certified as a Safe and Reclaiming School, write to Starr Commonwealth, No Disposable Kids, at 13725 Starr Commonwealth, Albion, MI 49224; call 800/837-5591; or visit the Web site (www.starr.org).

EDITORS' COMMENTARY

For years, teachers have been told how their behavior influences the behavior of their students. Although this statement is true, the corollary is also true: Troubled students can greatly influence the behavior of their teachers. Troubled students are proficient at provoking and pushing the "emotional buttons" of concerned, dedicated, warmhearted teachers, who can end up feeling and behaving in hostile and rejecting ways toward selected students. When this happens, many of these teachers feel surprised by and guilty about their reactions. One mild-mannered junior high school teacher expressed this problem in an open and honest way:

> Each night I promise myself I will not lose my temper with Gary; but by 11 A.M., after Gary has fallen out of his seat, teased a girl about being overweight, talked out loud during instruction time, and given the finger sign to a quick-tempered peer, I want to strangle the little SOB.

To understand why and how competent teachers find themselves in such self-defeating struggles with students, Nicholas Long developed the Conflict Cycle Paradigm. This model describes how the interaction between a student and a teacher follows a circular process in which the attitudes, feelings, and behaviors of the teacher are influenced by and, in turn, influence the attitudes, feelings, and behaviors of the student. During a stressful incident, this circular process creates additional problems for the student and the teacher. Once in operation, this negative interplay between a student and teacher is extremely difficult to interrupt. For example, students under stress behave emotionally rather than rationally. They are controlled more by feelings than by logic. They protect themselves from physical and psychological pain by becoming defensive, primitive, and regressive. When a teacher reacts to these inappropriate behaviors impulsively or with righteous indignation, a power struggle develops in which understanding and helping disappear, and "winning" becomes the only acceptable outcome for the teacher. When teachers react emotionally, they deny the issues and feelings behind the students' behavior and become part of the problem. The purpose of the Conflict Cycle is to help teachers (a) become aware of how their personal beliefs and values are challenged when helping troubled students and (b) develop effective strategies to prevent students from pushing their "emotional panic buttons." Teachers do not have complete control over student behavior, but they do have complete control over how they react to student behavior. The Conflict Cycle is an essential tool for teachers' success in helping troubled students.

THE next selection deals with the fascinating concept of how troubled students can get reasonable teachers to behave inappropriately during a student–teacher conflict.

THE CONFLICT CYCLE PARADIGM: HOW TROUBLED STUDENTS GET TEACHERS OUT OF CONTROL

Nicholas J. Long

The Conflict Cycle is a paradigm that describes the circular and escalating behavior of a student–teacher conflict.

Figure 6.2–1 presents the student's Conflict Cycle and its five interacting parts:

- Student's self-concept
- Stressful incident
- Student's feelings
- Student's observable behavior
- Adult/peer reactions

To help readers understand the dynamic nature of the Conflict Cycle Paradigm, I provide a detailed overview of the circular sequence of the Conflict Cycle (see Figure 6.2–2).

PART 1: STUDENT'S SELF-CONCEPT

The student's self-concept plays a central role in determining how he thinks about himself, how he relates to others, and what he believes will happen to him in the future (i.e., his self-fulfilling prophecy).

Developmentally, a child's self-concept is formed by the repetitive interactions of significant adults and peers in his life who give him ongoing feedback about his behavior and character. If a child receives clear and positive reinforcements, such as that he is lovable, curious, happy, smart, attractive, and strong, he will internalize these experiences and statements and slowly begin to attribute these characteristics to himself. If, however, he receives negative feedback and is told he is fearful, aggressive, sad, stupid, ugly, and rude, over time, the child will internalize a depreciating view of himself. As a result, how a child learns to think about himself is critical in determining his subsequent feelings and behaviors. For example, a student may score in the average range of intelligence, but if he thinks he is dumb, then his feelings and behaviors will be consistent with his thoughts about himself, regardless of the test results.

IRRATIONAL BELIEFS

In addition to developing a unique set of personal beliefs, the child concurrently develops a personal set of beliefs about her psychological world and the people in it. If the adults in her life are hostile, rejecting, negligent, depressed, helpless, ambivalent, perfectionistic, or inconsistent,

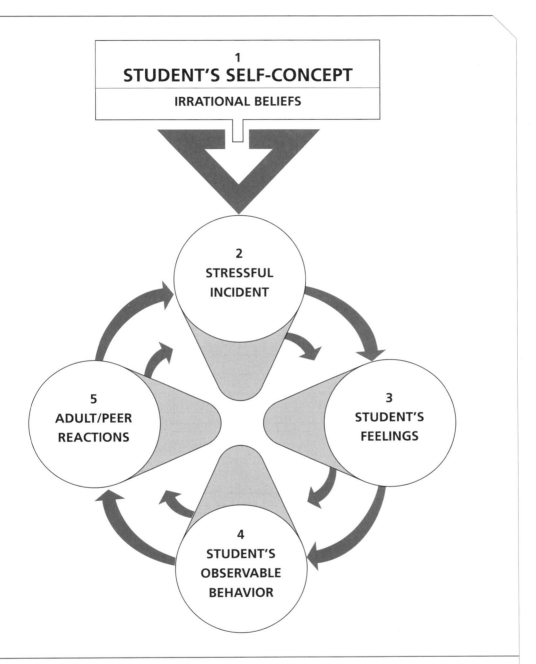

Figure 6.2–1. The Student's Conflict Cycle.

the child will learn to mistrust and to avoid interpersonal closeness with them. These negative beliefs about others in her world become the second active part of her self-concept. By early elementary school age, her beliefs about herself and her beliefs about others merge and become the major

THE SEQUENCE OF THE CONFLICT CYCLE

or

How a troubled student creates counteraggressive feelings in staff, which frequently leads to a mutual, self-defeating power struggle and reinforces the student's irrational beliefs (i.e., self-fulfilling prophecy).

1 A stressful incident occurs (i.e., frustration, failure), which **ACTIVATES** a troubled student's irrational beliefs (i.e., "Nothing good ever happens to me!" Adults are hostile!", etc.).

2 These negative thoughts determine and **TRIGGER** the student's feelings.

3 The student's negative feelings and not his or her rational forces **DRIVE** the student's inappropriate behavior.

4 The student's inappropriate behaviors (yelling, threatening, sarcasm, refusing to speak) **INCITE** staff.

5 Staff not only pick up the student's negative feelings but also frequently **MIRROR** the student's behavior (yelling, threatening, sarcasm and refusing to talk to the student).

This adverse staff **REACTION** increases the student's stress, triggers more intense feelings, and drives more inappropriate behaviors, thus causing even more staff anger and denunciation. Around and around it goes until the Conflict Cycle becomes a self-defeating power struggle.

Although the student may lose the initial battle (i.e., is punished or rejected), he or she wins the psychological war! The student's self-fulfiling prophesy (i.e., irrational belief) is **REINFORCED**, and there-fore the student has no motivation to change or alter the irrational beliefs or inappropriate behaviors.

Figure 6.2–2. The Conflict Cycle Paradigm.

motivating force of her emerging personality. This solidification of her self-concept results in the child's developing a characteristic way of per-ceiving, thinking, feeling, and behaving in all new situations. The child now has a predictable and functioning way of responding to most current and future life events. For example, just as a primitive tribe will explain a tidal wave or an exploding volcano as something the tribe had done to offend the gods, troubled children will explain why they were abused, neglected, or rejected. Their search for an explanation does not take place in reality, but in their irrational beliefs about their painful life experiences. This means all their life events are filtered by their thoughts, which are activated by their personal belief system.

RATIONAL VERSUS IRRATIONAL BELIEFS

How do we as helpers determine if a child's beliefs are rational or irrational? Irrational beliefs are not based on true reality conditions and operate to the detriment of the child's mental health. The distinction between rational and irrational beliefs becomes vague for troubled children who have experienced chronic abuse, neglect, and rejection. Initially, their negative beliefs about others are an accurate reflection of their life experiences.

What causes these reality-based beliefs to become irrational is the psychological process called *overgeneralization*. This is a specific way of thinking, which allows a troubled child to perceive any new relationship or experience in a negative way. This thinking is achieved by using the words *always* and *never* whenever an individual thinks about this person or event. For example, a troubled student neglected by his parents would say, "My parents always neglected me [fact]. I could never count on my parents to meet my needs [fact]. Therefore, I think all adults I meet in the future also will neglect my needs [irrational belief]."

The following lists describe some of the irrational beliefs commonly held by troubled students.

Irrational Beliefs About Self

- I should never express my anger openly and if I do I will be punished.
- I should be perfect at everything I do.
- I am stupid if I make mistakes.
- I am a terrible person.
- I am unworthy of love.
- I never have to listen to anyone except me.
- I have to be in control to survive.

Irrational Beliefs About Others

- Never depend on adults to meet your needs. They will always let you down.
- This world is filled with dangerous people and situations.
- People are too helpless and depressed to care about me.
- People will take advantage of me every time they can.

THE ADVANTAGES OF IRRATIONAL BELIEFS

Why are irrational beliefs maintained when they interfere with everyday, interpersonal relationships and psychological comfort? What are the internal rewards for holding on to pathological and self-defeating irrational beliefs? One explanation is that irrational beliefs provide troubled students with a sense of security and control. Irrational beliefs bring psychological order to the students' unstable and chaotic world. Irrational beliefs make their world predictable and manageable. Irrational beliefs allow students to know in advance what will happen to them in new relationships. Such beliefs also protect troubled students from moving beyond their feelings and becoming responsible for their behavior. Most important, irrational beliefs protect them from experiencing the dreaded and underlying feelings of helplessness and rage. As a result, troubled students feel there is no reason to change. In fact, they reinforce their irrational beliefs by projecting their belief system on others. They do this by engaging adults and peers in endless and absurd power struggles. This psychological process almost always guarantees the adult will confirm the student's self-fulfilling prophecy.

THE STUDENT'S SELF-FULFILLING PROPHECY

The self-fulfilling prophecy is the troubled student's way of validating irrational beliefs by getting staff or peers to act them out. Most staff and peers are unaware of this covert goal of a troubled student and end up fulfilling the student's prophecy about others. The following three examples demonstrate the effectiveness of students' self-fulfilling prophecies.

The Self-Fulfilling Prophecy of an Aggressive Student

This student believes he has the right to meet his needs regardless of the rights of others and to get back at any adult or peer who interferes with his pleasures. Concurrently, he believes adults are hostile and ultimately will reject and punish him. The question is, How can he maintain these irrational beliefs about all adults when his new teacher is kind, compassionate, skilled, and caring? Like a director of a play, his solution is to cast the teacher into the psychological role of a hostile adult, regardless of the teacher's personality, and to look for opportunities when he can accuse the teacher of being unfair and rejecting. The following classroom observation clearly highlights this process.

> Earl, a large 12-year-old boy, is sitting at his desk, completing his morning work. He raises his hand and asks for permission to get a drink of water. The teacher approves. Earl stands up, but instead of leaving the classroom, he walks over to Carl's desk and starts talking to him. Carl responds and Earl pats Carl on the head, laughs, and grabs his paper. Carl grabs it back and shouts, "Your sister!"
>
> The teacher intervenes and says, "Earl, you are more interested in causing trouble than getting a drink, so just forget it and return to your desk."
>
> Earl reacts as if he had been slapped, shouting, "What a gyp! You can't even get a damn drink in this school. This is not a school. It is a prison! I could die of thirst and you wouldn't care!" He walks back to his desk, slams a book closed, and looks sullen, and believes his teacher is hostile and rejecting like all the adults in his life.

The Self-Fulfilling Prophecy of a Passive–Aggressive Student

A passive–aggressive student believes the direct expression of anger is dangerous so she must hide and disguise her aggressive feelings and thoughts. It is common for a passive–aggressive student to say, "If adults ever found out how I really feel about them, terrible things would happen." Consequently, a passive–aggressive student learns to express her normal feelings of anger in indirect ways. She doesn't hear, see, or remember anything the teacher asks her to do. If she has to do something she doesn't want to do, she does it in a way that frustrates the teacher. If she is really angry with the teacher, she will get back at him by hiding some objects he needs, or by messing up the room without his knowledge. For example, Devon's indirect and subtle "drip- by-drip" frustrating behaviors begin to overwhelm the teacher. Over time he becomes emotionally loaded but psychologically unaware of his accumulated anger toward Devon. At the end of a difficult classroom lesson, Devon falls out of her chair, makes the teacher ask her three times before acknowledging him, and accidentally rips the teacher's newly designed bulletin board. This is the straw that breaks the camel's back, the spark that lights the fuse. The teacher explodes, yells, and threatens Devon. He has a 20-second intense temper tantrum.

Devon appears shocked, "Gee, it was an accident. I didn't really mean to do it." The teacher is also shocked by the intensity of anger he expressed. He begins to think, "Perhaps it was an accident. Perhaps I did overreact. This is not like me. After all, Devon is not the most difficult student in my class." He feels guilty and decides to apologize. "Devon," he says, "I'm sorry I yelled at you." Devon replies, "It's okay," but thinks: "Wow! Look at how crazy people get when they express their anger. It's a good thing I don't express my anger. My teacher needs to change, but I don't."

The Self-Fulfilling Prophecy of a Withdrawn, Abused Student

Mary, a 13-year-old student, believes she is a terrible person, unworthy of anyone's love. Her family consists of an alcoholic, abusive father; a subservient mother; and two younger sisters. Mary has been sexually abused since age 7. Her mother knew about it but never said or did anything to stop it. It was a family secret never to be told. Mary believes if she were a better person, these sexual assaults would not happen. Her irrational beliefs include, "I deserve what happened to me, and if others found out what I was really like, they would know how terrible I am and reject me." Mary's self-fulfilling prophecy is to avoid all meaningful relationships and attachments since she believes they would only cause her more pain, shame, and rejection. Mary's classroom teacher reports that Mary has no friends and appears to be uninterested and unresponsive to any peer and teacher who attempts to reach out to her. She is a loner, and if there were one word to describe her relationship with others, it would be "ignored." Clearly, Mary has created a social reality in school that maintains her irrational beliefs that she is unworthy of being a friend.

To understand and help a student, staff need to recognize the troubled student's self-fulfilling prophecy or pattern of self-defeating behavior.

PART 2: STRESSFUL INCIDENT

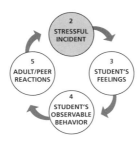

The second part of the Conflict Cycle is a stressful incident, defined as an external event that threatens the well-being of a student or activates his irrational beliefs. For example, a teacher may ask two students to come to the front of the class to read from a textbook. Gary thinks this request is a wonderful opportunity to demonstrate his reading skills and dramatic voice, believing it will improve his social status among his peers. Jason, however, thinks this same request is a disaster. He thinks he will mispronounce the words, stutter, and make a fool of himself in front of his peers. Whether this incident was stressful or not for each student depended on the specific meaning each student gave to the request to read aloud. In Jason's case, it triggered his irrational belief that "nothing ever works out for me," so it became a stressful incident for him. Gary, however, perceived it as a manageable challenge, so it became a positive experience for him.

THE PHYSIOLOGY OF STRESS

Once a student perceives an event as a stressful incident, a natural biological reaction follows: This response is automatic, unconscious, and predictable. Stress prepares the body for action. It does this by releasing a series of hormones into the bloodstream that activate the autonomic nervous system. This system controls the involuntary muscles and alters the blood pressure, respiration, and digestive systems. Anthropologically, stress has functioned as a personal alarm system enabling a person to survive a physical attack. During this stress state, all bodily senses are intensified. The person has an abundance of energy, creating increased levels of strength, agility, and endurance. The person can either attack a foe with new ferocity or escape by running great distances without tiring.

For primitive humans, stress served a very useful, specific, and important purpose. In many cases, it was the basis of life or death.

In today's complex society, however, there are many rules against attacking others or running away. Students must learn to control what their bodies are urging them to express. They must learn to manage a stressful event instead of acting out. Because self-control takes considerable skill and maturity, even "normal" students will behave inappropriately during a stressful event.

There are four types of student stress: developmental stress, economic/physical stress, psychological stress, and reality stress.

1. Developmental Stress

Developmental stress refers to the normal developmental stages from birth to death. For example, to be born is stressful. To be weaned from the breast or bottle is stressful. To be toilet-trained is stressful. To leave one's parents and home to go to school is stressful. Learning to read can be stressful. Learning to understand sex differences between boys and girls can be stressful. Learning to be part of a group can be stressful. For adolescents, there are numerous developmental stresses: watching one's body change, becoming independent, developing personal values as opposed to group values, understanding the excitement and confusion of one's own and others' sexuality, developing career courses, graduating from high school, and so on. Each of these developmental events can be stressful for all students regardless of races, ethnicity, creed, or socioeconomic level.

2. Economic/Physical Stress

Economic/physical stress is felt by millions of families in our society who are living on the brink of economic disaster. Not all of these families come from slums, ghettos, or disadvantaged groups. Many striving middle-class families are living beyond their financial resources and have extended their credit lines to the breaking point.

For chronically poor families, economic stress shows itself in poor diet and food; poor health habits; greater susceptibility to illness; lack of acceptable clothes; lack of privacy; lack of sleep; lack of opportunity to participate in social and school-related activities; and greater parent exhaustion, joblessness, and helplessness.

3. Psychological Stress

Psychological stress consists of an unconscious or deliberate attempt by parents, individuals, groups, and institutions to destroy the self-esteem of a student. For example, many students are told they are a financial and psychological burden to the family and the primary source of their parents' problems. They are told life would be better if they were not around. They are destroying the family and neighborhood because of their demanding and ungrateful behaviors. They are stupid, inconsiderate, mean, and useless to themselves and others. For some students, the stress does not come from open rejection but from trying to meet unrealistic parental standards. Students are told they must be successful to be loved. Whatever they do is not good enough. For other students, psychological stress is related to specific adults who are emotionally troubled—for example, the seductive parent who stimulates excessive sexual awareness and fantasy by showing unusual interest in sexual topics; the psychotic parent, who is suffering from a major mental illness and is not capable of carrying out adult responsibilities; the alcoholic or drug-abusing parent who creates a home where there is little emotional stability. In these homes children never know if their parents will care for them or expose them to more shame or terror. Other students must cope with overprotective or depressed parents. Moreover, any sibling, relative, or significant friend who is emotionally disturbed and active with these students will have a stressful impact on the mental health of these students and their ability to focus on classroom learning.

4. Reality Stress

Reality stress occurs when events happen to students that should not happen to them. These unplanned events are frustrating. They happen spontaneously and not from an organized attempt to frustrate the students. Reality stresses for troubled students seem to happen at a higher frequency than for regular students. Students begin to believe the world and the people in it are against them. The following are examples:

- A boy looks forward to wearing his favorite sweater only to discover that his brother wore it yesterday and spilled syrup on it.
- A girl lends her algebra book to a friend who forgets to bring it to school the next day.
- Two classmates are fooling around in class. One pushes the other into a third girl's desk, tearing her English composition, which is due in a few minutes.
- A teacher warns the class that the next student who talks will

be given a detention. The student next to Jason whispers to a friend, and the teacher points to Jason as the offender.

- A teenage boy is asked by a girl to go to the high school basketball game. At the game he discovers she has broken up with the school bully, who is staring at him.

In other words, things go wrong that should not go wrong. It is not anyone's fault, but the stress is very real, frequent, and intense.

For most troubled students, stress comes not from one source but from multiple sources. For example, a student may have the normal developmental stress of a final exam. The evening before the test, his parents have a violent argument, and he is unable to study or sleep. On the way to school, a hostile group of boys call him various racial and ethnic names. As he enters the classroom, a friend greets him by slapping him on the back, causing his glasses to fall and break. Finally, the teacher announces a new school policy that no exam can be taken over, regardless of the circumstances.

Teachers need to acknowledge that a student in a crisis needs to talk. Through mutual conversation, a greater appreciation of the students' stresses and a broader perspective of his or her behavior can be achieved. When teachers understand these multiple cycles of stress, they are more willing to help students rather than blame and punish them for their misfortune.

The following list represents some common classroom stresses.

Developmental Stress

- Student experiences group pressure to conform to their norms.
- Student experiences sexual attraction to a classmate.
- Student wasn't called on or selected for a group game.
- Student is teased by her peers.

Economic/Physical Stress

- Student is too tired to concentrate on the assignment.
- Student is too sick to concentrate on the assignment.
- Student is too hungry to concentrate on the assignment.
- Student has a handicapping condition that prevents him from competing with his peers.

Psychological Stress

- Student fails an examination.
- Student is racially depreciated.
- Student believes others have a higher expectation of her performance than she does.
- Student is deliberately rejected or scapegoated by peers.
- Student is too conflicted by his home problems to concentrate on classroom assignments.

Reality Stress

- Student is blamed for something she didn't do.
- Student doesn't have the appropriate textbook for class.
- Student doesn't understand the content of the assignment.
- Student doesn't understand the teacher's directions.
- Student cannot get his locker to open, which contains a report that is due next period.
- A friend accidentally tears the student's favorite shirt.

PART 3: STUDENT'S FEELINGS

There is considerable confusion among teachers and other helping professionals concerning the origin, awareness, accuracy, and expression of students' feelings. The following questions reflect the quandary many helping professionals have in determining how to work with the feelings of troubled students: What is the relationship between thinking and feeling? Are they independent of each other? Isn't it healthy for students to express their feelings and to get them out in the open so they can be understood? Is it accurate to describe feelings as "good feelings" and "bad feelings"? Should negative feelings be controlled? If feelings are swallowed or blocked, don't they come back as psychosomatic illnesses? Because feelings are real, are they an accurate assessment of the precipitating incident or are they an assessment of the student's current emotional state? Is there a difference between acknowledging feelings and expressing them? If the same feeling can be expressed in different ways are some expressions healthier than others? These questions corroborate the uncertainty, ambivalence, and fogginess that have developed around the concept of understanding and managing students' feelings.

THINKING CREATES FEELINGS

David Burns (1999), a cognitive therapist, wrote, "You feel the way you think." The source of feelings starts with thoughts and not with personal frustrations. It is how one *thinks* about an external event, and not the event itself, that triggers feelings. Positive thoughts about an event trigger positive feelings, and negative thoughts about an event trigger negative feelings, as in the previous example of the two students who were asked to read aloud. The process of thinking and feeling does not follow an independent path but is a continuous circular process. Thoughts trigger feelings, and negative feelings influence the way a person thinks about an event, creating a new cycle of negative feelings.

If the same external event happens frequently, the child will develop feelings that affect his or her thinking. For example, if a child is chronically yelled at by an adult, the child not only will have negative feelings such as anger or fear but also will be conditioned to respond automatically to all future acts of yelling. This will occur without the child's being aware of his thinking. For example, I once went to listen to a new student talk about a fight he just had with a classmate. Without saying a word, I entered the room and sat in the corner to observe the process. After 10 minutes I stood up and took off my jacket since the room was warm. Simultaneously, the student looked at me, panicked, and dove under the desk. The student was convinced that when the principal, or a man of authority, took off his jacket, the adult was preparing to hit the student. This reaction is called automatic thinking and explains the rapid negative behavior many troubled students demonstrate during conflict.

THE USEFULNESS OF FEELINGS

All feelings are real and powerful, and add excitement to life, but they are not always an accurate assessment of a situation. Emotions are not facts; they are feelings that are triggered by rational and irrational thoughts. If the feelings are triggered by irrational thoughts, then the subsequent feelings are real but self-defeating. When students act on these feelings, their behavior only makes the situation worse. However, if the feelings are triggered by rational thoughts, then the feelings are an accurate assessment of the situation and need to be accepted. This involves a complicated process of distinguishing between acknowledging one's feelings and learning to express these feelings in proper behavior. For example, it is healthy to feel upset and angry when one has been psychologically depreciated or discriminated against, but it is not acceptable to assault the offender. It is healthy to experience fear when someone threatens to hurt or abuse you, but it is not helpful to encourage it to happen. It is healthy to experience intense feelings of sadness when someone you love dies or moves away, but it is not healthy to withdraw from all relationships. It is healthy to feel guilty when you behave in an unacceptable way, but it is not useful to behave so others will punish you. It is normal to experience anxiety when you are anticipating a new experience or a new relationship, but it is not healthy to handle this anxiety through drinking or drug abuse. It is normal to feel happiness when you are in love, but it is not helpful to express blatant sexual feelings in front of others. The existence and importance of accepting one's feelings are irrefutable. The question is, How do students learn to express these feelings?

THREE WAYS OF EXPRESSING FEELINGS

The three ways children learn to express their feelings are to act them out, to defend against them, and to accept and own them.

Act Out Feelings

Many immature, impulsive, and unsocialized children express their feelings directly. There is no attempt to modify the direct expression of their feelings in behavior. If they are angry, they hit; if they are sad, they cry; if they are frightened, they run; and if they are happy, they giggle and laugh. There is an obvious one-to-one relationship between their feelings and behaviors. When students express their feelings directly in spontaneous classroom behavior, they almost always create more problems for themselves. Some students cannot distinguish between feeling angry and smashing a chair. For these students, the feeling and behavior are one response and not two.

Defend Against Feelings

Many children are socialized to believe that certain feelings, such as anger, sadness, or jealousy, are unacceptable for them to show. When these feelings occur, they create in the children a state of anxiety, discomfort, and inner conflict. The psychological goal for these children is to learn ways of avoiding or blocking these unacceptable feelings.

Anna Freud (1937) described these strategies of avoiding the pain of anxiety as defense mechanisms. This concept of defense mechanisms provides teachers with valuable insights on how children defend against anxiety. Children learn three ways of using defense mechanisms: (1) by denying these feelings, (2) by escaping from these unacceptable feelings, and (3) by shifting or substituting the unacceptable feelings to another person or object.

The most common defense mechanisms using denial are repression, projection, and rationalization; the most common defense mechanisms using escape are withdrawal and regression; and the most common defense mechanisms using substitution are displacement, compensation, and sublimation. Although defense mechanisms are successful in diminishing anxiety, they also use up the student's psychological energy, deny the real problem, and usually create new interpersonal problems with adults, peers, learning, and rules. This is like the adolescent driver who is concerned about running out of gas. His solution is to drive to the nearest gas station as quickly as possible, but in the process, he gets a speeding ticket, becomes frustrated, and also runs out of gas.

Accept and Own Feelings

Students who have learned to accept and own their feelings can use them to enrich their lives and to develop coping skills to manage their inevitable frustrations. These students have learned to distinguish between having the full range of feelings and being had by their feelings. When students are flooded by their feelings, their behavior is driven by their emotions and not by rational thought. If this pattern happens often, these students are labeled "emotionally disturbed" because their emotions drive their behavior. However, when students learn to own their feelings and think about them rationally, then the resulting behaviors usually are appropriate, logical, and realistic. Accepting one's feelings and learning how to be friends with them, including the unpleasant feelings such as sadness, anger, jealousy, envy, and rejection, is one goal of mental health.

PART 4: STUDENT'S OBSERVABLE BEHAVIOR

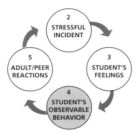

When students express their feelings directly or defend against them, they usually create additional problems for themselves. Inappropriate behaviors, such as hitting, running away, becoming ill, stealing, teasing, lying, becoming hyperactive, fighting, using drugs, inattention, and withdrawal, cause students to have difficulty with teachers, peers, learning, and school rules. For example, when a student displaces his feelings of hostility he has for his father on his teacher, an inevitable teacher–student conflict develops. When a student becomes depressed because her mother is ill or battered, the student may not be able to complete her assignments, and her grades drop. When this interpretation of behavior is accepted, one grasps the concept that the problems students cause in school are not always the causes of their problems. More accurately, the problems students cause in school are the result of the way they have learned to express their feelings.

Many professionals describe a student's behavior in general terms, such as "Jason hit Sam" or "Jason tore up his assignment." These are beginning statements, but to pinpoint the significance of a student's behavior, it needs to be described by answering the following questions: Where did the behavior occur? When did it happen? Who or what were the targets of this behavior? What was the duration of this behavior? What was the intensity of this behavior? What was the frequency of this behavior?

Notice the difference in meaning between these two statements:

Jason spit on Sam.

Jason and Sam were on the playground during recess playing tag. Sam tagged Jason by hitting him on the side of his face. Jason reacted by spitting on Sam's face, chest, and hands at least three times over a period of 2 minutes. The spits were intense and involved large amounts of saliva. This is the third time Jason has spit on another peer this week.

This second description of Jason's behavior provides a much clearer sense of the hostility Jason is expressing by spitting. The incident was not a simple, spontaneous act, but part of a destructive pattern of behavior he uses when he becomes angry.

PART 5: ADULT/PEER REACTIONS

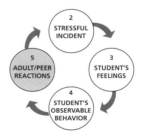

CATEGORIES OF INAPPROPRIATE STAFF RESPONSES

How a teacher reacts to inappropriate student behavior is the most critical part of the Conflict Cycle. Although a teacher does not have control over the student's thinking, feelings, and behaviors, a teacher does have complete control over how he or she reacts to the student's behavior. Unfortunately, staff members escalate too many student–staff conflicts when they respond in emotional, impulsive, and counteraggressive ways. An analysis of over 600 student–staff Conflict Cycles documented four categories of inappropriate staff responses to student behavior: (1) reacting in counteraggressive ways, (2) having rigid and unrealistic teacher expectations, (3) being caught in a bad mood, and (4) prejudging a troubled student.

Reacting in Counteraggressive Ways

One of the most important insights a teacher can gain from learning about the Conflict Cycle is awareness of how a troubled student can create negative feelings in a teacher. If the teacher is not trained to accept these negative feelings, he or she will act on them and mirror the troubled student's behavior. For example, when a student yells at a teacher, "I'm not going to do it," the normal impulse of a teacher is to shout back, "Yes you will!" Once the teacher behaves like the student, the Conflict Cycle is escalated into a self-defeating power struggle. Generally, an aggressive student will always create counteraggressive feelings in others, a depressed student will always cause others to feel sad and helpless, and a hyperactive student will always create feelings of impulsivity in others.

Staff do not start most Conflict Cycles; however, without training they keep the cycle going by reacting inappropriately. Initially, a teacher has no thoughts or intentions of yelling, threatening, or depreciating a troubled student, but once the cycle of teacher counteraggressive behavior begins, it is extremely difficult for the teacher to stop or to acknowledge his or her role in escalating the conflict. Usually, a teacher feels unjustly attacked and becomes flooded by feelings of righteous rage. These feelings seem to justify the teacher's retaliatory reaction or counteraggression. Reacting in counteraggressive ways account for 68% of school-based Conflict Cycles in our sample.

Having Rigid and Unrealistic Teacher Expectations Regarding Normal Developmental Student Behavior

Some teachers carry their own psychological luggage with them into the classroom. They are mean spirited, rigid, narrow minded, critical, and exacting about what kinds of behavior they will tolerate in their classrooms. These teachers believe students should be obedient to authorities, remain attentive to instruction, be motivated to excel, and use proper language and manners at all times. Problem behavior for them is defined as a discrepancy between what they expect and what they observe in their classrooms based on their personal histories. If there is a difference, it is because the student has a problem and needs to be disciplined. These teachers are unaware of how their forked tongues can become instruments of pain and how this contributes to escalating the crisis.

Over time, even "normal" students will react to an autocratic and repressive classroom atmosphere and begin to get back by becoming passive–aggressive toward the teacher. Troubled students in the classroom have even greater difficulties. These students react to the demeaning and critical behavior of the teacher by mirroring the teacher's behavior. In this instance of the Conflict Cycle in action, the teacher initiates the conflict and a student keeps it going. For example, a teacher may threaten a troubled student and say, "You better stop whispering or else!" only to hear him say, "You better stop talking or else!" After the class stops laughing, the student is labeled defiant and is sent out of the room. However, if the student refuses to leave the classroom, swears, or slams the door on the way out, the problem behavior escalates into a student–teacher crisis. The behavior of rigid teachers accounts for 7% of our sample of student–staff Conflict Cycles.

Being Caught in a Bad Mood

School staff are not robots. They have the same stresses as all adults. Occasionally, their personal or family life takes an emotional dip. As their level of stress increases, they become emotionally overwhelmed and exhausted. For example, their level of tolerance drops when they are dealing with their parents who are ill and need special care, when their children are having academic and interpersonal problems and need additional support, when they are having financial difficulties, and when they are angry with their mate or friends.

These teachers usually are competent, dedicated, and supportive of their students, but periodically something occurs that gives them a bitter attitude toward life. They cannot stomach the acid irritation of the normal and annoying developmental behavior of their students and are ready to spew out their exasperation on any student who upsets them. For example, Jamal decided it would be clever and fun if he added a little excitement to the classroom by making "burp" sounds with his armpits. The teacher overreacted to Jamal's attention-getting sounds by becoming punitive, and a crisis developed. Afterward, teachers who are caught in a bad mood usually can acknowledge their role in the crisis and respond positively to supportive confrontation. Teacher stress due to personal life situations accounts for approximately 20% of our sample of student–staff Conflict Cycles.

Prejudging a Troubled Student in a Crisis

In every school, a peer social structure exists in which students are assigned and assume specific group roles such as the leader, jock, nerd, mascot, lawyer, and clown. One group role is the instigator or troublemaker. Everyone knows who this student is. His reputation is acknowledged by the school staff and peers and follows him around like a shadow on a summer day.

If this student is involved in a crisis, and the sounds of trouble are all around him, there is a high probability this student will be prejudged. As the group instigator, he will be judged before all the relevant information is obtained. The staff who intervenes is likely to say, "I knew it would be you!" Call this process faulty clairvoyance or drawing of defective conclusions, but it happens to the nicest of people. Judgments are made that are not true, and the targeted student is accused of some act he did not do. In this sequence, the student becomes upset and the staff is convinced that the student is lying to protect himself. The result is an unfortunate incident that escalates into an ugly crisis. This process of prejudging a troubled student before all the facts are obtained accounts for 5% of our sample of student/staff Conflict Cycles.

These four categories of inappropriate staff reactions during a student–staff Conflict Cycle are helpful in identifying what additional skills adults need in order to break their own pattern of self-defeating behavior. Although the most frequent inappropriate teacher response category was reacting in counteraggressive ways, further analysis of our sample of student–staff Conflict Cycles revealed that staff in all four categories used "You Messages" when they were angry.

FUELING THE CONFLICT CYCLE WITH "YOU MESSAGES"

The following "You Messages" were recorded during student–staff Conflict Cycles that escalated into no-win power struggles:

- Can't you do anything right?
- You apologize immediately!
- Don't you dare use that language with me!
- You better start acting your age!
- You think you know everything. Should I call you Einstein?
- You have no respect for anyone or anything!
- You don't listen to anyone, do you?
- You better shape up because I have had it with you.
- You just never use your head.

The negative and blaming "You Messages" a student receives from a teacher frequently support the student's view of herself and confirm her self-fulfilling prophecy. This feeling creates more student stress, causing the student to feel and behave in more unacceptable ways. As the student's behavior deteriorates, the teacher becomes even more angry and disgusted with the student. As the teacher reacts in a negative, punitive way, this intensifies the student's stress, creating more negative feelings and primitive behaviors. The Conflict Cycle continues around and around until it escalates into a no-win power struggle. Logic, caring, and compassion are lost, and the only goal for each party is to win the power struggle. The teacher views the student as the source of the problem and tells the student to "shape up" and to improve her attitude and behavior. If she doesn't, the teacher labels her as disturbed, delinquent, dangerous, and disgusting. The student is usually suspended, transferred, or referred to a more restrictive, special education setting.

What is important to remember is that there are no winners when the Conflict Cycle reaches the level of a power struggle. Asking immature students to act maturely during intense states of stress cannot break this cycle. If change is going to occur, the staff must accept the first level of responsibility by responding in a more mature, professional manner. This means understanding how students in conflict can provoke concerned, reasonable, and dedicated teachers to act in impulsive, dispassionate, and rejecting ways.

In summary, the Conflict Cycle follows this self-defeating sequence for a troubled student:

1. External events arouse irrational beliefs.

2. These irrational beliefs trigger negative feelings.

3. Negative feelings drive inappropriate behavior.

4. Inappropriate behavior incites others.

5. Staff react in counteraggressive ways and create additional stress for the student, which fuels the student's next cycle of problems.

CASE STUDY

Example: How an Aggressive Student Successfully Creates Counteraggressive Behavior in a Student Teacher (Ms. Sarah Drue)

I did my student teaching at a city junior high and I was told there were specific rules and regulations that needed to be followed.

This incident occurred because of the tardy policy. When students are late for school without a legitimate written excuse, they must first report to the office to pick up a sign-in sheet, which is carried to homeroom. After the homeroom teachers sign this sheet, the students are required to stay in Tardy Hall from 3:00 to 4:00 P.M. Brian, a 16-year-old learning disabled student came in to my homeroom without his sign-in sheet at approximately 9:30. I had already filled his name in as absent for the day, but he requested that I change it immediately. He did not want to go to the office because he did not want to stay after school. This was my first day of student teaching the class. The regular teacher was in the classroom to observe me. Therefore, everything I did was being evaluated.

Of course, Brian insisted I change his name on my sheet from being "tardy" to "present." "Come on Ms. Drue, it won't hurt anything. I want to go to the game this afternoon and I can't stay in Tardy Hall."

"Well Brian, if I did this for you, I would have to do it for everyone else. Isn't that right, class?" Of course, the entire class agreed with me and began approaching my desk. One of my students had already been to the office because of being late; therefore, she insisted that if his was changed, then so should hers. I replied that I was not going to change anyone's and that Brian had better hurry to the main office before he's late for his first-period class.

Brian replied, "You're not my teacher anyway. I don't have to talk to you. Ms. Shell will do it for me." Ms. Shell was the "real" teacher for the Learning Center and she told Brian it was up to me since I was teaching for the rest of the semester. I had already decided not to make any changes. As much as I wanted to, I just could not.

Brian began raising "hell" after I had made my final decision and threatened he was going to "kick my ass" after school. Of course, I was scared. Brian stands at least 6 feet tall and is huge! Little ole' me was not used to this sort of outrage. He called me all sorts of "bitches" and "MF's," so I told him to wait in the office until I came down. Ms. Shell said I was to report this incident because this behavior cannot be tolerated. Brian again threatened Ms. Shell and me. She got up angrily, grabbed Brian by his collar and escorted him to the main office. "Bitch, you just wait," he continued to holler. "I'm going to flatten your tires along with your face." Well, I was in hysterics by now, but Ms. Shell told me to continue with the class.

By 10:30 A.M., Ms. Shell returned to the classroom without Brian. She informed me he had been sent home and could not return without his parents. I was very upset, but she informed me there wasn't more that could be done. "You did well! You didn't lose your temper. I'm used to seeing Brian go into these rages every now and then. Why, I am practically the only teacher who can do anything with him."

I tried to make my day go on as usual, but my mind kept thinking about what Brian said. I already had made up my mind to stay after school, so I could get away scot-free. I thought I would be safe. But by the time I checked my name out in the principal's office, I was sweating. I was scared! I proceeded down the hallway and out comes Brian! I should have turned around and gone back to the office, but if he knew I was afraid of him, he would probably provoke me for the rest of the semester. No way. I had to stand up to this kid. If I show him that I am not afraid, maybe he won't bother with me.

"Yea Bitch, I told you not to send my name to the office. Wait until you see your tires," Brian says.

"Aren't you supposed to be home by now? I thought you were sent home until your parents arrived back to school with you."

"Yea Bitch, I can tell, you ole' ho!"

"Okay, I'm a whore and you're a faggot. Now we're even." I continued toward my car.

"Faggot! Does this look like a faggot's dick?"

I wanted to faint. I hope he didn't actually pull his penis out! I surely wasn't going to turn around to find out either. "Brian, I am surprised at you. You have really disappointed me. I thought you were one of my better students. Say what you will, just make sure that you don't touch me. I am here to teach you, not to beat you."

Why did I say that? Brian then began throwing rocks and sticks at me outside of the school. I still didn't turn around, but I did warn him that if any of them hit me, I was going to forget about being his teacher and actually "KICK HIS ASS!" "Bang," a rock hit me in the back of my leg. I stopped and turned around to look at him. He began saying, "Kick my ass, come on, kick my ass." I proceeded toward my car but began telling him that I was going to call his parents tonight. "Bang," this rock hit me in the middle of my back, and I turned around and began walking toward him with full force. By now I had forgotten I was a teacher and I was aiming to kick his tail. When I got to him he looked so much larger than I but I was not going to back down. I began hollering and pointing my finger in his face, telling him that my brothers would love kicking his tail if he hurt me. He kept breathing real hard down on my face, just trying to provoke me even more. By now the assistant principal and two other teachers came running out of the school and grabbed Brian, dragging him to the office. I began crying and they questioned me about the entire incident. They wanted me to press charges. The school security guard stayed with Brian until his parents picked him up from the police precinct.

This student–staff conflict between Brian and Sara Drue demonstrates, with startling clarity, how quickly a Conflict Cycle can escalate into a no-win power struggle. The incident began with Brian experiencing a reality disappointment (being tardy), moved on to verbal threats, and proceeded to physical threats—throwing stones at Ms. Drue. This pattern of Brian's self-defeating behavior was not new to his regular teacher, Ms. Shell, who said, "I'm used to seeing Brian go into these rages," but it was a new and upsetting experience for Ms. Drue, even though she was commended by Ms. Shell as "doing well" and "not losing her temper."

The more Ms. Drue "thought" about Brian's threats, the more anxious and fearful she became. When she saw Brian, she had two thoughts: "I'll show him I'm not afraid of him" and "I need to walk back to the office and avoid this confrontation." She decided to take him on head to head, one to one, teacher against student. Brian started this new cycle by using sexual language, "Yea Bitch, I can tell, you ole' ho!" and discovered Ms. Drue's emotional panic button. She reacted by using similar sexual language, "Okay, I'm a whore and you're a faggot!" This remark only succeeded in escalating the situation. Brian retorted and started to throw stones at her. This triggered her feelings of righteous rage, and when he urged her to "kick his ass," she couldn't refuse. She threw away her professional skills and started toward him with aggressive intentions. If her colleagues had not arrived in time to rescue her, this situation could have resulted in serious injuries. The outcomes were predictable. Ms. Drue fulfilled her prophecy that Brian was a dangerous student. Brian fulfilled his prophecy that Ms. Drue was a hostile woman, and Brian ended up being totally responsible for this incident and was suspended with no insight into his pattern of self-defeating behavior.

Could this second student–staff incident have been avoided? If Ms. Drue understood the goal of the Conflict Cycle and was aware that Brian was trying to push her emotional buttons and to get her to act in unprofessional and counteraggressive ways, she would have selected her second option: avoiding Brian by walking back to the office. With this rational decision, Ms. Drue could have prevented the second cycle of craziness.

SUMMARY

The Conflict Cycle is a paradigm that explains why the management of student behavior begins with the staff and not the student. Unless staff members can control reactions to inappropriate student behavior and have an awareness of their "emotional buttons," staff will escalate the incident and only make it worse, like trying to put out a small fire by throwing gasoline on it. Knowing the dynamics of the Conflict Cycle not only helps staff understand their role in acting out the feelings of students, but also opens an array of new alternatives to school punishment. The skills involved in avoiding a power struggle with students help staff identify and address the important, underlying issues in a student's life rather than simply reacting to the student's annoying surface behavior. These skills give staff the ability to talk with troubled students and learning more about their lives, their struggles, and their beliefs about themselves and others. In this process, staff have an opportunity to teach troubled students better ways of behaving, being accepted, and becoming empowered.

Once teachers are knowledgeable about how troubled students can push their emotional buttons and create counteraggressive feelings in them, teachers can use this insight to accept these feelings. A conscious choice can be made not to engage in a power struggle with these students.

Once staff understand the dynamics of the Conflict Cycle, the next task is to learn the many successful ways of breaking the Conflict Cycle and turning it into a Coping Cycle. Once this occurs, student conflicts are an opportunity for the teacher to teach and for the student to learn.

REFERENCES

Burns, D. (1999). *Feeling Good.* New York: HarperCollins.

Freud, A. (1937). *The ego and its mechanisms of defense.* London: Hogarth.

ARTICLE 6.3

IN the next article, Nicholas Long and Ruth Newman have adapted Fritz Redl's (1951) four-notched scale of responding to student behavior to one of the essential concepts of effective discipline. This concept offers teachers specific guidelines for deciding when to *permit,* to *tolerate,* or to *stop* student behavior or when to *prevent* inappropriate behavior by reorganizing the classroom design or curriculum. The article also proposes eight reasons why teachers should intervene when inappropriate student behavior occurs.

THE FOUR CHOICES OF MANAGING SURFACE BEHAVIOR OF STUDENTS

Nicholas J. Long and Ruth G. Newman

There are four major alternatives to handling student behavior. They are permitting, tolerating, interfering, and preventive planning. Redl emphasizes that no one of these alternatives is better than any of the others. The task is to make the right choice for each student.

PERMITTING BEHAVIOR

Most rules in a school are made to inhibit and regulate the impulsive behavior of students. During the day, they are told in many ways to stop, slow down, and control their behavior. No one would argue against the importance of these rules in a group setting. If it is important for students to know what they cannot do, it is equally important for students to know what they can do. For example, students should be told that it is permissible to be messy when they are finger painting, to have some degree of movement within the classroom, to go to the lavatory when necessary, to show freedom of expression in their creative works, and to express an opposing view without being ridiculed or chastised. Students are reassured when they know in advance that their activities will not meet with adult frowns, shouts, or physical interference. More important, the sanctioning of behavior by teachers eliminates much of the students' unnecessary testing of limits. A teacher who permits students to leave their desks and go to the book corner after they have finished the assignment should make

Adapted from "A Differential Approach to the Management of Surface Behavior of Children in School," *Teachers' Handling of Children in Conflict,* Bulletin of the School of Education, Indiana University, *47* (July 1961), pp. 47–61. Adapted with permission.

this privilege clear. Then a student does not have to sneak a book and feel guilty or feel victorious about squeezing more freedom from the teacher than the student thinks he would expect. Teachers need to be clear and active in listing what behaviors they will applaud! This is another way of promoting positive student behavior.

TOLERATING BEHAVIOR

A lot of classroom behavior must be tolerated, but students should not have any reason to believe that teachers approve or sanction it. The more common basic assumptions behind tolerating behavior are (1) learner's leeway, (2) behavior that reflects a developmental stage, and (3) behavior that is symptomatic of a disease.

1. *Learner's leeway.* Whenever a student is learning a new skill, experimenting with new ideas, or trying to win status in the group, the teacher should expect the student to make mistakes. The teacher should not expect the student to do it correctly the first time. For example, many sensitive teachers tell their class they are not going to be upset when students err in trying to master new academic and social skills. With some teachers, the more mistakes students make, such as on an arithmetic assignment, the easier it is for the teacher to help them clarify and correct their misunderstandings. This was found to be true in the following incident:

> I have noticed that Carole (third grader) became very upset if she made a mistake on an assignment. The children were writing to a railroad company for some free material, but they did not know how to address the envelope. I went to the board and showed them the proper form and asked them to practice. In a little while I noticed that Carole had her head on her desk. When I asked her what was the matter, she said that she couldn't do it and that she already had made three mistakes. I asked her to show me her work. (She had misspelled one word, did not capitalize one of the words, and had the return address crowded up on the upper left-hand corner.) I told Carole that these are the kinds of mistakes that many students make and that I did not expect her or any of the other children to do it perfectly the first three or four times that they tried. With this encouragement, she started again.

Sometimes it is helpful to talk about "good mistakes" versus "poor mistakes." A good mistake is made when a student's answer reflects some personal logic. A poor mistake is one that rests on impulsive behavior with no semblance of logic.

2. *Behavior that reflects a developmental stage.* Some behavior is age typical and will change as the student becomes more mature. Any attempt on the part of the teacher to alter or inhibit this behavior results in such negligible changes it usually is not worth the inevitable fight. For example, students in the early grades are impulse-ridden and motor-oriented. Every kindergarten teacher knows this level of activity needs to be tolerated and channeled into activities. This concept of tolerance should not be confused with sanctioning it or permitting wild behavior. Another example is that students in the late third or early fourth grade, caught between group pressure and allegiance to the teacher, are notorious for tattling (e.g., "Miss Jones, Johnny hit Mary," or "Johnny pulled a leaf off your flower when you were in the hall"). Other illustrations of age-typical behavior are the unscrubbed, unhygienic appearance of the preadolescent boy, the primping of sixth-grade girls, the secrets of preadolescent girls, and the sex language and behavior of adolescent boys. A classroom example of age-typical behavior is presented below.

At noon, several third-grade girls came bursting into the room relating a story about the third-grade boys. The boys had discovered several pictures of nude women which were hidden in a bush on the playground. In small groups, they were examining the pictures in detail when a few of the third-grade girls "worked their way in" to see what was taking place. The girls screamed and found their way to my room. They related the story; then the bell rang.

The boys entered (without pictures), as though nothing had happened. Silence prevailed. They knew that I knew. Finally, I asked one of the boys where the pictures were. He explained that they had hidden them in the bathroom and planned to secure them after school for more detailed study. I asked another of the boys to bring the pictures into the room. This he did and I, *without looking,* threw them into the wastebasket.

The pictures remained in the wastebasket until after school. Several students sought me out at the teacher's desk, casting glances at the wastebasket all the while. Others, whom I had never seen before, entered the room and quickly left upon finding me there.

Next morning the wastebasket was empty; the pictures were gone. I didn't see them again until I entered the boiler room, where they were on the wall—property of the school janitor.

3. *Behavior that is symptomatic of an underlying illness.* When a child has a respiratory infection, the chances are he will cough in class and that the symptom (coughing) will continue until the child is well. This cause-and-effect relationship between an infection and a cough is accepted among teachers. However, when a student who is emotionally disturbed shows the symptoms of his illness, such as recurring temper tantrums, fights, and irrational fears, the student is likely to be rejected by his classmates, his teacher, and even by himself. A psychologically trained teacher realizes that, when a student suffers from emotional problems, the symptoms are rarely conscious forms of meanness but simply are a self-defeating way of expressing his feelings. For example:

> Some of the things that Martha did were fighting, tearing up other children's property, walking the floor constantly, tearing pages out of her book, name calling, and spitting. Although Martha makes me angry and caused all of us many problems, I feel we have grown a little in understanding that we all have problems and that the class is simply not divided into good and bad, accepted and unaccepted. Martha's behavior has improved during the year and, if I did anything to help it, I was doing it with kindness, firmness, and accepting her as an individual, rather than judging her on the basis of her actions.

Again, let's not confuse tolerating behavior with sanctioning it. This teacher's attitude toward Martha was more accepting because she didn't blame and punish Martha for her behavior.

INTERFERING WITH BEHAVIOR

Although a psychologically trained teacher is aware of long-range goals, the teacher still has to handle the spontaneous behavior that occurs in the classroom. Some behavior has to be stopped if classroom learning is to take place. A student cannot continue to act out his feelings. The task is to find a way of interfering with any inappropriate behavior so that the behavior does not disrupt the group but so the intervention technique still is helpful to the particular student. In *The Aggressive Child,* Redl and Wineman (1957) listed 21 specific staff techniques that they identified their work with aggressive boys.

Before suggesting ways of intervening, the question of when a teacher should intervene needs to be considered. While this question cannot be settled without considering many variables, school psychologists have observed that too many teachers never set limits or intervene until they are choked with counteraggressive feelings. When this happens, the teacher is likely to intervene in a way that is inappropriate and too severe. To remedy this situation teachers need to be given clear guidelines to help them with this difficult problem. Once again Redl (1959) provided direction by suggesting the following criteria for teacher intervention.

1. *Reality dangers.* Adults are more reality oriented than children and have more practice predicting the consequences of certain acts. If students are playing a dangerous game, fighting, or playing in a way that might result in injury to themselves or others, the teacher must move in and stop this behavior.

2. *Psychological protection.* Just as the adult protects the student from being physically hurt, the teacher also should protect the student from psychological injury. If a group of boys are ganging up on a student, bullying him, or using derogatory names, the teacher must intervene and stop it. The teacher must never support or condone this type of psychological abuse.

3. *Protection against too much excitement.* Sometimes a teacher intervenes to prevent the stimulation of too much excitement, anxiety, and guilt in students. For example, a group of students are playing a game of dodge ball, and the teacher foresees that it will likely get out of hand if it continues another 10 minutes. Based on previous experience, the teacher suspects that some student will be hit or start a fight. What started as a pleasant game can end up being an unpleasant experience. Once again, the teacher must intervene to protect students from this consequence.

4. *Protection of property.* This is almost too obvious to mention, but sometimes it can be overlooked. Students must care for

their belongings and school property. The teacher who sees some destructive act needs to move in quickly and stop it. Protecting school property and the building is a way of protecting the learning environment.

5. *Protection of an ongoing program.* Once a class is involved in learning and the students have an investment in its outcome, it is not fair to have it ruined by one student who is having some difficulty. In this case, the teacher intervenes and asks this student to take a time-out or to be nearer the teacher to ensure that the assignment or activity can continue without interference.

6. *Protection against negative contagion.* The teacher is aware of some unexpressed tension in the group, such as a racial issue or a group disappointment, and a student with high social influence begins tapping his desk with his pencil, the teacher needs to ask him to stop in order to prevent this behavior from spreading to the other students and disrupting the lesson.

7. *Highlighting a value area or school policy.* There are times when a teacher interferes in some behavior not because it is dangerous or disturbing but because the teacher wishes to illustrate a school policy or rule. For example, the teacher might want to demonstrate why it is impossible for everyone to be first in line, or to point out how a misunderstanding developed when there was no intent to lie or distort a situation.

What are some of the counterindications against interfering with a student's behavior when the behavior is not dangerous? (1) The fuss it would create at this time is not worth it! For example, the group is going on a trip or is about to have lunch. To stop this activity and talk about some behavior might create a negative group reaction. In such a situation it is better to wait for another similar incident. (2) The teacher decides to wait until the behavior deviates to the point where it is obvious not only to the student but also to the entire group. Then the student's typical defenses, such as projection (e.g., "You're always picking on me" or "I never get a fair deal"), are clearly inappropriate. (3) The teacher is in too good a mood today. He cannot work up enough genuine concern to impress the student or the group with the seriousness of the student's behavior. While this feeling does occur, it should not be the barometer for teacher intervention.

PREVENTIVE PLANNING

Redl's (1959) fourth alternative is preventive planning. Preventive planning should be considered whenever a chronic classroom problem exists. Sometimes this problem can be prevented by reorganizing the classroom, the curriculum, or the daily schedule. For example:

> The staff of an alternative school for troubled elementary students noticed an increase of off-task behavior around 11:30 A.M. A 10-day data-based study was initiated, and the findings confirmed the initial impressions. Three out of the four classrooms showed a significant increase in inappropriate behavior between 11:15 and 11:45 A.M. A staff meeting was called to discuss the findings and to propose ways of solving this problem. Staff suggestions included (a) providing more structured assignments, (b) increasing reinforcers to those students who were on task, (c) developing more appealing lessons, (d) using more audio-visual aids, (e) setting up a new contingency program that ties student recess to completed classroom assignments between 11:30 A.M. and noon. One staff member asked what time the students got up in the morning, whether they had breakfast, what time the special education bus picked them up, and how long they were on the bus. Much to everyone's surprise, the staff learned that most students had to get up between 6:15 and 6:30 A.M. Only 60% of the students had breakfast. They were picked up between 7:00 and 7:15 A.M. and had a bus ride that took from 40 to 75 minutes. The staff decided the off-task behaviors at 11:30 A.M. may be due to physical fatigue, so they moved the lunch period from noon to 11:30 A.M.
>
> The results of this simple change of schedule were most rewarding. The problem was not due to the teachers' personality, the type of assignment, the instructional method, or the reinforcers available to the students. The basic problem was physical stress. The students were hungry by 11:30. By moving the lunch period 30 minutes earlier, this schoolwide problem was prevented and everyone was happier.

Managing student behavior becomes an intellectual challenge for classroom teachers. Teachers need to ask themselves, Do I permit this behavior, do I tolerate this behavior, do I stop this behavior, or do I prevent this behavior from occurring? Remember, teachers have the choice over how they respond to student behavior.

Direct intervention is the third of four choices of responding to student behavior. We want to emphasize the importance of pairing teacher intervention with school values. This association between teacher intervention and school values is often neglected when behavior management skills are being taught, but it is a skill that enhances the teacher's effectiveness. For example, Mrs. Conner, a fifth-grade teacher, observes Brian making racial comments in her classroom. She decides to intervene so she walks up to Brian, gets his attention, and says, "Brian, your comments are inappropriate and need to stop!" Brian looks at her and replies, "Why?" Mrs. Conner doesn't respond with a "control statement," such as "I'm the adult or the boss in this class and you must be obedient to my authority" or "If you don't, you will lose your points." Instead, she uses this intervention as an opportunity to teach Brian an important value about how students in this school treat each other. Mrs. Conner is aware that whenever she stops student behavior she is saying there is a different and more rewarding way of living together. All direct teacher intervention can have three positive outcomes: (a) it interferes with undesirable student behavior, (b) it teaches an important school value, and (c) it models that teacher intervention is an act of professional protection and support and not an act of personal hostility and punishment. This third outcome confronts a predictable problem between troubled students and teachers. Many of these students have been socialized by parents who were volatile, hostile, and out of control. Like Pavlov's dogs, these students have been conditioned to associate adult intervention with adult aggression and hostility. Frequently, these students' initial reaction to any teacher intervention is to misinterpret it as a function of the teacher's personality (e.g., "She hates me," "He enjoys putting me down," "She's against me"), rather than recognizing it as a realistic adult response to inappropriate behavior. This type of thinking reinforces the students' resistance toward the teacher and can escalate the problem into a no-win Conflict Cycle. The teacher needs to counteract this distortion by removing his or her personality from the act of intervention. This removal can be accomplished by explaining the decision to interfere with the students' behaviors. Here are some examples of how this skill can be realized:

Brian, the reason I'm stopping your racial comments is that, in this school, we believe students have a right *to be protected* from verbal and psychological abuse. Whenever I hear any verbal abuse, it is my professional job to stop it.

Brian, the reason I'm asking you to take another seat [take a time-out, etc.] is that, in this school, we believe students have a right to learn without being disrupted. It is my job *to protect and maintain* the ongoing instructional program. Whenever I see or hear any student behaving in a manner that interferes with group learning, it is my professional job to stop this behavior.

Brian, the reason I want you to stop writing on the desk [wall, etc.] is that, in this school, we believe we should protect our learning environment. This is where we live and we need to make it as attractive and as comfortable as possible. Whenever I see anyone defacing or destroying our cared-for setting, it is my professional job to intervene and stop this behavior.

This skill of explaining teacher intervention as an act of *protection* is an effective way of confronting the students' belief that the teacher is hostile and rejecting. The teacher makes it abundantly clear that his or her actions have nothing to do with a student's personality or with liking or disliking the student. The teacher's response is a function of the student's behavior. Intervention is part of a professional commitment to enforce the school values by protecting the rights and responsibilities of all the students. Over time, this skill will promote teacher trust and respect among the students.

The skill of pairing teacher intervention with teacher protection of school values can be used for all circumstances in which teachers need to stop disruptive behavior. The pairing defines the teacher's role in stopping student behavior, identifies appropriate and inappropriate behaviors, provides an atmosphere of consistency and fairness, helps curb impulsive behavior, promotes a safer environment, and reinforces the rights of all the students. These rights can be translated into effective classroom rules. We make these suggestions for the development of classroom rules:

- Students should be involved in the writing of classroom rules.
- The rules should be short, precise, easy to understand, and written as positive statements.

- Classroom rules should be posted, throughout the year, in a prominent location where they cannot be overlooked or forgotten.
- Classroom rules should be reviewed frequently, especially after long holidays or absences.
- Classroom rules should be discussed by teachers and students when a new student joins the class.
- Different situations (cafeteria, gym, music, assemblies) may require a different set of rules.
- Classroom rules need to be reviewed with students to determine their effectiveness.
- Teachers must be sensitive to different cultural and family values when establishing class rules.

REFERENCES

Redl, F. (1959). The concept of the therapeutic milieu. *American Journal of Orthopsychiatry, 29,* 721–736.

Redl, F., & Wineman, D. (1957). *The aggressive child.* New York: Free Press.

ARTICLE 6.4

IN the next article, Mary Beth Hewitt discusses the emotional issue of teacher fairness. We have found many teachers want to be fair in their interactions with students. However, when a student responds to a teacher intervention by shouting out, "You are not being fair!" it can raise some personal doubt. This happens most frequently when a teacher tries to individualize his or her responses and tries to treat students according to their needs. Hewitt shares her concept of fairness and whether it means the same for all students.

BUT THAT'S NOT FAIR!

Mary Beth Hewitt

One of the most important discussions I had with my classes was on the topic of fairness. Children are wonderful attempting to control the decisions adults make by crying, "That's not fair!" What they are most often saying at these times is, "I don't like what I'm getting or not getting and I want you to change your mind." We rarely, if ever, hear children say, "that's not fair" when they like what they are getting.

As caring professionals, one of our most vulnerable emotional buttons is when we are accused of not being fair, as we pride ourselves on our ability to be impartial. What I discovered was that, when students made this accusation, it generally meant one of two things: they were genuinely confused as to the rationale behind differential treatment or I was not behaving the way *they* wanted me to and they were trying to "guilt" me into changing my mind.

Because many times we do not take the time to proactively examine our own belief systems regarding our rationale for differential treatment, we are more susceptible to falling into the trap of treating everyone the same because we are fearful of being perceived by others as being unfair. Furthermore, it is far easier to treat everyone the same as one does not have to consider a myriad of factors nor does one have to rigorously examine his/her own personal motivations and potential prejudices. Let's begin with the key points of the discussion I had with my students:

DOES FAIR MEAN THE SAME?

I began a discussion with my students by posing the question, "What is fair?" Usually, they came up with words such as same and equal. When asked, "What does the same mean?", the general response was, giving everyone the same thing. A physical analogy such as giving everyone the same size shoes seemed to illustrate the point that providing everyone with the same thing would definitely not be fair; only a few people would

From *CHOICES Newsletter, 1*, 1999, pp. 12–17. Reprinted with permission.

get what they needed and the rest would be uncomfortable. The students were able to come up with the idea that giving everyone a pair of shoes that fit would be the fair thing to do.

DOES FAIR MEAN EQUAL?

Then we discussed the issue of equality which takes into account the concept of value. One way I illustrated this was through the use of mathematically balanced equations. Giving one person one hundred pennies has the same value as giving another a dollar bill. However, because as individuals we have different preferences, we need to consider what is of value to each person in order to be equitable. To the student who has four pairs of shoes that fit, but no coat, another pair of shoes has little or no value. To the student who has no shoes, but has a coat, a pair of shoes is of great value. The students were able to see that individuals can receive different things, again according to their need, and still be treated fairly.

We then discussed factors among ourselves that might be different. The students acknowledged that they were different physically, emotionally, and intellectually; that they had a variety of different interests, personal preferences, skills, talents, strengths, and weaknesses. Since they were not alike in many ways, they had different needs in many areas. Ultimately, the first part of the definition my classes formulated to define fairness was: **Giving each student what they need and value....**

SO WHAT'S THE PROBLEM?

Ah, if only it were that simple! Now come the factors that really complicate the issue of fairness. Exactly who decides what an individual's needs are? The individual? The group? The teacher? An impartial person? On what criteria is that decision based? When the needs of the individual are in conflict with the needs of the group, what happens? Is there a difference between needs and wants?

I would like to tell you that we resolved these issues. I'd be lying. These are age old dilemmas which philosophers have argued for years. The students were able to keep it fairly simple by agreeing that decisions should be based on some criteria and that criteria should be applied without prejudice. (Actually, they said something more like, "Just don't give someone something because you like him/her better than someone else.") Prejudice being defined as the favoring of one person or group more than another *in disregard of the facts.* Our working definition of fairness became: **In this class we give each student what they need and value according to criteria which are implemented without prejudice.**

THE NOTION OF CRITERIA

It is important to expose the students to the idea that our decision making for how to treat each individual involves some form of criteria. Sometimes students can guess at the criteria. This is easiest when at least part of the reason for differential treatment is blatantly obvious, as in visible, physical handicaps. A student can deduce that *the reason John gets to use the elevator in school and I have to use the stairs is because John is in a wheelchair and he can't climb stairs. Although I'd like to use the elevator too, I don't meet the criteria.* It is much more difficult when the criteria for decision making is not as obvious.

In the cognitive realm, we have had more difficulty explaining individual differences because frequently the handicaps are "invisible" and the criteria can't be discerned by observation alone. A student who is learning disabled in reading has access to books on tape, in writing has access to a scribe, in language, access to ESL classes. Individualized Education Plans were designed to insure fairness, not sameness. These modifications are given to students who need them so that they can benefit from instruction. If, however, I am a student who is struggling with my mathematics and I look over and see my classmate using a calculator, I think that is not fair. When I tell my teacher that and ask, "Why does he get to use a calculator and I don't?", the teacher seems to get very uncomfortable.

Where does this discomfort come from? One of the chief sources is that frequently we have not systematically and rigorously examined our own criteria for making intervention decisions. So when someone questions whether or not we're being biased, we're not even sure, in our own minds, that we are not. Because we have not thought through a rational basis for our decisions, which we can clearly articulate to our students, we are more likely to become emotionally defensive when our decisions are questioned. Just having established criteria (which, by the way, is most effective if it is articulated to students up front) helps settle many issues of fairness.

Another source of discomfort comes from the fact that many times we are the agent for implementing criteria developed by others; as is with the case of providing augmentative devices and test modifications for learning disabled students. The problem with these "invisible" handicaps is that sometimes even the adults don't understand and/or truly believe in the need for modifications or they don't feel comfortable articulating the criteria for fear of breaking confidentiality. I recall talking to a teacher about problems she was having with a student. She related that the only time he really had serious behavior problems was when he was expected to write. I asked if he was learning disabled in written expression and she responded affirmatively. I inquired as to whether or not he had modifications in his IEP. She said that he did and that she allowed him to use them most of the day but every day he has to write for an hour. I asked her why. She looked at me with surprise and said, "Well, he has to learn to write!" I continued to question why he had to learn to write and she gave me reasons such as, "What if there is no one he can dictate to?" and "What if he doesn't have access to a tape recorder?" After a time, I asked her a question, "What if he had no hands?" She replied, "Well, *then* he wouldn't have to learn to write."

It's really difficult to explain to others why individualized treatment is fair when we do not have an explanation that is congruent with our own belief system. This staff member is not unique. To many people, the withholding of adaptive devices from physically challenged individuals would be unthinkable, however, those same individuals may see the withholding of a calculator from a mathematically challenged individual as being instructional. When handicaps are invisible, people erroneously believe that the student has the capacity to perform the task without external assistance if only they tried hard enough; that the disability isn't really that serious. Although some handicaps can be remediated, many times the remediation efforts cannot be successful because the student is at his/her frustration threshold and is expressing that frustration behaviorally. The inappropriate behavior is negating any chance that the student may benefit from the remediation. So much time is spent trying to remediate instead of compensate. Why is there such a focus on remediation? Remediation is based on the belief of the importance of sameness; that there is only one best way to accomplish a task. Compensation is based on recognizing and respecting the importance of differences; that there are many ways to skin the proverbial cat. Fairness, based on giving people what they need and value, is a compensatory concept.

What about the problem of informing students of criteria and how that affects confidentiality? Many times staff don't want to tell others the criteria because it might let the other students know that the student is different. Guess what, they already know he/she is different because he's using a calculator. Right now they think he's using a calculator because you like him better. What's wrong with informing students of the criteria for using a calculator? In order to qualify to use a calculator you have to be LD in Mathematics. The criteria for LD is … If you meet that criteria you would be allowed to use a calculator too. We let students know the criteria for other forms of differential treatment (Why does he get to go to honor's study hall? The criteria for an honor's pass is … when you meet that criteria you can have an honor's pass too) so why don't we let them know the criteria for augmentative devices? Is it because we deem handicaps as something that are bad, things to be hidden? By not sharing the criteria, we indirectly send the message that something is wrong as opposed to being different. (It is often not necessary, however, to go into great detail regarding criteria. Later in this article, I'll talk about what most students really mean when they ask "How come he gets to … and I don't?")

The problem becomes even more complicated when we start dealing with different behavioral expectations. So many times, in my workshops, when I suggest a behavioral modification for a student, staff immediately argue, "But the rest of the students will say that's not fair or everyone will want to do that." My immediate thought is, so what if everyone wanted to? Is the modification something that others might benefit from too?

Take my friend Mark. Mark was severely attention deficit disordered. He had enormous difficulty sitting still. Although Mark had many modifications in his classroom and was not required to sit for longer than 10 minutes at a time without a break, he had an hour and a half bus ride to and from school. Every day I would receive a bus report that Mark was "constantly out of his seat." I met with the driver and the bus monitor and asked them how frequently they stopped to pick up students. The answer, every 5 to 7 minutes. I suggested that they give Mark *permission* to stand up when the bus stopped to load or unload students; the condition being that he had to sit back down when the bus doors closed. At first they were resistant, voicing the belief that then everyone would want to stand up and the kids would think that they weren't being fair if only Mark could stand up. I suggested that they try to handle it as the problems came up. I speculated that about two-thirds of the group wouldn't notice or, if they did notice, they wouldn't care. About a third of the group would notice. Of these, some would be curious, whereas others would be looking for evidence of unfairness to add fuel to their "adults are jerks" belief system and still others would be wishing that they could stretch too. I hypothesized that if they handled questions like, "Why does Mark get to stand up?" by answering, "Do you *need* to stand up and stretch too?" and then giving permission with the condition that whoever stood up sat back down as soon as the door closed that the kids who just wanted to gather evidence against adults wouldn't even bother to stand up (and even if they did the novelty would soon wear off) and kids who truly needed to stretch would continue to do so. The feedback from the driver confirmed my hypothesis. Most students didn't notice, and those who did, once they were given permission to do the same thing, lost interest. Mark continued to stretch, when he needed to, within the given parameters, and stayed in his seat the remainder of the time. The bus reports stopped.

My next question is, "Is the modification needed by that individual?" and most often the answer is "yes." Then don't deny the individual access to that modification on the basis that others might get upset. Or don't feel pressured to give everyone a modification that they don't need (but may want). Just because other people do not understand the reason does that mean that we have to treat everyone the same when we know that it is not in anyone's best interest? That would be like giving everyone an aspirin because one person had a headache. I handled this conundrum with my students by having a discussion of the difference between wants and needs.

THE DIFFERENCE BETWEEN WANTS AND NEEDS

Handicapped parking spaces are an example that most individuals can relate to. I asked my students, "Is it fair that people with physical handicaps can park closer to a building?" They almost unanimously answered, "Yes." I'd go on, "Aren't there lots of other people who wish they could park closer too? Should we have no differential parking and make physically handicapped people walk or wheel their wheelchairs just as far as anyone else? Or should we let everyone park in handicapped spaces?" The class said "No, handicapped parking spaces should be for those people who need them." Occasionally, I'd run into some students who lacked empathy and felt that they had just as much right to park close to a building as a handicapped person did. In those cases I'd ask, "Would you rather be able-bodied and have to walk farther or would you prefer not to have the use of your legs and be able to park closer?" The answers, thus far, have been unanimous for the first choice. There is a definite difference between convenience and genuine need.

WE EACH RECEIVE DIFFERENT THINGS

For years I heard some staff members complain about the tremendous workload added by the use of behavior modification systems with whole classrooms. When questioned as to why the whole class was on a behavior modification program, generally it was because one or two students needed one, but it wouldn't be "fair" to the rest of the class not to have them on it. Why not? Don't the students who are behaving get rewarded for appropriate behavior in some way or another? They may not earn a tangible, material reward that goes on a chart (like a sticker), but they may earn the respect of their peers, be trusted and given more independence by their teachers. In my classroom, students knew from the beginning that they would be treated differently because they were different but that this differential treatment would be based on needs and not on favoritism. They could articulate: "Our rewards might be different but we'll all get rewards. Our punishments might be different, but we'll all get punishments. The type of help we receive might be different, but we'll all get help."

WHAT STUDENTS REALLY MEAN WHEN THEY SAY "IT'S NOT FAIR!"

Did having these discussions about fairness mean that my students stopped trying to "guilt" me into giving them things they may want instead of need? Of course not. They still tried. What was different is that I did not succumb to the pressure since I had clearly thought through my rationale for differential treatment and I was able to correctly interpret their messages. Generally, when students complain about unfairness by posing questions like: "Why does he get to use a calculator and I don't?"; "Why does he get to play first string and I don't?"; "Why did she win the prize at the Science fair and I didn't?"; "Why does she get to dictate to you and I don't?", etc. what they are really saying is, "My reason for bringing this up is because I want to be able to do or have that too." Most of the time the students really aren't primarily interested in knowing what the reasons are for differential treatment. I found that if I interpreted past their questions and said, for example, "You'd really like to have been picked for first string on the team and you're really disappointed you weren't. Are you interested in hearing the criteria for playing first string?" they did not even want to know the criteria.

Part of teaching about the issue of fairness is helping students come to grips with the difference between a disappointment and unfairness. One teacher shared with me a story about how a student in her class was enraged when his essay did not win a contest. He accused the judges of being unfair saying that they just picked the winner's essay because she was a girl and they liked her better. The teacher asked him what was the criteria for the essay. He stated the specified length, format, and content. She then asked him if he felt he had met the criteria. He looked at his paper, a few hastily scrawled sentences and sheepishly replied, "I guess not." Many times, individuals have not realistically considered the criteria on which decisions are based. One of the reasons individuals have difficulty with fairness is that most people come from an egocentric standpoint. Our agenda is getting our needs/wants met and frequently we don't consider other factors that weigh into the equation. The student who practices day and night and tries his best, may think it unfair that he has to sit on the bench while his naturally gifted teammate plays first string. However, if the criteria for picking the individuals to play in competitive sports is 'those players who consistently score the most points' not 'those players who practice the longest and try the hardest' and that criteria is implemented without regard for any other factors, then the coach's decision is fair. Individuals get upset when the criteria does not coincide with their own and they end up missing out on something they deem to be good for them. In reality, that is a disappointment, not unfairness.

HOW DO I KNOW IF I'M BEING FAIR?

People clamor for easy guidelines on which to base decisions. Black and white absolutes that will take the pain out of responsible decision making. The *easy* way is to treat everyone the same. There is no thought involved. Figuratively speaking, everyone gets the same size shoes. Some things I've learned:

- Being fair is not easy
- Being fair involves making difficult, sometimes unpopular, decisions
- Fairness is often in the eye of the beholder.

If trying to act in a fair manner is so complex, then why even bother to take the time to proactively explain it to the students? Two reasons: (1) Since, as the teacher, you are responsible for setting or implementing the criteria which classroom decisions will be made, students have a right to know what the criteria is (whether they agree with it or not); (2) If you can't explain your criteria to someone else you probably don't even know it yourself, thus opening yourself up to being unduly influenced by the reactions of others or your own personal moods and biases.

The good news is that you should feel a twinge whenever someone questions your decisions. Questions are designed to make us take a careful look at our own decision making process. In order to work toward being fair, we should question ourselves too. Careful thought, constant self-examination and a degree of doubt are probably going to help you behave in a fair manner. As Scott Peck says in his book, *A World Waiting To Be Reborn: Civility Rediscovered,* "Most of the evil in the world is done by people who are absolutely certain that what they are doing is right."

IN the next article Stanley Fagen presents a comprehensive and functional list of teacher skills for managing the surface behavior of students. These short-term and on-the-spot skills are essential for maintaining classroom order and learning. He describes seven skills for increasing desirable behavior and eight skills for reducing undesirable behavior. All these skills need to be learned and mastered so they become automatic responses to student behavior.

ARTICLE 6.5

FIFTEEN TEACHER INTERVENTION SKILLS FOR MANAGING CLASSROOM BEHAVIOR PROBLEMS
Stanley A. Fagen

Teachers' use of appropriate behavior management techniques is a basic responsibility for successful inclusion (Federico, Herrold, & Venn, 1999). Unfortunately, too many teachers have a limited range of techniques for reacting to deviant student behavior and quickly escalate problems to the point of exclusion. A common nightmare for special educators is when Billy returns to a regular class after a year of painful limit setting, contingency management, behavior rehearsal, and self-recording. The bad dream shows Billy muttering an obscenity upon being criticized by Mr. Meticulous, after which the teacher loses his temper and yells at Billy. This, of course, results in an exciting and nasty exchange of insults and the predictable banishment to the principal's office. Or, even worse, there is a dramatic suspension to emphasize the seriousness of Billy's "loss of control."

Disruptive student behavior should be dealt with in the simplest way possible to achieve the desirable outcome. The general rule is to use the least intensive strategy necessary to reduce or stop negative behavior and to increase positive behavior. This same point of view was advocated by Glasser (1977) in his "10 Steps to Good Discipline."

Table 6.5–1 presents a continuum of intervention strategies from least to most intensive in relation to undesirable and desirable behavior. These interventions have been shown to have significant value for improving classroom behavior (Algozzine & Ysseldyke, 1993; Nelson, Crabtree, Marchano-Martella, & Martella, 1998; Stage & Quiroz, 1997). This continuum of intervention strategies is applicable to elementary and secondary levels. In view of the large-scale concern about behavior in our secondary schools, however, specific illustrations and examples will focus on problems presented by adolescents.

BEHAVIOR PLANNING STEPS

Before discussing the intervention strategies, it is important to recognize that instruction in behavior requires careful planning in the same way that is true for academic instruction. Behavior planning involves four key steps: (1) establishing individual classroom behavior expectations, (2) identifying behavior deviations, (3) identifying incompatible desirable behaviors, and (4) selecting behavior intervention strategies.

Adapted and updated from "Least Intensive Interventions for Classroom Behavior Problems," *The Pointer, 31*(1), 1980, pp. 21–28. Copyright by Stanley A. Fagen. Adapted with permission.

CONTINUUM OF CLASSROOM BEHAVIOR INTERVENTION STRATEGIES

TABLE 6.5-1

Intensity	For Reducing Undesirable Behavior	For Increasing Desirable Behavior
Least Intensive	1. Planned ignoring	1. Stating expectations
	2. Modeling	2. Stating expectations
	3. Signaling	3. Structuring
	4. Restructuring	4. Positive reinforcement
	5. Conferencing	5. Regulated permission
	6. Warning	6. Contracting
	7. Enforcement of consequence	7. Token systems
Most Intensive	8. Life Space Crisis Intervention	

ESTABLISHING INDIVIDUAL CLASSROOM BEHAVIOR EXPECTATIONS

An individual classroom teacher's efforts to reduce problem behavior will be greatly enhanced if basic values have been defined in terms of *schoolwide behavior standards and limits* (i.e., expectations for behavior). It is widely recognized that consistency in stated expectations for behavior promotes adherence to those expectations, whereas ambiguity or inconsistency perpetuates disorder and limit testing. Desirable student behavior is directly related to the consistency of support of schoolwide standards and limits by all staff (e.g., counselors, cafeteria workers, maintenance personnel, arts teachers). If, however, adults turn their backs when a student scribbles his or her name on a wall or curses out another student, then instruction in discipline is undermined. There is a place for differing expectations by staff and for students to learn to respect differences between teachers. However, such differences should not exist in relation to agreed-upon schoolwide standards and limits. Examples of behaviors that are usually considered unacceptable by all school staff, as well as parents and students, are physical attacks on staff and students, verbal abuse, extortion, possessing dangerous weapons, vandalism, drug abuse, truancy, tardiness, profanity, and overt disruptiveness. These are all obvious examples of acting out. Examples of staff differences that are typically not schoolwide expectations are teacher preferences for being called by first or last names, amount of noise and movement in the classroom, and allowing questions about instructions or rules.

Thus, individual classroom expectations are established on the basis of schoolwide standards and limits plus additional personal values that do not conflict with total school norms.

IDENTIFYING BEHAVIOR DEVIATIONS

Before any problem behavior can be reduced or eliminated, the teacher must be sure that it is indeed a significant problem. Given 30 students in a class, the teacher can ill afford to spend time dealing with behaviors that reflect momentary deviations or minor irritations. Laughter at an inappropriate time or inattentiveness to a presentation may be very annoying but not worth serious intervention in comparison to physical aggression, verbal hostility, or loud interruptions. Two guidelines should be kept in mind in setting priorities for dealing with behavior problems: (1) *flagrant violations must be prioritized above other possible concerns* (e.g., threatening someone with a penpoint has to be addressed before modifying failure to complete assignments), and (2) *management of the disruptive behavior of several class members must precede attention to unique individual problems* (assuming the individual problems are *not* dangerous to self or others). It would be foolish to discuss the needs of one student for increased group participation when many members of the class shout out and walk around the room at will.

IDENTIFYING INCOMPATIBLE DESIRABLE BEHAVIORS

Once the teacher is clear on the undesirable individual or group behaviors that require priority attention, the next step is to specify desirable goals and objectives. A major weakness in many attempts to overcome behavior problems is the lack of positive or desirable behaviors to *replace* the negatives. Undesirable and desirable behavior should be seen as "two sides of a coin"—for every problem situation there are one or more desirable behaviors that are both preferable to and incompatible with the undesirable behavior. Finding incompatible desirable behaviors stems from asking oneself the question, "What can I teach the student to do instead of _____?" In other words, the undesirable behavior cannot be occurring at the same time as the new desirable behaviors. An incompatible relationship can be depicted as a seesaw—when the desirable behavior goes up, the undesirable goes down. Consider Table 6.5–2.

SELECTING BEHAVIOR INTERVENTION STRATEGIES

As shown in Table 6.5–1, a variety of behavior intervention strategies are available to the classroom teacher. However, the teacher should be sure that these strategies are sanctioned by the local board of education, the school principal, and the parent community before using them. It should be noted that the severity of the undesirable behavior will greatly influence the level of intervention required, particularly in regard to acting-out behaviors. For example, a student who starts throwing objects around the room must be stopped immediately and removed from the program until the disturbance can be understood and resolved. In this case, a less intensive intervention like planned ignoring would be totally inappropriate.

CONTRASTING UNDESIRABLE AND DESIRABLE BEHAVIORS

TABLE 6.5-2

Undesirable Behavior	Incompatible Desirable Behavior(s)
Making fun of others	• Cooperation with others • Helping others • Ignoring others who are not liked • Respectfully stating own feelings toward others
Fighting	• Expressing differences in words • Avoiding fighting while stating the negative consequences ("Hey man, I'm not gonna get in big trouble") • Avoiding antagonistic situations • Releasing physical energy in permissible ways • Taking a break to "cool off"
Loud, unrestrained talking	• Whispering or soft talking • Talking when permitted • Listening to others • Working independently
Disregarding rules	• Following an instruction • Expressing a difference of opinion or asking a question • Offering an alternative method • Restating rules before acting • Explaining rules to others

EIGHT TEACHER SKILLS FOR REDUCING UNDESIRABLE BEHAVIOR

1. The Skill of Planned Ignoring. Many students engage in negative behavior to receive attention from the teacher or peer group. For some, even this negative attention is preferable to being ignored. The decision to ignore or tolerate undesirable behavior so that it will drop out or be extinguished is planned ignoring. Part of the planfulness also includes giving positive attention (e.g., praise, privileges, recognition) to the incompatible desirable behavior. An example would be not attending to a student's daydreaming and facial grimaces, while complimenting him when he is working.

Planned ignoring is not as easy as it appears because it requires the teacher to withhold his or her usual response to a distraction and cope with some feelings of anxiety or frustration. It has the advantage of avoiding power struggles and suggesting confidence in the student's self-control. On the other hand, planned ignoring should not be used when the behavior is potentially dangerous to physical or psychological well-being, or when the group becomes confused or disorganized by the violation of limits.

2. The Skill of Stating Expectations. As noted earlier, individual classroom behavior expectations must be clearly established, preferably with student input and agreement. Most secondary schools publish a student handbook that contains rules and disciplinary actions. Each teacher is responsible to maintain these schoolwide rules in his or her own classroom. The teacher should develop a list of any additional standards or limits that will be emphasized in his or her own classroom. These expectations should be discussed with the class and posted conspicuously on a bulletin board.

It is best to keep stated expectations to a minimum and to word them positively. One classroom had the following standards mounted on poster board: Thou shalt listen to one another; Thou shalt ask permission for changes; Thou shalt let others learn; Thou shalt start and stop on time. With this common understanding, the teacher could effectively use direct reminders such as "too much noise," "we need to listen," "time to get to work," "we're supposed to be seated now," "people are trying to work."

3. The Skill of Signaling. Many nonverbal signals may be used to curb negative behavior, thus avoiding the pitfall of nagging or constantly naming particular students. Three major types of signals are available: (a) *facial expressions,* including eye contact; (b) *body movement, sounds, and gestures;* and (c) *mechanical devices.* A well-fixed glare or frown can be a relatively private and gentle way of redirecting behavior. Body movement, sounds, and gestures include rising from a seat, emphatically clearing one's throat, snapping the fingers, motioning with the hand, shaking the head, and using various postures. Mechanical aids are helpful for gaining attention of the class. With prior notification, switching the lights on and off, ringing a bell, or playing a note on the piano can provide the group with a clear message to desist.

A somewhat different but related form of signaling is called proximity control (Long & Newman, 1980). Five levels of proximity control may be employed: (a) orienting one's body toward a student, (b) walking toward a student, (c) putting one's hand on the student's desk, (d) touching or removing the object used by a student to create distraction, and (e) putting one's hand gently on a student's shoulder or arm. In the latter instance, caution is advised because some students resent being touched.

The essence of proximity control is the offer of teacher support for self-control without verbal reprimand or reminder. Teachers who are adept in the use of their physical presence can often reduce unacceptable behavior in an unobtrusive and humane manner.

4. The Skill of Restructuring the Situation. Undesirable behavior does not happen in a vacuum. The classroom is an extremely complex environment with many precipitating conditions for disruptiveness. A sensitive teacher can regulate the level of classroom disruption by restructuring or modifying the situation to bolster behavior control and attenuate stress. Modifications are possible in such areas as seating, grouping, degree of teacher assistance, nature of the task, format and complexity of the material, physical movement, degree of involvement, amount of recognition, extent of decision making, and personal feelings.

There are many examples of restructuring a situation, such as separating two boys who are continually fooling around *(seating change);* placing an immature, distractible student in a small group of responsible learners *(grouping change);* moving next to a student to offer assistance when the work becomes frustrating *(teacher assistance change);* modifying the assignment from completion of 20 problems to attempting 15 minutes worth of problems *(changing nature of task);* substituting a colorful, well-spaced workbook for an advanced textbook *(changing format and complexity of material);* asking a student who is angry at having been tripped to return a film to the school library *(physical movement change);* requesting that class members paraphrase another person's remarks before giving their own when there is a lack of group attentiveness *(change in degree of involvement);* providing opportunities for students who seek attention negatively (e.g., clowning, throwing paper, seat hopping) to take leadership roles (e.g., reading a part in a play, putting on a skit, giving a report) *(change in amount of recognition);* offering rebellious students a mixture of optional, required, and creative learning activities or centers *(change in extent of decision making);* reassuring students who are nervous about a test that it is okay to be anxious and to just relax and try their best *(change in personal feelings).*

5. The Skill of Conferencing. Arranging for a private conference with a problem student is a useful strategy for two reasons. First, it permits an exchange of views in a confidential manner. On occasion, both teacher and student gain in awareness of each other's interests, needs, and feelings. Second, it helps the student see that the teacher is concerned with him or her as an individual, despite the fact that classroom standards and limits must be protected. Individual conferencing can help to prevent reactive aggression for perceived unfair treatment, a common occurrence for students with behavior problems (Hartman & Stage, 2000). However, the teacher does need to be alert to the fact that individual conferences can become rewarding to some students and thereby perpetrate repetition of unacceptable behavior.

6. The Skill of Warning. Consequences for undesirable behavior should be established in advance of any enforcement. For example, constant talking during a lesson results in being sent to a time-out area; cursing the teacher necessitates a conference with the principal and parent notification; lateness to class causes an after-school detention. This does not require that all students receive identical consequences for similar behavior, because flexibility is important to meet learner differences. However, all students need to have a definite understanding that their negative behaviors *cause* unwanted consequences.

Many students lack a true realization that their own actions predictably determine what happens to them. Adolescents, in particular, greatly resent arbitrary or irrational treatment. Fair and direct consequences are important for the development of character and decision making. By providing a "warning"—that is, a reminder or restatement that a choice of continued unacceptable behavior will cause a negative outcome—the student has a clear and responsible decision to make. It should be recognized that by choosing to misbehave following a warning, a teenager may be saying "I don't believe you will follow through." On the other hand, the student is indicating that he or she is ready to accept the consequences that have been stated. One warning is preferred since more than that one usually results in more limit testing.

7. The Skill of Enforcement of Consequences. Follow-through on announced consequences for unacceptable behavior is critical to effective discipline. The consistent use of warnings and enforcement of consequences enhances cause-and-effect learning and establishes a structure for teacher authority. As long as consequences are considered fair by the group, enforcement is expected and psychologically appreciated. A teacher should remember that unacceptable behavior can spread rapidly and that the class (as well as the community) holds the teacher accountable for preserving basic behavior values, even if that requires punishment.

In enforcing consequences, the teacher should strive to be (a) immediate, (b) nonpunitive, and (c) consistent. Immediacy means trying to implement the consequence as close in time to the misbehavior as possible. In some situations (e.g., field trips, auditorium programs) it will be necessary to delay enforcement until a more opportune moment. It often is difficult to be nonpunitive, especially when the student's behavior has been flagrantly disrespectful. It is human to feel counterhostility toward students. At such times, the teacher would do best to count to 10 and then enforce a consequence in a tough, but not vindictive, manner.

The challenge of multiple misbehaviors, varying in intensity and frequency for different students, requires that all teachers have a range of negative consequences available at any time. Consequences will vary from those that can be administered in class to those that involve others in school and out of school. *Some common consequences that are available to the teacher and have been found to be effective are:* (a) use of soft reprimands, (b) in-class time-outs (e.g., sending to corner of room or outside door of room), (c) changing a preferred seat location, (d) taking away privileges (e.g., free time, class helper status), (e) taking away points or tokens (which may have been earned toward a reward), (f) during-school detentions (e.g., during activity or elective periods), (g) before- or after-school detentions, (h) restitution activities (e.g., repaint the room, repair a chair, replace a pen), (i) parent telephone calls or conferences, (j) time-outs or conferences with principal, (k) recording a poor score on behavior for grading class participation and/or work habits (Kerr & Nelson, 1983). In addition, the teacher can refer the child for further evaluation and recommend another placement.

Major infractions of school rules will usually result in an out-of-class consequence. For example, drug abuse may involve police notification and short suspension, and verbal attack on staff may require suspension or expulsion. Penalties for infractions of this magnitude are typically set forth in the board of education's discipline policy. The classroom teacher is responsible for accurately reporting such incidents so that out-of-class consequences may be properly enforced.

It is important to recognize that although many negative consequences may be enforced by the classroom teacher, their use should be carefully reviewed in the light of student progress. The teacher should keep in mind the strengths of the student and look for opportunities to praise or reward desirable behavior. *Where enforcement of consequences does not appear to be improving matters, the teacher should ask for help.* Resource or special class teachers, school counselors, psychologists, administrators, and other teachers can be emotionally supportive while helping to develop new approaches. In addition, it is widely recognized that a school-based team approach is necessary to address serious behavior problems (Dwyer, Osher, & Hoffman, 2000).

8. The Skill of Life Space Crisis Intervention. On occasion, a student will lose complete control and become a threat to himself or others. Intervention must be rapid to protect the student and the group from harm and to avert major escalation of the crisis. At these times, the goal is to reestablish order and control as soon as possible without hurting the student in crisis. Incidents such as a student threatening to commit suicide or attacking another student with scissors or smashing furniture and other property require quick backup for the classroom teacher. Specific staff roles and procedures should be defined in advance to provide for such crisis intervention, and the teacher should send an urgent message that assistance is needed. At such times the message can be delivered to the main office by another student. Long, Wood, and Fecser (2001) have developed a training program for teachers in this area.

In handling a crisis situation, the teacher must make every effort to appear outwardly calm. Signs of panic or hysteria will create more instability in an already tenuous situation.

An empathic appeal to the student's core values and inner strengths is most likely to prevent further breakdown of controls: "I know you're very upset but you're too important to hurt yourself "; "Tom, stop! You're furious but you can't attack him." The teacher can also use his or her relationship to halt dangerous or destructive actions, for example, "Betty, I don't want you to rip up your drawings."

The teacher may be able to position him- or herself so as to prevent the dangerous action. Physical restraint may be possible and should be carried out if it can successfully prevent attack or destructiveness. However, physical holding should only be attempted when a "clear and present danger" to person or property exists.

STRATEGIES FOR INCREASING DESIRABLE BEHAVIOR

1. The Skill of Stating Positive Expectations. Expectations for positive behavior (standards) should be specified for group and individual behavior, in the same way that limits are stated. Teachers need to highlight their list of Incompatible Desirable Behaviors (see Table 6.5–2).

2. The Skill of Modeling. This is a relatively easy and efficient way to promote positive behavior. To model desired behavior, the teacher should consistently display the behavior others are expected to exhibit, both in words and actions. Some examples are acting in a friendly and respectful manner to demonstrate a stated norm of "getting along with each other," allowing students to challenge their own ideas when advocating freedom of thought, and listening attentively to students to exemplify respect.

As simple as modeling appears to be, it is predicated on a congruence of teacher word and deed. One teacher was very surprised when a student refused to participate because "you don't want to hear what I have to say." The student was reading the teacher's nonverbal behavior (frowns, side glances, etc.) even though the class was being encouraged to speak freely.

Peer modeling can also be used. Thus, a teacher may have one student perform a certain behavior and then ask another student to try it, or the teacher may draw attention to the positive behaviors of some members of the class so that they may serve as positive models for others. For example, "I'm really pleased that some people are talking quietly, and not shouting." Another option is to group students so that a person needing improvement is placed with others who typically display the desirable behavior.

3. The Skill of Structuring the Situation. In contrast to restructuring to reduce negative behaviors (see earlier Strategy 4 for reducing undesirable behavior), structuring can be used to produce desired behaviors. As with restructuring, arrangements are possible in such areas as seating, grouping, degree of teacher assistance, nature of the task, format and complexity of the material, physical movement, degree of involvement, amount of recognition, extent of decision making, and personal feelings.

Some examples of structuring the situation include placing chairs in a circle for group discussion, setting up private cubicles to support concentrated seat-work, planning brief periods of work for students with a short attention span, pairing students with liked classmates to promote positive relationships, providing locker or cubby space to assure respect for property rights, and permitting verbal expression of emotions to foster self-awareness and responsibility.

4. The Skill of Positive Reinforcements. No strategy is more powerful or necessary than positive reinforcement for desirable behavior. Teachers and parents tend to take a child's achievements for granted and to focus on faults or needs for improvement. Amount of wealth, status, or education seems to matter little when one considers the lack of appreciation shown children for their sincere efforts. In fact, in upward-striving communities it is quite probable that offspring are less likely to satisfy parental expectations for success. By reinforcing desirable behavior, the classroom becomes a more positive environment—one in which accomplishments (behavioral and academic) are appropriately recognized and personal esteem is strengthened.

Positive reinforcement is defined as "a stimulus that, when presented as a consequence of a response, results in an increase or maintenance of that response" (Madsen & Madsen, 1974, p. 208). In other words, a stimulus becomes a positive reinforcer when it is valued or appreciated by the learner. However, the teacher cannot really know in advance what will be valued by a particular student.

As the student's interests, likes, and desires become known to the teacher, more positive reinforcers emerge. Whenever feasible, the teacher should try to find out from the student what would be rewarding or offer a choice of rewards, that is, positive reinforcers.

Several types of positive reinforcers are readily available to the classroom teacher, including activities and privileges, materials, food, parent recognition, leadership or prestige roles, physical proximity, awards, verbal approval, and nonverbal approval. Illustrations of these types of rewards for secondary students are shown in Table 6.5–3.

ILLUSTRATIVE REINFORCERS FOR SECONDARY STUDENTS

TABLE 6.5-3

Activities And Privileges

Operate equipment

Listen to records

Free time

Do a special project

Go on field trip

Help custodian, secretary, principal, teacher, etc.

Use typewriter

Play musical instrument

Choose own seat

Have work displayed

Exemption from a test

Exemption from an assignment

Doing errands

Leadership/Prestige Roles

Tutoring others

Peer counseling

Leadership/Prestige Roles *Continued.*

Representing group in some activity

Help teach class

Get materials ready for class

Lead opening exercises

Lead discussion groups or panel

Passing out exams

Helping grade papers

Present own hobby or collection

Awards

"Most improved"

"Teacher for a day"

Certificate of merit

Letter of commendation

"Super student"

Parent Recognition

Telephone call to parent

(continues)

TABLE 6.5–3

ILLUSTRATIVE REINFORCERS FOR SECONDARY STUDENTS *Continued.*

Parent Recognition *Continued.*

Take home letter

"We're proud" note, signed by parents

Nonverbal Approval

Smiling

Nodding

Laughing

Signaling OK

Saluting

Waving

Cheering

Winking

Materials

Books and magazines

Book markers

Bookcovers

Pencils with own name

Plants

Buttons

Address books

Stationery

Playing cards

Money

Records

Posters

Craft kits

Stamps

Food/Drinks

Soda

Potato chips

Ice cream

French fries

Peanuts/raisins

Fruit juice

Celery with spread

Flavored ice cubes

Sucking candy

Gum

Jaw breakers

Physical Proximity

Patting a shoulder

Sitting on desk near student

Walking alongside student

Special handshakes

Standing alongside student

Verbal And Written Approval

Good job

Super!

Outstanding

First rate

I'm proud of you

You did it

Real progress

Written compliments

Written comments on assigned work

Feedback stamps or stickers

5. The Skill of Regulated Permission. This strategy capitalizes on the momentum underlying a student's negative, unacceptable behaviors and calls for ingenuity on the part of the teacher. The goal is to channel basic impulses that are expressed disruptively into socially acceptable expressions. To implement this strategy, the teacher must first identify the likely impulse or motive behind the student's undesirable behavior. The next step is to find acceptable classroom alternatives for expression of this drive.

In many cases, the student can verify the motive behind his or her disruptive behavior, as might occur in a conference during which the teacher seeks to understand the student's feelings and perceptions of the class. For example, when asked how come she always called out answers to questions, Maria replied, "'Cause those dummies think I don't know anything." Hearing this, the teacher was able to think of ways for Maria to display her intelligence that did not interfere with her classmates' desire to answer questions. This process of regulating permission is shown in Figure 6.5–1.

Other examples of regulated permission are allowing an angry student to flatten clay, punch a boxing bag, or bang a blackboard eraser; enabling a dependent child to serve as a teacher aide; organizing a controlled debate when students want to assert their power toward one another;

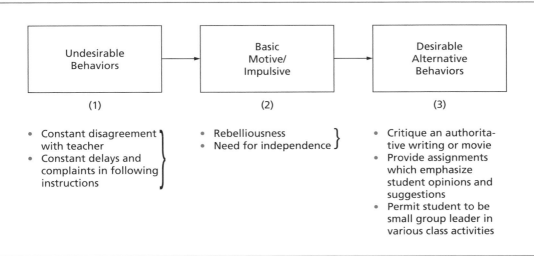

Figure 6.5–1. Changing Undesirable to Desirable Behavior.

and permitting structured small group discussion to meet needs for social contact during class.

6. The Skill of Contracting. Contracting is a process for establishing a written or verbal agreement with one or more students in which the teacher agrees to provide a particular service, reward, or outcome in return for a particular behavior or performance. Contracting often involves reinforcing desirable behavior, but adds a component of mutual goal-setting and negotiation. For example, Mrs. Smith and Robert agree that he can show his stamp collection if he first completes a class assignment.

The process for teacher–student contracting has four main steps (Fagen & Hill, 1977):

> **Step 1—Planning for the student conference.** Here the teacher selects a priority concern and considers a respectful way of communicating this concern to the student.

> **Step 2—Exploration with student.** During this step, the teacher shares his or her concern and listens to the student's reactions and views. Areas of agreement are identified for priority desirable behaviors, incentives for student effort, and responsibilities of student and teacher.

> **Step 3—Establish contract.** At this point, the actual terms of the contract are specified, including (a) desirable behaviors, (b) people involved and time period, (c) criteria for attainment, (d) responsibilities of people involved, and (e) consequences of behavior. Agreement is marked by a handshake or signatures.

> **Step 4—Review and revise contract.** This is a follow-up phase, at which time progress is checked and necessary adjustments are made.

A sample contract is shown in Figure 6.5–2. Some important guidelines for contracting are as follows:

(a) When other people have to be involved, let the student know that agreements are tentative and subject to others' approval.

(b) Use language the student can understand; use the student's words as much as possible.

(c) Written contracts offer the advantage of greater commitment; verbal contracts are quicker and more comfortable.

(d) Strive for as few objectives as possible; make them important and short term.

(e) Build in some items that have high probability for success.

(f) State objectives in positive terms, wherever possible. Negative phrases may be necessary, however, to assure specific understanding. For example, "*Carl* will not fight when mad but will

---

CONTRACT FOR: _____
(name of student)

I have decided to work on <u>"Staying on task"</u> (desirable behavior).

This will not always be easy, because I would often rather <u>talk or play with friends than concentrate on my school work</u> (undesirable behavior to be replaced by desirable behavior). However, I also know that I will earn the respect of teachers, parents, and friends by being a good student. There will always be a place for fun, too, at the right times.

Each day the teachers will rate me according to the following scale (indicate evaluation criteria):

    5—stayed on task all the time
    4—stayed on task most of the time
    3—stayed on task some of the time
    2—seldom on task
    1—off task all the time

When I achieve <u>5 contracts that average 4.0 or higher</u> (indicate criteria for specific reinforcement), I will then earn <u>a free interest period on Friday</u> (indicate specific reinforcement earned). This contract will be in effect for the period of _____ .

Signed: _____   Signed: _____
(student signature)   (teacher signature)

Date: _____   Date: _____

Figure 6.5–2. Sample Contract.

count to 10, walk away, or ask teacher permission to use the typewriter" (which helps him cool off).

7. Token Systems. Tokens are tangible objects or symbols that can be exchanged for a privilege, activity, or reward. They may include such things as points, chips, special cards, or homemade bills. Token systems usually include three features: (a) instructions to the class regarding behaviors that will be reinforced, (b) specifications about how tokens are earned as a result of producing desired behaviors, and (c) rules for exchanging the tokens for the backup reinforcers (Gallagher, 1979).

Token systems offer the following advantages (Kerr & Nelson, 1983):

(a)   whereas all students cannot receive the teacher's attention, they can all be involved with tokens;

(b)   positive reinforcement can be given quickly and consistently (through supplying tokens);

(c)   students can benefit from their responsibilities in record keeping; and

(d)   there is flexibility to vary items and costs for token exchange so that students begin to save for more expensive rewards. This results in longer periods of desirable behavior and greater ability to delay gratification.

REFERENCES

Algozzine, B., & Ysseldyke, J. (1993). *Strategies and tactics for effective instruction.* Longmont, CA: Sopris West.

Dwyer, K., Osher, D., & Hoffman, C. (2000). Creating responsive schools: Contextualizing early warning, timely response. *Exceptional Children, 66,* 247–365.

Fagen, S., & Hill, J. (1977). *Behavior management: A competency-based manual for inservice training.* Washington, DC: Psycho-educational Resources.

Federico, M., Herrold, W., & Venn, J. (1999). Helpful tips for succesful inclusion: A checklist for educators. *Teaching Exceptional Children, 32,* 76–82.

Gallagher, P. (1979). *Teaching students with behavior disorders: Techniques for classroom instruction.* Denver, CO: Love.

Glasser, W. (1977, November–December). 10 steps to good discipline. *Today's Education,* pp. 61–63.

Hartman, R., & Stage, S. (2000). The relationship between social information processing and in-school supervision for students with behavioral disorders. *Behavioral Disorders, 25,* 183–195.

Kerr, M., & Nelson, C. M. (1983). *Strategies for managing behavior problems in the classroom.* Columbus, OH: Merrill.

Long, N., Wood, M., & Fecser, F. (2001). *Life Space Crisis Intervention: Talking with students in conflict* (2nd ed.). Austin, TX: PRO-ED.

Madsen, C. H., & Madsen, C. (1974). *Teaching/discipline: A positive approach for educational development.* Boston: Allyn & Bacon.

Nelson, J., Crabtree, M., Marchano-Martella, N., & Martella, R. (1998). Teaching behavior in the whole school. *Teaching Exceptional Children, 30,* 4–9.

Stage, S., & Quiroz, D. (1997). A meta-analysis of interventions to decrease disruptive classroom behavior in public education settings. *School Psychology Review, 26,* 333–368.

EDITORS' COMMENTARY

In addition to the skills Fagen has described, teachers must master several other specific skills, including descriptive praise, decoding student behavior, therapeutic humor, and managing the school bully.

The Skill of Descriptive Praise

Behaviorists have taught that all behavior is learned and can be strengthened or weakened by the consequences that follow it. Positive reinforcers accelerate the behavior, and negative reinforcers decelerate the behavior.

The use of teacher praise is heralded as a positive way of building up or promoting a student's self-esteem and confidence. Teachers frequently use words such as *terrific, wonderful, excellent, outstanding, fantastic, perfect, very good, kind,* and *considerate* as positive reinforcers. When they use these terms to praise a student's conduct, teachers believe they are behaving as positive and effective teachers. *Unfortunately, this is not true when working with high-risk and troubled students.* Just as too much sunlight makes a desert and not an oasis, too much praise will "hothouse" troubled students' personalities and can have effects opposite to those intended. If a teacher tells one of these students he or she is "terrific," "wonderful," or "the best," the student may feel that the comments are not an accurate assessment. Instead of making the student feel better, they introduce additional pressure and cause feelings of guilt. The student might make any of the following conclusions:

1. My teacher is a poor judge of character and is lying to me.
2. I had a lucky day. I happened to hit the bulls-eye today, but it will never happen again.
3. I am unworthy of such glorious praises and I find it troublesome to own them.
4. I will have to show you I don't deserve such praise.

Descriptive praise is the skill of describing a student's motivation and accomplishments and not his or her personality. It addresses what is left over after the teacher pinpoints what the students were heard and seen doing today. Descriptive praise deals with only the students' efforts and behaviors, without interpreting them as "good," "better," or "best." The effect of the praise is the silent or verbal positive message a student self-delivers after evaluating the teacher's comments. If the student declares, "I am good," "terrific," "on task," or "considerate," then the teacher can reinforce it by saying, "I agree with you" or "I was just about to say the same thing."

Here are some actual classroom examples of effective (descriptive) and ineffective (personality) praise:

1. *Descriptive praise:* This room was a mess a few minutes ago, and now I look around and see everything is picked up and put away. What am I going to say to this class? (Answer: We are good at cleaning up our classroom.)

   Personality praise: You are priceless for cleaning up my classroom. What could I do without you! (Answer: I don't believe you. I am not priceless; I'm worth about a nickel. I could get along without you.)

2. *Descriptive praise:* Jerome, I noticed you worked at your desk for 15 minutes, and when you needed some help you raised your hand and waited until I could assist you. (Answer: I showed a lot of self-control today and I'm learning to follow the rules—good for me!)

   Personality praise: Jerome, you were wonderful to wait for me to come help you. You showed amazing self-control. This was the best day you had in weeks! (Good thing you got here when you did. I was about to yell at you for taking so long, and tomorrow I may end my 1-day streak of goodness.)

3. *Descriptive praise:* I can tell Susan is thinking by what she just said. (Answer: I am a competent thinker—I'm smart.)

Personality praise: I can tell Susan is a terrific, smart student by what she just said. (Answer: Yes, but I'm not as smart as Taylor.)

4. *Descriptive praise:* Stan, I noticed how you picked up all your resource materials, walked quietly to your desk, and started to work immediately. (Answer: I am a capable student—cheers for me.)

Personality praise: Stan, you were super today. You did everything perfectly. You are one of my best students. (Answer: I can't always be super or perfect. It is too much strain on me. I hope I won't mess up tomorrow.)

Remember, when a teacher tells students they are wonderful or terrific, it is not helpful praise. When students tell themselves they are resourceful, talented, and competent, the positive comments promote self-esteem and investment in learning.

The Skill of Decoding Student Behavior

Frequently, students in stress do not talk about their feelings; they act them out. They yell, run, cry, and withdraw, or they deny their feelings by saying, "I don't care" or "It doesn't matter to me." The skill is to learn how to decode their words, actions, and body language so they are connected to the students' feelings and initial source of stress. This skill is difficult to learn because it involves reading students' nonverbal behavior and reflecting what they are communicating in a clear and sympathetic way: "When I see you close your eyes and put your head on your desk, and I listen to you say, 'Nothing's wrong,' I get a different feeling. (Wait for reaction.) Perhaps you wish your problems would disappear, but you seem upset. (Wait for reaction.) A part of you knows that problems don't go away until you solve them. This is a difficult time for you. (Wait for reaction.) It is difficult and upsetting to talk about it, but perhaps in a few minutes you can begin to tell me what is troubling you."

Until students can accept their feelings and understand how feelings drive their behavior, they will never be able to accept the full responsibility for their behavior. Decoding skills (a) let students know their teachers are sensitive to their internal struggles and (b) offer them an invitation to talk about what is troubling them. This is an act of compassion and not a form of confrontation.

The Skill of Therapeutic Humor

There is nothing new about the skill of therapeutic humor. Everyone is aware of how a humorous comment is able to penetrate a tense and anxiety-producing situation. It clears the air and makes everyone feel more comfortable. The example below shows how one teacher used this technique to her advantage.

> I walked into my room after lunch period to find several pictures on the chalk board with "teacher" written under each one. I went to the board and picked up a piece of chalk, first looking at the pictures and then at the class. You could have heard a pin drop! Then I walked over to one of the pictures and said that this one looked the most like me but needed some more hair, which I added. Then I went to the next one and said that they had forgotten my glasses so I added them. On the next one I suggested adding a big nose, and on the last one a longer neck. By this time the class started to smile and then laugh. After a few seconds I said it was time to return to our lesson.

This example illustrates the phenomenon of group testing. The pictures were put on the board to test the vulnerability of the teacher. Some teachers could have reacted with sarcasm. They might have said that this was infantile behavior and not becoming of a fifth-grade class. Other teachers might have given the class extra work or administered a group punishment, such as denial of recess or free time. However, this teacher demonstrated she was secure, and a drawing could not cause her to regress or become counteraggressive. She turned a challenging moment into a therapeutic event and validated that she could be counted on during a stressful incident. She also was cognizant that therapeutic humor is a two-way experience in which both parties enjoy the situation. One-way humor is sarcasm, a put-down, a way of humiliating others, a form of social interaction in which one person has pleasure while the other person experiences psychological pain.

A common example of one-way humor is called "Playing the Dozens." This verbal game of peer insults probably has caused more fights in city schools than any other activity. The dozens has been called various names—*crackin', ribbin', dis-ing, rankin', mamma talk,* and *snaps.* The basic purpose is to deliver verbal abuse to a point where a peer gets out of control in front of the group. This form of verbal aggression depreciates the peer's family, mother, sister, or girlfriend. Its taunting has a clever twist and usually succeeds in winning group laughter and approval. Don't confuse it with two-way humor. Here are two examples: "Your mamma is so dumb she failed her urine test," and "Your sister works at a gas station because she likes to get pumped." This is a form of cruelty, not therapeutic humor.

MANAGING THE SCHOOL BULLY

Bullying is a new topic for us. It was not included in our last revision of *Conflict in the Classroom* or perceived as a serious problem for schools. Bullying was not sanctioned but was tolerated by the myth that "boys will be boys." Also, the bullying of other students usually took place at times and places where there was little staff supervision, such as in bathrooms, halls, the back of the school bus, and playgrounds. Now bullying is one of the most frequent topics of discussion among staff and at PTA meetings.

Time Magazine had a feature article on bullying titled, "The Bully Blight" (Lemonick, 2005). The lead sentence was, "Scientists find that getting picked on is more harmful than anyone knew." Bullying is defined as a persistent, aggressive, and deliberate act intended to scare or hurt a peer. Bullying behavior comes in many degrees and forms, ranging from name calling to sexual harassment to extortion. In one study, 47% of sixth graders reported they were the victims of a bully at least once during the course of 5 school days. This might explain a study by Fried and Fried (1996) who reported that 160,000 students missed school each day because they were afraid of what might happen to them.

The bully often selects two types of students: passive students and provocative students. The passive student, who usually is physically weaker than the bully, is cautious, withdrawn, and has low self-esteem. Passive students are reluctant to tell the staff or their parents about being picked on because they believe it will only make their life worse. This belief only reinforces their sense of helplessness and social isolation. The other target, the provocative student, is seen as hot tempered and socially offensive, and as having bad personal habits. Peers often feel the provocative student deserves the abuse he or she gets and will not come to his or her aid. Also, this student can be both a victim and a bully.

One interesting finding about bullying behavior is that it frequently takes place when other peers are available. This peer audience not only encourages the bully but also reduces his or her sense of wrong-doing. However, one study reported that 90% of students find bullying behavior disturbing to watch but choose to do nothing about it.

BULLYING is a serious problem to be solved, and schools are looking for proactive schoolwide bullying prevention programs that work. In the next article, Jerilyn Dufresne and Michael Dorn have a comprehensive discussion on the dynamic of bullying and how staff can bullyproof their schools.

ARTICLE 6.6

KEEPING STUDENTS AND SCHOOLS SAFE
Jerilyn Dufresne with Michael Dorn

This article is based on an interview with Michael Dorn, a noted expert on school violence who recently coauthored the book *Targeting Innocence: When Terrorism Comes to School*. Central to school safety are supportive bonds with adults who help create school climates free of bullying.

Q: A number of people claiming to be terrorism experts have been predicting a variety of types of terrorist attacks on American schools. Do you predict school terrorism incidents in American schools?

Michael Dorn: I'm seeing people waste a lot of time and energy on "what ifs," when they're ignoring what's right in front of them. It is impossible to make accurate predictions without access to current intelligence information, and the only people who have that, of course, are in government. Those of us who have actual experience in the field of anti-terrorism and experience in governmental school safety centers feel that most of the predictions that we've seen floating about the media are not likely scenarios. Our research shows that school terrorism events are extremely rare events. We have found only three incidents in U.S. history where schools were targeted by terrorists, and in all cases the terrorists were from the United States (Dorn & Dorn, 2005). Incidents in Wyoming and Alabama involved militia and the Beltway Sniper was in Maryland.

Q: Though school terrorism incidents are rare, they are very serious when they do occur. What do you recommend school and public safety officials do to try to prevent and prepare for acts of terrorism?

Michael Dorn: We recommend they do what they should already be doing—develop a comprehensive, four-phase school safety plan as recommended by the U.S. Department of Education (2003). And if they develop that four-phase, all-hazards plan, working closely with local officials, if they address traditional concerns, by and large, they will address terrorism concerns. For example, good access control to schools protects children from non-custodial abductions, child molesters who come to school on occasion, drug dealers and others who may trespass on campus, and also makes it harder for terrorists. They should have a proper emergency operations plan and address a wide range of hazards, including biological and chemical situations—which usually happen accidentally. Doing these things usually covers most terrorist concerns.

Q: What are some other current trends in school safety?

Michael Dorn: We're seeing a greater awareness; this is a major push for our non-profit safety center. School officials are becoming more aware that they have not been getting what they're paying for in some of their private consultant services. If they use a qualified training firm, consultant firm, or government agency, they find they can do a better job for less money. Government is putting out a lot of material to help schools do a better job without pouring money down an endless well. And I think that is going to continue. We're seeing schools right now that are in litigation and are losing because they relied on unqualified consultants four or five years ago. They purchased school safety plans, but those plans have failed and now the schools are getting sued. And the schools are losing. Simply paying people to do the work for you is not the best approach. It is better to train your staff and local officials to work together to write your school safety plans and emergency operations plans. Do your own site surveys instead of hiring consultants to do that for you.

Q: What are the most pressing issues for school safety today?

Michael Dorn: First is the more efficient use of safety resources, which covers a lot of things that I just talked about, but also available staff and available information. Some pressing issues have been around for 20 years, and I think will remain pressing issues for some time, like the failure of school and community safety officials to adequately identify and address risk. Another related issue is negligent supervision. I still think that proper supervision of school children is more elusive than people realize.

Q: What do you mean by "negligent supervision"?

Michael Dorn: It is a legal term, used when school districts are sued. For example, in most litigation against schools and with most deaths, whether from violence or accident, you find a common denominator: students were not being adequately supervised. Thus, if a child falls and dies because of being allowed to climb on something unsafe, or if someone brought a weapon in that led to a stabbing because we didn't properly supervise and control the environment.

A lot of people who think that just because a teacher, coach, or staff member is present that children are being supervised, which is not always true. Many adults do not understand that supervision is a top priority, and time and time again bullying can happen ten feet from a teacher. Every minute school is in session, we must supervise every child. We have to design our schools, conduct education, and interact with students in such a manner to minimize negligent supervision. That means students and others won't be in unsupervised places where they can do things they shouldn't do. Otherwise, problems develop, whether it is bullying, violent behavior, or sexual behavior.

Q: In your writing, you mention the importance of uncovering, reporting, and tracking school incidents.

Michael Dorn: Many have inaccurate assumptions of the threat level in a school. For example, if you ask middle school administrators about the level of bullying, they might cite a percentage; but, if they have not surveyed students, staff, and parents, they are just guessing. It's like not testing your students for math and presuming you know what their math ability is throughout your district. Many districts don't use proper survey instruments. They do not evaluate reported incident data and contrast it with self-reported information in surveys. They do not do an annual physical assessment of the facility to spot physical indications that they have incidents occurring on campus. Those are three ways to accurately determine threat levels. Often, schools did not think they had a problem until it hit them right between the eyes in a very big way.

Q: How can school personnel connect with youth who are vulnerable to gang influence, school failure, and delinquency?

Michael Dorn: First, on an environmental basis, you can design, structure, and operate schools in a manner that makes them warm and caring places where children can succeed. Academic success is critical when we talk about intervention strategies such as keeping kids out of gangs. We can do this through building design, through policies, through how we structure and design a school, and the way we operate it.

Second, on a personal level, we can constantly advocate for children and serve as cheerleaders for all who work with children. There are more people who may become too narrowly focused on one thing they are doing. We are not just teaching these kids math or English, but we are helping them succeed and overcome adversity.

The third thing we can do, again on a personal level, is reach out to individual children. A child who has a close connection with a caring responsible adult can often overcome incredible odds. Children are very resilient when they have this type of support. As we advocate for children, we can make a difference. When a student who has been bullied tells us, "I made it because of you. I stayed in school because of you," there may be 50 to 100 others who stayed in school because of that staff member but never said anything (Dorn, 2003). It is unbelievable sometimes how much of a difference a bus driver, a teacher, a teacher's aide, or someone who works in the cafeteria can make if they have the right attitude and reach out to help kids. It is absolutely astounding, but often they see the problems but do not realize the remarkable good they do.

Q: In your book, *Weakfish: Bullying Through the Eyes of a Child,* you talk about the need for those who work with children to be vigilant when it comes to bullying. How common is it for students to be severely bullied and not to tell an adult about it?

Michael Dorn: It is extremely common for children to go through the ordeal of being chronically bullied every day, to be close to dropping out of school, close to suicide, close to bringing a weapon and using it on someone, and for that student to never once tell an adult. The research shows that between 12–18% of children are bullied every day and don't tell an adult (Olweus, 1993). These are the children who are most at risk. They are also the most likely to never tell us they need help. We have to spot those indicators, to reach out to those children, and uncover that bullying. It's extraordinarily important.

Q: What is the danger for children who are not able to speak about bullying or do not have a supportive adult?

Michael Dorn: There is a dramatically increased risk of suicide, dropping out of school, greatly heightened risk of bringing weapons to school and using them, and problems after they have finished school. We have seen a number of studies that indicate they may have serious problems with their social life into their thirties (Dorn, 2003). We could do this whole interview on the horrible problems of chronic bullying. There are so many children who have taken their own lives, who have dropped out of school, who are in prison because of what they went through. The other side is it is not just the victim. It is pretty clear that chronic bullies have a much higher likelihood of serving prison time. We are doing them a disservice as well when we allow them to victimize these other children.

Q: What can teachers and other adults do to assist both the bullied and those doing the bullying?

Michael Dorn: The first thing is to care and be alert. The next is to become educated on issues of bullying; there is a lot of good information out there. But they need to take the right approach; bullying is a hot market, and many well-meaning attempts to try to address bullying have been very counter-productive. For example, peer mediation can be very effective in resolving some conflicts, but it should never be used for bullying situations. Peer mediation is for a conflict between two people. Bullying is not conflict. Bullying is victimization of one or more persons by another group of one or more persons. And there is a real inequality of power, real or perceived. Using peer mediation for bullying situations is like having a rapist apologize to a woman he has raped and asking the two of them to shake hands.

One should be mindful that we may see only the tip of the iceberg. Many children who are being chronically bullied are in that 12–18% who will not tell us. The next largest percentage includes the kids who will tell us once (Olweus, 1993); they will come to one adult and make one attempt. This may be a parent, a teacher, a custodian, or a school bus driver. They may report one incident but do not necessarily tell you what has been going on the last three months.

We have to investigate when we hear of bullying since in some cases there is a lot more to it than initially meets the eye. We have to ask a lot of questions and get more information before we act. What appears to be just an incident of hitting or name-calling may be far more serious than we think.

Q: What can community groups and churches do to keep their facilities safe, even while mentoring kids who may be gang-involved?

Michael Dorn: We do a lot of work with churches and youth organizations, such as the YMCA and, in particular, Boys and Girls Clubs of America. They face a lot of the same issues as schools, but they have a unique situation where they have to draw youth to them, in contrast to schools, where youth are told to go to them. When we think about creating that environment and atmosphere, we get into things like CPTED (Crime Prevention Through Environmental Design)—the use of murals, the use of colors, and the layout of an area.

For example, if we want to draw youth to a Sunday school class, we need to create a structured and safe environment, just like schools do. But we have to go further and make it a fun place where kids want to come. Boys and Girls Clubs put a lot of emphasis on this and have had dramatic success. And that is why some Clubs have incredible rates of usage by youth in their community. Safety is important for schools, but it is even more critical for voluntary organizations that don't have a compelled audience. Most of the same principles apply: reaching out to a child personally, making sure that all those organizations understand the difference they can make for those children. Close supervision is very important as bullying and assaults do happen, even in churches. One would be surprised at how much safety-related litigation churches face. Since they do not typically have qualified immunity as a government entity, they may be easier to sue. These safety-related issues range from people tripping to child molestation to outright physical assaults. Unfortunately, such things can happen in any setting, including a place of worship.

Q: What else would you like to tell our readers?

Michael Dorn: Never underestimate the absolutely profound impact they can have on the world by working with youth. Personally, I had child advocates reach out to me, and I went from an absolutely abysmal existence, where I would have just as soon died as take another breath, to someone who today works with people all over the world.

It is astounding what some of these folks have done. In the worst neighborhoods, with limited fiscal resources, they just have that burning desire to help children and they let nothing stand in their way. Miracles happen. I would encourage anybody who works with children to never give up. And never underestimate what they can do.

REFERENCES

Dorn, M. (2003). *Weakfish: Bullying through the eyes of a child*. Macon, GA: Safe Havens International.

Dorn, M., & Dorn, C. (2005). *Targeting innocence: When terrorism comes to school*. Macon, GA: Safe Havens International.

Olweus, D. (1993). *Bullying at school: What we know and what we can do*. Oxford, UK: Blackwell Publishers.

U.S. Department of Education, Office of Safe and Drug Free Schools. (2003). *Practical information on crisis planning: A guide for schools and communities*. Washington, DC: Author. Retrieved 3/17/05 from http://ww.ed.gov/admins/lead/safety/emergencyplan/ crisisplanning.pdf

SUMMARY

This chapter has presented the essential concepts and skills of effective classroom discipline. Typically, *classroom discipline* is defined as either maintaining student order or teaching students to be self-directed. Our definition is more inclusive and integrates the following four concepts and skills into a schoolwide positive behavior management program based on strength-based interventions.

1. Effective classroom discipline begins with teacher self-awareness and self-control, not with the students.

2. Effective classroom discipline teaches the democratic values of our society by providing students with opportunities to choose, regulate, and be accountable for their behavior. This long-range goal of discipline develops an internal locus of control.

3. Effective classroom discipline consists of a variety of short-range, on-the-spot, direct interventions based on school values and rules. These interventions either increase positive behaviors or decrease negative behaviors.

4. Effective classroom discipline is viewed as a professional philosophy of relating, teaching, and empowering students, and as a positive way of perceiving, thinking, feeling, and behaving toward students. It is not a bag of unrelated tricks.

EDITORS' REFERENCES

Fried, S., & Fried, P. (1996). *Bullies and victims: Helping your child survive the schoolyard battlefield.* New York: M. Evans.

Lemonick, M. D. (2005, April 11). The bully blight. *Time Magazine.*

McCurdy, B. (2003). Positive behavior support in urban schools. *Journal of Positive Behavior Intervention, 5,* 112–119.

Redl, F. (1951). *Children who hate.* New York: Free Press.

Rosenburg, M. (2003). The development, implementation, and sustainability of a comprehensive school wide behavior management system. *Intervention, 39,* 320–323.

Warren, J. (2003). Urban application of school-wide positive behavior support. *Journal of Behavior and Intervention, 5*(2), 30–91.

7 BEYOND STUDENT BEHAVIOR:
Strategies and Skills To Help Students Involved in Chronic Self-Defeating Patterns of Behavior

THIS chapter looks beyond students' behavior in order to make their personal problems more understandable and less mysterious. Personal problems are not temporary reactions to frustration; they are definable personality problems that are chronic and perplexing to teachers. As professional problem solvers, teachers are comfortable making decisions about how to help their students academically. However, when asked to help these same students deal with their personality problems, teachers seem reluctant to assume this responsibility. Their ambivalence often is reinforced by administrators, who may inform them that helping troubled students is not their area of professional competence and may instruct them to refer those students to the school counselor, psychologist, or social worker. This sounds like reasonable professional advice and a sensible division of labor. In fact, staff collaboration can result in an effective "team approach" to helping troubled students when adequate psychological staff and resources are available. When it works, it represents the best of interdisciplinary cooperation. Unfortunately, in the majority of public schools, including special and alternative schools, the psychological staff frequently are referred to as the "hidden faculty." They are rarely seen, are overloaded with cases and reports, and usually are not available when teachers need them. Meanwhile, the referring teacher continues to have the responsibility of providing the troubled students and their classmates with a safe, secure, and appropriate learning environment. Given this situation, what are the teacher's options and responsibilities? What should the teacher be doing to help these students and the class until professional help arrives? What if professional help never arrives? Should the teacher suffer through this frustration by saying, "That's life!" or "There is nothing I can do about this situation"?

Our recommendation is a resounding "No." Just as teachers are trained medically to administer CPR to a student who is not breathing and to perform the Heimlich maneuver when a student is choking, teachers need to integrate their instructional skills with specific mental health practices. This does not change a teacher into a psychologist any more than performing CPR turns a teacher into a physician. These additional skills simply acknowledge that the current conditions in many classrooms create a need for deeper and more effective understanding of the social–emotional problems of troubled students.

Looking for Causes

A basic principle of Gestalt psychology is that the whole or "personality" of a person is greater than the sum of its parts. Similarly, a student is psychologically more complex than the sum of his or her behaviors. Although inappropriate behavior needs to be managed, it is also important to look beyond the behavior of troubled students and to consider their unmet psychological needs. As professionals, teachers are naturally interested in understanding the underlying or causative reasons of chronic student problems. For example, teachers are aware that something is psychologically awry when a high-achieving student begins to fail exams, when a student becomes enraged and explodes when asked to carry out a routine classroom request, when a student enjoys bullying peers, or when a student becomes overstimulated and hyperactive during nonstructured times. Teachers also understand that there are underlying problems when a student escapes into silence and looks depressed; when a student is anxious, fearful, and helpless in normal situations; and when a student comes to school under the influence of alcohol and drugs or talks about ending his or her life. Rather than determining which students have chronic social–emotional problems, teachers are concerned with what insights and skills they can bring to these problems.

One way of learning about the underlying causes of personal problems is to review the various psychological need theories of personality development. A word of caution is offered at this time. When they study the needs of children and youth, teachers can become acutely troubled by the severity of a student's unmet psychological needs. It is important to emphasize that understanding a student's needs does not mean the teacher excuses the student's disruptive behaviors. An awareness of the emotional pain of a student's life can elicit a groundswell of teacher compassion, but this compassion must not be confused with sympathy. Teacher sympathy sends a message, "You poor child! I understand your emotional pain so I will not add to it by expecting the same standards for you. You have been treated unfairly by life and you have deep and justifiable reasons for being angry, confused, fearful, dependent, or depressed." Teacher sympathy reinforces a student's belief that he or she has been psychologically gypped and encourages more irresponsible student behavior. Any message of sympathy is a clear misuse of the concept of psychological acceptance. Compassion, however, sends a different message. It says, "Thank you for sharing some of your psychological struggles and feelings with me. They helped me better appreciate and understand you. Now, let's plan how we can use these difficult times to figure out what specific support and skills you need if you are to be emotionally strong, independent, and competent." Compassion emphasizes students' strengths rather than their weaknesses and promotes the beginning source of trust for the students while becoming a positive source of motivation for the teacher.

Maslow's Hierarchy of Needs

In 1943 Abraham Maslow wrote "A Theory of Human Motivation," in which he proposed the existence of a hierarchy of five human needs that motivate behavior believed the lowest level of need must be satisfied at a minimum level before the individual is motivated to seek out the next higher level of need.

Maslow's hierarchy is:

Level 1: *Physiological needs.* All the biological drives for survival and development—food, water, sleep, protection from heat/cold, and so on.

Level 2: *Safety needs.* All activities that protect the individual, such as physical and psychological security and personal safety.

Level 3: *Belongingness and love needs.* All activities that promote psychological attachment, trust, acceptance, and emotional security from others.

Level 4: *Esteem needs.* All activities that enhance the worth, recognition, achievements, and competitiveness of the individual.

Level 5: *Self-actualizing need.* The highest level of development—all activities that involve self-directed intellectual and aesthetic appreciation of life.

Maslow explained that the first four needs can only be satisfied by others (i.e., family, school, community); the individual is dependent on the skills of adult caregivers. Their quality of nurturing, attitudes, expectations, rules, and punishments govern and determine the extent to which the individual's needs are met. In contrast, the self-directed individual functioning at Level 5 has had the other four levels of needs met, is less dependent on others for approval, and can be more directed by inner capacities, talents, and goals.

Maslow's hierarchy of needs has been very instructional to educators. His theory represents a positive view of personality development. He described what needs must be met to foster the development of a well-adjusted individual. The theory also is useful in understanding the behavior of high-risk and troubled students. When students are deprived of their basic needs of food, shelter, sleep, and health; when students are frightened about their physical and psychological safety; when students are rejected and neglected; or when students are feeling worthless and inadequate, they will be driven to meet these unmet needs before they have the motivation and energy to achieve the higher level of academic success.

Glasser's Choice Theory

William Glasser is a child psychiatrist who has committed himself to finding more effective strategies of helping troubled students in school. In *Choice Theory in the Classroom* (1998), he presented the fundamental needs critical to a student's psychological welfare:

1. The need of survival

2. The need of belonging and love

3. The need for power

4. The need for fun

5. The need for freedom

The first two needs are similar to Maslow's needs. The need for power means a sense of achievement, success, and competence. The need for fun means the ability to experience some joy and pleasure from learning. The need for freedom means the opportunity to choose without violating the rights of others and to be free from autocratic control.

According to Glasser, educators who are teaching alienated and troubled students must be aware of these needs and must develop specific learning opportunities to meet these needs when designing daily school lessons and activities for these youth.

Brendtro, Brokenleg, and Van Bockern: The Circle of Courage

In 1990 Brendtro, Brokenleg, and Van Bockern wrote an inspiring book, *Reclaiming Youth at Risk.* Building on the history of traditional Native American child-rearing philosophies, they proposed a positive culture of caring to meet the four essential needs of developing children. Their model is based on a holistic concept characterized by the symbol of the Indian medical wheel or Circle of Courage and not a hierarchical system like Maslow's. They believe all children, regardless of their culture, will become healthy adults if the needs or "spirits" of belonging, mastery, independence, and generosity are met.

1. *The Spirit of Belonging.* All infants need nurturing parents, but all infants need to belong to the tribe, to have many mothers with many honored relationships and relatives. Children need to live in an extended family; over time, the children become a part of a shared community with a clear identity and sense of trust regarding their cultural roots and feelings of belongingness.

2. *The Spirit of Mastery.* Children are taught the importance of competency by observing and listening to the wisdom of their elders and by participating in tribal games, stories, and work. Each of these activities reflects the importance of mastering a skill, based on the value of co-operative achievement, personal persistence, creativity, and problem solving. This process of learning by doing becomes the basic educational experience of fostering the spirit of mastery in Native American youth.

3. *The Spirit of Independence.* To survive, to become brave, children are taught the importance of being autonomous, responsible, assertive, and self-disciplined. They are encouraged to hunt and trap on their own, to be accountable for their actions, and to take some risks by adventuring into the unknown. These expectations result in a sense of empowerment; therefore, this spirit is similar to Glasser's need for power.

4. *The Spirit of Generosity.* The spirit of generosity is a vital force in the socialization of Native American youth. They are taught the importance of giving and sharing their resources instead of accumulating and increasing their material wealth. Personal acts of generosity are a significant way of building the importance of helping others and of defining the quality of one's character. The emphasis on seeking intrinsic rather than extrinsic rewards is another way to enhance the spirit of generosity.

Using this theory, the authors advocate that special schools and treatment agencies can restructure their daily program and activities to reclaim troubled students by promoting their need to belong, to be competent, to be independent, and to be generous. This is the most positive model of helping troubled students, and it has an exciting future as these concepts become translated into specific psychoeducational strategies.

All three of the previous theories—Maslow's, Glasser's, and Brendtro et al.'s—describe underlying needs and environmental conditions required to promote the development of well-adjusted students. The next logical question is, What happens to children and youth when these psychological needs are not met by the adults in their environment? How do children and youth behave when they have been neglected, rejected, and depreciated? All three theories would predict that the unmet needs of these students for adult attention, approval, and acceptance would be greater and more difficult to meet in the classroom than the needs of other students. To make matters more frustrating, these troubled students have learned a variety of protective behaviors that are offensive to teachers and are less likely to result in a response of respect and approval. Like the adage, "the rich get richer and the poor get poorer," the students having the greatest need for teacher acceptance and approval usually end up getting the least, and the students having the least needs in these areas usually end up receiving the majority of teacher acceptance and approval. Dreikurs was one of the first child psychiatrists to write about this concept and to help teachers understand the meaning of student misbehavior.

Dreikurs's Four Goals of Misbehavior

In 1971 Dreikurs, Grunwold, and Pepper published an innovative textbook titled *Maintaining Sanity in the Classroom.* It was an immediate success. They proposed an original concept regarding student misbehavior. They believed misbehavior was motivated by four identifiable and underlying goals that teachers must learn before they attempt to correct or stop inappropriate student behavior. The four goals of misbehavior are motivated by the students' belief that these behaviors are in their best interests.

1. *Attention-getting mechanism.* Dreikurs documented that some troubled students believe they do not have any chance of being recognized by constructive behaviors so they take up a variety of attention-getting behaviors or mechanisms to engage the teacher's attention. The mechanisms of misbehavior include showing off in class, interrupting others, clowning around, becoming silly, and bullying others. For these students, it is more important to be noticed by the teacher and to tolerate his or her anger than to be ignored, forgotten, and excluded by the teacher. Behaviorists have acknowledged these same attention-getting behaviors and have taught teachers to ignore them while actively reinforcing any of the students' positive behaviors.

2. *The need for power seeking.* Some students try to get their needs met by becoming rebels with a cause. They try to master or control their immediate environment by being disobedient and stubborn, and by engaging the adults in power struggles (see Article 6.2). Their false beliefs are: "If I win this power struggle, I am in control of my life." "If I am successful, I am in charge of this situation, and if I'm in charge, I have real power in this group and have earned the respect of my peers."

   To maintain their feelings of power or self-worth, their goal is to outsmart the adults by knowing how to push their emotional panic buttons. Unfortunately, there are no winners in a power struggle, and this goal of misbehavior ultimately becomes self-defeating for the student.

3. *The need to compensate for feeling rejected and emotionally hurt by seeking revenge.* This goal of misbehavior is limited to a few very troubled students who have been damaged by their traumatic life experiences. They have given up trusting adults and are motivated by the desire for revenge. These students are so filled with hate at what has happened to them that they are controlled by the active thought: "You have hurt me, so I will find a way of hurting you!" They have lost their ability to discriminate between adults who care and adults who are exploitative. Consequently, during stressful times, they end up treating all adults alike. These students will need special education programs and perhaps an alternative school to provide them with an appropriate education.

4. *The need to express feelings of discouragement and hopelessness.* The goal of this misbehavior also is limited to a few students who have internalized their traumatic life experience and have concluded it is their fault. They do not seek revenge but have come to the conclusion that, because life is so overwhelmingly painful, they cannot manage the daily emotional stress. They have internalized a belief that they have failed, and they have given up the struggle to succeed. They don't want to try anymore. Their goals are to be left alone and to be able to turn to the nonrealities of drugs, alcohol, and passivity for relief and satisfaction.

According to Dreikurs, these four goals of misbehavior are not rigid categories. Instead, they are general diagnostic classifications that will help teachers understand the multiple meaning of troubled students' behavior.

Wood's Developmental Anxieties

Another important advocate of understanding the needs of students is Mary Wood. She has taken a developmental view of troubled students and believes that anxiety is a private, persistent reaction to unmet emotional needs.

In 1996 Wood described her theory in the third edition of her creative textbook, *Developmental Therapy—Developmental Teaching*. She stated that all children experience five developmental anxieties from birth through adolescence. These intrapsychic anxieties are feelings of abandonment, inadequacy, guilt, conflict, and identity. If a developmental anxiety is not resolved at the age-appropriate time, it will be carried into the next developmental stage and will create even more unmet emotional needs in the future. Like Maslow, Wood explained that many unresolved developmental anxieties will become the primary motivational force of the student at the next level and will interfere with all future relationships.

1. *The anxiety of abandonment.* Feelings of abandonment occur as a normal developmental crisis in infants and young children under the age of 2 years. If a young child bonds with parents or a significant adult and receives consistent love, care, and security, the feelings of abandonment will be resolved and a growing sense of trust will develop. However, if the child experiences early and prolonged physical or psychological neglect, the feelings of abandonment will become real and the child will likely develop superficial relationships, hoard objects, and have a gnawing desire to be accepted by others. This developmental anxiety is the opposite of Brendtro et al.'s (1990) spirit of belongingness.

2. *The anxiety of inadequacy.* Feelings of inadequacy become a normal developmental crisis of preschool children as they come to understand the needs and expectations of the important adults in their life. This developmental change generates additional feelings of self-doubt: Can I meet their expectations? Will I get it right? If the preschool child experiences chronic failure or is repetitively told that his or her behavior doesn't meet adult standards, the child will learn to deny or justify mistakes by blaming others, lying, or projecting feelings on others.

3. *The anxiety of guilt.* Feelings of guilt become a developmental crisis for children between 6 and 9 years of age. If these children have not resolved the previous developmental anxiety of inadequacy and think they are "no good" and "unworthy," they will actively put themselves down emotionally for not meeting their own standards. When this occurs, the merging of their feelings of inadequacy and guilt can result in such intense guilt that they actually seek out punishment. Troubled students have been observed stealing objects and breaking school rules so openly that they are guaranteeing they will be caught and punished. These students also can end up as group scapegoats and willing victims of exploitation. During stressful times, their behaviors are frequently examples of self-abuse due to personal guilt.

4. *The anxiety of conflict.* This developmental anxiety, which takes place between the ages of 9 and 12, emerges when the need for budding independence conflicts with the will of authorities. If this crisis is resolved, the preadolescent develops a new feeling of self-confidence and social flexibility. One of the significant outcomes of this developmental anxiety is the insight that with independence and freedom comes personal accountability for one's decisions and behaviors.

If this developmental crisis is not resolved, the preadolescent is likely to enter the adolescent years ill prepared to cope with the normal additional adolescent stresses. Fights with authority figures will continue and will ensure negative teacher reactions. A student may begin to believe there is status and power in being the "bad kid" in the classroom. This is very similar to Dreikurs et al.'s (1971) need for power seeking.

5. *The anxiety of identity.* Developmental anxiety for adolescents is illustrated by the psychological questions, "Who am I?" and "Will I be able to handle this crisis?" These questions reflect the dynamic interplay between new feelings of independence and residual feelings of dependency. This struggle increases as the adolescent's maturing body creates concerns about sexuality, attractiveness, and group acceptance. During this stage, adolescents experiment with new attitudes, appetites, and behaviors with the same interest as if they were buying a new pair of jeans. "Does it look right? Does it feel right? Am I comfortable wearing it?" As this anxiety about their identity is resolved and they feel more comfortable about themselves, they solidify their social and emotional skills and develop a direction for life after high school.

Wood's developmental therapy highlights the importance of understanding these five normal and predictable developmental anxieties in children and youth.

She wrote that this awareness can aid teachers in helping troubled students to identify their underlying anxieties and to recognize how they trigger their feelings, behaviors, and resulting teacher reactions.

Long's Concept of How Normal Developmental Needs of Very Troubled Students Get Turned Into Self-Defeating Fears

Long's (1993) study of reeducating seriously troubled students has provided teachers of emotionally disturbed students with additional insights into the dynamics of unmet needs. He claimed that because these students have experienced such early, intense, and prolonged neglect, abuse, and rejection, they no longer are motivated by personal trust or the spirit of human kindness. By the time these students are placed in special programs or alternative schools, they come to the classroom not only with a chip on their shoulders but also with an intent to avoid interpersonal closeness and academic learning. They view any therapeutic program as an intrusive and hostile life sentence. Their initial behaviors are centered on psychologically biting any hand that tries to feed them.

Their negative attitudes and rejecting behaviors are difficult to accept, particularly if the teachers are reaching out to them in a friendly way. Most caring teachers believe that if a student is cold, hungry, and tired, and if the adult provides that student a hot meal, warm clothes, and a good night's sleep, these caring conditions should improve the student's condition and disposition. Likewise, if a student has not experienced a nurturing adult, positive learning opportunities, and a chance to be empowered, and if these essential psychological needs are provided by a caring teacher, the student should respond with new hope, appreciation, and more appropriate behaviors. Long reported that this rarely happens with seriously troubled students. He has observed that emotionally disturbed students initially do not respond positively to interpersonal relationships or special programs. They seem to have developed psychological antibodies against the warmth of healthy relationships and supportive programs. They appear to be conditioned to consider close relationships as toxic rather than enriching experiences. Interpersonal closeness does not mean love, trust, and bonding, but a new cycle of rejection and abandonment. Interpersonal closeness is not something to seek and attain; it is a condition to avoid and fear. This reaction is particularly true when teachers begin to have some emotional meaning to them. The students' defense against adult closeness is to react with renewed resistance and rejection of the teacher. Similarly, academic competence for these students does not create a sense of mastery, but only a belief that adults will demand a greater and higher level of performance. These students are not motivated by success but by a fear of academic success since they believe they will only end up failing. Likewise, becoming independent does not lead to freedom of control but to a quagmire of new and overwhelming responsibilities. It appears much safer psychologically to manipulate others than to take charge of one's life. Independence also is something to fear and not a role to realize. Finally, generosity is not something that leads to altruism and sharing, but rather to another experience of personal deprivation. To give something away means that one has less of it for oneself. The goal is to hold on to whatever one has and protect it. Generosity is something to avoid.

Long has documented how these students have turned their healthy developmental needs into a fear of these needs. As infants, they were seriously abused, neglected, or rejected. As children, they still were motivated toward having their emotional needs met, but they frequently used a variety of inappropriate behaviors that resulted in more adult abuse. If this cycle of psychological and physical rejection continues into early adolescence, many of these seriously troubled students learn to fear their own healthy psychological needs and conclude that it is safer to avoid or deny them than to try again and suffer the pain of rejection. These seriously troubled students are not going to be helped in the regular classroom unless the teacher has many skills in seeing beyond their defensive behaviors. Many of them will need comprehensive and intensive therapeutic services and programs.

This chapter is organized for the reader to gain a better understanding of the unmet needs of troubled students. Topics include students who have low self-concepts and feelings of failure; who are silent in school; who are antisocial, aggressive, or passive–aggressive; who have attention deficits and hyperactivity disorders and/or learning disabilities; who have alcohol or drug problems; who are depressed; who have suicidal thoughts and actions; who are gay or lesbian; who have eating disorders (obesity or anorexia); or who perform self-mutilations.

The following behaviors may indicate that a student has an emotional problem:

- Sudden and pronounced behavioral changes
- Aggressive and harmful acts toward others
- Suicidal writings or artwork, and unexplained tears
- Self-destructive behaviors
- Withdrawal from activities and friends and a sense of depression
- Evidence of substance abuse such as alcohol or drugs
- Chronic lack of sleep or inability to eat
- Illogical language and general sense of confusion
- Signs of physical and sexual abuse

The articles in this chapter represent the best and the latest psychoeducational insights into how to understand and help students who are involved in chronic self-defeating patterns of behavior.

STUDENTS WITH LOW SELF-CONCEPTS AND FEELINGS OF FAILURE

The first article, "Masking the Feeling of Being Stupid," was written by Sally Smith, the founder and director of the Lab School of Washington, D.C., and a professor of the graduate program in learning disabilities at American University. The Lab School is recognized as a national model center for students with learning disabilties. This is a one-of-a-kind, innovative school in which the creative arts play a central role in the reeducation process. Smith's writings not only describe the needs and strategies of helping these special needs students but also have implications for all students who have academic problems and low self-esteem.

Self-esteem is defined as the student's feeling of self-worth and is an internal source of motivation that guides and directs behavior. Students with high self-esteem, in general, are confident, optimistic, and active; have little anxiety; and enjoy new challenges. Students with low self-esteem, in general, are fearful of angering others, dependent, anxious, and resistant to new challenges. Students with special needs are more likely to have low self-esteem and to develop ways of hiding their feelings of inadequacies.

We selected this article because it provides important insights into student behaviors. One concept to remember is that *the same underlying problem among students—in this case, the feelings of low self-esteem or the feelings of stupidity—can be expressed in many different behaviors.* There is rarely a one-to-one relationship between the cause of a student's behavior and its expression in behavior. The corollary statement of this concept is also true: *Different problem behaviors among students can all be motivated by the same underlying cause.*

IN this article, Smith describes 18 different masks or behaviors used by students with learning disabilities to defend against their feelings of stupidity and peer embarrassment. An awareness of these different protective masks may enable a teacher to see beyond these false images and to respond to these students by discovering the meaning behind their masks. When this connection is made and the teacher acknowledges their feelings, the possibility of genuine teacher support and help can develop.

ARTICLE 7.1

MASKING THE FEELING OF BEING STUPID
Sally L. Smith

I run a seminar with learning disabled adults every Tuesday evening at the Lab School of Washington. This is my current research. Learning disabled adults can tell you what our learning disabled children cannot. Through these seminars, I have been able to improve the teaching of our students and the training of special

From *The Pointer, 32*(3), 1988, pp. 18–22. Copyright by Sally L. Smith. Reprinted with permission of the Helen Dwight Reid Educational Foundation.

education teachers! The most important message they have given me is that the biggest battle of all with dyslexics is for their self-esteem. They feel stupid. They have been treated as stupid. School stands for mastery of academic disciplines. All through school for many years, they have felt defeated, worthless, dumb. They learned to mask their hurts.

One adult stated, "I learned to act a certain way so I couldn't be teased. I would appear bored, tired, eager to be of help, all knowing or funny, depending upon what was going on. In other words, I would do anything but let them know I couldn't read the material." Another adult shared that "I faked my way all through school. I had the gift of gab and an excellent memory."

"I masked my handicaps and saved my job."

"My ex-husband never knew."

"I masked my inability to write and used my wife to do all the correspondence and the billing."

"I don't want my own child to think I'm a dummy, so I hide it from him."

"When you don't know something or cannot read something and you feel you should be able to, then don't you mask this disability in front of people you respect? I do!"

Unfortunately, many of these learning disabled adults reported they started developing masks in first or second grade, when they could not read what others could. Few of our students ever received special education. They were not identified as learning disabled or dyslexic; their teachers usually identified them as lazy, when they were trying their hearts out. They were called "retarded" if they had any speech or language problems and "disturbed" if they were hyperactive, impulsive or had any of the behavioral manifestation of a learning disabled child. Often they were gifted, surely above average in intelligence, and could not bear their inability to accomplish the simplest of academic tasks. Here are some of the masks they wore:

THE MASK OF SUPER-COMPETENCE

"Easy!" "Oh, sure." "Everyone knows that." "I know, I know, I know …" With a great deal of bravado, everything is made to look simple. This person knows he can talk his way through anything. His logic is impeccable. He's good with people, with numbers, with problem-solving, trouble shooting. General George S. Patton assured his daughter that Napoleon couldn't spell either and he quoted Jefferson Davis as saying, "A man must have a pretty poor mind not to be able to think of several ways to spell a word."

THE MASK OF HELPLESSNESS

"I don't know." "I don't understand." "I can't do anything." "I'm such a failure." "I'm dyslexic." Through pity, this person gets everyone around him to help him, do his work, take on his responsibilities, so that he never fails; he refuses to risk any failure. However, he feels even worse inside because he knows he didn't do any of the work.

THE MASK OF INVISIBILITY

"I would hide in my shell, hold my neck like a turtle, my eyes bulging out, almost pleading with the teacher not to call upon me." Through looking frightened, whispering to teachers, acting terrified with peers, this person too has everyone else doing his work for him. "You can get through school by not talking, just repeating when necessary, and taking a low profile, no waves!" With head down, sitting quietly for a long time, nobody bothers this person. He has the talent of sitting in the back of the room, melting into the crowd, into nothingness … Teachers and supervisors realize they never got to know him; they barely know he was there.

THE MASK OF THE CLOWN

"Isn't that a riot!" "Ha, ha, ha …" "What a joke!" Everything is funny when this guy is around. Laughter will obfuscate the issue. The well known singer–actress Cher admits she was "the class clown" because she could not read, write, or do arithmetic at school even though she was exceedingly verbal and outstanding in all the arts. Her teacher proclaimed that she was not working hard enough. She felt dumb. She dropped out of school at 16 and wasn't tested for her learning disabilities until she was over 30. Another "class clown," for the same reasons, was Henry Winkler, The Fonz, who didn't discover his learning disabilities until his stepson was diagnosed as dyslexic.

THE MASK OF THE VICTIM

"It's not fair." "Everyone picks on me." "Why me?" "Look, she's not calling on the others, just me!" "There's no justice anywhere." Injustice collecting is a basic theme with this person. Often called "a jailhouse lawyer" because there's an argument for everything with this person, he truly feels victimized and takes on a "poor me" attitude. He assumes no responsibility for anything. He angers everyone around him.

THE MASK OF NOT CARING

"I don't care." "It doesn't matter." "Nothing matters." "Nobody cares about me. Who cares?" "Whatever you do, I don't care." With this mask, the person is never vulnerable. The person risks no failure. If he tries to succeed and fails, he says he never tried and it doesn't matter. It is a way of keeping others as distanced as possible from him and it makes them feel woefully inadequate. If nothing matters, then it's impossible to motivate somebody or get him to change.

THE MASK OF BOREDOM

"This is boring!" Yawn. "It certainly is not interesting." Yawn, yawn. "Boy, this is dull!" Yawn, yawn. "Can I go to the bathroom?" "What time is it now?" Yawn, yawn, yawn. With big yawns, loud sighs, tapping fingers and toes, this person lets his teacher, boss, supervisor, know how bored he is, which puts the other person on the defensive. Usually he is not bored, but frustrated, and can't do what he's been asked to do. Thomas Edison was kicked out of schools for not following instructions (he probably did not understand them because of his auditory problems and his severe learning disabilities prevented him from being able to write what he was told to). Often, the learning disabled make teachers feel terrible about themselves; feelings of inadequacy are catching.

THE MASK OF ACTIVITY

"Gotta run." "Have to make a call now." "Sorry, I'm in a hurry, can't talk now." "I'm late; I'm busy now; I'll do what ever you want later." "Later, later … no time now." This person is always on the move. Standing still may bring him close to others and he precludes any intimacy. Constant activity wards away others and keeps him from having to perform. This person frustrates everyone around him.

THE MASK OF OUTRAGEOUSNESS

"I'm way out." "I don't like conformists." "I believe in individualism to the extreme …" Through a wild choice of clothes, the color of hair, wigs, extraordinary glasses, stockings, boots, neckpieces, this person projects eccentricity and hides what he is worried about. Cher, extraordinarily talented as singer, dancer, actress, has drawn attention to herself through her bizarre clothing and incredible wigs. Robert Rauschenberg, the artist whose works are treasured all over the world and in virtually every important international collection of contemporary art, did outrageous, unheard of things. Many artists feel he expanded the definition of art for a generation of Americans by daring to innovate.

THE MASK OF THE GOOD SAMARITAN

"Let me help you." "Let me carry it for you." "What can I do for you?" "Where can I be of most help?" "Let me run your errands. Let me take care of your needs." This person wants to please at any cost. Frequently, he is too nice and too accommodating. He will echo what you say, work longer hours and be obsequiously helpful to get out of doing what he can't do or to achieve his goals. One Night School student spent 10th, 11th, and 12th grade in choir even though he detested it, because in his high school the choir teacher decided who graduated.

THE MASK OF CONTEMPT AND CUTTING EVERYTHING DOWN

"They don't know how to teach." "My glasses aren't right." "This whole place sucks." "I get all my information from TV—it's better." "Why go to church when I've been allowed to live with this much difficulty? They haven't helped me." Negativity encompasses this mask. This joyless person has a negative word for everything. If it's sunny out, it could be sunnier. This person wears out the people around him because nothing is ever good enough and he takes no pleasure in his small successes. He's angry at the whole world for making him feel stupid, and feels the world owes him something. He puts everybody else on the defensive.

THE MASK OF THE STRONG SILENT TYPE

"I'm Joe Cool." "Nobody comes too close to me but they follow me everywhere." "Get out of my face. Nobody moves on me." "Every sport is for me. I live for sports." "Life is like getting psyched for a wrestling match."

Personified by a sleek body and incredible prowess at sports, this person is revered by many and endowed, in their minds, with every fine feature. Bruce Jenner, Olympic Decathlon Champion, said that sports gave him his self esteem and that reading aloud in the classroom was much more frightening and harder for him than the decathlon. Tom Cruise, today's hot movie star, poured all his energies into sports because he suffered so from learning disabilities and needed to shine in an area. It was only when he became hurt, he auditioned for a school play, got the lead, ended up on Broadway and then in the movies, becoming a top star at age 23. Olympic gold medalist diver Greg Louganis said he turned to diving to show the world he was worth something since he was called "dumb and retarded" all through school. Ann Bancroft, one of the six explorers to reach the North Pole last year, found the grueling trip to the North Pole easier than getting through the University of Oregon in six years.

Sometimes The Strong Silent Type aches to open up and share his feelings, but can't. There is a wall that he creates often between him and those close to him.

THE MASK OF PERFECTION

"If they don't recognize my talents, it's their problem." "I have everything going for me." "If the world is a bunch of conformists, let them know I'm unique!" "Good artists don't have to read anyhow." "I'm doing fine, really well!"

Proclaiming loudly that there are machines to spell and write, secretaries to take dictation and lawyers to read for him, this person presents himself as perfection. He tolerates no mistakes in himself or others. Often carrying an impressive book or magazine he cannot read, he saunters into rooms looking completely pleased with life. He makes everyone around him feel miserable.

THE MASK OF ILLNESS, FRAIL HEALTH, VULNERABILITY

"My head." "My stomach." "My side." "My bladder." "My back." "My migraine." "My eyes." "My illness." "I'm weak in the knees."

To receive extra attention and to get out of the work he cannot do, this person calls in sick, leaves sick, constantly pretends to be sick and talks about his frailties. Given something to read, he uses his illnesses or fatigue as an excuse, or he cries if necessary. Expecting special attention, special privileges, while avoiding what he cannot do, this person confuses everyone around him and usually gets by with it.

THE MASK OF SEDUCTION

"Hey female, write this down for me. Men don't write." "Math is male stuff, baby doll can't do it." "Big man can."

This doll baby asks "Big Daddy" to do what she can't do and uses her feminine wile to make it all appear sexy. She hides behind the female mask while the macho chauvinist hides behind his mask in order for her to do for him what he can't do.

THE MASK OF BEING BAD

"Don't mess with me. You'll be sorry." "I don't care if she wants me to sit down, I won't." "I threw the book at him, so what?" "I'd rather be thought of as bad than dumb!"

Losers at school often become winners on the street. This person feels stupid, powerless, useless at school and often his frustration and anger get directed towards his teachers. His peers often enjoy his acting out and encourage more of it. Dallas real estate magnate, Rick Strauss, tells how he rode a cart down the school halls, played tricks on everyone, sold his Mom's good jewelry to neighborhood children for twenty-five cents apiece. He changed schools several times, always suffering the humiliation of not learning to read or write. He compounded his problems by cutting up, but at least he succeeded in getting the attention of the teachers off his poor work. Not until his last year at high school did he learn that his inability to read and write were due to his learning disabilities.

THE MASK OF "THE CON"

"My smarts got me by. I could sweet talk any teacher and be absent for all tests." "I could convince a teacher of any excuse—my dog died, my brother had my homework, my mother brutalized me, the hand that I wrote with had been operated on twice." "I learned to lie looking you straight in the face." "Hey, I'm a personality guy: I can out talk a salesman and make people like me."

This wheeler-dealer uses moxie. He negotiates how much work he will do and what the teacher will do for him. G. Chris Andersen, Managing Director of the Finance Department of one of Wall Street's biggest firms used his gift of gab to talk himself into or out of almost anything. He, who traveled through 38 states and 12 countries before he was eighteen years old, used every line and talent he had, to get through school. Even though he didn't know his left hand from his right and couldn't spell, he graduated from the University of Colorado and won a scholarship to obtain his MBA in finance from Northwestern University. Harry Anderson, TV's Judge Stone on "Night Court" each week, grew up on the streets learning card games and magic. He then conned and charmed his way through school. He was called brilliant in his early school years when large pictures accompany schoolbook texts. At age 16 he was Valedictorian at a Hollywood high school and only he knew that he could barely read!

THE MASK OF FANTASY

"I'm going to be a millionaire by 30! … The world will understand me soon." "I'll have a Ph.D. once I learn to read."

Characterized by a fertile imagination and, often, a great deal of creativity, this person tends to live more in his hopes and fantasies than with the daily frustrations. Hans Christian Anderson failed to learn to read and write even with the help of ten royal tutors of the Danish Court. He dictated his wonderful fairy tales to a scribe. His suffering came through in stories like "The Ugly Duckling." His mask protected him from continual pain. It is said that even at age 66 he woke up with nightmares of a schoolmaster trying to teach him to read.

Think of the energy spent on hiding, on masking the feeling of being stupid. It's an elaborate subterfuge that ends up making the person feel even worse about himself. The mask protects but, also it isolates a person from others. Often, it interferes with being able to learn.

The masks can be reduced or dropped when a certain comfort level has been achieved, when a person realizes he is not unintelligent, but learning disabled. There is enormous relief that comes from knowing what you know, knowing what you don't know and understanding why you don't know it.

In my mind, the purpose of research is to improve the quality of human life. What learning disabled adults have to say about their masks, heightens the need for all educators to reach children in the early years, identify those having trouble learning before they need to put on the masks, and teach them in ways they can succeed! This is my mission in teacher education!

STUDENTS WHO ARE SILENT AND DO NOT TALK IN SCHOOL

Teachers have been telling their students to be quiet and stop talking since the days of the one-room schoolhouse. Silence is still honored in many classrooms because talking is correlated with disruption, and classroom disruption is correlated with low academic achievement. Historically, students who sat at their desks quietly and completed their lessons were considered the "good students," the ones to be emulated. At the extreme end of these "good students" is a small group of students who are mute or who rarely talk in school. They come to class, complete their assignments, never volunteer, have no friends, are lonely, and are troubled by the demands in their life. A closer look at these students reveals that their decision to be silent is not a healthy response to classroom life, but rather a symptom of an underlying problem. A word of warning: Not all children who are quiet or shy are troubled. There is a difference between being alone and being lonely. A characteristic of a healthy student is his or her ability to enjoy peaceful, quiet times without feeling lonely. A troubled student can feel lonely even when surrounded by peers. The difference between these two students lies in the content of their thoughts. Both students can be observed to be silent, but this does not mean they are not thinking. The stream of consciousness is bombarding each of them with endless thoughts and messages. For the troubled student, listening to the thoughts and messages frequently causes feelings of anxiety, fearfulness, and preoccupation with upsetting events or fantasies. Unless these thoughts can be expressed verbally or symbolically, they will continue to dominate the student's inability to relate to others. We believe silence is an unexpressed thought that needs to be heard. Students who chronically withdraw from social interactions and are nonverbal are not developmentally shy but reflect feelings of being unacceptable and worthless to others.

ARTICLE 7.2

THE next article was written by Ralph Gemelli, a child psychiatrist who trained at Rose School, a psychoeducational day treatment center in Washington, D.C. Most of the students attending this school were aggressive, streetwise, and verbal. A few students were withdrawn, reluctant to talk, or selectively mute in school. Gemelli found these students fascinating and studied them.

His article provides teachers with helpful information regarding the developmental stages of speech, four underlying reasons why students do not talk, and four specific recommendations to help these nonverbal students. This article also highlights another important concept: *The same student behavior, silence, can be caused by different underlying problems.* The corollary statement is also true: *Different underlying causes can be expressed in the same behavior.* Once again, the complexity of student behavior is identified and the need for greater understanding is validated.

UNDERSTANDING AND HELPING CHILDREN WHO DO NOT TALK IN SCHOOL
Ralph J. Gemelli

A DEVELOPMENTAL APPROACH TO UNDERSTANDING THE MEANINGS OF SPEECH

SPEECH BRINGS LOVE AND A SENSE OF BEING VALUED

When a toddler begins his first vocalizations, all of his language is initially the language of others, most commonly the toddler's parents. In one view, every toddler is given the gift of speech by his parents and, in time, learns that to "give back" the words he has learned brings love and admiration from them.

Through his parents' speech, the child is responded to in a unique way, and hence through speech *his unique sense of self begins to develop.* In time, the developing child learns that speech is one of the *principal socially accepted ways of both receiving feedback about his uniqueness and his performances and of exhibiting his newly developing sense of being a separate self.* He learns that his words are valued and are responded to by his parents with love and support. As Helen Ross (1977) stated, "In the loved and responded to child, verbal communication and love begin to become synonymous."

SPEECH BRINGS RELIEF FROM FRUSTRATION
WHICH FACILITATES A SENSE OF MASTERY OF THE ENVIRONMENT

The developing child, in responding to his inner world (e.g., hunger) or his outer world (e.g., a stranger), reaches out through speech to relieve anxiety. When these signals are answered by an empathetic mother and/ or father, the child begins to equate the *activity of verbal communications with both a method of achieving relief from distress and a way of mastering his body as well as the environment. Speaking becomes a way of signaling distress* that the child learns will produce results; speech will produce responses from his parents that will take the distress away or at least lessen it significantly. When speech brings positive responses from his parents, the child begins to believe in the power, importance, and value of his words in influencing others and asking others to help him with his daily struggles and worries.

SPEECH BECOMES A FACILITATOR OF DEVELOPING INDEPENDENCE

When the child's first words and initial sentences are being spoken around age two, the child is in the midst of developing an internal image of his parents as basically good and protective. He "uses" this image, calls on it, for example, when he is left with the baby-sitter. He waits without overwhelming anxiety, remembers his parents as "good," and begins to listen to and trust their words that told him "We will be back later." *Words,* for the developing child, function in one sense then *as a means of tolerating separations and assist the individuation process.* As Eveloff (1971) hypothesizes, "the process of individuation both stimulates language development and reflects it." In other words, the individuating and separating child is encouraged to speak, to talk about his experiences and verbalize the worries he has about exploring and being away from his parents. At the same time, however, the degree of individuation and development of a sense of separateness in the child is reflected in the child's ability to produce speech to verbalize his needs, worries, and frustrations.

SPEECH BECOMES A MEANS TO CONTROL
AND UNDERSTAND FEELINGS

As speech develops, the child desires to verbalize what he perceives with his senses. When the child perceives and experiences feelings within himself, before he can verbalize the correct word for a feeling, his parents must correctly perceive the specific feeling state in the child. When they decode their child's behavior as sad and tell the child "You are sad right now," the child not only is given the correct word label for his inner feeling state but also is given permission to verbalize this word label—sad.

In order for speech to help the child control and modulate his feelings, Furman (1978) outlines a process in which feelings are initially dominated by action expression. That is, when angry, the child hits or runs, etc. *Dominance of action gives way to dominance of speech* when the child learns that he can control his feelings by putting them into words. He is told "You can say you are angry at your brother but you can't hit him." With increasing ability to verbalize feelings, the child slowly develops his ability to delay immediate gratification of a feeling. For example, a seven year old boy who was developing dominance of speech over action told his teacher he was angry at another boy and wanted to hit him. The teacher reminded him he couldn't hit in school. By the time recess arrived, the boy had used the time to think and subsequently decided on racing instead of hitting him. In delaying action (hitting) he was able to consider different options, that is, more socially acceptable ways of expressing angry feelings.

Ability to verbalize feelings also helps the child to develop the capacity to figure out why he is feeling a certain way in a particular situation. For example, a seven year old girl sat alone at a picnic. Her mother sensed her sadness and encouraged her to talk about her sad feelings by saying, "You look sad, tell me why?" The girl responded, "Because I want to play with my friends and Dad told me this morning that this is a new big park and that I should watch you and take care of you at the picnic." Mother smiled and explained to her that Dad was only encouraging her to be a big girl and help Mom if she needed help. She didn't have to worry about Mom, and she could go play with her friends. Her daughter smiled, looked relieved, and went to play with her friends.

FOUR REASONS WHY CHILDREN DON'T SPEAK IN SCHOOL

THE UNLOVED AND UNVALUED CHILD

The child who has parents who do not value him in any significant way enters the world of peers and school with excessive worry about offering or presenting himself to others. He is afraid that what he offers of himself will not be valued. Eric Erikson (1959) spoke of the developmental psychosocial task of the child of about six or seven. When grade school begins, the child struggles to attain *a sense of industry.* This is the ability *to produce among his peers,* and the child's words are his major production. When the unloved and unvalued child is asked by his teacher to produce words, he becomes *anxious* because he expects his words will not be welcomed, bring approval, or be seen as valued. He then will hide this anxiety by developing an outer shell in the form of shyness, or dumbness, or disinterest. In some children, stuttering will develop as the child's outer shell or defense to hide his anxiety about producing for others (Gemelli, 1982). In a graphic manner, stuttering becomes a visible expression of his conflict of wanting to give his words and, at the same time, wanting to hold them back. He wants the love and admiration of his teacher but is afraid his teacher will not value the words he produces. As a result, these children withdraw from any lesson or activity that involves talking.

THE ANXIOUS AND/OR SHOCKED CHILD

Every child has a threshold of how much tension and anxiety the child can tolerate *and still be able to speak.* The normal child learns that signaling his parents through speech brings responses from them that reduce his level of stress. Consequently, once speech has become a trusted signal of distress, the child will use words to communicate what is making him anxious, what is or has scared him, and what he wants his parents or his teacher to do at the moment. However, even the child who uses words as a distress signal has a limit to how much tension and anxiety he can tolerate. When he reaches his limit, he may regress to an earlier stage of development. As a result, speech is given up, and the child communicates his anxiety in other ways. For example, an eight year old girl used speech when anxious and communicated well to her teacher. Her father was killed suddenly when she was five years old. She adjusted reasonably well after his death and could speak about her father with fond memories. One day she arrived at school to find that the gerbils she cared for had been smothered under a towel and had died. She cried and told her teacher how sad and frightened she was that someone would kill her gerbils. That afternoon while she waited for her mother at her usual place outside school, the principal took her to her office to tell her that her mother had a car accident and was in the hospital but that she was doing fine. This day now had become too filled with loss, both real death (the gerbils) and the threat of possible death (her mother). She couldn't speak when the principal and her teacher told her it was okay to talk about how she felt. She could only cry for her favorite doll at home and whimpered that she wanted to be with her mother. Otherwise she refused to talk. She was too afraid to continue to be an eight year old; she was too afraid to put into words, to hear herself say what she was most afraid of, i.e., that her mother might really die just like her father had suddenly died three years before.

THE OVERPROTECTED OR ABUSED CHILD

The child's gradual development of a sense of autonomy (Erikson, 1959) and separateness is mediated and fueled by the child's development of speech. Separations from mother and father and other caretakers gradually are associated with less separation anxiety when the child is able, for example, to tell mother where he is going and what he will do, and mother tells him it's all right and that she will listen to what he tells her when he returns.

The parent who reacts with tension or sadness when the child says he wants to play at a friend's house communicates to her child that she needs to overprotect him, and that something bad might happen if he leaves her. Subsequently, this child's *words of wanting to leave mother* are sensed by the child as *an attack on mother.* After some time, this child may equate *speaking in general as a non-gratifying activity,* as an activity that causes mother and others to become upset, anxious, or depressed.

Similarly, the parent who is physically and/or emotionally abusive to a child produces in this child a beginning mental image of the parent as someone who is not to be trusted and not available to soothe if a sudden danger arises. This child will not view speaking as a way of announcing and sharing his explorations of the world away from his parent. To speak up could result in physical harm.

The child with an overprotective or abusive parent amazingly does not avoid the parents but tends to cling to them in an intense manner.

This child cannot tolerate a mental image of his parents as being bad because this creates unbearable anxiety. A "bad" parent is never available, etc. Instead, the child takes the badness onto himself and thinks of himself as bad and unlovable and consequently clings fiercely to his "good" parents. Such a child will abandon speech because he feels valueless and unlovable, and therefore expects that his speech—his verbal productions—will be ignored and unvalued (which often in reality they have been by his parents) or reacted to in a hostile way.

THE ANGRY OR SAD CHILD

All children when excessively angry or very sad may withhold their speech. The angry child wants to retaliate in some way, and if he senses that people want him to talk, he may refuse to speak as one manifestation of an "inner" temper tantrum. The child, however, who has just experienced the loss of someone or something of value will experience sad feelings. If the sadness is excessive, the child needs to withdraw and will not have the energy to engage in speaking with his teacher or his friends. He will often want to remain in school, but his energy level is low and he asks to be allowed to be quiet.

There are, however, other children who almost never talk when they are angry or sad. These children must be given the correct word labels for their different feelings, and permission by their parents to talk about these feelings. The parents can only do this when they can tolerate the same feelings in themselves and talk about them. For example, what if a mother says she is sad, then withdraws into a chair for hours? What if a mother looks sad but verbally denies she is sad while criticizing and nagging her child. For example, in an interview with the parents of a 7-year-old boy, I was asked to evaluate psychiatrically this child's listlessness in class, poor motivation, and unwillingness to talk in school. In the child psychiatry playroom he denied any feelings of sadness. In the interview with his parents, I stated that his mother looked sad. Father suddenly stated harshly, with much anger, "In my family no one gets sad, there is no time for sadness, it's just not allowed!" He then roughly grabbed his wife's arm and led her out of the room. He stated that he would only return if I called to apologize for "encouraging my wife to become sad and feel sorry for herself."

When the son of these parents stated that he was never sad, he believed it. *He had stopped perceiving within himself his sad feelings,* because to become aware of his sadness left him with a feeling that brought an angry attack from his father, and now also his mother. Incredibly his teacher could emphatically sense this boy's sadness, but when she told him he looked sad he reacted, much like his father had, as if he were being attacked by the teacher. On one occasion when his teacher said "You look sad, why don't you tell me about it," he responded with, "I don't get sad, it's wrong to be sad, I'm not sad, I don't feel sad, you say I'm sad when you want to say I'm bad."

WHAT THE TEACHER CAN DO
FOR THE STUDENT WHO IS NOT TALKING

Four recommendations are offered which may help the teacher formulate a helping plan for these children. The child who periodically does not talk is somewhat easier to help than the child who is almost continually unwilling or unable to speak. For this latter group, an evaluation by a speech–language pathologist and a child psychiatrist should be arranged. Regardless of the diagnosis, if the child remains in class, the following recommendations will help these silent children to talk more in school.

Recommendation No. 1. Suggest to the child that he has good reasons of his own, from his own point of view, for not wanting to talk. Tell the child that if he can talk about his reasons for not wanting to talk, he might learn what is frightening him about talking. He might then reveal his fear that his words are "not smart enough," or that the teacher will not like him despite what he says, etc.

For example, the child who has grown up in a family where his words have never received much attention or positive feedback initially will not believe his teacher when she tells him, "*I'd* like to hear what you have to say about what just happened in the school yard." The teacher must convey the message that she realizes the child wants to talk, but doesn't want to talk because he expects the teacher not to be interested. The child, however, in time will sense the teacher's empathy for his conflict. On the teacher's side is the developmental force present in all children to interact and engage with new people. With time, children are people seekers. This is a major reason why some children with unloving, abusing, or hateful parents will nevertheless develop good self-esteem through their emotional interaction with teachers, coaches, relatives, and other adults. Once this process is set into motion, the teacher provides the conditions that permit the child to have the gift of speech. The child will accept this gift slowly and hesitantly because once before the child, after being given "the gift of speech" by his parents, discovered that his use of this gift was fraught with anxiety, conflict, and shame.

Recommendation No. 2. Allow yourself to empathize with the child. Allow yourself to observe how you feel in the child's presence in order to become aware of the feeling(s) the child is experiencing but unable or unwilling to put into words. For example, the sad non-talking child will produce a similar feeling of sadness in the empathic teacher.

Once the teacher senses a feeling the child is not talking about, it is useful for the teacher to tell the child, "*I* know you think it won't help or make you feel better if you tell me how sad you feel, but you'll have to take a chance to see what happens. If you give talking a try, you'll feel better and the feelings you have inside won't feel so scary or make you feel you are not a nice boy." When the teacher speaks in this manner to a child, she must be prepared to be suddenly perceived by the child as a "re-incarnation" of one of the child's parents. The child may say, for example, "*I* don't believe you; I know you'll yell at me if I tell you I'm sad." At that moment the child is mis-perceiving the teacher as being the reincarnation of his mother. His mother did indeed yell at him when he spoke of being sad. If the teacher is aware of the "transference" of fears and feelings associated with mother onto the teacher, the teacher will not respond to the child's view of the teacher as a personal attack. In time, the child may indeed take a chance and talk to the teacher despite his fear that the teacher will yell at him the way his mother often did.

Recommendation No. 3. Encourage and suggest to the child that she can communicate in other ways other than through speech. A child not speaking can be asked to "draw a picture that tells a story about children at school," etc. Another useful technique is to engage the child in some form of play. While playing with the teacher, some children will feel less pressure to produce speech. In play, the child will often communicate a message about what conflict the child is experiencing about talking.

For example, a seven year old girl came to school looking upset and angry. She would not talk about what was wrong or how she felt. Her teacher at recess spent a quiet time with the child encouraging her to play in the corner of the classroom where dolls and puppets were kept. While holding a doll the little girl stated, "My baby had a hard time making up her mind; if she could make up her mind she would be happier. I want her to talk to me, but she can't make up her mind to talk to me or not talk to me." The teacher later found out from the child's mother that the girl had been recently nagging and clinging to her mother because her mother was spending a great deal of time with this little girl's new baby sister. Her mother admitted that she had not been able to give her seven year old much time lately and didn't find talking to her a joy but more of a chore and responsibility.

Recommendation No. 4. Ask yourself, and then decide, if you are able and/or willing to give to the non-talking child a little more attention, patience, feed-back, and kindness. This recommendation is listed to emphasize what observational data from child research tells us. Speech unfolding follows, more or less, a maturational sequence, but speech blossoms through the child's loving interaction with his caretakers. When the child's caretakers, usually the child's parents, fail the child in all the functions listed earlier in this paper, the child's speech is in great jeopardy. A recrudescence of speech development can often only take place through the child's close interaction with an empathic and admiring adult who can accept the child's productions, of which speech is only one, but a very crucial, production of childhood. Perhaps one of the most gratifying experiences for a teacher is helping a non-talking child to talk. When this occurs, the child begins to blossom in many other areas of development because speech is not only very highly valued in our culture, but through speech children learn, adapt, and build positive self-esteem.

SUMMARY

Children need and want to talk. It is their way of reaching out and relating to others. With some children their feelings are so intense that they retreat into a world of silence. Teachers can play a significant role in identifying these students, developing trusting relationships, referring them to helping professionals, and supporting their team program.

REFERENCES

Erikson, E. Identity and the life cycle. *Psycho-logical Issues,* 1959, 1, 101–172.

Eveloff, H. Some cognitive and affective aspects of early language development. *Child Development,* 1971, 1895–1907.

Furman, R. Some developmental aspects of the verbalization of affects. *Psycho-analytic Study of the Child,* 1978, 187–213.

Gemelli, R. Classification of child stuttering: Part I. Transient developmental, neurogenic acquired, and persistent child stuttering. *Child Psychiatry and Human Development,* 1982, *12* (4), 220–253.

Richmond, M. Personal communication, 1976.

Ross, Helen. Personal communication, 1977.

THE ANTISOCIAL OR AGGRESSIVE STUDENT

Antisocial or aggressive behavior among students has increased significantly in recent years. The frequency and intensity of student aggression have led to popular use of the phrase "school violence," which is a generic and not a diagnostic term. School violence is also a popular and appealing topic for television news shows, radio talk shows, endless newspaper articles, and national conferences. Most of these media programs are advertised as violence prevention programs, but their underlying intent is to shock the audience with the latest and most frightening statistics about school violence. Schools are portrayed as intimidating blackboard jungles populated with roaming streetwise delinquents organized in gangs, armed with guns, and confronted by naive and ineffective teachers. John Wayne–like principals might be wielding a baseball bat and using a cellular communication system as they walk through dimly lighted halls.

These media messages rarely provide in-depth understanding of the nature of anger in students, but they do succeed in stirring up strong adult feelings of helplessness and counteraggression. Messages such as these describe spontaneous fights between students as a potential life-threatening school event: "Fights no longer consist of name calling, verbal threats, and shoving, but quickly escalate into physical assault and the use of lethal weapons, and the switchblade has been replaced by the 9-mm gun as the weapon of choice."

A media study of the New York City public schools reported a 35% increase in the number of reported student assaults over a 5-year period, and identified junior high school students as the most likely targets of peer assaults. During this same period of time, acts of larceny against other students increased 24%, and the number of reported attempted and actual school rapes escalated. As if these figures were not shocking enough to upset law-abiding citizens, the study also reported a substantial increase in the number of teacher assaults by students and circulated a new diagnostic term: "battered teacher syndrome." This syndrome was described as being similar to battered spouse syndrome because of its concomitant feelings of anxiety, sleep problems, physical ailments, and depression. This medical condition was viewed as a painful example of the deteriorating role of teacher authority and the impulsive behavior of angry students. Undeserved teacher assaults do happen, but we have observed some battered teachers who clearly lacked the skills to deescalate an angry student and inadvertently fueled the attack.

Another way of dramatizing school violence is to document the national increase in school vandalism. Broken windows; damaged lockers, walls, and ceilings; trashed classrooms and bathrooms; and destroyed school equipment are all examples of malicious vandalism and expressions of students' anger. The economic costs to taxpayers of repairing and replacing damaged or destroyed school property has reached multimillion-dollar figures. This money could have been used to build more effective educational programs; instead, it was needed to repair and replace school buildings and equipment. School vandalism is used as a powerful illustration of how angry students displace their hostility toward schools in a blatant and destructive way.

We do not deny that antisocial student behaviors have increased in select schools and are a concern of students, staff, and parents. If one's only source of information is TV talk shows or the tabloid news stories, it appears that America is preoccupied with school violence. However, we do not believe antisocial student behaviors are out of control, unmanageable, or unsolvable. Aggressive behaviors toward students, staff, and property can be stopped, controlled, and prevented. Contrary to media hype, American schools are basically a normal civilized place.

The problem of student violence is complicated and distorted by lack of accurate and useful information regarding the nature and expression of student anger and staff counteraggression. When students behave aggressively, teachers can spend too much time trying to decide *who* is right in this conflict instead of judging *what* is the right thing to do professionally.

Teachers are not to be blamed or to be made the professional scapegoats for the rise of aggression in schools. Most teachers have not received adequate training in anger management and, without it, teachers are forced to act like firefighters trying to put out a blaze without having an adequate water supply. To be successful in a volatile situation, teachers need many resources and intervention skills.

We believe teachers need to understand the nature of anger, as well as the difference between angry feelings and antisocial behaviors. They need to acknowledge how their counteraggressive feelings can escalate an aggressive student incident. They need to know what short- and long-term teaching strategies are effective in deescalating antisocial behaviors, and how to help students learn more appropriate ways of expressing their anger. To begin this discussion, a brief summary of basic terms, concepts, and strategies is presented.

What Are the Differences Among Feelings of Anger, Hate, and Rage?

Anger is a temporary internal neurophysiological feeling or an emotional state triggered by how one thinks about life events that are perceived as frustrating, painful, and fearful. Anger can have a rational or irrational base. It can be triggered by an accurate perception or a misperception of a life event. The feeling of anger exists in all persons as an automatic survival response, a learned habit, and a personal choice. Anger is always a feeling and should not be confused with aggression. Aggression is a behavior and is only one of several ways anger can be expressed.

Hate is an internal neurophysiological feeling and is a more intense and focused state of anger. Hate is like frozen anger that rarely melts. Hate usually has a specific target and develops when one feels depreciated or is betrayed by a friend or group. Unfortunately, hate is contagious and easy to pass on from one generation to the next or from one group to another. Religious, racial, ethnic, and national conflicts and wars are examples of what can happen when hate is taught to others and how others can internalize a feelings of hatred toward another group without ever having any reality experiences with that group. Hate is deliberate, identifiable, and unresponsive to logic or rational thinking. Hate is a feeling and should not be confused with hostility, which is a behavior.

Rage is an explosive feeling of uncontrollable anger or hate. The current behavior of terrorists toward the Western world is an example of rage. It is a final response to overwhelming feelings of revenge. Rage is the biological beast or primitive feeling that exists in all of us. Rage is mindless, runaway anger. It serves as the voluble fuel for violent and destructive behaviors.

Anger, hate, and rage are all internal feelings and should be distinguished from their corresponding behaviors of aggression, hostility, and violence.

What Triggers Feelings of Anger in Students?

Anger in students is triggered by the way they have learned to think about specific life events and by the subsequent negative thoughts they have. If they fail an exam, are rejected or criticized, or lose an object, they might send themselves negative messages such as, "This is unfair!" "I have been gypped!" "No one should treat me like this!" "I will never let anyone know about my limitations!" "This is hopeless!" "I will get back at you!" "People are making fun of me!" When these negative messages occur, students end up feeling the way they think.

The following 12 conditions, emotional needs, fears, events, and reactions have been documented to trigger in students negative thoughts that result in angry feelings.

1. Student anger can be triggered by altered states. The use of alcohol, marijuana, amphetamines, barbiturates, heroin, and opium has the physiological effect of dissolving the rational part of the mind and causing altered states of reality. The student's ability to misperceive a normal event as a threatening one or to have a delusional experience can create angry feelings.

2. Student anger can be triggered by mental illnesses such as psychotic conditions that result in altered perceptions of reality, active negative thoughts, and angry feelings.

3. Student anger can be triggered by brain trauma. Only an intact and healthy brain can perceive and think rationally and sort out the differences between real and imaginary threats. Dr. Robert Hunt, a research

psychiatrist, observed that in children who have prefrontal cortical deficits, the slightest irritation can cause intense feelings of anger or rage.

4. Student anger can be triggered by personal frustration ranging in degree and intensity from dropping a pencil to experiencing overwhelming and multiple physical, psychological, and reality stresses that bring on feelings of helplessness, anger, and rage. Personal frustrations are probably the most frequent triggering events that result in negative thoughts and angry feelings.

5. Student anger can be triggered by a need for attention. As described earlier in this chapter, Dreikurs, Grunwold, and Pepper (1971) pointed out in their concept of the attention-getting mechanisms that some students decide it is more effective to act up and receive negative attention than to be ignored or neglected.

6. Student anger can be triggered by a need to maintain group power and status or to respond to group pressure. Some students' anger is triggered more often by their group role and the dynamics of the group, such as a group contagion or group scapegoating, than by individual forces.

7. Student anger can be triggered by a need to be punished. Students who are abused, deprived, and abandoned commonly have blamed themselves for their emotional plight. They may use emotional reasoning that says, "Bad things happen to me because I'm a bad person. Bad people need to be punished. When I do bad things, I need to be punished." These students will almost always succeed in being punished if they act aggressively and violate class rules by cheating, stealing, and fighting.

8. Student anger can be triggered as a defense against failure. A psychological defense is one way a student can protect against experiencing a painful feeling. Some troubled students will become angry and disrupt the learning process or argue with the teacher as a way of avoiding their fear of impending failure. Sally Smith (Article 7.1, earlier in this chapter) described how this feeling of failure can be acted out in various ways, including antisocial behavior.

9. Student anger can be triggered as a defense against closeness. Some troubled students have been so traumatized by their primary adult relationships that any new nurturing adult relationship triggers their fear of closeness. To trust someone means they will become vulnerable to more rejection. The solution is to respond to interpersonal acceptance by becoming angry and oppositional.

10. Student anger can be triggered as a defense against sadness and depression. Many children find it difficult to acknowledge their sad or depressed feelings. They have discovered that they can mask their feelings of depression by becoming angry and aggressive. In one study of incarcerated delinquent youth, one third of the sample groups were diagnosed as having an underlying diagnosis of depression, and all of them were involved in antisocial behaviors. Acting out one's angry feelings is easier than talking about one's feelings of sadness.

11. Student anger can be triggered as a reaction to watching violent movies, television shows, and sporting events. The visual stimulation of observing violent acts of vandalism, extortion, torture, sexual perversion, murder, and the excitement of the home team's winning or losing a game can create vicarious stimulating experiences that trigger angry feelings and riotous behavior.

12. Student anger can be triggered by feelings of revenge. This anger, triggered by a conscious choice to get back at the hated person or group, probably represents the most heinous expression of hate.

These 12 conditions, needs, psychological defenses, reactions to frustration and overstimulating events represent the most common motivations of angry feelings in students.

How Are the Feelings of Anger, Hate, and Rage Expressed in Behavior?

Feelings of anger can be expressed in three different ways: (a) as overt behavior in the forms of aggression; (b) as covert behavior, for example, passive–aggression, in which the feelings of anger are masked and indirect; or (c) as a reaction to be swallowed and turned inward, resulting in psychosomatic illnesses, pain, rashes, and so on.

For our purposes, it is important to understand the differences among aggressive behavior, hostile behavior, and violent behavior. These differences are diagnostically important because certain intervention strategies that are effective in controlling student aggression are not effective in controlling hostile or violent behaviors.

Aggressive Behavior

Aggressive behavior is most frequently triggered by stressful life events or personal frustrations and is an unplanned spontaneous expression of anger. Aggressive behavior is usually the result of a sudden impulse breakthrough or a loss of self-control skills. Often, students are not aware of their aggressive behavior until they hear themselves shout, swear, slam a book down, run out of a room, or hit someone. After an aggressive outburst, some students feel guilty about their behavior and redirect their anger into self-punishment. Other students find ways of rationalizing or justifying their aggressive behavior by saying, "He started it" or "I was only defending myself." Student aggression is the most frequent expression of anger and is the easiest to modify and prevent.

Hostile Behavior

Hostile behavior is characterized as a deliberate expression of hate. It is a conscious, calculated act of revenge that is thoughtfully planned to intimidate, injure, or hurt a person or to take, steal, or destroy specific properties. Hostile behavior is not a function of an impulse breakthrough or a loss of self-control. It is cruel behavior directed at a particular person, group, or country. The bombing of the Twin Towers in New York City is an example of hostile behavior. Gang wars and targeted killings are all forms of hostility, not aggression. War is always an act of hostility, not an act of aggression.

Violence

Violent behavior is anger and hate that have gone out of control and turned into rage. All expressions of rage are violent and mindless. Violence is like a volcano that has erupted. Everyone in its path will be hurt. Violent behavior does not discriminate between friends and foes, and it often results in hurting, injuring, or killing everyone in the target area. Terrorists who blow themselves up in a restaurant or at a marketplace are demonstrating violent behavior.

Understanding the Dynamics of Student Aggression

Although aggressive behavior is driven by anger and triggered by many different causes, the dynamics of aggression are predictable. An aggressive student has never learned to tolerate normal amounts of frustration, disappointment, or anxiety. Instead of owning these feelings, the student gives them away by attacking or depreciating everyone in sight. The student knows how to engage staff by using provocative words or actions that upset them. While the aggressive behavior reduces the internal level of anxiety, the impulsive behavior simultaneously creates normal counteraggressive feelings among the staff. If the staff are not trained to understand the dynamics of aggression, they not only will pick up the student's aggressive feelings but also will mirror similar behavior, thus escalating the aggressive conflict. For example, when a student shouts, "I'm not going to do it! Don't you hear me?" and a teacher shouts back, "Yes, you will! Do you hear me?" this is a counteraggressive staff response. By mirroring the student's behavior, the response creates more psychological stress for the student. The student's angry feelings become more intense, and his or her behavior becomes more primitive. At this point, the teacher and student become locked in a power struggle, and the problem escalates. What is surprising about the dynamics of aggression is that, even if the student loses the power struggle and is suspended or physically restrained, his or her basic assumption that adults are hostile are reinforced. There are no winners in a power struggle with aggressive students.

The teacher's psychological position, however, is complicated by the fact that teacher anger seems entirely justified, and this seems like an ideal time to teach this arrogant, aggressive student a "lesson." If the teacher acts out these feelings, does what comes naturally, and decides "to take the student on" by returning a verbal attack, then the teacher will perpetuate the aggressive cycle. The statement "aggression elicits counteraggression" becomes true, and the aggressive student has been successful in controlling the teacher's behavior.

Insight occurs when the teacher begins to understand the nature of this aggressive cycle and realizes that making an aggressive response is only going to make a bad situation worse. To continue any counteraggressive behavior with an aggressive student is self-defeating. To break this cycle, the teacher must make a conscious decision to break off the fight, disconnect from the struggle, and abandon feelings of righteous rage, primitive revenge, and an infantile wish to win.

Basic Concepts Essential to Managing Aggressive Student Behavior

The following list describes important concepts that are basic to managing aggressive student behavior. The knowledge of the dynamics of aggression

1. Raises staff consciousness about conflict. Staff will know in advance that a student in stress will create in them normal counteraggressive feelings. "To be forewarned is to be forearmed."

2. Enables staff to accept and "own" their counteraggressive feelings toward a student and to use them as useful information regarding how the student is feeling.

3. Enables staff not to act on their counteraggressive feelings. Personal insight comes when staff can say "yes" to acknowledging their angry feelings and "no" to the expression of their counteraggressive feelings through behaviors. Thus, both parts of their life—the emotional part and the behavioral part—can live in harmony.

4. Helps staff to make a conscious choice not to join in a power struggle with a student.

5. Helps staff to stop all "you" messages, which escalate the aggressive cycle (e.g., "You apologize," "You'd better use your head").

6. Helps staff to use "I" messages as a way of expressing their feelings while reducing the pressure of a "double struggle" (controlling one's own feelings and avoiding loss of self-control while simultaneously trying to manage the aggressive student's inappropriate behaviors).

7. Helps staff to focus their energies on what a student needs instead of on what staff members are feeling.

8. Helps staff remember that, although feelings are real and powerful, they may not reflect an accurate assessment of any aggressive conflict. Feelings are not rational functions and should not be used to determine what is helpful to a student at a particular time.

9. Enables staff to decode aggressive behavior into the student's angry feelings.

10. Enables staff to help an aggressive student connect the inappropriate behavior and angry feelings with the original stressful incident or life event.

Specific Guidelines for Managing Aggressive Student Behavior

Once a staff member has successfully controlled his or her counteraggressive behaviors and has substituted "I" messages for "you" messages, the staff can focus on the student's needs by responding to the aggressive behavior as an opportunity to protect, model, and teach.

- Begin by using the various strategies for reducing inappropriate behaviors (see Article 6.5).
- State clearly and firmly the positive, expected behaviors.
- Accept the student's angry feelings but not the aggressive behavior.
- Refer to specific classroom rules that are appropriate for aggressive behavior.
- Encourage the student to make a good decision to solve this problem.
- Make sure the student, not the staff, is responsible for the choice of behavior.
- If the student's behavior improves, affirm the efforts made (e.g., "That was a difficult choice to make, but you made the right decision this time!").
- If the aggressive behavior does not improve, intervene quickly with a time-out or a stated logical consequence for the aggressive behavior.
- Explain the reasons (or values) why the staff had to stop the behavior (e.g., "My job is to protect the learning process. Your behavior was interfering with classroom learning so I had to stop it.").
- If possible, set up with the student a behavioral contract that reinforces the expected behavior. Make the conflict a learning experience.

These guidelines are offered as immediate strategies for managing aggressive behavior. The long-term goal is to teach students acceptable ways of expressing their angry feelings using appropriate social skills.

A Strategy of Using Self-Talk as a Way of Controlling Staff Anger

Eggert (1994) developed an Anger Management for Youth Program that includes teaching troubled students and staff a cognitive self-talk strategy for controlling their anger. A brief excerpt of this approach is included here to demonstrate this important skill (Eggert, 1994, pp. 95–97):

PREPARING FOR ANGER TRIGGERS: THINGS THAT PUSH MY BUTTON

This is going to be upsetting, but I can handle it. This doesn't have to be a catastrophe. Stop! Figure out what I have to do ... work out a plan. I can manage this. I know how to control my anger. I'll know what to do if I find myself getting upset ... relax, take a deep breath, remember my plan. Don't overreact. Don't blow this out of proportion. This could be a sticky situation, but I believe in myself.... Feel comfortable, relaxed, at ease. Easy does it. Remember to keep your sense of humor. Easy does it. Remember your lines.

WHEN CONFRONTED: WHEN MY BUTTON IS PUSHED

Stop! Stay calm. Think! Don't jump to conclusions.... Count to ten. Don't blow things out of proportion. So it hurts! There's no use stretching it into an AWFUL, DREADFUL, TERRIBLE situation. As long as I keep my cool, I'm in control. Don't get bent out of shape. Stick with the plan. You don't need to prove yourself. You know you're OK. There is no point in getting out of control. Don't make more of this than you have to. Look for the positives. Don't assume the worst. If I start to get mad, I'll just be banging my head against the wall. So I might as well just relax. There is no need to doubt myself. I can handle this! I'm on top of the situation and it's under control.

COPING WHEN I'M ALREADY ANGRY OR STARTING TO FUME

My muscles are starting to tense.... Slow things down. "Catastrophizing" won't help. Think straight! I'm angry ... that's a signal of what I need to do. Time to instruct myself. Lower the tone, lower the volume, speak slower. Getting upset won't help. It gets me into trouble. Negatives lead to more negatives. Work constructively. Reason it out. Take the issue point by point. Try the cooperative approach. Maybe we're both right. Ask that we treat each other with respect. I can't expect people to act the way I want them to. Take it easy, don't get pushy! Negotiate.

REFLECTING: AFTER THE EVENT

When Conflict Is Unresolved

Forget about it. Thinking about it makes you more upset ... at a minimum, don't stretch the situation into AWFUL! This is a difficult situation that will take time to heal. Try to shake it off. Don't let it outweigh the positives. Remember relaxation, exercise. It's better than depression. Can you laugh about it? It's probably not so serious! Don't take it personally. You did the best you could ... better than last time! It takes two to resolve things. You did your part! I'll get better at this with more practice.

When Conflict Is Resolved or Coping Is Successful

I handled that pretty well. It worked! That wasn't as hard as I thought. It could have been a lot worse. Nice going! I could have gotten more upset than it was worth. I actually got through that without "losing my cool!" My pride gets me into trouble, but when I don't "blow it," I'm better off. I guess I've been getting upset for too long when it wasn't even necessary. I'm getting better at this all the time.

Curriculum Resources for Teaching Anger Management, Anger Replacement, or Self-Control Skills

The goals of the following curricula are to help students learn to manage their anger by allowing them to be assertive, to stand up for their beliefs, to resist peer and adult pressure, and to become independent and responsible for their decisions and behaviors without becoming aggressive, hostile, or violent.

1. *The Walker Social Skills Curriculum* (Walker et al., 1988):

- The ACCEPTS Program: A Curriculum for Children's Effective Peer and Teacher Skills (K–6)

- The ACCESS Program: Adolescent Curriculum for Communication and Effective Social Skills (Secondary)

2. *Aggression Replacement Training: A Comprehensive Intervention for Aggressive Youth* (Goldstein, Glick, & Gibbs, 1987).

3. *Teaching Self Control* (Henley, 2003). This social skills program is organized around five goals: (a) to control impulses, (b) to follow school routines, (c) to manage group situations, (d) to manage stress, and (e) to solve social problems.

4. *Anger Management for Youth: Stemming Aggression and Violence* (Eggert, 1994). This is an award-winning cognitive model of teaching anger management in a well-structured small group. The activities are realistic and appealing to small groups of troubled adolescents.

5. *Personal Growth Class: A Group Approach for Youth* (Eggert & Nichols, 1996). This personal growth class is a therapeutic program designed to help students reconnect with school and with particular skills to decrease drug involvement, depression, anger, and suicidal risk.

ARTICLE 7.3

IN the next article, Fred Tully and Larry Brendtro describe the characteristics of angry and unattached youth who respond poorly to traditional methods of helping. The authors present a comprehensive reclaiming strategy for these resistant students.

REACHING ANGRY AND UNATTACHED KIDS
Fred G. Tully and Larry K. Brendtro

BROKEN BELONGINGS

Two hundred years ago, Swiss educational reformer Johann Pestalozzi started homes and schools for unwanted street urchins. He based the philosophy of these places on the creed that love, rather than teaching, was the core of education. During the past half century, the foremost pioneer in researching this "love thesis" has been John Bowlby of England. His writings are childcare classics—from a 1944 study on the home lives of juvenile thieves through tomes on separation, anxiety, and anger (e.g., Bowlby, 1973). Bowlby's contributions have shaped our understanding of the power that a child's need for affection can have and the despair, rage, and delinquency that ensue when the bond of belonging is broken.

Bowlby's work dovetailed with Harlow's (1958) research on affectional patterns in monkeys separated from their mothers. Subsequently, Bowlby's colleague Mary Ainsworth (1978) developed novel research methods for experimentally studying the effects of separation on young children. We now have available a considerable body of research on the psychology of attachment and separation.

A range of serious behavior problems can best be understood as growing from absent or impaired relationships with caregiving adults. In his description of separation reaction in children, Bowlby (1973) identified the typical sequence as follows:

1. **Initial protest,** which was characterized by crying, screaming, and general activity;

2. **Despair and depression,** seen in the forms of stupor, decreased activity, and withdrawal; and

3. **Detachment or angry responses** when reunited with the separated parent.

Children seem to be most vulnerable to long-term separation or loss from the ages of 7 months to 3 years (Yarrow, 1965). The effects vary for individual children, depending on the time of occurrence, the nature of the previous relationships with the parents or other adults, and the quality of subsequent care. Traumatic events such as physical or sexual abuse and overt or subtle rejection also create or complicate attachment difficulties.

Children rejected by parent figures develop significant behavior problems, including hostility, attention-seeking, aggression, and slow development of a conscience (Sears, Maccoby, & Levin, 1957). Many such children exhibit problems in verbal and conceptual development and don't seem to learn from experience; they also resist submitting to adult authority. There is evidence that over half of delinquent young people with serious patterns of recidivism have experienced persistent threats of abandonment by parents or other caregivers (Stott, 1980). To an emotionally malnourished child, there can be no greater fear than further affectional deprivation. Bowlby (1973) contended that rejection probably produces the most violent, angry, and dysfunctional responses of all, particularly in children subjected to repeated threats of being sent away. This is particularly troubling because threats of exclusion or expulsion are common behavior-control methods in programs for troubled students. When they are at their worst, these children need to experience claiming behaviors (e.g., "We won't give up on you") rather than threats of impending banishment (Fahlberg, 1991).

The mindset of professionals makes a big difference as to how these attachment problems are interpreted or framed. Early pioneers in childhood behavior research viewed children from a developmental perspective and employed relatively benign terms, such as *wayward youth, affect hunger,* or *relatively affectionless.* These labels suggested the need for guidance and nurturance. In contrast, adults who focused on behavioral deviance and conscience deficits often employed pejorative labels, such as *sociopath* or *psychopath.* Currently, when unattached and angry youth enter adolescence, the prevailing response no longer is to see them as damaged or rejected children, but as societal predators who need to be locked away. Some researchers contribute to this professional pessimism by contending that antisocial personality disorders are essentially untreatable and require lifelong external sanctions and restraints.

Negative labels can create self-fulfilling prophecies and confine the stigmatized person to a "dumping ground." Once such persons are classed as hopeless, we shunt them aside like the terminally wounded in a battlefield triage situation. Although terms such as *sociopath* have little scientific standing, they continue in common use—often by politicians and prosecutors, but sometimes by professionals as well. In currently accepted clinical terminology, "reactive attachment disorder" describes children who have problems bonding with adults. We prefer the term *adult wary,* which avoids the connotation of disease.

CAN ATTACHMENT DISORDERS BE CORRECTED?

Harlow's (1961) research on monkeys suggested there is a critical window of opportunity for bonding that, when missed, cannot be revisited. Findings regarding this situation for humans are less absolute. In spite of rejection or abuse, many children continue to make some attempts to gain attention from parents, even though those parents may offer only marginal nurturance on a very intermittent schedule. Just as starving persons migrate to forage for food, so children deprived of attachment often seek out substitute attachments with other adults or even peers.

In their book *The Sibling Bond,* Bank and Kahn (1997) showed that although the parent is the preferred stable figure for attachment, siblings can play a significant role in the early development of a child's personality. Siblings can cuddle, feed, clothe, and protect, but they seldom have the maturity to provide adequate care. Children will also form close attachments to animals or inanimate objects such as stuffed toys, which provide some comfort in times of stress; however, like Harlow's terry-cloth substitute monkey mothers, these are inadequate replacements for nurturing parents.

Because attachment behavior is brain-based, it is not surprising that neurological impairment could interfere with its normal development. Children with brain damage caused by fetal exposure to alcohol, crack-cocaine, or other drugs often exhibit attachment problems. Fetal alcohol syndrome and fetal alcohol effect are major problems for significant numbers of Native American children who come into our care, a phenomenon that was given broad recognition by Michael Dorris (1990). Based on our experience, however, we believe it is reckless to assume irreversibility, even in these cases. From a life-span perspective, many such children who receive long-term supportive relationships will be able to overcome—by middle adulthood—some effects of the early developmental damage.

UNDERSTANDING ATTACHMENT PROBLEMS

Clinicians and educators grounded in the developmental psychology of attachment have identified three types of attachment in children:

Secure Attachment. Paradoxically, meeting dependency needs actually fosters responsible independence. Children who are securely attached are able to explore the world while operating from the safe base of caregivers who can be counted on to meet their needs.

Anxious Attachment. Youngsters who are anxiously attached demonstrate high insecurity and show distress in the absence of attachment figures. They are overly hungry for affection and seek closeness but often cling and exhibit a passive–aggressive form of anger.

Avoidant and Adult-Wary Children. Children who are avoidant behave as if they are indifferent or aversive to adults. They shun overtures from nurturing adults and build coercive internal patterns; at the slightest provocation, they rage or run.

Anxiously attached children are generally passive and more inclined to have internalizing problems such as self-abuse, depression, and suicidal thoughts; however, they usually have a developed conscience. Avoidant children, on the other hand, are likely to develop a hostile approach to life. Because they have not been provided with a protective environment, they do not have even a minimal amount of trust in the adults who are supposed to care for them. They are commonly described as self-centered and antisocial, and many become involved in criminal activities. Therapy for these children involves restoration of a positive cycle where a key adult builds trust and a secure bond and then seeks to generalize this attachment to other adults and peers.

The powerful genetically based survival mechanism that triggers attachment behaviors is activated during stressful conditions. However, the common adult response to an antisocial youth in crisis is to avoid or punish him or her. This is exactly the opposite of what the youth needs. He or she will never internalize positive values from adults who reject him or her. Contrary to common belief, a crisis, temper tantrums, or even a delinquent act can be used as an opportunity for bonding. Children are genetically programmed to seek out support during stressful periods, and adults should not squander such an opportunity.

Among the strongest voices against giving up on angry and adult-avoidant youth are adults who have specialized in the area of resilience. Waln Brown, for example, is a former delinquent who founded the William Gladden Foundation and publishes resources on at-risk youth. He contends that clinicians who assume solely on the basis of office interviews that a youth is untreatable are often only describing their own inability to bond to resistant clients in that setting. In reconstructing his own case history as a troubled child in psychiatric and correctional programs, Brown (1981) summed up his encounters with most treatment professionals this way: "Our eyes seldom met."

Dr. John Seita of the Kellogg Foundation displayed severe attachment problems in his own childhood, moving through a dozen failed foster care and institutional placements. Seita posited that youth need what he termed "Connectedness, Continuity, Dignity, and Opportunity" if they are to develop to their potential (Seita, Mitchell, & Tobin, 1995). Seita identified a dozen practical strategies for "reclaiming unreclaimable children," which are summarized in the sidebar. Seita himself was reclaimed by "tenacious caring," and he contends that professionals who are more concerned about boundaries than bonding are unlikely to reach troubled youth.

PROFILES IN COURAGE AND DISCOURAGEMENT

Who are these children who carry diagnoses of reactive attachment disorder? Many of them might better be called "resilient" and "courageous." By the age of 11, Denise had experienced years of abuse by both parents. Her father regularly took her and a smaller sister to a darkened basement filled with rats to assault them sexually. The girls hated the sexual abuse but always got it over with quickly to escape from the dark and the rats. Finally, when one day her little sister extracted five of her own teeth with her fingers to distract herself from the emotional pain, Denise spoke up in spite of enormous pressures to remain silent. She testified against both parents in court. They went to prison, but how would she and her sister be able to trust new caregivers?

A 5-year-old boy who recently came to our setting is out of control and attacks adults when told "no." He digs his nails into the adult's arms, kicks him or her, and attempts to bite. He is a primitive little being. He

THE PATH FOR CONNECTING WITH DIFFICULT KIDS

by John Seita and Larry Brendtro

1. **Recast all problems as learning opportunity.** "Please coach me, don't scold me."

2. **Provide fail-safe relationships.** "A person like me really needs a fan club."

3. **Increase dosages of nurturance.** "I need to believe that you really care."

4. **Don't crowd.** "When you get too close, I will back away for a while."

5. **Use the back door.** "If you can help me do well, you are important."

6. **Decode the meaning of behavior.** "I try to hide what I really think."

7. **Be authoritative, not authoritarian.** "Help me learn to control me."

8. **Model respect to the disrespectful.** "Your respect helps build mine."

9. **Enlist youth as colleagues**. "We are the only real experts on ourselves."

10. **Touch in small ways.** "I watch little things you do to discover who you are."

11. **Keep positive expectations alive.** "I look in your eyes to see if there is hope."

12. **Give seeds time to grow.** "Please be patient with me—I am still under construction."

Note. John Seita, the lead author of this list, was a troubled boy who had sabotaged a dozen court-ordered placements by the time he was 12 years old. From ages 12 to 18, John was a student at Starr Commonwealth and a "colleague" (for definition, see #9) to Dr. Larry Brendtro, who then headed this youth facility. Today they are still colleagues, but John is now getting paid for his work. Dr. John Seita is director of Youth Development Initiatives for the W. K. Kellogg Foundation. This list is adapted from an article they wrote, "Reclaiming the Unreclaimable" which was first published in 1995 in the journal *Reclaiming Children and Youth*, 4(3). Copyright 1998 by the authors.

has had 30 placements out of his home, away from an alcoholic mom—30 formal placements! He never knows where he will be or who will take care of him. Seething with rage, he is devoid of any sense of self-worth.

Or consider Bill, who was brutally abused by his father both physically and sexually. He refused to go home at night, preferring to sleep under a railroad trestle with alcoholic men because they wouldn't hurt him. One night, one of his fellow bridge dwellers died. Bill discovered the man's stiff body the next morning. He thought the man had frozen to death and was fearful that he, too, would freeze. He continued to return to the trestle each night, however, risking death rather than a return to his own home.

Such children require extensive treatment, and some have even been adopted successfully. At the Children's Home Society, where the first author is a clinical director, they receive controls and discipline that provide parameters and boundaries for their exaggerated behaviors. They also receive nurturance and education that give them a reason to believe in themselves.

THE STAGES OF TREATMENT

Many troubled children are extremely angry and wary of any adult. We conceptualize our treatment approach as 10 steps designed to address the issues that caused these children to rage at or retreat from adults.

1. CREATING A SAFE ENVIRONMENT—"YOU WON'T GET HURT HERE"

With a child who is abused, the first and most critical step in the treatment process is to convey to the child that he or she is entering a safe environment. We stress that because of adequate teachering and our philosophy, no adult will use corporal punishment or physically injure a child in any way. At first, children assume that adults are not truthful, so we rely upon children who have been in residence for a while to provide testimonials to the truth of our assurances. Distrustful children may actively try to elicit physical abuse, testing us again and again. They look for our weaknesses and "push our buttons." They are masterful at testing our patience, at trying to push us over the edge. Although staff members are patient, we are not devoid of emotions. We learn not to overreact to testing, but our strong feelings are legitimate if children hurt one another or are willfully destroying property. The children must feel our unhappiness and our anger in such circumstances and yet see that we are able to control ourselves. Although staff members have emotions and may be upset, we will not hurt a child, become petty, or indulge in name-calling. Children need such proof that adults can be trusted to behave responsibly toward them.

The new child may be quite fearful and attempt to ingratiate him- or herself with adults through smiles and a compliant attitude. This honeymoon is often short-lived and then the rage erupts. If a child must be physically managed to protect him- or herself—or others—we need to have adequate numbers of adults available to provide protection and control. Additionally, children are not allowed to be out of sight of adult supervision in this treatment environment, which offers high levels of both structure and nurturance.

2. EXPERIENCING THE CHILD'S RAGE—"BOY, ARE YOU MAD!"

For children who are aggressive, rage comes easily. They constantly encounter people or objects in their environment to attack, and they explode over the most minute incidents. A direction to pick up a pair of socks may create a reaction akin to being bludgeoned by the adult. Tantrums may last minutes or hours, with infantile screaming, sobbing, and highly negative, repetitive statements such as, "You hate me." The child attempts to scratch, bite, kick, break items, or run away. Just as the infection in a sick body may produce vomiting, these children are vomiting out their rage from previous rejections and emotional wounds. Staff members learn to maintain a calm demeanor, even in the presence of verbal and physical attacks. Still, they are ever vigilant to prevent injury to the raging child, as they are constantly being reminded of this by the vivid protests of the child, who may honestly believe he or she is under attack. With children who hate, our temporary external controls send a therapeutic message: "Adults will take care of you, and soon you will be able to take care of yourself."

3. CONNECTING RAGE TO ITS SOURCE—"WHO ARE YOU MAD AT?"

During a behavioral crisis, we have an opportunity to address the source of a child's rage. We recognize that this outburst is not connected to our direction to pick up a pair of socks; it signals something else entirely. Perhaps an expected phone call from a parent, which did not occur, has reopened old rejections? Might it be the news that the stepfather is moving home again? We explore a variety of the child's emotions, often touching a raw nerve that raises emphatic denials wrapped in profanity. Repeated sessions eventually may yield results: The child discloses that the source of his or her anger is past abuse. He or she may burst forth with a specific outburst directed toward an abusive adult or a parent who did not protect or provide for the child.

Pearlman (1979) described children who had been severely abused as vessels with narrow, constricted openings that only allow small drops of nurturing at a time; smothering affection only spills over. Adults therefore should look for times when children are more receptive to affection. For some children, this is at bedtime or when swimming or playing. In crisis, children may cuddle close to the adult—crying and sobbing, and in regression. During these moments, they are susceptible to our warmth.

It is our philosophy not to isolate youth in time-out procedures. It is particularly important to maintain a close proximity to adult-wary children, who must learn that no amount of anger will drive the adults away. Instead, we stay with them through the storm, responding to the messages implicit in their behavior and conveying the message that we care about how much they are hurting.

4. ENHANCING SELF-WORTH—"YOU ARE A PERSON OF GREAT VALUE"

Healthy childhoods are made up of mental images that recall holidays at the grandparents' home, sports activities with neighbor children, an important achievement, and other positive, happy memories. Our children are void of many of these images, and we must help to create some for them during their stay. We begin building positive memories from the moment the child arrives. Attention is paid to the child's physical appearance, including personal grooming, haircuts, well-fitting clothing, and communications to help the child understand that he or she is beautiful.

Photography can assist in remolding a child's self-concept. We capture moments of individual and group happiness, thus "freezing" memories of joy. Most of our children believe they are physically unattractive, so we take photographs that show them at their best to counter those inner negative messages. An album is kept for each child in which pictures are inserted to establish a visual history of his or her progress in the program. These albums offer proof of good times, are testimonials to friendship, and demonstrate that each child is loved. Any child who feels alone can be reassured by spending time with these photographs.

Hobbs (1982) indicated that troubled children need to feel some joy in each day to offset the hopelessness of their lives. We are "party people"—we use just about any occasion as an excuse for celebration. Birthdays, Valentine's Day, Thanksgiving, Easter, May Day, Christmas, Halloween, or even invented holidays enable children to sing songs, have secret friends to whom to send gifts, do things anonymously for others, have parades, receive awards, feel the warmth of applause, feel success as a performer, and be valued as a member of a team.

For many of our children, school has been a "bad" experience that has damaged their self-concept. They have felt "stupid" in the classroom, and our task is to create the opposite feeling—that learning is fun, challenging, and within their grasp. They must discover the delight and joy of "knowing" an answer. We believe that each child is on a quest for mastery but is sometimes held back by the fear of failure. As our children create beauty with colors, grasp the power of stories, experience success with numbers, or complete a hard assignment, they are taking charge of their lives.

Encouragement is a powerful tool in healing damaged spirits. To be told, for example, that you are beautiful, you are talented, you are tall, or your hair is radiant makes one feel distinctive. Nothing must ever be done to attack the child's positive sense of self-worth. To a child who assumes the worst about herself, one cutting remark, one piece of sarcasm, one time of name calling by an adult can erase hundreds of instances of validation.

5. RETRACING THE ABUSE—
"RETURNING TO THE SCENE OF THE CRIME"

As the abused child reveals feelings of hurt and identifies those who have been the source of his or her pain, we attempt to draw out the specifics for an accurate recollection of the timeline of the destructive event. With the child who has been sexually abused, understanding of what happened may be diminished, due to his or her feeling of responsibility for the act, confused emotions, and embarrassment. If the child says, "It only happened once," we realize this may mean it happened numerous times and the act that is being described may not be the most horrendous one experienced.

As we process the specifics of those acts, the child returns mentally to the scene, and the moments of fear and strong anxiety are vividly recreated. His or her body wrenches with discomfort, he or she sobs deeply and becomes sick to the stomach as the adult pushes the child to describe the specific circumstances. It must be emphasized that this is done cautiously and in the context of a trusting relationship. We reassure the child that we are there to protect him or her and that this will not happen again. As a child learns to talk about the horror felt, he or she conquers fear and gains control over the previous abuse. Thus, the child can overcome injury, reframe what really happened, and perhaps eventually even forgive.

6. RELIEVING THE FEELING OF RESPONSIBILITY— "IT'S NOT YOUR FAULT"

It is an axiom in treatment that children who have had terrible things happen to them usually assume they must be terrible persons. Individuals who have been physically abused believe that they are inherently bad and can give great evidence as to why the parent needed to use physical pain to "teach you a lesson" or to punish them for their misdeeds. They have learned that they are worthless and deserve only the harshest treatment from the adults of this world. As the burden of self-blame is lifted, we unleash great reservoirs of rage. Managing anger is a common focus throughout the treatment process as the child consolidates gains made in each stage of the treatment process.

Individuals who have been sexually abused often harbor feelings that they are inherently bad and assume that they have always been sexually damaged. They also feel guilt if they felt any pleasure during sexual acts. If they were given any gifts by the offending adult, they will feel as if they had been prostitutes. We explain that they do not have control over the physical pleasure their body experiences when stimulated and that their perpetrators were just using them. Expressions of anger toward the assailant is the foundation of healing. Repeatedly, the child must be told that the terrible things that were done could never have been his or her fault—the adult carried full responsibility.

7. ATTACHMENT—"FALLING IN LOVE"

Our next element of treatment involves attachment of the child to a healthy adult. This is actually also a part of all the treatment stages. However, the attachment process usually solidifies after a child has been relieved of responsibility for his or her own rejection or abuse. From the first day, we immerse the child in a variety of interactions with numerous caring persons. The cook may form a special relationship with the child to help to "break the ice" and to begin the formation of trust. The maintenance worker, secretary, speech therapist, or family therapist might be the one person the child can trust and idealize. The foundation of all that we do is to enhance relationship building between an adult and the child.

The individual who has the closest relationship with a child does not have interactions that are always pleasurable and momentous. The depth of the relationship allows this adult to admonish the child for misbehavior and have an enormous impact upon him or her. The displeasure of this adult toward negative behaviors motivates the child to extinguish them out of fear of disappointing this significant other. Disciplining the child is important to his or her development, but the discipline needs to be from a caring adult.

Our colleague, the late psychologist Albert Trieschman, used to tell childcare professionals that the most important observation they would ever make is when they saw the adult become a glimmer in the eyes of a child and the child become a glimmer in the eyes of the adult. The intensity of the bonds that can develop between caring adults and children who have never known real attachments can make some professionals nervous, particularly those persons who work in organizations or roles where "professional distance" is the norm. We sometimes simplistically describe the bonding process as "a child falling in love with us." As we become hero or heroine, the child begins to quote our wisdom, imitate our physical gestures, and glory in the knowledge that he or she is special to us. Because genuine relationships are reciprocal, this bonding also enables the adult to see the child as especially engaging, humorous, and bright, and as the possessor of extraordinary potential. The adult communicates these positive qualities to the child, who begins to really believe that he or she is lovable.

Although adults may develop strong feelings toward the child, the goal of the relationship is not to meet the adult's needs for affection. Boundary problems arise not because adults become close to a child, but because they use the power of this bond for some reason other than helping the young person. The primary developmental need of youth with attachment problems is to extend this fledgling trust to other significant adults and peers.

Some adults contend that a child should not get overly attached to us because we are temporary figures in his or her life. But most adults can recall powerful short-term attachments that were very meaningful, such as bonding to a camp counselor. When the relationship ended, we were saddened but not rejected. Just as we would provide food to a hungry child, so we are generous with attachments for a lonely child. Children benefit from many close relationships in their lives. When they leave those relationships, they feel a sense of loss and sadness, and they cry and grieve. This is a measure of how much they have been loved.

8. FAMILY DECISIONS—"TO GO HOME OR FIND A NEW HOME"

For the child who will return to his or her own family, intensive work must be done to create change within the family, deal with the unhealthiness of certain family members, and ensure that the family can provide for the child. Frequently, the offending parent must make an admission of responsibility for his or her own behavior if progress is to be made. Our work with natural parents is directive and confrontational but also warm and nonrejecting. We may argue that a child should not return to a parent's home, but we do not reject the parent as a person. We must clearly establish that the child will be in a safe environment, that he or she will not be abused again, before he or she can return. The parent must understand the extent of the injury that occurred to the child and the resulting anger.

In the United States, there is considerable pressure to preserve the family in virtually all cases. Some authorities seem to assume that even the worst family is better than the best foster home—which, of course, is not true. We must be an advocate for the family as long as that unit is viable and meeting the child's needs without the presence of danger. However, if safety cannot be assured or the parents cannot provide for the basic needs of the child, a healthier family must be sought. Children are *not the property* of any adult. If termination of parental rights is required, we try to make the separation as positive as possible. We tell the parents that the greatest gift they can give to their offspring is a healthy farewell and permission for the child to have another family.

9. TRANSITION TO A FAMILY—"GO SLOWLY"

The transition from treatment to family is done in a very careful and deliberate manner. If this is a new family, we use the six steps of placement developed by Katheryn S. Donley (1989) of New York Spaulding for Children:

1. Linking—a specific child is selected as appropriate for placement with a particular family;

2. Presenting—information on a specific child is provided to a particular family in order to make the critical decision to proceed to the next step in placement;

3. Showing—the specific child and particular family are brought together in a situation designed to offer the family an opportunity to observe the child's appearance or behavior without risk of rejection;

4. Introducing—child and family meet face to face for the first time;

5. Visiting—a series of contacts, usually of progressive duration, are carefully planned to move the child and family toward placement; and

6. Moving in—the child is physically placed with the new family.

We address all of the potential behaviors that may be exhibited, and we communicate to the parental figures the difficulty this child can present throughout the remainder of childhood and perhaps even into adulthood. We talk of the need for assistance through the various stages of development and of the particular issues that will arise in adolescence. In the past, some children were depicted to potential families as tiny cherubs who merely needed love, which ultimately was damaging to both the child and the parents.

10. HEALTHY FAREWELLS—"CRYING TIME"

A final—but very significant—stage of treatment is to provide a healthy farewell as we "send along" a child to his or her family. We celebrate this passage with a ceremony: We use candles, recollections of our good and bad times spent together, messages of love, and an affirmation that the child has the strength to do well. It is an open expression of feelings. Tears are common in this ritual and enable our recent admissions to see the emotional investment that we have in the child and that the child has in us. It is a time for us to give permission for the child to move on, to attach to other adults. It is a time for us to model for the children the necessity of formally saying good-bye.

RAMON

Ramon was born in Columbia and abandoned by his birth mother as a boy. He was placed in a Catholic orphanage and then adopted by a single woman from the United States who did not even speak his language. His adoption failed when his mother became weary of his anger and his limited ability to reciprocate her affection. After 2 years in the stable setting of the Children's Home, he was able to bond to several peers and significant adults, and he was succeeding in school. We prepared Ramon for a transitional placement that would help him approach independence. When the time came for his departure ceremony, a favorite staff member read aloud the story of his life. As his attachments were chronicled, a candle was lit for each one. Ramon first lit a flame for his birth mother, then another for the priests from the orphanage, and one for his adoptive mother. Ramon himself had chosen three peers and three staff members to light candles signifying his bonds to this place and its people. The final candle lit symbolized his new foster family, and everyone present sang the refrains of "Friends Are Friends Forever." Hugs and tears were plentiful, and Ramon knew that this separation was a rite of passage instead of another rejection. If Ramon keeps alive the flames of love ignited here, he may in the future find a real family, perhaps in the home he one day will create for his own children.

REFERENCES

Ainsworth, M. (1978). *Patterned attachment: A psychological study of the strange solution.* Hillsdale, NJ: Erlbaum.

Banks, S. P., & Kahn, M. D. (1992). *The sibling bond* (15th ed.). New York: Basic Books.

Bowlby, J. (1973). *Separation: Anxiety and anger.* New York: Basic Books.

Brown, W. (1981). *The other side of delinquency.* Cameron, WV: William Gladden Foundation.

Donley, K. S. (1989). *Opening new doors.* New York: State Mutual Books and Periodical Service.

Dorris, M. (1990). *The broken cord.* New York: HarperCollins.

Fahlberg. (1991). *A child's journey through placement.* Indianapolis, IN: Perspective Press.

Harlow. (1958). The nature of love. *The American Psychologist, 3,* 673–685.

Hobbs, N. (1982). *The troubled and troubling child.* San Francisco: Jossey-Bass.

Pearlman, H. H. (1979). *Relationship: The heart of helping people.* Chicago: University of Chicago Press.

Sears, R., McCoby, E., & Levin, H. (1957). *Patterns of child rearing.* Evanston, IL: Row, Peterson.

Seita, J., Mitchell, M., & Tobin, C. (1995). *In whose best interest?* Elizabethtown, PA: Continental Press.

Stott, D. H. (1980). *Delinquency and human nature* (2nd ed.). Baltimore: University Park Press.

Yarrow, L. J. (1965). Research in dimensions of early maternal care. *Merrill-Palmer Quarterly,* 101–114.

THE PASSIVE–AGGRESSIVE STUDENT

ARTICLE 7.4

THE passive–aggressive student is rarely studied or understood, although he or she is skilled in frustrating teachers in subtle ways. In the next article, Jody and Nicholas Long present a dynamic overview of this student, with new insights into behavior and specific recommendations for management. This article will make a difference to all teachers who work with passive–aggressive students, colleagues, and parents.

UNDERSTANDING AND MANAGING THE PASSIVE–AGGRESSIVE STUDENT

Jody E. Long and Nicholas J. Long

Passive–aggressive behavior exists in all cultures, and passive–aggressive students and staff exists in every school. Passive–aggressive behavior is an indirect and socialized form of aggression, but it is equally as destructive as aggressive behavior. Passive–aggressive behavior has escaped the scrutiny of professional study, perhaps for the same reason a passive–aggressive student has escaped being detected by a classroom teacher. Teachers know when an aggressive student is mad at them, but they may not be aware of the indirect "drip-by-drip" water torture skills of a passive–aggressive student.

For example, do you have a student in your classroom who irritates and annoys you in endless and insignificant ways, and over time you have had the impulse to place your hands around his or her neck? If you answer "yes" to this question, the chances are you have identified a passive–aggressive student. You are not alone in having this urge. In a survey of 300 special educators, over 75% said they would prefer to work with an aggressive student than a passive–aggressive student (Institute of Psychoeducational Training, 2000). A typical comment from this group was, "When we work with an aggressive student, at least we know where the anger is coming from. It's out in the open and we can deal with it. It is not like those sneaky, arrogant, sulky, passive–aggressive students." It is clear that passive–aggressive students stir up strong feelings in staff.

This article describes the five major questions teachers have about understanding and managing a passive–aggressive student.

1. How does a student become a passive–aggressive personality?

2. What are the dynamic beliefs of a passive–aggressive student?

3. What passive–aggressive behaviors frustrate teachers?

4. How do staff react to a passive–aggressive student?

5. What concepts and skills are needed to alter a passive–aggressive student's dysfunctional ways of relating to others?

HOW DOES A STUDENT BECOME A PASSIVE–AGGRESSIVE PERSONALITY?

Two very different early socializing experiences appear to promote the development of a passive–aggressive student. The first developmental pattern involves a child's psychological reaction to early and prolonged verbal and physical parental aggression. For thousands of children, home is not a secure, protected environment, but instead an emotional nightmare. Their parents are intermittently out of control; are under the destructive influence of drugs, alcohol, mental illness, or sadism; or are hell-bent on making their children obedient to their authority and wishes. These children are threatened, intimidated, hit, punished, and made to feel guilty over normal developmental issues. They are frightened and in a chronic state of anxiety. If these children continue to be exposed to their hostile,

explosive, and unpredictable parents, the children frequently either identify with their aggressive parents and become aggressive students or learn
to survive in their volatile world and become passive–aggressive students.
Just like a child learns not to put his hands on a hot stove, these children learn not to express their angry feelings out loud. Instead, they learn
to express their feelings under their breath and in their thoughts. They
fantasize, "I will get back at you—not now, but I will find a way. And
when I do, you won't even know about it." Nothing grows stronger or
becomes more powerful than an unexpressed hostile thought. Over time
these abused and exploited students often grow up learning a passive–
aggressive way of relating to hostile adults. Unfortunately, this indirect or
insidious way of expressing personal anger can spill over to any adult who
makes demands on these students regardless of whether the adult demand
is reasonable or irrational.

The second developmental pattern that may result in a passive–
aggressive personality seems paradoxical. It involves nurturing parents
who love their children and want them to be socially and professionally
successful. These parents have worked hard for what they achieved and
want their children to be well liked and accepted because social approval
will enhance their children's chances for success, such as making good
grades, winning scholarships, finding a professional career, or attracting
useful friends. These parents also believe their children are an extension
of their values and goals. If their children turn out to be "good children,"
then they can take pride in their parenting skills. To achieve this, these
parents systematically teach their children that "good children" are not
angry children. Good children are never hostile or sarcastic. Good children have pleasant thoughts and pleasant behaviors. Good children never
think or speak in negative terms. The socialization forces of these parents
are effective not only in controlling their children's aggressive behaviors,
but also in teaching them that negative thoughts and angry feelings must
be suppressed. Inadvertently, the goal of developing "proper and well-
behaved children" ends up as a grievous form of mind control. These children learn they must not express their angry thoughts even though they
feel guilty for having them. For example, Susan, age 8, tells her mother
she was angry at her friend Nancy at school and told Nancy she hated her.
The mother's reaction is predictable:

> Susan, I'm surprised you said that. It is not nice to hate your friends!
> I want you to stop all those hateful words. There is too much hate in

this world! Everybody seems to be hating someone, and the only way to prevent all this hate is to stop those hateful thoughts in our heads. I want you to think about yourself like an artesian well that bubbles up only pure, good, and nice thoughts and behaviors. So today, no more hate—only love, joy, and happiness.

What Susan learns, however, is to experience personal anger as an enemy to be conquered and not as a feeling to be accepted as a normal and natural part of one's life.

These two socializing patterns that promote a passive–aggressive personality are significantly different from each other, but they have a similar outcome. Children learn that anger is evil and must be hidden.

WHAT ARE THE DYNAMIC BELIEFS OF A PASSIVE–AGGRESSIVE STUDENT?

The passive–aggressive student believes that the direct expression of anger is both dangerous and destructive. As a result, this student has had to learn to hide, conceal, or mask his or her anger behind a facade of socially approved behavior. Like the tip of an iceberg, the real size and power of his anger is out of sight. For a passive–aggressive student, the expression of anger is not a misdemeanor, but a felony. Here are some statements that passive–aggressive students told us:

- Angry feelings are upsetting. When people are angry they yell, scream, and are scary.
- When people get angry, terrible things can happen.
- I don't let people know when I am angry. If they knew what I was thinking, they would want to kill me.
- Thinking about anger is wrong, but exciting.
- When I'm treated unfairly by my teacher, I'm smart enough to know how to upset her so she can suffer like she made me suffer.

These statements express the intensity and strength of some of their internalized beliefs about anger and aggression.

Once a student has internalized a passive–aggressive way of perceiving, thinking, feeling, and behaving, then he will maintain his beliefs about anger by creating a self-fulfilling prophecy as he relates to other adults. The following sequence has been documented by numerous clinical observations during a student–staff Conflict Cycle:

1. The passive–aggressive student is upset at the teacher.

2. The passive–aggressive student behaves in indirect and subtle ways, which frustrates the teacher.

3. Over time, the teacher is unaware of the amount of accumulated anger she has absorbed from the passive–aggressive student.

4. During a stressful classroom incident, the passive–aggressive student falls out of his seat, burps, or malingers. This small incident becomes the straw that breaks the camel's back, the spark that lights the fuse, the pin that pops the balloon, or the final incident that causes the teacher to explode.

5. The teacher has a 30-second temper tantrum or, in clinical terms, a brief impulse breakthrough.

6. The passive–aggressive student responds with alarm and says to himself, "Wow! Look how crazy people get when they express their anger. Isn't it wonderful I don't express my anger directly."

7. Afterwards, the teacher usually feels guilty for overreacting to such a minor event. She feels sorry for losing her self-control and, in some cases, actually apologizes to the passive–aggressive student.

The self-fulfilling prophecy of the passive–aggressive student has been achieved. The adult lost control, acted improperly, and reinforced the passive–aggressive student's belief that anger is dangerous and there is no need to change his way of thinking or his behavior.

WHAT PASSIVE–AGGRESSIVE BEHAVIORS FRUSTATE TEACHERS?

Our observations of passive–aggressive students have identified four levels or patterns of behavior, ranging from normal or "age-appropriate" behaviors to pathological behaviors.

> *Level 1.* The teacher makes a request, and the student agrees to do it but then doesn't do it. This is the most common passive–aggressive

behavior. The student does not want to comply with the teacher's request, because of other interests, boredom, fatigue, frustration, and so on. Unlike the aggressive student, this student agrees to do it but then demonstrates selective vision ("I can't find it"); selective deafness ("Oh, I'm sorry, I didn't hear you"); selective memory ("Oh, I forgot, but I will do it in a minute"); or a slowdown tactic, "I'm coming!" These passive–aggressive behaviors inevitably frustrate the teacher, who frequently completes the requested task with resentment. To some degree, all students use these tactics as a way of reacting to authority figures.

> *Level 2.* This is a slightly more sophisticated form of passive–aggressive behavior. The teacher makes a request, and the passive–aggressive student doesn't want to do it but decides to do it in a way that will upset the teacher. This is also called "intentional efficiency." The following are demonstrations of this level of behavior:

- cleaning up by making a mess
- turning in an assignment that is difficult to read or is incomplete
- asking for help but not listening (e.g., by looking at the ceiling)
- singing too loud or off key during music class
- following the wrong procedures during science class
- deciding to read with one eye closed during remedial reading class
- talking so softly that the teacher can't hear
- overwatering the teacher's plants
- greeting the teacher by playfully punching him on the arm and then, when confronted, replying, "Oh, I'm sorry, I was just trying to be friendly."

This level of reacting to authority figures is conscious and more characteristic of a passive–aggressive personality.

> *Level 3.* The passive–aggressive student at this level has hostile feelings toward the teacher and decides to get back at her at a later time or without her awareness. This is a conscious decision and a damaging way of expressing hostile feelings toward the teacher. This

is a form of indirect revenge. Demonstrations of passive–aggressive behavior at this level include the following:

- giving the teacher the "finger sign," sticking out one's tongue, or making sexual gestures behind the teacher's back
- hiding the teacher's belongings and resources, such as the grade book, keys, erasers, or science equipment
- being aware of a pending crisis but letting it happen (e.g., not warning the teacher when the student knows that the overhead projector has an electrical short or that an insect has dropped into the teacher's water glass at lunch)
- forgetting to tell the teacher about an important phone call

This level of passive–aggressive behavior is inappropriate but is intrinsically reinforcing, so the passive–aggressive student is not motivated to learn other ways of expressing anger.

> *Level 4.* This is a pathological form of passive–aggression in which a student becomes self-destructive, unattractive, and repulsive in exchange for the pleasure of getting back at selected adults, most often parents. The following demonstrations have been observed in a variety of students, including students who are very intelligent and come from professional, upward-mobile families:

- dressing weirdly, or in a cult fashion
- refusing to turn in a final report because it is stupid
- eating in a gross manner
- refusing to bathe or brush teeth
- soiling oneself in class, creating a stink with a smile

Levels 3 and 4 are examples of passive–aggressive behaviors that are dysfunctional and harmful to healthy interpersonal relationships, and they need to be confronted therapeutically.

HOW DO STAFF REACT TO A PASSIVE–AGGRESSIVE STUDENT?

The typical staff reaction to a passive–aggressive student is to become counter–passive–aggressive. This reaction is a basic principle of the Conflict Cycle. A student in stress—in this scenario, a passive–aggressive student—will create in a teacher his or her feelings, and, if the teacher is not trained, the teacher will mirror the student's passive–aggressive behavior.

Our observations of classroom teachers, who are not passive–aggressive personalities but are teaching passive–aggressive students, verify this principle. These teachers initially respond to passive–aggressive students by demonstrating selective hearing, memory, and visual problems. They forget to return a passive–aggressive student's paper or grade it more vigorously than other papers.

WHAT CONCEPTS AND SKILLS ARE NEEDED TO ALTER PASSIVE–AGGRESSIVE STUDENTS' BEHAVIOR?

The following concepts and skills are necessary and effective when helping a passive–aggressive student. This student is not going to change over night, but staff needs to learn not to reinforce the student's passive–aggressive behaviors.

1. The teacher knows in advance that passive–aggressive students will create counter–passive–aggressive feelings in her, with the goal of getting her to blow up, lose control, and fulfill the prophecy that the expression of anger is dangerous. To be forewarned is to be forearmed.

2. The teacher understands that all passive–aggressive behaviors are inappropriate ways of expressing anger. The teacher should never empower a passive–aggressive student by saying, for example, "The entire class will remain seated until Pat (the passive–aggressive student) gets off the floor." The passive–aggressive student will be pleased if the teacher gives him or her the power to control the class and all the attention.

3. The teacher decodes the passive–aggressive student's behavior by using the Detective Columbo technique of wondering out loud why the student is using this passive–aggressive tactic. A monologue might be as follows: "Hmm. I just don't understand this. William has good hearing. I mean, he can hear all the way across the playing field when I call him to come and take a turn at bat. And he seems to be able to hear without any problems when he talks with his friends. So I wonder why it is that he doesn't hear me when I ask him to start cleaning up. Hmm … this is very strange. I'll bet he really doesn't want to hear me and is only pretending not to hear. Maybe he's angry

at me for some reason, and this is his way of trying to make me angry and frustrated. Let me think about this." Because most passive–aggressive students believe staff are not aware of their passive–aggressive behavior, they usually shape up spontaneously after hearing this monologue.

4. The teacher decodes the passive–aggressive student's behavior by using benign confrontation. The teacher meets with the student and shares her concerns about his passive–aggressive behaviors. Because the student will deny his anger, the teacher can arrange for a personal signal such as pointing to her ear when she feels he is being passive–aggressive and then hold the student responsible for his behavior.

5. The teacher holds a group discussion in which the teacher encourages the student's peers to talk about how they handle their feelings of anger. It is important to emphasize how normal and acceptable it is to have angry feelings and how satisfying it is to talk about them rather than act them out. The goal is to learn to say "yes" to one's angry feelings and to say "no" to expressing them in indirect or aggressive ways.

6. If a student uses Level 3 or 4 behaviors as primary ways of relating to adults, the teacher refers the student to the school psychologist or counselor.

7. The teacher evaluates his or her style of showing anger to make sure that he or she is not modeling passive–aggressive strategies.

SUMMARY

Passive–aggressive behavior exists in all cultures and classrooms but is less understood, examined, or researched than other inappropriate types of behavior. The passive–aggressive student is skilled in annoying the teacher (and others) in endless, seemingly insignificant ways. The teacher, unaware of his or her increasing anger over these accumulated irritants, suddenly blows up over a seemingly minor incident. Quite often the teacher feels guilty about the overreaction because he or she does not understand the dynamics of passive–aggressive behavior. This article has examined the socializing influences that promote the development of passive–

aggression, the destructive nature of passive–aggressive behavior, and specific concepts and skills to help passive–aggressive students.

REFERENCE

Institute of Psychoeducational Training. (2000). *Survey of special educators.* Hagerstown, MD: Author.

STUDENTS WHO HAVE ATTENTION DEFICITS AND HYPERACTIVITY DISORDERS AND/OR LEARNING DISABILITIES

Every teacher has struggled with intelligent, well-motivated students who seem incapable of maintaining their attention, organizing their materials, remembering instructions, and completing their assignments. Their disorganization and confusion frustrate not only the students but everyone around them. The following analogy characterizes the futile and unproductive behavior of a student with attention-deficit/hyperactivity disorder (ADHD). Imagine a driver of a car stuck in a ditch on a country road miles from the closest town and tow truck. Feeling isolated, anxious, and concerned, his plan to solve this situation is to walk around the car, kick the tires, swear, and jump back into the driver's seat. He starts the engine and floors the gas pedal. This impulsive behavior causes the engine to roar, the rear wheels to spin, and ample amounts of dirt, stone, and mud to be thrown onto the road. He has expended considerable energy, but his situation has not improved. The car is still stuck in the ditch, and all his activity has only made the situation worse. The car has sunk deeper into the ditch and is spattered with mud. The driver is now frustrated, angry, and baffled by the lack of forward progress. Students with ADHD and/or learning disabilities (LD), like the driver of this car, often find themselves in similar situations. They are aware they have a problem in school, but they seem unable to do anything to better their situation.

The following letter was written by an 11-year-old boy to his teacher as an attempt to explain his frustrations and confusion when he is unable to listen to or remember his classroom assignments. This is an honest, painful, from-the-heart letter that depicts the psychological suffering many of these misunderstood students experience.

I try to tell the truth and not lie, but my problem is that I can't seem to remember anything or that I'm just not listening. I understand that already but I don't know why I just start listening or just start remembering. Most people think that sounds easy to do, but I wonder why I can't start doing that. Not listening and not remembering has just about got me in trouble every time. I've been in trouble since I've been alive (and take my word for it, I've been in a lot of trouble!) I don't mean I've only been in trouble at school, but at home too. When I was in first grade I got strait A's and I've gotten worse every year until now unexceptable! I think I would be happier if I could finish my work and relax. I wish I could just dump every paper out of my binder and start out fresh and see the change. I bet it would be a good one chances are they'd be good changes (90% to 10!). I'd have better holiday's weekends and even in and out of school.

This student was diagnosed later as having an attention-deficit disorder with specific learning disabilities.

Approximately 10% to 20% of all school-age children have learning disabilities. Of those with LD, about 20% to 25% also have ADHD. LD and ADHD are two separate problems; however, because they occur together so frequently, it is useful to consider them related. In addition, most children and adolescents with LD and/or ADHD develop emotional, social, and family difficulties. These result from frustrations and failures experienced with family and peers and at school. They are the consequence of the academic problems, not the cause.

A Brief Overview of the Changing Diagnostic Names

Over time, professionals have used different diagnostic names to describe the conditions of these students. Many of these terms are still used by different professionals, causing professional confusion.

Prior to the 1940s, students who had difficulty learning or paying attention were considered *mentally retarded, emotionally disturbed,* or *culturally disadvantaged.* Research during the 1940s identified a fourth group of children: those who had difficulty because of the way their nervous system worked. Their problems were described as "neurologically based." Initially, this disorder was called *minimal brain damage;* later, the name was changed to *minimal brain dysfunction.* These terms described students with neurologically base academic problems, hyperactivity, a short attention span, impulsivity, and emotional problems.

Since the 1940s, this group of problems has been a separate focus of study. First, the neurologically based academic problems were identified and named to reflect the primary area of skill difficulty: *dyslexia* for reading problems, *dysgraphia* for writing problems, and *dyscalculia* for math problems. Later, the term learning disability was applied to the types of learning difficulties that underlie the skill problems.

Hyperactivity, distractibility, and impulsivity were initially called *hyperkinetic disorder of childhood* (thus, the "hyperactive child"). By 1980 the name had been changed to *attention deficit disorder* (ADD) to emphasize that the attentional problem was the major issue, not hyperactivity. In 1987 the name was changed again to reflect the reality that all of the problems were significant. The newest term is *attention-deficit/hyperactivity disorder* (ADHD).

The latest terms, therefore, are ADHD and LD. If colleagues use other terms, teachers should not be confused. They are not seeing a different problem; they are merely using older terms to describe it.

If a student has ADHD and/or LD, he or she will probably have emotional problems (anger, sadness, anxiety, or disruptive behavior), social problems (immaturity, poor relationships with same-age children), and/or family problems. To understand this student, the teacher must evaluate these difficulties from all angles to see how they affect every aspect of life—not only in school but also with other children and with the family. In addition to interfering with reading, writing, and math, learning disabilities affect, for example, recess and physical education—baseball, basketball, and hopscotch. They also may interfere with art, music, or related activities. Likewise, ADHD does not interfere only with classroom behavior; it also affects peer-related behavior and family life. Teachers must become knowledgeable about these students so that they can help them both inside and outside the classroom.[1]

ARTICLE 7.5

THE next article was written by Larry Silver, a child and adolescent psychiatrist who has specialized in studying students with ADHD and LD. His article, updated for the 6th edition of this book, represents the latest and most comprehensive overview of ADHD and gives specific and realistic recommendations for classroom teachers to accommodate their teaching and managing skills to help a hyperactive, inattentive, and impulsive student.

HELPING THE STUDENT WITH ATTENTION-DEFICIT/ HYPERACTIVITY DISORDER IN THE REGULAR CLASSROOM
Larry B. Silver

WHAT IS ADHD?

Attention-deficit/hyperactivity disorder (ADHD) is a neurologically based disorder manifested by hyperactivity, inattention (distractibility), and impulsivity. Individuals with this disorder might have one, two, or all three of these behaviors. They need not have all three. ADHD is usually apparent by age 6 years and is estimated to be present in about 1% to 3% of school-age individuals. About 50% appear to mature out of their ADHD by puberty; 50% will continue into adolescence. Approximately 30% of children will continue past adolescence into adulthood.

---

[1]These introductory remarks include excerpts from Larry B. Silver, *ADHD,* 1990, pp. 1–2, Ch. ADD (pamphlet).

Hyperactivity refers to an increased activity level, often reflective in fidgety behavior. The individual typically is not wild, running around the room, but is more likely to be tapping fingers, playing with something, swinging legs, wiggling, or getting in and out of the seat. *Inattention* or *distractibility* refers to an inability to block out unimportant stimuli, resulting in difficulty staying on task and a short attention span. This distractibility might be with auditory stimuli (reacting to subtle sounds or noises that others ignore), with visual stimuli (reacting to movement or items others ignore), or with both types of stimuli. Starting with older adolescents and continuing into adulthood, another form of inattention might be noted: difficulty blocking out thoughts to focus on what is important. This student will daydream or tune out in class. *Impulsivity* refers to an inability to stop and think before speaking or acting. This individual might interrupt or call out in class without raising his or her hand, interrupt parents, act without thinking of the consequences, and answer work tasks before thinking through the problem.

Current research strongly suggests that ADHD is caused by a deficiency of a particular neurotransmitter (norepinephrine) in specific pathways within the lower brain stem area (the ascending reticular activating system).

HOW IS ADHD DIAGNOSED?

The formal criteria for ADHD are noted in the *Diagnostic and Statistical Manual of Mental Disorders–Fourth Edition* (1994; see box). Behaviors are listed that describe hyperactivity, inattention, and impulsivity. Professionals are to document a certain percentage of these criteria to establish that one or more of the three behaviors exists. Although there are no formal tests or evaluations that establish the diagnosis of ADHD, several types of behavioral rating scales are available and often used by school systems to document these behaviors. Once the behaviors are documented, it is necessary to show that the behaviors are chronic and pervasive. Many other difficulties may result in a student's being hyperactive, inattentive, or impulsive. Thus, as will be explained, the only way to establish the diagnosis is by the clinical history.

Anxiety or depression can result in a student's being restless, not on task, or irritable. Certain learning disabilities also can result in a student's appearing to be off task or unable to complete assignments. The hyperactivity, inattention, or impulsivity observed in these situations would not be considered to be ADHD.

Only a clinical history of the problems can clarify the diagnosis. If the behavior(s) observed occurred only during a certain time in the person's life or occur in certain situations, one must think of an emotional problem or a learning disability. ADHD is a neurological disorder, probably present from birth. Thus, if the behavior(s) have been present since early childhood (i.e., are chronic) and are present during all parts of the student's life, at school, home, and various activities (i.e., are pervasive), the diagnosis of ADHD is made.

If the classroom teacher suspects that a student has ADHD, he or she should discuss this concern with the parents, who should then discuss the concerns with the student's family physician. Members of the special education professional team can participate in finalizing the diagnosis of ADHD. In most areas, the diagnosis is not considered official until diagnosed by a physician (e.g., family practitioner, pediatrician, child and adolescent psychiatrist).

HOW IS ADHD ADDRESSED WITHIN SCHOOL SYSTEMS?

If a child or adolescent has ADHD, the public school system can recognize and service the student under education law or under civil law. The education law is the Individuals with Disabilities Education Act (IDEA) (P.L. 101-476), passed by Congress in 1990 as the reauthorization of the Education for all Handicapped Children Act (P.L. 94-142). The civil law used is Section 504 of the Rehabilitation Act of 1973 (P.L. 93-112).

Part B of IDEA defines the categories of disability recognized for special education by the U.S. Department of Education. ADHD is not identified as a separate disability. Thus, in 1991 the U.S. Department of Education issued a memorandum clarifying how students with ADHD could be eligible for special education services. If the student with ADHD also has a Learning Disability, he or she could be identified as having this disability; If the student also has a significant emotional problem, he or she could be identified as Seriously Emotionally Disturbed; or if the student does not meet the criteria for these two disabilities, he or she could be identified under the Other Health Impaired category. Any of these three classifications would make the student with ADHD eligible for special education services.

DIAGNOSTIC CRITERIA FOR ATTENTION-DEFICIT/HYPERACTIVITY DISORDER

A. Either (1) or (2)

(1) Six (or more) of the following symptoms of **inattention** have persisted for at least 6 months to a degree that is maladaptive and inconsistent with developmental level:

Inattention
(a) often fails to give close attention to details or makes careless mistakes in schoolwork, work, or other activities
(b) often has difficulty sustaining attention in tasks or play activities
(c) often does not seem to listen when spoken to directly
(d) often does not follow through on instructions and fails to finish schoolwork, chores, or duties in the workplace (not due to oppositional behavior or failure to understand instructions)
(e) often has difficulty organizing tasks and activities
(f) often avoids, dislikes, or is reluctant to engage in tasks that require sustained mental effort (such as schoolwork or homework)
(g) often loses things necessary for tasks or activities (e.g., toys, school assignments, pencils, books, or tools)
(h) is often easily distracted by extraneous stimuli
(i) is often forgetful in daily activities

(2) Six (or more) of the following symptoms of **hyperactivity–impulsivity** have persisted for at least 6 months to a degree that is maladaptive and inconsistent with developmental level:

Hyperactivity
(a) often fidgets with hands or feet or squirms in seat
(b) often leaves seat in classroom or in other situations in which remaining seated is expected
(c) often runs about or climbs excessively in situations in which it is inappropriate (in adolescents or adults, may be limited to subjective feelings of restlessness)
(d) often has difficulty playing or engaging in leisure activities quietly
(e) is often "on the go" or often acts as if "driven by a motor"

This same U.S. Department of Education memorandum clarifies that students with ADHD can also be served under Section 504 of the Rehabilitation Act of 1973 if their condition is severe enough to be considered a handicap. In this law, a disorder is considered a handicap if the disability "substantially limits a major life activity," such as learning. Thus,

(f) often talks excessively

Impulsivity

(g) often blurts out answers before questions have been completed

(h) often has difficulty awaiting turn

(i) often interrupts or intrudes on others (e.g., butts into conversations or games)

B. Some hyperactive–impulsive or inattentive symptoms that cause impairment were present before age 7 years.

C. Some impairment from the symptoms is present in two or more settings (e.g., at school [or work] and at home).

D. There must be clear evidence of clinically significant impairment in social, academic, or occupational functioning.

E. The symptoms do not occur exclusively during the course of a Pervasive Developmental Disorder, Schizophrenia, or other Psychotic Disorder and are not better accounted for by another mental disorder (Mood Disorder, Anxiety Disorder, Dissociative Disorder, or Personality Disorder).

Code Is Based on Type

314.01: Attention-Deficit/Hyperactivity Disorder, Combined Type

314.00: Attention-Deficit/Hyperactivity Disorder, Predominantly Inattentive Type

314.07: Attention-Deficit/Hyperactivity Disorder, Predominantly Hyperactive–Impulsive Type

314.09: Attention-Deficit/Hyperactivity Disorder Not Otherwise Specified (This category is for disorders with prominent symptoms of inattention or hyperactivity–impulsivity that do not meet criteria for Attention-Deficit/Hyperactivity Disorder.)

Note. From *Diagnostic and Statistical Manual of Mental Disorders* (4th edition), by American Psychiatric Association, 1994, Washington, DC: Author.

under Section 504, children and adolescents with ADHD may be eligible for accommodations in the regular classroom to meet their educational needs.

Many students with ADHD may not qualify for services within a school district's severe eligibility specifications for learning disabilities but can meet the criteria to be serviced under Section 504. Eligible students under Section 504, like students receiving services under IDEA, are entitled to reasonable accommodations in order to benefit from the educational process. These accommodations are to be made by the teacher within the regular classroom.

HEALTH/MENTAL HEALTH TREATMENTS FOR ADHD

ADHD is a neurological disorder resulting from a deficiency of a specific neurotransmitter in a specific area of the brain. The primary approach to treatment focuses on the use of specific medications that increase the amount of this neurotransmitter in this area of the brain. Once the level is where it should be, the student becomes significantly less hyperactive, inattentive, and/or impulsive. The most frequently used medications are methylphenidate (Ritalin), dextroamphetamine (Dexedrine), pemoline (Cylert), and imipramine (Tofranil).

In addition to the use of medications, other services might be needed depending on the remaining problems once the medication is working. Some children or adolescents may need individual therapy or counseling. Parents might need help addressing behavioral or family issues. Social skills training might also be helpful.

With all aspects of this treatment plan, it is essential that health and mental health professionals work closely with the special education team and the classroom teacher. When a student is on medication, feedback from teachers is critical to learning how the medication is working or what adjustments are needed. Behavioral programs may have to be integrated into a school-based program to have the best impact.

The focus of this chapter is the role of the classroom teacher in addressing the special needs of the student with ADHD. There are two such needs: (1) the ability to adjust the classroom, curriculum, and teaching approaches to accommodate to the needs of this student and (2) the need to understand the effects and side effects of the medications needed in order to report the student's progress or lack of progress as medications are started and doses are adjusted and to recognize side effects so that this information can be forwarded to the physician managing the medication.

The general role of the school in addressing the needs of the student with ADHD will be reviewed first. Then the role of the regular classroom teacher will be discussed.

THE GENERAL ROLE OF THE SCHOOL IN ADDRESSING ADHD

When planning for the placement, curriculum, and classroom strategies needed for a student with ADHD, two important factors must be considered. Each influences the individualized plan developed. The first factor is whether the student also has a learning disability. Studies show that between 50% and 70% of students with ADHD also have a learning disability; thus, whenever the diagnosis of ADHD is made, it is essential that the possibility of a learning disability be explored. The second factor is whether this student is successfully on medication or not.

If the student has a learning disability, these processing problems must be addressed through appropriate special education services as well as accommodations provided within the regular classroom. For some students with ADHD, no learning disability is found; however, the student might have areas of deficit in specific skills or less than grade-appropriate knowledge in certain areas because he or she may not have been available for learning during the years in school before the diagnosis was made and treatment started.

If on appropriate medications at the correct dose, about 85% of students with ADHD will no longer be hyperactive, inattentive, and/or impulsive in the classroom. Thus, no special interventions may be needed. If parents refuse medication, the physician does not recommend medication, or the use and dosage of the medication is not optimum, interventions must be designed to address the specific behaviors that the student has in the school settings.

If the learning disabilities result in the student's needing more services than can be provided in the regular classroom, the possibility of a special education program to address these needs may have to be considered. If the student is not on medication and the resulting hyperactivity, inattention, and/or impulsivity result in behaviors that make the student unavailable for learning in the regular classroom or result in behaviors that make the classroom unavailable for the other students to learn, the child or adolescent might need a special education program for students with serious emotional problems.

The regular classroom teacher should be able to accommodate to the general educational needs of the student with ADHD. He or she should not be expected to address the full special educational needs for the student with ADHD who also has significant learning disabilities or serious emotional problems.

THE ROLE OF THE REGULAR CLASSROOM TEACHER

The teacher should be prepared to address two major issues in the regular classroom: (1) adjusting the classroom, curriculum, and teaching strategy to address the behaviors of ADHD and (2) recognizing the side effects of the different medications used to treat ADHD so that this information can be forwarded to the prescribing physician.

ADDRESSING THE BEHAVIORS OF ADHD

It is not possible to provide a specific list of things to do in the classroom. Each student is different and each needs a specially designed approach. It is important to understand which of the many behaviors of ADHD a specific student has and to accommodate for his or her specific needs. The following are possible behaviors:

1. Hyperactivity (fidgety behaviors)

2. Inattention (distractibility)
   (a) auditory distractibility
   (b) visual distractibility
   (c) internal distractibility

3. Impulsivity
   (a) does not stop to think before speaking
   (b) does not stop to think before acting

In addition to addressing the specific behaviors, it is important to know where the student is academically. If knowledge or skills that should have been learned in an earlier grade are weak or absent because the student was not available for learning at that time, these areas will need to be addressed. Often, once the student is diagnosed and treated with medication, he or she will be available to catch up in these areas.

To successfully work with students who have ADHD in the regular classroom requires a competent teacher who has a positive attitude toward mainstreaming and inclusion. In addition, this teacher needs to have the ability to collaborate as part of an interdisciplinary team and to have knowledge of behavioral management techniques. Teachers who work well with special needs students in the regular classroom are fair, firm, warm, and responsive. They have patience and a sense of humor and are able to establish rapport with students.

ACCOMMODATIONS FOR HYPERACTIVITY

Students who are hyperactive are most challenging. They have difficulty sitting in their seat for prolonged periods. They may get up to sharpen their pencils frequently. They fidget with pencils, pens, or paper clips, appearing never to be calm and relaxed. A student's need for physical movement and activity must be taken into account in planning classroom accommodations. Teachers should try to channel this excessive activity into acceptable activities. Simply telling the child or adolescent to stop his or her disruptive hyperactive behaviors will not work. This student needs to find ways of channeling this excessive activity into acceptable behaviors. The other students will have to be told why this student will be permitted to do some things that the class in general will not. The following are examples of accommodations:

- Allow nondisruptive, directed movement in the classroom.
- Allow standing during seatwork if the student wishes to do so.
- Use activity as a reward. Permit specific activities (running an errand, cleaning the board, organizing materials) as an individual reward for improvement.
- Use teaching activities that encourage active responding (talking, moving, working at the board).
- Encourage diary writing, note taking, painting, and other meaningful work-related activities.
- Consider having this student sit near the teacher. If the student begins to fidget with objects on the desk, tap feet, rock the chair, or do other disruptive behaviors, the teacher can reach over and remind the student what is happening. Perhaps a hand signal could be developed that says "You are too hyper. Relax." Since the student may not be aware of the behaviors, this signal might be all that is needed to stop.

ACCOMMODATIONS FOR INATTENTION OR DISTRACTIBILITY

Students who are inattentive or distractible will have a short attention span and frequently not complete assignments. Some accommodations help with all forms of this problem, and others are most appropriate for a specific type of distractibility.

General accommodations to prolong a student's concentration on tasks might include:

1. Shorten the task.
   (a) Break one task into smaller parts to be completed at different times.
   (b) Give two tasks, with the task the student prefers to be completed after the less preferred task.
   (c) Assign fewer problems (spelling words, math problems).
   (d) For rote tasks, set up more short, spaced practice sessions rather than fewer but longer and more concentrated sessions.
   (e) Give fewer and shorter homework assignments.

2. Make tasks more interesting.
   (a) When possible, encourage the student to work with partners in small groups.
   (b) Alternate highly interesting and less interesting tasks.
   (c) Try to create novel ways of teaching a task.

3. Improve the student's ability to focus and listen.
   (a) Be sure to have the student's attention before speaking. Ask for the class's attention and watch for eye contact from this student.
   (b) Give clues that it is important to attend. Use key phrases ("This is important" or "Listen carefully").
   (c) Use short, simple sentences.
   (d) Give one instruction at a time.
   (e) Prompt the student to repeat instructions after listening to them.
   (f) Write a short outline or summary of the directions on the board.
   (g) Use visual aids (charts, pictures, graphs).

4. Have the student sit next to the teacher's desk. When instructions are to be given, the teacher might walk over to his or her desk or reach out and touch the desk. If the student appears not to be focused or to be distracted, the teacher can reach out and help him or her attend. Again, a hand signal might work well as a reminder that the student is distracted and needs to refocus.

Specific accommodations for students who have *auditory distractibility* would start with all of the above ideas. In addition, the student should be working in the quietest place in the room, away from the door, window, air conditioner, and high-traffic areas. For some assignments or tests, it might be helpful if this student went to the library or another quiet place to work.

Specific accommodations for students who have *visual distractibility* also include the general interventions. In addition, this student might do best in the least visually active part of the room, away from doors, windows, traffic, posters, and pictures. Sometimes a cubicle can be placed on the desk. She or he might be asked to work in a corner facing the wall. If this is done, the student and the others in the class need to understand that this place is not being used as a punishment. This student might do best sitting in the front row. By doing this, much of the possible visual distraction caused by the other students will be decreased. (Do not use this idea for the student with auditory distractibility; he or she will continually turn around to see what the activity or noise is about.) Try to keep the desktop free of clutter. If only the task to be done is visible, the student is less likely to be distracted.

Specific accommodations for students who are *distracted by their own thoughts* include having their desk near the teacher. When they appear to be daydreaming or staring off, a gentle touch or word can bring them back. Once the student looks at the teacher, a hand signal might be used to remind the student what is happening.

ACCOMMODATIONS FOR STUDENTS WHO ARE IMPULSIVE

Students who are impulsive will call out answers without raising a hand or waiting to be called on. They might make comments that are inappropriate or that hurt feelings because these students do not think before speaking. They might act before they think, resulting in pushing, yelling, or hitting. Or, they might turn to do something so fast that they bump into other students or knock things over. Some may rush through assignments and tests, putting down the first thought or answer that enters their head. Younger children may have difficulty learning to wait (for their turn to do something, for a toy, for attention).

Behavioral approaches for helping the student become aware of his or her impulsivity should be combined with both accommodating the teaching style and activities and teaching the student techniques for delaying responses or actions. It might be helpful to consult with the school psychologist or other mental health professional when designing specific strategies for helping these students.

Accommodations for helping this student learn to wait include the following:

1. Teaching substitute verbal or motor responses to use while waiting.

2. Instructing the student to work on easier parts of tasks while waiting for the teacher's help on harder parts.

3. Allowing this student to doodle or play with clay, paper clips, or other items while waiting or listening to instructions.

4. Letting the child participate in setting the pace for activities when possible.

The following are accommodations for helping the student who calls out or interrupts:

1. Suggesting and reinforcing alternative ways for getting attention (being a line leader or paper passer).

2. Teaching these children to recognize pauses in conversations so that they can learn when to speak and how to hold onto ideas while listening for these pauses.

3. Letting the child know about upcoming transitions or difficult times or tasks for which he or she will need extra control.

4. Teaching and practicing social routines (saying hello, goodbye, please).

MEDICATION MANAGEMENT IN THE CLASSROOM

Two groups of medications are used to treat ADHD. The most frequently used medications in each group will be discussed. The first group consists of methylphenidate (Ritalin), dextroamphetamine (Dexedrine), and pemoline (Cylert). Each increases the production of the deficient neurotransmitter in the lower brain stem area. The second group of medications consists of imipramine (Tofranil), desipramine (Norpramine), and

Clonidine. Each increases the level of the deficient neurotransmitter not by producing more but by slowing down the breakdown of the existing amount.

Ritalin, Dexedrine, and Cylert are safe and effective medications. There are few side effects. The most frequent ones are loss of appetite and difficulty falling asleep at night. Less frequent side effects are complaints of headaches or stomachaches. A very uncommon side effect is the development of motor tics (twitching of eyelids, facial muscles, shoulder muscles). If the muscles in the back of the throat develop tics, the teacher will hear sniffing, snorting, or coughing sounds. If other difficulties are observed and the teacher is not sure what these mean, the physician should be called.

Tofranil and Norpramine can make a student sleepy and tired. In addition, less common side effects are constipation, dry mouth, or blurred vision. Clonidine can make the student very tired, sometimes resulting in falling asleep in the classroom.

If any of these side effects are noted, they should be told to parents, who should inform the prescribing physician. As with the other medications, if any behaviors are noted that are of concern, the teacher should err on the side of being overcautious and inform the physician.

IN CLOSING

Most children and adolescents with ADHD can be educated in the regular classroom setting. Some of these students who also have significant learning disabilities or significant emotional problems may need supplemental services within the classroom or placement in a special education program. Also, some students with ADHD who are not on medication will experience hyperactivity, inattention, and/or impulsivity that prevent them from being available for learning in the regular classroom or cause them to be so disruptive in the classroom that other students are not able to learn. These students may need a special education placement not necessarily because of the ADHD but because the ADHD is not being treated.

Students with ADHD do not want to be hyperactive, inattentive, or impulsive. They do not want to be bad or get into trouble. They do want to learn. By providing the appropriate accommodations in the classroom, with the curriculum, and with teaching strategies, this child or adolescent can be a happy, productive, successful student in the regular classroom.

REFERENCE

American Psychiatric Association. (1994). *Diagnostic and statistical manual of mental disorders* (4th ed.). Washington, DC: Author.

STUDENTS WHO HAVE ALCOHOL OR DRUG PROBLEMS

Alcohol use by children and youth is much more than a "gateway" to other drug abuse. Alcohol is inexorably intertwined with a myriad of serious emotional, behavioral, and learning difficulties confronting young persons today. In a poll by the National Association of Student Councils, 46% of respondents ranked alcohol as today's most serious school problem. By 10th grade, 90% of youth have tried alcohol; of these, 69% report first use by the eighth grade. One third of 12th-grade students engage in binge drinking at least semiweekly. Drinking is strongly related to promiscuous sexual activity and date rape; among sexually active teens, those averaging five or more drinks daily were three times less likely to use condoms, thus placing them at risk for HIV (Office of Substance Abuse Prevention, 1991). Such statistics caused pollster George Gallup, Jr. to conclude that America does not have a crime problem, a teenage pregnancy problem, a worker productivity problem, or a problem of broken homes. Instead, says Gallup, America has an alcohol and drug problem.

Cheers to the Drug of Choice

Fueling the alcohol crisis among modern youth is a virtual alcohol immersion campaign waged by the media. A multibillion-dollar "beverage" industry feigns responsibility by counseling teens to "wait until you are mature" while simultaneously crafting commercials that tantalize youth. Advertisers employ a deceptive Orwellian "Newspeak," where beer drinking is paired with all the "good things in life." Drinking is associated with images of wild stallions running free (masculinity), a rugby or touch football game (fellowship), an exciting sports event (athletic prowess), a beach party, a volleyball game, or a bar scene involving beautiful women (sexuality). In this make-believe world, real men and women hurry off after a hard day's work—not to meet their families but to reward themselves with a drink. The adolescent readily reaches the intended conclusion: "I can't wait for Happy Hour."

Contrary to popular opinion, the misuse of alcohol by children and youth is a more serious and pervasive problem in our society than the use of other drugs. Although alcohol is illegal for children and youth to purchase, it is cheap and easily obtained from home and from older peers, through falsified ID cards, and through the complicity of merchants. Even parents often wink at youthful binges: "Thank heavens it is only alcohol and not drugs!" they exclaim, blinded by a culture in which alcohol is the drug of choice. This comment reflects the curious inconsistency in parental expectations about alcohol compared to other drugs.

Drinking is deeply rooted in our cultural traditions. In the days of small frontier towns, the mark of moral safety was achieved when the number of churches equaled or exceeded the number of bars. Because spirits are not a recent invention, it is not surprising that the abuse of alcohol was widespread among Europeans who first settled in North America. Many imbibing pioneers could outdrink their modern barroom counterparts. Alcoholics among the poor squandered their weekly wages on liquor, ignoring the needs of their starving families. But this was also the time of Calvinistic revivalism in America. The immorality of alcohol was clear—good was warring against evil, and there was no confusion between them. A dipsomaniac was a tool in the hands of the Prince of Darkness. A popular Currier lithograph in the 1800s offered vivid and painful images of the nine stages of alcoholism:

The Drunkard Progresses from the First Drink to the Grave

Step 1. A glass with a friend.

Step 2. A glass to keep the cold out.

Step 3. A glass too much.

Step 4. Drunk and riotous.

Step 5. The summit attained: jolly companions—a certified drunk.

Step 6. Poverty and disease.

Step 7. Forsaken by friends.

Step 8. Depression and crime.

Step 9. Death by suicide.

The 12-Step Program of Alcoholics Anonymous might well have had its origins as a restorative alternative to the ruinous steps of Currier's lithograph.

Ideally, language is designed to clarify ideas and thoughts and to communicate the core values of a civilization. However, when describing alcohol use in Western culture, language is used to deny, minimize, and rationalize the destructive effects of this drug. Notice, for example, how very few words in the English language are available to describe sobriety, and how stiff and lifeless they sound: abstinence, prohibition, temperance, and teetotalism. However, when it comes to describing drinking or drunkenness, the dictionary offers a virtual frolic of light-hearted euphemisms: binge, smashed, inebriated, boozer, lush, plastered, pickled, crocked, polluted, stewed, soused, soaked, ranked, bombed, loaded, in the bag, stinko, skunk drunk, blind drunk, three sheets to the wind, high, tipsy, having a drop, a spot, a jigger, a snort, a round, an eye-opener, one for the road, hooch, rotgut, wetting one's whistle, raising one's elbow, or becoming mellow, giddy, or relaxed.

Facing Our Alcohol Problem

Beer is the most consumed drug among children and youth. Adolescents who drink frequently believe that alcohol will not affect their lives. They convince themselves they drink only to relax and loosen up for social activities. They rationalize that drinking beer and wine is not as destructive as drinking hard liquor. However, beer can lead to binge drinking, addiction, lowered academic motivation, sexual promiscuity, dangerous driving, violence, and self-destruction. Alcohol has an insidious effect on a young person's mood, thinking, judgment, and behaviors. It floods the self-control system, rendering intoxicated children victims of their own impulses.

Alcohol is a principal cause of physical and sexual abuse of children and the burgeoning rates of youth suicide. Thirty years ago, the term *fetal alcohol syndrome* (FAS) was first introduced to describe a pattern of birth defects observed in children born to alcoholic mothers (National Institute on Alcohol Abuse and Alcoholism, 1991). FAS children are subjected to chemical abuse *in utero,* which leads to severe impairments in learning, human attachment, and social functioning. Between the ages of 6 and 33, traffic crashes are the leading cause of death, and almost half of these are alcohol related. In fact, the correlation between alcohol abuse and a host of other antisocial behaviors is so strong that prevention programs often use indexes of disordered behavior to screen for possible alcohol abuse.

Drinking also can be used to deny serious family problems, peer problems, and school problems. Drinking is an immature and unsuccessful way of dealing with feelings of frustration, humiliation, and depression. Unfortunately, drinking can help children or youth believe that relief is easy to attain. When they drink, they feel they can overcome their feelings of unhappiness. Alcohol creates a pattern of thinking errors in which youth delude themselves into believing that they are in control, likable, and competent, when in reality they are out of control, disgusting, and dysfunctional. Additionally, we need to recognize that the denial of alcohol abuse not only is an individual defense mechanism but also applies to our society. We deny the destructive impact that alcoholic parents have on their children. Fifty percent of today's alcoholics are children of alcoholic parents (Russell, Henderson, & Blum, 1984). Children of alcoholic parents are two times more likely to become future alcoholics than their peers, have a higher risk of using illegal drugs, and are more likely to marry into alcoholic families.

As we confront our massive problems with alcohol in contemporary society, every educator needs to reflect deeply on these issues, at both the personal and academic levels, and to develop realistic interventions to take the thrills, the sex, and the feelings of comfort out of adolescent drinking.

THE next article, by Jamie Chambers and Teresa Henrickson, describes the powerful relationship youth develop with drugs. The authors clarify the underlying psychological reasons for drug dependency and offer four strength-based principles that teachers can use to help these students.

ARTICLE 7.6

"DRUGSHIPS": HOW KIDS MAKE RELATIONSHIPS WITH ADDICTIVE BEHAVIORS

Jamie C. Chambers and Teresa Henrickson

Raymond enters the group for the first time, head down, dragging his feet. When asked why he's there, he says, "It wasn't my idea to come here, it was my mom's. These groups have done me no good. They're a waste of my time!"

This is Ray's third referral to a drug-use prevention program. Marijuana is the love of his life. He has replaced friendships with a "drugship." The challenge is to reclaim this young man from a life of sex, drugs, and crime. The question is: How do you engage a youth who enjoys drugs and thinks he has no problem? Raymond believes his main difficulty is the adults in his life who demand he quit using drugs simply because he failed his last urinalysis.

Youth like Ray are truly enchanted by substance abuse and other mood-altering behaviors. To build therapeutic alliances with them, we must understand the drug-use culture with which they feel a deep connection. The challenge is nothing less than extricating them from captivity in a subculture that operates outside of mainstream America.

DRUGSHIPS AS PART OF A GREATER YOUTH CULTURE

In *The Disconnected Generation,* Josh McDowell (2000) writes that adolescent aloofness is more than a passing identity crisis, but is becoming an entrenched cultural condition. When the alienation and aloneness of youth is not addressed, the distance they feel from adults is a relational gulf. Ron Taffel (2001) describes peer drug subcultures as a second family.

> Starting in late elementary school, youngsters tend to move away from their own siblings and parents. They surround themselves instead with friends, forming a second family, a separate but equally important system. As kids become more and more attached to their friends and to the common interests they share, by early adolescence it is a natural, easy step to divorce themselves not only from their first families but, often, from other significant adults as well. (p. 17)

When they enter schools and treatment programs, such youth drag with them their drug-use culture. It is often ignored or countered by oppressive treatment cultures that shame and confront kids into submission. This powerful subculture can undo our efforts to help these youth change.

Negative youth subcultures and gangs are found worldwide. Embracing values of freedom without responsibility, they cannot be reached by either permissive or authoritarian approaches (Brendtro, Brokenleg, & Van Bockern, 2002). Adults can argue, threaten, and pound their chests all they want. The only effective methods involve respectful confrontation and relationship-building (Schwebel, 2002).

Youth like Raymond enter our world committed to a counterculture. The government may be waging a war on drugs and drug users, but its influence is often invisible to the drug-using youth we meet. Drug use and its lifestyle of cutting school, chasing sex, and committing crimes can be seen as a third person entering the room. In order to personify Ray's "partner," we look at the hold that the drug culture has on such a youth.

THE ENCHANTED SUBCULTURE

To those who embrace it, drugship behavior has both rewarding and negative features. The drug subculture offers a place where youth are accepted and claimed. Its many benefits include:

- A shared language
- Rites that become transforming rituals
- Common contacts

- Universal symbols and artifacts
- Shared ideas, beliefs, and core values

Youth wrapped in drugships dare you to challenge their passionate practice of drug-use rituals. Becca, a 16 year old, urges us to "understand before you attempt to help me." Understanding requires a therapeutic alliance. But Becca does not come alone, for this coalition is a triad involving the helper, the youth, and the drugship (Pedersen, 2000). The drugship is treated as a third party in the conversation. The power and influence of the drugship over the lives of students can be assessed and changed. Through this coalition, we help youth reformulate and reach their goals.

THE ANATOMY OF A DRUGSHIP

Alexia and her group were discussing the definition of a friendship versus the kind of destructive relationships she was involved in while using. They defined a friendship as "a relationship between two people where their relationship with each other is primary." She and her group came up with the term "drugship," and they defined it as "a relationship between two or more kids where drug use and drug-use activity are primary." We have elaborated on the concept of drugships based on conversations with several drug-using youth:

- "I date her/him because she/he will get me high, drunk, or stoned."
- "I hang out with them because they always have something to use."
- "I have sex with people so I won't have to pay for my alcohol and drugs."
- "I hang out with people who use because I know I'll be accepted and admired."
- "Drugs seem to be more important than those people or events that used to be important to me."

Psychiatrist William Glasser (1998) characterized drug-using youth as unhappy people who have abandoned relationships for nonhuman pleasure. They pursue quick, intense pleasure, which requires nothing more than getting the drug in their bloodstreams. Other people are only useful as a conduit for drugs. In a drugship, youth trade relationships with people for relationships with things. Eighteen-year-old Marty reported, "Being committed to getting high is like being in an abusive marriage." He tearfully confessed, "And it's just as hard for me to get out of as it is for a woman to leave a violent man."

ELEMENTS OF A DRUGSHIP

The first clue that a young person is becoming enchanted with chemicals is that drug use becomes one of life's organizing principles. Robert and Mary McAuliffe (1975) have described the pervasiveness of these drugships. Table 7.6–1 is adapted from their work.

Youth in drugships have a host of related concerns including health, sexual orientation, employment, living conditions, and involvement with the mental health or criminal justice system. They do not do well in traditional deficit-oriented treatment programs. Therefore, treatment providers or educators must attend to the many factors that contribute to the young person's current situation (Winters, 1999). This entails moving away from finding pathology and fixing flaws to approaches that build on strengths and potentials.

UNRAVELING THE DRUGSHIP

Before treatment happens, a youth must be motivated to change. Tammy Bell (1990) identifies ways to help kids see that chemical use is a problem:

1. Examining problems in living

2. Examining the development of substance abuse or dependence

3. Exploring the relationship between problems and substance abuse

4. Using crisis situations to motivate requests for help

Once the "marriage," as Marty described it, is recognized as abusive and uninhabitable, we can begin to facilitate a divorce. This is a challenge because youth caught in the web of a drugship often react in ways that confirm the belief that the drug trance is better than the painful relationship problems that triggered their addictive behavior. Unraveling the power of drugships involves changing entrenched patterns of thinking, feeling, and behaving. Dealing with youth usually requires family involvement. Family treatment can also give parents the optimism and skills to cope with challenges in raising their teens (Winters, 1999).

ETHNOGRAPHIC INTERVENTIONS

The science of anthropology offers a model for respectfully entering the world created by our young clients. The use of ethnography literally creates a picture of our study group's way of life. The ethnographer's tools are vital to youth workers, teachers, and counselors. They are: participation–observation, interviewing, utilizing written records and analysis, and collecting nonwritten records (Wolcott, 1988). Active participation gives us a chance to be an influence. As ethnographic interventionists, we can rely on these strategies when engaging youth who are caught in drugships:

> 1. One-Downsmanship

Most youth captivated by drugships will approach us from adversarial positions. It is not acceptable to respond in the same manner. As adults, we must disengage from our tendency to rely on our power. Instead, we must use our curiosity about the youth's story. She becomes the teacher on the subject of her experience in developing a drugship. We become the students, asking questions and reflecting what we see. Our job is to make observations and form tentative hypotheses about the meaning of drug-related behaviors.

> 2. Unearthing Strengths

Behavior can be best understood in its social context (Dinkmeyer, Dinkmeyer, & Sperry, 1987). Seen in context, all behavior is purposeful or goal directed. Alfred Adler talked about the importance of understanding goals: "If we know the goal of a person, we can undertake to explain and to understand … how his character traits, his feelings and emotions, and his logic, must be constituted" (Ansbacher & Ansbacher, 1956, p. 196).

(text continues on p. 486)

TABLE 7.6–1

ELEMENTS OF A DRUGSHIP (ADAPTED FROM MCAULIFFE, 1975)

Elements	Definitions	Resulting Conditions
Unmanageability	Loss of control. Youth can't change, quit, or see that substance abuse is harmful. Sees no connection between using and negative effects on life.	1. Belief in personal control over situations. 2. Guilt, anxiety, depression, intentional or accidental suicidal behavior. 3. Occasional awareness results in fear. 4. Periods of ambivalence, ambiguity, indecisiveness, procrastination.
Distorting	Lies of commission or omission and twisted details are intended to convince both the youth and others that life is under control.	1. Physical and emotional feelings blocked. 2. Contact with reality, including intellectual perception, understanding, reasoning, forethought, decision-making, and judgment is impaired. 3. Reality shaped to fit twisted perspective and pushed further from the youth's grasp.
Protectiveness	Defensive of type, extent of involvement. Distrustful of those who don't use or who interfere with using. Elaborate defenses, attitudes, cognitive traps, disguises.	1. Nondrug-using relationships bombarded with poisonous projections. 2. Family members and straight friends feel guilt, remorse. 3. Confusing, infrequent displays of remorse. 4. Separation from others. 5. Youth locked in drugship culture.
Addict's Identity	Declining moral behavior. Nagging awareness of guilt, anxiety. Defensive of irresponsible, disrespectful behavior. Enjoys idolization, idolizing others with Addict's Identity.	1. Severe internal conflict between personal values and conduct. 2. Self-alienation. 3. Sociopathic coping style. 4. Uncaring, disqualifying behavior, attitudes. 5. Moral anxiety, feelings of worthlessness.
Compulsiveness	Strong emotional urge to use chemicals. Rituals of using have an almost hypnotic power.	1. Impulsive loss of control over drug use, drug activities. 2. Self-destructiveness. 3. Impaired ability to detect damage. 4. Unconscious thrust toward negativism, suicide.

(continues)

ELEMENTS OF A DRUGSHIP *Continued.*

Elements	Definitions	Resulting Conditions
Addict's Attitude	Negative, suspicious, distrustful. Negative emotions lead to negative behavior and responses. Attitude helps justify hurtful behavior.	1. Desocialization. 2. Disoriented, disordered, disintegrated relationships. 3. Paranoia, self-centeredness, negativism. 4. Withdrawal from community life. 5. Depersonalized situation. 6. Obsessed with negative ideas, judgments, opinions, fantasies, and memories. 7. Negating, nullifying feelings toward self, others. 8. Self- and other-destructive.
Preoccupation	Thinking is characterized by remembering past good times or imagining future good and better drug-using times. Day-to-day thinking involves preparing for, enjoying, or recovering from using. "I have lost interest in other activities, and I'm not as effective at doing other things besides using."	1. Intellect, memory, perception, insight, understanding, reasoning impaired. 2. Rational forethought, judgment, decision-making impaired. 3. Apathy, indecision, procrastination. 4. Recollections of drug use experiences dominate memories. 5. Imagination loses dynamic creative power, bombarded with fantasies of future drug use experiences.
Spell-Based Beliefs	Drug use takes priority as user imagines abilities are enhanced by chemicals. Beliefs about using, users and non-users affect emotions, thoughts, behavior.	1. Depersonalization of all life tasks. 2. Loss of self-awareness, self-respect, self-esteem, positive self-identity. 3. Desocialization, irresponsibility. 4. Other areas of life unmanageable. 5. Responsibilities shifted to others.

Recognizing that behavior follows this socially goal-directed thrust, we seek to unearth strengths using the technique of reframing. Even shabby drugship behavior serves some social purpose which provides a clue to positive alternative behavior (Watzlawick, Weakland, & Fisch, 1974; Fisch, Weakland, & Segal, 1982).

> ### 3. Storytelling and Re-Authoring Kids' Stories

Looking at substance abuse as a relationship helps a youth create an external identity separate from addiction. We ask kids to imagine their drug use as a person. Pete, a blond-haired 16-year-old retorted, "You want me to do what?" We restate the request, "If your drinking was a person, what would his or her name be?" Pete, with an understanding grin, snapped, "It's Bud!" His drug of choice was beer, and his favorite was Budweiser. For the first time, Pete could see himself in a relationship.

Using this metaphor sharpens awareness of the invasive control drugships have over one's life. With this recognition, we also now have the chance to cooperate with the young person in developing a new story or reauthoring their story (White & Epston, 1990; Smith & Nylund, 1997). We later asked Pete how his life would change if he could get away from "Bud." He responded, "Maybe I could do school and make something of myself. I wouldn't be tired during the day and violent at night."

> ### 4. Decoding the Meaning of Behavior

Kids are the philosophers of our times. They purposefully move and interact with their world, always mapping meaning. Sometimes their behavior makes sense to them, but those in drugships often report having no rhyme or reason for their behavior. Decoding involves teaching students to recognize specific thoughts and feelings that drive their inappropriate behaviors and building their strength and confidence to break free from self-defeating patterns (Long, Wood, & Fecser, 2001).

The first level of decoding is reflecting the emotion hidden beneath the youth's words and behavior. The second level is connecting feelings to specific actions. The third level of decoding, which is crucial in unraveling drugships, is recognizing denial and distortion. We must help youth get beyond their pain and defensive behavior.

Searching together for the meaning of behavior enhances trust between youth and adult. The young person learns that the adult is understanding and willing to suspend judgment. Youth begin to recognize how their thinking and feelings are related to their drug-use behavior and destructive behavior. As they become disentangled from drugships, they discover they are worthy of friendships.

REFERENCES

Ansbacher, H., & Ansbacher, R. (Eds.). (1956). *The individual psychology of Alfred Adler: A systematic presentation in selections from his writings.* New York: Harper Torchbooks.

Bell, T. (1990). *Preventing adolescent relapse.* Independence, MO: Herald House/Independence Press.

Brendtro, L. K., Brokenleg, M., & Van Bockern, S. (2002). *Reclaiming youth at risk: Our hope for the future.* Bloomington, IN: National Educational Service.

Dinkmeyer, D., Dinkmeyer, D., & Sperry, L. (1987). *Adlerian counseling and psychotherapy.* Columbus, OH: Merrill Publishing Company.

Fisch, R., Weakland, J., & Segal, L. (1982). *The tactics of change.* San Francisco: Jossey-Bass.

Glasser, W. (1998). *Choice Theory: A new psychology of personal freedom.* New York: HarperPerennial.

Long, N., Wood, M., & Fecser, F. (2001*). Life space crisis intervention: Talking with students in conflict.* Austin, TX: PRO-ED.

McAuliffe, R., & McAuliffe, M. (1975). *The essentials of chemical dependency.* Minneapolis: The American Chemical Dependency Society.

McDowell, J. (2000). *The disconnected generation: Saving our youth from self-destruction.* Nashville: Word Publishing.

Pedersen, P. (2000). *Hidden messages in culture-centered counseling: A triad training model.* Thousand Oaks, CA: Sage.

Schwebel, R. (2002). Drug courts and adolescents. *Counselor, 3*(1), 14–19.

Smith, C., & Nylund, D. (Eds.). (1997). *Narrative therapies with children and adolescents.* New York: Guilford Press.

Taffel, R. (2001). *The second family: How adolescent power is challenging the American family.* New York: St. Martin's Press.

Watzlawick, P., Weakland, J., & Fisch, R. (1974). *Change: Principles of problem formation and problem resolution.* New York: Norton.

White, M., & Epston, D. (1990). *Narrative means to therapeutic ends.* New York: Guilford Press.

Winters, K. (1999). *Treatment of adolescents with substance use disorders.* Rockville, MD: U.S. Department of Health and Human Services, Public Health Service, Substance Abuse and Mental Health Services Administration, and Center for Substance Abuse Treatment.

Wolcott, H. (1988). Ethnographic research in education. In R. M. Jaeger (Ed.), *Complementary methods for research in education.* Washington, DC: American Educational Research Association.

STUDENTS WHO ARE DEPRESSED

Depression is a complex term that can be used to describe a fleeting feeling of sadness, the blues, or a chronic state of withdrawal from the everyday activities of life. Depression can be characterized as a feeling, a mood, a negative state of mind, or a severe form of psychopathology. Prior to 1970, most psychiatrists believed that depression was only an adult disease and that children were immune to this form of mental illness. Now, depression in children and youth is recognized as a valid diagnosis by the American Psychiatric Association's *Diagnostic and Statistical Manual of Mental Disorders–Fourth Edition* (American Psychiatric Association, 1994) and has two classifications: Major Depressive Disorder and Dysthymic Disorder. It is estimated that 20% of adolescents in treatment centers have one of these two diagnoses.

The U.S. Surgeon General (2003) reported that 5% of all teenagers, or approximately 3 million, suffer from depression at one time. Girls are twice as likely to develop depression as boys. Boys, however, are more likely to commit suicide than girls. Adolescents who are depressed do not look like the typical adult who is depressed. Adolescents more often are irritable and moody, and their behaviors are viewed as typical of this stage of development. Perhaps this explains why some depressed adolescents go unnoticed.

Depression also has been called the wordless scream for help and is the precipitative cause of suicide. Cognitive therapists believe that most depressed students have internalized a negative way of thinking about themselves. Their irrational thoughts trigger pervasive feelings of guilt, grief, pessimism, and worthlessness, which are expressed in behaviors that have debilitating effects on their academic, social, and personal skills. Psychologically, they are like a flower trying to return to a seed. They block out all the sunlight in their lives and are drawn to the dark magnetism of their thoughts. Their negative statements—"Nothing ever is going to get better or change," "I hate life," "I'm too tired to do anything—just let me rest," "No one really cares about me ... I don't really care what happens to me," "There is nothing you can do to help me; this is the way it will always be and I only want to be left alone"— make it extremely difficult for staff to be motivated to help them.

Another problem for staff is that depression can be as contagious as a noxious virus. Even the healthiest of staff can be affected and will then reflect the students' feelings of irritability, negativism, and hopelessness. This sequence is a perfect example of the dynamics of the Conflict Cycle in action (see Article 6.2): A student in a depression will create in the staff his or her feelings, and if the staff is not adequately trained, the staff will end up feeling and behaving like the depressed student. A more direct way of stating this principle is to say that a depressed student will create counterdepression in the staff.

Once the staff begins to feel uncomfortable and frustrated by lack of progress, a common reaction is to withdraw and to accommodate the student's wish "to be left alone." If this happens, the depressed student will be successful in taking another step backward into his or her inner world of sadness.

Another variation of depression occurs when a student is able to mask feelings of depression by becoming irritable, anxious, and aggressive. Not all depressed students are withdrawn and tearful. A few find it more comfortable to direct their anger at people than to talk about their sad feelings. One student at Rose School, who had tears rolling down his cheeks, quickly said to the crisis teacher, "I'm not sad—that's just water!"

Historically, depressed students have been seen as the professional responsibility of psychiatry. Now, educators have a professional responsibility to work with these students—ideally, in a collaborative team model. Unfortunately, teachers (even teachers of students with emotional disturbances) have little or no training or experience in this area. Despite the popular use of the term *depression* in television shows, magazines, and everyday language, there are more myths about depression in children and youth than there are facts about this personality problem.

IN the next article, Norman Alessi, a child and adolescent psychiatrist and director of the Children and Adolescent Mood Clinic at the University of Michigan, Department of Psychiatry, exposes 10 myths regarding depression among children and youth. Alessi represents the new breed of psychiatrists who are willing to leave the security of a medical center and address the multiple social and emotional problems of helping depressed students at home, in schools, and in the community.

ARTICLE 7.7

DESPAIR AT ANY AGE
Norman Alessi

MYTHS ABOUT DEPRESSED CHILDREN AND ADOLESCENTS

It has been only 23 years since the publication of the first papers identifying depression in children. Since that time, we have made significant progress in understanding the scope of this problem. Nevertheless, childhood and adolescent depression often goes unrecognized. Frequently teachers who have daily contact with children and adolescents often either fail to recognize this serious disturbance, or mislabel the youth as having a behavioral problem. Possibly, the greatest sources of confusion about childhood and adolescent depression are various "myths" we maintain about childhood that, ultimately, determine our perceptions and actions. What are these myths, and what are the facts about child and adolescent depression?

> **Myth 1: Childhood Is a Happy Time**

Fact: Everyone experiences difficulties in childhood and adolescence that can have lifelong impact: loss, failure, an inability to live up to one's own or others' expectations. But the plight of our children and adolescents is much worse. Child abuse, poverty, and homelessness are only a few factors that make the lives of a growing portion of our children miserable at best and chronically impaired at worst. No longer can or should we harbor the notion of childhood as being pristine, without pain and suffering.

> **Myth 2: Children and Adolescents Are Unable To Talk About Their Feelings**

Fact: Children as young as three and four have been shown to demonstrate an understanding of their affective states. The ability to identify one's affect and communicate about it has less to do with age than with innate ability. Not surprisingly, there are some children who are far better able to discuss their feelings than are most adults. When approaching a child or adolescent, one should assume that they can express their feelings and communicate with you.

An important source of difficulty is the potential presence of speech and language disorders among children and adolescents with psychopathology. This is not a rare phenomenon, but a rarely noted phenomenon. Studies clearly have noted that up to 75% of inpatient populations and 45% of outpatient populations have some form of communication disturbance, with the majority never being identified.

> ### Myth 3: Prepubertal Children Are Too Young To Be Depressed

Fact: Toddlers as young as four years old have been identified as being depressed, though at a rate less than among adults and adolescents. These children are not just unhappy or sad; they have major depressive disorders. This should not come as a surprise, given the early work of Spitz and his identification of "anaclitic depression" among infants. The limiting factor is not the age of the child, but the ability of the observer to identify the depression.

When depression is seen in such a young child, it is often asked, "What could a child that young have experienced that would make him or her depressed?" There are three answers: First, even extremely young children can experience severe trauma, the consequence of which is depression. Second, because of genetic disposition, some children will be more sensitive to stress than other children; and even the normal stresses of life can result in depression for these children. Third, with enough loading, these children may have a spontaneous onset of depression.

> ### Myth 4: Depression in Children and Adolescents Is Always Due to Something

Fact: This idea presupposes that a trauma or conflict in an individual's life is the "factor" that leads to depression. The problem with this assumption is that not all children, adolescents, or, for that matter, even adults will experience depression as a consequence of a "trauma." Also, there are those who will not experience relief even if a "trauma" is identified. This often is seen when patients are in psychotherapy or family therapy for protracted periods of time without progress.

> ### Myth 5: Expressed Sadness Always Accompanies Depression

Fact: One would assume that a depressed person should look sad or "depressed." Nothing could be further from the truth, especially in children and adolescents. A number of studies have demonstrated that "depression" in children and adolescents often is seen as anxiety (especially separation anxiety in younger children), phobias (often of school), opposition, aggression, or irritability, which then is labeled as either an oppositional disorder or a conduct disorder. These symptoms, not the depression, then become the main target for treatment.

One may ask, "Isn't this masked depression?" No! If the depression is not identified, then it is an unidentified depression, not a masked depression. The mislabeling of aggression or other symptoms leads one to apply a "therapy" that does not deal specifically with the problem of depression. Given the new diagnostic procedures, there is no reason to assume that a child, regardless of his or her symptoms, cannot be diagnosed, if depression exists.

> ### Myth 6: Depressed and Sad Feelings Are Short-Lived

Fact: For some, they are. But for those with a mood disorder, they are not. Often, children and adolescents will describe having been depressed for a number of years, with extremely severe periods and extended times of boredom, poor concentration, and irritability. Yet they are repeatedly told, "This will pass with time." It is often this statement that makes the child or adolescent feel embittered and hopeless; it can and does lead these youths to question the value of life and to desire that life come to an end.

> ### Myth 7: They Will Outgrow the Depression. It's Nothing To Worry About

Fact: Several longitudinal studies have shown that if a child has a major depressive disorder, the likelihood is greater than 60% that they will have a recurrence within five years. And if a dysthymic disorder is present, the child is more than 75% likely to have a Major Depressive Disorder within 5 years. If a child or adolescent has either of these depressive conditions, they should be monitored closely for either recurrence or relapses. For some children, adolescents, and their families, depression is a way of life, not a passing phase.

> ### Myth 8: Withdrawal Is Just a Part of Being an Adolescent

Fact: At one time, it was thought that all adolescents experienced "adolescent turmoil" and, as a consequence, were not able to be diagnosed as having a major psychiatric disorder. Whether called "adolescent turmoil" or "adolescent crazies," this undermines the ability to adequately assess adolescents, and when necessary, administer needed care. Social withdrawal is an issue of significance, and to mislabel it as a matter of normal development will unquestionably have lifelong impact.

When a child becomes withdrawn, it is important to assess why. Following a traumatic event, the adolescent may have the onset of a major depressive disorder, a psychotic disorder, or a substance abuse disorder. It is important to not turn your back on them or ignore them.

> ### Myth 9: Mad Versus Sad

Fact: Irritability is one of the most frequent symptoms seen in this population. It is most disconcerting when it is expressed as overt aggression, such as verbal outbursts, the destruction of property, or in extreme situations, physical aggression toward self or others.

Children and adolescents with depressive disorders often have "conduct disorders" or "oppositional defiant disorders" as well. The presence of diagnostic disorders occurring together is referred to as "comorbid disorders." Research has shown several disorders occurring frequently in children and adolescents with depression. In their order of frequency of co-occurrence are anxiety disorders (separation anxiety, phobias, panic attacks, and general anxiety), then disruptive behavioral disorders (attention deficit hyperactive disorders, oppositional defiant disorders, or conduct disorders).

Certainly, the hallmark of the disruptive behavioral disorder is the presence of aggressive symptoms that are extremely bothersome to those professionals who interact with depressed children and youth. One of the most difficult features of this complex illness is the ability to empathize with a chronically angry person who is depressed. Therefore, the therapist, rather than providing a bridge for children and youth to return from their depression, can get caught up in the chronic anger and end up also alienating them.

> ### Myth 10: All It Takes To Make a Depressed Child or Adolescent Better Is Kindness

Fact: This myth may be rephrased as "love will make it all better" or, when medications are suggested, "Hugs not drugs." One should not assume that these children will respond to kindness, nor should therapists be disappointed when their kindness is not rewarded. Many of these patients are unable to respond to the attempts of the therapist to be empathic. In fact, being with these children often can produce within their caregivers enormous feelings of pain, lethargy, and actual fatigue. Until a therapist becomes acutely aware that these conditions exist in himself, he will unconsciously withdraw from the patient, causing the patient to sense rejection.

The ability to make oneself aware of these myths and their consequences is of utmost importance if one wishes to be of help to these children and adolescents. We all harbor myths. It is the ability to rise above these myths in the pursuit of truth that determines the true worth of any profession and its professionals.

DIAGNOSTIC CRITERIA—*DSM–III–R*

The most frequently used diagnostic criteria, developed by the American Psychiatric Association, are published in the *Diagnostic and Statistical Manual, Fourth Edition (DSM–III–R)*. These diagnostic criteria, a group of signs and symptoms used to identify the syndrome of depression, have proven invaluable in the identification and treatment of depressed children, adolescents, and adults. A significant feature of the *DSM–III–R* is the classification of several types of depressive disorders. This classification allows for the study of patients in groups, rather than as individuals, thereby allowing the testing of hypotheses to determine the validity of our treatments. When a treatment is of "proven" value for a group of patients, there is some confidence in putting it to use. The two most frequently identified depressive disorders in children and adolescents are major depressive disorder and dysthymic disorder.

The following is the *DSM–III–R* diagnostic criteria for a Major Depressive Disorder:

- The presence of at least 5 of the following symptoms during a two-week period, at least one of which is symptom 1 or 2 listed below.
  1. Depressed mood or, in some cases, irritable mood.

2. Diminished interest or pleasure in all or almost all activities.
3. Significant weight gain or weight loss (when not dieting), increase or decrease in appetite, or failure to make expected weight gain in children.
4. Insomnia or hypersomnia.
5. Psychomotor retardation or agitation.
6. Fatigue or loss of energy.
7. Feelings of worthlessness or excessive guilt.
8. Diminished ability to think or concentrate; indecisiveness.
9. Morbid ideation, suicidal ideation, or a specific plan or attempt at suicide.

- Exclusion criteria. These symptoms and signs, if present, would exclude the diagnosis of a depressive disorder:
  1. Not initiated or maintained by an organic factor. If a medical disorder has been identified, or if the person is taking drugs, using alcohol, or taking prescription medications, a depressive disorder cannot be identified.
  2. A nonnormal reaction to death of a loved one.
  3. At no time have there been delusions or hallucinations for as long as two weeks in the absence of depressive symptoms. This is meant to exclude those with a primary "psychotic" disorder, such as schizophrenia.
  4. Not superimposed on schizophrenia, a delusion disorder, or other forms of psychotic disorder. Modifications of this criterion, such as the presence of the symptoms for prolonged periods, make the diagnosis one of a depressive disorder, recurrent or chronic. Also, there are degrees of major depressive disorders and noted seasonal variability.

Following is the *DSM–III–R* diagnostic criteria for a Dysthymic Disorder:

- Depressed mood (can be an irritable mood in children and adolescents) for most of the day, more days than not, as indicated either by subjective account or observation by others, for at least two years (one year for children and adolescents).
- Presence, while depressed, of at least two of the following:
  —Poor appetite or overeating.

—Insomnia or hypersomnia.

—Low energy or fatigue.

—Low self-esteem.

—Poor concentration or difficulty making decisions.

—Feelings of hopelessness.

- No evidence of an unequivocal major depressive episode during the first year of the disturbance. Never had a manic episode or hypermanic episode.
- Not superimposed on a chronic psychotic disorder, such as schizophrenia.
- Organic factor is not the basis of the disturbance, such as a chronic illness or a reaction to a medication.

One of the most challenging difficulties is identifying the presence of a depressive disorder when it occurs in a child or adolescent with possibly numerous emotional, behavioral, or cognitive disturbances. But, after the identification of a depressive disorder and after the child or adolescent receives treatment, some of these comorbid disturbances, such as separation anxiety or attention deficit disorders, may be seen as secondary. Others, such as learning disabilities or conduct disorders, may demand further case conceptualization and therapeutic intervention....

HOW FREQUENT ARE THESE DISORDERS?

There have been numerous studies attempting to determine the frequency of these disorders in children and adolescents. There are no broad epidemiological studies; this will have to await the completion of the Epidemiological Child Investigation recently begun by the National Institute of Mental Health. Most of the studies that have been completed have involved those who have been identified as having psychiatric difficulties, such as psychiatrically hospitalized children and adolescents. The exceptions have been the studies by Kashani, which focused on the identification of depression in those with physical or presumed physical illnesses. These have demonstrated that between 2% and 10% of children may have major depressive disorders, and this number increases significantly at adolescence to greater than 20%.

CONCLUSIONS

They are frequent, disabling, affect development, and possibly have irreversible consequences, yet depressive disorders among children and adolescents go unnoticed. They are true silent killers, potentially of the body, certainly of the human spirit.

Too often, these children and adolescents are mislabeled and rejected by the people to whom they come for help. Before presuming to care for these children and adolescents, we must admit our own myths about childhood and depression. Then, and only then, will the care for these youths be improved.

REFERENCES

American Psychiatric Association. (1987). *Diagnostic and statistical manual of mental disorders* (3rd ed., rev.). Washington, DC: American Psychiatric Association.

Bromberger, J. T., & Costello, E. J. (1992). Epidemiology of depression for clinicians. *Social Work, 37*(2), 120–126.

Burke, P. (1991). Depression in pediatric illness. *Behavior Modification, 5*(4), 486–500.

Carlson, G. A., & Kashani, J. H. (1988). Phenomenology of major depression from childhood through adulthood: Analysis of three studies. *American Journal of Psychiatry, 145,* 1222–1225.

Keller, M. B., Lavori, P. W., Beardslee, W. R., et al. (1991). Depression in children and adolescents: New data on "undertreatment" and a literature review on the efficacy of available treatments. *Journal of Affective Disorders, 21,* 163–171.

Kovacs, M., Feinberg, T. L., Crouse-Novak, M. A., et al. (1984). Depressive disorders in childhood: I. A longitudinal prospective study of characteristics and recovery. *Archives of General Psychiatry, 41,* 229–237.

Kovacs, M., Feinberg, T. L., Crouse-Novak, M. A., et al. (1984). Depressive disorders in childhood: II. A longitudinal study of the risk for a subsequent major depression. *Archives of General Psychiatry, 41,* 643–649.

Ryan, N. D., Puig-Antich, J., Ambrosini, P., et al. (1987). The clinical picture of major depression in children and adolescents. *Archives of General Psychiatry, 44*(10), 854–861.

Spitz, R., & Wolf, K. M. (1946). Anaclitic depression: An inquiry into the genesis of psychiatric conditions in early childhood. *Psychoanalytic Study of the Child, 2*(3), 313–342.

Weissman, M. M., Gammon, D., John, K., et al. (1987). Children of depressed parents. *Archives of General Psychiatry, 44,* 847–853.

STUDENTS WITH SUICIDAL THOUGHTS AND ACTIONS

Suicide is deadly and suicidal attempts are risky. The only way to prevent a suicide is to prevent a suicidal attempt. This statement implies that teachers can be taught the risk factors of suicidal students and the accompanying life events that precipitate their behaviors. Research studies have confirmed that suicidal behavior is more often observed in troubled students who have been abused, traumatized, or abandoned, or are depressed or on drugs. These high-risk students may be experiencing unbearable emotional stress and may think of suicide as a way out of a painful world.

In the past, educators didn't have a mandate to intervene. Now, a growing number of states have passed comprehensive laws regarding attempted suicidal behaviors. Florida legislators have mandated training for all high school teachers in the areas of suicide detection, interventions, and referral skills. Although the schools are not totally responsible for suicidal acts or behaviors, they can serve as the first line of defense in recognizing and supporting these at-risk students. McGee and Guetzloe (1988) have summarized the relevant research findings in this area and have made the following recommendations to teachers:

1. Be ready to take drastic action if you think a student is in danger. Let the student know you care. It is far better to err in the direction of doing too much than too little.

2. Be ready to talk about suicidal behavior without being shocked. There are no inconvenient times to talk about suicidal thoughts and plans.

3. Never take a suicidal threat or gesture casually. Do something. Mobilize your available resources.

4. Don't be afraid to bring up the topic and question the student closely and carefully about any possible suicidal plan.

5. Encourage the student to talk (i.e., "You seem troubled. Tell me what you are thinking and I might understand how difficult it is for you at this time.").

6. Don't leave a suicidal student alone. Stay with the student until another adult arrives.

7. Get rid of any object in the immediate environment which the student could use in a hurtful manner.

8. Do not promise to keep a student's suicidal behavior secret.

9. Try to get a commitment from the student not to inflict self-harm. If possible, get the student to sign a contract with you. The following wording can be modified as necessary:

1. I, _____, agree not to kill myself, attempt to kill myself, or bring any harm to myself during the period from _____ to _____ (dates).

2. I agree to get enough sleep and to eat regularly and well.

3. I agree to get rid of things I could use to kill myself.

4. I agree that if I have a bad time and feel that I might hurt myself, I will call _____ at _____ (telephone number) or the Suicide and Crisis Center at _____ (telephone number).

Signed _____

Witness _____

Date _____

10. Be sure to connect the student with a crisis counselor or suicide prevention worker.

THE next article was written by Eleanor Guetzloe, a professor of special education at the University of Southern Florida and a national expert in suicide prevention training. Guetzloe presents an extensive and thorough overview of suicide risk factors, precipitating events, and intervention. This article should be read periodically, as a reminder of the seriousness of this widespread problem.

ARTICLE 7.8

ANSWERING THE CRY FOR HELP—
SUICIDAL THOUGHTS AND ACTIONS

Eleanor C. Guetzloe

Suicide accounts for the deaths of more than 5,000 young people each year in the United States alone. Authorities estimate that for every completed suicide, there are probably from 100 to 350 attempts and many more threats and thoughts. Estimates of attempts among children and adolescents usually range from 50,000 to 500,000 per year (Allen, 1987).

According to the results of a recent Gallup Poll, one-third of American 15- to 19-year-olds had thought about suicide, 15% had seriously considered killing themselves, and 6% had made actual attempts (Peterson, 1991). In other studies, 8% to 9% of high school students admitted to one or more attempts, and up to 63% reported some degree of suicidal ideation (Harkavy-Friedman et al., 1987; Smith & Crawford, 1986).

Suicidal behavior also has been noted in very young children. In a sample of 16 preschoolers who had been referred to a child psychiatry outpatient clinic after seriously injuring themselves or attempting to do so, 13 had made multiple suicide attempts and expressed specific reasons for wanting to die (Rosenthal & Rosenthal, 1984).

Suicide attempts lead to the hospitalization of an estimated 12,000 youngsters ages 14 and under in the United States each year (Berman, 1986; Matter & Matter, 1984). Many other attempts (as many as 7 out of 8 in this age group) do not require medical treatment and are therefore not included in this estimate (Berman, 1986).

Among high-school-age youngsters, approximately one-fourth of attempts require emergency treatment. However, most suicide attempts by children and adolescents are never reported to mental health professionals or school personnel. Hospital personnel often learn of previous attempts only when a more serious attempt requires hospitalization.

RISK FACTORS FOR SUICIDAL BEHAVIOR

Risk factors specifically associated with completed suicide in young people include the following (Kupfer, 1991):

- Psychiatric disorders, including affective disorder (particularly depression), schizophrenia, borderline personality disorder, conduct disorder, and substance abuse.

- Parental loss and family disruption.

- Familial characteristics, such as predisposition to affective illness or being the biological relative of a suicide victim.

- Biological correlates, such as low concentrations of a serotonin metabolite and a dopamine metabolite in the cerebrospinal fluid.

- Certain personality traits, including impulsivity, aggressivity, cognitive rigidity, excessive perfectionism, and hopelessness.

- Other factors, including homosexuality, being a friend of a suicide victim, access to lethal weapons, and previous suicidal behavior.

Among children and adolescents who have been treated in emergency rooms for suicide attempts, the following individual and family factors, similar to those listed above, have been noted: (a) past history of psychotherapy; (b) aggressiveness and hostility; and (c) current psychiatric diagnosis. The families of these youngsters had histories of mental illness, suicide, drug and alcohol abuse, group or foster placement, unemployment of father, and father absence (Kovacs & Puig-Antich, 1991).

PRECIPITATING EVENTS

The presence of a situational crisis is an important warning sign of potential suicide in a child or adolescent. Among the most common events that precipitate suicide attempts are losses resulting from disruptions of relationships with girlfriends or boyfriends, problems at school or in the community, and conflicts within the family. Among younger children, precipitating events include (a) severe punishment (or fear of punishment), (b) a desire to join a dead relative (or pet), (c) feeling guilty over parents' divorce, and (d) modeling of media events. Any event that contributes to feelings of stress, depression, helplessness, hopelessness, and low self-esteem may in turn lead to suicidal behavior in young people.

EXAMPLES OF SUICIDAL THOUGHTS, THREATS, AND ATTEMPTS

The following actual cases illustrate the suicidal verbalizations and behaviors of children ages 5 to 17 who were hospitalized in the same facility because of suicidal attempts, threats, or thoughts. Each of these youngsters suffered from loss, humiliation, real or perceived rejection or neglect, physical or sexual abuse, or psychiatric disorders. All of them expressed very specific reasons for their suicidal behavior, as follows (Guetzloe, 1993):

- A five-year-old explained that he sees cars and guns on the walls and the ceiling. "The cars tell me to hurt myself—dead." The child tried to jump from a balcony.
- A six-year-old, who had been abandoned by both his parents and foster parents, said that he was "sick and tired of everyone leaving" him. He tried to drown himself in the bathtub.
- A seven-year-old was angry with his mother for remarrying. He stated, "I'm going to kill my mom and then me so Dad won't see her with that man."
- An eight-year-old "felt sad" because his grandfather had died and wanted to join him in Heaven.
- A nine-year-old, who had been sexually abused for years, expressed sadness "about all the bad people in the world who hurt children." She threatened suicide by pointing a knife at her stomach. Her mother took the knife away.
- A nine-year-old was angry because his mother would not let him go to the movies with his friend. He put the entire contents of a bottle of Tylenol in his mouth. He then spit it out and asked, "Can I go now?"
- "I was feeling depressed and like there was no way out. Last resort is how I felt at the time … either raise my grades or kill myself. I decided to raise my grades. Other things also was upsetting. I have many girl problems. Sometimes I feel like an outcast. I don't want to be gay. People should give other people a chance to prove themselves so if you ever feel the last resort, think about it hard first. People say that I'm different. Maybe they are mad because they're not like me, but they talk about

me every day about something. Just be yourself. Something very good will happen to you."

- A ten-year-old, who had been sexually abused, said that she hated herself and tried to strangle herself with a shoestring while in the psychiatric unit.
- A 13-year-old female tried to hang herself with a bed-sheet. Her mother found her while she was still breathing. "I see Beth and hear her voice telling me to kill myself." Beth is the girl's invisible friend.
- "I want to feel the pain because I can't feel anything anymore." The 13-year-old, a victim of abuse, attempted to asphyxiate herself with carbon monoxide emitted by an automobile.
- "I wish my life was over!" The 15-year-old's identity as a lesbian had "leaked out" at her high school. She attempted suicide by cutting her wrist and swallowing her prescription pills.
- A 17-year-old was driving while drinking and ran his car into a tree. He suffered severe head injuries but lived to tell of his anger over his parents' divorce.
- A 17-year-old swallowed "a few pills" (not a lethal dose) to "get back at Mom" for not letting her date a 30-year-old man.

ASSESSMENT OF SUICIDE RISK

The assessment of suicidal risk in young people consists of an evaluation of the degree to which the various risk factors and/or precipitating events listed above are present in their lives at that specific time. It should be noted that it is not the type of loss that is critical, but rather how much the specific loss means to the individual. For example, many children are not concerned about grades, but a child with a high grade point average may agonize over a B.

Informal assessment of risk may be carried out in the school or other facility by an internal team of professionals, but only a trained professional should conduct a formal assessment and make judgments regarding the seriousness of suicidal behavior. It is important that nonprofessionals (a) recognize the limits of their competence and (b) make appropriate referrals to professionals with skills and experience in working with young people and with knowledge about suicide.

RESPONSIBILITIES OF PERSONNEL IN SCHOOL AND TREATMENT FACILITIES

The primary responsibilities of teachers, counselors, and other staff include:

- To be aware of the risk factors for suicide.
- To detect the signs of potential suicide, including suicidal threats and ideation.
- To report such behavior to the contact person or crisis team within the facility or program.
- To secure emergency medical services, if necessary.
- To make immediate referrals to child study teams or other personnel for further assessment.
- To provide immediate and continuing emotional support and supervision for the suicidal youngster.
- To report to parents and/or other appropriate individuals and agencies (and to document these reports).
- To help parents in securing assistance from school and community resources.
- To provide long-term follow-up services within the program. (Guetzloe, 1989, 1991)

PROVIDING EMOTIONAL SUPPORT AND SUPERVISION

All members of the staff in the school or treatment facility who come in contact with a suicidal child or adolescent should be informed of a suicide threat so they can help provide supervision and support. It is important to have the youngster understand that the adults in the setting are deeply concerned about his or her welfare, and staff should be prepared to respond quickly to verbalizations of suicidal intent. Youngsters who are depressed or suicidal may misinterpret uncertainty or failure to respond to be lack of caring. Staff should practice (in role play) what they would say to a student who expresses thoughts of worthlessness, despair, or suicide, so they will be prepared when the situation presents itself.

The most commonly cited warning signs of potential suicide include (a) extreme changes in behavior, (b) signs of depression, (c) making final arrangements or "saying good-bye," and (d) procuring the means (for example, a gun or pills). Most crucial of all is the presence of a detailed, feasible, and lethal plan. Any staff member should not be afraid to ask a youngster directly about a suicide plan, using such questions as: "Are you planning to hurt yourself? How do you plan to do this? Do you have a gun or pills? When do you plan to do this?" In addition to the questions, the staff member should express his or her concern and caring, continue to listen, and indicate his or her willingness to help in any way possible. The young person should be kept under close supervision and must not be left alone.

SUGGESTED INTERVENTIONS BY SCHOOL AND TREATMENT STAFF

Some positive change in the youngster's life, no matter how small, should be affirmed immediately to prove that the situation is not hopeless. Schneidman (1985), who recommends such action for therapists, has called this a "J. N. D." or "Just Noticeable Difference." The major stresses that led to the suicidal behavior should be identified, and steps should be taken to reduce those stresses. For example, dropping a class, changing a schedule, providing a tutor, or removing a threat of punishment may provide hope for a student who is experiencing problems at school.

> The 17-year-old youth was a good student, but he had been placed (through "computer error") in a class in which he was failing. His grade point average would be ruined, and his choices for college would be limited. He had become increasingly despondent and had told his counselor he would rather die than lose his chances for the college he wanted. When the counselor requested a schedule change, the principal's response was, "If we changed one student's schedule, we'd have another hundred requests. One failing grade won't hurt him."

This story had a happy ending. Upon receipt of a written memorandum from the counselor outlining the student's symptoms, the risk of suicide, and the principal's responsibility in this regard, the principal reversed her position. The obvious point is that it was possible to make the change (Guetzloe, 1989).

Berman and Jobes (1991) have discussed the themes of escape, relief, control, and power that appear during therapy with suicidal youth. They suggest that the intended goals of suicidal behavior involve attempts to replace pain, helplessness, hopelessness, or powerlessness, feelings and cognitions that are common to the suicidal state. The immediate tasks of a teacher, counselor, or therapist are to provide hope and to instill in the youngster some feeling of being in control. However, it is important not to promise any change that cannot be accomplished; a suicidal child should not be subjected to further disappointment. The focus of the changes, therefore, is on provisions that are under the control of the staff in that setting—whether school or treatment facility.

WORKING WITH THE FAMILY

One of the primary responsibilities of the school or treatment facility is to maintain communication with parents or guardians. Parents may not be aware of problems with school, peers, or community. They must be notified immediately of any signs of suicidal behavior so they can provide support and seek assistance.

Parents also should be advised of their responsibility for securing emergency evaluation, treatment, or other intervention for a suicidal child. It is crucial that they understand that all suicidal behavior must be taken seriously.

A 15-year-old girl shot herself in the abdomen during an agriculture class at a junior high school. Police said that she had brought the 22-caliber handgun from home. The girl was transported to a local hospital, where she was listed in stable condition. The girl's stepfather said that she was upset about problems with her boyfriend. Her mother said that the shooting "wasn't really a suicide attempt … she just wanted attention."

Ignoring or belittling suicidal verbalizations or actions may be misinterpreted by a young person as an invitation to die.

Further attempts may occur. Without the desired "attention," the child may try again—and succeed (Guetzloe, 1989).

REFERRALS TO OTHER PROFESSIONALS

Within the school, internal referrals can be made to counselors, school psychologists, and special education assessment teams. Berman and Jobes (1991) have suggested that schools should maintain lists of therapists who are skilled in working with suicidal youth, so that this information can be available quickly to parents and guardians.

Intervention in the home, school, and community requires considerable interagency cooperation. To ensure that services have been sought and are being furnished, a designated member of the staff in the school or treatment facility should maintain contact with the other individuals, organizations, and institutions that are working with the suicidal youngster and the family.

FOLLOW-UP WITH A SUICIDAL YOUNGSTER

After the immediate crisis has been resolved, a suicidal youngster still requires supervision and support for an extended period of time. An intervention plan should be developed for a suicidal child that includes the following (Guetzloe, 1989):

- Some immediate and positive change in the young person's life—at home, in school, and in the community.
- Provision of therapy, counseling, and contact with supportive individuals.
- Continuing supervision and support.
- Delivery of whatever has been promised.

SUMMARY

This discussion has focused on (a) the risk factors associated with suicide attempts, threats, and ideation in children and adolescents and (b) suggested interventions for faculty and staff of schools and treatment facilities. Other information regarding the problem of suicide in young people is available from the resources listed below.

REFERENCES

Allen, B. (1987). Youth suicide. *Adolescence, 22,* 271–290.

Berman, A. L. (1986). *Epidemiology of youth suicide.* Unpublished manuscript.

Berman, A. L., & Jobes, D. A. (1991). *Adolescent suicide assessment and intervention.* Washington, DC: American Psychological Association.

Cohen-Sandler, R., Berman, A. L., & King, R. A. (1982). A follow-up study of hospitalized suicidal children. *Journal of the American Academy of Child Psychiatry, 21,* 398–403.

Garfinkel, B. D., Froese, A., & Hood, J. (1972). Suicide attempts in children and adolescents. *American Journal of Psychiatry, 139,* 1257–1261.

Guetzloe, E. (1991). *Depression and suicide: Special education students at risk.* Reston, VA: The Council for Exceptional Children.

Guetzloe, E. C. (1989). *Youth suicide: What the educator should know.* Reston, VA: The Council for Exceptional Children.

Harkavy-Friedman, J. M., Asnis, G. M., Boeck, M., & DiFiore, J. (1987). Prevalence of specific suicidal behaviors in a high school sample. *American Journal of Psychiatry, 16,* 313–325.

Kovacs, M., & Puig-Antich, J. (1991). Major psychiatric disorders as risk factors in youth suicide. In L. Davidson & M. Linnoila (Eds.), *Risk factors for youth suicide* (pp. 27–143). New York: Hemisphere Publishing Corporation.

Kupfer, D. J. (1991). Summary of the national conference on risk factors for youth suicide. In L. Davidson & M. Linnoila (Eds.), *Risk factors for youth suicide* (pp. xv–xxii). New York: Hemisphere Publishing Corporation.

Matter, D., & Matter, R. (1984). Suicide among elementary school children: A serious concern for counselors. *Elementary School Guidance and Counseling, 18,* 260–267.

Otto, U. (1972). Suicidal acts by children and adolescents, a follow-up study. *Acta Psychiatrica Scandinavia.* Supplement 233, 7–123. (see p. 141, #31).

Peterson, K. S. (1991, April 2). Suicide by older teens on upswing. *USA Today,* p. 1.

Pfeffer, C. R. (1986). *The suicidal child.* New York: The Guilford Press.

Rosenthal, P. A., & Rosenthal, S. (1984). Suicidal behavior by preschool children. *American Journal of Psychiatry, 141,* 520–525.

Shneidman, E. S. (1985). *Definition of suicide.* New York: Wiley.

Smith, K., & Crawford, S. (1986). Suicidal behavior among "normal" high school students. *Suicide and Life-Threatening Behavior, 16,* 313–325.

GAY AND LESBIAN STUDENTS

There are open and hostile differences within and between school boards, educators, parents, and community leaders regarding how students who are gay or lesbian should be treated in schools. Adult attitudes toward homosexuality range from a belief that it is a personal sinful choice against the will of God to a belief that it is an innate biological process over which the individual has little control. This latter group advocates that homosexuality needs to be recognized as a development difference and not a form of sexual deviancy or pathology.

One reason this topic is difficult to resolve in schools is the existence of homophobic feelings among the staff. Although many educators are traditionalists, they are expected to model and pass on the acceptable behaviors, values, and beliefs of the community. Students who are gay and lesbian can stir up strong negative feelings in staff that make it difficult for them to reach out to these students in a caring way.

We believe that public schools have a legal and ethical mandate to provide a safe and accepting school environment for all students. We also believe that all significant change begins with staff and not with students. We feel that the behavior of staff who ridicule students and perpetuate negative stereotypes should not be tolerated. Just as we encourage peers to speak up against the actions of a bully, we encourage staff to speak up and confront their colleagues when they depreciate gay and lesbian students. This will take some courage. The January 2005 issue of *Youth Today* published a study by the Gay, Lesbian and Straight Education Network. Eighty-one percent of gay students reported that teachers did not intervene when they witnessed homophobic comments by students or staff.

It is not uncommon for gay and lesbian adolescents to want to tell their parents about their sexual thoughts but to fear "coming out." They fear that their parents and friends will alienate them. This may explain why too many of these students end up running away or being rejected from their home. They become homeless and are at high risk of becoming exploited and victimized by other adults.

One active and powerful support group is Parents, Families and Friends of Lesbians and Gays (www.pflag.org), a national organization with chapters in every major city. It is a safe, inclusive support group with the goal of reaching out and providing needed services.

IN the next article, Kathy Gill discusses the Gay and Lesbian Education Commission of Los Angeles's program to curb discrimination and sexual harassment of all students.

ARTICLE 7.9

MAINTAINING THE DIGNITY AND RIGHTS OF GAY AND LESBIAN STUDENTS

Kathy J. Gill

PROTECTION FROM HARASSMENT

School districts are public institutions that have an obligation to serve all children and parents. In 1992, the Los Angeles Unified School District Board of Education established the Gay and

Lesbian Education Commission to uphold Title IX, a federal law that prohibits discrimination against, and sexual harassment of, all students. Educators have a responsibility to provide a safe environment conducive to learning. A school's failure to live up to its responsibilities now has greater legal and financial implications. Legal action can also be taken against individual teachers and administrators.

Effective implementation of policies regarding discrimination and harassment requires the involvement of all stakeholders in their creation and distribution. Workshops and staff training are essential for communicating the organization's stance on and concern about issues of safety and equal access. Establishing a reporting and monitoring system signals to involved individuals the importance of compliance, and having an office, such as an Equity Compliance Office, is tangible evidence that harassment and discrimination will not be tolerated.

Sexual harassment is not a new issue, but it has become a crucial factor in dealing with vulnerable adolescents. A national study on sexual harassment of K–12 students documented the overarching existence of such harassment (American Association of University Women [AAUW], 1993): Four out of five students (81%) had experienced some form of sexual harassment in their school life. Such harassment usually occurred openly in classrooms and hallways rather than in secluded areas of the school. Girls were more likely to be targeted in public places, whereas boys were more likely to be harassed in less public places such as the locker room or boys' bathroom. According to the study, a majority of boys (76%) and girls (85%) had been harassed at school. One third of these students had first experienced sexual harassment in Grade 6 or earlier. The most common harassers of students were other students, but 18% had been harassed by adults in the school. Most students didn't know if their schools had a sexual harassment policy.

Students rarely told a teacher or school adult when they'd been harassed. In the AAUW study, *male students noted that being called gay was the most upsetting form of harassment.* Girls were nearly five times as likely as boys to be afraid at school following sexual harassment. Although sexual harassment at school has serious negative impacts on the education of all students, girls, who were harassed more frequently, reported a more negative impact on their academic life.

From *Reclaimnig Children and Youth,* 7(1), 1998, pp. 25–27. Copyright by Reclaiming Children and Youth, Inc. Reprinted with permission.

A SEXUAL HARASSMENT CHECKLIST

One of the challenges facing educators is translating theories regarding sexual harassment into identifiable, observable acts. The following checklist for assisting staff in identifying and reporting acts of sexual harassment was developed by Deanne Neeman, director for education equity compliance, and approved by the leadership of the Los Angeles Unified School District.

- Being the target of sexual comments, jokes, gestures, or looks: direct degrading sexual remarks and sexual putdowns; body comments; and public catcalls, grunts, and/or whistles
- Being forced to kiss someone
- Being forced to do something sexual other than kissing
- Being touched, grabbed, and/or pinched in a sexual way: groping, fondling
- Being subjected to mooning and flashing
- Being the target of sexual rumors: constant sexual innuendo
- Having clothing pulled or pulled down: skirt flip-ups, spiking or pulling down pants
- Being shown, given, or left unwanted sexual pictures or notes: sexually explicit pictures and magazines, use of sexual computer files or disks, and passing "dirty" notes
- Being blocked or cornered in a sexual way
- Being called gay or lesbian
- Being the target of written sexual messages or graffiti (on bathroom walls, lockers, etc.)
- Being spied on while dressing or showering at school

Because gay and lesbian students receive a disproportionate amount of psychological and physical abuse, they often need additional protection and support. It has been said that one of the loneliest and most conflicted adolescents in any high school is the gay or lesbian student.

A great many schools do not adequately protect gay youth, and teachers often are reluctant to stop harassment or rebut homophobic remarks. Gibson (1989) reported that 28% of gay and lesbian youth drop out of school because of discomfort in the school environment. Eighty percent of gay and lesbian youth are victims of insults and 40% reported being threatened by physical attack. Twenty-two percent of boys and 29%

of girls reported being physically attacked by other students. Seven percent reported being physically hurt by a teacher (Pilkington & D'Augelli, 1995).

The leading cause of deaths in the gay and lesbian youth group is suicide. Lesbian, gay, and bisexual youth suicides represent 30% of all teen suicides. These youth are two to six times more likely than heterosexual peers to attempt suicide (Gibson, 1989; Marino, 1995). Anti-gay discrimination also has serious effects upon non-gay youth: They learn to hate and discriminate (Hunter & Schaecher, 1995).

When adolescents do "come out," they are usually alienated from peer and other social groups. Even the adult gay population often turns a cold shoulder in fear that they will be perceived as "recruiters" if they offer assistance. Lesbian, gay, and bisexual teens are often hesitant to seek help from school counselors or teachers (Marino, 1995).

LACK OF ACCURATE INFORMATION
ABOUT GAY AND LESBIAN STUDENTS

Unfortunately, many education staff members have inaccurate or distorted information regarding gay and lesbian students. As part of our mission to address staff education on issues of sexual orientation, we developed two basic documents, which contain the following information:

USEFUL DEFINITIONS

Bisexuality: Sexual attraction to and/or sexual behavior with both sexes.

Coming Out: The process of becoming aware of one's sexual orientation, accepting it, and telling others about it. Coming out is a never-ending process.

What might lesbians/gays be afraid of?

- Rejection, loss of relationships
- Harassment/abuse
- Being thrown out of the family and/or house
- Being forced to undergo psychotherapy
- Having their lover arrested
- Loss of financial support

- Losing their job
- Physical violence

Why might lesbians/gays want to come out?

- End the hiding game
- Live honestly
- Feel closer to family and friends
- Be able to feel "whole" around others
- Stop wasting energy by hiding all of the time
- Feel a sense of integrity
- Make a statement that "gay is ok"

Gay: Men and women who accept their homosexual orientation and identify themselves as being gay. There are gay people in every sector of society and among every ethnic and racial group.

Homophobia: The intolerance of homosexuality, bisexuality, and lesbians and gays. Homophobia is the root of anti-gay violence.

Homosexuality: Sexual attraction to a person of the same sex. It is normal, has no known cause, and is not an illness.

In the Closet: Being secret about one's sexual orientation. This means having to avoid or elude the truth in order to protect oneself from discrimination and anti-gay violence.

SPECIAL CONSIDERATIONS FOR WORKING WITH GAY AND LESBIAN STUDENTS

- Be yourself
- Be aware of your comfort level as well as your personal biases
- Establish trust
- Use vocabulary that the student uses (i.e., if the student uses "gay" or "lesbian" to identify themselves, use that term)
- Show respect for the sensitivities of students
- Do not make assumptions or attempt to generalize about or label a student's orientation
- Be aware that students may be experiencing grief issues due to rejection by family, church, classmates, and/or friends

- Be aware that parents may or may not know about the student's sexual orientation
- Know when and where to seek help
- Help the student build a support system (critical)

In addition to developing a comprehensive system of recognizing, reporting, and dealing with student sexual harassment and sexual orientation issues, the Los Angeles Unified School District has developed inclusive lesson plans at the elementary and secondary levels on the following topics:

- Name Calling
- Targets of Hate
- Heroes and Role Models: They Defied the Odds
- Family Diversity
- Fighting Hate Crimes

The Gay and Lesbian Education Commission of the Los Angeles Unified School District is an example of how a public school district can be proactive by reaching out and protecting the dignity and rights of gay and lesbian students. Probably the most effective strategies for assisting students with sexual orientation issues is Project 10, a support group for gay, lesbian, bisexual, transgender, and questioning youth. Project 10 is a unique dropout-prevention program founded in 1984 by Dr. Virginia Uribe. It is used on most Los Angeles high school campuses.

REFERENCES

American Association of University Women. (1993). *Hostile hallways: The AAUW survey on sexual harassment in American schools.* Washington, DC: The Foundation.

Gibson, P. (1989). *Report of the Secretary's Task Force on Youth Suicide.* Washington, DC: Department of Health and Human Services.

Hunter, J., & Schaecher, R. (1995). Gay and lesbian adolescents. In R. L.

Edwards et al. (Eds.), *Encyclopedia of social work* (19th ed., pp. 1055, 1059). New York: NASW Press.

Marino, T. W. (1995, May). To be young and gay in America. *Counseling Today,* *37*(11).

Pilkington, N. W., & D'Augelli, A. R. (1995). Victimization of gay, lesbian, and bisexual youth in community settings. *Journal of Community Psychology,* *23*(1), 34–36.

STUDENTS WITH EATING DISORDERS

The next two articles discuss the weighty problem of two eating disorders, obesity and anorexia nervosa. Although the latter is considered the most deadly of all psychiatric disorders, obesity increasingly threatens public health and individuals' quality of life, with consequences that include cardiorespiratory disease, diabetes, some cancers, gall bladder disease, osteoarthritis, and threats to mental well-being. One root cause is societal "advancement," which has produced abundant and cheap energy-dense food and surrounded us with energy-saving devices and attractive sedentary leisure activities, such as television and movies. The film *Supersize Me,* directed by Morgan Spurlock (2004), exemplifies the overabundance in our society.

Perhaps the media also are to blame as they spend over $30 billion a year in advertising. Not only do mouth-watering images of pizza and deluxe sandwiches bombard us daily, but also beautiful bodies seem to be marketing tools for everything from cars to beer. When women (and some men) are dissatisfied with bodies that do not match up to their ideal, they spend billions on cosmetics, diet plans, and plastic surgery. Perhaps Nikki, described Article 7.11, fell prey to this cruel commercialized society as she attempted to be accepted by her family, friends, and self.

From 1970 to 2000, the percentage of overweight school-age children increased by 15.3% (National Center for Health Statistics, 2002). One of every 10 American females at some time in their life suffer from the eating disorders anorexia nervosa or bulimia nervosa. Parents and teachers must be aware of these serious disorders before a healthy food and lifestyle plan can begin. In severe cases, physician consultations or comprehensive treatment programs will be necessary.

THE following two articles will help teachers better understand the world of the "fat kid" and that of young girls who choose to go on starvation diets, risking their lives.

ARTICLE 7.10

UNDERSTANDING THE WORLD OF THE "FAT KID": CAN SCHOOLS HELP PROVIDE A BETTER EXPERIENCE?

Kenneth R. Fox and Laurel D. Edmunds

One of the most worrying threats to public health and life quality … is obesity. This is a serious illness that affects approximately 1 in 5 adults in most Westernized countries. Ironically, as many people in the world suffer from obesity as suffer from starvation. In the United States and the United Kingdom more than 50% of the adult population is now seriously overweight.… Genetics plays an important role, because individuals who have inherited a predisposition to storing fat will become most susceptible in what has become a toxic environment for obesity. For those persons with a strong predisposition, obesity can be considered a disability.

Unfortunately, our children have not escaped this epidemic. Evidence from the National Health and Nutrition Examination Surveys (NHANES) in the United States and the National Study of Health and Growth (NSHG) in the United Kingdom has shown that children, as well as adults, are becoming seriously fatter (Flegal, 1999; Hughes, Li, Chinn, & Rona, 1997). In addition, the most affected people seem to be children who are already overweight—The fat seem to be getting fatter while the thin remain the same!

Obesity has both short- and long-term consequences for youngsters. For instance, the chances of becoming an obese adult increase the earlier that a youngster becomes fat and the longer that he or she remains that way (Flegal, 1999). The belief is that these children may be developing habits that perpetuate long-term obesity. Also, many overweight children begin to display early risk indicators for coronary heart disease, even symptoms of *adult-onset diabetes,* and to suffer from respiratory problems. Due to these factors, overweight children are at a short-term risk for ill health. Of particular significance to this article is the fact that overweight children also are at an increased risk for psychological problems. Fatness, which is seen as highly undesirable, is also associated with negative per-

From *Reclaiming Children and Youth, 9*(3), 2000, pp. 177–181. Copyright by Reclaiming Children and Youth, Inc. Reprinted with permission. *Note.* The data discussed in this article are from Laurel Edmunds's doctoral dissertation, which was conducted under the supervision of Ken Fox. As yet, they have been published only in abstract form.

sonal characteristics such as laziness and greediness to such an extent that many children report they would prefer to have a physical disability than be viewed as fat. Fat children thus are more likely to be ostracized, to suffer rejection, to become socially isolated, or to acquire a distorted body image.

Clearly, it is up to professionals and parents to help these children through their difficulties so that they can develop into healthy and happy adults, even if they do not reach optimal weight. Because children spend up to 45% of their waking time in school or at school-related activities, teachers and school administrators have the potential to contribute positively to better health.

FAT CHILDREN'S PERCEPTIONS

Clearly, we adults would be able to prepare a more helpful and friendlier school environment for children who are fat if we better understood how they feel about their fatness. Recently, we conducted 30 interviews with extremely overweight 9- to 10-year-olds in the United Kingdom that provided us with important insights into how they psychologically process their condition (Edmunds & Fox, 1997).

DO FAT CHILDREN KNOW THEY ARE FAT?

Based on the findings from our interviews, it is evident that fat children are aware of their condition. Nearly all the overweight children appeared to be acutely aware of either their own fatness or that of others. They became aware of this once they displayed a significantly greater amount of body fat than the average-weight child (> 35mm summed triceps and calf), which amounts to being considered "chubby" for most. This acquisition of knowledge occurred in several ways:

1. Direct self-observation: "When I get up in the morning, my belly's poking out and I can see."

2. Comparisons with photographs of their body from earlier times: "I just look a lot bigger now; it's horrible."

3. Older clothes no longer fitting or new ones being too small, so that all clothes are tight: "They don't look good on me because they show my fatness."

4. Comparisons with others' bodies: "I don't look very nice. When I'm dressed up, I look all right … slimmer.… but I feel and look different to the others."

Weight related name-calling or teasing from other children is very potent. Children reported that name-calling occurred while they were walking to school, at recess, and in class. As a great majority of overweight children mentioned this problem, it would appear that name-calling is pervasive. Performance comparisons often provided the basis for derogatory comments. One normal-weight boy mentioned that name-calling was worse for an overweight boy during breaks at school:

If you're overweight, you're going to be made fun of. People say he (overweight boy) can't even see his feet and make fun of him like that. I hear it a lot when I'm playing football.

These experiences extend into physical education activities, where performance is public, participation is required, and the opportunities for social comparison are heightened. A perception of poor physical ability is often the key. Overweight children of this age have become aware that they are not performing as well as other, less obese children. One girl could no longer do backward rolls and said that her fat "got in the way," and one of the boys wanted to be able to walk and swim "without getting worn out." "I can't run as fast as my friends," another child confessed sadly. They realize that they have to work harder in physical education (P.E.) classes because they see their red faces and feel their labored breathing. Comments from other children confirm these self-perceptions: "When I run, people take the mickey [are sarcastic with me] and say my belly wobbles." "When I'm running 'round and everybody runs past and shouts 'fatty' and all that, it makes me feel bad."

Changing clothes was an important reason for disliking P.E., particularly for the heavier girls: "It makes me look bad." Other contributory factors were wearing the same clothes (P.E. uniform) and performing the same tasks as average-weight children, both of which are unintentionally ideal for making negative comparisons. The result is that the overweight children in our study preferred to participate in activities *outside* the school environment, where they were able to make their own choices:

I don't really like sports ... it's my worst subject. I like playing out of school best because you can do what you want.... you have to do what the teacher says and you have to try and at home you don't have to try; I like doing games 'n that, but I'd rather walk and ride my bike and swim than do it in school. It's easier, not so many people annoying me (name calling).

Surprisingly, in general, most overweight children remained positive about physical activity and were aware of the associated health benefits, despite their trying experiences.

HOW DOES BEING OVERWEIGHT AFFECT CHILDREN?

Results for overweight children on the Self-Perception Profile for Children (Halter, 1985) indicated that the majority scored lower in positive perceptions of physical appearance and athletic ability than average-weight children. However, for the majority, an awareness of being fat did not seem to negatively affect self-esteem or perceptions of social acceptance. Although some children experienced a lower sense of worth, for most of the group in the Halter study, their excess fatness did not seem to be of central importance. It may be that youngsters of 9 or 10 are still rather optimistic in their self-vision or that their experiences have not devastated them. Perhaps, other aspects of their lives compensate for the troubles brought on by being overweight. Regardless, their awareness of their obesity clearly shapes their attitudes toward physical activity, and evidence from research (Gortmaker et al., 1996) has indicated that by the early teen years, youngsters who are overweight are less likely to take part in sports and more likely to watch TV, thereby worsening the problem.

HOW DO CHILDREN MANAGE THEIR FATNESS?

Overweight children, particularly girls, usually report engaging in a variety of weight-loss strategies. In our study of more than 300 elementary-age children, fatness was *negatively* related to self-reported intake of fatty foods and snacks and TV watching and *positively* related to physical activity (Edmunds & Fox, 1999). In other words, the fatter the children were, the more likely they were to say that they were doing the right things to reduce their weight. Girls reported replacing high-fat foods with healthier options, and more than half talked about increasing the amount of exercise as a result of feeling overweight. "I run around the block about four times when I get home," one girl reported. "I do lots of exercise because of my stomach," a boy stated. However, our objective measures of physical activity (using accelerometers) did not back up these claims. We believe that these children reported their *intentions,* rather than *actual behaviors,* or they provided socially desirable answers. Nonetheless, it does appear that most fat children know what they *should* be doing. Further assistance is needed to translate this knowledge into changed behavior.

We found 9- and 10-year-old children who were developing coping strategies. For instance, they tried to ignore the name-calling: "I take no notice." They also removed themselves from the situation: "I just walk away." Some types of responses may be unhelpful in the long term. Whereas girls tended to be more able to openly express their hurt, boys were more likely to respond in a more insular or negative way: "Sometimes I eat (crisps, biscuits, toast) when I feel miserable.... I just sit down in a corner and do nothing."

HOW DO OTHERS AFFECT CHILDREN'S COPING WITH THEIR FATNESS?

Parental approval is a robust predictor of self-esteem in children and has more impact than peer approval until early adolescence (Halter, 1996). The children in our study openly discussed parental reactions to their weight. There appeared to be at least two approaches adopted by parents:

1. Some tried to build confidence through encouraging self-acceptance: "My mum says ... I look good as I am now. She's proud of me. My mum reckons I should be proud of what I am, and I am."

2. Others denied the existence of a problem, possibly in order to protect the child's feelings: "My mum tells me that I'm not overweight, but I know I am."

Children frequently reported that they received mixed messages from parents, and there was little evidence from the interviews that parents were able to provide consistent help with strategies to manage weight or deal with weight problems. In addition, the children had very little to say about the influence of their teachers. In fact, some children commented

CONCLUSIONS ABOUT FAT CHILDREN'S PERCEPTIONS

- By age 9 or 10, fat children are acutely aware of being fat.

- For the majority of these children, their fatness has not yet become central to their priorities nor had a deeply detrimental effect on their mental well-being.

- They are beginning to demonstrate coping strategies to deal with the negative aspects of being fat.

- They believe that they are attempting to make changes in their eating and activity to resolve the problem.

- These changes may be intentions only and probably have not been translated into consistent behaviors.

- They are receiving little assistance from parents and teachers about how to deal with their problem.

- They see friends as an important element of support.

about teachers' ineffectiveness in preventing name-calling: "They don't do very much about it."

Friends provided an important source of support for overweight children. One teenage girl illustrated the role of friends this way:

> Friends say that I'm pretty ... I'm not overweight. Some people that I don't like take the mickey, and it makes me all upset and I start thinking that I'm overweight ... my friends help me. They make me laugh.

On the other hand, overweight children were aware that being fat interfered with making friends: "It's not very easy ... some people don't really like me ... 'cuz of my weight." It is clear that friends can be an important buffer for fat youngsters.

HOW CAN SCHOOLS HELP?

Schools are only one element in the world of the overweight youngster. However, through its policies, curriculum, and teacher input, the school can make a positive contribution. Although there is not enough room in this article to list specifics, we can offer guiding principles for schools to judge how their policies and rules might affect overweight and obese children:

- Does the school experience undermine or improve the self-esteem of overweight children? The way that physical education classes are delivered is particularly crucial, and teachers are not seen as particularly helpful.
- Does the school help or hinder the need of overweight children to develop healthy activities and eating habits? This depends on matters such as the range of foods and activity experiences offered, the provision of health-related education through the curriculum, and the way each are presented by staff. It would be relatively easy for schools to develop a checklist to assess these areas.

As with parents, teachers often find issues related to weight difficult to deal with. Many teachers are themselves overweight and are reluctant to openly discuss it. A problem also arises with what may seem on the surface as conflicting objectives. On one hand, there is a need to maintain a child's confidence and self-esteem. This might lead to downplaying, ignoring, or even denying the problem. On the other hand, there is a need to break into the behavioral cycle that contributes to the obesity. This may suggest overt advice. The data provided here suggest that this apparent conflict may be invalid. By the age of 9 or 10, children are already very aware of their fatness, and many of them may be making rather uneducated attempts to independently do something about it. What youngsters need is a friendly and nonthreatening setting where there is unconditional acceptance of the condition and support to adopt strategies to slowly address the problem. Teachers and leaders need simply to take a low-key, matter-of-fact approach that does the following things:

- focuses on and rewards self-improvement rather than compares children;
- develops mutual respect among youngsters, regardless of their appearance, physical abilities, or intellectual performance; and
- empowers youth to assess their weaknesses through the provision of accurate information and the teaching of effective strategies to match individual needs.

MULTICHOICE QUIZ:

Which Would You Choose?

When a child makes fun of a fat youngster in gym, the teacher should:

1. Make the youngster apologize in front of the class and say why it is wrong.
2. Take the offending youngster to one side after class and explain the effect the comment had.
3. Ignore the event and explain to the fat youngster after class why you let it go.

Your Suggestion? _____

_____

You want to get across the importance of avoiding obesity in a health class, so you should:

1. Provide lots of information about the diseases associated with obesity.
2. Use sixfold calipers to measure each youngster's fatness during a class session.
3. Talk about what constitutes healthy eating and good physical activity to help avoid gaining weight.

Your Suggestion? _____

You are trying to motivate children to be more active outside class, so you should:

1. Run the class through a series of fitness tests to show them where they need to improve.
2. Suggest in the class that all the fatter children should come to special afterschool sessions.
3. Pin scores up in the gym to show who is the fittest.

Your Suggestion? _____

_____

You want to encourage healthy eating habits, so you should:

1. Take away all high-calorie foods in the tuckshop [snack shop at school] and canteen.
2. Offer healthier options alongside the usual high-calorie foods and drinks.
3. Provide eating advice in class to help youngsters diet.

Your Suggestion? _____

_____

You want to seriously help overweight children at school to lose weight, so you should:

1. Each morning offer a special program for overweight children that includes advice about activities and eating.
2. Adopt a schoolwide policy that is passed to teachers and children about how to treat children who are overweight.
3. Bring parents into school and teach them how to deal with the causes of obesity in the home.

Your Suggestion? _____

_____

Good teachers and leaders already operate under these conditions, which are similar to how professionals deal with children experiencing other physical or mental disabilities. However, obesity is more likely to be viewed as a result of personal failings, rather than as a disability that requires special consideration. Each child needs to be regarded as possessing equal worth, to be seen as special and as presenting unique challenges. Actions that violate or ignore these principles will invite embarrassment, discouragement, and alienation, which only add to these children's problems rather than help solve them. Ultimately, we want all fat youngsters to be as optimistic as one lad, who said, "I know I am fat, but I think I'm pretty good at playing sports. When I play games, I feel happy, and I just want to do more of it." Encouraging a positive outlook, a sense of self-worth and behaviors that promote the right energy balance can be the only way forward.

The quiz in the sidebar illustrates the plight of overweight children in school. To lessen stigma from the unintentional consequences of some teacher's behaviors, we have written this as a lighthearted way to raise awareness on behalf of these children. The suggestions are not necessarily right or wrong, although some are more appropriate than others. A guiding principle might be the following: "Which would you choose if you were that fat child?"

REFERENCES

Edmunds, L. D., & Fox, K. R. (1997, October). *"My Mum tells me that I'm not overweight, but I know I am" Jodie (aged 9): Children's perceptions and processing of their fatness.* Paper presented at the Eurobesitas Conference, London.

Edmunds, L. D., & Fox, K. R. (1999). A preliminary investigation into the physical activity and fatness of 9- to 10-year-old children at risk of obesity as adults. *International Journal of Obesity, 23*(Suppl. 3), S76.

Flegal, K. M. (1999). The obesity epidemic in children and adults: Current evidence and research issues. *Medicine and Science in Sports and Exercise, 31*(Special Suppl.), S509–S514.

Gortmaker, S. H., Must, A., Sobol, A. M., Peterson, K., Coldite, G. A., & Dietz, W. H. (1996). Television viewing as a cause of increasing obesity among children in the United States, 1986–1990. *Archives of Pediatric Adolescent Medicine, 150,* 356–362.

Halter, S. (1985). *Manual for the Self-Perception Profile for Children.* Denver: University of Denver.

Halter, S. (1996). Historical roots of contemporary issues involving self-concept. In B. Bracken (Ed.), *Handbook of self-concept* (pp. 1–37). New York: Wiley.

Hughes, J. M., Li, L., Chinn, S., & Rona, R. J. (1997). Trends in growth in England and Scotland, 1972 to 1994. *Archives of Disease in Childhood, 76,* 182–189.

ARTICLE 7.11

IN the next article, we move to the other extreme, the complex issue of anorexia nervosa. Roger Vernon's article, adapted from his book with the same title, follows a seventh grader through her education and treatment at the Eating Disorders Program at Menninger Clinic.

MIRROR, MIRROR, ON THE WALL, WHO IS THE THINNEST OF THEM ALL?

Roger Verdon

Eating disorders consume health one bite at a time in the quest for a "perfect" body.

When Nikki arrived at Menninger, she was a good student and a fine daughter from a loving family. In Nikki's view, she had only one problem: she was too fat. Never mind that she had shed 30 pounds in recent months from her already thin frame. What she saw in the mirror was an imperfect body. She feared getting fatter; consequently, she was reluctant to eat.

Her arrival at Menninger earned her a certain notoriety. She would now be counted among a select and growing group throughout the nation whose members have an eating disorder: 10 out of every 100 American females at some time in their life, according to the American Academy of Child and Adolescent Psychiatry (1992). Boys also suffer the disorders, but much less often.

That Nikki's disorder was diagnosed as anorexia nervosa is notable, since it has among the highest mortality and morbidity rates of all psychiatric illnesses. "That means," said Dr. Mae Sokol, a Menninger eating disorders expert who would treat Nikki, "that more people die of it or derive medical problems from it than any other psychiatric disorder. It is a very deadly disease." Among other things, a major initial concern for Nikki's Menninger treaters was to halt her increasing emaciation and get her weight up. That would be the course of treatment if everything went smoothly, and if Nikki's aversion to food didn't defeat her own best efforts and those of her therapists.

Nikki's family voiced high hopes. So did her treatment team, whose members were prepared to do whatever was required to save her life. But the situation posed its own conundrum, as do so many physical and mental disorders. If Nikki didn't eat, she could die. And Nikki's greatest fear was gaining weight. Nikki, herself, would have to play a major role in her own recovery. Everyone was counting on her. In her whole life, Nikki might never confront such a difficult challenge, an enormous task for anyone at any age, but perhaps especially for Nikki, who was all of 13 years old.

EARLY IS BETTER

Most eating disorders are treatable, and many young people have been placed back on the road to health. But swift action is called for. An eating disorder left untreated is a dangerous condition.

Comprehensive treatment is recommended and requires a multidisciplinary team approach that may involve individual, cognitive–behavioral and family therapies, direct work with psychiatrists and psychotherapists, group psychotherapy, biofeedback, nutrition, and medication. The Menninger Eating Disorders Program, now in its 17th year, is a completely individualized treatment. The goal is to stabilize medical symptoms, examine underlying biological, emotional, social, spiritual, and mental issues, and develop a healthier lifestyle. The program diagnoses and treats children, adolescents, and young adults of both sexes evidencing the following disorders:

- *Anorexia nervosa,* which is characterized by self-starvation and often some form of overactivity or overexercise. A person with anorexia has a disturbed body image, an intense fear of becoming obese, and an inability to maintain normal body weight.
- *Bulimia nervosa,* signified by recurrent episodes of binge eating followed by purging. A person with bulimia tends to binge on high-calorie, easily ingested foods, and is preoccupied with body shape and weight. Regular purging behavior (such as self-induced vomiting, use of laxatives or diuretics, strict dieting or fasting), or rigorous exercise in order to prevent weight gain, accompanies this disorder.
- *Compulsive overeating,* distinguished by eating more than is nutritionally necessary, resulting in obesity. Many medical and psychological consequences often accompany compulsive overeating.
- *Activity disorders* entail sole reliance on excessive exercise to maintain desired weight, self-esteem, or calmness. Health, school, and relationships are often compromised as the individual pursues unrealistic goals for "fitness."

Lengths of stay differ with each patient, and a full continuum of care is available, including inpatient, day hospital, and outpatient services. Because of the severe nature of Nikki's condition, she required inpatient care. Since the average healthy range for a supervised weight gain is about 2 pounds per week, and she required a minimum weight gain of at least 20 pounds, Nikki and her family could anticipate 10 to 12 weeks of treatment, perhaps more, depending on her response and the severity of her physical and mental condition.

STARVATION DIET

Dr. Mae Sokol has been examining the mental and physical effects of eating disorders for years. As the director of the Eating Disorders Program at Menninger, her work has resulted in important breakthroughs in the field, but even she finds her mostly young, mostly female anorexia nervosa patients somewhat mystifying: "Even when they are emaciated, these kids keep up their grades. They tend to be straight A students, perfect little girls quietly starving themselves to death. That's the stereotype. Their condition affects their cognitive abilities but not their abilities to do math and schoolwork. It's a different kind of cognition. It doesn't make any sense."

Solving the puzzle of how to treat each patient individually is how Dr. Sokol and her team spend their day. The rise of eating disorders has given Menninger clinicians a breadth of experience in some of the most extreme cases. Yet, identifying the best treatment method can still be as challenging as interpreting an ancient script.

LONG-TERM EFFECTS

Too often in the short-term, the appearance of eating disorder symptoms may trouble a family, but not enough for them to intrude into a young girl's obsession with weight control. Some parents may simply write off such behavior as a phase in the developing life of a young person. That, of course, would be, and is, a grave mistake. Ignoring the signs of anorexia nervosa and bulimia may have long-term and devastating effects on a young person's developing body.

"If you don't grow normally when you're 12 or 14 years old, you may never have that window of opportunity to do it again," Dr. Sokol said, "and your reproductive organs may not develop normally, your bones may not have enough calcium, and these may turn out to be lifelong problems. There is a window of opportunity for human growth and no one knows what it is. It's different for each individual. The best thing to do is treat an eating disorder early and treat it aggressively. The vast majority of cases improve. The individual is then likely not to relapse in the future. Treatment will limit long-term damage to a developing body."

MALNUTRITION, BRAIN FUNCTION

Unfortunately, the practice of starving oneself may be only the beginning of a vicious cycle. In fact, the disorder points to a shift in which the mind is concentrated on the body's outer appearance, to the exclusion of the entire landscape of the inner self. That's not a surprising consequence of abstaining from food. Improper nutrition results in a reduction of physical and mental functioning. That can mean impaired thinking and the eventual unraveling of a myriad of defenses that would otherwise stem the course of self-inflicted starvation. "We really think that malnutrition causes some brain damage," Dr. Sokol said, "and people can't think straight or it causes brain dysfunction. A lot of the behaviors our patients have is from the malnutrition created by their disorder." That can drastically alter how people—whether it's a 13-year-old girl or an adult male—view themselves and their world.

A GOVERNMENT STUDY

Research can be instructive about how malnutrition, as a consequence of starvation, affects mood and behavior. Dr. Ansel Keys, the man who developed and gave his name to K-rations, the military's field food supplies, spent 3 months overseeing the supervised starvation of a volunteer group of conscientious objectors in order to learn the effects of starvation on the human body and mind. Conducted in the waning days of World War II, the objectives of the government study were not meant to be punitive. There was a humanitarian and scientific interest in learning the effects of human starvation to better understand and treat returning prisoners of war and Holocaust survivors.

As recounted in Menninger psychiatrist Dr. Kathryn Zerbe's landmark book, *The Body Betrayed: Women, Eating Disorders, and Treatment* (1995), Dr. Keys guided the healthy male subjects in losing one quarter of their body weight, which resulted in slowing down individual heart rate, respiration, and body temperature, conditions that replicate symptoms experienced by eating disorder patients. As they starved, their main topic of discussion became food, a common behavior among anorectic patients. But there were other similar behaviors, as well. Mealtime for the test participants became the focal point of the day, to the exclusion of all other activities. When they did eat, the men spiced their food excessively or mixed food groups on their plates. Some of the men, who occasionally slipped in self-control and overate, endured great guilt. Others who slipped developed a bingeing–purging disorder in an effort to remain loyal to the goals of the study.

At the onset of starvation, the research subjects grew irritable and angry and were beset by emotional difficulties, including depression, anxiety, and a general physical malaise. One participant became so depressed over food that he exhibited suicidal tendencies and was removed from the study. "These men cut their food up into little pieces," Dr. Sokol said. "They did a lot of the same things our patients do. The thought is that a lot of the behaviors of these men was from the malnutrition."

Months after the conclusion of the 90-day experiment, the men were consumed with concerns over body shape and fat. "The parallel between anorexia nervosa and these experimental findings with volunteers shows how much starvation alone affects mood and behavior," Dr. Zerbe stated. "Consequently, any treatment must begin with gaining weight and changing nutritional patterns, because some of the apparently psychological effects may really be the result of starvation."

FIRST THINGS FIRST

At Menninger, Dr. Sokol set down the rules for Nikki, a seventh-grader who was able to continue her education throughout her treatment. She was initially given the conventional treatment applied to most patients. As Dr. Sokol said,

> with treatment team members trying to lovingly get her to eat. Telling her how important it was. Telling her we know it's hard, but at the same time being very structured about it, setting limits. Saying things like: "Look, you need to take care of your body to live. We're not going to let you let yourself die, so if you don't eat and drink food we're going to give you oral supplements. If you don't drink that and you become medically compromised, we will give you an NG tube.

A "nasal-gastric" tube is inserted up the nose and into the throat. It is uncomfortable, and for patients concerned about their outer appearance, it looks awful. (In visually focused anorexia nervosa patients such concerns are not taken lightly.)

In the collegial group environment that exists among inpatients in the eating disorders program, veteran patients will always advise newcomers like Nikki that eating anything is preferable to coming within proximity of an NG tube. The peer pressure that can be brought to bear is a useful weapon the clinician exploits as often as possible. "One of the things that helps us in treatment is the group of kids together," Dr. Sokol said, "the pressure the kids put on one another. That's one of the things I love about my work. You put all these kids with anorexia together and they really get each other better. The kids who are in advanced treatment will help the ones who are struggling and they get positive results."

Among fellow high achievers, Nikki was encouraged to use her own competitive energies in a positive direction. Instead of seeking approval from her anorectic peers as the thinnest patient, for instance, her efforts might be redirected into becoming a volunteer member of the "junior staff," which entitles the recipient to help fellow patients who are not doing as well. The sense of purpose derived from such an exercise pays dividends in self-esteem and affirms the program's goals.

"Nikki was given the basic limits most eating disorder patients are presented," said Dr. Sokol, "eat, don't throw up, make sure no one throws food away, you need to gain weight in a structured environment, and you need to follow the structure to get better." Nikki went through the motions of conforming to the discipline, eventually gaining 20 pounds, despite holding firm to her radical ideas about eating. She remained horrified about gaining weight. On her plate she carefully put food at positions equivalent to an hour hand on a clock, placing morsels at the 3-, 6-, 9-, and 12-o'clock positions. She ate one piece at a time. Of 20 pieces of macaroni on her plate, she would have to eat 1 piece from each hour, and then go around the plate once again.

"That was very obsessive ideation," Dr. Sokol said. "Our patients are very similar to people with obsessive–compulsive disorder. They have obsessions about food and compulsions about exercise and about calories and how they eat their food. They tend to cut up their food into tiny pieces and Nikki did this too. It could take her 2 hours to eat a meal." Consequently, Nikki's progress was minimal. "You could tell she was going to relapse the moment she got home," Dr. Sokol concluded. And the underlying cause of her condition remained elusive.

THE WHY BEHIND THE DISORDER

Pick any of a hundred reasons why an American teenager living in the most bountiful country on earth would restrain from eating, and you might not even come close. Eating disorders do not surface out of thin air; they have roots, and often they can be traced to various branches sprouting from the family tree. In addition to genetics as a factor behind the disorder, there may be underlying biochemical, behavioral, or environmental factors, or any combination thereof.

Anorexia nervosa may be the expression of conflicts over sexuality or a reaction to grief, or a way of expressing feelings during stressful or changing times. People with eating disorders share common traits: fear of getting fat, low self-esteem, helplessness. Many are perfectionists in an imperfect world, and the disorder manifests itself as a means of assuming some control over one aspect of life, or as a means of handling anxiety. Dr. Sokol and the treatment team continued to search for the motivation behind Nikki's loss of appetite. Something else had to be causing her aversion to food, maybe something that wasn't even in the medical literature. Dr. Sokol would have to probe deeper. What she found would not only change Nikki's life, it would also change Dr. Sokol's life.

REVIEWING THE PAST

When her parents were asked when the eating disorders began, their answers were very specific. They gave dates concerning the onset of the disorder that were only days apart. "They agreed what made the moment memorable was the sudden onset of Nikki's worry over food." And not just the remarkable onset of worry, but the dramatic change in Nikki's appreciation of food. This attitude seemed to have appeared in an instant. Her behavior was an anomaly. Most eating disorders are gradual in nature.

"In the past, according to her parents, she was a little bit worried about food and calories," Dr. Sokol recalled.

> Like other young girls in our society she would say "Oh, I'd like to lose a few pounds, I want to be thin, I want to look like the models," but nothing unusual. And then, suddenly, she became very afraid of eating. She thought if she ate too much she would become extremely fat, and actually thought she was fat at the time. She was very, very upset.

Before arriving at Menninger, Nikki's poor eating habits had put her in a hospital several times for dehydration. Pediatricians fed her fluids intravenously and treated her but missed the eating problem. Consequently, Nikki would return home and relapse. Eventually, Nikki's parents put her in the psychiatric unit of a hospital. "They didn't know what to do with her," Dr. Sokol recounted. "They don't have the kind of structure we have. They did talk to her about her thoughts and feelings, but that's not all it's about. And at the point where they're not eating, and they're so terrified of eating, you can't really talk to them about their thoughts and feelings, anyway."

Then the parents mentioned a part of the story they hadn't previously disclosed. Three to 4 weeks prior to the onset of Nikki's eating disorder, everyone in her family had suffered sore throats. The flu-like symptoms kept everyone home. At the time, no one in the family received medical attention. The news set off warning bells. Dr. Sokol performed lab tests. Nikki's physical condition was consistent with strep.

A VERY BAD TRIP

Normally, when strep throat arises, the body's infection-fighting apparatus prepares to set sail. White blood cells produce antibodies which are directed to the infection in a natural process. But sometimes those same cells fall victim to "molecular mimicry," an incidence of navigational mischief that misdirects their geography off-course and toward molecules in the body disguised as the targeted infection. Once deceived by this "mimicry," if the heart is the mistaken destination, rheumatic fever results, which can then lead to rheumatic heart disease, a condition that attacks the heart. Once there, what began as a well-intentioned trip becomes an invasion of the brain's center—the basal ganglia—where human emotions are centered and influenced and psychiatric symptoms result. The long-winded theory behind this case of "mistaken identity" is called Pediatric Autoimmune Neuropsychiatric Disorders Associated with Streptococcus, also known by the acronym PANDAS.

When Dr. Sokol and her treatment team detected the proximity in time between the illness in Nikki and her family with the onset of Nikki's psychiatric symptoms, antibiotics were prescribed. "It was very interesting," Dr. Sokol said. "She didn't appear to have an acute infection, but just by taking the antibiotics she started getting better. Within 2 weeks, her thinking cleared up." In some rare cases, like Nikki's, PANDAS has been linked with anorexia nervosa, obsessive–compulsive disorders, and tics or abnormal body movements. As Nikki improved physically and mentally, she began to benefit from intensive individual psychotherapy.

ONE MORE TIME

Although the cause of Nikki's anorexia nervosa may have been novel, the condition manifested itself in all its conventional phases. After her release from Menninger, she eventually went off antibiotics. Months later, she again came down with strep, and the same thoughts that plagued her under the daunting grip of anorexia nervosa returned. Fortunately, she didn't stop eating. In fact, she was so worried about a relapse that she overate to compensate for her troubling thoughts. After consulting with

Dr. Sokol, who prescribed antibiotics to Nikki and reassurance to her family, the strep cleared up, and so did Nikki's fears.

While anorexia nervosa's origins can be traced to the complexity of individual and family dynamics, conflicts and struggles, the cultural desire for a "perfect" body shape, infections, or a plethora of other causes, the research is only beginning. Dr. Sokol's solution to Nikki's case has become a part of medical literature, accepted as one cause for anorexia nervosa under the practice guidelines of the American Psychiatric Association. Meanwhile, Menninger research into the causes and treatment of eating disorders continues. "We don't have—and we're unlikely to find—any single cure," Dr. Sokol said. "We don't have a medicine that will take anorexia nervosa or any of the eating disorders away, and we don't have a single treatment that will take it away. We're really at a frontier."

REFERENCES

American Academy of Child and Adolescent Psychiatry. (1992). *Teenagers with eating disorders* [Fact Sheet #2]. Washington, DC: Author.

Zerbe, K. J. (1995). *The body betrayed: Women, eating disorders, and treatment.* Carlsbad, CA: Gurze Books.

STUDENTS WHO PERFORM SELF-MUTILATIONS

A discussion of self-defeating behaviors would not be complete without mentioning the growing incidence of deliberate body injury. Nichols (2000) writes that 85% of self-mutilations are carried out by girls and occur most frequently after the onset of menstruation. Adolescents who pride themselves on being independent are likely to copy the behavior of their peers. It is a personal experiment and not an expression of sexual confusion, an interpersonal loss, or an eating disorder. However, self-mutilation can be a serious problem. The motivating reasons for this type of self-abuse include low self-esteem, an irrational belief that punishing one's body will release the unbearable feelings of stress, and a nonverbal way of expressing feelings of independence that is bound to attract the attention of adults. Nichols emphasizes that helping these students requires managing our personal feelings of shock and anger at the student for making such a poor decision. Self-mutilation is not a behavior that is easy to accept or understand. The first step is to get the student to tell why and when this self-abuse took place. Only then can a decision be made whether to intervene in a therapeutic way.

USEFUL WEB SITES

For more information on the patterns of self-defeating behaviors described in this chapter, one can consult the following Web sites.

Advocates for Youth
www.advocatesforyouth.org

Al-Anon/Alateen
www.al-anon.alateen.org

American Academy of Child and Adolescent Psychiatry
www.aacap.org

American Association of Suicidology
www.suicidology.org

American Orthopsychiatric Association
www.amerortho.org

American Psychological Association
www.apa.org

Children and Adults with Attention Deficit Disorders (Ch.A.D.D.)
www.chadd.org

Children of Alcoholics Foundation
www.coaf.org

Learning Disabilities Association of America
www.ldaamerica.org

Life Space Crisis Intervention
www.lsci.org

National Alliance for the Mentally Ill
www.nami.org

National Association for Children of Alcoholics
www.nacoa.org

National Black Alcoholism & Addictions Council
www.nbacinc.org

National Center on Addiction and Substance Abuse
www.casacolumbia.org

National Council on Alcoholism and Drug Dependence
www.ncaddnj.org

National Depressive and Manic-Depressive Association
www.ndmda.org

National Eating Disorders Association
www.nationaleatingdisorders.org

National Institute of Mental Health
www.nimh.nih.gov

National Mental Health Association
www.nmha.org

Suicide Prevention Center
www.suicidepreventioncenter.org

Youth Violence Prevention Resource Center
www.safeyouth.org

SUMMARY

The articles in this chapter were compiled to take the mystery out of helping students with self-defeating psychological problems. To understand the behavior of these students, the teacher must look beyond the students' behavior and understand the source of their unmet needs. Each of these behavioral and emotional problems is a student's psychological solution to stressful life events. Specific recommendations about how to help these students in the classroom have been offered. The purpose of this chapter is not to turn a teacher into a psychologist but to help the teacher recognize these student problems and to help the teacher understand and manage these students until they can be referred to psychological services.

EDITORS' REFERENCES

American Psychiatric Association. (1994). *Diagnostic and statistical manual of mental disorders* (4th ed.). Washington, DC: Author.

Brendtro, L. K., Brokenleg, M., Van Bockern, S. V. (1990). *Reclaiming youth at risk: Our hope for the future.* Bloomington, IN: National Educational Service.

Dreikurs, R., Grunwold, B. B., & Pepper, F. C. (1971). *Maintaining sanity in the classroom: Illustrated teaching techniques.* New York: Harper & Row.

Eggert, L. (1994). *Anger management in youth: Stemming aggression and violence.* Bloomington, IN: National Educational Service.

Eggert, L., & Nichols, L. (1996). *Personal growth class: A group approach for youth.* Bloomington, IN: National Educational Service.

Glasser, W. (1998). *Choice theory in the classroom.* New York: Harper & Row.

Goldstein, A. P., Glick, B., & Gibbs, J. C. (1987). *Aggression replacement training: A comprehensive intervention for aggressive youth.* Champaign, IL: Research Press.

Henley, M. (2003). *Teaching self control.* Bloomington, IN: National Educational Service.

Long, N. J. (1993, Spring). Stages of helping emotionally disturbed students through the reeducation process. *The Pointer, 30*(1).

Maslow, A. H. (1943). A theory of human motivation. *Psychological Review, 50,* 370–396.

McGee, K., Guetzloe, E. (1988). Suicidal emotionally handicapped students: Tips for teachers. *Pointer, 32*(4), 7–10.

National Center for Health Statistics. (2002). *Prevalence of overweight in U.S. children and adolescents.* Washington, DC: Author.

National Institute on Alcohol Abuse and Alcoholism. (1991). Fetal alcohol syndrome. *Alcohol Alert,* No. 13, PH 297. Rockville, MD: Author.

Nichols, P. (2000). Bad body fever and deliberate self-injury. *Reclaiming Children and Youth, 9,* 151–157.

Office of Substance Abuse Prevention. (1991). *Too many young people drink and know too little about the consequences.* Rockville, MD: Author.

Russell, M., Henderson, C., & Blum, S. (1984). *Children of alcoholics.* New York: Children of Alcoholics Foundation.

U.S. Surgeon General. (2003). *Mental health: A report of the Surgeon General.* Rockville, MD: U.S. Department of Health and Human Services.

Walker, H. M., McConnell, S., Holmes, D., Todis, B., Walker, J., & Golden, N. (1988). *The Walker social skills curriculum.* Austin, TX: PRO-ED.

Wood, M. (1996). *Developmental therapy—Developmental teaching* (3rd ed.). Austin, TX: PRO-ED.

8 CLASSROOM CRISIS AS AN OPPORTUNITY:

Strategies and Skills
of Life Space Crisis Intervention

DURING NASA's Apollo 13 flight in 1970, the equipment in the space capsule malfunctioned and caused severe damage to the navigational and life support systems: Staff members at the Houston Command Center were alarmed by the magnitude of these technical problems and feared for the ultimate safety of the three astronauts. After assessing the damage, the mission engineers reported that they were unable to predict the outcome of the space flight. They were concerned that the damaged heat shield of the space capsule would not protect the astronauts from being burned up during the reentry stage, that the three parachutes would not open to protect them from crashing into the sea and drowning, and that the supply of oxygen would not be sufficient to protect them from suffocating. A senior administrator, hearing these statements and reacting to his feelings of panic and doom, said, "This could be the darkest day in the history of NASA." The command flight director turned to him and replied, "This also could be our finest hour, so let's focus on solutions."

These different reactions to an emergency were expressed centuries ago by the Chinese. The word *crisis* is written with two characters that mean "an opportunity for change" and "disaster or destruction."

We believe that a student crisis is a unique opportunity for adults to teach and for students to experience some insight into their pattern of self-defeating behaviors, learn more effective social skills to manage volatile emotional situations, and improve their trust in the teaching staff.

This chapter describes the essential concepts and skills of managing a student crisis, with particular attention to Life Space Crisis Intervention (LSCI) strategies.

The Need for Crisis Intervention

Student crises do not happen by appointment, nor are they scheduled into the school day. Student crises seem to happen at the most inconvenient times for staff—at the beginning of the school day, during transitional periods, and during activities such as lunch when staff are not available or didn't see the precipitating events. During these crises, tempers flare and behaviors become more primitive, disruptive, and dangerous. Something needs to be done immediately, and the staff cannot postpone intervening until they can understand the underlying causes of the crisis. Like firefighters, staff must act quickly to put out the blaze, to protect the endangered, and to save property. Later, they will use their professional skills to identify the source and reasons for the fire. Although the need for staff action is important, it does not justify impulsive and unprofessional staff behaviors. During a crisis, it is common for staff to be quick to speak and slow to listen. With training, staff can learn to be quick to listen; and when they talk, it should be in a nonthreatening way that is intended to deescalate the student crisis as well as provide the student with protection, support, and respect.

ARTICLE 8.1

IN the first article, William Morse details the changing conditions in the public schools and the need to use a student crisis as a positive and powerful medium for understanding and modifying the behavior of troubled students. Morse believes that school staff members are slowly recognizing that their authority base has eroded and they no longer can make students change their behavior or conform to school rules. Staff cannot maintain their authority and use fear of failure, transfer, or exclusion to enforce their decisions. These threats are not effective with troubled students. Morse senses that society has moved away from the divine rights of institution to a new base of persuasion based on values. The old power of authority in schools has vanished, and the new theory of crisis intervention provides schools with a significant opportunity to view a crisis not as a disaster to be avoided, but as another chance to have a positive and profound impact on the students' way of thinking, feeling, and behaving. Crises are an essential part of student life. If used therapeutically, they can result in new coping skills, an improved ability to adapt, and better student–staff relationships.

CRISIS INTERVENTION IN SCHOOLS

William C. Morse

The currently popular concept of crisis intervention has been espoused as an innovation and a central core in the new mental health movement.

Crises are not new, nor is the concept of intervention. Schools have used many different interventions. The problem is, they are usually of a reflexive and haphazard resource. Since they usually lack an awareness of the underlying conditions, they are reactions to symptoms, often with a curbing intention. For example, a student who skipped a day of school is excluded for several days as a corrective intervention, and the more he skips the longer become the exclusions, the further behind he gets, and the more escape becomes necessary. Frequently a teacher–student confrontation is born of a long gestation period of marginal aggravations. Suddenly a minor incident appears catastrophic and there is a reaction. These confrontations are usually quite one-sided, with no attempt to explore the genesis of the situation or the meaning to the particular student. Why do these interventions tend to be so primitive? Are we still seeking instant change, the non-existent silver bullet? Sometimes a passage of time serves as a huge sponge absorbing the true nature of the incident and we have only a charade in the after school detention. In the past there has been considerable support for cooling-off periods, which is the opposite of crisis intervention or confrontation, and the cooling-off may extend to the point where usable psychological material has been completely dissipated. Often the person with power to determine the intervention is remote from the circumstances which generated the problem. Rather than reality—which is the essential ingredient of crisis intervention—the once or twice removed person deals with second-hand, frequently distorted perceptions of what really happened. The teacher is so often group bound that leaving the class to participate in the necessary discussion would require a new federal grant. When they do desert the classroom for a quick discussion, they are anxious over what may be developing back in the classroom. Time again makes the decision. Frequently the student crisis centers around a teacher who is responsible for the classroom and yet a third party, the principal, many times controls the outcome of the crisis.

The principal is in a very awkward situation. Not knowing exactly what happened, and having past experience or a perception regarding the teacher as well as the student involved, he may make certain judgments about the depth of the problem. He is also by role a "fixer" person. This role demands that he *do something* about the incident. As the superior in the command chain and given the obligation by the teacher for some corrective influence, he is, in fact, often without the resources needed to obtain a change. But this does not allow an escape from the reality problem of doing *something* about the situation. Usually after a dressing down which may be done politely or more vigorously, the student is returned to the original setting, often with the realization he will be back soon for more of the same. Of course the teacher who sent him out does not know what has happened with the authority person either.

The importance of all of this for contemporary mental health ideology is as follows. Studies of life histories of those making successful adjustments differ from those who make unsuccessful adjustments less in the amount of stress they have faced in their lives than in how well they learned to cope with the stress. Thus, we can have two "identical" case histories as far as the supposed genesis of pathology is concerned, but one turns out to be reasonably well-adjusted while the other does not. Corrective influence and good mental health are the result of satisfactory solutions to crises rather than a simple sentence passed upon a person by his life experience. Some turn out well under very poor odds; others had little to sustain them but managed. While the more life adversity the more risk, it is not a simple arithmetic addition. Some learn to cope much more effectively than others.

Thus it follows, we teach how to cope by providing the proper intervention at the time of a crisis, while the student is in the process of learning how to cope. This is not to say that people are always particularly "teachable" at a time of their crises, in the sense that they stand there awaiting help in learning how to cope with a particular situation in a socially acceptable fashion. It merely means that at the point of crisis a person is in turmoil and seeking some resolution. The object of crisis intervention is to provide coping styles which will have long-term utility. In this way it becomes clear that the typical reflective response as now practiced in schools frequently "teaches" coping which is of a nature we do not wish at all. But we cannot avoid teaching something at the time of crisis because the student is always learning some means. The Harvard group which dealt with this problem has been interested in studying overwhelming crisis situations such as accidents, bereavement, and other catastrophic life events. Caplan states that during such a period a person is more susceptible to being influenced by others than in times of relative psychological equilibrium. A particular insight we could gain from their studies of major crises is to avoid conceiving every event in a student's life as catastrophic.

One of the first questions which teachers ask is a definition of a crisis. The reason is obvious. So much happens in certain classes of normal or disturbed students that almost everything could be considered a crisis. An event which may have a great deal of explosiveness in it is not necessarily a significant crisis if it is unrelated to the nature of the group's or individual's abiding problem.

His research points out a very interesting kind of dilemma: Is the crisis in the eye of the student experiencing the "crisis" or in the eye of others around him, particularly the teacher? Thus many crisis situations may have no meaning as far as the individual primarily involved is concerned. It is a crisis to the teacher who is the consumer of the behavior. Parenthetically, the type of crisis consultation which many of us attempt takes this into consideration: the teacher is most eager to engage in a problem-solving effort at such a time. The issue of what comprises a crisis is of great importance and many interventions fail because they are poised with an inadequate awareness of the fact that the one being helped must sense a crisis. Many events which are crises to us are satisfying, ego building, and gratifying to the student. Hence, there is no crisis except to ward off any effort to make it one. Stated in simple terms, a crisis is precipitated by overloading the student's capacity to cope. It may be generated by external demands in the environment such as the academic or behavioral tasks he is given. Or it may be in consequence of internal perceptions, distorted or accurate. The student's coping failure is of such an intensity that he cannot be supported by the typical supporting tactics which teachers use day in and day out. The crises take many forms. For example a student acts out and becomes a critical management problem. A teacher may recognize a peak of depression sometimes under the guise of clowning. A sharp and noticeable erosion of self-esteem can be the basis of an approach. It may be generated by academic failure or frustration. Frequently, crises are a consequence of contaging social stimulations. Often evaluation experience such as an examination coming up or grades being given precipitates a crisis. Thus, a crisis is a psychological condition of duress which may be accompanied by overt signs but may not. In another article, Gerald Caplan states that a crisis is a relatively sudden onset of disequilibrium in a student where previous functioning was known to be stable. These are states of turmoil. Caplan points out that many students who are facing an identity crisis will have a period of this type but are not necessarily emotionally disturbed unless this develops into a chronic negative pattern.

Caplan also differentiates between developmental and accidental crises. Developmental crises are the transitional periods one anticipates in both normal and disturbed students. For example, the onset of adolescence constitutes a developmental crisis period. We usually think of the third grade and beginning of school as significant periods. The accidental crises are like accidents in general. You can predict there will be a certain number in a population but not when they are liable to occur. These are conditions precipitated by loss of basic support or some threat or challenge which puts heightened demands on an individual. Caplan sees both of these as pathways leading to increased or decreased capacity to cope with one's environment. In his own experience these people are ready for increased help and are more easily influenced.

The important point, from Caplan's point of view, is that the critically correct small force acting for a short time during the period of acute crisis can produce drastic changes which would otherwise be impossible. This is the most central concept of the whole procedure. From my own point of view it becomes important to recognize that interventions must be thought of not only as verbal but as consideration of all aspects of the external environment as well. But the idea remains: an effective solving of today's problem is a most promising way of neutralizing the impact of an unfortunate past. This immediacy with which one attempts to deal with issues is in contrast to the traditional "cool down" theory. Many institutions use a quiet room or have a student quiet down before anyone will talk to him. This is not to say that one would never want some reduction of intensity, but the essential nature of crisis intervention is to use the emotional potency of the contemporary charged situation to help the youngster understand what he is feeling and what can be done. When you let a student "cool down," he has lost the impetus for change. It is particularly amusing to think of expecting a student in a crisis to have his problem ready for discussion when he comes in for his therapy hour the next day. As a matter of fact, if one examines counseling with students, after the precipitating event has passed, it will be clear that a good deal of time is spent in rationalizing the problem to be discussed. One of the reasons so much of the student–teacher interaction is nothing more than hollow moralizing is because the student at that point in time has no feeling of an issue about which he has to do something. A teacher working with a student who has a reading difficulty but who denies it may get him to actually read and thus demonstrate an issue in order to be able to work with him.

The use of the crisis implies keen understanding of the appropriate interventions. This means knowledge in depth—psychological, sociological, and educational—applied at the correct point in time. Actually it requires more rather than less insight in these domains. Inappropriate interventions result in faulty learning rather than real help.

In our own experience there are four places the crisis concept has changed procedures rather radically. One is in consultation, which has changed from supervisory or case analysis of a historical nature to strategic planning for the student. Roles cease to determine function when solutions are sought. No one knows enough to resolve all difficulties. Second is the use of the crisis or helping teacher who is available to operate at the time of severe difficulty and breakdown by handling disturbed students taken from the regular class at the time when they flounder. This teacher works with both emotional and academic aspects in teaching the student to cope. The third major use in working with disturbed students is in the style of interviewing developed by Redl and others entitled Life Space Interviewing [now known as Life Space Crisis Intervention]. This presumes that working with a student through interviews around the particular difficulty he faces in the contemporary life scene is an effective way to help him learn long-term coping. The last is a conceptual system to handle the confrontation situations which are more and more frequent in secondary education today. If these are seen as crises resulting from a failure to meet situational demands, there will be less repressive action, which solves little.

We are a long way from really understanding how to make constructive use of severe trouble points, but at least we have a theory to explore. One hopes that it will be taken seriously and not as another verbal gimmick with a catchy sound. We need to school ourselves relative to the theory involved and train ourselves in practice.

REFERENCES

Bernard L. Bloom, "Definitional aspects of a crisis concept," Journal of Consulting Psychology, 1963, Vol. 27, #6, 498–502.

Gerald Caplan, Prevention of Mental Disorders in Children, New York: Basic Books, 1961.

Gerald Caplan "Opportunities for School Psychologists in the Primary Prevention," Mental Hygiene, Vol. 47, #4, Oct. 1963, pp. 525–539.

Harold Renaud and Floyd Estess, "Life History Interviews with One Hundred Normal American Males: Pathogenicity of Childhood," American Journal of Orthopsychiatry. October 1961, Vol. 31, No. 4, 786–803.

Long, Wood, and Fecser's Crisis Cycle Model

Long et al.'s (2001) model of understanding crisis is based on the Conflict Cycle (see Article 6.2), which becomes the Crisis Cycle when the needs of a student clash against the expectations of others. Figure 8.1 illustrates the circular nature of the Conflict Cycle and how, if it is uninterrupted, it will unleash intense feelings and oppositional behaviors and incite staff anger. Most student crises begin with a minor event, move into a problem incident, and expand into a personal crisis for the student and a school wide crisis for staff. The Conflict Cycle is explained in detail in Chapter 6.

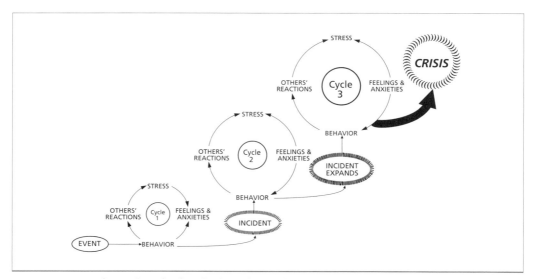

Figure 8.1. If Left Unbroken, the Conflict Cycle Spirals into Crisis.

The Three Generic Categories of a Student Crisis

A student crisis can be triggered by any of the following: (a) a developmental crisis, (b) a destructive personal life event crisis, or (c) a situational crisis. All three types of student crises happen in school, and an awareness of these different types becomes helpful in improving the effectiveness of adult intervention.

A Developmental Crisis

Caplan (1961) documented that all individuals, from birth to death, go through a series of predictable stress periods or transitional stages that can lead to personal crisis. Developmental crises can include leaving home and going to school, learning how to read, making friends, belonging to groups, becoming independent, accepting physical development and sexual identity, developing values and beliefs, selecting a profession, and so on. At each of these developmental stages, a student can become temporarily flooded by feelings of anger, excitement, shame, guilt, fury, or fear, and will need the assistance of an adult to resolve the conflict or confusion. According to Wineman (1959), all children and youth can profit at times from crisis intervention, and teachers should broaden their view that crisis intervention is a strategy designed only for troubled students.

> The idea that normal and healthy children don't need any therapy is basically correct. The further assumption that being normal and healthy also means freedom from the danger of being overwhelmed by the complexities of life is a naive illusion. Most healthy and normal kids are equipped with a considerable amount of resilience. They can handle many experiences that would send their more disturbed compatriots into psychotic blow-ups or neurotic convulsions. This, however, does not mean they can manage all of them. Take any child, no matter how well matured, healthy, wonderful, and at some time during some phase of his life, he will find himself in predicaments in which he will need an adult to stand by. Indeed, during such a time it will make a lot of difference just how well this adult handles himself during this crisis. (pp. 3–7)

Developmental crises are particularly active and plentiful during the junior high or middle school years.

A Destructive Personal Life Event Crisis

Destructive personal life event crises are triggered by events over which the student has no control but which drastically affect his or her ability to function in school. Unplanned traumatic events might include the shooting of a friend, the death of a family member, a paralyzing illness, sexual and psychological abuse, a sudden move to a new city, or physical threats by people in the community. Students experiencing these types of crises will need abundant support and clarity to help them focus on the "real" problem and get control over their lives.

A Situational Crisis

Redl and Wineman (1957) concluded that a number of crises occur in every on-going group situation for children and youth, and these crises can be used in therapeutic ways to help children and youth cope with their reality frustrations, interpersonal conflicts, and personal problems. Redl and Wineman called this type of crisis intervention Life Space Interviewing (LSI).

A Brief Overview of Life Space Interviewing

In 1959 Redl proposed an exciting and effective way of talking with troubled children and youth about some behavior that they could not manage appropriately. This reality-based verbal technique, called Life Space Interviewing (LSI), differs significantly from the structured office interview used by clinicians, although it has similar goals. Most important, LSI provides the staff, who have worked directly and have had the most contact hours with troubled children and youth, with a therapeutic technique that enables them to be more active and professional as contributors to the treatment team.

The Two Outcome Goals of LSI

Every student crisis begins with an issue or a life event that triggers the crisis. Each LSI can focus on one of two outcomes: Emotional First Aid on the Spot or Clinical Exploitation of Life Events. The decision about how a crisis is to be managed does not depend on the instigating issue but is determined by a set of staff criteria. If the staff decides the goal is to support this student emotionally by draining off his or her feelings and returning the student to the program ASAP, then the staff outcome goal involves Emotional First Aid on the Spot.

If the staff decides to use the student issue to clarify a pattern of self-defeating behavior that is in need of repair or change, then the staff's outcome goal involves Clinical Exploitation of Life Events. Redl (1959) provided an excellent example of the choice involved in deciding what to do about a crisis issue:

> Let's assume that a group of children are just about ready to go out on that excursion they have anticipated with eagerness for quite a while. Let's assume there is, due to our fault, somewhat more delay at the door because of a last-minute search for lost shoes, footballs, etc., so that irritability mounts in the gang that is already assembled and raring to go. Let's further assume that in the ensuing melee of irritated bickering two of our youngsters get into a flare-up, which ends up with Johnny's getting socked more vehemently than he can take, furiously running back to his room, cursing his tormentor and the world at large, all educators in particular, swearing that he will "never go on no trip no more in his whole life." We find him just about to soak himself in a pleasurable bath of self-pity, nursing his grudge against people in general and adding up new evidence for his theory that life is no good, people are mean "so-and-so's" anyway, and that autistic daydreaming is the only safe way out. (p. 4)

If the decision is made to be with John during his unhappiness and to help him sort out his many emotions in order to get himself back in shape and to go on the trip, then the appropriate choice is Emotional First Aid on the Spot. However, if the decision is made to use this issue as an opportunity to help John become aware of a pattern of behavior he does not recognize, then the goal of returning John to the group is given up in order to use Clinical Exploitation of Life Events to introduce some personal insight and behavioral changes. The goal of this interview is to use this incident—and previous ones the staff and John have experienced—to demonstrate how John's rude, impulsive, and provocative behavior invites peer rejection, although he may not be aware of this pattern. It is important to remember that, although staff may begin with one goal in mind, new information or reality factors can force the staff to switch to the other category.

IN the next article, Carol Merritt-Petrashek describes Redl's five specific strategies of Emotional First Aid on the Spot. Teachers can use these strategies to patch up a student emotionally and keep the student in the program. These five strategies are similar to surface management techniques and to Stanley Fagen's techniques (see Article 6.5) for reducing undesirable behavior. Merritt-Petrashek has developed an effective way of teaching these five strategies, and has offered a teacher quiz.

ARTICLE 8.2

EMOTIONAL FIRST AID: BANDAIDS FOR THE BUMPS

Carol A. Merritt-Petrashek

Emotional First Aid is one of the strategies of life space interviewing (LSI) characterized by the multiple skills of active listening, decoding behaviors, advocating and sanctioning students' feelings, and supportive decision making by the interviewer. Often a student will require immediate help when his coping skills break down while dealing with a particularly stressful situation. At these painful times, one or more of the five subcategories of Emotional First Aid can be used.

From *The Pointer,* 25(2), 1981, pp. 16–19. Copyright by Carol A. Merritt. Reprinted with permission.

SUBCATEGORIES OF EMOTIONAL FIRST AID

1. *Drain-off of Frustration Acidity or "Look Out, I'm Going to Explode."* Life is frustrating. The release of emotional stress due to frustration is termed a "drain off." Broadly, release of stress is accomplished by the use of sympathetic listening and the decoding of feelings and behavior. In plain language, all the angry feelings must be drained off verbally before the student is able to look at his behavior and the situation rationally. The interviewer encourages this process by sharing and supporting the student's feelings with statements such as, "What you are saying is …," and "I can see you are feeling _____ ('angry,' 'confused,' 'sad,' 'lonely,' 'scared,' etc.) about …"

Sympathetic listening is also used to reassure a student of the interviewer's understanding of the frustrating situation. Saying nothing—simply listening—an interviewer can communicate acceptance by nodding, touching, and facial expression. Many students need this quiet acceptance in order to control their intense feelings. At these times, the interviewer does not want to risk decoding prematurely or decoding irrelevant information because it could create a power struggle with the student.

Through the use of these two skills—sympathetic listening to convey acceptance and decoding to focus—the student begins to release the whys, hows, and when of the stressful incident. The more information released or "drained off" by the student, the less confusing and disappointing the painful incident becomes.

"I Can't Take It Anymore!" In the middle of English class, Bob throws his pencil down and yells, "The hell with this! How do you expect me to do this stuff? I hate this goddamn class anyway!" As Bob talks, he rips the paper in front of him and throws it across the room. Angry with his disruptive behavior, his teacher tells Bob to pick up the paper and observes that the work would have been easier if he had only listened to the directions initially. Bob, furious and insulted, seeks revenge by flipping over his desk and chair. He then leaves the room shouting obscenities.

What technique would have been effective yet not disruptive to others in the class? What form of release could be useful? The next paragraph may provide some suggestions.

The first step is to label the cause for the behavior and anger—in this case frustration with the task and perhaps fear of failure. The second step is to realize that a surface technique, as opposed to an in-depth technique, is needed because of situational factors (i.e., the class is in session, time to deal with the problem is limited, or the issue producing frustration can be remediated rapidly). The third step is the approach. At this point, the teacher has indicated a need to interfere with the student's frustration, release the emotional pressure, and return the student to the program as soon as possible. A possible approach could be as follows:

The teacher should move toward the student instantly, sending up a flag stating, "I hear you." To convey acceptance rather than anger share the understanding rapidly: "This English assignment is frustrating."

Sympathize with the student by decoding what you see and hear. Usually, if a teacher is successful in "draining off" the frustration, both physical and verbal release are quite visible. At this point, both teacher and student should develop a way to tackle the original task without creating a new conflict cycle.

2. *Support for Management of Panic, Fury, and Guilt, or "Let Me Know You Care."* Often, when a student becomes overloaded with, or flooded by, guilt, panic, or fury, interpersonal confusion surfaces. In this frenzied state, the student is capable of losing total self-control. At this time, it is essential for the interviewer to provide *protection for the student and others around him.* A message whether stated verbally and/or physically to a student must convey, "I will be your controls until your own controls take over." This message when communicated gently yet confidently helps the student feel secure and protected as he gathers his internal control. Once the student can endure and control his intense feelings, the interviewer's task is to return him to the daily schedule as soon as possible.

"It's Unfair!" One morning, Chris entered the class in a highly aggressive state. (Chris was suspended from the bus because the driver said he was uncooperative.) He burst through the door of the classroom screaming and yelling obscenities. Running around the room, he threw chairs, knocked over desks, and pitched small objects. With tears running down his face, he screamed over and over again, "That's no fair!" His teacher stood with hands on hips yelling, "Chris, stop this instant!" Unfortunately, Chris did not stop but threw a block, hitting another entering student. The entering student promptly launched a physical attack on Chris. The teacher was rendered practically helpless in attempts to end the struggle.

Did the teacher's behavior escalate Chris's stress? If the teacher had moved toward Chris instantly, could the fight have been prevented? A suggested technique follows.

The student is obviously in a severe state of panic and fury. His behavior should be an immediate signal of needed "support for management of panic, fury, and guilt." The emphasis is placed on the word "support."

The first step requires the teacher to reach the student as fast as possible. Isolate the student's space gently with your own body and words, e.g., "Calm down, Chris" or "I will help you through this, Chris." If the student's behavior decreases, physical restraint is not necessary. Support the student in every way possible, remembering to speak softly and accept all feelings at this time.

The second step occurs if, after verbal controls, the student is still unable to manage his frenzied state. Physical restraint is then used to protect the student, his peers, and oneself from his aggressive behavior. Be prepared for physical and verbal aggression to escalate during the restraint, followed by tears and silence.

3. *Maintenance of Communication in Moments of Relationship Decay; or "I Can't Hear You and You Can't Make Me Listen!"* After an intense conflict, some students are so overwhelmed by their feelings that they withdraw into fantasy or go into a prolonged anger, sulk, and refuse to talk. Unless these reactions can be penetrated, the silent world of fantasy or anger can be more destructive than the world of reality.

A withdrawal into fantasy is best dealt with by engaging the student in any kind of conversation or activities. A quick change of subject to the student's interests, followed by questioning in a non-threatening way, can be helpful. The use of something manipulable may be helpful at this point, or the quiet use of an art medium may lure the student back to words.

"I Deserve More Points." Cathy and her teacher had a disagreement about the number of points earned on a daily behavioral program. Infuriated with the outcome of the total, Cathy glares at her teacher and says, "I hate you." When the teacher ignores this remark, Cathy begins to breathe deeply, folds her arms across her chest, and tilts her chair back. Cathy's eyes become fixed on a decided point on the wall, and her sulk begins. She does not speak, nor does she make or hear any attempts to resolve the issue. This retreat from reality usually continues for ten minutes to an hour, depending on the intensity of the previous conflict. Deciding that

the behavior is purely attention seeking, Cathy's teacher chooses totally to ignore Cathy for whatever length of time her stubborn withdrawal lasts.

Does the teacher alter Cathy's behavior effectively? Is Cathy's withdrawal from reality simply a conscious sulk? The following technique may help to answer these questions.

The first step in "Communication maintenance in times of relationship decay" is to decide whether the student is truly withdrawing from reality or seeking attention from the adult. An obvious way of identifying attention-seeking behavior is to gauge the intensity, duration, and frequency of this behavior.

If the student is showing evidence of listening to others but not to you or if the student responds to your direction in one modality but not others, she is obviously in touch with reality. If clarification of reality versus fantasy is still warranted, the following simple method may be helpful. Use a convincing act to entice the student to respond, e.g., say, "Oh, look what's outside the window!" If the student does not budge or blink, he or she has retreated into fantasy.

Once the interviewer has identified the fact that the student is truly losing contact with reality, the reinstatement of communication can begin. Discussion of "safe" and comforting people is helpful, along with the use of favored objects. When successful, this nonthreatening approach usually registers in the student's face. Blinking, smiling, and relaxing of the facial muscles are typical reactions prior to speech. Maintain communication at a gentle pace, ending the discussion only when assured the student is once again based in reality.

When the student enters the world of reality, he or she feels more comfortable with his thoughts. Discussion of the initial conflict can occur after a safe amount of time has passed.

4. *Regulation of Social and Behavioral Traffic, or "Policing the Area."* Although most students understand the rules and regulations of a school, they need to be reminded frequently of where, when, and what they should be doing. The task is to keep the activities, lessons, and transitional periods as free as possible from interpersonal traffic jams by monitoring the pupils' behavior.

"Strike Three, and You're Out!" It is 8:30 A.M. when Bus 305 pulls up to the school. Tom steps off the bus, laughing with John, Bill, and Rodney. Tom begins to flex his muscles, taking playful jabs at Bill. Rodney turns to John and punches him in the shoulder. He is imitating Tom,

saying, "Look at me, I'm real tough." The four boys laugh. Tom turns and begins to take playful jabs at Rodney. "Who can hit harder" begins. The supervising adult has been more concerned up to this point with unloading the bus than interfering with four playful boys. Rodney takes a powerful and painful slug from Tom, bringing tears to his eyes. Rodney says, "You bastard, Tom," while John and Bill announce to all arriving students, "Rodney's a baby, look at those tears." "What did you just call me, punk?" Tom demands. Rodney launches a rage-filled attack on Tom, and four adults are needed to separate the fight. What seemed like playful amusement became a brawl. How could this have been avoided?

In the "regulation of social and behavioral traffic," a teacher must always be predicting outcomes of interactions. This foresight provides positive support to students by warning them of the possible hazardous outcome.

When the students began the playful boxing, the following sequence might have been helpful. First, an organizing comment could be used, such as, "All right, guys, on into school." This message reminds them of what should be occurring. If this approach is ineffective, try a clear verbal warning, e.g., "Playful hitting can sometimes become painful. Stop, please." As you are speaking, emphasize your point by moving closer to the students. Your presence, with the use of words, may have altered the playful punching, thus refocusing their attention to appropriate school behavior.

5. *Umpire Service, or "Safe or Out, That Is the Question."* This technique is required in two instances: in umpiring a student's initial conflict with self or in umpiring for several students as you would in a team sport. Both types of problems surface when a conflict causes a student to lose self-control. The interviewer's task in these situations is to appeal to the values of fairness. Also remember umpires are not always cherished people.

"A Quick Hand When Trouble Strikes!" Sue was a rather heavy child, constantly struggling for peer acceptance and often rejected because of her appearance. One day, in the lunch line, after several days of dieting, Sue grabbed a piece of pie and a package of cookies. As she tried to sneak by her teacher in the lunch line, several of her classmates announced her actions. "Sue's breaking her diet!" Sue looked up at her teacher, hoping for a decision. Her teacher simply stated, "You've been doing a great job on

your diet, and I notice some weight loss." Smiling, Sue promptly removed the desserts from her tray. The other students were equally supportive.

In this incident, Sue's teacher simply appealed to her "better" self to encourage an appropriate decision. The teacher's remark was supportive, not critical, and helped Sue to feel great about the eventual outcome.

"Let's Change the Rules!" A class of twelve boys were outside playing softball. All members of the two teams agreed on two outs. In the third inning, one team was losing by seven runs. Bob said, "Our team should have three outs to catch up!" All members of his team looked at the teacher for the verdict while the other team protested quite loudly. The teacher simply stated, "How many outs were originally agreed upon?" After the answer had been given, several of Bob's team members said, "We can catch up, Bob! Let's leave it as is." The game went on with two outs.

In this incident, the teacher realized any change in the rules would contribute to chaos. Acting as umpire, the teacher refocused on the original decision allowing better selves to shine here and there on the two teams. The outcome has the appearance of the majority wanting to stick with the original rules.

All the methods mentioned under Emotional First Aid are used on the spot. Immediate attention is offered in the student's present surroundings. Supportive measures are given when coping mechanisms become inadequate or overburdened by life's reality demands.

The emergence of new information through the interview process may cause the interviewer to switch goals to pinpoint the student's needs. Furthermore, as this new information is discussed, the need for in-depth interviewing may become applicable. In this case, the Clinical Exploitation of Life Events offers an interviewer a more extensive interviewing capacity.

Because students in stress create similar feelings in teachers, what emotional first aid techniques can a teacher use to get through the day?

TEACHER'S EMOTIONAL FIRST AID NEEDS: A QUIZ

1. You have just spent several hours developing what you consider to be a wonderful lesson. As you present it to the class, a majority of the students begin to say, "That's dumb!" "We're

not doing it!" With time passing, it becomes more and more apparent that you will be unable even to try your lesson. Your stomach tightens, and your face turns purple. All you can think of is how much time and effort you spent. Which method of Emotional First Aid would be helpful in providing ego support for you? (Hint: Identify how you are feeling.)

a. Regulation of behavior and social traffic
b. Umpiring
c. Drain-off of frustration acidity
d. Communication maintenance in times of relationship decay
e. Support for management of panic, fury, and guilt

2. You are angry at a student who has been off-task and disruptive all day. However, you notice he has earned just enough points to have free time. Your anger makes you really want to take away his free time; yet he has earned it. When you mention the problem to a fellow teacher, his response is, "Hey, he has earned the points. Maybe you need to tighten up your behavioral system in the future." What form of Emotional First Aid can be offered to this angry teacher?

a. Drain-off of frustration acidity
b. Support for management of panic, fury, and guilt
c. Communication maintenance in times of relationship decay
d. Regulation of behavioral and social traffic
e. Umpire services

3. John has been quite verbally abusive and disruptive off and on during the day. It seems no matter what you try, this behavior continues. You feel a tightening in your stomach as John begins again. Enraged by his actions, you confront him. John spits in your face. What technique of support do you need immediately?

a. Umpire service
b. Drain-off of frustration acidity
c. Regulation of behavioral and social traffic
d. Support for management of panic, fury, and guilt
e. Communication maintenance in time of relationship decay

4. All students are working independently at their desks on an assignment. Suddenly, it seems each student requires your help now. You hear and feel the anger in the words as you try to meet each student's needs. You can feel yourself becoming overwhelmed and wanting to be somewhere else; consequently, you begin to withdraw slowly. What form of support do you need?

   a. Drain-off of frustration acidity
   b. Support for management of panic, fury, and guilt
   c. Communication maintenance in times of relationship decay
   d. Regulation of behavioral and social traffic
   e. Umpire service

5. All staff members are attending an important meeting. Time is running out, and a decision has not been made. Mrs. Jones raises her hand. Contributing nothing, she talks at a tangent. Members of the staff become irritated. The director of the program interrupts Mrs. Jones and redirects the group to the task by saying, "Remember, we must reach a decision about our new policy today." What is the method the director used? (Hint: The director used the word "remember.")

   a. Support for management of panic, fury, and guilt
   b. Umpire services
   c. Drain-off of frustration acidity
   d. Communication maintenance in times of relationship decay
   e. Regulation of behavioral and social traffic

ANSWERS: 1. c 2. c 3. d 4. c 5. e

EDITORS' COMMENTARY

In the previous article, Merritt-Petrashek described the first category of LSI— Emotional First Aid on the Spot. The second category of LSI is the Clinical Exploitation of Life Events.

Subcategories of Clinical Exploitation of Life Events

To achieve this second category of LSI, Redl (1959) proposed five different types of interviews for student insight and behavioral changes.

1. *Reality Rub-in Interview.* This interview is used with students who distort reality and have social blindness because of their level of anxiety. They perceive reality not as it is but as they are emotionally. They frequently hear things, see things, and remember events during a crisis that are not accurate, but they believe their distortions.

2. *Symptom Estrangement Interview.* This interview deals with students who are comfortable with their aggressive, hostile behaviors and believe nothing is wrong with them. They are not motivated to change, and they have no awareness that their behavior is deviant or pathological. They may assault a peer and justify their behavior by saying, "He started it" or "I warned him" and assume the role of the victim and not the victimizer.

3. *Massaging Numb Values Crises.* This interview is conducted with students who act out and then become so guilty they put themselves down emotionally and show self-abusive behavior, such as tearing up their work or hurting themselves. This interview focuses on students' self-worth and self-control, and attacks their irrational beliefs that they deserve to be punished. This interview also avoids any guilt-inducing statements.

4. *New Tools Salesmanship.* This interview focuses on a student's lack of social skills, which, in turn, creates new social problems for the student. The interview is the precursor of social skills training curricula developed in the 1980s.

5. *Manipulation of Body Boundaries.* This interview helps a student understand how manipulation by "group forces" or a "false friend" encourages him or her to act out the group's wishes in exchange for personal acceptance.

These five clinical interviews involve knowledge of group dynamics, developmental psychology, and psychodynamic theory, and are based on the following beliefs:

1. When a student crisis occurs, it is to be perceived by staff as a unique opportunity for change and not as a disaster to be avoided. It is a time for benign instruction and not a time for punishment and student alienation.

2. LSI is a verbal firefighting strategy that leads to developing fireproofing skills. It takes place in the student "here and now."

3. LSI is a humanistic approach in which the staff serves as the student's advocate.

4. LSI is initially nonjudgmental, but if the student is not motivated to change the inappropriate behaviors, further staff intervention is grounded on clear ethical values about how people live and treat each other in group situations.

5. LSI assumes that a student in a crisis initially will deny, project, and rationalize any responsibility for the aberrant behavior. During this time, the student is his or her own worst enemy and will make the situation worse.

6. If logic, order, responsibility, and resolution are to happen during a crisis, the staff must be well trained to understand and manage a student's inner thoughts, feelings, and behaviors.

7. A successful LSI will have the following benefits for the student, staff, and school district.

The student will learn that:

- A crisis doesn't mean adult rejection or estrangement.

- An adult can accept a student at his or her worst and still extend respect.

- There is an important relationship between one's thinking, feeling, behaving, and consequences.

- Change begins when the student identifies a chronic pattern of self-defeating behavior.

- Accepting responsibility for personal behaviors leads to personal growth.

- Learning more appropriate social skills leads to new ways of managing frustrations.

- Adults can be trusted to help.

The staff will benefit by:

- Feeling empowered as professionals.

- Learning successful ways of deescalating a crisis.

- Learning different strategies of responding to a crisis therapeutically.

- Developing more supportive staff relationships.

- Providing a safer school environment.

The school district will benefit by:

- Providing a more successful resource for "high-risk" and "troubled" students.

- Reducing the level of violence in schools.

- Reducing the number of lawsuits filed against the school system.

- Improving public relations with the community.

The Translation of LSI for Educators

Morse (1980) was the first educational psychologist to adapt the LSI concept into an understandable process for school staff use. In his "Worksheet on Life Space Interviewing for Teachers," he described a seven-step process for carrying out a successful LSI. His translation of the LSI made the clinical issues of LSI more understandable and teachable to educators. Table 8.1 delineates the differences among LSI, psychodynamic, and traditional approaches to conflict resolution.

The Evolution of Life Space Interviewing to Life Space Crisis Intervention

From 1970 to 1980, behavior modification theory and programs dominated special education practices, and, in the majority of the teacher training programs, LSI instruction faded into disuse.

In 1981 Long and Fagen published a new monograph on LSI to promote its use among special educators as they struggled to mainstream students with emotional and behavioral problems into the regular classroom. LSI had a fresh and important role in special education but still lacked a teacher-friendly instructional model. In 1991 Wood and Long published *Life Space Intervention* and filled this void. In 1992 Long and Fecser took LSI to the next step and developed a certification program in Life Space Crisis Intervention (LSCI), sponsored by the Institute of Psychoeducational Training. These two resources provided professional structure and the standards for trainer preparation in LSCI, which resulted in an unprecedented resurgence of this concept.

The Five Modifications of Life Space Interviewing to Life Space Crisis Intervention

LSCI developed out of the LSI theory proposed by Redl, Wineman, and Morse in the 1950s and 1960s. The basic concepts of LSI have not changed, but they have been upgraded, expanded, and made more functional. Just as a modernized fire department has improved its effectiveness by integrating new technology into its firefighting tactics by using better heat-resistant apparel, more reliable

TABLE 8.1

MORSE'S WORKSHEET ON CONCEPTUAL VARIATIONS IN INTERVIEW DESIGNS WITH CHILDREN

	Pyschodynamic	Life Space or Reality	Traditional
1. Instigating condition	General personality problem, long- term, not responding to supportive and growth correctional effort	Specific incident (or series) of behavior usually calling for "on the spot" managerial interference	Both implied, but interpreted as moral issue
2. Goal	Long-term expectations of gradual emergence of more healthy personality, possible regression followed by integration and eventual independence	Degree of behavioral compliance accompanied by life space relief fostering adjustment	Induce an immediate character change, exterior change
3. Setting	Office isolation away from immediate life pressures, formal setting, sequence timed	Direct use of milieu reality aspects; choice of time and place to enforce or mitigate as needed	Isolated, integrated, frequent use of group or setting for pressure
4. Relationship	Classical transference, resistance to interpersonal relationship	Emphatic, child identified role by adult	Adult role of authority; paternalistic, autocratic
5. Content	Conscious and unconscious, fantasy, early conflicts, projection, focus on feeling, impulse exploration	What went on, reality exploration, reconstruction with attached feelings and impulses recognized and accepted	Emphasis on the standard morality interpretation of event
6. Processes	Transference, resistance interpretations, insight, identification, acceptance of impulses (interpretations of unconscious material), high verbal permissiveness, acting out interpreted	Causal behavior "accepted," clinical exploitation of life space events, ego-level interpretation, impulse-control balance critical, support given, explanations fostered, ego support, hurdle help, "skills" depicted, behavior implications faced	Appeal to value system, threats, admonition, exhortations, denial of impulses
7. Resolution	Eventual transfer to life situations	Support and milieu planning to mitigate critical conditions	Surface compliance or rejection

oxygen-breathing apparatus, and more effective water nozzles, LSCI has been enhanced and intensified to meet the new social concerns about the increase of student aggression, hostility, and violence in schools. The following five significant updates have been made (Long, Wood, & Fecser, 2001). The modifications of LSI that created LSCI have maintained the theory of LSI while also making LSCI a significant and critical skill for all professionals who provide direct service to troubled students.

1. The name Life Space Interviewing was modified to Life Space Crisis Intervention (LSCI). LSI originally was used in clinical settings with seriously disturbed students. LSCI is now used more frequently in educational programs, correctional facilities, and residential settings. The word *interview* seemed too restrictive and gave the impression of interrogating or extracting information from a student to obtain admission of some wrongdoing. Also, the notion of "interview" appeared to be a one-time experience in a highly structured, adult-dominated setting. Finally, the pervasive emotional needs of many troubled students required more support and help than could be provided by the psychodynamic model. In response to these concerns, the words *crisis intervention* were substituted to indicate that LSCI also involves the integration of many theoretical concepts and skills, including psychodynamic theory, cognitive theory, social learning theory, and behavioral theory. The word *intervention* is a broader and more realistic term than *interview* in describing how LSCI is currently being taught and used in schools during a crisis.

2. LSI was based on sophisticated clinical insights and skills. All too often, they reflected the personality of the interviewer. As a result, LSI was difficult to teach and often was misinterpreted and misused by new staff. The appeal of this concept was so magnetic that learners believed they knew about LSI before they understood it. LSI sounds easy to learn and practice, but it is a highly complex and demanding skill. To counter these concerns, Long and Fecser (2007) analyzed the LSI process and identified 26 baseline competencies that are necessary to learn before one is qualified to practice LSCI. These 26 foundation concepts and skills took the mystery out of LSI and provided a quality control standard for LSCI training while emphasizing the importance of the "helping staff" to enter the student's world relatively uncontaminated by their own life history.

3. One of the problems with LSI is the ease with which the helper can get lost, sidetracked, and confused by the irrational, defensive, and disorganized world of a troubled student in a crisis. Too many staff begin an LSI appropriately, only to become bewildered and perplexed by the intensity of the student's feelings and issues.

To clarify the LSCI process, a cognitive map was developed to "cue" the staff to specific student and staff stages. Morse's worksheet on LSI was modified, and the new LSCI guidelines propose six sequential stages of the process with identifiable student and staff issues. The first three stages are considered "diagnostic," as the interviewer is gathering information to determine next steps. The final three stages are "reclaiming" as the interviewer takes the student through a process that allows him or her to examine patterns of perceiving, thinking, feeling, and behaving.

Stage 1: Student Crisis Stage and Staff's Deescalation Skills

The goal of this stage is to drain off the student's angry feelings to the point where his or her behavior is driven by rational processes and not by emotions.

- *Drain off emotional intensity.* Reduce the amount of emotion around the incident; acknowledge that the emotions the student feels are acceptable.
- *Support a student engulfed in intense emotion.* Use time-out when a student is so flooded by emotion that his or her behavior is out of control; protect the student and others from his or her temporary rage; communicate that an adult will temporarily protect the student.
- *Use all deescalation and affirmation skills to maintain communications.* Beware of staff counteraggression.

Stage 2: Student Timeline Stage and Staff's Relationship Skills

Assist the student in a detailed step-by-step recounting of the entire incident, beginning with a point in time when the problem did not exist. Use attending, active listening, observing, and responding skills.

- Frequently validate or *affirm* and acknowledge feelings and behaviors that were "appropriate" under the circumstances.
- *Clarify* "questionable" points. "What you are saying is very important and I want to be sure I have it right." See the sequence of behavior from the student's point of view.
- *Watch for "red flags,"* seemingly insignificant comments or asides that may signal a personal issue. If one appears, try repeating the key word or phrase, or try a follow-up question. Don't push it if the student doesn't want to continue, but remember the comment and return to it at another time.
- Observe the student's *body language* very carefully. Denial, agitation, interest, or silence is sometimes indicative of being on a meaningful track.
- Use *reflecting* often, to clarify, signal support, and keep the conversation going.
- *Decode* or interpret the student's comments.
- *Stop and summarize* what you have heard so that the student can see the sequence of his or her thoughts, feelings, behaviors, and reactions. Use the Conflict Cycle model whenever possible.

Stage 3: Student Central-Issue Stage and Staff's Differential Diagnosis Skills

- *Find the central issue.* Decide whether the issue is representative of the student's chronic patterns of perceiving, thinking, feeling, and behaving or is merely a situational conflict.

- *Assess the student's perception, insight, and motivation to change.* Decide whether the student is capable of participating in an LSCI.
- *Select the appropriate therapeutic goal.* This will decide whether the focus of the interview will be Emotional First Aid or one of the seven reclaiming interventions.

Stage 4: Student Insight Stage and Staff's Clinical Skills

- *Carry out the appropriate reclaiming intervention*—should lead to some student insight regarding one's pattern of self-defeating behavior and to learn more effective social skills.
- *Get a commitment.* Help the student to commit to the solution. What will the student see as a satisfactory solution that can be "owned"?

Stage 5: Student New-Skill Stage and Staff's Empowering Skills
This is the prosocial teaching time.

- *Rehearse new behaviors.* Role-play under as realistic conditions as possible.
- *Anticipate consequences.* Discuss the possibility of discomfort when the student tries out the new behavior for the first time. How will the student deal with the possibility of a less-than-desired outcome?
- *Affirm potential benefits.* Review the commitment and the positive results hard work can bring.

Stage 6: Student Transfer-of-Training Stage and Staff's Follow-up Skills

- Set the expectation to participate with the group. What is the ongoing activity that the student will be expected to join? What rules and expectations are in place?
- Prepare for reactions of the peer group. Anticipate how peers will receive the student as he or she enters the room. How will the student handle possible problems?
- Support and follow-up. Do what you can to help the student make a successful attempt at using the new behavior modification plan. Speak with colleagues to let them know what to expect and how to encourage the new behavior. Check in with the student and show that the new plan is important to you.

4. To more accurately reflect the goal of LSCI in contemporary settings, the term *clinical interview* was replaced by *reclaiming intervention* (Long et al., 2001). In addition, descriptive terms were added to the names of the reclaiming interventions to clarify their meanings, as listed below.

5. In the final change, the five clinical interviews, now reclaiming interventions, have been expanded to seven identifiable patterns of self-defeating behavior. This decision was based on an analysis of over 300 school crises in which two new clinical interventions emerged: (a) *the Red Flag Reclaiming Intervention,* in which a student carries in or expresses an explosive personal issue in school, and (b) the *Double Struggle Reclaiming Intervention,* in which a staff inadvertently misperceives or mishandles the student's crisis and ends up making the conflict worse. The seven reclaiming interventions follow:

1. Reality Rub (Errors in Perception)
2. Red Flag (Imported Problems)
3. Symptom Estrangement (Comfort with Antisocial Behavior)
4. Massaging Numb Values (Overwhelmed by Guilt)
5. New Tools (Poor Social Skills)
6. Manipulation of Body Boundaries (Manipulation of Peers)
7. Double Struggle (Intervention with Staff)

To help improve the clarity of these patterns of self-defeating behaviors, we describe each of the seven reclaiming interventions in greater detail according to the student's perception, indicators for use of the reclaiming intervention, the outcome goal, the focus of the intervention, and the student's new insight.

RECLAIMING INTERVENTION 1: REALITY RUB (ERRORS IN PERCEPTION)

Student's Perception: "No one agrees with what I know happened!"

Uses: With students who demonstrate any of the following patterns:

1. Blocked perceptions of reality due to intense feelings
2. Misperceptions of reality due to triggering of personal emotional sensitivities
3. Restricted perceptions of reality due to perseveration on a single event in the sequence leading to the crisis
4. Private reconstruction of reality as events are interpreted through rigid perceptual filters derived from personal history
5. Manipulation of reality to test limits

Goal: To help the student organize his or her thinking so that a more accurate perception of reality emerges; to bring the student to the realization that there is "more than meets the eye"; to help the student begin to understand his or her contribution to the problem.

Focus: Organizes students' perceptions and sequence of time and events; developmentally the most rudimentary of the therapeutic goals.

Student's New Insight: "Maybe there is another way to look at this situation; I can see how I might have made it worse, and what I need to do about it."

RECLAIMING INTERVENTION 2: RED FLAG (IMPORTED PROBLEMS)

Student's Perception: "Everybody is against me! No one understands what's going on with me and no one cares! I can't take it any more!"

Uses: With students who overreact to normal rules and procedures with emotional outbursts; they attempt to create a "no-win" situation by engaging staff in a power struggle, which ultimately results in more rejection and feelings of alienation.

Goal: To identify the source of the problem: Is it a "Carry In" problem from another setting, a "Carry Over" problem from another place within the current setting, or a "Tap In" to a personal unresolved emotional conflict?

Focus: Helps the student recognize that he or she is displacing feelings on others and alienating the sources of support the students needs to help him or her handle the stress.

Student's New Insight: "Someone does understand my real problems and can read beyond my behavior. I need to talk to staff about my real problems and not create new ones here."

RECLAIMING INTERVENTION 3: SYMPTOM ESTRANGEMENT (COMFORT WITH ANTISOCIAL BEHAVIOR)

Student's Perceptions: "I do what I have to do even if it hurts others." "I have to take care of 'Number One.'" "I have a reputation to maintain. I have no need to change."

Uses: With students who are too comfortable with their deviant behavior and receive too much gratification from it; those who practice aggression, passive–aggression, manipulation, or exploitation of others.

Goal: To make a particular behavior uncomfortable, by confronting the rationalizations and decoding the self-serving narcissism and distorted pleasure the student receives from the unacceptable behavior.

Focus: Helps student realize that he or she is paying a high price for justifying his or her exploitation of others and that he or she is tricking him- or herself into believing his or her cause is just.

Student's New Insight: "Maybe I'm not as smart as I tell myself." "Maybe I've been cruel." "Maybe I've been tricking myself."

RECLAIMING INTERVENTION 4: MASSAGING NUMB VALUES (OVERWHELMED BY GUILT)

Student's Perception: "Even when I'm upset, a part of me is saying, 'Control! Stop yourself,' but I don't."

Uses: With students who, after acting out, are burdened by remorse, shame, inadequacy, or guilt about their own failures or unworthiness; those with a destructive self-image; and those who have a negative social role.

Goal: To relieve some of the burden by emphasizing a student's positive qualities; to strengthen self-control and self-confidence as an able and valued person with qualities like fairness, kindness, friendship, or leadership potential.

Focus: Expand student's self-control and confidence through abundant affirmations and reflections about existing socially desirable attributes and potential for future acclaim by peers; developmentally, this goal requires a shift in source of responsibility from adult to student.

Student's New Insight: "Even under tempting situations or group pressure, I have the capacity to control myself."

RECLAIMING INTERVENTION 5: NEW TOOLS (POOR SOCIAL SKILLS)

Student's Perception: "I want to do the right thing, but it always comes out wrong."

Uses: With students seeking approval of adults or peers but lacking appropriate social behaviors to accomplish this.

Goal: To teach new social behaviors that student can use for immediate positive gain.

Focus: Instruct in specific social behaviors that will have immediate payback in desired responses from others; developmentally reflects emerging independence and responsibility.

Student's New Insight: "I have the right intention, but I need help to learn the skills that will help me make friends, achieve, and get along with adults."

RECLAIMING INTERVENTION 6: MANIPULATION OF BODY BOUNDARIES (MANIPULATION OF PEERS)

Student's Perception: "It's important to have a friend even if the friend gets me into trouble"; or "I'm going to teach him a lesson!"

Uses: With students who are neglected, abused, scapegoated, or isolated, or who seek out destructive friendships by acting out for them; or with students who are unwittingly "set up" by passive–aggressive peers to act out.

Goal: To help a student see that another student (or adult) is manipulating events in a way that is working against the student's best interest.

Focus: Provide insight into reasons for the behavior of others; view social interactions from the perspective of motivations and

behaviors of others; developmentally, this goal requires considerable maturity on the student's part, as the student learns
to understand how others think, feel, and behave.

Student's New Insight: "A friend is someone who helps you solve
problems and feel good rather than someone who gets you
into trouble"; or "I can make my own decisions; I don't need to
'take the bait' when someone is trying to get me in trouble."

RECLAIMING INTERVENTION 7: DOUBLE STRUGGLE (INTERVENTION WITH STAFF)

Staff's Perception:

1. "I'm not going to take his abuse! If he wants to challenge me, I'm
ready!"
2. "He'll conform to my demands with a smile or he's out!"
3. "That's the last straw! I won't take any more of his garbage behavior!"
4. "I knew it would be him again!"

Uses: With staff who inadvertently fuel conflict for any of the following reasons:

1. They become caught in the student's Conflict Cycle.
2. They hold rigid and unrealistic expectations regarding normal developmental student behavior.
3. They are caught in a bad mood.
4. They are caught in prejudging a problem student in a crisis.

Focus: To benignly confront the staff by using the Conflict Cycle to
help the adult gain insight into his or her role in the incident.

Goals:

1. To acknowledge the adult's good intentions in dealing with the crisis.
2. To share information about the student or the incident that the adult
may not have had at the time of the crisis.
3. To correct misperceptions about the student's role in the crisis.
4. To use the Conflict Cycle as a way of understanding student and adult
stress during a crisis.
5. To support the adult with affirming statements rather than blame him
or her.

6. To help the adult accept a new and accurate perception of the incident.

7. To help the adult understand the situation from the student's point of view.

8. To facilitate reconciliation and problem resolution.

Staff's New Insights: "Now I understand the situation from the student's point of view and I recognize how I contributed to the problem."

THE skills involved in carrying out these seven different interventions can be learned, but the first task is to understand the differences among them. A differential spot quiz follows to help readers explore the differences among these interventions.

The Differential Diagnosis of the Seven LSCI Interventions: A Quiz

Read the following seven crisis situations documented by Beck and Beck (2006). Identify the central issue of the crisis, and then select the appropriate reclaiming intervention:

A. Reality Rub
B. Red Flag
C. Symptom Estrangement
D. Massaging Numb Values
E. New Tools
F. Manipulation of Body Boundaries
G. Double Struggle

1. In an eighth-grade homeroom, Christopher and Louis were seated together at the computer. Christopher was seen whispering to Louis, who seemed pretty much unconcerned. A few minutes later, Latanya, who had a rough morning, entered the room. As she was walking to her seat, Chrisopher was heard saying to Louis, "You're not going to do anything; you're such a punk!" He continued by saying, "I can't believe you're going to let a girl talk about you like that." Louis, feeling the pressure of his classmate, responded by asking Latanya why she was talking shit about him. Latanya immediately became loud and began walking toward Louis, telling him to shut the fuck up. Louis responded by caller her a bitch. The two were in each other's faces and began pushing. Staff intervened,

but not before punches were thrown. Christopher remained seated while Louis and Latanya were separated and taken to time-out rooms.

2. Tommy, an anxious seventh-grade student, suddenly became very disruptive during language arts class. He began singing and playing the drums on his desk, disturbing the other students. The teacher, Ms. Foster, redirected him to his assignment and told him that if he continued, he would lose points and owe time after class. Tommy continued and was directed to leave the classroom. While in the hall, Ms. Foster reminded him of behavioral expectations, but Tommy ignored her and started to lightly kick the wall and pace up and down the hall. He was told that if he continued, he would need to go to a quiet room for time-out. Tommy's behavior began to escalate, and he became disruptive to the surrounding classrooms. Ms. Foster directed him to the quiet room, and Tommy responded by running out of the area and down the stairwell. Tommy was stopped by security and escorted to the quiet room, but he began to struggle and lightly kick staff. He was placed in a physical restraint. As he deescalated, he was released, but he began to lightly hit the wall with this fist and to kick. Staff started to tell him expectations for serving a quiet time-out, and he quickly sat down, saying he was ready to start his time-out. As staff affirmed his good decision, Tommy became angry, targeting staff by calling them names. Staff used planned ignoring, and Tommy gradually calmed down, then began to cry and mumble to himself.

3. Monty, a second-grade student with a chaotic home life, typically enjoys recess. On the day in question, there weren't any significant problems throughout the midday recess period. Monty seemed to enjoy playing soccer and basketball with his peers. As the class was lining up to go inside, Monty had a conflict with a classmate. Apparently, Monty put his hand on the other boy's arm. The other boy then pushed his hand off. While the playground supervisor was asking about the problem, Monty began repeatedly punching the other boy in the stomach as hard and violently as he could to the point where the boy fell to the ground. Monty had to be pulled off the other boy.

4. James is a 10-year-old boy who demands a great deal of attention from both his special education and regular classroom teachers. The following incident occurred during a science class in which James participates with nonhandicapped peers. The students had been given small seeds which they were to plant and observe growth. James had been attempting to join in with a group at another table. He was especially trying to get the attention of a particular girl. Mr. Byrd, the science teacher, had redirected James twice to return to his own table, but James continually attempted to interact with the girl. In an effort to get her attention by being funny, he began to do a rap and dance. In the process, he accidentally knocked the girl's seeds out of her hand and onto the floor. Mr. Byrd, now impatient, directed James to give his seeds to the girl, who was quite upset. The class was watching the interaction between Mr. Byrd and James, who responded by yelling profanities at the teacher and screaming embarrassing remarks at the female student.

5. Joe, an eighth-grade student, was disheveled and out of breath as he entered the special education classroom for his first-period class. This was particularly odd since Joe's father had called the school earlier and reported that Joe would not be in because he was ill. Joe was heard in the hallway yelling things at other students, attempting to engage them in arguments. As Joe came into the room, he began yelling at students who were already at their seats. He then approached the teacher and stated loudly that he was in big trouble and he was going to be big trouble for everyone today.

6. Christina, a troubled high school student, had been counting on gaining some employment experience through school. She had been looking forward to her appointment with the guidance counselor for some time. On the day of the meeting, Christina entered the building and, without checking in with her homeroom teacher, started on her way to the counselor's office. She was stopped by security and asked to produce an ID and a pass. She told the guard that she had an appointment and didn't need a pass, but the guard insisted that she must have written permission. Ignoring the guard, Christina continued on her way to the counselor's office. As the guard took her by the arm, Christina pulled away and screamed obscenities at her. The scene in the hallway attracted a lot of attention, and Christina was escorted to the assistant principal's office, where she was promptly suspended. She never made it to the counselor's office for her appointment.

7. David, a seventh-grade student who is known for his turbulent behavior, was sitting at a table with six other boys during lunch. Two of the other students began teasing one another in a popular game known as "the dozens" in which two students exchange derogatory remarks in an effort to outwit the other. This often escalates into a conflict as remarks become increasingly personal. On this day, Jemaul and Eric were engaged in such a match when it suddenly erupted into a food fight. In the melee, David was splattered as well, even though he was, for once, just a bystander. As the lunchroom staff intervened, David found himself being hauled out of his seat and read the riot act. Staff told him he was going to serve detentions because they had had enough of his outrageous behavior. David responded at first by trying to claim he had nothing to do with the food fight, but staff were not listening. David began to swear and was taken to the office for disciplinary action.

ANSWERS: 1. F 2. D 3. C 4. E 5. B 6. A 7. C

ARTICLE 8.3

IN the next article, John Hill and Nicholas Long provide a comprehensive illustration of an actual Life Space Crisis Intervention. This example demonstrates the many skills required to enter a crisis and turn it into a rewarding experience for the student and staff.

HOME FOR THE HOLIDAYS: A RED-FLAG, CARRY-IN, RECLAIMING INTERVENTION

John W. Hill and Nicholas J. Long

In the terminology of Life Space Crisis Intervention, a "Red-Flag Carry-In Crisis" occurs when a youngster overreacts because of stress he or she brings in from another setting. For example, many students bring problems from home or the street into the school. This article describes the diagnosis and resolution of such a carry-in problem when a student's fear of abuse at home triggered major dysfunctional behavior at school.

Although our students come to our learning disabilities clinic after school, we greet them as though they were just beginning the school day. This decision helps us to be ready to identify any significant problems brought from home and school. Brandon is a 9-year-old third grader who was diagnosed as having emotional disturbance and a reading disability. One day, prior to coming to our clinic, Brandon received a letter from Robert, his physically abusive 16-year-old brother. Brandon was convinced this letter was a statement that Robert was coming home for the holidays.

BACKGROUND

Brandon has been hospitalized twice over the past year for violent and uncontrollable emotional outbursts. He lives at home with his mother; he has two older brothers who do not live with them. Robert resides in a distant court-mandated residential ranch treatment program. David, age 13, lives in a court-ordered community-based group home for youth.

Brandon attends a general education public school. He has remedial reading activities that take place in the resource room, but he is included in regular classroom activities throughout the remainder of his school day. At our clinic, Brandon usually is well motivated, even when reading tasks are difficult for him, and he enjoys teacher praise that focuses on his accomplishments. Aside from his rare emotional rages, Brandon would be considered a gentle, vulnerable student. Recently, Brandon began taking violin lessons, and he is demonstrating pleasure and pride in his new violin and his ability to play it.

THE INCIDENT

Before the incident, Brandon had attended the learning disabilities clinic for 5 months for intensive reading and decoding instruction. Students attend clinic classes from 4:30 P.M. to 6:30 P.M. On the evening of the incident, Brandon completed his regular school day and spent time at home before getting a ride from his mother to our clinic. When Brandon arrived for class, he was visibly upset, lying in the back seat of the car with tears streaming down his cheeks and refusing to leave the car. Thirty minutes later, Brandon finally got out of the car and walked to the classroom. When his teachers asked him if he was ready to begin his reading activities, Brandon stiffened, folded his arms over his chest, and began shaking his head from side to side, saying, "No! Reading sucks! This school sucks! You suck!" At this point, his teacher became concerned about the possibility of prolonged confrontation and escalation. She asked if I [John Hill] would talk with him because Brandon and I have a comfortable relationship. I agreed.

DRAIN-OFF STAGE

Kneeling next to Brandon's desk to establish eye contact, I waited several minutes in silence. When Brandon finally looked at me, I asked him if he would please come with me to the back of the room for a drink of water. Without comment, Brandon stood up, arms still folded tightly across his chest, and walked to the fountain. I thanked Brandon for coming with me and found two chairs so we could face each other.

> **Interviewer:** Brandon, it is clear you are upset today. I see your tears, but I don't know what is causing them.
>
> **Brandon:** I don't want to read.
>
> **Interviewer:** Okay, I hear you. But I'm also concerned because usually you come to class ready to read. Today seems different for you. Can you share with me what you have been thinking about?
>
> **Brandon:** It's just different today. You don't know anything.

Interviewer: *(ignoring the personal comment)* By different, do you mean you are having different feelings today than usual?

Brandon: Yes!

Interviewer: So you are feeling different today, but you still got out of the car and came to class all by yourself. That must have been difficult to do when you were upset.

Brandon: Yes, I did!

Interviewer: And now you are talking and not fighting with me.

Brandon: Yes, I am!

Brandon then unfolded his arms from around himself and asked me if he could get another drink of water. After sitting together a few more minutes, Brandon dried his eyes on his shirtsleeve and gave a weak little smile, seeming more relaxed.

TIMELINE STAGE

Interviewer: So, how was school today?

Brandon: Okay.

Interviewer: Did you wake up this morning in time for breakfast?

Brandon: Yes. Then my mom drove me to school.

Interviewer: Did you have to do a lot of reading today?

Brandon: I read and wrote stuff, and I also got to play my violin. Then I went home to get my snack.

Interviewer: So, it sounds like you had a pretty good day.

Brandon: Yes. *(pause)* But guess what. I got a letter.

Interviewer: *(I recalled from my Life Space Crisis Intervention [LSCI] training the importance of exploring any new object about which a student displays emotion.)* Tell me about this letter.

Brandon: Do you want to see it?

Interviewer: I sure do!

Brandon jumped up from his chair and went over to his jacket, removing an envelope from the pocket.

Brandon: Here it is.

Interviewer: So this is the letter you want me to see.

Brandon: Yes. *(frowning)* It's from my brother Robert.

Interviewer: It is addressed to you—your very own letter. Did you read it?

Brandon: No. I can't. But my mom read it to me before I left home to come here. Do you want to read it?

Interviewer: This letter seems very important to you. Do you want me to read it to you?

Brandon: Yes!

Interviewer: Okay. Here goes.

> Dear Brandon,
>
> How are things going for you there? There's not much to do here. I have to go to class. They have horses here, but I'm not sure when I can ride them. I can't come home for the holidays. Tell Mom to buy me a cheap camera, and I will send you some pictures of this place.
>
> (signed) Robert

Brandon: Read the part about coming home again.

Interviewer: "I can't come home for the holidays."

Brandon: Oh.

Interviewer: Are you disappointed that Robert won't be coming home?

Brandon: No way!

Interviewer: "No way!" You said that in a strong way. Tell me about Robert.

Brandon: I'm glad he won't be coming. He hurts me. He hits my mother and he steals cars.

Interviewer: You're glad your brother won't be coming home because in the past he hurt you and your mom. How has he hurt you?

Brandon: He takes my stuff from my room and hits me hard until I cry. Mom too. That's why he's gone.

Interviewer: So Robert is very aggressive and hurtful to his family, and you feel better knowing that he won't be coming home.

Brandon: Yes.

Interviewer: Safer?

Brandon: Yes. *(After a long pause)* Do you think Robert is safe, too?

Interviewer: Robert is away and won't be coming home. You are safe now. He can't hurt you from far away. He is safe, also, because he can't hurt you and is getting help with his anger. You were brave to tell me what you really felt. Let's read this letter together out loud so you can learn the words and read it to yourself any time you want.

We read the letter twice.

Brandon: Thanks. Guess where I'm going to keep my letter?

Interviewer: Where? Do you have a special place in mind?

Brandon: Yes. In the inside compartment of my violin case.

Interviewer: That's a very special and safe place for your letter. Safe and in control, just like you are now. Do you want to put your letter in the violin case now?

Brandon: Yes.

CENTRAL ISSUE AND INSIGHT STAGES

Clearly the letter from Robert tapped into Brandon's fear of his brother, which he displaced onto his mother and teacher as refusal to come to class and to read. Once Brandon understood that his older brother was not coming home, he began to feel safe and more in control, even deciding to put the object of his crisis, the letter, in a symbolically contained and "safe" place. Reviewing the timeline in my mind, I selected a Red-Flag, Carry-In, Reclaiming Intervention to help Brandon understand his pattern of self-defeating behavior.

Interviewer: Before returning to reading lessons, can you tell me again what upset you?

Brandon: My brother coming home and hitting me.

Interviewer: That's right, but who had to deal with your upset?

Brandon: My mom and my teacher.

Interviewer: So let's review this sequence. You were actually upset with your brother, but you got upset with your mother and teacher instead. Is that the way it was? Did that help your problem with the letter?

Brandon: No. Reading the letter helped.

Interviewer: And now that your private worry about your brother coming home is over and you are safe, how will you behave in class?

Brandon: Okay.

Interviewer: Sure, because once you talked about your problem, you were able to solve it, so now you are ready to return to class.

NEW SKILLS STAGE

Interviewer: What can you do the next time you're upset or afraid of a letter from your brother?

Brandon: Tell my mom.

Interviewer: That sounds like a good idea. Now let me ask you a question. What will you say to your mom or to your teacher in order to get help next time you receive a letter from your brother?

Brandon: Read the letter to me.

Interviewer: That is very clear. Can you tell your mother or teacher that so they can talk with you?

Brandon: Yes.

Interviewer: Thank you for talking with me. I also think you learned something important from this problem. Are you ready to go back to reading class?

Brandon: Yes. Do you think my teacher will let me play my violin for the class?

Interviewer: I don't know, but it sounds like a good idea. Let's ask her.

During snack break, Brandon played his violin for the class, thus ending his afternoon on a very positive note.

TRANSFER OF TRAINING STAGE

I talked with Brandon's mother about this incident. Brandon will continue family therapy to deal with his brother's abuse and his own explosive episodes. Brandon's teachers agreed to listen to his attempts to tell us his feelings because Brandon's self-defeating behaviors may occur again if he receives mail from his brother. It also was agreed that Brandon should "check in" at the beginning of each class session with his teacher, whom he trusts and is the most comfortable in talking to.

INSTRUCTIONAL COMMENTS
—NICHOLAS J. LONG

I selected this Red-Flag, Carry-In Crisis because not only is it an excellent instructional example, but it also offers an opportunity to respond to some common and significant criticisms regarding using LSCI in public schools.

CRITICISM 1

"The determination of the student's pattern of self-defeating behavior is too ambiguous a concept to be valid and reliable. Many of the students I have seen in a crisis could fit at least two of six proposed patterns of self-defeating behavior. It appears to me the diagnosis is more a function of the staff than the behavior of the student."

RESPONSE TO CRITICISM 1

This criticism reflects only partial understanding of the LSCI diagnostic process of identifying any one of the six student patterns of self-defeating behaviors. The confusion begins whenever a staff person has difficulty distinguishing between the student's presenting pattern of self-defeating behaviors and the precipitating source of his or her problem. A differential diagnosis of a student's pattern of self-defeating behavior is based on an analysis of the student's presenting behaviors, not on his or her underlying issues. Let me explain.

The diagnostic pattern of a Manipulation of Body Boundaries–Crisis Type 1 is based on the dynamics of "false friendship." The presenting pattern involves a relationship in which a manipulative student offers his or her friendship to a student who is emotionally needy only if the latter carries out the wishes of the former. Ultimately, this friendship is not in the best interest of the student with emotional problems, because he or she will end up being exploited and in trouble for acting out the suggestions of his or her "friend." Once this pattern of behavior is identified, the diagnosis of the Manipulations of Body Boundaries–Crisis Type 1 can be made during the timeline stage, followed by specific reclaiming interventions to alter this destructive relationship.

A second look at the behavior of the two students in this example, however, may cause some persons to wonder if the correct diagnosis was made. For example, the manipulative student may appear to be too comfortable with his or her devious behaviors and perhaps could benefit from a Symptom Estrangement Intervention. Likewise, the student who is emotionally needy may appear to lack adequate social skills for making friends and perhaps could profit from a New Tool Intervention. These conclusions are logical, but there are secondary issues. The primary diagnostic issue is the presenting behavior of "false friendship," not these students' underlying issues, which are addressed during the reclaiming intervention, not during the diagnostic process.

To clarify the distinction between a student's presenting behaviors and his or her underlying concerns, I will review the diagnostic process Brandon's behaviors took. Brandon's presenting behaviors were (a) his initial refusal to get out of the car and (b) his continued negativism once he was in the classroom. The staff members who knew Brandon realized his behavior was unusual and out of proportion to the situation. This was the diagnostic behavior or clue that Dr. Hill needed to consider. After draining off Brandon's intense feeling and obtaining his story about his brother's letter, Dr. Hill was able to confirm his diagnosis of a Red-Flag, Carry-In Crisis. A staff member could argue, however, that Brandon's crisis was also an example of a Red-Flag, Tap-In Crisis and/or a Reality Rub Crisis. The evidence justifying these diagnostic interpretations is as follows:

- This is a Red-Flag, Tap-In Crisis because Brandon's belief that his abusive brother was coming home tapped into Brandon's unresolved feelings of fear, and this sequence triggered massive feelings of anxiety in Brandon, resulting in his subsequent dysfunctional behavior.
- This is a Reality Rub Crisis because Brandon misperceived what he had heard when he listened to his mother read Robert's letter. This distortion triggered his fear of Robert and drove his subsequent dysfunctional behavior.

Both of these interpretations are correct, but they became secondary issues once Brandon carried his problem from home to the remedial reading clinic. Brandon's presenting pattern of self-defeating behavior, which was unusual and an overreaction to a reasonable situation, determined that this was a Red-Flag, Carry-In Crisis and not a Red-Flag, Tap-In Crisis or a Reality Rub Crisis. These additional underlying issues—distortion of reality and unresolved fear of Robert—would be addressed during the reclaiming interventions and not during the diagnostic process.

Evaluating a student's pattern of self-defeating behavior to determine if it represents one of the six LSCI diagnostic crises is a learned skill. Based on my experience, a correct or valid diagnosis will emerge if a staff person is certified in LSCI, has a positive relationship with the student, is able to obtain a complete and honest timeline of the crisis, and concentrates on the student's presenting pattern of self-defeating behaviors.

CRITICISM 2

"I'm confused about the relationship between the six steps of the LSCI process and the six LSCI diagnostic crises and reclaiming skills."

RESPONSE TO CRITICISM 2

Much of this confusion is legitimate and is due to our ongoing refinement of LSCI. Over the past 3 years, we have expanded and improved the teaching and skills of LSCI, which caused us to add and change some terms and concepts. Unfortunately, not everyone interested in LSCI is aware of these changes, so let me review the major ones:

Developing a Cognitive Map of the Six LSCI Stages

To help staff members know where they are during an LSCI, a cognitive map was developed for each stage, delineating student's role, staff person's role, and specific skills needed to complete each of the six sequential stages. The stages are as follows:

1. The Student Crisis Stage

2. The Student Timeline Stage

3. The Student Central Issue Stage

4. The Student Insight Stage

5. The Student New Skills Stage

6. The Student Transfer of Training Stage

The first three stages will contain the information needed in the diagnostic process to determine if the student's presenting pattern of self-defeating behavior fits one of the six LSCI diagnostic crises:

1. The Red-Flag, Carry-In, Tap-In, or Carry-Over Crisis–Imported Problems

2. The Reality Rub Crisis–Errors of Perception

3. The Symptom Estrangement Crisis–Delinquent Pride

4. The New Tools Crisis–Limited Social Skills

5. The Massaging Numb Values Crisis–Impulsivity and Guilt

6. The Manipulation of Body Boundaries Crisis: Type I or II—Vulnerability to Peer Influence

The last three stages of the LSCI process, consisting of the Insight stage, the New Skills stage, and the Transfer of Training stage, represent the LSCI reclaiming intervention. For each LSCI diagnostic crisis there are corresponding reclaiming interventions to turn the problem into an opportunity for insight, change, and responsibility. The LSCI process consists of determining the proper diagnosis (Stages 1, 2, and 3) and then determining the appropriate reclaiming interventions (Stages 4, 5, and 6).

CRITICISM 3

"We are not a fancy therapeutic school, loaded with clinical staff who have the time to talk with a student in a crisis. As a counselor, I see 10 to 15 problem students a day. If I spend more than 15 minutes with them, I cause more problems for the staff because my services would not be available to them. LSCI may be great, but it would never work in our school. We have too much to do, and LSCI is too complicated and takes up too much time!"

RESPONSE TO CRITICISM 3

This criticism of LSCI is wrapped in a rigid, ironfisted rationalization that prevents and depreciates any new behavior management strategy from ever being considered. This rationalization usually is based on staff member feelings of being overworked and underappreciated, which leads to a sense of helplessness about their situations. Once this type of thinking settles in, any hope that life in this school will get any better is squashed. There is no easy way to penetrate such self-reinforcing rationalization, but some common misperceptions about LSCI can be identified and clarified.

Example 1: LSCI Is an Add-On and Not a Replacement Strategy

LSCI is designed as an advanced, specific strategy for students involved in chronic self-defeating school behavior patterns. It is not a panacea for all student problems. Just as we would not put out a match with a fire extinguisher or give antibiotic medicine when fluids and rest would be effective, we would not engage a student in the LSCI process unless his or her behavior was severe. In general, we believe less-demanding behavior management techniques would be appropriate in 85% of student problems.

Example 2: Successful Implementation of LSCI Practices in a School Does Not Involve Great Expense or Schoolwide Commitment

With all of the demands on staff members, many times we suggest it is better to begin LSCI quietly and slowly, without any fanfare. One plan we have found successful is to have two staff persons (one must be a counselor, school psychologist, social worker, or administrator) become certified in LSCI during the summer. These two people need to be volunteers. Once school starts in the fall, they will have the skills and the enthusiasm to work effectively with difficult students in a crisis. Inevitably, their success with these students will attract other teachers' interest in LSCI. This is what we call our "build a better mousetrap" philosophy of change.

Example 3: LSCI Can Save Staff Member Time and the School's Reputation

Student crises cannot be scheduled. Once they occur, staff members *have* to respond. In our study of school crises in District 75 of the New York Public Schools, we found that staff members did not start or initiate the majority of student conflicts, but they often responded to the crisis in a way that fueled it and kept it going. They thus escalated the crisis into an explosive situation where the student ended up attacking a staff member, injuring him- or herself, and having to be restrained. Occasionally the crisis involved calling the police, which often generated television and newspaper stories about more student violence in the public schools.

Example 4: LSCI Is Not Complicated or Time-Consuming if One Is Trained

LSCI is not easy, but once you learn it, the skill will allow you to participate in more rewarding and more diverse life experiences. Dr. Hill was trained in LSCI, and the example in this article illustrates the effectiveness of his training. The entire LSCI took no more than 15 minutes, but its impact on Brandon was a significant and meaningful life experience, which I believe he will never forget. Instead of feeling rejected, punished, and/or alienated, Brandon walked out of his crisis having new insight into his pattern of self-defeating behavior and feeling respected and cared for by adults in the school. Life got better for Brandon because Dr. Hill had the necessary skills to turn Brandon's crisis into an opportunity for personal growth, responsibility, and a more trusting relationship with him.

EDITORS' COMMENTARY

In summary, students experiencing the Red Flag Carry-In Crisis are more resistant to help than students with other self-defeating behaviors. However, the Red Flag Carry-In Crisis is becoming the number-one source of crises in schools, and staff need to be trained to help these students. With training, staff can quickly see the tip of the iceberg and avoid the fatal crash!

How LSCI Can Be Integrated Into the Schools

If the schools are serious about meeting the needs of high-risk students and including students with special needs in the regular classroom, then the schools must have well-trained staff who are responsible for handling student crises. We believe that every school should have at least two staff members—a special education teacher, a school counselor, a school psychologist, or the school principal—who are certified in LSCI.

IN the next article, Carol Dawson discusses a study she conducted in New York schools. Using two junior high schools, one experimental and the other control, she found that the school in which staff were trained in LSCI had significant positive outcomes. The frequency of crises was lower, suspension rates decreased, students were mainstreamed into regular education classes more often, and staff reported feeling competent in their ability to manage crises.

ARTICLE 8.4

A STUDY ON THE EFFECTIVENESS OF LIFE SPACE CRISIS INTERVENTION FOR STUDENTS IDENTIFIED WITH EMOTIONAL DISTURBANCES

Carol A. Dawson

This research reports the effects of Life Space Crisis Intervention (LSCI) training with staff in a junior high school serving students with emotional disturbance. An experimental and a control school were selected from a large city where students came from neighborhoods in which abuse, poverty, violence, gangs, and drugs were prevalent. The schools were located a few miles apart in fairly new facilities, and each served over 40 students with a staff of counselors, teachers, and paraprofessionals. Students had similar backgrounds, and the schools both used behavior management programs based on points and levels with students presenting significant behavior problems being sent to staff in Crisis Resolution Rooms. Experimental school staff received LSCI training as a solution strategy for crisis, while control school staff received regular support in developing their own solutions for crisis. Data were gathered to compare specific outcomes related to these two interventions. Frequency of crises decreased significantly in the LSCI school while increasing significantly in the control school. In addition, there was a significant difference in the frequency of crises between the LSCI school and the control school at post-test. There was a greater decrease in suspensions in the LSCI school than in the control school. More students in the LSCI school were mainstreamed and transferred to less restrictive settings. Students in the LSCI school also had higher attendance rates. All staff in the LSCI school reported that they felt able to manage crises, while only 2 of 16 staff in the control school reported this competence. The author offers recommendations for use of LSCI with troubled students and for future research.

THE SETTING

This article summarizes research on the implementation of Life Space Crisis Intervention in a school for troubled students in New York City. New York operates the largest public school system in the United States with an enrollment of over one million students. Approximately 161,000 of these students are identified as needing special education services. Of these, 21,600 more seriously disabled students are served by a special District 75, which has over 9,000 educational staff and provides alternative programs of special educational services in 63 school organizations, located in 324 buildings spread across all five boroughs of New York City. Approximately 12,000 of these students are identified as emotionally disturbed and have multiple needs, which require more intensive special education services. These troubled students represent the full range of trauma and social problems that challenge the professional skills of the most competent educators and schools.

The administrative staff of District 75 is committed to providing teachers with the support and the skills to develop effective interventions

From *Reclaiming Children and Youth*, *11*(4), 2003, pp. 223–230. Copyright by Reclaiming Children and Youth, Inc. Reprinted with permission.

for their students. While considerable resources are available, an unacceptable number of student crises continued to occur. In 1992, District 75 contracted with the Life Space Crisis Intervention Institute to develop a five-day certification program in Life Space Crisis Intervention (LSCI) for selected principals, administrators, clinical, and educational staff. The goal was to reduce the frequency and intensity of student crises. The evaluations of the LSCI program were strongly positive and a new series of LSCI certification programs were offered over the next four years to District 75 staff. The staff evaluations following these training sessions supported the need for expanding LSCI training. District 75's response was to develop and staff the Office of Positive Behavior Support, with the goal of providing inservice training programs based on best practices. In 1997, three staff members from the Office of Positive Behavior Support and one administrator from District 75 were certified as Senior Trainers of LSCI. In the following three years, more than 600 staff were certified in LSCI.

LSCI is a therapeutic, strength-based strategy using a student's crisis as an opportunity for personal insight and accountability. It goes beyond the narrow focus of containment, coercion, and control common in some crisis management models. LSCI involves strategies for connecting with and teaching children and youth in crisis. It helps youth understand and change chronic patterns of self-defeating thinking and behavior that have proven difficult to address with traditional behavior management strategies. This comprehensive, multi-modal intervention is based on 26 specific staff competencies. The theory and research foundation of LSCI is an integration of psychodynamic, developmental, behavioral, cognitive, and social learning principles.

Evaluations by frontline staff who received LSCI training in District 75 found this model of intervention to be well-received. While staff ratings are important, there was little empirical evidence on the efficacy of LSCI with emotionally disturbed students. For LSCI to be accepted as "best practice" with troubled students, research based on student outcome measures was needed. Experimental studies rarely happen in public school systems because of legal, financial, administrative, staff, and parental issues. Securing the administrative support and approval procedures to develop and implement such research in the public schools is a complex and time consuming task. District 75 needs to be commended for its professional willingness to oversee this study of the efficacy of LSCI training on a school with troubled students.

THE STUDY

This research used a quasi-experimental design with two matched school populations. Staff in one school received the LSCI model of crisis training, while staff in a second school received support in developing their own strategies for managing crisis. Pre- and post-intervention results were compared with an emphasis on student outcomes as displayed in more positive behavior in the school setting.

THE SCHOOLS AND STUDENTS

Two inner city junior high school special education sites serving emotionally disturbed students between the ages of 11 to 15 were selected for this study. Both sites were located in the wings of buildings separated from the general education students. The experimental group (JHS-1) was selected by a coin toss, leaving the other site to be designated as the control group (JHS-2). Both programs had been formed the previous year and were located 14 miles from each other. All students received federally funded, free breakfast and lunch. Both programs were administered, funded, and staffed by District 75 Alternative Programs. Both programs had 17 licensed educational staff. Each classroom consisted of a special education teacher and a full-time paraprofessional assistant and was limited to a maximum of 12 students. The educational staff of both programs were evaluated and found to be similar in educational, ethnic, teaching experience, and racial backgrounds. Therefore, the condition of matched settings and staff was accepted.

The experimental group (JHS-1) had 44 students and the control group (JHS-2) had 47 students. The experimental group consisted of 27 African-American and 17 Hispanic students. Thirty-eight of the students were males and six were females.

The control group consisted of 29 African-American and 18 Hispanic students. Thirty-six of the students were males and 11 were females. The students of both groups were compared on key demographic variables such as age, gender, racial distribution, social economic status, and level of emotional disability. No significant differences were found between the two groups on any of these variables. The assumption that these troubled junior high school students were representative of the same population was supported.

ORGANIZATION OF THE STUDY

This research took place over three school semesters and involved three separate phases. Phase One took place during the spring semester of 1999 (January–May), when all baseline or pre-test data were collected. Phase Two took place during the fall semester of 1999 (September–December) and was used to train and certify all staff in the experimental group in the skills of LSCI. Staff in the control school received consultation support during this period. Phase Three took place during the spring semester of 2000 (January–May), when all post-test data were collected.

Both groups had similar behavior management programs based on a level and point system. Both also employed crisis management rooms and staff for more serious behavior problems. They differed on the methodology for dealing with students in crisis. In the fall semester of 1999, staff in the Life Space Crisis Intervention program participated in a prescriptive, 40-hour course in Life Space Crisis Intervention principles and skills. Staff in the control school were provided consultation enabling them to develop their own approach to challenging student behavior. Students in the experimental group who had a crisis were seen immediately and were involved in the reclaiming stages of the LSCI process. Students in the control groups who had a crisis were managed by the current special education guidelines and faculty-designed strategies for crisis intervention.

HYPOTHESIZED OUTCOMES OF INTERVENTIONS

Prior research led us to hypothesize differential outcomes for various interventions with emotionally troubled students. A national study by the Bank Street College of Education (Knitzer, Steinberg, & Fleisch, 1990) characterized the prevailing behavior management strategies employed in special schools for disturbed students as a curriculum of control. These students have been removed to segregated settings because their emotional and behavioral problems interfere with school performance. When placed together with other challenging students, high levels of conflict may overtax the capacity of even trained special educators.

Surprisingly, most special educators lack formal training in working with students in crisis. This was apparent in the current study where fully 90% of staff in both schools initially reported that they did not believe they were competent in managing crises presented by students. Adults who feel overwhelmed by student crises can be expected to either retreat from dealing with problems or revert to coercive interventions. When adults cannot effectively manage crisis and stress in the school setting, this negatively impacts faculty effectiveness (Stempein & Loeb, 2002), which is likely related to the poor outcomes for this population of special education students. Thus, it was hypothesized that staff, left to their own inclinations, might be unable to deal effectively with their most difficult students, and problems would escalate.

In contrast to the curriculum of control, Life Space Crisis Intervention trains staff to use naturally occurring problems to teach youth more effective coping skills. A crisis is reframed as an opportunity to help youth learn alternatives to aggressive, disrespectful, or discouraged behavior. In LSCI parlance, staff zero-in on specific behaviors with laser-like focus. LSCI interventions are designed to target chronic problems related to poor student outcomes, such as recurrent conflict, poor attendance, school suspension, and escalation of problem behavior leading to more restrictive placements. The goal in LSCI is to teach youth positive alternatives to self-defeating patterns of thinking, feeling, and behaving. If effective, LSCI intervention would be expected to increase positive behavior support and provide youth with proactive skills.

Thus, it was hypothesized that there would be significant differences between schools in these outcomes related to crisis in schools:

1. The number of student crises based on records kept by crisis room staff

2. The number of student suspensions based on administrative records

3. The student attendance rates recorded in administrative records

4. The number of students transferred to more restrictive placements

5. The number of students transferred to less restrictive placements

6. The number of students partially mainstreamed to general education

7. Staff ratings of their own perceived ability to manage student crisis

Experimental and control schools were compared on these seven dependent variables through pre- and post-intervention analysis.

THE FINDINGS

Below we briefly summarize key results of this study. For a more exhaustive analysis of the data and methodology, see the original study (Dawson, 2001). Here we organize our discussion around seven questions related to the study hypotheses.

1. Did the number of student crises decrease in the LSCI program?

Figure 8.4–1 compares the frequency of pre- and post-test student crises of the experimental and control groups.

The experimental group had a total of 167 student crises, and the control group had a total of 376 student crises during the four-month, pre-test data collection period. The reasons for this initial difference are unclear, but in each case, the direction of change could be measured.

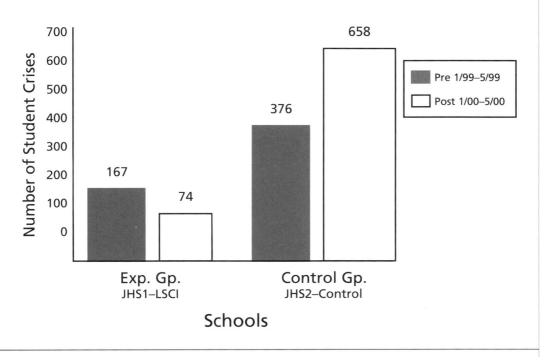

Figure 8.4–1. Number of Pre- and Post-Test Student Crises.

During the four-month, post-test period, crises in the experimental group decreased by more than half. In the control group, the number of crises increased to a total of 658. Are these changes between and within groups significant? An Analysis of Variance [ANOVA] test of significance was calculated by converting the total number of student crises per semester into a mean average crisis score per student per month over the four months of the pre- and post-test data collection periods. Figure 8.4–2 presents these converted mean average student scores.

During the pre-test period, the experimental group had a mean average score of 0.95 student crises per student per month and a post-test mean average score of 0.42 student crises per month. During the pre-test period, the control group had a mean average score of two crises per student per month, and a mean average score of 3.5 crises per student per month during the post-test period. An ANOVA analysis of the mean average crises scores resulted in two significant findings:

1. The experimental group had a significant decrease in the number of student crises in comparison to the control group. ($F[1,102] = 40.61$, $p < .001$).

2. There was a significant within-group interaction between the two groups. The experimental group significantly decreased the number of student crises over time, while the control group

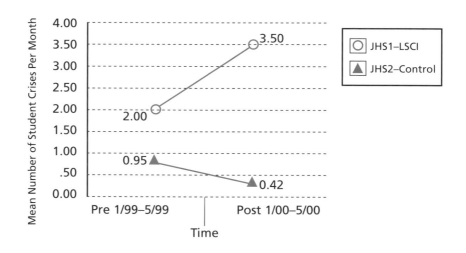

Figure 8.4–2. Mean Number of Student Crises Per Month.

significantly increased the number of student crises over time. $(F[1,102] = 7.00, p < .01)$.

In sum, the number of student crises was significantly reduced in the LSCI program.

2. Did student suspensions decrease in the LSCI program?
Figure 8.4–3 presents a bar graph of the percentage of students in the experimental and control groups who were suspended because of unacceptable behavior: 15% of the 47 students in the control group were suspended during the pre-test period, while 25% of the 44 students in the experimental group were suspended.

During the post-test period, 5% of the students in the experimental group and 9% of the students in the control group were suspended.

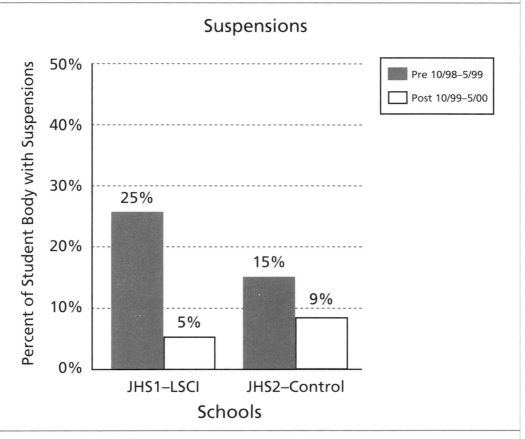

Figure 8.4–3. Suspensions.

While both groups decreased the number of pre- and post-test student suspensions, the experimental group showed a decrease of 20% and the control group showed a decrease of 6%. Thus, the experimental group had a greater reduction in the number of student suspensions than the control group.

3. Was student attendance better in the LSCI Program?

Figure 8.4–4 presents a bar graph of the daily attendance rate of students at school during the experimental period (1/00–5/00).

An examination of the attendance data revealed that the attendance rate for the students in the experimental group was 86%, while the attendance rate for the students in the control group was 74%. The experimental group had a 12% greater attendance rate than the control group.

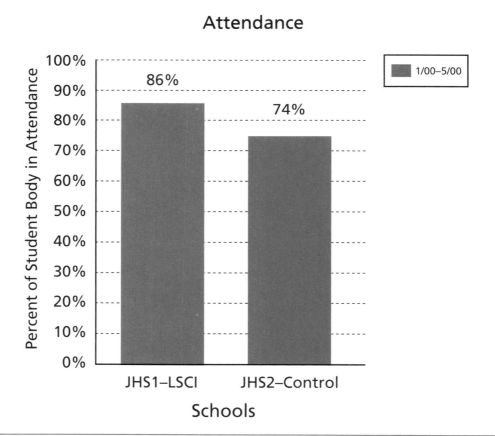

Figure 8.4–4. Attendance.

4. Was transfer to more restrictive programs prevented in the LSCI program?

Figure 8.4–5 presents a bar graph of the percentage of students in the experimental and control groups who were transferred to a more restrictive program.

During the pre-test period, neither group transferred any students to a more restrictive program. However, during the post-test period, the control group transferred 3 of their 47 students (6%), while the experimental group transferred none of their students to a more restrictive program. These data indicate that the experimental group was successful in maintaining students in the program.

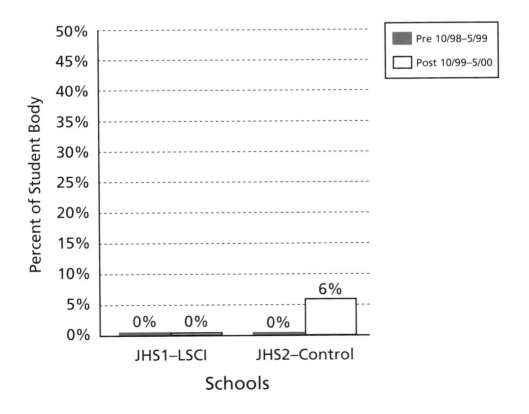

Figure 8.4–5. Transfers to More Restrictive Environment.

5. Did transfer of students to less restrictive programs increase in the LSCI program?

Figure 8.4–6 presents a bar graph of the percentage of students in the experimental and control groups who were transferred to a less restrictive program.

During the pre-test period, neither of the groups transferred any student to a less restrictive program. However, during the post-test period, the experimental group transferred 12 of the 44 students (27%) to a less restrictive program, while the control group transferred 1 of the 47 students (2%) to a less restrictive program. Thus, the experimental group increased the number of students transferred to a less restrictive program over the control group by 25%.

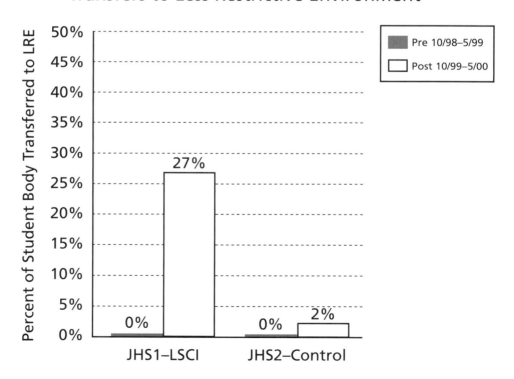

Figure 8.4–6. Transfers to Less Restrictive Environment.

6. Did mainstreaming in general education increase in the LSCI program?

Figure 8.4–7 presents a bar graph of the number of students in the experimental group and control group who were partially mainstreamed to a general education program.

During the post-test period, 41% of the students in the experimental group and 9% of the students in the control were partially mainstreamed. The pre- and post-test data of the experimental group documented a 28% increase in the number of students partially mainstreamed. A pre- and post-test comparison between the experimental and control groups showed that the experimental group partially mainstreamed 19% more of its students than the control group (28% in the experimental group versus 9% in the control group).

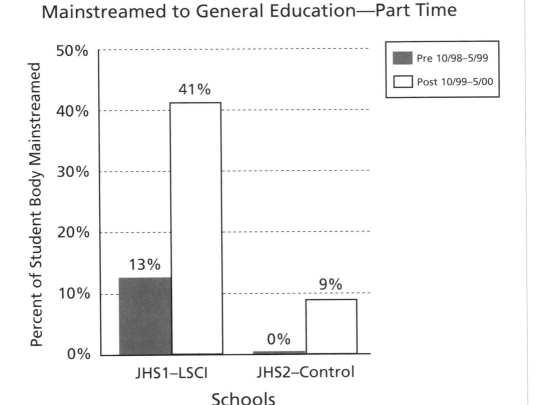

Figure 8.4–7. Percent of Student Body Mainstreamed.

7. Did staff who received the LSCI training report improve crisis intervention skills?

Figure 8.4–8 presents the pre–post staff ratings of crisis intervention skills of the experimental and control groups. During the pre-test period, both groups had 2 of 16 staff members (12.5%) who indicated they felt competent to manage a student crisis successfully. At the end of the study, 16 staff members (100%) of the experimental group felt they had the skills and confidence to manage a student crisis successfully. Concurrently, there was no improvement in perceived crisis skills among the staff of the control group. However, 87.5% of the experimental staff reported improvement in their crisis intervention skills.

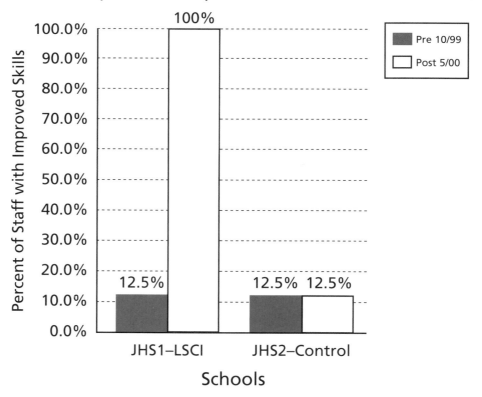

Figure 8.4–8. Staff Perception of Improved Crisis Intervention Skills.

DISCUSSION

The results of this experimental study of Life Space Crisis Intervention consistently support all seven hypotheses about improved student and staff outcomes. There were significant reductions in the number of student crises, and there were fewer suspensions. While transfers to less restrictive settings increased, there were no transfers to more restrictive settings. There were also higher rates of student attendance and improvement in the number of students partially mainstreamed in general education. Finally, staff certified in LSCI felt more confident in their abilities to deal with student crises.

These findings are consistent with qualitative data suggesting that Life Space Crisis Intervention enables staff to gain a sense of personal efficacy. One paraprofessional commented, "I used to be afraid of the students and not know what to say or do. I was very quiet and avoided contact with them. Now I am confident in my abilities. I find that every time I use Life Space Crisis Intervention, I become closer to the students, and now they come to me when they have problems. It feels good to make a difference in their lives." In contrast, staff from the control group became increasingly exasperated by the "revolving door" of crisis situations. When disruption continued, the philosophy frequently was "students need more discipline," which took the form of phone calls home, additional time out of the classroom, and more punishment and alienation.

Students also offered their perspective on the programs. At the end of the study, several youth at each school who had emotional outbursts resulting in removal from the classroom were interviewed. They were asked, "What do you need from teachers when you are most upset?" A typical student at the LSCI school replied, "Kids have a lot on their minds. Sometimes I can't think at school when I am upset. It helps to talk to teachers." In contrast, a youth at the control school answered, "Nothing. Teachers can't help me with my problems. I have to take care of myself."

At its core, LSCI offers a new mindset about problems as opportunities and about troubled students possessing untapped strength and resilience to change. The LSCI process allows the students to connect stressful life events with their thinking, feeling, and behaving and to see the connection between their behaviors and the reactions of others. The students are treated with respect, even in times of crisis, learn to understand and own their behavior, and gain more appropriate coping strategies. Youth and adults experience each other in a more trusting way. Over time, these students no longer find school a hostile and alienating experience but a place where they are accepted, nurtured, and taught new skills. Equally important, staff no longer feel helpless or believe that nothing works with these troubled students. They are empowered with a new sense of professional confidence and skill in helping these challenging students.

RECOMMENDATIONS

The following proposals for future studies and actions are offered:

a. Staff working directly with students with emotional and behavioral disorders should be trained in LSCI as part of a comprehensive approach that also includes consistent school-wide and classroom-level behavior management systems.

b. To insure fidelity, LSCI training should include ongoing support and supervision by an individual proficient in the LSCI philosophy and strategies. The goal should be to integrate a consistent, comprehensive crisis team approach throughout the school setting, augmented by ongoing consultation and periodic refresher workshops.

c. LSCI reveals not only the observable data of a self-defeating behavior; it also taps the private logic of youth. This provides key information regarding chronic behavior problems that interfere with learning. This information can be incorporated into a Functional Behavioral Assessment (FBA) and a positive behavior support plan. Training programs in this area are being developed (McGowan, 2002).

d. Crisis training must become a part of pre-service teacher education. LSCI can be a core component in training, providing new teachers prerequisite skills for success with these challenging students. Colleges and universities are strong partners in this joint effort.

e. Further studies need to be conducted using LSCI with other populations, settings, and longer time periods. Research needs to be pursued regarding populations other than students with emotional and behavioral disorders, different age groups, and settings beyond segregated instructional environments. The potential value of LSCI in an early intervention and prevention program is most intriguing.

f. The effects of LSCI on academic achievement, self-esteem, and behavioral and emotional strengths need to be the subject of future experimental research.

REFERENCES

Dawson, C. A. (2001). *Crisis intervention training and support for school staff of junior high school special education students with emotional disturbances.* Unpublished doctoral dissertation, Nova Southeastern University.

Knitzer, J., Steinberg, Z., & Fleisch, B. (1990). *At the schoolhouse door.* New York: Bank Street College of Education.

McGowan, L. (2002). Life Space Crisis Intervention and Functional Behavioral Assessment: The guiding models. *Reclaiming Children and Youth, 11*(3), 156–161.

Stempien, R. L., & Loeb, R. C. (2002). Difference in job satisfaction between general education teachers and special education teachers: Implications for retention. *Remedial and Special Education, 23*(5), 258–267.

SUMMARY

This chapter was organized to describe the essential concepts and skills of managing a student crisis using the concept of Life Space Crisis Intervention. LSCI is an effective and therapeutic concept involving staff who are a natural part of the students' school experience. LSCI provides staff with the skills to talk with students about specific target behaviors and personal problems that frequently escalate into destructive experiences. Finally, the LSCI dramatizes the value of assisting students to talk about themselves, how they see life, and how they view their troubles in the context of school. LSCI supports a powerful and insightful approach to problem solving by singling out the student's difficulty for instant, unmuddled, and undisguised supportive handling—at the time and place that the difficulty occurs. What makes LSCI a powerful and effective strategy is the knowledge that students in a crisis, regardless of how angry, depressed, fearful, or anxious they are, want to tell their story.

REFERENCES

Beck M., & Beck, B. (2006). *Life space crisis intervention: A series of case studies.* Unpublished manuscript.

Caplan, C. (1961). *Preventing mental disorders in children.* New York: Basic Books.

Long, N., & Fagen, S. (1981). Life space interviewing [Monograph]. *The Pointer, 25*(2).

Long, N., & Fecser, F. (1992). *Life space crisis intervention training manual.* Hagerstown, MD: Institute of Psychoeducational Training.

Long, N., & Fecser, F. (2007). *Life space crisis intervention training manual.* Hagerstown, MD: Institute of Psychoeducational Training.

Long, N. J., Wood, M. M., & Fecser, F. A. (2001). *Life space crisis intervention* (2nd ed.). Austin, TX: PRO-ED.

Morse, W. (1980). Worksheet on life space interviewing for teachers. In *Conflict in the Classroom* (4th ed., pp. 267–271). Belmont, CO: Wadsworth.

Redl, F. (1959). The concept of life space interviewing. *American Journal of Orthopsychiatry, 29,* 1–18.

Redl, F., & Wineman, D. (1957). *The aggressive child.* Glencoe, IL: Free Press.

Wineman, D. (1959). The life space interview. *Social Work, 4*(1), 3–7.

Wood, M., & Long, N. (1991). *Life space intervention.* Austin, TX: PRO-ED.

9 NEW VISIONS, CONCEPTS, AND SKILLS FOR TEACHERS OF AT-RISK AND TROUBLED STUDENTS

THERE are significant differences of opinion within our profession regarding the future ability to reclaim troubled students. Some advocates are committed pessimists who point out that the problems involved in helping these students are increasing faster than the proposed solutions. They highlight the growing political, social, and economic problems of our society. They emphasize that family divorce, neglect, physical and psychological abuse, drug and alcohol use, health problems, teen pregnancies, and school violence have a destructive impact and result in a growing number of severely emotionally disturbed children and youth. They play up the lack of adequate financial support for buildings, programs, and in-service teacher training; for mandated federal and state programs; and for needed disciplinary action for disruptive students.

We acknowledge that the problems of helping these students are real and cannot be denied. However, we believe in the power of positive strength-based relationships and programs. We believe that every problem is an opportunity for new understanding and change. We believe in the new emphasis on positive psychology, Nicholas Hobbs and his 12 principles of Re-Education, the Psychoeducational Model, the Circle of Courage, early intervention and prevention programs, and the dedication and compassion of caring staff. This is an exciting time to work in this field. This is not the pessimistic field of the past. Many positive changes are taking place. The future contains many new visions, concepts, programs, and plans to improve the skills of teachers and the lives of troubled students.

This chapter includes an overview of these new visions, including the proposed skills of the teacher–counselor or psychoeducational teacher, innovative programs to promote student resiliency, neuropsychology, and early and primary prevention programs.

WE begin this odyssey with a futuristic article written by James Kauffman. As one of the most prolific writers, behaviorists, and leaders in the field of education of troubled students, he proposes future directions for this field. He ends with a surprising recommendation that all future professional practices should be organized around the positive attributes of the Circle of Courage which promote the sense of Belonging, Mastery, Independence, and Generosity.

FUTURE DIRECTIONS WITH TROUBLED CHILDREN
James M. Kauffman

FOUR COMPONENTS OF A HAPPIER FUTURE

Because what lies over the horizon is anybody's guess, I will concentrate here on what I hope we will see and what I think we need to guard against if my hopes are to become realities. I'm going to focus on just four things that I think are most important to a happier future:

1. recognition that antisocial behavior is disabling and requires special education intervention,

2. widespread implementation of effective prevention procedures,

3. establishment of the multicultural education priority of finding and embracing the common or universal, and

From *Reclaiming Children and Youth,* 9(2), 2000, pp. 119–124. Copyright by Reclaiming Children and Youth, Inc. Reprinted with permission. *Note.* Portions of this article are adapted from "Future Directions—Part II," by J. M. Kauffman, in *Educating Students with Emotional and Behavioral Disorders: Historical Perspective and Future Directions* (pp. 39–54, 56), by R. J. Whelan and J. M. Kauffman, 1999, Reston, VA: Council for Children with Behavioral Disorders. (Part of the series *What Works for Children and Youth with E/BD: Linking Yesterday and Today with Tomorrow,* by L. M. Bullock and R. A. Gable, series editors.) Adapted with permission.

4. commitment to finding and using scientific or common knowledge as the basis for promoting best practices.

RECOGNIZING THAT ANTISOCIAL BEHAVIOR IS DISABLING

My first hope is that we will recognize that antisocial behavior is disabling and requires special education intervention. For the past quarter-century, we have been stuck with a federal definition that fosters a disinclination to serve children and youth who exhibit behavior that can be considered maladjusted or a conduct disorder. Many school authorities—including some in special education—use the social maladjustment exclusion in the federal definition to avoid taking any responsibility for youngsters with one of the most serious, devastating disorders of childhood. In my view, school administrators and legislators have been leading the way toward denial of educators' responsibility for disability of a type that angers people instead of making them sympathetic, and too many of us in special education have been inclined to follow. Neither logical arguments nor reliable empirical studies support the distinction between social maladjustment and emotional disturbance (Costenbader & Buntaine, 1999; Kauffman, 1997).

Our society does not like children with conduct disorder, and, in fact, we do not want to be tolerant of such conduct. We want better understanding of behavior and valuing of kids, but we certainly don't want people to think that conduct disorder is acceptable. We want people to recognize that conduct disorder is a bad thing and that we want these children changed. Tolerance for the behavior is not what we want, any more than we want acceptance of any other disease or disability as a welcome condition. What we want is recognition of the fact that we could and should avoid a lot of the deviant behavior known as conduct disorder or social maladjustment. We want the understanding that such behavior is disabling, and that special education interventions applied early and consistently to the children who begin exhibiting such conduct are among the strategies we need to practice.

I hope that just over the horizon we will see the National Mental Health and Special Education Coalition's definition accepted into federal law and regulation. It would be a great leap forward if the powerful in our society were to recognize social maladjustment or conduct disorder as a condition needing early correction by special education rather than later correction by juvenile justice. It would be progress if our society were to see the role of juvenile justice as education and rehabilitation rather than merely as containment and punishment.

What I think we need to avoid is assuming that we can somehow discriminate the emotional from the behavioral, the inner turmoil from the external manifestations of it. What I hope we will stop is saying that the behavior is not the problem, not the disorder, not the disability. We are going to be able to take effective preventive action only if we avoid the assumption that behavior is only a manifestation of something inside, only if we start recognizing that serious misconduct in its many varieties is itself a disability.

IMPLEMENTING PREVENTIVE PRACTICES

The second hope I have is that we will see the widespread implementation of effective preventive practices at all levels—primary, secondary, and tertiary. We need to intervene early and effectively in schools to keep behavioral disorders from developing at all, if we can, or to catch problems in their earliest stages and reverse their trajectory so that they do not get worse. For children who are already exhibiting behavioral disorders, I hope we will learn more about how to step in early in the chain of events so that they have fewer serious episodes of misconduct. I expanded on this idea in an article recently published in *Exceptional Children* (Kauffman, 1999a).

Everybody I have ever talked to says, "Oh, yes, we should practice prevention," and the reasons they give are obvious: Prevention would save a lot of money, not to mention human misery. And yet, although everybody seems to be in agreement that we should do prevention, we do not do it consistently in our schools. In fact, what I have come to understand is that we are not going to do much prevention unless we change our thinking significantly. Our actions say that we believe that, in the end, other things are more important.

I want to list and comment briefly on what I see as some of the forces running counter to prevention. Remember that prevention means early identification and early, effective intervention. But we raise objections that have some legitimacy, and in the end we decide that these concerns override our desire for prevention. Therefore, we fail to take preventive action. Here are a dozen ways we do it—that is, a dozen ways we prevent prevention:

1. We express overriding concern for labels and stigma. Now, you can treat everybody the same without labels, but you cannot address individual needs without labels. So, for any child who needs something atypical, no label means no special services and no prevention.

2. We object to a medical model and failure-driven services. But prevention is, by definition, focusing on the avoidance of failure. If we do not anticipate a failure, we will not do prevention.

3. We prefer false negatives to false positives. We would rather risk the disaster of doing nothing about a behavioral disorder than risk doing something unnecessary, maybe because we feel we actually do more harm than good or believe that prevention is impossible.

4. We propose a paradigm shift. The upshot is that we abandon our ability to discriminate better practices from those that are not so good, so we end up saying we do not know what to do anyway.

5. We call special education ineffective, saying that it does not work. If you conclude that special education does not work, you will not suggest it except as a last resort under pain of legal penalty, so prevention does not have a chance.

6. We misconstrue the least restrictive environment (LRE) and least restrictive intervention (LRI). We think LRE or LRI means doing the least we can, so our interventions are always too little, too late, or both.

7. We protest the percentage of children receiving special services. Prevention requires identifying and serving more children. If we want to stop the growth of special education, we are not going to do prevention. We will say it's not a job for special educators; it's a job for general education.

8. We complain that special education already costs too much. Prevention may save money in the long run, but it is going to require spending more money now, and that is something most politicians and most taxpayers do not want to do now.

9. We maintain developmental optimism. We say that it is just a phase, not to worry; this one will grow out of it no doubt. Again, we do not step in with preventive practices.

10. We denounce disproportional identification of students from ethnically and culturally diverse backgrounds. We know that minorities in the United States have been discriminated against and that in some cases cultural difference is misinterpreted as deviance. So, in the case of a child from a diverse background, we may refuse to step in early and preventively for fear of being unfairly discriminatory or viewing ourselves as racist or being called racist.

11. We defend diversity or disability. We keep extending the range of the permissible under the guise of tolerance, and our tolerance for misbehavior keeps us from practicing prevention. After all, we're not going to prevent what we see as different but OK.

12. We deny or dodge deviance. We say that deviance is a social construct and deny the reality of the consequences for the person who exhibits deviant behavior, or we simply say that behavior is different but not deviant, unacceptable but not a disability. It is much easier to say something is not deviant or to disclaim responsibility for it than to prevent it.

I think we need to guard against letting these rationalizations keep us from practicing prevention.

FINDING AND EMBRACING THE COMMONALITIES

The third thing I hope for is making our priority in multicultural education finding and embracing the common or universal. I highlight this hope because I see multicultural education as one of the most important facets of our work now and in the new millennium. Currently, what I see in our approach to multiculturalism is an emphasis on diversity, on the different, the unique, the things that set cultures and people apart from each other. I am aware of the importance of understanding that people and cultures are different, but to my way of thinking, there is a far more important concept that we ought to be highlighting: the ways in which we are the same, the commonalities across all cultures.

It is the failure to see our common humanity that allows, if not justifies, slavery and racism and sexism. It was not any lack of recognition of difference but a lack of appreciation for sameness, for the common thread of humanity, that allowed and justified the Holocaust, apartheid, and the continuing horrors of civil wars in some of the Balkan states and some African nations. I think it is losing sight of our common humanity, our shared culture, that allows the continuation of revolting acts of violence against minorities in the United States. An emphasis on the ways people are alike, not the difference in the color of their skin or their genetic heritage, was the hallmark of Martin Luther King's civil rights movement, and that is the mark of any movement for human rights.

Today, the current is against finding and accentuating the common. It is acceptable and laudable in today's social environment to say that rules, expectations, curricula, management strategies, and so on do not apply to Group A or Group B because of their cultural differences. It is not yet seen as critical to seek and apply what is common. There is great resistance to the idea of any universal, and this rejection of the universal in favor of claiming the personal and unique is being spurred on by postmodern philosophies that reject the very idea of common knowledge or universal principles.

Two of my favorite editorial writers have commented on this notion. Ellen Goodman remarked how, in marketing, the assumption is that gender differences are more important than differences in interests, which may be shared across gender lines. She said, "The danger now is that the marketing moguls choose the safe route, exaggerate the differences between boys and girls, and try to mass-market by gender instead of interests" (Goodman, 1999, p. A8). According to Goodman, we need diversity in approaches, a diversity of options, but this diversity should not be achieved by assuming stereotypical differences based on gender, color, or nation of origin.

William Raspberry wrote about how common language is getting lost in the obsession with linguistic differences. He noted, "But when we have no common shorthand—worse, when we, black and white, have two separate shorthands—it isn't just our language that gets weaker. So does some of the glue that binds us together and makes us American" (Raspberry, 1999, p. A23).

I do not want to be misunderstood. Again, I know that we can be too quick to call our own ideas or behavior patterns or expectations universal. We do need to recognize differences and welcome all differences that are not destructive. My point is that in our focus on diversity we are in danger of neglecting what we share and things that are, in fact, universal or nearly so. The price we will pay for this is very dear, and it will include losing the very possibility of a multicultural society that does not come apart at the seams. It is as if we have finally noticed that our cultural garment has different parts joined at the seams, and now our focus is on the seams and how each part is distinctive, not the wholeness of the garment that makes the society attractive. Pulling constantly at the seams will either result in the garment's coming apart at the seams or in it's becoming misshapen and ill-fitting—something we will not want to wear. The loss of wholeness, the division into separate parts, might reduce something that could be beautiful to a pile of rags. Overemphasis on diversity and neglect of commonality—this is what we need to guard against.

USING SCIENTIFIC OR COMMON KNOWLEDGE TO PROMOTE BEST PRACTICES

The fourth thing I hope for is our recommitment to finding and using scientific or common knowledge as the basis for promoting best practices. I want to make clear that I do not reject all new ideas or different perspectives. But ideas are not good or helpful simply because they are new or different, nor is an idea wrong just because it is old or familiar or dominant.

Today, antiscientific sentiment is popular among many academics in the humanities and in the social sciences. *Postmodernism* and *deconstructionism* are terms often used to describe this antiscientific philosophy. I commented on this in the article I published in *The Journal of Special Education* (Kauffman, 1999) and in a recent article in *Behavioral Disorders* (Kauffman, 1999b), but I will reiterate briefly what I see as the essence of the problem. I think the postmodern view of things has two severe and unacceptable negative consequences for our profession. First, it offers no better solutions to problems; that is, it gives us no better tools for finding out how to improve the practice of special education or anything else. Second, and even worse, it rejects the assumption that we can actually find out that some ways of doing things are more effective than others, that there are best practices and generally ineffective practices. As I understand it, postmodernism is a call to abandon scientific understanding for the notion that there is no objective truth.

Some readers may think that I misunderstand or misinterpret, or they may conclude that I am needlessly, inappropriately argumentative. Maybe I am and maybe not. Let me share with you the words of someone who identifies himself as taking the postmodern view and claims he is able to explain the postmodern perspective in special education. Read carefully; think about what it means.

> What postmodern philosophy does, among other things, is question the ability of social scientists using ANY research paradigm to "discover the truth." Basically, postmodernists hold that the idea of a neutral, disinterested research producing unbiased knowledge is unbelievable ...
>
> What postmodernists would say, and what I said in regard to [facilitated communication] FC, is that since the social scientists are unable to determine the general effectiveness of a given professional practice across cases and situations, then we should allow the served persons (students and families) the largest role possible in the decision-making process. Basically, if they want to try FC, we help them do so while making no promises about effectiveness. Try it and find out. Some find this helpful and some do not. (Source unknown)

I see this postmodern or deconstructivist position as an abdication of both science and professional responsibility. If we embrace this point of view, then we have nothing to offer the children and families we serve but hand holding. This is not the way to achieve greater social justice but a certain way of adding insult to injury. I think it is worth remembering that scientific or common knowledge and its pursuit are among the best tools we have for fighting for social justice. I imagine that the parents and children we serve are going to want functional assistance in learning, that they will ultimately condemn (and rightly, in my opinion) the academic puffery that does not provide us with better tools for solving problems. I think parents will tell us—in fact, I think they are telling us now—"Show us the results."

As I understand postmodernism, it is a rejection of the very idea that we can create and use functional tools that are generally effective. It seems to be (a) the denial of our ability to know when something works better or does not work at all and (b) a refusal to take professional responsibility. Unfortunately, postmodernism and deconstructivism are all the rage in academic circles. The people marketing these ideas want us to buy into them. If we buy them, I believe we will have bought the greatest lemon sold. And if we buy this lemon, we will have a worthless vehicle for helping children and their families. I readily admit—and I think most people do—that science does not and cannot answer every important question. But to deny the answers that science does or can give us is to embrace a philosophy that does no good and can do great harm.

THE CIRCLE OF COURAGE

So, with these hopes and cautions in mind, what do I see as most important? Maybe the most important thing for us to do is to practice in our own professional lives the four principles Martin Brokenleg and his colleagues have described as the Circle of Courage (Brendtro & Brokenleg, 1993). The Circle of Courage comes from American Indian culture, but that is not why it is helpful. It is a useful way of looking at things because it applies across cultures. It is universal, or nearly so. When the Circle of Courage is the basis of education, then we have what Brokenleg has called a reclaiming environment—the kind of environment we want not only for the children with whom we work but also for ourselves. The Circle of Courage has four parts: belonging, mastery, independence, and generosity. I will comment briefly about each aspect of the circle.

BELONGING

There are two important things to remember about belonging. First, the most significant groups to which we belong are the smallest, the ones in which we play the clearest roles, the ones in which relationships are closest and most intimate. This is why family is so important and why those without blood kin to whom they feel they belong need surrogate families. This is why small classes and schools, special classes, and professional specialties with distinctive concerns and methods are more attractive for many people than the larger, more amorphous or ambiguously defined groups. Second, a sense of belonging is based on perceived similarities or commonalities, not on differences or diversities. To the extent that we see that sameness overshadows difference in our group, we will feel that we belong. This is why I have such hope that we will see multicultural education as something that emphasizes commonality more than diversity.

MASTERY

We know that the children we are concerned about really need to feel a sense of achievement; to perceive that they are making progress in learning important and useful skills; to see the world as a stable, predictable, and understandable place. It should come as no surprise that we adults who work with these children have the same need, that our emotional well-being and professional behavior will be enhanced by our mastery. What undermines the achievement of mastery? I suggest that mastery is undermined by anything that makes the world unnecessarily complex, unpredictable, or not understandable, including the notion that you cannot really know anything or make progress. Think about how many of our students believe this—they see the world as unknowable and unpredictable, as chaotic. The postmodern view undermines the very sense of mastery and predictability that we need for ourselves and our students.

INDEPENDENCE

Independence does not mean isolation or lack of connection or belonging, but it does mean that there are important things we can do regardless of the actions of others. This is what we call autonomy. Reformers who say that the improvement of special education depends on the reform of general education undermine our need for independence. As I have suggested elsewhere, we need to focus on what we can change, what we can do as special educators to improve the education of students with disabilities, regardless of the direction general education takes. Again, this does not mean that we fail to recognize the importance of general education and its improvement, but simply that we know to which professional group we belong most clearly, that we master the tasks of special educators and then act as independently or autonomously as necessary to accomplish our purposes.

GENEROSITY

Generosity does not just mean giving stuff to others; it means being generous enough in spirit to endure slights or offenses without retaliation. It means developing empathy and a forgiving spirit. It means abandoning the desire for payback or getback. I have spoken and written previously about civility in our culture and in our schools (Kauffman & Burbach, 1997), mentioning the "group offense patrol" and the "slight trigger disease." The former means that you have your antennae out for any possible offense to your group. The latter means that the smallest perceived slight will trigger in you a reaction to get back at, pay back, or cost the other person, making him or her suffer in some way. Generosity of spirit means being slow to anger toward other people because we have a sense of humor about ourselves and can practice self-restraint.

… My hope is that as we enter the new millennium we will be proud to belong to special education, achieve mastery of our science and craft, act autonomously, and increase our generosity of spirit. If we do, then we will make our own lives and the lives of the children and families we serve significantly better.

REFERENCES

Brendtro, L. K., & Brokenleg, M. (1993). Beyond the curriculum of control. *Journal of Emotional and Behavioral Problems, 1*(4), 5–11.

Costenbader, V., & Buntaine, R. (1999). Diagnostic discrimination between social maladjustment and emotional disturbance: An empirical study. *Journal of Emotional and Behavioral Disorders, 7,* 2–10.

Goodman, E. (1999, March 26). Computer games for girls maintain old stereotypes. *The Charlottesville (VA) Daily Progress,* p. A8.

Gould, S. J. (1997). *Questioning the millennium: A rationalist's guide to a precisely arbitrary countdown.* New York: Harmony.

Kauffman, J. M. (1997). *Characteristics of emotional and behavioral disorders of children and youth* (6th ed.). Upper Saddle River, NJ: Prentice Hall.

Kauffman, J. M. (1999). Commentary: Today's special education and its messages for tomorrow. *The Journal of Special Education, 32,* 244–254.

Kauffman, J. M. (1999a). How we prevent the prevention of emotional and behavioral disorders. *Exceptional Children, 65,* 448–468.

Kauffman, J. M. (1999b). The role of science in behavioral disorders. *Behavioral Disorders, 24,* 265–272.

Kauffman, J. M., & Burbach, H. J. (1997). On creating a climate of classroom civility. *Phi Delta Kappan, 79,* 320–325.

Raspberry, W. (1999, April 12). An end to our American argot? *The Charlottesville (VA) Daily Progress,* p. A23.

NEW CONCEPTS AND SKILLS FOR TEACHERS

At one time teachers were teachers and therapists were therapists and the twain rarely overlapped. Teachers were professionals distinct from therapists. Times have changed, and the distinctions are blurred. School is now recognized as a natural place where children and youth learn for many hours a day and for student many years. Federal laws mandate that public schools provide an adequate education for students with emotional problems, as well as counseling and parent services. As a result, the schools function as a logical place where the new therapeutic concepts of helping troubled students can best be practiced. This does not mean that a teacher becomes a therapist, but it implies that a teacher of troubled students must accept the dual responsibilities of providing both educational and social–emotional support to troubled students. For a minority of special education teachers, this is not a new responsibility. Hobbs (1982) adopted the French educator model, which is a blend of training between education and social work. This concept later became the model of the teacher–counselor of Re-ED. Morse, Rhodes, Long, and Fagen proposed a similar concept called the psychoeducational teacher.

THE PSYCHOEDUCATIONAL APPROACH TO TEACHER TRAINING

We have used the terms teacher–counselor and psychoeducational teacher interchangeably throughout this book. Both terms identify teachers with professional training in the helping skills of psychology and special education. Furthermore, both terms acknowledge that staff working with troubled students need to integrate the strength-based skills of positive psychology and remedial education into their interpersonal skills. We predict that teacher training colleges will acknowledge the need for these teachers and will modify their teacher training curricula to better prepare the next generation of helping teachers to reclaim troubled students.

Teaching Troubled Students Is More Complicated Than Having a Positive Attitude

A good attitude is necessary when teaching troubled students, but self-awareness skills make a difference in the helping process. Remember, the students do not select their teacher, and in turn a teacher does not get to select only those students who complement or enrich his or her personality. This is a Russian Roulette arrangement that is predicted to explode sometime in the future. Expecting the teacher to help the full range of troubled students makes as much sense as expecting a physician to treat the total range of medical problems without any additional help. It simply cannot be done.

IN the following article, Nicholas Long describes the personal struggles involved in working with troubled students. He documents three primary reasons why it is difficult for teachers to help all troubled students assigned to their classrooms. These reasons are presented with frank insight into the dynamics of the student–teacher relationship. Fortunately, he ends by recommending four useful strategies to acknowledge and cope with these realistic issues. This is a must read article for beginning teachers.

ARTICLE 9.2

PERSONAL STRUGGLES IN RECLAIMING TROUBLED STUDENTS

Nicholas J. Long

Special education professionals are aware that their students may be neglected, rejected, or abused and that they may have identifiable social and psychological problems. What makes the task of educating these troubled students difficult is the reality that we can no longer separate their school problems from their home/community problems. A growing number of families are frightened by the powerful influence of gangs, guns, and drugs in their community. We have to acknowledge the existence of a new level of student deviancy that has never before existed in the public schools. For more than 20 years, I directed residential and mental health programs in Washington, D.C. Today, educators from around the country describe student behavior as being as primitive, pathological, and inappropriate as anything they have ever witnessed in residential settings.

Let me offer a suggestion. Every city has emergency rooms to handle medical emergencies. Why doesn't every public school develop an "emergency room" for students in emotional crisis? In New York City, District 75 is the psychological emergency room for troubled children and youth. Students are placed in special education classrooms not only to be educated but also to get help with their troubling thoughts, their intense feelings, and their inappropriate behaviors. Given this difficult task, we become more than just special educators. I am suggesting that we call ourselves "Emotional firefighters," because we need to be our very best when life in the classroom gets emotionally hot.

SOME GENERAL OBSERVATIONS ABOUT STUDENT CRISES

Over the past 5 years, I have had the privilege of working with select staff members involved in a crisis intervention program called Life Space Crisis Intervention (LSCI). During this time we have analyzed more than 140 schoolwide crises. As we reviewed these crises, two major conclusions emerged. First, schoolwide crises did not happen by accident nor did they happen by appointment. In fact, what we learned is that these crises happened at the most inappropriate times. They occurred within the first 30 to 45 minutes of the school day, during transitional periods when students are moving from one activity to another and when the staff was not there and didn't see the precipitating incident, making it difficult to know what really happened. Second, the vast majority of crises begin with a minor issue, such as students talking without permission, walking around the classroom, refusing to do work, using inappropriate language, or teasing other peers. Let me emphasize this next point: In 100% of these crises, the staff members did not initiate the crisis, but in approximately 60% of these crises, they kept it going. They refueled it—they reinforced it—they escalated the conflict into a no-win power struggle between the students and themselves. We also discovered that during crises, staff members were quick to speak, slow to listen, and relied primarily on their authority and consequences, which were ineffective. This led us to explore some underlying reasons for these behaviors.

WHY IS IT DIFFICULT TO HELP TROUBLED STUDENTS?

The concept of caring for others is not new. In most religions, caring for the needy is described as a rewarding and necessary experience involving the simple process of personal giving. For example, if a child is hungry, you feed him; if she is cold, you clothe her; if he is tired, you provide him with a place to rest; and if she is lonely, you offer her your friendship. Usually a needy child responds positively to your giving, thanking you for your kindness and leaving you with an enhanced feeling of altruism and self-worth. What makes this process of helping so appealing is that it does not take any specialized skills other than having an open and compassionate heart. Unfortunately, the process of helping troubled students goes far beyond the concepts of love, dedication, and charity. Helping troubled students is a complicated process involving many dynamic intrapsychic and interpersonal concepts and skills. At the end of this article, I will propose four specific concepts and skills on how to improve our relationship with troubled students by 5% to 10%. But now I want to describe three specific reasons why it is frustrating and difficult to help troubled students.

REASON 1: AVOIDANCE MOTIVATION

Troubled Students Initially Are Motivated
To Avoid Interpersonal Closeness, Learning, and New Social Skills

Most troubled students enter our classrooms with an emotional chip on their shoulder toward all of the educational goals we want to promote for them. Often, these students have been damaged developmentally in their ability to learn from adults or to feel close to and protected by adults without experiencing neglect, inconsistency, unrealistic expectations, or psychological and physical abuse. Consequently, they have learned not to trust adults, which means that they do not want any part of us or the classroom. They do not trust us and will resist all of our attempts to help them. Although these troubled students have periods of intense emotional pain, they do not want to change. In fact, they defend their behaviors while eschewing our help. Simultaneously, they are searching for our Achilles' heel so they can depreciate us. The ultimate goal of their behaviors is to create personal rejection in us so that we will end up saying, "Nothing works with this student! I have tried everything and he is impossible! He has stripped away my professional skills and I am feeling helpless around him." Whenever I hear a competent teacher express this feeling, I become concerned because imprisoned behind this feeling of helplessness lurks the destructive feeling of rage. Rage is powerful and is not a therapeutic emotion. The expression of teacher rage only fulfills the troubled student's belief that the teacher is hostile and rejecting and cannot be trusted. It also reinforces the initial conviction that it was wise not to get involved in a relationship with the teacher. This *fear of closeness* is one reason why it is difficult to help troubled students.

REASON 2: PSYCHOLOGICAL FIT

We Don't Have a Natural or Comfortable
Psychological Fit with Certain Troubled Students

Somewhere in our sugar-coated teacher training program, we were convinced that we should like all our students—it was the correct attitude to have as a professional educator. This fantasy was expanded into the conviction that we could become "Great Teachers" skilled and wonderful with all students. What nonsense! There are no great teachers, social workers, psychologists, and so forth, only ordinary people who have chosen to help troubled students. As a result, we have very different individual relationships with each student. Some of us are comfortable helping students with dependency issues, but we are not comfortable helping students with depression. Some of us are terrific with aggressive students but not with passive–aggressive young people. Remember, we do not choose the students in our classrooms, and the students do not choose us.

Based on my observations and clinical experiences, I would say that, fortunately, we have a good psychological fit with about 60% of our students. The ways we perceive, think, feel, and behave are similar to the ways these students perceive, think, feel, and behave. As a result, we understand them. With 25% of the students, psychological fit is moderate, and we rely on our professional training to keep us on task. But with 10% of students, our psychological fit is marginal, and we need the support of our team members to help us understand these students. Now for the painful news: Based on my own experience, I believe that there is one student in every classroom whose ways of thinking, feeling, and behaving are so significantly different from mine that I have a dysfunctional relationship with him or her. We adults will label the student as "crazy" because we don't understand how he or she thinks, feels, and behaves. This reminds me of the social studies teacher who said, "If I had but one life to give for my country, it would be Jason in my fourth period."

REASON 3: THE CONFLICT CYCLE

We Are Caught in the Conflict Cycle,
or Doing What Comes Naturally

The Conflict Cycle Paradigm was developed to help competent teachers understand why they end up in painful and self-defeating struggles with troubled students. The Conflict Cycle describes how the interactions between a troubled student and a teacher follow a circular process in which irrational beliefs, feelings, and behaviors of the student influence—and are influenced by—the beliefs, feelings, and behaviors of the teacher (see Figure 9.2–1). Once in operation, this negative and escalating interplay is difficult to interrupt.

For example, a student experiences disappointment and frustration, which activates negative thoughts or irrational beliefs such as "Nothing ever works out for me." In turn, these irrational beliefs *trigger* feelings of anger, and those feelings *drive* his or her behavior. The student shouts, threatens, and throws books on the floor. These inappropriate behaviors *incite* the teacher, who reacts by mirroring the student's feelings and, at times, his or her behavior. The negative adult reaction creates more student stress, more intense feelings, and more deviant behavior, which results in more punishment, thereby continuing the cycle.

Let me say it another way: When we help a student in stress, we experience frustration and, if we're not aware of this dynamic, we will do what comes naturally and mirror the student's inappropriate behavior. This means that when we're working with an aggressive student, we will have counteraggressive feelings, which are normal. We need to acknowledge the existence of these feelings but learn to say "no" to expressing them in our behaviors. What often happens in the Conflict Cycle, however, is that we *escalate* the conflict. When a student becomes angry and says, "I'm not doing that," we say, "Yes, you are," and the battle is on. Although our behavior can be classified as a learned habit or a personal choice, once we are caught in the Conflict Cycle, it becomes an automatic response. We therefore cannot rely on our natural feelings to make good judgments. An example of this would be when we are talking to a student with depression who says, "Listen, nothing is ever going to get better for me. This is the way I am. Just leave me alone. That's all I want

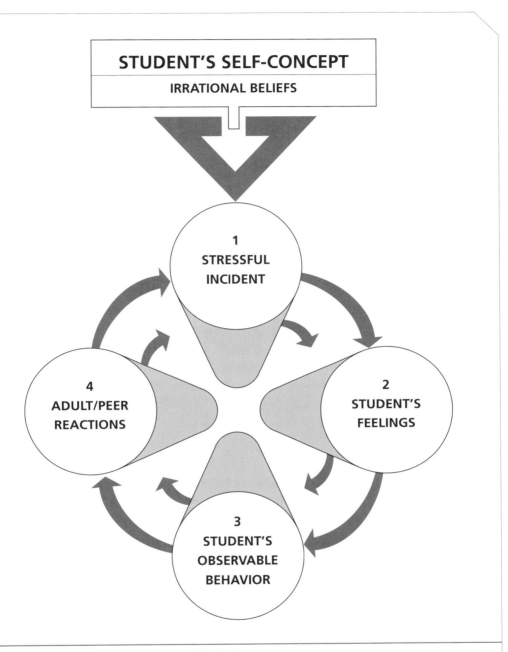

Figure 9.2–1. The Student's Conflict Cycle.

you to do—leave me alone." After about 5 minutes of listening to these comments we think, "Maybe that's not a bad idea. I'm getting depressed around this student. I woke up this morning feeling pretty good, but this student is bringing me down." What we have to realize is that when we are around a student who is depressed, we are going to feel depressed. But if we act on these feelings and walk away and leave the student alone, we will not have helped him or her.

RECOMMENDATIONS

1. BE A THERMOSTAT, NOT A THERMOMETER

We need to be aware of what is happening to us during the process of helping these students. Our behavior management strategies must begin with us and not with our students. To start, we have to make a personal choice not to fight or get into power struggles with troubled students. This does not mean that we are going to be "punching bags" or permissive. Instead, we are making a decision to see ourselves more like a thermostat than a thermometer. A thermometer reflects the temperature around it. If we are working with a student who gets hot, we also get hot. If we are working with a student who gets cold, we get cold. The student determines how we feel and, frequently, how we behave. If we see ourselves as a thermostat, we will set our emotional temperature to 98.6 degrees. When a student gets hot, we are going to cool him or her down, and when a student withdraws, we are going to heat him or her up.

Let me illustrate this with a story. A parent was sitting outside the office of Mr. Miller, the school guidance counselor, when she heard him say, "Take it easy, Donald, just relax. I know it's difficult, but in a few minutes you'll feel better. Take some deep breaths, Donald." The door opened and Mr. Miller stepped out. The parent said, "Mr. Miller, you sure know how to talk to Donald. I'm impressed." He replied, "Thank you, ma'am, but I think you should know that my first name is Donald." Mr. Miller realized that until he could control his own counteraggressive behavior, all his skills and techniques would be useless. He understood the Conflict Cycle and the need for anger management skills.

2. PUT KIDS FIRST

We need to put our personal needs last. Our first responsibility must be to try to understand and meet the needs of our students. Let me offer an example: Imagine that you are a nurse who is responsible for a patient who is vomiting. Now that may upset you—even disgust or make you angry—but a nurse doesn't make professional decisions based on how she or he feels. She or he has to make professional decisions predicated on what helps the patient.

I have been in the hospital a lot this last year, and I would have been upset if the nurse had said to me, "All right, Dr. Long, you throw up one more time, you're out of here. I run a good ward. You're messing it up. You're not a good example for the other patients!" I'm not saying this is easy, but our personal needs have to come last. Our first priority is our students, then the group, then the ongoing program, and, finally, our personal needs. Harry Truman said it best: "If you can't stand the heat, get out of the kitchen." In our business, we have to learn to feel comfortable with being uncomfortable.

3. LEARN FROM YOUNG PEOPLE

We need to identify the most difficult student in our classroom and make him or her our teacher. Fritz Redl taught me this, and I have always appreciated my time with him. One time I was having difficulty with a delinquent boy and was complaining about his behavior to Dr. Redl, who replied, "Nicholas, make him your teacher, because Tom has the ability to stir up strong feelings in you and to tap into some of your unfinished emotional business. In fact, Tom probably has the key to your psychological baggage and is willing to open it at the most inconvenient times for you."

4. USE MANY TOOLS FOR CULTIVATING STRENGTHS

We need to go beyond our current theoretical method of helping. Many of us see ourselves as advocates of behavioral theory, cognitive theory, social learning theory, or psychodynamic or psychoeducational theory, depending on what university we attended. However, times have changed. We cannot fit the complex needs of our troubled students into one theoretical model. It doesn't work anymore. We need to learn as many new intervention skills as possible from as many theories as possible. We need to use strength-based strategies and teach the behavior we want to promote, not the behavior we want to eliminate. Most important, we need to say what we mean and mean what we say, but not say it in a mean way.

Let me close with a 13th-century Muslim story:

A man looked up to the sky and said, "I saw a crippled woman try to walk. I saw a blind beggar ask for food. I saw a father beat his son. And I saw a soldier kill an infant. And I said, 'All powerful and merciful God, how can you see such atrocities and sadness and evil, and yet, do nothing about it?' " There was a silence, and then God spoke to the man. God said, "I did do something. I made you."

This is our task—not to say something needs to be done, but to do something about it.

Maintaining a Healthy Psychological Self

A teacher–counselor working with seriously troubled students inevitably will experience a high level of personal stress. This is the nature of the profession. The skill is not to deny the existence of these feelings but to learn new strategies of managing personal negative talk. All too often the teacher's lounge becomes the bitching room of negative talk about the frustrations of teaching. Negative talk involves self-deluding ways of projecting the blame on others or circumstances beyond one's reach.

ARTICLE 9.3

JO Webber, in the next article, explains the process of negative mind-sets in adults and how these irrational beliefs can be replaced by using the skill of cognitive restructuring. As you read this article, you might think how to apply this cognitive skill to your personal and professional life. This article could be a helpful topic for inservice discussion.

MIND-SETS FOR A HAPPIER LIFE
Jo Webber

Working and living with children and youth with emotional and behavioral problems can be an exhausting endeavor because they are often demanding, irrational, ungrateful, and aggressive. It takes constant vigilance and practice to establish and maintain positive relationships with these young people, and a tremendous amount of energy, empathy, and emotional health to be consistently effective. Because of the challenges these youth present, adults have a tendency to avoid the experience completely, begin to feel helpless and depressed, maybe learn to perversely enjoy chaos and craziness, or also become angry and aggressive. Sometimes, under extremely stressful situations, adults may become as troubled as the children they are trying to help.

Only when adults remain psychologically resilient and behave in appropriate and healthy ways can they meet the challenges presented by individuals with emotional and behavioral problems. One of the best descriptions of the attributes that facilitate living and working with these troubled children was provided by Nicholas Hobbs (1982). He suggested that successful adults must be competent, self-assured, and resilient, and that they view each day as a rewarding experience. Furthermore, they must be

> able to give and receive affection, to live relaxed, and to be firm; a person with private resources for the nourishment and refreshment of his own life; … a person with a sense of the significance of time, of the usefulness of today and the promise of tomorrow; a person of hope, quiet confidence, and joy; one who has committed himself to children and to the proposition that children who are disturbed can be helped. (p. 82)

It is also thought that adults can be more effective when they engage in active problem solving with children; remain calm and act appropriately in crisis situations; and display openness, optimism, and empathy (Fink & Janssen, 1992). How does one manage to remain psychologically sound, emotionally resilient, self-assured, affectionate, self-nurturing, hopeful, committed, empathetic, optimistic, and full of quiet confidence and joy in a context of anxiety and irrationality? One method for maintaining mental health is found in the cognitive restructuring theory.

COGNITIVE RESTRUCTURING THEORY

Cognitive restructuring theory posits that psychological soundness is a function of how we view the world (e.g., Beck, 1964; Ellis, 1962): People

---

can choose to interpret events in a way that can cause anxiety, anger, fear, or depression, or they can choose to think in a way that results in a sense of well-being. Adults can remain psychologically sound by refusing to engage in self-defeating thinking, disputing irrational thinking, and adopting healthy belief systems. Sometimes seeing the world through "rose-colored glasses" is even helpful for avoiding emotional distress. If you find yourself reacting in unhealthy ways while dealing with troubled young people, you might want to examine your own cognitions.

Thinking about your thought processes and recognizing the thoughts that block healthy emotional and behavioral responses is the first step to developing psychological well-being. Changing the way you interpret events may lead to changes in your emotional reactions and behavioral responses to children with emotional and behavioral problems. Your altered emotional reactions and behavioral responses may, in turn, affect children's emotions and behaviors. For example, a teacher who thinks that she can't stand these students talking back to her might glare at her class with arms crossed and sternly say, "Let's get to work." Conversely, a teacher who thinks about how much she enjoys her job might have open arms, a kind smile, and a laugh when she says, "Let's get to work." The first teacher's attitude may elicit inappropriate behavior from students while the second teacher may be met with student smiles and compliance. The smiles and compliance, in turn, cue the teacher to think positively, feel affectionate, and behave in a friendly way. Positive thinking seems related to greater happiness, higher levels of achievement, and better health. Conversely, persons who engage in negative thinking are more prone to suffer from depression, lack of productivity, and illness (McAuliffe, 1992).

CHANGING UNHEALTHY THOUGHTS

Several times in the preceding section, I alluded to the impact of positive versus negative thinking. In general, we consider positive thinking as facilitative and negative thinking as inhibitory. At a more specific level, Beck (1976) described negative thinking in terms of certain *cognitive distortions* that make a person more prone to inappropriate behavior. He arranged these distortions into three levels:

1. *Automatic thoughts* that portray one as helpless, the environment as frightening, and the future as hopeless, for ex-

ample, a parent whose *pervasive* view of his child is "My son will never amount to anything";

2. *Biased thinking* that results in overgeneralizing conclusions drawn from one event, for example, a teacher who, upon being called names by a student, thinks, *"No one* ever cares about my feelings";

3. *Dysfunctional belief constructs* used to make sense of one's environment, for example, adults who may think, "The *only* way for me to be happy is to be successful."

An example of an automatic thought could be a teacher who hopes that no one observes him today because he believes his students are always disruptive. If he were to think instead that he is going to use powerful reinforcers today to ensure that his students work well, his feelings may change from fear to anticipation, and his withdrawn behavior will probably become active and firm.

A mother who engages in biased thinking might believe that she is a terrible mother because she lost her temper one day. This thought might cause her to feel inadequate, depressed, helpless, or frustrated. In turn, these feelings might cause her to behave in a passive or aggressive manner. A more rational view might be that she did not get enough sleep the previous night and had little energy to effectively manage her child's behavior. This rational perception may change her feeling to mild regret and result in more assertive behavior.

Beck's notion of cognitive restructuring compliments that of Rational Emotive Behavioral Therapy [REBT] set forth by Ellis and Bernard (1985). As Zionts and Zionts (1997) stated, the premise of REBT is that it is not really the event but your belief systems, learned early in life, that cause intense feelings and inappropriate behavior. They described three basic irrational beliefs that cause people trouble:

1. The belief that *"I must be loved by everyone or else I am totally unlovable."* This type of thinking might lead a teacher to become terribly upset if a student acts aggressively toward him or her because it has just been proven that he or she is a horrible and unlovable person (i.e., the student doesn't love him or her).

2. The belief that *"I must be perfect and never make mistakes or else I am a failure and a generally rotten person."* An individual engaging in this thinking might become extremely defensive and blame others when it is pointed out that he or she should have handled a crisis differently.

3. The belief that *"Life should be easy, I should be comfortable, and people should act the way I want them to or else I should be very upset and punish them."* Someone engaging in this irrational belief will have low frustration tolerance, will complain and whine incessantly, and in general will blame everyone else for his or her own misery.

Finally, Seligman, in his work on attributions and optimism, stated that many people who accurately assess reality are often at its mercy (see McAuliffe, 1992). He recommended viewing the world from a positive perspective by learning to overestimate your own ability, attractiveness, and talents while not dwelling on losses and failures. By viewing the world as "rosy," you can protect yourself from depression and anxiety and maintain good cheer and health. By taking control of thinking and belief patterns, teachers and parents can become optimistic and mentally strong. The three most commonly recommended ways to do this are *disputation, semantics,* and *adoption of alternate mind-sets.*

DISPUTATION

Once unhealthy, negative, or irrational thinking is recognized, the next step is to use disputation—a method of self-questioning—on specific thoughts. For example, if you have overgeneralized and assume you are a bad mother, ask yourself, "Where is the evidence that what I'm thinking is true? Factually prove that I am a bad mother. Is it really impossible to make changes in my life?"

Teachers can use this same technique. For example, a teacher who thinks no one cares about his or her feelings may dispute this thought: "Why should the actions of one student dictate whether people in general are concerned with my well-being? My family and friends are interested in how I feel. My principal asked me yesterday if I needed help. Not everyone is concerned about my feelings, but some significant people are!"

The key component for effective disputation is to use "prove it" questions. You want to be hard-nosed, literal, factual, and precise to dispute unrealistic assumptions, overgeneralizations, rigid thinking patterns, and irrational beliefs. For example, where is it written that life should be easy and you should be perfect and loved by everyone? View the world as it is and refuse to be terribly unhappy about the hand you have been dealt.

SEMANTICS

Semantics is the language component that addresses meaning and interpretation (e.g., nonliteral and literal meanings). We can make use of semantics through our overt and covert speech to facilitate healthy thinking. Cognitive psychologists encourage people to talk to themselves and to others as though they were talking to a friend—in a realistic, kind, and respectful manner. When using self-talk, you should employ words that best describe true conditions, and avoid words that accompany all-or-nothing thinking and demands. For example, replace demand statements ("I must," "I should," "I ought to") with nondemand statements ("I prefer," "It would be better if …," "I would do well to …"). Pressure that you place on yourself to perform, and the stress that accompanies it, is reduced as demands are changed to preferences. The biggest semantic change occurs when what were once believed to be "needs" simply become "wants." A need is something without which you will die. A want is everything else. There is no choice involved with thwarted "needs"—a semantic aspect of language that can lead to feelings of helplessness. On the other hand, there are choices involved when desires are not met, which may lead to feelings of empowerment.

When someone thinks, "I *should* not have lost my temper," the implication is that because he or she did not comply with that demand, he or she must be a failure. It is almost as if saying "should" magically changes the outcome of a previous situation. Although this thinking is erroneous, nevertheless, it is prevalent. On the other hand, if someone thinks, "I *wish* I hadn't lost my temper, and *it would have been better* to deal with Olivia in a quieter fashion," then the worst that happened is that a preference was not met. In fact, the person has identified something else that might work better in the future. The first thinking pattern may be followed by severe self-criticism or even depression; the latter may be followed by problem solving.

Additional words that reflect dichotomous (all-or-nothing) thinking, such as *always, never, no one,* and *everyone,* can also be eliminated from the vocabulary to enhance emotional well-being. Seldom do events or conditions take on such all-or-nothing considerations. Using words such as *usually, sometimes, some people,* or *few people* to depict the real state of affairs (e.g., "Sometimes Charlie acts aggressively toward me" rather than "Charlie is always hitting me!") may result in fewer negative feelings and more productive behaviors.

ADOPTING ALTERNATIVE MIND-SETS

The next step after disputing unproductive thought patterns and using more realistic self-talk is to adopt alternative thinking patterns, or mind-sets, that may trigger positive feelings and productive behavior. Learn to view the world in ways that allow happiness and goal achievement. Healthy thinking provides a means for becoming self-nurturing and self-assured. The following are 10 mind-sets that might help teachers and parents who are exposed to other people's irrational behavior on a daily basis. Read about each mind-set, then practice reciting each as a daily affirmation. If unhealthy thoughts return, examine your self-talk for *should*s and absolutes, dispute irrational thinking, and practice reciting the mind-sets.

I Think I Can, I Think I Can

The first mind-set has to do with believing in one's own capacity to perform. As a parent or teacher working with children with emotional and behavioral problems, you need to believe that, in most instances, you have the power to change situations. You are at risk for becoming a victim if you do not, and you may learn to be helpless, hopeless, and inept at obtaining desired outcomes. Being a victim results in resentment and ineffectiveness, and undermines future motivation to change things. Believing in your own ability to make changes, no matter how difficult, sets the stage for positive, effective action. Refuse to quit, think that you can, and keep trying.

I Will Persist

Closely related to the first mind-set is the notion that persistence may result in finding solutions to problems. People who persist at solving problems reject the notion that they must be perfect on the first try, which allows them to ask for help and resist helplessness, depression, and shame if a solution fails. The following are some effective problem-solving strategies: (a) objectively identify problems, (b) develop many possible solutions, (c) pick solutions and seek help when necessary, (d) try the solutions, (e) evaluate the results, and (f) choose other solutions when one does not work. Someone who is a persistent problem solver usually looks forward to new challenges as opportunities to be creative. Persistent problem solvers will have more self-confidence and be better able to resist defeat and recuperate from stressful situations.

I Have Hope

Looking on the bright side instead of seeing yourself in a negative light and the world as a frightening place can result in better health, more energy, fewer fears, more trust, more self-confidence, and higher achievement. Optimists believe that their efforts cause their successes, and they believe in future success at everything they try (McAuliffe, 1992). If something bad happens to optimists, they do not blame themselves, and the thought of future failure is not an issue. In certain stressful situations, it may even be good to think in terms of subtle, self-aggrandizing lies that "foster the illusion that we can achieve positive outcomes in our lives" (McAuliffe, 1992, p. 59). Although a true assessment of reality (pessimistic thinking) is usually recommended as a rational thinking strategy, optimism often is more effective. The key is to find a balance between optimistic and realistic thinking and to avoid overly catastrophic thoughts.

Another recommendation for learning to think optimistically is to avoid "overthinking" (i.e., crying over spilled milk), particularly right after a negative event occurs. Engage yourself in a pleasurable and distracting activity. You can tackle the problem later when you are in a better mood, which may enhance creative problem solving.

My Self-Worth Is Separate From Other People's Behavior

The ability to "disengage" and not take others' behavior personally will do much to boost your mental health. Children and youth with emotional and behavioral problems suffer from faulty learning, unsatisfied desires, and thwarted expectations; they probably are not astute judges of one's character. What they say in a fit of anger about adults is very probably not true. It is self-defeating to think that you are a failure just because a child insults or criticizes you. The child's actions probably mean he or she is scared, sad, frustrated, or in want of attention.

A second part of this cognition is to practice "no-strings-attached" caring. Care for these young people freely without expectation of anything in return. Youngsters with emotional and behavioral problems sometimes take what they can without giving much in return, which often is a result of past learning. Adults need to detach their own needs from those of the student, view the world through the student's perspective, and analyze each situation.

I Am Allowed to Make Mistakes

Closely related to separating self-worth from children's behavior is the belief that making mistakes is part of learning and might even be something to celebrate. People who believe that "I must be perfect in order to be happy," or "If I make a mistake, it means I am inept," or "My value as a person depends on what others think of me," are at risk for depression and neurosis (Ellis & Bernard, 1985). In addition, people who are very demanding of themselves tend to be very demanding of others and often give up easily in the face of failure. Learn to view mistakes and foolish acts for what they are—a one-time occurrence. As fear of failure or of appearing foolish subsides, you will become more self-assured and self-confident. Changing perfectionist demands to preferences for "doing a good job" can alleviate self-induced stress, feelings of shame, and fear of failure.

Gosh Darn It, I Did a Good Job

Negative self-appraisals are linked to depression and anxiety (Beck, 1976). Beck claimed that evaluating yourself in a negative fashion may lead to feelings of sadness or fear. Dealing with individuals who are difficult to teach and often in conflict may set the stage for thinking "this is going to be a failure," which can become a habit and cause self-defeating behavior. Thinking "I have done well at this in the past and I will do well again" will more likely lead to self-assurance, self-confidence, and assertiveness.

A way to increase the frequency of positive self-appraisals is to learn to recognize progress. Because we live in a goal-oriented society, progress often is measured by completion. Parents and school personnel usually have neither the resources nor the time to complete goals; therefore, they need to recognize that every step toward a goal is a victory. Two steps forward and one step back is occasion for celebration. In fact, overestimating one's accomplishments may even be healthier!

I Can Manage Conflict

To be a conflict-avoider while living or working with children and youth who are aggressive might be a fast track to a mental breakdown. For individuals who are emotionally disturbed, conflict is often a first response to a problem. You may quickly find yourself in a spiral of fear, guilt, and self-damnation if you avoid conflict because you believe you may have caused it, or if you feel *obligated* to prevent it from ever happening again.

One person cannot control all conflict, and not all conflict *should* be avoided. Some can be healthy and productive—actually stimulating interest and creativity in people, or facilitating valuable insight. Believing that conflict is manageable and accepting it as a growth experience can be a very useful mind-set.

I Can Travel New Roads

Rigid beliefs have been linked to negative feelings and inappropriate behavior (Beck, 1964). Believing that "My way is the only way," or "I've always done it this way and cannot change," or "I'm just that kind of person" is indicative of the "global" and "stable" attributions that can cause depression and anxiety. Individuals with a flexible mind-set usually are open to new ideas and suggestions, and they may be willing to work through initial discomfort toward new and unfamiliar strategies. Subsequently, more opportunities for success and for fun become available. As more successful events occur, fear of change decreases, allowing for more effective communication and better relationships with others.

Flexible thinking also includes the ability to choose how to think in given situations. You need not become a slave to some irrational beliefs that often are promoted through media, family, or religious teachings. Thinking "There is a clear right and wrong in every situation," or "Children must respect me or they must be punished," or "I must be who my parents want me to be or else I am a failure," or "If this person does not love me, I must cease to exist," is self-defeating and will lead to excessive frustration, anxiety, and possible depression (Ellis & Harper, 1975). Dispute inaccurate beliefs and replace them with more rational ones.

I Can Find Joy in Hard Work

Living and working with individuals who may be demanding, aggressive, and violent is strenuous and stressful. It thus is counterproductive to get overly upset at the slightest inconvenience and complain about the daily demands of parenting and/or teaching. You would do better to accept that life is difficult and learn to find joy in hard work. Why should life be easy? Maslow (1954) alluded to this "hard work–joy" principle by writing that "optimal living" involves working instead of stagnating and devoting yourself to a mission or vocation. Accepting the challenge, believing in the ability to do it well, recognizing progress, and positively appraising that progress will result in feelings of a job well done, joy, and well-being. Coping with the demands of life and living up to reasonable performance standards will improve self-confidence and mental health.

Life Is Bizarre and Funny

Surviving in any difficult situation requires that one be able to accept and laugh at one's own foolish behavior and life's bizarre twists (Ellis & Harper, 1975). Humor may relieve or prevent depression, anxiety, and hopelessness. The task is not to minimize serious events, but to find humor in people's foolishness and an imperfect world. Bringing humor to the home or classroom can also have therapeutic value for children and youth with emotional and behavioral disorders. Young people will find it more difficult to persist in noncompliant, aggressive, or destructive behavior when they are laughing. Humor can act to disarm potentially explosive situations, relieve stress, and change how you view things. Laughing about something previously perceived to be frightening or hurtful changes its power over your feelings. Refuse to hold onto anger and hurt. See the world and people as fallible and imperfect. Forgive mistakes and thoughtless acts.

SUMMARY

What teachers and parents believe and think about the world around them has an impact on their feelings about their job and their behavior toward others. Adults who are humane, confident, and hopeful; who are persistent and creative problem solvers; who plan to prevent crises but are not afraid of them; who can occasionally wear "rose-colored glasses"; and who refuse to think and act in crazy ways, instead believing in their own ability to make changes, will best be able to survive in strenuous situations.

By disputing negative thinking and using vocabulary that indicates preferences (not demands) and possibilities (not probabilities), you can change your thinking. You can also help yourself by adopting as part of a general philosophy the 10 mind-sets provided in this article. Everyone is free to choose how to think and can learn new ways of doing so. Developing ways of thinking that involve positive self-evaluation, promote self-assurance and confidence, enhance interpersonal relationships, and are based on a somewhat accurate perception of reality will make for happier living This type of psychological immunization can last for a life-time.

REFERENCES

Beck, A. T. (1964). Thinking and depression: II. Theory and therapy. *Archives of General Psychiatry, 10,* 561–571.

Beck, A. T. (1976). *Cognitive therapy and the emotional disorders.* New York: International Universities Press.

Ellis, A. (1962). *Reason and emotion in psychotherapy.* New York: Lyle Stuart.

Ellis, A., & Bernard, M. E. (1985). What is rational emotive therapy (RET)? In A. Ellis & M. E. Bernard (Eds.), *Clinical applications of rational emotive therapy* (pp. 1–30). New York: Plenum.

Ellis, A., & Harper, R. A. (1975). *A new guide to rational living.* Englewood Cliffs: NJ: Prentice-Hall.

Fink, A. H., & Janssen, K. N. (1992). Competencies for teaching students with emotional-behavioral disabilities. *Preventing School Failure, 37*(2), 11–15.

Hobbs, N. (1982). *The troubled and troubling child.* San Francisco: Jossey-Bass.

McAuliffe, K. (1992, September). Interview: Martin Seligman. *Omni,* pp. 59–61, 81–85.

Maslow, A. H. (1954). *Motivation and personality.* New York: Harper & Row.

Zionts, P., & Zionts, L. (1997) Rational emotive behavior therapy in troubled children. *Reclaiming Children and Youth, 6*(2), 103–108.

HOW TO MAKE A DIFFERENCE IN THE LIVES OF TROUBLED STUDENTS

ARTICLE 9.4

AFTER presenting all the theories, strategies, concepts, and techniques of helping troubled students, it all comes down to the teacher's ability to connect with students and make a difference in their lives. Bonnie Benard discusses how these unique teachers, called "turnaround teachers," are successful in turning students in a right direction. They create transformations in students rather than mere behavioral changes. In the following article, she describes the approaches and strategies that turnaround teachers use with high-risk youth. This article also can serve as an example of a set of best practices in the classrooms.

HOW TO BE A TURNAROUND TEACHER
Bonnie Benard

For over a decade, public and educational discourse has been steeped in the language of risk. Between 1989 and 1994 alone, more than 2,500 articles were published on "children and families at risk" (Swadener & Lubeck, 1995, p. 1). Over 40 years of social science research has clearly identified poverty—the direct result of public abdication of responsibility for human welfare—as the factor most likely to put a person "at risk" for social ills such as drug abuse, teen pregnancy, child abuse, violence, and school failure.

Yet policymakers, politicians, the media, and often researchers themselves have personalized "at-riskness" by locating it in youth, their families, and cultures—perhaps providing a convenient smokescreen for the naming and blaming of poverty. Even when its use is well intentioned (e.g., when used to secure needed services for children and families), this approach has increasingly led to harmful, isolating practices such as stereotyping, labeling, tracking, and reduced expectations for a growing number of students in urban schools.

Most dangerous of all, this risk focus has encouraged teachers and other helping professionals to see children and families only through a deficit lens. This "glass-as-half-empty" perspective blocks our vision to see the whole person and hear the "real story"—often one filled with strengths and capacity. Wehmiller (1992) warns, "When we don't know each other's stories, we substitute our own myth about who that person is. When we are operating with only a myth, none of that person's truth will ever be known to us, and we will injure them—mostly without ever meaning to" (p. 380).

RESILIENCE: AN ALTERNATIVE WAY OF SEEING

Indeed, this "mythical" lens *is* injurious, quickly translating into a racist, classist, sexist, or ageist perspective. While our common sense alone cautions us against such an approach, there is an even more concrete reason to reject it. We now have the most rigorous scientific research on human development—prospective longitudinal studies—that should put our preoccupation with risk to rest permanently. These studies on how individuals develop successfully despite risk and adversity certainly prove the lack of predictive power of risk factors. Researchers worldwide have documented the amazing finding that, when tracked into adulthood, at least 50 percent, and usually closer to 70 percent, of "high-risk" children grow up to be not only successful by societal indicators but also "confident, competent, and caring" persons (Werner & Smith, 1992).

The personal attitudes and competencies most often associated with these resilient individuals include the broad categories of social competence, metacognition, autonomy, and a sense of purpose and belief in a bright future. While many researchers and practitioners have latched onto these personal attributes, creating a myriad of social- and life-skills programs to teach them directly, the strong message of resilience research is that these attributes are expressions—not causes—of resilience. Werner and Smith (1992) refer to resilience as an *innate* "self-righting mechanism" (p. 202), and Lifton (1994) identifies resilience as the human capacity of *all* individuals to transform and change—no matter their risks. Human beings are genetically hard-wired to form relationships (social competence), to problem-solve (metacognition), to develop a sense of identity (autonomy), and to plan and hope (a sense of purpose and future). These are the growth capacities which have enabled survival throughout human history.

However, even though some individuals can express these capacities in the absence of a facilitative environment, it is clearly the presence of a *nurturing* climate that draws them forth and encourages their expression. This finding is perhaps the most important and prescriptive for educators. The research shows that, contrary to much popular belief, teachers and schools actually do have the power to tip the scales from risk to resilience.

Werner and Smith (1989) found that "among the most frequently encountered positive role models in the lives of the children … outside of the family circle, was a favorite teacher, For the resilient youngster, a special teacher was not just an instructor for academic skills, but also a confidant and positive model for personal identification" (p. 162). Repeatedly, these turnaround teachers and mentors are described as building, in their own personal styles and ways, three crucial environmental protective factors: connection, competence, and contribution.

TURNAROUND TEACHERS PROVIDE *CONNECTION*

Turnaround teachers are characterized, first and foremost, as caring individuals who develop relationships with their students. They convey the message that they are "there for" a youth through trust and unconditional love. To the greatest extent possible, they help meet the basic survival needs of overwhelmed students and their families. On a basic level, this may mean that they have extra school supplies on hand, as well as other necessities such as hats, mittens, and personal hygiene items. On a more comprehensive level, they may connect students and their families to outside community resources in order to find food, shelter, clothing, counseling, treatment, and mentoring.

Providing connection also translates into meeting emotional safety needs. Resilient survivors talk about teachers' "quiet availability," "fundamental positive regard," and "simple sustained kindness," such as a touch on the shoulder, a smile, or a greeting (Higgins, 1994, pp. 324–325). Being interested in, actively listening to, and validating the feelings of struggling young people, as well as getting to know their strengths and gifts, conveys the message, "You matter." According to renowned urban educator Deborah Meier (1995), this kind of respect—having a person "acknowledge us, see us for who we are, as their equal in value and importance" (p. 120)—figures high in turnaround relationships.

Finally, these teachers connect with their students by showing compassion—nonjudgmental support that looks beneath the students' negative behavior and sees their pain and suffering. They do not take the students' behavior personally, no matter how negative it may be, but understand instead that the student is doing the best he or she can, given his or her life experiences. Sandy McBrayer, founder of an alternative school for homeless youth and 1994 National Teacher of the Year, declares, "People ask me what my 'methods' are. I don't have a method. But I believe one of the things that makes me an adequate or proficient teacher is that I never judge ... and I tell my kids I love them every day" (Bacon, 1995, p. 44). This rapport is also the critical motivational foundation for successful learning. As Noddings (1988) points out, "It is obvious that children will work harder and do things—even odd things like adding fractions—for people they love and trust" (p. 4).

TURNAROUND TEACHERS BUILD *COMPETENCE*

At the core of caring relationships are positive and high expectations that not only structure and guide behavior, but also challenge students to perform beyond what they believe they can do. These expectations reflect the teacher's deep belief in the student's innate competence and self-righting capacities. A consistent description of turnaround teachers is that they see the possibility: "They held visions of us that we could not imagine for ourselves" (Delpit, 1996, p. 199).

However, turnaround teachers not only see the possibilities, they also recognize existing competencies and mirror them back, helping students appreciate where they are already strong. When they use these strengths, interests, goals, and dreams as the beginning point for learning, they tap the students' intrinsic motivation and existing, innate drive for learning. Positive and high expectations then become easier for students to meet.

This identification of strengths can especially assist overwhelmed, labeled, and oppressed youth in reframing their life narratives from "damaged victims" to "resilient survivors." Turnaround teachers help youth to avoid:

- Taking *personally* the adversity in their lives ("You aren't the cause—nor can you control—your father's drinking")
- Seeing adversity as *permanent* ("This too shall pass"; "Your future will be different")
- Seeing setbacks as *pervasive* ("You can rise above this"; "This is only one part of your life experience") (adapted from Seligman, 1995)

Instead, they build their students' sense of competency by teaching metacognition—the understanding of how thoughts influence feelings and behaviors. When students recognize their own conditioned thinking—the environmental messages they have internalized that they are not good enough, smart enough, thin enough, and so on—they can remove blocks to their innate resilience. For example, in a Miami, Florida, study, the dropout rate for youth from a public housing community fell to nearly zero when they were taught they had this power to construct the meaning they gave to everything that happened to them (Mills, 1991).

TURNAROUND TEACHERS LET STUDENTS *CONTRIBUTE*

Rutter and his colleagues (1979), in their seminal research on effective urban schools in poor communities—schools in which the rates of delinquency and dropping out actually declined the longer students were in them—found a striking similarity among them. All of the schools gave students "a lot of responsibility. [Students] participated very actively in all sorts of things that went on in the school; they were treated as responsible people and they reacted accordingly" (1984, p. 65).

Indeed, providing outlets for student contribution is a natural outgrowth of working from this strengths-based perspective. In a physically and psychologically safe and structured environment, opportunities for participation can include:

- Asking questions that encourage self-reflection, critical thinking, and dialogue (especially around salient social and personal issues)
- Making learning more experiential, as in service learning
- Helping others through community service, peer helping, and cooperative learning
- Involving students in curriculum planning and giving them choices in their learning experiences
- Using participatory evaluation strategies
- Involving students in creating the governing rules of the classroom

Even in such classroom discipline issues, student participation can have surprising benefits. "Bring the kids in on it!" Alfie Kohn (1993) urges. "Instead of reaching for coercion, engage children and youth in a conversation about the underlying causes of what is happening and work together to negotiate a solution" (p. 14). When we invite students to help create the classroom rules and school policies, we ensure their buy-in, ownership, and sense of belonging. Perhaps more importantly, we also build their ability to make responsible choices. "It is in classrooms and families where participation is valued above adult control that students have the chance to learn *self-control"* (Kohn, 1993, p. 18).

THE BELIEFS OF TURNAROUND TEACHERS

> Perhaps more significant than what [our teachers] taught is what they believed…. They held visions of us that we could not imagine for ourselves. And they held those visions even when they themselves were denied entry into the larger white world. They were determined that, despite all odds, we would achieve.
>
> —Lisa Delpit in *City Kids, City Teachers,* 1996

Certain programmatic approaches such as those described in "How To Support Turnaround Teachers" [in the box] have proven particularly effective in providing opportunities for active participation and contribution. However, resilience research points out over and over that transformational power exists not in programmatic approaches *per se,* but at the deeper level of relationships, beliefs and expectations, and the willingness to share power. In other words, it is *how* we do what we do that counts.

Asa Hilliard (1991) advises that "to restructure we must first look deeply at the goals that we set for our children and the beliefs that we have about them. Once we are on the right track there, then we must turn our attention to the delivery systems, as we have begun to do. Cooperative learning is right. Technology access for all is right. Multiculturalism is right. *But none of these approaches or strategies will mean anything if the fundamental belief system does not fit the new structures that are being created"* (p. 36).

The starting point for creating both classrooms and schools that tap students' capacities is the deep belief of all school staff that every youth is resilient. This means that every adult in the school community must personally grapple with questions like "What tapped my resilience? What occurred in my life that brought out my strength and capacity? How am I connecting this knowledge to what I do in the classroom?"

Believing in our students' resilience requires foremost that we believe in our own innate capacity to transform and change. Our walk

HOW TO SUPPORT TURNAROUND TEACHERS

The characteristics and beliefs of turnaround teachers can be amplified when they are supported by colleagues and administration staff in a school building or organization. The following suggestions can help create classrooms and schools that are more likely to help students turn their lives around from risk to resilience.

Reflect on and discuss as a staff your beliefs about innate resilience. What does it mean in our classrooms and school if *all* kids are resilient? Answering this question as an individual and then coming to a consensus on the answer as a staff is the first step in creating a classroom or school that taps into its students' resilience.

Form a resiliency study group. Read the research on resiliency, including the studies of successful city schools. Share stories—both personal and literary—of individuals who successfully overcame the odds. "It is important to read about struggles that lead to empowerment and to successful advocacy, for resilient voices are critical to hear within the at-risk wasteland" (Polakow, 1995, p. 269). When working against the dominant risk paradigm, we need the support and "shelter of each other."

Focus on climate. Schools and classrooms that have been turnaround experiences for stressed young people are continually described as being like "a family," "a home," "a community"—even "a sanctuary." "School was my church, my religion. It was constant, the only thing that I could count on every day.... I would not be here if it was not for school" (Children's Express, 1993). Creating these safe havens requires a collective focus on building inclusive communities through relation-

always speaks louder than our talk. So to teach our students about their internal power, we first must see that we have the power—no matter what external stresses we face—to let go of our conditioned thinking and access our innate capacities for compassion, intuition, self-efficacy, and hope. Only when this belief is in place are we truly able to create the connections, point out the competence, and invite the contribution that will engage the innate resilience in our students.

RESILIENCY RESEARCH OF YOUR OWN

In the coming weeks or months, try an initial experiment of your own ships and responsibilities that invite back our disconnected and disenfranchised youth—and their families.

Foster school–community collaboration to coordinate needed services for children and families. Meeting the needs of the whole child necessitates school, family, and community collaboration. Develop a list of community agencies, including after-school neighborhood-based organizations. Match the needs of your students and families with the services of these organizations.

Provide for teachers what students need. Nurturing and sustaining a belief in resilience is not only the critical task of teachers; it should be the main focus of administrators. Resilience applies to all of us. What has sustained youth in the face of adversity is equally what enables teachers and administrators to overcome the incredible stresses they face in schools today. Teachers need the same good stuff as their students: caring relationships with colleagues; positive beliefs, expectations, and trust on the part of the administration; and ongoing opportunities to reflect, engage in dialogue, and make decisions together. A wise administrator once remarked, "If you don't feed the teachers, they'll eat the students." Research has shown that providing teachers with the time and opportunity to work collegially together, and thus build a sense of professional community, is critical in both sustaining school change efforts and raising students' academic scores (McLaughlin & Talbert, 1993).

Self-assess. Make an assessment tool from the best practices describing turnaround teachers and schools. Assess your classroom and school and ask your students to do the same. Identify both areas of strength and areas of challenge.

using the resiliency approach. Choose one of your most challenging students. Spend at least a few minutes each day building your connection with that student. Look for and identify all of his or her competencies. Mirror back those strengths. Teach that student that he or she has the power to create his or her own reality. Create opportunities to have the student participate and contribute his or her strengths. Be patient. Focus on small victories—they often grow into major transformations.

But in the meanwhile, relax, have fun, and trust the process! Working from our own innate resilience and well-being engages the same elements in our students. Thus, teaching becomes much more effortless and enjoyable. Resiliency research, as well as studies on nurturing teachers and successful schools, give us all the *proof* we need of the benefits of lightening up, letting go of our tight control, being patient, and trusting the process.

Finally, know that you are making a difference. When you care, believe in, and "invite back" our most precious resource—our children and youth—you are not only enabling their healthy development and successful learning. You are, indeed, creating inside-out social change, building the compassionate and creative citizenry of the future that will restore our lost vision of social and economic justice.

REFERENCES

Bacon, J. (1995). The place for life and learning: National Teacher of the Year, Sandra McBrayer. *Journal of Emotional and Behavioral Problems, 3*(4), 42–45.

Children's Express. (1993). *Voices from the future: Children tell us about violence in America.* New York: Crown.

Delpit, L. (1996). The politics of teaching literate discourse. In W. Ayers & P. Ford (Eds.), *City kids, city teachers: Reports from the front row.* New York: New Press.

Higgins, G. (1994). *Resilient adults: Overcoming a cruel past.* San Francisco: Jossey-Bass.

Hilliard, A. (1991). Do we have the will to educate all children? *Educational Leadership, 49*(1), 31–36.

Kohn, A. (1993, September). Choices for children: Why and how to let students decide. *Phi Delta Kappan.*

Lifton, R. (1994). *The protean self: Human resilience in an age of fragmentation.* New York: Basic Books.

McLaughlin, M., & Talbert, J. (1993). *Contexts that matter for teaching and learning.* Stanford, CA: Stanford University Press.

Meier, D. (1995). *The power of their ideas.* Boston: Beacon Press.

Mills, R. (1991). A new understanding of self: The role of affect, state of mind, self-understanding, and intrinsic motivation. *Journal of Experimental Education, 60*(1), 67–81.

Noddings, N. (1988, December 7). Schools face crisis in caring. *Education Week*, p. 32.

Polakow, V. (1995). Naming and blaming: Beyond a pedagogy of the poor. In B. Swadener & S. Lubeck (Eds.), *Children and families at promise: Deconstructing the discourse of risk*. Albany: State University of New York Press.

Rutter, M. (1984, March). Resilient children. *Psychology Today*, pp. 57–65.

Rutter, M., Maughan, B., Mortimore, P., Ouston, J., & Smith, A. (1979). *Fifteen thousand hours*. Cambridge, MA: Harvard University Press.

Seligman, M. (1995). *The optimistic child*. Boston: Houghton Mifflin.

Swadener, B., & Lubeck, S. (Eds.). (1995). *Children and families at promise: Deconstructing the discourse of risk*. Albany: State University of New York Press.

Wehmiller, P. (1992). When the walls come tumbling down. *Harvard Educational Review, 62*(3), 373–383.

Werner, E., & Smith, R. (1989). *Vulnerable but invincible: A longitudinal study of resilient children and youth*. New York: Adams, Bannister, and Cox.

Werner, E., & Smith, R. (1992). *Overcoming the odds: High-risk children from birth to adulthood*. New York: Cornell University Press.

INNOVATIVE PROGRAMS FOR TROUBLED STUDENTS

ARTICLE 9.5

WHAT exactly does a teacher do to create a strength-based approach to reclaiming troubled students? The goal is to develop student resiliency. *Resiliency* is the ability of a student to bounce back from painful life experiences without being emotionally damaged. Larry Brendtro and Scott Larson believe that students gain resiliency by experiencing the personal strengths of belonging, mastery, independence, and generosity in their lives. In the next article these authors not only provide a brief historical overview of the psychology of strengths but also integrate these research-validated principles into the Circle of Courage. They provide teachers with a new road map for promoting resiliency in troubled students.

THE RESILIENCE CODE: FINDING GREATNESS IN YOUTH
Larry Brendtro and Scott Larson

> What we want to achieve in our work with young people is to find and strengthen the positive and healthy elements, no matter how deeply they are hidden. We enthusiastically believe in the existence of those elements even in the seemingly worst of our adolescents.
>
> —Karl Wilker, 1920[1]

Long before the terms "resilience" and "risk" came into common use, Alfred Adler (1930) used the words "courage" and "discouragement" to express similar ideas. Thinkers since Plato have tried to define courage. In the classic book, *The Courage to Be,* Paul Tillich (1952) notes that courage is necessary to surmount life's difficulties, but courage only comes from experiencing adversity. Thus, adults should not shelter children from all difficulties, nor allow them to become discouraged. The goal is to support children as they develop courage to cope with the challenges and problems of life.

Resilience science is a relatively recent arrival on the psychological scene. A leading researcher, Emily Werner (1995), described resilience as achieving positive life outcomes in spite of risk. Resilience also involves the ability to rebound from adversity with greater strength to meet future challenges (Walsh, 1998). Clinical research shows that even serious disruptions in a child's life can offer unexpected opportunities for growth (Flach, 1988). How do we develop resilience in children? Research on positive youth de-

From *Reclaiming Children and Youth, 12*(4), 2004, pp. 194–200. Copyright by Reclaiming Children and Youth, Inc. Reprinted with permission.

[1]Karl Wilker was a physician and educator who transformed Berlin's worst juvenile institution into a model of mutual respect between youth and adults. He wrote *Der Lindenhof,* which was a rallying cry for the Wandervogel youth movement. When Hitler came to power, Wilker's books were burned and he fled to South Africa, where he taught in schools for Black students. This quotation is from: Wilker, K. (1920). *Der Lindenhof.* Translated in 1993 by Stephan Lhotzky. Sioux Falls, SD: Augustana College, p. 69.

velopment is providing a growing body of data about the factors that give kids the courage to thrive, even in the face of great adversity.

When the concept of resilience first was studied, the view of some was that this was a rare and remarkable trait of a few invulnerable super kids. Now we realize that humans by nature are resilient, for we are the descendants of survivors. Even children exposed to great trauma can turn their lives around, if they can develop certain inner strengths and rely on supports from caring persons in their lives. The other side of the coin is that there are no invulnerable humans, for if our basic needs are frustrated, we all are at risk.

DEFICITS OR STRENGTHS?

Glance at problems, gaze at strengths.

—J. C. Chambers

Eminent psychiatrist Karl Menninger (1893–1990) believed that building strengths was the foundation of mental health. When he was well into his nineties, Dr. Karl was asked which of his many books would have the most enduring impact. He quickly chose *The Vital Balance,* which he had written in 1963. That work described three stages in the history of mental health:

- Yesterday marked the discovery of mental illness.
- Today's research focuses on methods for prevention and treatment.
- Tomorrow will show how persons can become weller than well.

Dr. Menninger accurately foretold a science of resilience, where even life's disruptions could strengthen human character. His prototype of "weller than well" was William James, who overcame serious personal problems to achieve eminence in both psychology and philosophy. In 1902, in a classic treatise on religion, James wrote: "The potentialities of development in human souls are unfathomable" (cited in Menninger, 1963, p. 412).

In contrast to the optimism of James, the two prevailing views about how to deal best with youth problems are both pessimistic. The first is to punish behavior. The second is to treat disorders. Punitive models describe wayward youth as deviant and disruptive. Treatment models cast them as disturbed and disordered. We encountered yet another strain of pessimistic professionalism on a visit to a Russian children's home. Our professional hosts proudly introduced themselves as "defectologists." We have tried to stop using such deficit words, because they mask the needs and potential greatness of young persons. Sharing this repugnance to the deficit mindset is Australian therapist Michael White who writes, *"Pathology. The word makes me wince"* (White, 1995, p. 5).

During the last half of the twentieth century, psychology was preoccupied with the study of pathology (Aspinwall & Staudinger, 2002). Tomes were written about anger, guilt, depression, and trauma. Locked in this deficit mindset, little attention was given to human strengths like hope, courage, friendship, and kindness. This is rapidly changing as resilience science has sparked a new positive psychology.

THE RESILIENCE REVOLUTION

After decades of dwelling on the dark side of human behavior, a psychology of human strengths is emerging. Researchers are now exploring how to cultivate qualities such as courage, responsibility, and hope. In the words of leaders in this revolution: "Much of the task of prevention in this new century will be to understand and learn how to foster these virtues in young people" (Seligman & Peterson, 2003, p. 314).

In many ways, the move to strengths is the blossoming of seeds planted over the past century. In spite of the dominance of the deficit model, there have always been powerful advocates for the strengths perspective. Following is a quick 100-year sample of contributions to a psychology of strength and resilience in work with troubled children:

- **1900** — Sociologist Ellen Key of Sweden writes *The Century of the Child* and predicts that science and democracy will unleash a new positive approach to education and treatment of youth.
- **1917** — Physician Karl Wilker turns Berlin's worst facility for delinquents into a model of self-governance, searching for positive qualities in the most troubled young persons.
- **1925** — Austrian educator August Aichhorn pens the classic book, *Wayward Youth,* explaining how those who act out against

authority are often those who inwardly most fiercely long to be loved.

- **1939** — Psychologist Carl Rogers concludes that children from difficult backgrounds are able to gain insight into their circumstances and take responsibility for their problems.

- **1942** — Janusz Korczak of Poland accompanies 200 Jewish children to the Nazi gas chambers. In his *Ghetto Diary*, he predicts that in 50 years the world will finally recognize a child's right to respect.

- **1951** — Anna Freud forms an experimental group of Jewish orphans from concentration camps. Wildly defying adults, they show amazing loyalty, concern, and self-sacrifice towards peers.

- **1965** — Paul Torrance summarizes research on healthy personal development and concludes that mental health involves developing skills and resources to deal constructively with life stresses.

- **1972** — Urie Bronfenbrenner attacks research on "strange behavior in strange situations," calling for ecological study of the child's natural relationships in family, school, peer group, and community.

- **1989** — The United Nations ratifies the Rights of the Child, recognizing that even youth growing up in difficult situations are entitled to care in environments of happiness, love, and understanding.

- **1995** — Pioneering resilience researcher Emmy Werner has followed high-risk Hawaiian children into adulthood finding most show positive outcomes, in spite of troubled backgrounds.

- **2000** — The American Psychological Association (APA) calls for the creation of a positive psychology, which would shift from a preoccupation with deficits to focus on the development of strengths.

At the millennium, Martin Seligman used his presidency of APA to bring human strengths to the forefront of psychology. This is now a robust movement where researchers are providing exciting new studies on the psychology of strength and resilience (Aspinwall & Staudinger, 2002). As the narrowness of the deficit mindset is exposed, even the established DSM system of diagnostic labels for mental disorders is being questioned (Buetler & Malik, 2002). An alternative view is that most interpersonal problems of children and youth result from the absence of essential human strengths (Seligman & Peterson, 2003). Following this premise, researchers are seeking to identify and classify the key strengths that lead to successful life outcomes.

One may not need psychologists to identify strengths, since they have been known throughout human history. Strengths are valuable because they contribute to personal balance and interpersonal harmony. Even cultures without a written language pass on stories of heroes who embodied the key virtues elders seek to instill in children. For example, the parables of the Bible and the stories of Native Americans are both rich with inspiring accounts of generosity. The recent attention given to developing virtues and character in children is yet another example of the importance placed on teaching positive strengths (Lickona, 2001).

It is reasonable to believe that those strengths that insure the survival of individuals and communities are built into both human nature and culture. While strengths are probably universal, certain groups more highly prize particular virtues (Seligman & Peterson, 2003). Thus, *belonging* is the centerpiece of kinship cultures, while *independence* is a highly valued trait in competitive, materialistic societies. If strengths are wired into the human DNA, children would be expected to show natural variations in these, as is the case with any human trait.

DECODING RESILIENCE

After years of listing disorders, there is great interest in cataloguing strengths. For starters, we could reread Allport and Odbert who, in 1936, identified 18,000 English words for human traits, some positive and some negative. But long lists of strengths would be just as unwieldy as 900 pages of disorders in the DSM manual of psychiatric diagnoses. Einstein advised that the important ideas of any field should be stated in terms "as simple as possible but not simpler." Following his advice, we seek to distill the myriad of human strengths into a practical and manageable set of concepts.

One promising system of categorizing strengths is the Developmental Assets model, produced by researchers from the Search Institute (Benson, 1997). This is a list of 40 assets that lead to positive outcomes. Twenty are internal assets (e.g., achievement motivation) and 20 are external assets (e.g., positive peers). Youth with many assets usually turn out well. But those with limited assets are at risk for a host of bad outcomes, including substance abuse, reckless sexuality, school problems, emotional problems, and delinquency. Remarkably, 60% of youth in the United States have less than 20 of these protective assets. Across the country, the Search Institute is helping communities increase assets for children and youth of all ages.

In South Africa, Nelson Mandela's Inter-ministerial Commission on Young People at Risk had a unique opportunity to reconstruct child and youth care programs. Rejecting the bitter legacy of apartheid, they embraced a strengths perspective. The Circle of Courage, first identified in *Reclaiming Youth at Risk* (Brendtro, Brokenleg, & Van Bockern, 1990), was adopted as the basic model of organizing developmental assessment and strength-building interventions. This model focuses attention on the four principles of belonging, mastery, independence, and generosity. When youth have opportunities to develop these strengths, they thrive. When these are lacking, children are at risk. The commitment to this positive philosophy is expressed by Archbishop Desmond Tutu in the foreword to the latest revision of *Reclaiming Youth at Risk:*

> We must look on children in need not as problems but as individuals with potential to share if they are given the opportunity. Even when they are really troublesome, there is some good in them, for, after all, they were created by God. I would hope we could find creative ways to draw out of our children the good that is there in each of them. (Tutu, 2002)

For some time, we have been intrigued at the close connection between the 40 Developmental Assets of the Search Institute and the Circle of Courage dimensions of belonging, mastery, independence, and generosity (Brendtro, Brokenleg, & Van Bockern, 2002). The 20 internal assets seemed to describe nuances of the four global strengths included in the Circle of Courage. The 20 external assets identified a range of environmental supports that help youth develop these strengths.

While the Search Institute labeled 40 assets, researchers in positive psychology have developed a tentative list of over 50 strengths, which they place in six categories (Seligman & Peterson, 2003). Once again, most of these seem to be extensions of the four Circle of Courage strengths.

We thought it would be illustrative to take key studies of resilience and overlay them on the Circle of Courage. There is richness in the longer lists. There is simplicity in being able to interpret these as exemplars of belonging, mastery, independence, and generosity. We believe that the reason the Circle of Courage has a goodness of fit with so many other data sets is that it is tied to universal developmental needs, namely attachment, achievement, autonomy, and altruism.

In Table 9.5–1 we sort four other lists of strengths into Circle of Courage categories. These are drawn from leading researchers on resilience and self-worth. The Circle of Courage provides a unifying tool to integrate the complex factors identified by diverse researchers. A perusal of these concepts clarifies just what is involved in building Circles of Courage.

The Resilience Code translates and clarifies a mass of important research on the psychology of human strengths. It places the focus on core needs of children and provides a roadmap for supporting youth in their sometimes painful journey through the hazards of human existence. An emphasis on resilience does not mean that we throw children to their own resources. Youth cannot thrive on strengths alone, but need concerned adults and peers who embrace them in both good and difficult times.

CHILDREN AS ACORNS

A remarkable blending of scientific and spiritual worlds comes from research on resilience. Psychiatrist Robert Coles (1990) studied the spiritual life of children. He concluded that youngsters ask the same eternal spiritual questions as thinkers like Tolstoy and Gaugin: "Where do we come from? Who are we? Where are we going?" (p. 299).

Youth whose lives are in pain and turmoil are those most likely to wrestle with deeply spiritual questions, such as, "Why was I born?" and "What is the reason for living?" Many studies show that resilient youth are able to find meaning in their lives by investing in a purpose beyond themselves (Larson & Brendtro, 2000). We once asked teens in a detention center if they had any hopes or dreams for their future. One boy responded, "No. That's why we're here."

As young people gain an understanding of who they have been uniquely created to be, they discover a sense of calling for their lives. A youth returning from a week-long volunteer service project exclaimed, "I finally found the reason I was born!" Suddenly he had something bigger to live for than his self-gratification. But without a sense of purpose, the lives of these young people are mostly about deviance control or "sin management." Helping young people discover their dreams involves more

THE RESILIENCE CODE
CIRCLE OF COURAGE PRINCIPLES AND RESILIENCE SCIENCE FINDINGS

TABLE 9.5-1

Attachment: This growth need is met by opportunities for **Belonging.**

Coopersmith:	Significance, acceptance, attention, and affection of others.
Flach:	A network of friends, a community where one is respected, humor.
Werner:	Caring and attentive family environments; if parents are absent or inattentive, extended family, siblings, and other adults provide counsel, safety, and suppport; participation in school and community programs.
Wolin:	Relationships, humor, intimate and fulfilling ties to others.

Achievement: This growth need is met by opportunities for **Mastery.**

Coopersmith:	Competence, success in meeting demands for achievement.
Flach:	Creativity, open-mindedness, receptive to new ideas, wide range of interests, recognizes one's gifts and talents, willing to dream, finds novel solutions to meet goals, redefines assumptions and problems to find solutions.
Werner:	High expectations, academic success, communication skills.
Wolin:	Insight, initiative, creativity, stretches self in demanding tasks, asks tough questions, gives honest answers, brings order and purpose to chaos.

Autonomy: This growth need is met by opportunities for **Independence.**

Coopersmith:	Power, the ability to be in charge of self and to be able to influence others.
Flach:	Autonomy, independence of thought and action, personal discipline and responsibility, insight into one's own feelings, high tolerance of distress, distances oneself from destructive relationships.
Werner:	Sense of personal efficacy or control over one's environment.
Wolin:	Independence, keeps boundaries and emotional distance from troubled persons, initiative, takes charge of problems, exerts control.

Altruism: This growth need is met by opportunities for **Generosity.**

Coopersmith:	Virtue, adherence to moral and ethical standards.
Flach:	Insight into the feelings of others, hope, commitment, the search for meaning, purpose, faith, a sense of destiny.

(continues)

TABLE 9.5–1

THE RESILIENCE CODE *Continued.*

Werner:	Empathy and caring, productive roles in family and community life.
Wolin:	Relationships of empathy, capacity to give, morality with an informed conscience, judges right from wrong, values decency, compassion, honesty, fair play, responds to needs and suffering of others.

Research Sources

Stanley Coopersmith. (1967). *The Antecedents of Self Esteem.* San Francisco: W. H. Freeman.

Frederic Flach. (1989). *Resilience: Discovering a New Strength at Times of Stress.* New York: Fawcett Columbine.

Emmy Werner and Ruth Smith. (1992). *Overcoming the Odds: High Risk Children from Birth to Adulthood.* Ithaca, NY: Cornell University Press.

Steven Wolin and Sybil Wolin. (1993). *The Resilient Self.* New York: Villard.

than simply saying, "You can do whatever you put your mind to. Go for it!" That's just another set-up for failure. We need to help kids think realistically, yet boldly, about who and what they could become. And then we walk with them one step at a time to get there.

Writing in *The Soul's Code,* James Hillman (1996) uses the metaphor of an acorn to describe each child's unique hidden potential. A tiny acorn carries coded instructions for becoming a mighty oak. All children are endowed with the seed for some unique "genius." In the struggle to find their purpose, they make missteps and show many problems. Our task is to provide opportunities so children can discover their destiny and calling.

> It is amateur night at the Harlem Opera House. Ella, an awkward skinny teen, fearfully goes on stage. The announcer first tells the audience that this next contestant will dance for them. "Hold it, hold it. Now what's your problem honey?" Ella has just changed her mind so he announces her decision to the crowd: "She's not gonna dance, she's gonna sing...." (Hillman, 1996, p. 10)

That night, a shy girl found her calling, taking a new pathway to become the legendary singer, Ella Fitzgerald.

Some children show their destiny and genius very young. Golda launched into leadership in fourth grade in Milwaukee, Wisconsin, public schools. She organized a protest against requiring poor children to purchase schoolbooks. She rented a hall to stage a meeting, raised funds, enlisted a group of girls to help, and then addressed the assembly. Young Golda Meir was well on the way to her destiny of becoming prime minister of Israel.

Robert Perry who crossed the Arctic and "discovered" the North Pole was the only child of a widow. He stayed close to his mother to escape the neighborhood boys who called him skinny and bullied him about his fearfulness. Mohandas K. Gandhi was a short, thin, sickly, ugly, and frightened child, afraid of snakes, ghosts, and the dark. His stand against racism in South Africa was a rehearsal for his nonviolent protest in India that confounded the power of the British Empire.

As children struggle to find their calling, along the way they often create grief for themselves and others. By current standards, Eleanor needed therapy. Before nine, she had lost a mother, younger brother, and father. In school, she was sullen and stubborn and threw tantrums. Because of school failure, she was taught for years by a tutor whom she hated. Deprived of normal relationships, she would fantasize and dream of the day when she would do great acts of compassion. The destiny of Eleanor was to care for a family and to be the strength behind her disabled husband, Franklin Roosevelt, as he served as governor of New York and president of the United States.

Psychologists sometimes describe high-achieving young persons as "compensating" for their weakness. But this is a pessimistic view, since obviously the potential was always lying within the acorn. Hardship and difficulty only brought it to the fore. Reframing these lives in resilience theory, the challenges, frustrations, and disruptions of life are essential to develop character and strength.

On their way to achieving their destiny, many youngsters are obstinate, frustrated, and angry. If one checks off lists of "symptoms," they might qualify for one or more psychiatric labels from the *Diagnostic and Statistical Manual* (DSM). The DSM is so named because it uses statistical standards of "normal" to label those deemed "abnormal." Hillman prefers the term "extraordinary" and challenges us to diagnose the encoded greatness in children, rather than some disorder. On the search for their destiny, children strive and defend, and stubbornly persist. They should be expected to show problems when their needs and potentials are ignored. The new psychology calls for identifying those conditions that enable youth to achieve important life goals (Stokols, 2003).

CONCLUSION

Two centuries ago, Goethe declared that the job of the educator was to find the germ of virtue concealed in the kernel of every fault. The resilience revolution has brought us full circle, back to the wisdom of early pioneers who saw positive qualities in even the most challenging youth.

One of today's leading experts on resilience is John Seita. His credentials began when he was removed from his family at age eight. In the next four years, he was kicked out of 15 court-ordered placements, as he battled all who crossed his path. Soon his case file was heavy with pessimistic assessments of deficit and disorder. But along the way, he found adults who engaged in "talent hunts" to uncover and unleash his hidden potentials. He also bonded to positive peers who shared his pain and his dreams. His journey of resilience led him to his current role as professor of social work at Michigan State University. He views troubled kids as possessing a unique but distorted courage, even as they struggle to outwit adults (Seita & Brendtro, 2002). In a book describing his own battles with adults (Seita, Mitchell, & Tobin, 1996), he offers this straightforward advice to all who dare to care for difficult kids:

> I personally challenge all of you to take the bold, brave steps to reclaim every child. My message to you is to use your hidden resources to summon courage, compassion, wisdom, strength and tenacity so that all children of today may have a tomorrow. No longer should we expect children to navigate without a map, steer without a rudder, or seek without a friend. (p. 62)

BIBLIOGRAPHY

Adler, A. (1930). *Die seele des schwererzeihbaren schulkinde [The Problem Child].* Translated by G. Daniels into English in 1963. New York: G. P. Putnam's Sons.

Allport, G. W., & Odbert, H. S. (1936). Trait-names: A psycho-lexical study. *Psychological Monographs, 47*(Whole No. 211).

Aspinwall, L. G., & Staudinger, U. M. (Eds.). (2002). *A psychology of human strengths.* Washington, DC: American Psychological Association.

Benson, P. (1997). *All kids are our kids: What communities must do to raise caring and responsible children and adolescents.* San Francisco: Jossey-Bass.

Brendtro, L., Brokenleg, M., & Van Bockern, S. (1990). *Reclaiming youth at risk: Our hope for the future.* Bloomington, IN: National Educational Service.

Brendtro, L., Brokenleg, M., & Van Bockern, S. (2002). *Reclaiming youth at risk: Our hope for the future* (Rev. ed.). Bloomington, IN: National Educational Service.

Buetler, M., & Malik, M. (Eds.). (2002). *Rethinking DSM.* Washington, DC: American Psychological Association.

Coles, R. (1990). *The spiritual life of children.* Boston: Houghton Mifflin.

Coopersmith, S. (1967). *The antecedents of self-esteem.* San Francisco: W. H. Freeman.

Flach, F. (1988). *Resilience: Discovering a new strength at times of stress.* New York: Fawcett Columbine.

Hillman, J. (1996). *The soul's code: In search of character and calling.* New York: Random House.

Larson, S., & Brendtro, L. (2000). *Reclaiming our prodigal sons and daughters.* Bloomington, IN: National Educational Service.

Lickona, T. (2001). What good is character and how can we develop it in our children? *Reclaiming Children and Youth, 9*(4), 239–251.

Menninger, K. (1963). *The vital balance.* New York: The Viking Press.

Seita, J. R., & Brendtro, L. K. (2002). *Kids who outwit adults.* Longmont, CO: Sopris West.

Seita, J., Mitchell, M., & Tobin, C. (1996). *In whose best interest?* Elizabethtown, PA: Continental Press.

Seligman, M., & Peterson, C. (2003). Positive clinical psychology. In L. G. Aspinwall & U. M. Staudinger (Eds.), *A psychology of human strengths* (pp. 305–318). Washington, DC: American Psychological Association.

Stokols, D. (2003). The ecology of human strengths. In L. G. Aspinwall & U. M. Staudinger (Eds.), *A psychology of human strengths* (pp. 331–343). Washington, DC: American Psychological Association.

Tillich, P. (1952). *The courage to be.* New Haven: Yale University Press.

Tutu, D. (2002). Our hope for the future. In L. Brendtro, M. Brokenleg, & S. Van Bockern, *Reclaiming youth at risk* (Rev. ed.). Bloomington, IN: National Educational Service.

Walsh, F. (1998). *Strengthening family resilience.* New York: Guilford Press.

Werner, E. (1995). Resilience and development. *American Psychological Society,* *4,* 81–85.

White, M. (1995). *Re-authoring lives.* Adelaide, Australia: Dulwich Centre Publications.

Wolin, S., & Wolin, S. (1993). *The resilient self.* New York: Villard.

PREVENTION PROGRAMS

ARTICLE 9.6

IN the next article David Moore describes an innovative program from the Puget Sound school district in Washington state. This model program was designed for students at risk for alcohol and other drug problems. The creative aspect of this program is the successful way the researchers involved the school staff, families, community agencies, and youth to create a school environment free of substance abuse and violence. This is a prototype design that can be duplicated to correct any school problem.

NEW DIRECTIONS IN PREVENTION WITH AT-RISK STUDENTS
David D. Moore

Since the United States Congress enacted the Education for All Handicapped Children Act in 1976, an entire service delivery system has developed to aid disabled students. A decade later, in 1986, Congress passed Public Law 99-570, the Drug-Free Schools and Communities Act (DFSC). Over the last seven years, this act has stimulated the development of new services for at-risk students, much as earlier legislation did for the handicapped.

The DFSC Act established "Drug-Free Schools and Cam-

From *The Journal of Emotional and Behavioral Problems,* 1993, pp. 28–32. Copyright by The Journal of Emotional and Behavioral Problems, Inc. Reprinted with permission.

puses Regulations" (34 CFR, part 86, subpart 86.200) to guide the development of prevention programs. These are key legislative mandates that schools must address:

1. Provide alcohol and other drug-prevention programs from early childhood level through grade 12. Schools responded quickly to this mandate, and alcohol and other drug-abuse prevention curricula have proliferated (Klitzner, 1987). The Department of Education provided guidelines for selecting materials and training staff.

2. Establish student codes of conduct with clear disciplinary consequences for use or possession of alcohol and illicit drugs on school premises or at school activities. School districts have attached sanctions for substance use and possession to existing codes of conduct. Model disciplinary policies were widely disseminated (Anderson, 1986).

3. Use student drug and alcohol counseling programs as a component of education and/or disciplinary reentry contracts. This mandate for rehabilitative counseling clearly fell outside of traditional school services. Government regulations called for school–community–family partnerships (Bennett, 1986), but schools were provided very few specific methods for accomplishing this task.

The Department of Education designated five regional training centers to disseminate alcohol and other drug-abuse prevention programming to schools. These regional centers have compiled research that has shaped an extensive national training system.

THE SEARCH FOR NEW APPROACHES

The University of Washington Center for the Study and Teaching of At-Risk Students conducted a meta-analysis of the DFSC research projects conducted between 1989 and 1991 (Moore, 1992). The center also has drawn insights from more than 1,000 school district staff who participated in focus groups during on-campus training activities.

Two interconnected service models for assisting students at-risk of, or involved in, substance abuse emerged in this review: The interdisciplinary "case management model" and the "student assistance model," which often are used in combination.

The "Case Management Model" (Rothman, 1992) was developed to meet the need for holistic service planning involving schools with other social, health, and community service agencies. Unlike special education programs based mainly within schools, case management involves interdisciplinary programs where many (if not most) services are provided by community agencies. The technology of case management is designed to make these interdisciplinary systems operate smoothly and efficiently.

The "Student Assistance Model" (Moore & Forster, 1993), like the Employee Assistance approach for adults, operates from the premise that persons abusing alcohol or other drugs are likely to resist receiving help because of "problem denial" (Kinney & Leaton, 1987). Whether substance abuse is present in the family, among peers, or isolated to the student, self-referral is unlikely. Student Assistance Program methods penetrate problem denial, motivate referral into a service plan, and maintain ongoing involvement with the service system.

Certain principles consistently underlie effective programs that combine interdisciplinary case management technology with student assistance programs. This is what we have learned about these programs:

Following are five structural principles which undergird successful programs for students at-risk of, or involved in, substance abuse.

1. *Clear school district policies.* Problems in student functioning are viewed as a school responsibility. Serious health and safety issues (for example, substance use and physical aggression) are immediately addressed from two perspectives: (a) emergency expulsion; and (b) a health and social services plan that, when possible, brings the student back into the school system. This response mirrors the DFSC mandate. Often an interdisciplinary task force or technical review panel develops these policies. Involving parents and community agencies in the task force broadens program advocacy.

2. *Site-based student assistance teams.* These teams serve students whose identified behavioral problems place them at risk for substance abuse and/or school failure. These teams are analogous to the IEP team in special education, which matches

students' needs with school and community resources. The student assistance team initiates on-campus interventions, which usually include group counseling. The team also locates community counseling, health, and social services to augment services available at the school. Finally, the team provides faculty with a student referral process and often has overlapping membership with the special education team.

3. *The student assistance case manager.* In order to coordinate community services with school services, at least one person from a community agency is brought into the system. This individual typically provides assessment and service planning and often is called the student assistance case manager. In intervention strategies, it is necessary for responsibility to be delineated clearly. However, case management is a team process, and other personnel also play pivotal roles in serving referred students.

4. *A standardized service menu.* There must be a range of options for developing service plans, particularly when the case management student assistance program will be used for disciplinary referrals. This menu of possible interventions is often written directly into the facilitating policies (Moore, 1992).

5. *A standardized evaluation process.* A method must be established to match client needs to related resources. Because problem denial is likely with student and family substance abuse, a sophisticated evaluation may be required. Standardized evaluation using a multiple gates approach might include these steps:

   a. *Identify a problem* using a brief initial screening test with a follow-up interview.
   b. *Match the problem to a service* employing a comprehensive diagnostic test and a 60-minute clinical interview.
   c. *Develop a comprehensive treatment plan* through multiple assessments and ongoing student and family contacts.

The student assistance case management model incorporates these five principles to provide a range of innovative services for students and families. Table 9.6–1 summarizes the service activities identified in our study.

TABLE 9.6–1

CASE MANAGEMENT ACTIVITIES (ROTHMAN, 1992)

1. Family Identification and Outreach: Identify families needing services and reach out to those who do not seek help.

2. Assessment: Provide evaluation of youth and family including social supports, service needs, and attitudes toward service.

3. Service Planning: Develop individualized service plan including steps for service delivery, monitoring, and evaluation.

4. Service Linkage and Coordination: Connect families with services ensuring that agency interactions benefit families.

5. Follow-up, Monitoring, and Evaluation: Assure that the family is receiving the expected and appropriate services.

6. Advocacy: Work to advance the best interests of the family in meeting its needs.

7. Family Mentoring Self-Management: Families are encouraged to develop self-efficacy skills and assume their own case management.

THE PUGET SOUND PROGRAMS IN ACTION

The U.S. Department of Education awarded a three-year demonstration grant to study the Case Management Student Assistance Program in four Puget Sound (Washington) area school districts with a combined enrollment of 59,000 students and a 23% minority population. One district was rural, one was urban, and two were urban-suburban. The University of Washington's Center for the Study and Teaching of At-Risk Students provided the technical assistance; and its associate community service agency, Olympic Counseling Services, provided agency personnel to all four districts. Approximately 3,000 students were referred into the Case Management Student Assistance Program each year. The following discussion summarizes the operation of the Puget Sound programs.

Each of the four school districts selected referral policies from the University of Washington's Mastery Educator Institute's manual (Moore, 1992), which corresponded to the DFSC mandates. In addition to disciplinary referrals for substance use, cases are referred to the Student Assistance Team in such problem situations as:

1. a health care concern, corroborated by the school nurse,

2. an acute social or family problem, corroborated by the school counselor, or

3. behavior indicating a chronic maladaptive response to stress, corroborated by the classroom teacher.

Besides using standard behavior checklists (for example, Anderson, 1986; Newsam, 1992), teachers look for the five patterns of behavior summarized in Table 9.6–2. These patterns indicate high levels of personal discomfort and are predictive of both school failure and substance use.

Each school assembled a student assistance team that represented the potential referral sources: school administrator (discipline), teacher representative (classroom behavior profile), school counselor (family and emotional crisis), and nurse (health problems). In some schools without a full-time counselor or nurse, other personnel represent these referral areas. Support groups in each school are operated by trained faculty or

MALADAPTIVE STRESS RESPONSE PROFILES (CHANDLER, 1986)

TABLE 9.6-2

Profile Description	Developmental Risk
Acting-Out Student	
Socially non-conforming, aggressive to others	Juvenile delinquency, conduct disorder
Over-Active Student	
Impulsive, off-task, inability to concentrate or maintain control, immature	Attention deficit disorders in adolescence, social skills delay
Passive–Aggressive Student	
Fails to meet adult requests, rejects standard goals, forms alternate internal reward system	Narcissistic, potentially exploitive, may progress to an acting-out profile
Repressive Student	
Over-involved, low level of relaxation and leisure, compulsive behavior with low recognition of feelings	Anxiety or panic disorders, eating disorders, and other obsessive–compulsive behavior patterns
Dependent Student	
Withdrawn, passive, little social interaction, resignation	Depression, thought disorders, dysfunctional intimate relationships

para-professionals. The student assistance teams contacted various community agencies to augment these on-campus groups.

The next step in the process was to develop a service menu for developing individualized student plans (see Table 9.6–3). This comprehensive list of possible services includes school-based groups and mentoring activities, agency-based youth development and treatment programs, family empowerment and counseling programs, and other services individualized to student and family needs.

When students first are referred to the program, the student assistance case manager uses a standardized screening to identify risk profiles and substance use problems. The results of this screening help determine which interventions from the service menu will be used.

The students' risk profiles are identified through Chandler's Stress Response Scale (1986). Initial substance use disorders are identified by a group of items excerpted from the Client Substance Index (Moore, 1989), used by the National Center for Juvenile Justice as a screening instrument (Thomas, 1992). Measurements were keyed to one of three diagnostic levels:

> **Level I:** Substance MISUSE. Developmental delay due to using substances in a culturally inappropriate manner (WHO, 1957).

> **Level II:** Substance ABUSE. Person continues substance use despite recurring threats to physical or psychological well-being (APA, 1987).

> **Level III:** Chemical DEPENDENCY. Substance abuse with the addition of loss of control and/or tolerance (APA, 1987).

When the service plan includes the use of community agencies, an agency specialist completes a more extensive evaluation for planning treatment. The school counselor or school social worker monitors the on-campus components of the service plan, and the student assistance case manager monitors the overall plan and facilitates the community service components.

VISION FOR THE FUTURE

Initial data confirm the operational effectiveness of Case Management Student Assistance Programs. The four participating Puget Sound districts

MENU OF STUDENT ASSISTANCE SERVICES

TABLE 9.6-3

I. School-Based Services	**Diagnostic Profile**
a. "Boundaries" group for children of alcoholics	Risk profile and alcoholic home
b. "Transitions" group for divorce or remarriage	Risk profile and family change
c. "Pass insurance" group for students in conflict with school rules	Passive–aggressive, acting out, and overactive risk profiles
d. "Good grief" group for students experiencing dependent, repressive profiles	Any student experiencing serious loss, particularly death
e. "Candle" group for sexual victimization	Any sexually victimized student
f. "Insight" group for students evaluating their own substance use or risk (can also be agency based)	Students who are too defensive to evaluate
g. "Bridges" group for students in or returning from community substance use treatment (can also be agency based)	Students who are substance abusers or are chemically dependent
h. Individualized mentoring	Dependent risk profile; others as available

II. Agency-Based Services	**Diagnostic Profile**
i. "Adolescent Development" group for youth who have misused substances	Families needing information and intensive prevention education
j. Young Men's or Women's groups for youth or their partners	Substance-abusing youth disengaging from the substance abuse subculture
k. Intensive Outpatient workshops for substance-abusing or chemically dependent youth	Substance abuse or chemical dependency diagnosis
l. Residential treatment for serious mental health and/or substance use disorders	Middle-stage chemical dependency or multiple diagnoses
m. Family counseling	All risk profiles and substance use disorders
n. Family Empowerment Program. Multifamily support group offering parent training, babysitting, and free meals from community service/ church groups	All risk profiles and substance use disorders
o. Medical, nutritional, housing, services	Site specific, individualized to family needs and other social/health services

represent only 30% of the student population in the training cooperative, but they identified and referred 62% of all students who received services in 1990–1991.

A focus group of school, community, and university staff conducted a formative evaluation of the program to identify areas for further refinement. The major identified need for staff skills was the area of multicultural competence. Five other areas of projected need for staff development were:

- self-care/wellness planning for professionals
- confidentiality/legal issues
- group facilitation/group work
- supervision and supervisory process
- staffing for difficult/complex family situations

One district (Tacoma Schools) involved school, community, university, and agency leaders in a strategic planning process. The vision statement prepared by this group can serve as a guide for all schools starting similar programs:

> We envision a systemic change inclusive of students, school personnel, families, and communities working in partnership to advocate, cooperate, and coordinate services for the community's children and youth. This effort will empower students to attend school ready to learn, thereby enabling them to contribute to society with respect for diversity and hope for the future.

BIBLIOGRAPHY

American Psychiatric Association. (1987). *Diagnostic and statistical manual,* third edition. Washington, DC: APA.

Anderson, Gary L. (1987). *When chemicals come to school: The student assistance program model.* Milwaukee, WI: Community Recovery Press.

Benishek, L. A. (1989). A summary of adolescent substance abuse assessment instruments. *Health Care Study Project.* Lansing, MI: Michigan State University, Department of Psychiatry.

Bennett, William J. (1986). *What works: Schools without drugs.* Washington, DC: U.S. Department of Education.

Chandler, L. A. (1986). *The stress response scale.* Pittsburgh, PA: University of Pittsburgh, The Psychoeducational Clinic.

Hawkins, J. D., Lishner, D., & Catalano, R. F. (1985). Childhood predictors and the prevention of adolescent substance abuse. In: Jones, C.L. and Battjes, R.J. (Eds.), *Etiology of drug abuse: Implications for prevention.* NIDA Research Monograph No. 56, DHHS Publication (ADM) 85-1335. Washington, DC: U.S. Government Printing Office. 75-126.

Kinney, Jean & Leaton, Gwen (1987). *Loosening the grip,* third edition. St. Louis: Times Mirror/Mosby College Publishing.

Klitzner, M. D. (1987). Report to Congress on the nature and effectiveness of federal, state, and local drug prevention/education programs. Part 2: An assessment of the research on school-based prevention programs. Prepared for U.S. Department of Education, Office of Planning, Budget and Evaluation.

Moore, David D. (1989). *The client substance index.* Tacoma, WA: Olympic Counseling Services.

Moore, David D. (1992). *Mastery educator institute for K-12 drug and alcohol programs.* Seattle, WA: University of Washington's Center for the Study and Teaching of At-Risk Students.

Moore, David D. & Forster, Jerald R. (1993). Student Assistance Programs: New approaches for reducing adolescent substance abuse. *Journal of Counseling & Development,* Jan-Feb;71:326–329.

Newsam, Barbara Sprague (1992). *Complete Student Assistance Program handbook: Techniques and materials for alcohol/drug prevention and intervention in grades 7–12.* West Nyack, NY: The Center for Applied Research in Education.

Rothman, Jack (1992). *Guidelines for case management: Putting research to professional use.* Itasca, IL: F.E. Peacock Publishers, Inc.

Seligman, Milton (Ed.). (1975). *The family with a handicapped child: Understanding and treatment.* Orlando, FL: Grune & Stratton, Inc.

Thomas, Doug (1992). *Implementation manual: Substance abuse screening protocol.* Pittsburgh, PA: National Center for Juvenile Justice.

U.S. Department of Education (1992). Progress report and year three continuation grant proposal re: USDOE Grant No. S201C12560 entitled "Washington State coordinated service initiative for at-risk youth and families" (CFDA No. 84.201). Seattle, WA: University of Washington's Center for the Study and Teaching of At-Risk Students.

World Health Organization. (1957). *Producing drugs: Seventh report.* W.H.O. Technical Report Service, 116:9.

Wright, B. D. (1991). *Rasch analysis for all two facet models: Person measurement, item & step calibration, person & item fit analysis.* Chicago, IL: Mesa Press.

THE SEARCH FOR PREVENTIVE PROGRAMS

Dr. Karl Menninger (1893–1990), an eminent American psychiatrist for over six decades, wrote,

> Most of my life has been spent treating persons one by one. But as I became increasingly aware of the extent of misery and hopelessness in our society, I think more of preventing unnecessary suffering at the source before individuals take or are forced to take the wrong road. (1938, p. 37)

Menninger spent the beginning years of his career providing early treatment to mental patients. The remainder of his life was dedicated to promoting the idea of primary prevention. He defined mental health in humanistic terms. He wrote,

> Mental health is the adjustment of human beings to the world and each other with a maximum of effectiveness and happiness. Not just efficiency, or just contentment or the grace of obeying the rules of the game cheerfully. It is all these things together. It is the ability to maintain an even temper, an alert intelligence, socially considerate behavior, and a happy disposition. This I think is a healthy mind. (1938, p. 37)

Menninger would be pleased to see the new paradigm change from psychopathology, deviancy, and dysfunction to the strength-based programs of today. He would not be satisfied, however, that the philosophy of primary prevention is still at the beginning stage of acceptance.

PETER Benson of the Search Institute (www.search-institute.org) in Minneapolis, Minnesota, has developed the concept of developmental assets to describe the healthy development of children and youth. The next article introduces the importance of his work and the impact it will have on future school and community goals.

ARTICLE 9.7

WHAT WORKS IN PREVENTION: THE SEARCH CONTINUES

Peter L. Benson

DEVELOPMENTAL ASSETS

An ongoing research project at Search Institute examines the promotion of programs for a more general population of adolescents, not just those exposed to certain risk factors. This research demonstrates the strong link between social–psychological well-being and the avoidance of various negative behaviors, for example, using alcohol, tobacco, or illicit drugs and violence and promiscuous sex. This work defines healthy development in terms of developmental assets (Benson, 1993). Assets are understood as the building blocks of healthy development, and each asset is useful, and perhaps necessary for promoting psychosocial well-being.

Positive development requires constant exposure to interlocking systems of support, control, and structure. Ideally, young people would interact constantly in schools, families, community organizations, and religious institutions with caring, principled adults. These patterns of support, control, and structure function as external assets, providing youth with the webs of safety and love that stimulate and nurture healthy development.

During childhood a person is surrounded by networks of external support. But beginning in adolescence, these networks are partially supplanted by the internal checks and balances that enable the individual to make wise choices. It is of primary importance, particularly during adolescence, to nourish a range of internal assets. These are the commitments, values, and competencies that help an individual thrive competently and responsibly when "on one's own."

Table 9.7–1 lists 16 external assets, grouped into the categories of support, control, and structured time use. Table 9.7–2 lists 14 internal assets, grouped into educational commitment, positive values, and social competencies.

These 30 assets emerged from a review of the literature on children and adolescents and synthesize a range of concepts from the fields of human development and social and clinical psychology. The assets provide systems of social support, mechanisms of control (both internal and external), structure, meaning, and competency that inoculate youth against negative peer pressure, decrease opportunities for risk taking, and provide a kind of personal "centeredness," which both enhances prosocial behavior and reduces health-compromising choices.

These 30 assets are among the constructs measured and reported in *The Troubled Journey* (Benson, 1993). This study has provided some of the first clues about the distribution of assets among public school students and their connection to multiple forms of risk taking.

Among the nearly 47,000 students included in the study, the mean number of assets is 16.3, with a decline from grade 6 (17.4) to grade 12 (15.9). Aggregating students within communities reveals that 89% of communities have asset averages for 6th- to 12th-grade students in the range of 15 to 17, with relatively little variability as a function of town size.

AT-RISK BEHAVIOR

The term "at risk" has a fairly short history. It was first used as an adjective describing national life in the federal report, *A Nation At Risk: The Imperative for School Reform*. Since that time, it has become a term that describes individuals, as in "at-risk youth." Its primary use is in reference to those who are raised in poverty or have dropped out (or are likely to drop out) of school.

In this study, we have used the term "at risk" to cover 20 behaviors. The working definition is that at-risk behaviors are choices that potentially limit psychological, physical, or economic well-being during adolescence or adulthood. Many of the behaviors can have negative, long-term consequences.

16 EXTERNAL ASSETS: DEFINITIONS

TABLE 9.7-1

Asset Type	Asset Name	Asset Definition
Support	1. Family support	Family life provides high levels of love and support
	2. Parent(s) as social resources	Student views parent(s) as accessible resources for advice and support
	3. Parent communication	Student has frequent, in-depth conversations with parent(s)
	4. Other adult resources	Student has access to non-parent adults for advice and support
	5. Other adult communication	Student has frequent, in-depth conversations with non-parent adults
	6. Parent involvement in schooling	Parent(s) are involved in helping student succeed in school
	7. Positive school climate	School provides a caring, encouraging environment
Control	8. Parental standards	Parent(s) have standards for appropriate conduct
	9. Parental discipline	Parent(s) discipline student when a rule is violated
	10. Parental monitoring	Parent(s) monitor "where I am going and with whom I will be"
	11. Time at home	Student goes out for "fun and recreation" 3 or fewer nights per week
	12. Positive peer influence	Student's best friends model responsible behavior
Structured Time Use	13. Involved in music	Student spends 1 hour or more per week in music training or practice
	14. Involved in school extracurricular activities	Student spends 1 hour or more per week in school sports, clubs, or organizations
	15. Involved in community organizations or activities	Student spends 1 hour or more per week in organizations or clubs outside of school
	16. Involved in worship	Student spends 1 hour or more per week attending programs or services

TABLE 9.7–2

14 INTERNAL ASSETS: DEFINITIONS

Asset Type	Asset Name	Asset Definition
Educational Commitment	1. Achievement motivation	Student is motivated to do well in school
	2. Educational aspiration	Student aspires to pursue post-high school education (e.g., trade school, college)
	3. School performance	Student reports school performance is above average
	4. Homework	Student reports 6 hours or more of homework per week
Positive Values	5. Values helping people	Student places high personal value on helping other people
	6. Is concerned about world hunger	Student reports interest in helping to reduce world hunger
	7. Cares about people's feelings	Student cares about other people's feelings
	8. Values sexual restraint	Student values postponing sexual activity
Social Competence	9. Assertiveness skills	Student reports ability to "stand up for what I believe"
	10. Decision-making skills	Student reports "I am good at making decisions"
	11. Friendship-making skills	Student reports "I am good at making friends"
	12. Planning skills	Student reports "I am good at planning ahead"
	13. Self-esteem	Student reports high self-esteem
	14. Positive view of personal future	Student is optimistic about his/her personal future

To some extent, the choice of these at-risk indicators is based on speculative and incomplete knowledge, for there is little firm evidence about the actual long-term consequences of certain choices during the first 18 years of life. We rely on informed hunches, choosing indicators that one could reasonably argue are possible precursors to later difficulties. An example is daily cigarette use, which is one of the 20 at-risk indicators. The assumption is that smoking regularly during adolescence increases the probability of nicotine addiction in adulthood. Another case is binge drinking, defined as consuming "5 or more drinks in a row." This kind of behavior may increase the probability of either misuse of alcohol during adulthood or physical injury (as in automobile accidents).

The 20 forms of at riskness measured in *The Troubled Journey* are grouped into 9 categories or domains: alcohol, tobacco, illicit drugs, sexuality, depression/suicide, antisocial behavior, school failure, vehicle safety, and others (for example, bulimia).

Among the almost 47,000 public school students in the national sample, the average number of at-risk indicators (out of the 20 forms) is as follows:

Grade 6 — 1.47
Grade 7 — 1.69
Grade 8 — 2.21
Grade 9 — 2.71
Grade 10 — 3.13
Grade 11 — 3.79
Grade 12 — 4.18

The average for all students combined is 2.85. For grades 9 to 12, 31% are at-risk in the area of alcohol use (defined as use of alcohol 6 or more times in the last 30 days or binge drinking once or more in the last 2 weeks). Twenty percent are at risk in the area of tobacco (defined as daily cigarette use or using chewing tobacco 20 or more times in the last 12 months). And 11% of high school students are at risk in the area of illicit drug use (defined as using an illicit substance 6 or more times in the last year).

THE RELATIONSHIP OF DEVELOPMENTAL ASSETS TO AT-RISK BEHAVIOR

The students were placed in four categories based on the number of assets evidenced: 0–10, 11–20, 21–25, and 26–30. Figure 9.7–1 shows a powerful connection between assets and at-risk behavior. For both grades 6 to 8 and 9 to 12, each incremental increase in assets tends to cut the total number of at-risk behaviors in half. Among those in grades 6 to 8, for example, those with 10 or fewer assets average 4.1 of the 20 at-risk indicators. The average drops to 2.0 for those with 11 to 20 assets, to .9 for those with 21 to 25 assets, and to .4 for those with 26 to 30 assets.

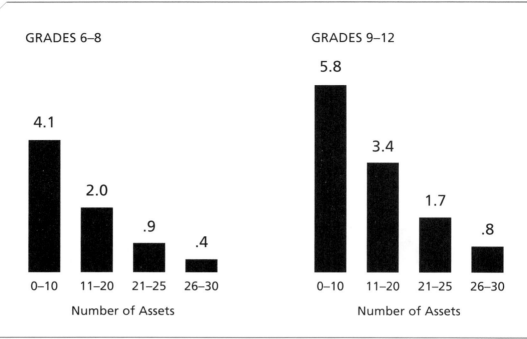

Figure 9.7–1. Average Number of 20 At-Risk Indicators, by Number of Assets.

Equally important is the relationship of assets to each of the individual at-risk domains. As shown in Figure 9.7–2, there is a strong linear association between the number of assets and the alcohol and tobacco at-risk indicators. For example, 46% of all the students with 10 or fewer assets are at risk in the alcohol domain. This falls to 25% for those with 11 to 20 assets, 10% for those with 21 to 25 assets, and 3% for those with 26 to 30 assets. Similar linear trends occur for the illicit drug, sexuality, school failure, and antisocial behavior at-risk indicators.

These strong relationships between assets and at-risk behavior suggest that positive youth development, understood as asset promotion, represents a potentially powerful approach to the prevention of at-risk behavior in multiple domains. However, further research, employing both experimental and longitudinal designs, is needed to more fully explicate the role of asset promotion in prevention.

IMPLICATION FOR COMMUNITIES

This study suggests that a rather serious rupture has occurred in the developmental infrastructure for youth in general. The national average for

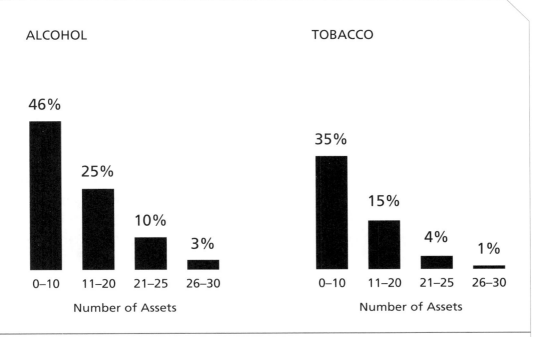

ALCOHOL

TOBACCO

Figure 9.7–2. Percent At-Risk by Number of Assets.

the number of assets is 16; of the communities studied to date, the range is from 13 to 19.[1] Only about 30% of public school students evidence 20 or more of the 30 assets. Thus every community has major work to do to rebuild the asset base. It is not only a central-city problem; it also affects suburbs and small agricultural towns. The simple fact is that communities no longer do well what they are designed to do.

Rebuilding the asset infrastructure in communities needs to involve many sectors of community life. Such community transformation ought to be driven by five principles.

The first is the *principle of service expansion,* through which communities put into operation all of the programs and strategies that we know can enhance assets. These positive youth-development programs cover a wide spectrum: mentoring programs, parks and recreation, libraries, after-school care, peer counseling, church-based youth programs, and youth-serving organizations. The guiding concept is to surround every

[1]Since the writing of *The Troubled Journey,* this research program has extended to 500 communities involving 230,000 6th–12th grade students. In this expanded data set, the average number of assets is 16.5.

student with principled, caring adults in settings where peers model responsible behavior.

Second is the *principle of mission expansion*. It is not enough to put into operation multiple programs. Equally important is training youth-serving leaders in expanding their mission to include the full range of these assets. Schools, somewhat begrudgingly, tend to function in most or all of these asset arenas. But so, too, should athletic coaches and mentors and congregations.

The third principle is *duplication*. Developmental assets are best nurtured when young people receive multiple socialization exposures to the assets. That is, each of the assets is more likely to blossom if all are nurtured simultaneously by parents, schools, and youth organizations and programs.

The fourth guiding principle is *consistency*. In *Building Community* (1991), John Gardner says: "Families and communities are the ground-level generators and preservers of values and ethical systems. No society can remain vital or even survive without a reasonable base of shared values—and such values are not established by edict from lofty levels of the society. They are generated chiefly in the family, school, church, and other intimate settings in which people deal with one another face to face. The ideals of justice and compassion are nurtured in communities." The problem in many communities is that there is no consensus on values. There is no task more important than developing a measure of value consensus and exposing the young to consistent, multi-sector efforts to nurture these shared values.

The fifth principle is *coordination*. Each of the four principles described above—service expansion, mission expansion, duplication, and consistency—are most likely to occur in an atmosphere of community coordination and collaboration in which all positive youth-development resources work hand in hand, through both formal and informal mechanisms, to develop a shared vision, build a sense of team, raise public consciousness, and provide support to each other.

A goal in all communities should be to surround all young people with multiple circles of love and support; provide consistent and multiple systems of control and discipline; give consistent attention to shared values; build and reward social competencies; connect the young to multiple forms of adult-led, supervised group activities; and build and reward a commitment to learning. The community that coordinates this effort to strengthen the asset infrastructure will see major progress in the prevention not only of alcohol and other drug use, but also a wide range of health-compromising and future-jeopardizing choices.

There is a synergy between classic prevention programs and promotion of personal assets. It could well be that a primary reason why prevention effects evaporate over time is that most American children and teenagers lack the requisite assets to make consistently wise and responsible choices when they are out of the reach of prevention programs. Accordingly, the best strategy is a dual strategy: reshape communities to surround the young with developmental assets, and reshape communities to provide consistent and coherent messages about alcohol and other drugs. In both cases, the challenge is for every community to mobilize the commitment and resources necessary to enhance the life chances for all of its young.

BIBLIOGRAPHY

Benson, P. L. (1993). *The troubled journey: A portrait of 6th–12th grade youth.* Minneapolis: Search Institute.

Gardner, J. W. (1991). *Building community.* Washington, DC: Independent Sector.

ANOTHER colleague who has dedicated her life to prevention programs in schools is Linda Lantieri, founding director of the Resolving Conflict Creatively Program (RCCP) and The National Center of Educators for Social Responsibility. She has been successful in involving 400 schools in these programs, and RCCP is one of the longest running research-based school programs (K–12) in social and emotional learning. In the next article she describes how a school in Anchorage, Alaska, chose to wage peace in their school instead of installing metal detectors to find weapons.

ARTICLE 9.8

AN OUNCE OF PREVENTION IS WORTH A POUND OF METAL DETECTORS

Linda Lantieri

> I do not want a new generation of children with high intelligence quotients and low caring quotients; with sharp competitive edges and dull cooperative instincts; with highly developed computer skills, but poorly developed consciences; with gigantic commitment to the big "I," but little sense of responsibility to the bigger "we."
>
> —Marian Wright Edelman, president, Children's Defense Fund
> (Children's Defense Fund, 2000, p. 11)

Who could predict that the 20th century would end with the senseless stream of violence in our schools and communities that has touched all of our young people, from the poorest to the most privileged? As we enter a new century, we are faced with a great challenge—how to reclaim our schools, homes, and communities as violence-free growing zones for our children. How will we ensure that our young people feel so cared for that they would never wish to do harm to themselves or anyone else?

These challenges offer an unprecedented opportunity. The choices we make now about how to nurture the youth at highest risk will have critical implications for generations to come. At this time, we seem to be doing the least harm to the most privileged (Comer, 1999). Yet, one U.S. government study found that 25% of teenagers, privileged or not, are at risk for failing to cope with the demands in their lives (National Research Council, Panel on High-Risk Youth, 1995).

From *Reclaiming Children and Youth, 10*(1), 2001, pp. 33–38. Copyright by Reclaiming Children and Youth, Inc. Reprinted with permission. *Note.* Adapted from the book *Schools with Spirit: Nurturing the Inner Lives of Children and Teachers,* edited by Linda Lantieri, 2001, Boston: Beacon Press. Copyright 2001 by Linda Lantieri. Adapted with permission.

In our society is a deep current—a belief that something is not okay with the way we are living. In the midst of huge advances in technology and brain research, we are struggling to rescue a whole generation of young people who are growing up without the supports they need. We are facing a deep crisis concerning how to rediscover meaningfulness and purpose, and although we are aware of the void, we have few ideas about what to do.

SCHOOLS PLAY A VITAL ROLE

For more than three decades, I have devoted my life to the important role schools can play in nurturing the emotional, social, and ethical development of young people. I have been attempting to answer the following question: How can schools help reclaim the souls of some of our most troubled youth? I have used my experiences as a former teacher and school administrator while working with a particular initiative—the Resolving Conflict Creatively Program (RCCP)—which I co-founded in 1985 with the nonprofit organization Educators for Social Responsibility.

The 175,000 young people in RCCP are not armed with the thousands of guns that are still brought into schools on a daily basis or the daily taunts that so many young people wield like weapons. They use weapons of the spirit—nonviolent communication, appreciation for diversity, the ability to center themselves and manage their anger, and skills to resolve conflict creatively. These young people attend schools with an educational vision that recognizes that the ability to manage emotions, resolve conflict, and interrupt bias are fundamental skills—skills that can and must be taught. Our work seems to be making a critical difference in the lives of children at high and low risk and of both genders.

A recently completed study of the Resolving Conflict Creatively Program provides new evidence of the potential of school-based programs for preventing violence and reaching out to angry and hostile youth (National Center for Children in Poverty, Joseph L. Mailman School of Public Health, Columbia University, 1999). We have found that when schools are willing to sustain a comprehensive and systematic approach to nurturing the social, emotional, and ethical development of young people as a basic part of their education, students not only do well academically, they also learn how to be gentle and caring. At a time when our schools are scrambling for ways to stop violence and aggression, the RCCP study provides compelling evidence that school-based violence prevention programs are an effective way to curb student aggression and teach youngsters positive new skills they can use for a lifetime. We have known for years that RCCP can transform classrooms and schools—we've seen it with our own eyes. However, it is extremely gratifying to have our experiences backed up by one of the most comprehensive, scientific studies ever conducted in the field.

As the principal investigator, Dr. Lawrence Aber, said, "We found out that an ounce of prevention is worth a pound of metal detectors" (Aber, 1999). Two years of teaching the 5,000 young people in this study concrete skills in managing their emotions and resolving conflict actually deterred the developmental pathways that could lead to later violence and aggression. When I had the privilege of being on a panel with Archbishop Desmund Tutu at the International Hague Appeal for Peace, he smiled joyously when he heard of the study results and said,

> By the looks of things, we could be in deep trouble. Imagine these peacemaking skills being incorporated throughout a child's entire education. I'm not sure we would have enough people in the world who would be willing to kill or be killed in wars or even would want the job that has the power to press the button that could cause a nuclear holocaust. (Tutu, 1999)

What an elegant and powerful vision of our evaluation results! Being anointed by his words strengthened my convictions about what we can imagine and create for young people.

Until now, however, RCCP's success in nurturing an ethic of caring and nonviolence had been most striking in the elementary and middle schools we serve, but not in the high schools. So, in the shadow of the first anniversary of the tragedy at Columbine High School in Littleton, Colorado, I was eager to accept an invitation to visit a high school in Alaska that was engaged in this work. I was told that the concept of a "peaceable school" was taking hold at Chugiak High School on the outskirts of Anchorage, Alaska. I also had heard that the principal, teachers, and young people at Chugiak had responded to the tragedy at Columbine quite differently from other high schools across the country. They had not spent the year turning their school into an armed fortress, where electronic searches of students and lockers are the norm and armed police and surveillance cameras define the landscape. They chose instead to courageously wage peace in their school and reclaim it as a place of learning and growth. I was eager to find out how they went about working as partners in developing a caring community of learning.

NURTURING A CULTURE OF NONVIOLENCE

I was not quite prepared for the first glimpse of Chugiak High School, even as the pristine Chugiak mountain range silhouetted the tan, sprawling edifice. To my surprise, the Chugiak campus was laid out almost identically to that of Columbine. My psyche could not help but be flooded with the riveting images of students breaking through windows to escape the carnage in Littleton. As I walked through the entrance of the school, I realized that even the school colors were the same. Chugiak, like Columbine, is a typical U.S. high school in many respects: The average teacher sees 150 students a day, S.A.T. scores are important, and athletics appear to occupy a high rung on the prestige ladder.

As I was greeted by one of the teachers and brought into a room to meet with staff members and students, I realized that everyone present had not missed the ironic similarity in appearance to Columbine High School. As people introduced themselves, most expressed, in some form or another, "but for the grace of God, it could have been us." The more I listened, however, the more I began to understand that such a tragedy was not likely to happen at Chugiak. Instead of elaborate security hardware, I witnessed touching gestures of kindness and forgiveness. A spirit of belonging was evident in the way in which each person shared his or her story with me, talking about settling arguments by talking things out and asking and seeking forgiveness. The focus did not seem to be on how schools fail to identify the warning signs that perpetrators exhibit but rather on the context in which these acts can occur.

Concentrating on looking for the warning signs of individuals who will be perpetrators and victims diverts us from looking for the warning signs of an entire social climate where bullying, intolerance, and violence are the acceptable norms. Before Chugiak High School embarked on this school culture shift, they had begun to notice that a more important warning sign was when one young person wouldn't let another young person be different without taunting or bullying him or her. Other warning signs: students could not speak openly about issues that concerned them, and adults did not have the time or the resources to connect to young people personally. Chugiak staff members wanted to know how they could nurture students' social, emotional, and inner lives and move beyond conflict resolution into healing and reconciliation. Staff members and students shared how their work was not about attempting to stop individual violent acts or identify the next "young predator" but rather about dismantling the cycle of violence they saw every day.

They were not talking about preventing a shooting from happening in their school. Unlike the 71% of Americans who believe a shooting is likely to occur in their school—despite the fact that there was actually only a 1 in 2 million chance of anyone being killed in a school in 1998–1999 and there has been a 40% nationwide decline in school-associated deaths from violence (Center on Juvenile and Criminal Justice, 1999/2000)—they did not believe that violence was a necessary risk in going to school. Instead, these folks were talking about the way in which they were creating "a culture of nonviolence" in which there was the realization that the most important skills needed to navigate their social world were being able to engage in thoughtful decision making, understanding signs of one's own and others' feelings, listening accurately, communicating effectively, and respecting differences. They were struggling with the kind of school reform and renewal that changes school culture by addressing relationships.

So how exactly did Chugiak High School go about becoming such a model of nonviolence? The staff members and students were guided through this process by Carol Lieber, Educators for Social Responsibility's (ESR) director of Partners in Learning (ESR's program for high schools). In the early stages of her work with Chugiak staff members, Lieber expounded on a key concept—high school students are developmentally ready to think on their own and work collaboratively with others. Adolescents are becoming autonomous and need to feel they have a stake in their actions and in the community they create. Because high school cultures are often shaped by content choices and subject matter, adolescents usually are not given the chance to contribute to their classrooms in any significant way. Lieber believes that this status quo can be changed. She has seen that treating teenagers with respect, expressing a personal interest in them, and giving them choices increases their ability to become peacefully engaged in their community, whether it is the school or the larger society. Stated Lieber,

> One important student/teacher outcome I look for is the building of more positive student/teacher relationships—especially with young

people who are not the star students, who are used to being ignored or invisible. Imagine that youth are like Web sites. There are some young people in every high school who are getting positive social and academic "hits." Then there is the invisible middle: the young people who get no "hits" at all. I ask my teachers, what can you do to give a young person a 10-second hit? Comment on their clothes, ask about their family, or anything personal. Relationships mean everything, in terms of motivation. Students want to mean more to you than just their grade. They want you to know them. (C. Lieber, personal communication, March 14, 2000)

During our sharing time, I noticed that the Chugiak teachers understood that each student is a unique individual, and they knew how important this was in building a peaceable community. Allowing students the autonomy to make choices about the things that will affect their daily lives is another crucial component. Lieber believes that part of building social and emotional competency is building greater social responsibility among students:

When you empower young people to make more choices and to take more responsibility for learning, they inevitably need to use more effective communication and problem-solving skills to do that. In the process, the teacher/student relationship is improved, because youth begin to like and trust the person who respects them enough to give them a chance. What emerges is the beginning of a collaborative learning community. (C. Lieber, personal communication, March 14, 2000)

It was evident in talking to Jan Christensen, principal of Chugiak High School, that under her leadership both students and teachers had a sense of fairness, belonging, and the ability to effect change. The school safety committee that was created also played a critical role in change. Made up of teachers, students, parents, and representatives of other key constituencies, this committee made recommendations that were taken seriously and often adopted. The morale of staff members and students was high, partly due to democratic processes in place at Chugiak.

The safety committee is committed to openly seeking information from everyone regarding the functioning of the school as they identify problems and concerns. Through a school climate assessment process, the committee secured feedback from the school community and attempted to prioritize issues and determine which concerns needed the most attention. The community of collaboration that is created when students share responsibility with teachers for the way their school feels and operates is also mirrored in the teachers' collaborative relationships. The teachers at Chugiak model many of the collaborative techniques they encourage their students to use. Teachers share agendas and instructional strategies with one another, problem solve together, and team teach.

THE CURRENT EDUCATIONAL CLIMATE

As some of us attempt to create in other schools this new version of places that educate the heart and spirit along with the mind, we can't forget that there is a dramatic social and political climate that deeply affects the likelihood of this vision becoming the norm. The equation currently operating in schools could be stated as follows:

education reform = state standards = high-stakes tests.

Clearly, a struggle is under way in this country about what it means to be an educated person and, therefore, about what a good education entails. This debate is being carried out on the terrain of school curriculum and pedagogy. Back is an emphasis on cognitive development that places primary value on mastering skills and the content of traditional academic subject areas. This translates to a movement toward state standards and testing, which are determining what can and cannot be done in schools.

It is not that explicit standards in and of themselves are problematic. In fact, the school reform movement, as well as the whole field of social and emotional learning, is about standards. Setting clear, compelling, and measurable improvement goals that guide our actions is always helpful to the learning process.

The problem lies in determining whether children are learning solely through testing of easily measurable and easily forgettable extraneous knowledge, which emphasizes memorization over critical thinking. This knowledge has very little connection to what employers want or need, or for that matter, what young people need to be personally and professionally successful. The use of testing has become a large national industry that has greatly influenced what happens in classrooms today. This is a problem! Social and emotional learning, conflict resolution, and violence prevention can play an important role in helping to define what young people really need to thrive.

In the midst of this struggle to redefine the basics of a good education, it is the courageous few like Deborah Meier, one of my "she-roes" and principal at the Mission Hill School in Boston, who is able bravely to say to her students' parents: "We don't intend to teach your child the things they will be examined on, because we have more important things to teach them" (Bogen, 1999, p. 11). Meier's past experience as principal at Central Park East High School in East Harlem confirmed to her that her students wouldn't be penalized for this kind of education philosophy. Central Park East still has better than a 90% graduation rate, with more than 90% of its students going on to college.

EMOTIONAL INTELLIGENCE IS IMPORTANT

What skills do our young people need to be successful in the 21st century? In his groundbreaking 1995 book, *Emotional Intelligence,* Daniel Goleman, social psychologist and mental health writer for *The New York Times,* made the convincing argument that EQ, or "emotional quotient"—a way of describing people's human skills—may be as important as IQ for success in life. Well-implemented programs such as RCCP effectively give young people the social and emotional skills they need, preparing them for both work and life. This new kind of schooling is possible. Amidst the despair, I find great hope.

In my long-term vision for this work we are doing in schools, I see children entering kindergarten and immediately beginning to learn that differences are accepted, feelings are okay, and nonviolent approaches to conflict are the norm. By the time they are in first or second grade, they will almost automatically choose to use conflict resolution skills to mediate disputes among classmates. As they enter high school, they have the courage and skills to stand up to bigotry and violence and to work for a more peaceful, just, and caring society.

We adults have to dramatically change our education priorities for this to happen. We are a country that has let its priorities become so skewed that we spend $4 billion in medical care each year to take care of gunshot wounds and still don't guarantee every child health coverage. In fact, among all the industrial countries, the United States ranks first in military exports and defense expenditures and last in protecting children against gun violence. A gun still takes the life of a child in this country every 2 hours. We are living in a country that spends millions of dollars on national security rather than investing in the support communities need to decrease the statistic of one out of five children growing up poor: In other words, 13.5 million children in this country grow up in poverty. We are living in a country that spends more money on prisons than on education, that guarantees young people the availability of a prison cell but not a college education. And the wealth of only three of the richest people in the United States exceeds the gross national product of the 32 least-developed countries. The annual budget of the Head Start programs is equal to 1 week of military spending (Children's Defense Fund, 2000).

What would happen if we took the $4 billion we spend each year treating gunshot wounds and instead used it to implement a comprehensive program in the approximately 90,000 U.S. schools to nurture the social, ethical, and emotional development of our children as a regular, natural part of a young person's educational experience? That $4 billion would allow us to implement a comprehensive violence program in every school in this country for 1 year.

Will we learn from the mistakes of the past so that we can avoid losing more of our young people? More and more schools are making significant long-term commitments to creating cultures that emphasize caring, respect, and safety. Our willingness to turn schools into caring communities rather than armed fortresses may determine the future of young people in far greater ways than we know. As 1999 drew to a close, I had the extraordinary opportunity to be present at the final meeting of the century of the United Nations' General Assembly. It was inspiring to witness the Assembly declare the first decade of the new millennium would be the Decade of the Culture of Peace and Nonviolence for the Children of the World. Our work is clearly cut out for us in meeting this challenge.

While visiting one of our RCCP elementary schools recently, I witnessed two fourth-grade boys in an intense conversation as they were walking in front of me, oblivious that I was behind them. One of the boys had his arm around the shoulder of the other boy, who was visibly upset. "He said those mean words to you?" asked the one boy. "Yes," the other one nodded. "And he even almost hit you?" Another affirmative nod from the troubled youngster. "I know what must be happening," said his friend. "That mean boy is probably new to the school. He doesn't know that we don't do things like that around here." The power of nonviolence had taken hold so strongly that these students could not imagine why someone had been acting mean except that "he was new to the school." What we need is to give peace not only a chance but also the resources, time, and commitment it will take to create peaceable schools all over this world that are the norm, not the exception.

REFERENCES

Aber, L. (1999, September 25). *Morning edition* (radio broadcast). Washington, DC: National Public Radio.

Bogen, M. (1999, Fall). The power that comes from real standards: An interview with Deborah Meier. *Forum, The Newsletter of Educators for Social Responsibility.* 4–5, 11. (Available from Educators for Social Responsibility, 23 Garden Street, Cambridge, MA 02138)

Children's Defense Fund. (2000). *The state of America's children 2000.* Washington, DC: Author.

Comer, J. (1999, Nov. 6). *Social and emotional learning and digital technologies: New means and methods.* Remarks at the Social and Emotional Learning Fall 1999 Conference. New York: Teachers College, Project for Social and Emotional Learning.

Goleman, D. (1995). *Emotional intelligence.* New York: Bantam.

National Center for Children in Poverty, Joseph L. Mailman School of Public Health, Columbia University. (1999). *The evaluation of the Resolving Conflict Creatively Program: Teaching conflict resolution, an effective school-based approach to violence prevention.* New York: Columbia University Press. (The full text of the research may be downloaded at www.nccp.org)

National Research Council, Panel on High-Risk Youth. (1995). *Losing generations.* Washington, DC: National Academy Press.

Tutu, D. (1999, May 12). Remarks made at the Panel for Peace Education Efforts, Hague Appeal for Peace International Conference, The Hague, The Netherlands.

ARTICLE 9.9

THE U.S. Department of Education, in conjunction with other federal agencies, has funded major resource centers and technical assistance systems to promote new programs and best practices throughout the country. These are national resources you need to know and use to reinforce your future psychoeducational plans. The next article explains these federal resources and is written by the Center for Effective Collaboration and Practice.

IMPROVING SERVICES FOR CHILDREN WITH EMOTIONAL AND BEHAVIORAL PROBLEMS
Center for Effective Collaboration and Practice

As we prepare to enter a new millennium, all eyes seem to be on the U.S. education system. The schooling of our nation's children has been, and will continue to be, a major issue, both in Congress and in the upcoming election season. Beyond the headline debates about school safety and class size, many adults are thinking about the needs of our children and youth with emotional and behavioral problems. How can we provide them with improved services and ensure better outcomes? How can we support the parents, teachers, mental health counselors, child welfare workers, juvenile justice personnel, and others who care for and work with these young people? The U.S. Department of Education, in conjunction with other federal agencies, has funded a number of centers and projects to address these questions. This article describes some of the new and ongoing efforts and explains how you can make use of them.

CENTER FOR EFFECTIVE COLLABORATION AND PRACTICE

The Center for Effective Collaboration and Practice (CECP) is in the fourth year of a 5-year cooperative agreement with the Office of Special Education Programs (OSEP), Office of Special Education and Rehabilitative Services, U.S. Department of Education.

The CECP receives additional support from the Child, Adolescent, and Family Branch, Center for Mental Health Services, Substance Abuse and Mental Health Administration, of the U.S. Department of Health and Human Services. CECP efforts focus on (a) facilitating and expanding interagency collaboration, (b) identifying and developing useful information regarding how to serve children and youth with emotional and behavioral problems, and (c) fostering the exchange of such information. Intended as a resource for child-serving professionals across disciplines, as well as for family members of children with emotional and behavioral problems, this project works toward accomplishing its mission in a variety of ways.

WORLD WIDE WEB SITE

The CECP hosts a Web site containing a good deal of research on a variety of topics, frequent online discussions with authors and other professionals on current issues of interest, and an extensive collection of links to other organizations and resources. The CECP also maintains several e-mail listservs to connect people and enable them to ask questions and share resources on a wide variety of related subjects. Because not everyone has access to a computer and a modem, it also operates a toll-free telephone line through which callers can order publications, find out about its resources, and speak directly to CECP staff.

IDENTIFYING PROMISING PRACTICES

The CECP maintains lists of effective and promising programs for serving children and youth with serious emotional disturbance. Although, due to the newness of some of these programs, research concerning their effectiveness is not yet available, they hold promise nonetheless. These are places where the "seeds" of effective practice have been planted, and CECP staff call them our "nurseries." Programs that are very well-established and have a strong evidence base are called our "greenhouses." The CECP lists contact information for all of these programs on its Web site.

FACILITATING HUMAN CONNECTIONS

The CECP has a lengthy list of strategic "partners"—organizations and individuals who may offer particular expertise or resources for those seeking further information relating to working with children with emotional and behavioral problems. Areas of expertise for a number of researchers, family members, and national organizations that can serve as resources for people seeking information are provided.

PUBLICATIONS

The CECP also develops and disseminates research-based publications on topics such as safe and drug-free schools, promising practices in children's mental health, functional behavioral assessment, and prevention of school failure and antisocial behavior. These publications are available by contacting the CECP through the Web site, the toll-free phone number, or regular mail.

ELECTRONIC DISCUSSIONS

As noted earlier, the CECP maintains both e-mail listservs and online discussion groups. The listservs are focused on a particular topic, and anyone on the list can e-mail a question to a group of people, many of whom have expertise in that particular area. The Web site–based online discussion groups allow people to write in with questions or comments regarding a particular topic or journal article. Those questions and comments are then addressed by a researcher or another "online expert" in a timely manner.

OSEP CENTER ON POSITIVE BEHAVIORAL INTERVENTIONS AND SUPPORTS

The OSEP Center on Positive Behavioral Interventions and Supports (PBIS) is a new initiative funded by the U.S. Department of Education, Office of Special Education Programs, and the Safe and Drug-Free Schools Program. It is administered by the University of Oregon in Eugene. The Center represents a collaboration of several universities: the University of Oregon, the University of Kansas, the University of Kentucky, the University of Missouri, and the University of South Florida. This Center was established to provide schools with information and technical assistance that increases their capacity to identify, adapt, and sustain effective school-wide disciplinary practices. The Center has two mandates: to broadly disseminate information about schoolwide positive behavioral interventions and supports to schools, families, and communities and to demonstrate that these interventions and supports are feasible and effective.

The Center hopes to accomplish the following:

- enhance the schools' capacity (systems and practices) to address a range and diversity of behavioral challenges,
- diminish disruptions that impede teaching and learning,
- create teaching and learning communities that establish and sustain positive school climates,
- reclaim instructional time previously lost to behavioral disruptions,
- maximize use of time and learning opportunities, and
- enhance the quality and efficiency of instruction.

The Center focuses on dissemination of research-validated schoolwide disciplinary practices and systems that foster positive learning and teaching environments, including schoolwide discipline; classroom management; functional behavioral assessment; positive behavioral interventions and supports; discipline and behavior support; and family, school, and community partnerships. This dissemination occurs through publications, Web sites, training materials, and presentations. In addition, the Center provides technical assistance to establish effective systems of positive behavioral interventions and supports at the school, district, and state levels.

For more information, contact Positive Behavioral Interventions and Supports Technical Assistance Center, Behavioral Research and Training, 5262 University of Oregon, Eugene, OR 97403-5262; 541/346-2505; Fax: 541/346-5689; Web site: http://pbis.org; e-mail: pbis@ oregon.uoregon.edu

NATIONAL EARLY CHILDHOOD TECHNICAL ASSISTANCE SYSTEM

The National Early Childhood Technical Assistance System (NECTAS) was funded in 1996 by the Office of Special Education Programs, Office of Special Education and Rehabilitative Services, U.S. Department of

Education. NECTAS is a national technical assistance consortium working to improve services and results for young people with disabilities and their families. The consortium is composed of the following six organizations:

- Frank Porter Graham Child Development Center at the University of North Carolina in Chapel Hill (the NECTAS coordinating office)
- Center on Disability Studies at the University of Hawaii at Manoa
- Federation for Children with Special Needs in Boston
- Georgetown University Child Development Center in Washington, D.C.
- National Association of State Directors of Special Education (NASDSE) in Alexandria, Virginia
- ZERO TO THREE in Washington, D.C.

Each partner brings a different area of expertise to NECTAS activities. Because NECTAS serves as a central repository of knowledge on national early childhood policies, research, and practices, members must have diverse capabilities and be able to take on multiple roles. The consortium provides an identified single source for information on and support for state and jurisdictional programs under IDEA. NECTAS is also involved in (a) identifying critical challenges that are common across states and jurisdictions and that hinder policy development and program implementation, and (b) reducing unnecessary duplication of efforts among states working on similar policy and implementation issues. The consortium tries to match state program needs with the innovative solutions developed by a national network of model early childhood programs. To meet these ends, NECTAS employs a variety of technical assistance strategies.

For more information, contact National Early Childhood Technical Assistance System, Frank Porter Graham Child Development Center, University of North Carolina at Chapel Hill, Chapel Hill, NC 27599; Voice: 919/962-2001; TTY: 919/966-4041; Fax: 919/966-7463; e-mail: Pat_Trohanis@unc.edu; Web site: http://www.nectas.unc.edu

ELEMENTARY AND MIDDLE SCHOOLS TECHNICAL ASSISTANCE CENTER

The Elementary and Middle Schools Technical Assistance Center (EMSTAC) was funded in 1996 by the Office of Special Education Programs, Office of Special Education and Rehabilitative Services, U.S. Department of Education. EMSTAC was created to develop a comprehensive national technical assistance approach that would improve outcomes for children with disabilities in elementary and middle schools. This approach relies heavily on the expertise of "linking agents"—officials from within a particular school district whose knowledge of existing resources and effective practices can help other school districts evaluate problems, identify solutions, work through change, and critically reflect on their own organization and practices. EMSTAC is testing technical assistance strategies by assessing the effects of varying the type of training and degree of support offered to the linking agent and school district. It will progressively scale up activities to become more national in scope and thoroughly assess the strategies in order to design a comprehensive national model of technical assistance delivery.

Interested persons can become involved with EMSTAC by becoming a linking agent. Through training offered by EMSTAC, linking agents learn how to systematically move through the change process and how to choose a technical assistance topic by conducting a district-wide needs assessment. They also learn how to coordinate and implement technical assistance, evaluate and monitor the impact of such assistance on children with disabilities, and use EMSTAC support. Linking agents can access research-based information regarding best practices for students with disabilities through EMSTAC's Web site. In addition, they can communicate with other linking agents in other school districts through EMSTAC's e-mail listserv, which operates as a forum for discussing programs being implemented in the school districts and for discussing and critiquing innovations in research-based practice.

For more information, contact Elementary and Middle Schools Technical Assistance Center, 1000 Thomas Jefferson St., NW, Suite 400, Washington, DC 20007; Phone: 202/944-5300; Fax: 202/944-5454; TTY: 877/334-3499; e-mail: emstac@dc.air.org; Web site: http://www.emstac.org

NATIONAL TRANSITION ALLIANCE FOR YOUTH WITH DISABILITIES

The National Transition Alliance (NTA) was funded in 1995 by the U.S. Departments of Education and Labor. The mission of the NTA is to ensure that youth with disabilities, including those with severe disabilities, acquire skills and knowledge, gain experience, and receive services and supports necessary to achieve successful postschool results, including postsecondary education, gainful employment, independent living, community living, social integration, and lifelong learning. An aim of the NTA is the formation of a national education system that contains the best elements of special, general, and vocational education. This alliance is a collaboration of universities, nonprofit service and business organizations, and national education associations.

The NTA has three main goals:

1. Improve transition services and results for youth with disabilities,

2. Build state capacity to plan and implement effective school-to-work practices for youth with disabilities, and

3. Build integrated systems that recognize the importance of aligning structures, policies, and procedures to support youth with disabilities and their families.

To these ends, the NTA acts as a technical assistance "bridge" among personnel responsible for providing transition services, particularly individuals who are planning and implementing school-to-work opportunities systems and a broad range of model programs, such as those funded by the Office of Special Education and Rehabilitative Services (OSERS). In addition, the NTA prepares information on how best to fulfill the secondary education needs of youth and establishes linkages to universally available communication systems that promote dissemination of such information.

Through the NTA, people can access information sources via the Web, e-mail, or telephone to request publications, including a directory of innovative approaches for providing transition services for youth with disabilities (Kohler & Troesken, 1999). The NTA also operates a network of more than 270 professionals, practitioners, parents, and students nationwide who are interested in transition issues. A third function of the

NTA is maintaining project and bibliographic databases regarding strategies, interventions, and people working with students who have emotional and behavioral disorders.

For more information, contact: National Transition Alliance for Youth with Disabilities, c/o Transition Research Institute at the University of Illinois, 117 Children's Research Institute, 51 Gerty Drive, Champaign, IL 61820; Phone: 217/333-2325; Fax: 217/244-0851; Web site: http://www.dssc.org/nta

The Center for Effective Collaboration and Practice: Improving Services for Children and Youth with Emotional and Behavioral Problems *is funded under a cooperative agreement (Grant No. H237T60005) with the Office of Special Education Programs, U.S. Department of Education, and with additional support from the Child, Adolescent, and Family Branch; Center for Mental Health Services; and Substance Abuse and Mental Health Administration, all of the U.S. Department of Health and Human Services. The Center can be contacted at: The American Institutes for Research, 1000 Thomas Jefferson Street, NW, Suite 400, Washington, DC 20007. Center staff can be reached toll-free at 888/457-1551 (in DC, call 202/944-5400), via e-mail at center@air.org or through our Web site at www.cecp.air.org*

REFERENCE

Kohler, P. D., & Troesken, B. J. (1999). *Improving student outcomes: Promising practices and programs.* Champaign, IL: Transition Research Institute.

IN the next article, Paul Baker, a neuropsychologist, writes a provocative article describing the role of brain research in working with troubled students. Baker not only spent years directing a psychoeducational treatment program in Georgia but also is an outstanding Senior LSCI trainer. He challenges the basic assumption of cognitive psychology that thought precedes feeling and behavior. Based on

ARTICLE 9.10

current brain research findings, he believes that this sequence is more complicated. He also predicts that future clinical findings of brain research will significantly change the way educators are teaching and managing troubled students. This article is a thought-provoking professional look into the future. Read it with open eyes and a critical mind, because the earth might be flat.

NEUROSCIENCE AND THE HELPING PROCESS

Paul W. Baker

Compassion Associates International

Therapeutic helpers once thought that neuroscience stood in conflict to the basic mission of the helping fields, strengthening the countertherapeutic view that temperament and mental health are genetic and change very little after birth. Recently, however, neuroscience research has found evidence of the plasticity of the human brain, the fact that the brain actually does change and leaves open many doors of opportunity throughout one's life.

Previously, scientists thought the number of neurons and their interconnections were permanently fixed and the brain one was born with was physically the same brain one died with. Now the ultimate of neuroscience counterpoints has become generally accepted: The brain, shaped as much by experience as a genetic code, produces brand new cells throughout the life span. This means that every experienced sensation, everything we learn, every human contact we make causes millions of neurons to fire together, forming physical interconnections called neural maps or networks, the official map of all our experiences. These maps become the literal pathways that guide our lives, through good and bad experiences.

Studies using advanced techniques have begun to examine the neurological impact of psychotherapeutic interaction. In 2001 Brody et al. established that patients treated with either medications or psychotherapy showed clinical improvement and more normal metabolic activity in the prefrontal cortex and temporal lobe—regions associated with depression. A 1996 positron-emission tomography study of patients suffering from obsessive–compulsive disorder (OCD), led by Schwartz (2002), demonstrated that cognitive–behavioral therapy worked as effectively as medications: Both kinds of treatment normalized metabolism in the caudate nucleus, an area correlated with OCD symptoms.

Encouraged by breakthroughs in mapping the brain and a newfound belief in its plasticity, some in the helping professions are incorporating neurobiology findings into their everyday work. In essence, they're taking the brain out of its black box and opening it up for discussion. Psychiatrist Daniel Siegel (1999), author of *The Developing Mind,* wrote,

> I do things differently in my office every day because of what I know about the brain. I not only have a model of the brain that I must take out maybe three or four times a week with different individuals, but I have a chalkboard I constantly use to draw brain diagrams to help people see their problems in a different light. People keep telling me things like, "You know last week when you drew that picture of the brain? I finally understood my amygdala (the area primarily associated with our fear-based fight or flight responses). It's changed my whole view of what's been going on with me all these years." (pp. 134–135)

Much like clinical professionals, classroom teachers will benefit from understanding the brain and teaching how it works to their students. Students will, in turn, understand their individual dilemmas more clearly and be more apt to comply with a variety of treatment approaches.

Critics argue that the incorporation of a neurobiological perspective into talk therapies is premature. The danger, they insist, is a popularization of complicated findings that misrepresent the science of the brain and could lead to a neurobiological reductionism that ignores the complexities unearthed over the past century of clinical practice. In response, the growing element of brain-smart therapists argues that the nature of talk therapy has always been to move more quickly than formal science. Most insist they use neurobiology to complement existing clinical models, not to supersede them. It appears that neuroscience is in some form shaping the way therapists interact with those they are charged to help. This involves understanding four new concepts.

1. THE BRAIN IS SOCIAL

Historically, helping professionals have assumed that the brain is nothing more than a "master switchboard." However, neuroscientists are finding that much of our brain function is an interpersonal phenomenon. We are a social species who require teaching to learn life's "rules of the road." Not only do brain structures and functions provide the means by which we connect with and make sense of one another, but through relational experience, parts of the brain literally grow. In fact, the brain, as we know it, is inconceivable without social relationships: "The traditional idea of the brain has been the single-skull view—an organ encased inside us whose functioning is determined primarily by our inborn biology," says Siegel (1999, p. 18). He coined the term *interpersonal neurobiology* to describe how advances in research have created a conceptual bridge among biology, attachment research, development psychology, brain science, and systems theory. "But we survived as a species not so much because of our physical brawn, but due to our interpersonal capacity. More and more, we're realizing our brain is being shaped by our interpersonal environment" (p. 19).

Siegel (1999) proposes a "multiskull view" of the brain, a way of understanding that brain processes take place through people's interactions with one another. Siegel wrote,

> The best way to define the mind is as the flow of energy and information. That flow can happen between neurons in a person's skull, as well as between two people. Without being reductionistic, the cultural transmission of meaning ultimately comes down to a neuronal process. (p.64)

The most clearly studied example of interpersonal brain "connectedness" in social relationships comes from attachment research. Scientists have long accepted that a significant deficiency of relationships early in life lead to psychological gaps, but we're now learning how a lack of quality relationships can create parallel physiological deficits within the infant's brain. How two brains interact—say, a parent and child, or a teacher and student, in an intense, emotional relationship—determines the magnitude of the neuronal connections through which we "feel" our feelings and form emotional bonds with others. This research has given us the clearest picture of how physical structures of the brain depend on social connections.

Of particular scientific focus is the brain's orbitofrontal cortex, an area strategically located behind the eyes, between the "higher" (i.e., thinking) areas and the "lower" (i.e., emotional) areas. This region integrates and coordinates cognitive and emotional processes, helping us to regulate emotional arousal and control our impulses. Sometimes called the "center of free will," this region enables us to think before we act. But just as important for the parent–child bond is the fact that the orbitofrontal cortex is wired to read facial expressions and is uniquely sensitive to face-to-face communication. Thus, it enables us to evaluate signals from other people and respond appropriately to them. Some scientists think that one reason autistic children cannot connect with other people may be that they have abnormalities in this area.

A responsive parent helps the connections in this part of the infant's brain to grow by communicating—or "collaborating," as Siegel calls it—with the baby, via eye contact, facial expression, gestures, tone of voice, and so on. The baby gurgles to its mother, and the mother picks it up and "answers" with a smile and a joyful, "Now, everything will be all right, Mommy's here"; or the baby cries in pain or frustration and the father soothes and consoles it; or the parent gradually calms down an overexcited child at bedtime. These interactions—ordinary, routine, and repeated innumerable times—stimulate the growth of synapses in the orbitofrontal cortex that enable children to moderate their frustration, rage, and fear, and to respond flexibly to other people. The securely attached child develops the neural pathways for resilience. Even when a caregiver is upset or impatient, due to the brain's wiring, the child "knows" from experience the caregiver won't abandon her and will reconnect after the storm has passed. Kids who don't get this kind of mutual parental attention may grow up more or less at the mercy of their emotions, unable to manage their rage and aggression, calm their anxieties, console themselves in their sadness, or tolerate high levels of pleasure and excitement. They'll be more likely to suffer social disconnection. They are unable to interpret others' social cues because of deficits in their orbitofrontal cortexes, and they'll have trouble joining in the rhythm of relational exchange. In short, from the beginning, relating isn't a discretionary activity, something we can do without. The brain must make human connections to develop a healthy, working mind.

Challenged by limited training and old perceptions of the brain, clinicians typically avoid the role that neurobiology plays in social relationships and presenting difficulties. Helping others to become aware of their own brain styles can sometimes short-circuit years of insight-based therapeutic work. What seemed like intractable resistance or deep-seated pathology can often be a function of a brain's information-processing style.

The shift from a purely psychological to a more biopsychosocial paradigm can strengthen the skills of both student and helping professional.

2. THE BRAIN IS EMOTIONAL

Historically, emotions were deemed too vague, too daunting, too much the realm of touchy-feely types, to be worthy of serious scientific study. With the advent of brief therapies and the emphasis on behavioral strategies, many helping professionals have come to regard emotions as a professional minefield and fear even trying to navigate such a tricky pathway.

However, in the field of neuroscience, emotions are very much in fashion. Over the last decade, neuroscientists have learned that, on a neurobiological level, emotions are integral to such mental processes as cognition, perception, memory, and physical action. Instead of being tidily housed in the limbic system, emotions are regulated along the same brain circuits that govern social relationships and the processes of making meaning. Emotions are neurologically intertwined with the experience of "selfhood."

In adaptive terms, emotions are absolutely crucial to our survival (Damasio, 1999). Emotion connects not only the mind and body of one individual but minds and bodies between individuals. The need to appraise and respond to a potential threat comes up too fast to address consciously, so before we're aware of what we're responding to, we respond emotionally, priming the brain and body for action. Hence, in a quite real sense, we're always in the process of catching up with our emotions.

One reason emotions are in vogue is that it's now possible to do microscopic experiments that reveal brain processes down to the smallest levels of neurons and synapses. The development of these techniques, with sci-fi names like PET (positron-emission tomography), QEEG (quantitative electroencephalography), and SPECT (single positron-emission tomography), have for the first time literally put emotions on the map of the brain. Today's scientists can study emotional changes in the brain of living animals and humans in real time. Using chemicals to trace the neural circuits that produce fear in behaviorally conditioned mice, one can observe how the brain processes emotions on the scale of individual neurons.

Emotions can be regarded as dynamic processes that interact continuously with other emotions, with cognition and perception, with the social environment, during the therapeutic interaction, and, just as significantly, with bodily states. It's doubtful that we'd even experience emotions without the body, for emotions are basically bodily responses triggered by brain circuitry. Our heads are held hostage to our bodies. As every helping professional knows, our body-driven emotions—fear, anxiety, depression—regularly consume rational thought.

A person or thing that elicits fear (e.g., a sight, sound, taste, touch, or smell) bypasses the cognitive centers and goes straight to the amygdala, an almond-shaped structure deep within the brain in an area known as the limbic brain, a structure that might be called the brain's "early warning" area—a place of no words, no thought, no consciousness. The amygdala sets off a full-body response that can bypass the conscious brain, and is experienced physically as overwhelming, irrational, uncontrollable fear.

After the first amygdala-produced shock, the frontal cortex engages, reinforcing the original visceral fear or letting the individual know that the "dangerous stranger" is only a businessman carrying a briefcase. The fear process reverses, and the individual calms down. Therapy with clients subject to phobias, anxiety attacks, or post-traumatic stress disorder instructs people, in part, how to fortify the frontal cortex—making them more thoughtful, better able to bring reason to use on their fears, and less liable to lose control when they approach a fear.

Reflection, however, takes a person only so far. A crucial feature of brain anatomy is that more connections run from the amygdala to the cortex than the other way around, which means that the amygdala has more power to control the cortex than vice versa. Worry, anxiety, and stress, all close relatives of fear, probably stem from the amygdala and are notoriously resistant to one's attempts to reason oneself out of them. Once fearful reactions or traumatic memories are stamped into the amygdala, they tend to lock the mind and body into a recurring pattern of arousal, flooding with stress hormones and irrational fear.

The human brain has difficulty restraining an excited amygdala. Noted neuroscientist Joseph LeDoux (1996), author of *The Emotional Brain,* argues that phobias and neurotic fears—indeed, all strong emotional memories—are neurobiologically indelible. Therapies that "extinguish" phobias or help patients "work through" irrational fears can stop the symptoms and gain the person some freedom from them, but whatever the conscious experience, the neuronal residue of the fear remains intact in the amygdala and may someday return to stalk again—a phenomenon observed by many clinicians treating previously traumatized clients in the wake of 9/11. "A phobia can be in remission (the sight of a snake no longer elicits paralyzing anxiety) and then the patient's mother dies and snakes regain their propensity for producing terror," says LeDoux (p. 189).

In fact, the difficulty of the therapeutic interaction may reflect the fact that some neural networks that maintain dysfunctional behavior record fears set down at a young age in the amygdala, the one part of the brain that never forgets. That's why therapy is seldom successfully done in a session or two, and is never simply a matter of "explaining" to people how irrational their thinking is or how counterproductive their behavior. Therapy can be "such a long and difficult process," says LeDoux (1996), "because the neocortex is using imperfect channels of communication to try and grab hold of the amygdala and control it" (p. 101).

What all this means is that the old therapeutic thoughts about helping others "feel" their feelings is right on target: Emotions are powerful forces in the service of reason. Therapy isn't just about behavioral change. In brain terms, that would be incomplete. Choice, self-determination, and personal freedom unimpeded by crippling fears and hidden motives all depend on a healthy appreciation of one's emotional roots. It isn't that emotions are better than reason or that feelings say more than words, but, as neuroscience suggests, the expression of emotion and the use of reason are each manacled without the other.

Recognizing the centrality of emotion in brain functioning underlines the struggle for meaning. By weaving stories and airing grievances, therapist and patient are interacting neural net to neural net. As stated by Nobel Prize–winning neuroscientist Eric Kandel (1998), also a psychiatrist and a vigorous champion of psychotherapy,

> When a teacher speaks to a student and the student listens, the teacher is not only making eye contact and voice contact, but the action of neuronal machinery in the therapist's brain is having an indirect and, one hopes, long-lasting effect on the neuronal machinery in the patient's brain, and quite likely, vice versa. (p. 139)

Some therapists studying the interplay of biology and psychology suggest that therapy works primarily via emotion on procedural memory circuits—the implicit, nonconscious memory that governs automatic habits of behavior and thinking, as well as involuntary emotional responses. To understand how these changes occur, we need to grapple with neuromodularity. According to Siegel (1999), "neuromodularity creates a state in which neuron connectivity is more likely to happen and [therefore] the brain is more plastic. This happens through the release of neurotransmitters like serotonin and norepinephrine" (p. 121). In simple terms, this means that the more brain networks engaged (especially those involved in emotion), the more pliable the circuitry. Imagine rigging a model of the brain with tiny light bulbs: The more bright spots you see, the more ripe for change the brain is.

> As a teacher I use this basic brain principle all the time. You have to make something personally relevant to the students or their brains won't be engaged. It's not just about students repeating things or listening to a lecture. They have to get emotionally involved in a context of psychological safety. The same thing holds for therapy. (Siegel, 1999, p. 143)

Though good parenting gives rise to healthy brain organization and development, a nurturing therapeutic relationship allows for reorganization and development where structure and development may have been lacking. When a therapist emotionally resonates with a client, clinicians like Siegel (1999) believe that the emotional bonding reproduces the unconscious, supportive, nonverbal bond that well-attached infants and parents share.

> The most consistent finding in psychotherapy research is that when a relationship of trust and acceptance develops between therapist and client, regardless of clinical method, therapy works. The openness and emotional availability of the therapist seems to be the triggering mechanism. Openness and emotional availability are also the prime features of secure attachment. You take those three areas of research—psychotherapy, attachment, and neurobiology—and you can make the following statement: psychotherapy which works is using an interpersonal relationship to change self-regulatory circuits of the brain. It isn't just that a person temporarily feels better. At the level of the brain, therapy changes the mind by changing neuronal connections. (p. 157)

3. UNDERSTANDING THE BRAIN HELPS TO UNDERSTAND OTHERS

As attentive individuals know, many students are more at home in irrational, nonverbal modes of communication, particularly with the material that therapy seeks to explore. Although the science of brain styles and brain dominance has a long way to go, a small number of clinicians are already crafting innovative strategies that reflect this new knowledge. Harvard associate psychiatry professor John Ratey (2001), author of *A User's Guide to the Brain,* has made this observation:

> As therapists learn more about the brain and how it takes in and processes information, it will change the kinds of questions they ask patients. Instead of reflexively asking, "How do you feel?" therapists will increasingly try to find out about how clients perceive the world. They'll find out more not only about how clients feel, but also how they fear, see, and even smell things. They'll tune into their clients' movement habits and other aspects of their behavior that show how their brains work and how to communicate with them. (p. 213)

For some clinicians, an interest in brain style is the next step in developing the postmodern notion that meaning is individually constructed. What could have a greater effect on how someone constructs reality than how that person's brain processes information? They insist that you needn't subscribe to any specific therapeutic model to add brain-friendly interventions to your skills. All you need is an openness to observing clients more closely and a curiosity about what brain science can teach us about how to understand their experiential world. The attempt to incorporate brain research expands the traditional theoretical framework of therapy and invites a range of new approaches and methods.

4. THE PERSON'S STORY IS IMPORTANT IN THERAPY

Perhaps the real revolution in neuroscience lies in the way it illuminates some old and paradoxical truths about human nature. Our brains are shaped by experience, but they also shape our experiences. We're buffeted by our "animal" emotions, but our emotions also drive human will and choice. Our brains determine who we are as individuals, but the way individual brains develop is determined by relationships with others. The greatest paradox seems to be that our brains are biologically programmed to program themselves, to create and recreate themselves throughout life.

There's no greater example of the brain's innate powers of self-creation than the universal human practice of constructing personal narratives. This ability to draw from one's conscious and unconscious experiences the stories with which our brain explains itself is unique. According to Siegel (1999), who believes the neurological subplot of the well-made story involves the integration of the brain's left and right hemispheres,

> Storytelling is central to every culture, and when you find that kind of universality, you know it's not just social learning but reflects something deep-seated in our genes. Coherent stories are an integration of the left hemisphere's drive to tell a logical story about events and the right brain's ability to grasp emotionally the mental processes of the people in those events. (p.103)

Storytelling also relies on the prefrontal short- and long-term memory systems and the cerebellum—once thought to coordinate only physical movement, but now believed to coordinate different emotional and cognitive functions. Storytelling involves planning, sequencing ideas, using language coherently, shifting attention, and interacting appropriately with other people. The ability to tell a good story is a measure of mental health and a well-functioning brain.

The most striking empirical indication of storytelling's role in mental health and development may come from a series of studies involving the Adult Attachment Interview (AAI), a research protocol that assesses the level of relational attachment. In 1993 Mary Main found that a child's attachment to a parent could be better predicted by listening to how a pregnant couple related their autobiographical narrative than by measures of intellectual function, personality assessment, or socioeconomic status. A year after the initial assessment, children's attachment to their parent could be predicted with 75% accuracy, based on the AAI assessment. The idea of measuring the "coherence" with which people describe their life story, its emotional content, plausibility, completeness, relevance, brevity, and clarity, can determine how securely bonded their child will be. Additional research suggests that secure children will then develop the capacity for coherent narrative themselves—good narrative is, literally, something their parents can pass on to their children.

Why is storytelling paramount? Stories link the factual to the emotional, the specific to the universal, the past to the present. A child hearing a story thinks, "There are others like me." A storytelling parent models coping skills and provides a template for self-expression, logic, and prioritizing. In sharing stories, parent and child are connected at many levels of mind, which translates to many levels of the brain. Siegel (1995) speculates,

> For a parent to engage in the process of telling a coherent story about his or her life reflects a fundamental capacity for that parent's brain to integrate memory, knowledge, and feeling. It appears that this ability in the parents' brain nurtures their children's own neural integration. (p.146)

That process of integration then guides their capacity for self-regulation and full adult development.

People tell their stories in therapeutic interactions. This is how they explain themselves. But they also *learn* to tell stories—to organize and make something whole from sometimes chaotic feelings of pain and confusion. The enterprise of therapy is itself a kind of story: There are psychoanalytic stories, cognitive–behavioral stories, family therapy stories. Different stories resonate with the brains of different patients. According to Cozolino (2002)

> Therapy evolved because language organizes the brain in some primary, fundamental way. What we know of the brain suggests that therapy is successful to the degree to which it builds and integrates neural networks. In therapy, we teach clients that the more ways they have of interacting with others, experiencing themselves, and understanding life, the more likely they are to find new ways of approaching their problems. Therapy is a process of helping clients rewrite the story of their lives while simultaneously building neural networks and reorganizing neural integration. (p. 207)

Talk therapy is perhaps the only therapeutic technique where the human brain's capacity for storytelling is most deeply engaged—not only telling old stories but also making sense of what has always seemed irrational, and making up newer, better stories, with better plotlines, stronger characters, and more promising outcomes. Even the reduction of the mind to "nothing but" the physical brain, even the way the physical brain functions, *become* stories we tell ourselves about ourselves, providing meaning, worldviews, and political and social agendas.

Neuroscience researcher Jaak Panksepp of Bowling Green State University posits what he calls a "seeking system" in the brain—the inner urge to find and get, to discover and learn, to understand, and to satisfy curiosity (Cozolino, 2002; Kandel, 1998). This system underpins primitive urges, like the urge to hunt. It informs complex behaviors, like the search for knowledge, spiritual connection, and love. The need to satisfy curiosity about ourselves—where we come from, who we are, how we developed, what we're made of—compels the creation of the evolving story of the brain and how it grows. As John Ratey (2001) puts it, "Whatever the advances of neurobiology and our ability to relieve symptoms, I don't think that we'll ever undo the need for understanding people's history" (p. 141).

For future generations of therapists, training will certainly change: Curricula will have to face the accumulation of knowledge coming from neuroscientists.

Louis Cozolino (2002) writes, "Most of us have been indoctrinated into particular theories and methods based on the accidents of our training. But the one thing all perspectives have in common is that they're ultimately the underlying operating principles of the human brain" (p. 134). In the future, we'll develop a common language within mental health based on the impact that different interventions have on specific neural circuits. Mental health might look like a wheel, with our many theories as the spokes and the brain as the hub. The science of studying the brain and its relationship to human behavior will continue to bring new useful insights, and those responsible for educating children and youth will have to integrate more and more of this fascinating knowledge into their everyday helping strategies.

REFERENCES

Brody, A. L., Saxena, S., Stossel, P., Gillies, L. A., Fairbanks, L. A., Alborzian, S., et al. (2001). Regional brain metabolic changes in patients with major depression treated with either paroxetine or interpersonal therapy. *Archive of General Psychiatry, 58*, 631–640.

Cozolino, L. (2002). *The neuroscience of psychotherapy.* New York: Norton.

Damasio, A. (1999). *The feeling of what happens: Body and emotion in the making of consciousness.* New York: Harcourt Brace.

Kandel, E. (1998). A new intellectual framework for psychiatry. *American Journal of Psychiatry, 155*(4), 457–468.

LeDoux, J. (1996). *The emotional brain.* New York: Simon & Schuster.

Main, M. (1993). Discourse predictions and recent studies in attachment: Implications for psychoanalysis. *The Journal of the American Psychoanalytic Association, 415,* 209–244.

Ratey, J. (2001). *A user's guide to the brain.* New York: Pantheon.

ARTICLE 9.11

THE book closes with Frank Fecser's description of a Re-ED program called Positive Education Program, in Cleveland Ohio. This program supports its students and staff and is a gratifying place to work. It is the kind of program that exudes hope. Like Fecser, the other editors of this book have experienced the challenge of developing a school staff into a cohesive team to create a therapeutic milieu. It can be done.

THE SPIRIT OF RE-EDUCATION
Frank A. Fecser

It is said that Re-ED is hard to describe. That is true. Re-ED is a state of heart as much as a state of mind—as much spiritual as it is intellectual. It begins with an attitude of unconditional caring—not just for troubled and troubling children, but for all people. It incorporates a sense of limitless hope sprinkled with naiveté and energized by boundless enthusiasm. When it comes to children, Re-ED is blind in one eye and has stars in the other. Re-ED never says never. Re-ED is not good at finding the disease or sickness or weakness in people. Re-ED targets personal strengths and builds on them. Re-ED sizes up what's working, what's resilient, and then nurtures that part so that it takes up more and more space in a child's life.

Re-ED doesn't blame kids for their problems. Rather, it recognizes that the problems kids cause are not the causes of their problems. Kids can never feel completely whole if they are not gaining knowledge and skill academically, because, as Hobbs noted, that is the business of children.

Re-ED understands that in the life of a child, problems are temporary; that the group, the community, the family, the ecology are all important. Re-ED does not stop at the four walls of the classroom; and when at its best, Re-ED is infinite, carrying its influence far into the child's future. Re-ED is a talisman crafted carefully by the loving, patient hands of teacher/counselors and gifted to the spirit of the child. It is unforgettable, irreversible, and enduring. It is the backbone of our past, it nourishes our daily work, and it guides our future.

SUMMARY

We close this chapter not because the topic has been covered to our satisfaction but because we have to accept the limitations of assigned space. There are additonal articles and topics that we wanted to include but could not. We have spoken of the leaders who have inspired us, but our primary inspiration has come from teachers who have shared their insights and wisdom with us. We constantly asked ourselves how this concept or paragraph would resonate with teachers who help troubled students. We share their battles and their battle scars. All of us owe the greatest debt to our troubled students, who have taught us so much about what it is like to live a troubled life.

EDITORS' REFERENCES

Hobbs, N. (1982). *Troubled and troubling children.* San Francisco: Jossey-Bass.

Menniger, K. (1938). *Man against himself.* Harest Books.

INDEX

ABOUT THE EDITORS

Frank A. Fecser, PhD, is the Chief Executive Officer of Positive Education Program (PEP), a multiservice, special education and mental health program serving over 3,000 troubled children, youth, and families throughout Greater Cleveland. During his career, Dr. Fecser has held a number of direct service and administrative positions including classroom teacher, case manager, building administrator, quality assurance director, and CEO. He has provided numerous LSCI Training Institutes and served as a national consultant to many programs in the U.S. He has authored articles and monographs on positive approaches to working with troubled and troubling children and youth. He cofounded the Life Space Crisis Intervention Institute and coproduced the LSCI video series with Dr. Nicholas J. Long.

Nicholas J. Long, PhD, graduated from the University of Michigan in 1956 and was Dr. Morse's graduate assistant. Dr. Long held leadership positions in psychiatric research hospitals, schools, mental health centers, and universities, and continues to contribute to the knowledge base in special education and mental health. He is Professor Emeritus at American University. Throughout his career, he worked directly with troubled students, serving as a model for his graduate students. Dr. Long has published major works in special education and psychology, and developed and directed the Rose School, the first interagency treatment program for seriously emotionally disturbed students who were excluded from the DC public schools. In 1988, Dr. Long cofounded the Life Space Crisis Intervention (LSCI) Institute in order to train professionals in effective strength-based approaches to working with troubled students. Today, there are 27 national training sites. Dr. Long's work has been published in several languages, and professionals on four continents have benefited from his insights into the minds and hearts of troubled and troubling children and youth.

Dr. William C. Morse, PhD, is Professor Emeritus of Educational Psychology and Psychology at the University of Michigan, where he taught for 31 years. During his distinguished career he has written seven major textbooks and received numerous national awards, including the CEC's highest professional honor, The Wallin Award, for his ingenious teaching and dynamic leadership. He is credited as the founder of the humanistic psychoeducational theory in special education, the originator of the Crisis Teacher concept, and the director of the first interdisciplinary clinical training program for special educators, psychologists, and social workers at the University of Michigan's Fresh Air Camp. He continues to make significant contributions to understanding and teaching emotionally disturbed children and youth.

Dr. Ruth G. Newman, PhD, had a distinguished career for 40 years in the fields of education and psychology. After receiving her PhD in 1956 from the University of Maryland, she had major leadership roles at the Washington School of Psychiatry, the National Institutes of Health, and numerous children's centers in the Washington, DC, area as well as the William Allenson White Institute in New York. She was a recognized and vocal advocate for emotionally disturbed and troubled youth and taught at both American University and the University of Maryland at Baltimore. She authored a number of articles and books on education and troubled youth, including *Psychological Consultations in the Schools* (Basic Books, 1967) and *Groups in Schools* (Simon and Schuster, 1974). She died in 1996.